AUGUSTINE'S IDEAL OF THE RELIGIOUS LIFE

AUGUSTINE'S IDEAL OF THE RELIGIOUS LIFE

ADOLAR ZUMKELLER, O.S.A.

Translated by
EDMUND COLLEDGE, O.S.A.

New York
FORDHAM UNIVERSITY PRESS
1986

LC 85–70093
ISBN 0–8232–1105–3 (*clothbound*)
ISBN 0–8232 1106–1 (*paperback*)

Translated from the second, revised edition of *Das Mönchtum des heiligen Augustinus* (Würzburg: Augustinus-Verlag, 1968). The German has been translated by Edmund Colledge, O.S.A., and Adolar Zumkeller's German versions of Augustine have been replaced by Janet Blow's new translations from the original Latin.

Printed in the United States of America

CONTENTS

PREFACE TO THE ENGLISH TRANSLATION

In 1955 Ambrose Roche, O.S.A., of the English Vice-Province (now Province) of the Augustinian Order translated the first German edition of this book; this translation never reached the printer. The present one is based on the second, greatly enlarged and revised, edition which was published by the Augustinus-Verlag, in Würzburg, in 1968.

Since then, a number of books and articles have been written on the subject of Augustinian monasticism. But no essentially new aspects and results demanding special attention have come to light. The most important work of the last decade—Luc Verheijen's two-volume *La Règle de Saint Augustin*, published in Paris in 1967—was available to the author in manuscript form.

Among the other works worthy of special attention are:

A. Manrique, "Nuevas aportaciones al problema de la *Regula S. Augustini*," CD, 181 (1968), 707–46.

R. J. Halliburton, "Fact and Fiction in the Life of St. Augustine: An Essay in Mediaeval Monastic History and Seventeenth-Century Exegesis," *Recherches Augustiniennes*, 5 (1968), 19–40.

L. Cilleruelo, "Conclusiones sobre la *Regula Augustini*," RAE, 10 (1969), 49–86.

A. Sage, *La Règle de Saint Augustin: Traduction et commentaire* (Paris, 1969).

L. Cilleruelo, *El monacato de San Agustín*, 2nd ed. (Valladolid, 1970).

J. Fernández, *La pobreza en la espiritualidad agustiniana* (Madrid, 1970).

L. Rubio, "La norma fundamental de la vida monástica segun Agustín," CD, 183 (1970), 189–235.

J. Fernández, "San Agustín y la espiritualidad sacerdotal," RAE, 12 (1970), 97–139.

A. Trapè, *S. Agostino: La Regola* (Milan, 1971).

L. Verheijen, "Eléments d'un commentaire de la Règle de Saint Augustin," *Augustiniana*, 21 (1971)–27 (1977).

R. Arbesmann, *Aurelius Augustinus: Die Handarbeit der Mönche, Übersetzung mit Einführung und Erläuterungen* (Würzburg, 1972).

A. Sage, *La Vie religieuse selon Saint Augustin* (Paris, 1972).

A. Manrique, "Espiritu de pobreza y humildad en la regla de S. Agustín," in *Scientia Augustiniana* (Würzburg, 1975), pp. 92–106.

T. J. Van Bavel, "The Evangelical Inspiration of the Rule of St. Augustine," *The Downside Review*, 93 (1975), 83–99.

L. Verheijen, " 'Non sint servi sub lege, sed sint liberi sub gratia constituti': La 'date ancienne' et la 'date récente' du *Praeceptum*," in *Scientia Augustiniana* (Würzburg, 1975), pp. 76–91.

On the Feast of St. Augustine 1978 — ADOLAR ZUMKELLER, O.S.A.

FROM THE PREFACE TO THE FIRST GERMAN EDITION

Modern man sees in St. Augustine a seeker after God, a bishop, and a great theologian. The monasticism of the saint has largely been forgotten. And yet, his personality can be fully understood and appreciated only in the light of his life and work as a monk. From the time of his conversion his only desire was to live as a "servant of God," i.e., a monk. As bishop, too, Augustine lived and died as "a poor man of Christ."

Not only did Augustine personally live as a monk, but, like the other great founders of monasteries and orders in later centuries, he has given the monastic ideal a special style and stamp. In fact, he holds a super-eminent position in the development of Western monasticism. Just as the religious life in the Catholic Church is unthinkable without St. Benedict of Nursia, so it cannot be conceived without St. Augustine. It was he who pointed the way for Western monasticism before St. Benedict. A father of Western monasticism could hardly proceed without taking note of St. Augustine.

Charity (love), the very heart of Christianity, is the center of Augustine's thought, especially of his monastic ideal. For this very reason, Augustinian monasticism is up-to-date in all Christian centuries. Augustine wanted his monasteries to be communities of love by which all social relations of men could ever and again be formed and renewed in the spirit of the first Christians. His monasteries were to further the realization of his deepest desire and ideal: i.e., the formation of the City of God (*Civitas Dei*)—the community of men under God—here on earth.

March 1949 ADOLAR ZUMKELLER, O.S.A.

ABBREVIATIONS

AA	*Analecta Augustiniana.*
AH	Arbesmann, R., and Hümpfner, W. *Jordani de Saxonia Liber Vitasfratrum.* New York, 1943.
AM	*Augustinus Magister.* 3 vols. Paris, 1954.
ArA	*Archivo Agustiniano.*
AVSM	*Sanctus Augustinus vitae spiritualis magister.* 2 vols. Rome, 1958.
BMS	*Benediktinische Monatsschrift.*
Butler	Butler, C. *Sancti Benedicti Regula monasteriorum.* 3rd ed. Freiburg, 1935.
CCL	*Corpus Christianorum,* Series Latina.
CD	*La Ciudad de Dios.*
CSEL	*Corpus Scriptorum Ecclesiasticorum Latinorum.*
Linderbauer	Linderbauer B. *S. Benedicti Regula monachorum.* Metten, 1922.
LThK	*Lexikon für Theologie und Kirche.* 10 vols. 1st ed. Freiburg, 1930. 2nd ed. 1957.
MA	*Miscellanea Agostiniana.* 2 vols. Rome, 1930, 1931.
Morin	Morin, G. *Sermones S. Augustini post Maurinos reperti* (= MA I).
PG	*Patrologia Graeca.*
PL	*Patrologia Latina.*
Possidius	*Vita Sancti Aurelii Augustini, Hipponensis episcopi, auctore Possidio* (PL 32.33–66).
RAE	*Revista Agustiniana de Espiritualidad.*
REA	*Revue des Etudes Augustiniennes.*
Steidle	Steidle, B. *Die Benediktusregel.* Beuron, 1963.

AUGUSTINE'S IDEAL OF THE RELIGIOUS LIFE

I

Augustine's Monastic Ideal in Its Development and Maturity

IN THE EARLIEST CHRISTIAN TIMES there were believers in the Church who made a total dedication of themselves to God's service, according to the counsel of the Lord and the Apostles. Imitating Christ closely, and awaiting the fulfillment of His promises for the Last Days, they rejected marriage and possessions and practiced fasting and various kinds of abstinence. Their way of life also showed a growing effort to free themselves from the "world." Very soon, such ascetics, and virgins dedicated to God, formed a distinct class within the Church.

St. Anthony of Egypt (d. 356) ranks as the true Father of Christian monasticism. In the second half of the third century he withdrew into the Libyan desert as a hermit, as many before him had also done. A larger settlement of hermits grew up around him, and he emerged as their spiritual leader. Monasticism entered a new phase when St. Pachomius, beginning about A.D. 320, united many hermit-monks in a single large monastery at Tabennisi in the Theban desert. Soon other foundations were made, so that at the time of Pachomius' death, in 347, this association of monasteries, which he himself had governed, comprised nine houses of men and two of women. The monks were said to number several thousand. Pachomius' Rule, the complete text of which is preserved only in a Latin translation by St. Jerome, influenced many later monastic rules.

The new movement took hold very rapidly. It was not long before monasticism, in its two forms, eremitic and cenobitic, acclimated itself in Palestine, Syria, Mesopotamia, and Asia Minor. The most important spiritual instructor of Eastern monasticism was St. Basil the Great. When he died in 379 as archbishop of Caesarea in Cappadocia, he himself had visited monasteries in Egypt and Palestine and had lived as a monk for a considerable length of time amidst like-minded men in Neocaesarea in Pontus. His spiritual instructions for monks, which were collected as questions and answers in the so-called 55 "Longer Rules" and 313 "Shorter Rules," were of crucial importance for the spread of the cenobitic way of life in the East. This *asketikon* by a Father of the Church contributed notably to the withdrawal of Eastern monasticism from contact with the world, and influenced the formation of monastic life in the West.

Almost simultaneously with this spread in Palestine, Syria, Mesopotamia, and Asia Minor, the ideals of the anchorites and cenobites began to gain a foothold in the West. It was probably St. Athanasius of Alexandria (d. 373), before the middle of the fourth century, who, on his way into exile, introduced the first monks into the West. St. Martin, bishop of Tours (d. 397), was a pioneer of the developments that extended from Gaul. In Italy, too, a chain of monasteries was already established before the end of the fourth century. Clearly, this early monasticism in the West was broadly marked with the form and outlook of the monastic life of the East. Western monasticism, properly speaking, still had to be created.

Thus, the ideal of Christian monasticism had already undergone a significant development by the time Augustine encountered it for the first time at the crucial turning point in his life. This encounter was to be of pivotal importance for the rest of his life. But it also exercised a normative influence on the subsequent development of monastic life in the West.

1

Groundwork

AURELIUS AUGUSTINUS was born on November 13, 354, at Tagaste in Numidia. The character of the growing child to some extent reflected his very different parents. His mother, Monica, was a faithful Christian, distinguished by her moral strictness, her piety, and the uprightness of her life. His father, by contrast, with his religious indifference, his sensuality—which he did little to bridle—and his passionate disposition, embodied the lifestyle of a dying paganism. Augustine himself was richly endowed with understanding, spirit, and imagination, and even when young manifested genuine religious feeling and a passion for education. But as he grew toward maturity the mastering of his impulses caused him considerable difficulties; it seemed as if he were completely devoid of certain predispositions necessary for the life of Christian asceticism. And yet, he possessed characteristics that grace could build upon.

NATURAL PREDISPOSITIONS

From his early youth, Augustine showed marked inclinations toward companionship and friendship. The company of friends was a great necessity for him, and with them he sought intellectual exchange and spiritual growth. This penchant toward friendship was one of the natural predispositions for the ideals of his later life. When he lived in the monastic communities at Tagaste and Hippo, he found a type of ultimate fulfillment; but even so, his concepts of friendship first had to undergo many changes.

One event of great significance for his later development showed that he retained a deep longing for the "beauty of the soul" through all the aberrations of his youthful years. He was in his nineteenth year. He enrolled in the academy at Carthage for the study of rhetoric. In the course of the standard curriculum, Cicero's *Hortensius* came into his hands. The book, a call to the philosophic life, impressed him deeply. He himself acknowledges that it redirected his desires and fundamentally changed the nature of his aspirations: "Suddenly, all my vain ambition counted for naught, and with an immeasurable fervor in my heart, I yearned for the immortality of Wisdom, and I started to rise, that I might return to You."[1] "A certain metaphysical Eros awoke in him, which sought true joy, the *vita beata*, in philosophy and in immortal Wisdom."[2]

The obstacles that stood in the way of achieving this goal were plain to him. Whoever labors for Wisdom must for the love of it renounce all longing for riches, honor, and sensual satisfaction. This is what Cicero demanded in his book. For the first time, a notion of ascetic living entered Augustine's mind. Though he had not yet found the strength to make such a philosophical renunciation a reality, he certainly was deeply moved when he read the book and was filled with longing for Wisdom. Yet later he had to confess that he could not free himself "from the sickness of concupiscence";[3] nor did he have success in putting up serious opposition to his ambition and to his desire for fame.[4]

When he looked back, there was only one particular in which he did not need to reproach himself. After he had read the *Hortensius*, the desire for temporal goods was almost wholly extinguished in him, giving way to his longing for Wisdom.[5] But there was something else that was to be even more significant for his spiritual development: the consciousness persisted that riches, honor, and sensual satisfaction were not ultimate values and did not bring contentment. Through his reading of the *Hortensius* a chord had been struck which would never again fall silent.

The reading of the *Hortensius* also gave Augustine's youthful friendships a nobility and a spiritual quality. Even if the friendships of his adolescence had been captive to sensuality, the friendly relations which the budding rhetorician established at the beginning of his studies in Tagaste with his fellow-countryman and pupil Alypius manifested from the very start a significant maturity. This was a friendship that would last a lifetime. It found its fulfillment as each promoted the other's spiritual growth, as they advanced toward moral perfection, as they both longed for Truth and for Wisdom. It was in Milan that this friendship grew into a true community of life when Augustine found in Alypius the "brother of his heart." It was then, too, that it developed, in a constantly growing circle of their friends. In addition to Augustine's colleague Verecundus, there were old acquaintances from Africa who sought Augustine's company, such as the well-to-do Romanianus, Evodius, a native of Tagaste, and Nebridius, who was especially close to him spiritually.[6]

In the midst of these friends in Milan, there ripened in the thirty-year-old Augustine a philosophical ideal of living which represented, as it were, a natural first step toward the later communal life of the monasteries. For many years Augustine had longed for a life far away from the hustle and bustle of a great city and free of anxieties for his material existence. Now he formed the plan of abandoning his hopes of an appointment as a teacher of rhetoric at the Milan academy, which would have gained him such esteem. Instead, he and his friends would withdraw from public life and dedicate their lives to the "love of Wisdom" alone.[7] They would provide for the material needs of this communal life by pooling their possessions, and they proposed to entrust to two of this circle of friends each year the administration and direction of the community, while the others would live solely for their muse, Philosophy. Models from pagan antiquity may have inspired this plan.[8] In the end, the proposal came to nothing since, as Augustine explains, several of the friends were already married, and others were approaching the time of their weddings.[9]

ENCOUNTER WITH MONASTICISM

When he was thirty-two years old, Augustine experienced that deep spiritual crisis which preceded his return to the religion of his childhood and his baptism.[10] More than anything else, the preaching of Bishop Ambrose of Milan, a certain Christian Neoplatonic circle there,[11] and his reading of Plotinus and Porphyry[12] influenced his intellectual and religious development. Years before he had experienced disappointment in the content and language of the Scriptures.[13] Now St. Ambrose's allegorical explanations of Scripture and the influence of this Christian Neoplatonism helped him to find an approach to the Bible and to overcome his difficulties with his childhood religion.[14] Another important consequence of Neoplatonic spirituality was that he came to see that the road of perfect continence, forswearing marriage, was the only way to live wholly for the search for Truth and to attain happiness in this life.[15]

Augustine's encounter with Christian monasticism was an additional decisive element in the history of his *conversio*. It occurred on the very day when his hesitations gave way to decision. An African compatriot called Pontitianus, an influential leader at the imperial court, was visiting Augustine and Alypius, who were both his friends. He was leafing through a book, which by chance was lying on a table, and to his astonishment he discovered that it contained the Epistles of the Apostle Paul. He himself was a Christian believer, and he congratulated Augustine on his choice of reading. Soon he steered the conversation to the subject of the Egyptian hermit Anthony, who at the time was the occasion both of much wonder and of much esteem in Christian circles. He recounted the life of this Desert Father, and he was surprised that his friends had heard nothing of it. He informed the two friends about the anchorites and cenobites in the Egyptian desert regions and, to their amazement, told them that even in Milan, outside the city walls, a monastery had recently been established under the direction of Bishop Ambrose. Then he described an incident in which he himself had taken part, years before, as an imperial official at Trier. He was taking a walk in the gardens surrounding the town walls with three friends who were also in the emperor's service. Two of them chanced to enter a monk's dwelling, and there they found an account of Anthony's life.[16] One of them began to read it, and he was so swept along by what he read that on the spot he renounced all his worldly plans, the emperor's friendship, and the marriage which he was proposing, and he convinced his friend to do the same. They wanted to dedicate themselves wholly to the service of God. When Pontitianus and his companion had searched for them for a long time and had found them both in the monk's hut, they had come to an irrevocable decision. On that very day they set about changing their way of life.[17]

Pontitianus' anecdote affected Augustine profoundly. "You, Lord, . . . put me before my eyes, so that I might see how shameful, how deformed and befouled, how bespotted and ulcerous I was." He was seized by a violent longing to do as these uneducated men had done.[18] In his turmoil he went out into the adjoining garden. The fear of abandoning his old ways and a longing to gain what was new struggled within him. Then he heard a voice calling, like that of a child: "Take and read" ("*Tolle, lege*"). This, too, was an echo of Pontitianus' narrative, which was working upon him in his moment of decision. Pontitianus had told a story about Anthony —how he once, apparently by chance, came upon the saying in Holy Scripture: "Go, sell all that you have, and give it to the poor. Then you will have treasure in heaven. Then come, follow me" (Matt. 19:21). In this, Anthony recognized the call of God. Similarly now Augustine took up Paul's epistle. In silence he read the first words on which his glance fell: "Not in rioting and drunkenness, not in debauchery and wantonness, . . . but put on the Lord Jesus Christ, and make no provision for the concupiscence of your flesh" (Rom. 13:13–14). Illumination and peace came to his soul too. He writes that he had no need to read further.[19]

For Augustine the decisive battle in that hour was a conflict, not over the truth of the Christian faith—for in his heart he had already made a complete act of assent to that faith[20]—but over the ideal of continence. Nourished by his encounter with Neoplatonic philosophy, he had for a long time had as a wavering object a life of complete ascetic denial, lived with those of like mind and wholly dedicated to the search for Wisdom, but up to that time the ideal had seemed unattainable. Now what Pontitianus had told him suggested that that realization was a possibility. So, at that moment, for him becoming a Christian meant a striving after perfection and Wisdom in complete self-denial.[21] From the beginning, that was how he and Monica had regarded *conversio*. God had given him far more than his mother had dared to ask for him in the long years of her weeping and prayers. God had so "converted" him that he "never again sought a wife or any other ambition this world has to offer."[22]

It was of importance for Augustine that his African countryman had shown him Christian ideas about monasticism in the twofold form in which they had been realized in history: in Anthony's life as an anchorite, and in the communal living of the cenobites.[23] Augustine had always admired the lonely high road which St. Anthony had taken, and defended it.[24] And yet this way of life seemed to him to exceed that measure of renunciation which the average man could sustain.[25] Augustine was no friend of solitude. He loved a contemplative peace, it is true, but he always sought it in the company of the like-minded. From the beginning therefore his esteem for the cenobitic ideal was unbounded.[26]

CASSICIACUM

At once, Augustine's decision was fixed. He would resign his post as a teacher of rhetoric in Milan. Although the position offered him an assured financial standing and, more than that, the prospect of promotion to high office in the state, still the purely formal duties of an old-time rhetorician could bring no lasting contentment to Augustine's spirit. He writes in his *Confessions* (not, it is true, wholly without exaggeration) that he could no longer reconcile his convictions with continuing to occupy a chair of garrulity and lying, instructing young men in the folly, untruths, and bickering of the market place.[27]

Augustine's decision to abandon teaching and to withdraw from public life was clearly influenced by his models, who in earlier times had drawn up plans for a life lived in common in philosophic leisure. Recently it has been observed that in the writings he was composing at this time Augustine shows an inclination, typical of the philosophies of late antiquity, toward a life of retirement. This retirement manifests itself in him in two ways, as he withdraws from public life, and as he retreats, spiritually, into himself (ἀναχώρησις εἰς ἑαυτόν).[28] As Plotinus and his pupils had once done, Augustine retreated with his friends, in order, as he writes, "to gather the mind into itself and hold it fast there," and so to attain knowledge of "God and soul."[29]

Still there can be no doubt that Pontitianus' description of the life of the monks had its own influence on Augustine's decision to withdraw from the world.[30] It is clear that Augustine regarded the philosophical life of retirement advocated by Neoplatonic philosophers whom by this time he was interpreting in a Christian sense as in no way antithetical to the retreat from the world represented by Christian monasticism. Rather he saw both as expressions of the same striving for a "life of happiness" (*vita beata*), lived in the contemplation of divine Truth and Beauty.[31] His compatriot's report on the life of the monks was constantly on Augustine's mind. This fact bears witness to the great interest he showed in monasticism, as does his treatise on *The Ways of the Catholic Church*, written shortly after his baptism.[32] But in the *Confessions* Augustine specifically insists that even at Cassiciacum he had decided that he would serve God.[33] It is significant that in relating Pontitianus' story he attributes almost the same words, a few pages earlier, to one of the imperial officials who suddenly entered the monastic life in Trier: "I have made up my mind to serve God."[34] Then he described the new ideal of life of the two court officials as *militia*, that is, a military service of the spirit.[35] Now he sees no objection, after he has recounted the scene in the garden in Milan, to applying to himself the term *militia Domini*: serving in the army of the Lord.[36]

So Augustine broke with the past; and yet he avoided everything that might have excited needless attention. He waited until the fall vacation, and then handed in his resignation. It was easy to make his weakened physical condition the excuse. He not only had worked too hard at his job but, perhaps because he was unaccustomed to the climate, had developed a bronchial complaint. Breathing difficulties, chest pains, and a persistent hoarseness made a lengthy convalescence necessary.[37] After the storm through which his spirit had passed in the previous weeks, he longed for peace and relaxation. He found them at Cassiciacum, the country estate of his Milanese friend and colleague Verecundus. After spending the fall and winter there, he was baptized at the Easter Vigil in the year 387.[38]

Perhaps the days at Cassiciacum can be counted among the happiest in Augustine's life. Sharing the weeks of recovery and reflection with him were Alypius, the "brother of his heart," his mother, Monica, his son, Adeodatus, his brother Navigius, his cousins Lastidianus and Rusticus, and two young African friends and pupils, Licentius, the son of Romanianus, and Trygetius, who had seen service in the imperial army.[39]

The precise location of Cassiciacum can no longer be established with certainty, but even today in the vicinity of Milan there is a small market town with the name "Cassago." It lies in the fertile Brianza hill district, a good day's march north of Milan. This region is still called "the garden of Lombardy" because of its mild climate, small lakes, rich orchards, and plantations of vines and mulberry trees. It is probably here that we should look for ancient Cassiciacum.[40] Verecundus' country house, though not particularly large,[41] was comfortably arranged. There was even a small Roman bath. Here they spent the following months as a family. Everyone rose at daybreak,[42] and assembled for morning prayers in common,[43] after which everyone went off to his chores. Monica was in charge of the housekeeping.[44] Augustine assumed the supervision of the estate business, in order to repay to some extent Verecundus' hospitality, and he was assisted in this by his friend Alypius, who had had some management experience.[45] If there was urgent work to do in the fields, the vacation guests also lent a hand.[46] In addition, there was a great deal of correspondence for Augustine.[47] Shortly before the midday meal he was accustomed to read a few pages of Vergil with his two pupils and to comment on them in schoolmaster's style.[48] The meal at midday, which they ate in common, was simple, for it was Augustine's opinion that any overeating was a hindrance to the work of the spirit.[49]

In their leisure hours, Augustine and his friends conducted lengthy discussions on philosophical questions, in which his mother at times also participated.[50] These conversations were inspired with that yearning for Wisdom and happiness which the new convert hoped and longed to attain not only by his faithful acceptance of Truth but also by his rational understanding of it.[51] He himself said that his philosophical ideal of the "life of happiness" consisted in "perceiving, piously and completely, Him by Whom you are led to the Truth, the nature of the Truth you enjoy, and the bond that connects you with Him in the fullest degree."[52]

When the weather was fine, these discussions took place outdoors; the participants sat around in a small meadow in the shade of a tree. But if it was cold or rainy, they met, according to ancient custom, in the bath quarters.[53] The well-heated apartments, furnished with couches, provided a suitable place for philosophical conversation in the cold weather.[54] The interchanges were recorded, and have come down to us in Augustine's early works *Against the Academics*, *The Happy Life*, and *Of Order*. In the evenings they went to bed early. Augustine shared his bedroom with his two pupils. Study was not permitted at night, and conversation then was a rare exception. He did not wish to deprive his pupils of their necessary sleep.[55]

Cassiciacum was a time of transition. There was still in Augustine's lifestyle much that mirrored the style of the ancient philosophers. Fourteen years later, in the *Confessions*, he describes his academic work at Cassiciacum. It had indeed been consecrated to God's service, but still much was inspired by the vanity of the schools.[56] And in the early writings I have just mentioned, there are many expressions, many sentiments, which Augustine, when he was almost seventy years old, repudiated in his *Retractations* as a residue from the pagan schools of rhetoric. Among these were his use of such concepts as *fortuna*, *omen*, and the *Musae*, and of the pagan tale of the twin sisters Philocalia and Philosophia, his enthusiasm at the time for the liberal arts, and his high esteem for non-Christian philosophy and its representatives.[57] For example, at the end of his life he deplored how in his early treatise *Against the Academics* he had regarded man's highest good (*summum bonum*) as being in his spirit, and the ideal of the happy life as living (*beate vivere*) in accordance with this spirit.[58] In rejecting this typically Stoic teaching, he demonstrates in the *Retractations* that God is man's highest good, and he finds the ideal of living happily (*beate vivere*) realized when man lives "in accordance with God."[59] Augustine's view in *The Happy Life* that the life of happiness is anticipated in this world in the soul of the wise man, whatever the condition of his body,[60] is also of Stoic origin. In his critical retrospect this opinion he likewise corrected; for one can designate as a *beata vita* only the life to come, in which the body will possess incorruptibility and immortality, and will be subordinated to the spirit, without any grudging or conflict.[61]

If in these early works Augustine is still no more than a philosopher, his philosophy is nonetheless directed toward the truth of the faith, and his philosophical thinking is governed by the principle that "Never will I reject Christ's authority, for I can find none better on which I can rely."[62]

Plotinus' teaching has led him to Christ.[63] Some people have with justification written of a synthesis between Christianity and Neoplatonism in the young Augustine.[64] He draws a clear dividing line between the philosophy of this world and that other philosophy in which true Wisdom manifests itself.[65] His thinking is supported by Christian ethics, and is directed to the formation of Christian living.[66] To be sure, the ideal life which Augustine is outlining in these early works is that of the wise man. The highest goal is Truth, in which man unveils for himself the face of God.[67] But the Church is the lofty school in which one learns this Wisdom.[68] The wise man's portrait already has a certain Christian tint.

But more than anything else, Cassiciacum was a time of inner growth for Augustine. Though the dialogues which he composed there do not cast much light on his spiritual disposition at the time, there is still enough to enable us to understand what he later reports in the *Confessions* about the months he spent there.[69] His soul was filled with gratitude and joy, yet there was deep contrition as he thought of the years that were past and of his present "wounds" and "misery."[70] He prayed that these wounds of his might find complete healing, as he once admitted, "almost daily as I wept."[71] Nightly meditating was a practice which had grown dear to him,[72] and a fruit of the meditations of these months is his *Soliloquies*—in particular the ardent prayers of praise and intercession at the opening of this early work.[73] At this time, the Psalter provided rich material for his private prayer.[74] Thus the sojourn at Cassiciacum was rich for Augustine in God's "great benefits," as he thankfully recalls in the *Confessions*.[75] In retrospect, those vacation days appeared to Augustine the bishop as a rest in God's presence from the turmoil of the world.[76] "Sweet it is to me, O Lord," he writes, "to confess with what internal goads You thoroughly subdued me, how You brought low the mountains of my meanness and the hills of my thought, how You straightened what was crooked in me and made my rough places smooth."[77]

Furthermore, at Cassiciacum Augustine strove to take the ascetical renunciation, on which he had decided at the moment of his conversion, with utmost seriousness. In keeping with his inward disposition, he had by then completed his rejection "of the tumult of transient things."[78] In the dialogue which he pretends, in the *Soliloquies*, to conduct with his reason, he calculates precisely why he had forsaken all longing for riches, honor, marriage, and the pleasures of the table, regarding this renunciation as an indispensable condition if he is to realize his hopes for a Neoplatonic Christian Wisdom. He says that he had abandoned his strivings for riches once he had read the *Hortensius*. Now he felt himself free of ambition. The preservation of his health was one reason which had decided him in favor of abstinence in eating, drinking, and satisfying his other physical needs.[79] Then he had firmly decided to renounce forever any thought of marriage. Giving the grounds for his decision, as it were, he writes: "The more the hope grows in me of looking upon that beauty for which I long so violently, the more all my love and my yearning are turned toward it."[80] It may seem here as if Augustine's only motives for embracing this ascetic way of life were philosophical; but the emphasis with which in these meditative soliloquies he calls himself "the servant of God"[81] (*famulus Dei, servus Dei*) indicates that he was concerned with more than the realization of the philosophers' ideals of the wise man. The strong religious and Christian tone is unmistakable:[82] "Now I love You alone," he writes in his prayer; "I follow only You, I seek only You, ready to serve only You. . . . I long to be possessed by You."[83] So, during these weeks of quiet on the estate at Cassiciacum, Augustine's *conversio*—his turning away from the world to a life of asceticism, but to an asceticism that had more than Neoplatonic ideals to nourish it—was completed.

Yet with all this, it is highly characteristic of Augustine that he very consciously avoided a break with the world around him, and that from the beginning he aspired to a life lived in the company of men of like mind.[84] In his *Soliloquies* he acknowledges to himself the reasons why he had taken his relatives and friends with him into solitude: so that he could with them reflect upon "God and the soul," and thus help them as well in the search for Wisdom.[85]

But what they had sought together was not mere knowledge. Augustine tried to make the lives of his pupils and friends embody a Christian mode of thought and conduct.[86] His friend Alypius was to be included in this. He was a shining example for them all in his ascetic zeal, carrying his own mortifications so far that even in winter he proposed walking barefoot on the frozen ground.[87]

These friends, striving together in Cassiciacum for Wisdom, were Christians, however much their piety was still permeated with Neoplatonic ideas.[88] The day's work began and ended with prayer in common.[89] The chanting of psalms in church had become so much a part of them that Licentius incurred reproof from Monica for singing the sacred texts in unsuitable places.[90] Even in their philosophical discussions there was place for a common prayer of thanksgiving.[91] Augustine loved to make frequent intercession for absent friends, and he encouraged the others in this.[92] The ideals of friendship of the years in Milan, which had been secular, however much spiritualized, had been replaced by a common way of life which was Christian.[93]

Certainly, the circle of friends at Cassiciacum was not yet a monastic community, but the groundwork had been laid for the new way of life which was to be established at Tagaste and Hippo. The echo of Pontitianus' account, the philosophic–religious meditations and dialogues, even the daily association with friends who thought as he did, and the example of his mother's deep faith may have helped to make Cassiciacum for Augustine into more than a place of ascetic resolution in the spirit of ancient philosophy—into a vital Christian community in which his intention of "serving God" (*servire Deo*) could go on ripening.

A SECOND STAY IN ROME

This encounter of the friends in God which took place at Cassiciacum was sealed when they all were received into the bosom of the Church. During the Easter celebration of 387, Augustine, together with his friend Alypius, and his son, Adeodatus, were baptized in Milan by Bishop Ambrose.[94] Evodius had already taken this step,[95] and when Nebridius entered the Church about the same time or shortly afterward,[96] their community was confirmed and ennobled in the "true friendship" which, as the *Confessions* states, can exist only in the "love poured out in our hearts through the Holy Spirit, Who is given to us" (Rom. 5:5).[97]

It was also in Milan at that time that Augustine made his first personal acquaintance with Christian monasticism. Immediately after he was baptized, the plan for a permanent community life lived with his friends took hold in his soul. He felt compelled to visit the "monastery" outside the city walls which his countryman Pontitianus had mentioned to him in his hour of decision. The monks' withdrawn life, totally dedicated to prayer, the reading of the Scriptures, and manual labor, and, in particular, the learning of the superior, a priest, deeply impressed the newly baptized Augustine.[98] We have good reason to surmise that St. Ambrose's conception of monastic life, which was embodied in this convent, was not without influence on Augustine, even if we cannot be more precise.[99]

Monica was now playing a special role in her son's proposals for his monastic life. From the beginning she had wholeheartedly welcomed his plan to forswear marriage and worldly advancement, and now she did all she could to contribute to the realization of the "community in God."

Augustine pays this tribute to her: "For all of us who can by Your grace call ourselves Your servants and who . . . lived together, united in You, after we had received the grace of Your baptism, she cared as if she were the mother of us all, and she served us as if she were everyone's child." [100]

When Augustine left Milan in the fall, he had made his decision. He proposed to return to his homeland with his mother and his friends, and there they would carry out their "holy enterprise" (*placitum sanctum*),[101] consecrating themselves together to the service of God. But the journey home was much delayed, by an unexpected affliction. The little band of travelers had proceeded as far as Ostia and were making the final preparations for their crossing to Africa when Monica was attacked by a violent fever and died within a few days.[102] Augustine was inconsolable. His mother's sudden death, and perhaps the political uncertainties created by the usurper Maximus as well, prompted him to postpone their voyage until the fall of the following year.[103] He spent the nine months with his friends in Rome, busily writing. Two works from this period, *The Greatness of the Soul* and the first book of *The Freedom of the Will*,[104] indicate that he was still thinking along Neoplatonic lines. Yet his philosophical attitudes were shaping themselves according to the truths of the Christian faith, notably more so than they had at Cassiciacum.[105]

Once before, Augustine had spent a year (383–384) in Rome, after his sudden departure from Africa, in the hopes of finding better prospects as a rhetorician in the imperial metropolis than in Carthage.[106] But this time he arrived with different interests. On the earlier visit he had been a disciple of Mani, even though he had secretly become estranged from the sect and had joined the ranks of the skeptics. Now he was writing his first great work against the Manichaeans, in which he extols the life of the Catholic Church, the crown of which, it seemed to him, was monasticism. In the old days he had despised Christian Rome, and had courted the favor of the pagan prefect Symmachus; now he frequented Christian monastic circles, and wanted only to be a servant of Jesus Christ.

The work I have just mentioned, *The Ways of the Catholic Church*, which he was writing in Rome[107] but did not complete before he returned to Africa,[108] offers abundant evidence of what his attitude toward monasticism then was. He gives detailed descriptions of the city's monastic communities,[109] which he had visited. They were places of Christian love and holiness, headed by respected and intelligent superiors. According to Eastern custom, which imitated the example of the Apostle Paul, the monks dedicated themselves to manual labor in order to provide for their needs and to be a burden to no one. Augustine writes admiringly of the Roman monks' severe penances, for he had observed for himself that many of them worked for three days or even longer without nourishment.

It was also here in Rome that Augustine became acquainted with his first monastic communities of women. Widows and virgins had joined them to live a common life, earning their livelihoods by spinning and weaving. Augustine praises the intelligence and experience of the women who presided over them and who knew well not only how to guide their charges in a Christian way of life but also how to contribute to their spiritual and religious formation.[110]

It is hard to overestimate the importance Augustine's second stay in Rome had for the maturing of his ideas about monasticism. Here he had the opportunity not only to study first hand for nearly a year the basic theory of Christian monastic asceticism but also to observe its practical application.

It was in Rome as well, a few years earlier (382–385), that St. Jerome had decided on the monastic way of life. In the midst of a pleasure-seeking world, a strongly ascetic movement was developing, as the spirit of Christian asceticism was asserting itself in the city, especially among its women, and penetrating the ranks of the nobility. Considerable numbers were entering monastic houses.[111] We do not know if Augustine at this time sought personal acquaintance with the hermit of Bethlehem—that would, in any case, happen a few years later—but it is certain at least that Jerome's ascetic ideals, and those of the Roman monasteries under his influence, were not without effect on Augustine.[112] It must have been chiefly from Jerome's writings that Augustine learned more about Eastern monasticism at this time.[113]

In the enthusiastic account of the life of the Eastern monks, which Augustine gives in *The Ways of the Catholic Church*, he likewise relies on Jerome.[114] He touches only in brief on the lives of the Desert Fathers, who in the extraordinary severity of their penances and their contempt for the world, had found satisfaction even in the solitude of the wilderness; and he admiringly gazes up to this "peak of holiness." He knows that there are those who reproach the anchorites for being useless members of human society, but he denies the justice of their accusation; such critics are blind to the benefits which prayer and the exemplary lives of the hermits bring to Christendom. Still Augustine concedes that this way of life exceeds men's normal capacities.

His report of the cenobites' lives is highly idealized. They strove for

Christian perfection in poverty, obedience, continence, and penitential zeal. Their daily occupations consisted in prayer, the reading of Scripture, manual labor, and pious conversation. In what he wrote we can detect not only how much Augustine saw in this common life of concord and love what he himself had been longing for, but also what he had learned about the organization of the Eastern monastic communities: their superiors, the so-called "Fathers," the deacons who bore the economic responsibilities, and the conferences held every evening, as well as the monasteries' beneficence—they were said to have sent entire shiploads of food and other products of their industry to regions in want.

Thus, because of these closer contacts with monasticism, Augustine's feelings about Christian living ordered to a rule were surfacing in his writings. When he came to write *The Ways of the Catholic Church*, Christian asceticism was shown as the ideal for the true sage.[115]

NOTES

1. *Confessions* 3.4.7f.
2. E. Hendrikx, "Augustinus," LThK, I², 1095.
3. *Confessions* 6.11.18ff., 8.7.17.
4. Ibid., 6.6.9f.; cf. also *Soliloquies* 1.10.29.
5. *Soliloquies* 1.10.17.
6. Cf. *Confessions* 4.4–9, 6.7–12, 7.2, 9.3, 9.8. Cf., in addition, H. H. Lesaar, "Alypius," in *Miscellanea Augustiniana* (Rotterdam, 1930), pp. 220–32; F. Lang, "Des heiligen Augustinus Jugendfreundschaften," *Der Fels*, 24 (1929–1930), 250–64; and V. Nolte, *Augustins Freundschaftsideal in seinen Briefen* (Würzburg, 1939).
7. See *Confessions* 3.4.
8. Nolte (*Augustins Freundschaftsideal*, pp. 30f.) is reminded of Plotinus' circle of friends. In Rome, in the house of a certain Constantinus, a Manichaean "monastery" had been founded (*The Ways of the Catholic Church* 2.20.74; *Against Faustus* 5.5; see also A. Manrique, *La vida monastica en San Agustín: Enchiridion historico-doctrinal y regla* [El Escorial & Salamanca, 1959], pp. 52, 60f.). But it is less than probable that this influenced Augustine's plan, since his own inner rejection of Manichaeanism had progressed so far. See also P. Courcelle, *Recherches sur les Confessions de Saint Augustin* (Paris, 1950), pp. 178ff.; and R. J. Halliburton, "The Inclination to Retirement—The Retreat of Cassiciacum and the 'Monastery' of Tagaste," in *Studia Patristica* V, ed. F. L. Cross (Berlin, 1962), pp. 330f.
9. *Confessions* 6.14. In the work which he composed fourteen years earlier, *Against the Academics* (2.2.4), Augustine indicates the same plan.
10. The historical trustworthiness of the *Confessions* as they concern Augustine's conversion experience has been questioned repeatedly since Adolf von

Harnack's *Augustins Konfessionen*, published in 1887, particularly by P. Alfaric (*L'Evolution intellectuelle de Saint Augustin* [Paris, 1918], pp. 364ff., 391ff.) and, more recently, by R. Reitzenstein (*Augustin als antiker und als mittelalterlicher Mensch*, Vorträge der Bibliothek Warburg 1922–1923 [Leipzig & Berlin, 1924], p. 30). Now, thanks to a series of fundamental studies of the sources, their reliability can be regarded as assured. Cf. J. Nörregaard, *Augustins Bekehrung*, trans. A. Spelmeyer (Tübingen, 1923); C. Boyer, *Christianisme et Néo-Platonisme dans la formation de Saint Augustin* (Paris, 1920; 2nd ed. Rome, 1953); K. Holl, "Augustins innere Entwicklung," in *Gesammelte Aufsätze zur Kirchengeschichte* III, ed. K. Holl., pp. 54–116; M. Wundt, "Augustins *Konfessionen*," *Zeitschrift für neutestamentliche Wissenschaft*, 22 (1923), 161–206; B. Legewie, *Augustinus: Eine Psychographie* (Bonn, 1925); J. Mausbach, "Zur inneren Entwicklung des heiligen Augustinus," *Theologische Revue*, 25 (1926), 1ff.; idem, *Die Ethik des heiligen Augustinus*, 2nd ed., 2 vols. (Freiburg, 1929), II 390ff.; F. Billicsich, *Studien zu den Bekenntnissen des heiligen Augustinus* (Vienna, 1929); G. Wunderle, *Einführung in Augustins Konfessionen* (Augsburg, 1930); F. Hofmann, *Der Kirchenbegriff des heiligen Augustinus* (Munich, 1933), pp. 9ff.; P. Courcelle, *Recherches sur les Confessions de Saint Augustin* (Paris, 1950), pp. 29ff.; J. J. O'Meara, *The Young Augustine* (London, 1954), pp. 6ff.; L. Rodríguez, "La conversión de San Agustín a través de los diálogos de Casiciaco," CD, 176 (1963), 303–18.

Harnack himself, in his anthology of the writings of the Church Father *Augustin: Reflexionen und Maximen* (Tübingen, 1922), pp. xvif., corrected his earlier point of view.

11. Cf. Courcelle, *Recherches*, pp. 153ff. He also produces weighty arguments (pp. 93ff.) for the view that certain of St. Ambrose's sermon sequences brought Augustine's Neoplatonic philosophy closer to a Christian standpoint.

12. *Confessions* 7.9.13ff. Cf., in addition, O'Meara, *Young Augustine*, pp. 131ff. and 143ff.; and P. Courcelle, "Litiges sur la lecture des *Libri Platonicorum* par Saint Augustin," *Augustiniana*, 4 (1954), 225–39.

13. *Confessions* 3.5.9.

14. Ibid. 5.14.24, 6.4.5f., 7.21.27.

15. Cf. ibid. 8.1.2.

16. Monasticism arrived relatively early in Trier, perhaps through St. Athanasius of Alexandria, who lived there in exile for a number of years. The *Life of St. Anthony*, which is mentioned, refers to the account written by Athanasius, ca. 357, which was very quickly translated into Latin by Evagrius of Antioch. See P. Monceaux, "Saint Augustin et Saint Antoine: Contribution à l'histoire du monachisme," MA II, pp. 62f., and B. Altaner, *Patrologie*, 6th ed. (Freiburg, 1960), pp. 245f.

17. *Confessions* 8.6.14f. Courcelle, *Recherches*, pp. 181ff., assumes, and tries on solid reasons to prove, that these two imperial "men of affairs" (*agentes in rebus*) mentioned by Pontitianus, who chose a life of asceticism in Trier, were Jerome and his friend Bonosus.

18. *Confessions* 8.7f.16ff. Cf. Billicsich, *Studien*, p. 99.

19. *Confessions* 8.8.19, 8.11f.25ff. On the historical character of the scene, cf. P. Courcelle, *Les Confessions de Saint Augustin dans la tradition littéraire* (Paris, 1963), pp. 191ff. It is indeed his opinion that the "*Tolle, lege*" represents nothing more than "the translation of an interior happening" (p. 613).

20. Cf. *Confessions* 8.7.18. See also Legewie, *Augustinus*, pp. 40ff.; Billicsich, *Studien*, pp. 87ff., 155f.; K. Adam, *Die geistige Entwicklung des heiligen Augustinus* (Augsburg, 1931), p. 21; Hofmann, *Kirchenbegriff*, p. 16; R. Guardini, *Die Bekehrung des Aurelius Augustinus* (Leipzig, 1935), p. 272. The contrary reasons adduced by Mausbach, "Entwicklung," 7, and *Ethik*, II 396f., are unsound.

21. *Confessions* 8.11.25. On the other hand, it is an exaggeration for Adam (*Entwicklung*, p. 23), followed by Hofmann (*Kirchenbegriff*, p. 16), to maintain that at that time Augustine saw Christianity in a light so Neoplatonic that he believed that he must "follow the way of complete liberation from the senses in order to become a Christian." Cf. Nörregaard, *Augustins Bekehrung*, p. 80, and Holl, "Entwicklung," p. 83.

22. *Confessions* 8.12.30. Cf. also Possidius 2.

23. It is of course true that according to the report in the *Confessions* (8.6.15) Pontitianus was more reticent in his description of the life of the cenobites (cf. Monceaux, "Saint Augustin et Saint Antoine," p. 66), yet without doubt they too were mentioned. Augustine specifically states that his African compatriot had told him about "companies of monasteries" (*monasteriorum greges*).

24. In *The Ways of the Catholic Church* 1.31.66, he takes issue with the reproach that the anchorites are useless members of human society, from which they have excluded themselves. He rejoins by showing the significance of their prayer and example for their fellow-men.

25. "Hoc excedit nostram tolerantiam" (ibid. 1.31.67).

26. Ibid. 1.31.67f. Cf. Monceaux, "Saint Augustin et Saint Antoine," pp. 68f.

27. *Confessions* 9.2.2ff. H. I. Marrou has a thoroughgoing description of the ideal of education of those days, "the eloquent and learned man" with all his manifest deficiencies; see *Saint Augustin et la fin de la culture antique*, 4th ed. (Paris, 1958), pp. 1–157.

28. Halliburton, "Inclination to Retirement," p. 333.

29. *Of Order* 1.1.3 and *Soliloquies* 1.2.7. Halliburton supposes ("Inclination to Retirement," pp. 334f.) that the chief influence on Augustine's decision to withdraw himself was the Neoplatonist Manlius Theodorus, who is thought also to have been a type of this life of retirement. But it must be stressed that in the case of Theodorus the circle of friends which provided so strong an impetus to Augustine, when he was living at Cassiciacum, was lacking.

30. Halliburton (ibid., p. 339) specifically contradicts this; and he believes that there is no proof, even for the foundation in Tagaste, "that St. Augustine was any more involved in the monastic life of the Church." But his chief argument—that "Nowhere in the whole of the literature which refers to this period

is the society formed there described as a *monasterium*"—is untenable. During this period, even when he was plainly writing about monasteries and the Christian monastic life, Augustine avoided the word *monasterium* (cf. *The Ways of the Catholic Church* 1.31ff., 66ff.). Thus, the fact that the word *monasterium* was not used does not tell against Tagaste's monastic character. See also below, chap. 2, note 52.

31. Augustine says this in so many words about the monks of Egypt: "What is it, I ask, that those people see . . .? Certainly, it is superior to human affairs, whatever it is which enables man as he contemplates it to live without other men. . . . Enjoying to the full their converse with God, they adhere to Him with pure minds, and they are most blessed in the contemplation of His beauty . . ." (*The Ways of the Catholic Church* 1.31.65, 66).

32. He visited the monastery in Milan and the monastic communities in Rome (ibid., 1.33.70), and collected more information about the life of the Egyptian monks (ibid., 1.31.66–68). See below, pp. 13–15. One is somewhat surprised to read the words with which Halliburton seeks to vitiate these early witnesses to Augustine's personal interest in Christian monasticism: "Of his later interest in Christian monasticism the position of his discussion of this subject in the framework of the *De moribus ecclesiae catholicae* [*The Ways of the Catholic Church*] would suggest that this was for him, to quote Professor Burnaby, 'in itself admirable only as a living organization of charity' " ("Inclination to Retirement," p. 339). It would be difficult for anyone, after an unprejudiced reading of Augustine's report, to confirm this interpretation.

33. " 'Renuntiavi, . . . quod et tibi ego servire delegissem' " (*Confessions* 9.5.13). In Augustine's usage at that time (cf. the treatise composed in the same period, *The Works of Monks*), this "to serve God" means nothing other than to become a monk. Possidius, too (chap. 2), in what he writes about the recent convert does not understand his "to serve God" (*Deo servire*) and "my intention of serving God" (*propositum serviendi Deo*) any differently. And the significance of the titles "servant of God" (*famulus Dei*) and "slave of God" (*servus Dei*) which Augustine attributes to himself in the *Soliloquies* (1.1.15 and 1.15.30), an early work, can in my opinion be rightly interpreted only in the light of Pontitianus' account of monasticism.

34. " '. . . et Deo servire statui . . .' " (*Confessions* 8.6.15).

35. "Respondit ille adhaerere se socium tantae mercedis tantaeque militiae" (ibid.).

36. ". . . quod iam pleno corde militia tua . . ." (*Confessions* 9.2.4).

37. Ibid. See B. Legewie, "Die körperliche Konstitution und die Krankheit Augustin's," MA II, pp. 19ff. His physical ailments were not the decisive reasons for resigning his post, but merely a pretext. His representations in the *Confessions* are, on this point too, trustworthy. We hear the first rumors of these religious and moral motives in his earliest writings (see Billicsich, *Studien*, p. 110, and Hofmann, *Kirchenbegriff*, pp. 17f.). C. J. Perl (*Aurelius Augustinus: Die Ordnung*, 2nd ed. [Paderborn, 1947], p. xiii) puts forward another motive for Augustine's resigning of his state appointment; the Arian

court at Milan is supposed to have been so full of hatred and hostility toward Bishop Ambrose at that time that it was exceptionally difficult for any state official to be reconciled to the Catholic Church.

38. *Confessions* 9.2f.2ff.

39. *The Happy Life* 1.6.

40. For the site of Cassiciacum, see F. Meda, "La controversia sul Rus Cassiciacum," MA II, pp. 49–59.

41. It must be because of this that Augustine shared a bedroom with his pupils. Cf. *Of Order* 1.3.6.

42. *Against the Academics* 2.4.10.

43. *Of Order* 1.8.25.

44. *Against the Academics* 2.5.13.

45. Cf. E. R. von Kienitz, *Augustinus: Genius des Abendlandes* (Wuppertal, 1947), pp. 132f.

46. *Against the Academics* 1.5.15, 2.4.10.

47. Ibid. 2.11.25.

48. *Of Order* 1.8.26. Cf. also *Against the Academics* 1.5.15, 2.4.10.

49. *Against the Academics* 2.6.14, 3.4.7; *The Happy Life* 1.6.

50. *Of Order* 1.11.31. Cf. also J. J. Gavigan, "The Mother of St. Augustine," *The American Ecclesiastical Review*, 119 (1948), 271ff. The historical content of these dialogues is not to be doubted; cf. P. Keseling, *Gottes Weltregiment: Des Aurelius Augustinus "Zwei Bücher von der Ordnung"* (Münster, 1939), pp. 39ff.

51. ". . . ut quid sit verum, non credendo solum, sed etiam intelligendo apprehendere impatienter desiderem" (*Against the Academics* 3.20.43).

52. *The Happy Life* 4.35.

53. *Against the Academics* 2.11.25, 3.1.1; *The Happy Life* 1.6, 4.23; *Of Order* 1.8.25, 2.1.1, 2.6.19.

54. Cf. Perl, *Die Ordnung*, p. 99.

55. *Of Order* 1.3.6.

56. *Confessions* 9.4.7.

57. *Retractations* 1.1–3.

58. *Against the Academics* 3.12.27, 1.2.5.

59. *Retractations* 1.1.2 and 4. On Augustine's Stoicism, it is the judgment of G. Verbeke ("Augustin et le stoïcisme," *Recherches Augustiniennes* I [Paris, 1958], p. 88) that "With no profound knowledge of Stoic philosophy, St. Augustine was exposed to its influence, chiefly in his earliest works." On the Stoic passages mentioned here, see ibid., p. 74.

60. Cf. *Retractations* 1.2.

61. Ibid. Cf. also Verbeke, "Augustin et le stoïcisme," p. 74.

62. *Against the Academics* 3.20.43.

63. Cf. Billicsich, *Studien*, p. 113, and J. Barion, *Plotin und Augustinus: Untersuchungen zum Gottesproblem* (Berlin, 1935), p. 166.

64. J. J. O'Meara, "Augustine and Neo-Platonism," *Recherches Augustiniennes* I (Paris, 1958), p. 101.

65. *Of Order* 1.11.32.

66. Wunderle, *Einführung*, pp. 43, 60.
67. *Of Order* 1.8.23.
68. *Against the Academics* 2.2.5. Cf. Hofmann, *Kirchenbegriff*, pp. 21f.
69. Cf. A. Trapè, *San Agostino* (Rome, 1961), pp. 42f. Without a doubt, the *Confessions* were made to agree with the early writings, including this description of the stay at Cassiciacum. Cf. Boyer, *Christianisme et Néo-Platonisme*, pp. 135ff.; Holl, "Entwicklung," pp. 81ff.; Nörregaard, *Augustins Bekehrung*, pp. 1–18; Billicsich, *Studien*, pp. 110ff.; and O'Meara, "Augustine and Neo-Platonism," pp. 91–111.
70. Cf. *Soliloquies* 1.1.5f., 1.14.26; *Of Order* 1.10.29. See also Billicsich, *Studien*, p. 104, and Hofmann, *Kirchenbegriff*, p. 19.
71. *Of Order* 1.10.29. See also 1.8.22.
72. *Of Order* 1.3.6. See also *Letter 3* 1.
73. *Soliloquies* 1.1.2–6.
74. *Confessions* 9.4.8.
75. Ibid. 9.4.7.
76. ". . . ubi ab aestu saeculi requievimus in te . . ." (ibid. 9.3.5).
77. Ibid. 9.4.7.
78. *Letter 10* 2.
79. *Soliloquies* 1.10.17. Cf. also *Confessions* 3.4.7f., 6.11.18f.; and *Of Order* 2.20.52
80. *Soliloquies* 1.10.17.
81. Ibid. 1.1.5, 1.15.30. Cf. also note 33, above.
82. Cf. Hofmann, *Kirchenbegriff*, pp. 23ff. See also how Augustine painstakingly delineated his concept of asceticism in *The Ways of the Catholic Church* a year and a half later.
83. *Soliloquies* 1.1.5.
84. ". . . I look for many who will long for [the love of Beauty] with me, possess it with me, and enjoy it with me . . ." (*Soliloquies* 1.13.22). Cf. also S. Alvarez Turienzo, "San Agustín y la soledad," *Giornale di Metafisica*, 9 (1954), 377–406.
85. *Soliloquies* 1.12.20.
86. Cf. *Of Order* 1.10.29f. Here Augustine reprimands his pupils sharply for their ambition and their jealousy. Cf. Nörregaard, *Augustins Bekehrung*, p. 192.
87. *Confessions* 9.6.14.
88. Cf. Nörregaard, *Augustins Bekehrung*, p. 95.
89. Cf. above, note 43; see also *Letter 3* 4.
90. *Of Order* 1.8.22.
91. *The Happy Life* 4.36.
92. *Against the Academics* 1.1.1., 2.1.2; *Of Order* 2.20.52.
93. Cf. Nolte, *Augustins Freundschaftsideal*, pp. 33ff.
94. *Confessions* 9.6.14.
95. Ibid. 9.8.17.
96. Ibid. 9.3.6. Cf. J. J. Gavigan, "St. Augustine's Friend Nebridius," *The Catholic Historical Review*, 32 (1946), 50.

97. *Confessions* 4.4.7.

98. *The Ways of the Catholic Church* 1.33.70. When at this point Augustine mentions that the monastery's superior was a priest ("quibus unus presbyter praeerat"), there is no contradiction with the statement in *Confessions* 8.6.15 that the monastery is "under the fostering care of Ambrose" ("sub Ambrosio nutritore"). E. Spreitzenhofer's assumption (*Entwicklung des alten Mönchtums in Italien* [Vienna 1894], p. 18) that Augustine had two different monasteries in mind is thus unfounded. Nor can Ambrose's monastery have been a "bishop's monastery," such as St. Eusebius of Vercelli organized, as Spreitzenhofer believes, because it was not in the leastwise located within the city walls.

99. Cf. also D. Sanchis, "Pauvreté monastique et charité fraternelle chez Saint Augustin: Le commentaire Augustinien de Actes 4, 32–35 entre 393 et 403," *Studia Monastica*, 4 (1962), 26–29, who points to pertinent texts in the writings of St. Ambrose.

100. *Confessions* 9.9.22.

101. Ibid. 9.8.17.

102. Ibid.

103. In *Against the Writings of Petilian the Donatist* 3.25.30, Augustine specifically testifies that it was only after the assassination of Maximus, which took place in the late summer of 388, that he undertook the return journey.

104. Cf. *Retractations* 1.7–9 (6–8).

105. E. Hendrikx, *Augustins Verhältnis zur Mystik* (Würzburg, 1936), pp. 71ff.

106. *Confessions* 5.8.14f.

107. *Retractations* 1.7 (6).

108. See the Maurist Fathers' *Life of St. Augustine* 2.14.1 (PL 32.155f.). Cf. also O. Bardenhewer, *Geschichte der altkirchlichen Literatur* IV (Freiburg, 1924), p. 464; and P. Keseling, *Das Ethos der Christen: Des Aurelius Augustinus Buch "Von den Sitten der katholischen Kirche"* (Münster, 1948), pp. 31–33.

109. For the communities of monks and nuns in Rome at that time, see Spreitzenhofer, *Entwicklung des alten Mönchtums*, pp. 5ff., 27ff.; G. D. Gordini, "Origine e sviluppo del monachesimo a Roma," *Gregorianum*, 37 (1956), 220–60; G. Penco, *Storia del monachesimo in Italia* (Rome, 1961), pp. 15ff.; idem, "La vita monastica in Italia all'epoca di S. Martino di Tours," *Studia Anselmiana*, 46 (1961), 69f.; and R. Lorenz, "Die Anfänge des abendländischen Mönchtums in 4. Jahrhundert," *Zeitschrift für Kirchengeschichte*, 77 (1966), 3ff.

110. *The Ways of the Catholic Church* 1.33.70f.

111. Cf. M. Viller, *Aszese und Mystik in der Väterzeit*, trans. K. Rahner (Freiburg, 1939), pp. 181f.; M. Rothenhäusler, "Hieronymus als Mönch," BMS (1920), 382f.; Penco, *Storia*, pp. 16–18.

112. J. de Vathaire ("Les relations de Saint Augustin et de Saint Jérome," in *Miscellanea Augustiniana* [Rotterdam, 1930], pp. 484–99) has nothing whatsoever to say about Jerome's influence on Augustine's monastic thought.

113. It can be shown that of the other monastic writings of his day Augus-

tine knew Sulpicius Severus' *Life of St. Martin* and the translation by Rufinus of Eusebius of Caesarea's *Historia monachorum.* Since both works were composed and translated around the year 400, Augustine received his earliest knowledge of them at a time when his own notions of monastic life had already been formed. Cf. Lorenz, "Anfänge," 38*n*6.

114. *The Ways of the Catholic Church* 1.31.66–68. The description of the life of the cenobites in these chapters markedly resembles Jerome's *Letter* 22 34–36, composed in 384.

115. *The Ways of the Catholic Church* 1.31.66. Cf. Hofmann, *Kirchenbegriff*, pp. 53f.

2

Realization

IN THE FALL OF THE YEAR 388, after five years' absence, Augustine, with his son, Adeodatus, and his friends Alypius and Evodius, once again set foot on African soil. When he left home he had been searching and struggling; now he returned home, having found his peace with God. His plan for the future, his holy enterprise (*placitum sanctum*),[1] was now formulated. He intended to found, for himself and his friends, a monastic community, resembling those he had learned about in Italy, and yet in many respects with a flavor and style of its own. It was his inclination, encouraged in his Neoplatonic days, to a life of retirement, dedicated to study and lived in a circle of friends, which from the beginning gave his enterprise a personal character.

First, Augustine made a brief stopover at Carthage, the provincial capital, at the home of an acquaintance named Innocentius,[2] to allow himself and his friends a short rest, after the arduous sea voyage. Then, too, the final preparations for the establishment of the communal life they were planning had to be made. Perhaps he was seeking yet other companions for their undertaking; indeed, it is not impossible that it was only then that they saw clearly where they should make their settlement. For this, they chose Augustine's father's property at Tagaste, the three friends' home.

THE FIRST MONASTERY

Augustine's native town, Tagaste, was in the Roman province of Numidia (the modern Algeria), a good hundred kilometers inland, about a day's march from the present border with Tunisia.

Tagaste was not without its military and commercial importance. The hilly region abounds with springs and creeks, and the Medjerda River flows nearby. Pasture lands and wooded mountains, intersected with deep valleys, give the landscape its peculiar characteristics. Augustine's birthplace now has the name Souk Ahras. Today the exact location of the Christian basilica, the episcopal church of ancient Tagaste, where Augustine and his first companions attended services, and where a few years later Alypius was to occupy the episcopal throne, cannot be determined; and the place where the monastery was to rise is similarly lost to oblivion. The only remains of the town's prosperity in Roman imperial times are the ruins of an ancient bath.

In the small Numidian town Augustine first saw the light of day, on November 13, 354. It was here that his pious mother first told him about Jesus Christ, and here he spent his childhood under his parents' protection. But it was also here that the sixteen-year-old boy took up a life of idleness. Later, Tagaste would bear witness as the young rhetorician returned from the school at Carthage, a Manichaean, and as his mother, for that reason, expelled him from her home. Afterward he practiced his rhetor's profession in this provincial town for a good while; perhaps ten to twelve years may have passed before he left home to seek a position of honor in Carthage, and then in Rome and Milan. Now he had returned, a different person. Augustine had become a convinced Christian. What was more, he had decided to dedicate himself fully, with his friends, to the service of God, and was losing no time in putting this decision into practice.

Possidius, the saint's biographer, accounts for the years at Tagaste in one meaningful sentence: "He had abandoned all worldly cares, and served God with those who were one with him, in fasting, praying, and good works, while day and night he meditated upon the law of the Lord, passing along in what he said and in what he wrote whatever God had revealed to him in study and in prayer."[3]

Here in Tagaste something of the spirit of the cenobitism of the Eastern monasteries was revived.[4] And yet Augustine immediately introduced new aspects to this form of living. Manual labor was no longer the companions' sole occupation. Possidius describes Augustine's curriculum: study, teaching, and writing. From the beginning, Augustine devoted much time to study, viewing as his special vocation the reconciling of the Church's asceticism with scientific knowledge and literature.

The writings of these years in part owe their origin, as do those at Cassiciacum, to his lively exchanges of ideas with his brethren. In Tagaste, too, conversation on spiritual and religious topics filled many leisure hours.[5] Most of the literary works of this period are dedicated in some fashion to the service of the Church and of its great salvific work. Augustine's activity as an author in Tagaste begins to foreshadow some of the apostolic zeal of the spiritual director he was to become.[6] Thus a work which I have already mentioned, *The Ways of the Catholic Church*, which Augustine finished at this time, is a form of apologia for the Church against the Manichaeans, and bears witness to his deep love for her.[7] Augustine believed, as he wrote in the *Retractations*, that he could no longer "endure in silence the Manichaeans' vauntings over their feigned and misleading temperance or abstinence";[8] and in numerous other writings of this period he was deeply concerned to be of help to "his fellow-men and neighbors," to arrive "where God in His wisdom calls us."[9]

The notion of Christian *caritas*, too, was no longer an alien notion. We have observed his detailed account in *The Ways of the Catholic Church* of the charitable undertakings of the Egyptian monks.[10] He was now beginning to grasp the meaning for the Christian life of the love of one's neighbor.[11] However much he might go on attempting to harmonize this love of neighbor with the Stoic ideal of ἀπάθεια, the soul's repose in a freedom from feeling, he was now insisting that man's loving gift of himself to God must find expression in his practical love for his neighbor, and that the love of our neighbor is our surest way to the love of God.[12] Thus, more and more, the conduct of his life at Tagaste acquired a Catholic dimension.

We also find this dimension expressed in the letters which he wrote in these years. They surely must have been directed to people of every kind: for friends and strangers, zealous Catholics and those of other faiths, and even a pagan philosopher are among the addressees of letters that have survived. Certain thoughts occur repeatedly. We should free ourselves of vain cares about things of transient value, so that we may be attached only to what is profitable and of abiding worth.[13] This idea comes in Neoplatonic guise; nonetheless, Augustine's call for a Christian and ascetic idealism is plain. "Whoever believes in Christ," he wrote, "does not love what is lowest, does not remain complacently satisfied with middle things, and thus becomes able to cling to the highest. And this is the whole of what we are commanded, admonished, and urged to do."[14] In one of these letters we encounter Antoninus, a married Christian full of admiration for the life of continence consecrated to God which Augustine and his brethren were living. He had commended himself to the prayers of the community; and Augustine for his part asks him to remember them.[15]

Of the letters of this period those exchanged with the friend of his youth, Nebridius, occupy a special place. Like Augustine, he had determined after his baptism to live chastely for the love of God. About the year 388 he came home to Africa, and withdrew to his family's estate near Carthage.[16] He would greatly have liked to live in Augustine's community, but his health was so uncertain—he was sick, and could have traveled only in a litter—that his mother would not permit him to leave. As for Augustine, he could not come to Nebridius, and did not wish to. He hated all this traveling, which went on robbing his soul of the peace it longed for, imperiled the salvation of the brethrens' souls, and, what was more, would do nothing to promote what he and Nebridius alike regarded as the ideal of their lifestyle.[17]

But what Augustine found to say to console Nebridius, who was lamenting his loneliness and his solitude, are among the finest things he has written about community. He directs his mind to that holy union in God which surpasses any physical propinquity. "Withdraw into your soul, and lift it up to God with all your might. Beyond doubt, you will find us there too, not through the bodily images of your imagination, . . . but through the perception that will make you see that we are together, wherever we may be."[18] Not even Nebridius' death, which occurred during the Tagaste years,[19] could remove him from this company of friends. Now, as Augustine wrote in the *Confessions*, Nebridius could drink from God's Wisdom and at last quench his thirst for the Truth. And Augustine believed that, in so doing, he would not forget his friends on earth: "For You, O, Lord, Whom he drinks, You, too, are mindful of us."[20]

Nebridius once expressed his opinion about the letters Augustine was writing to him: "Now you will tell me about Christ, now about Plato, now about Plotinus."[21] It is true that when Augustine describes for his friend the spiritual joy that Tagaste has brought to him he uses the concepts and the modes of expression of Neoplatonic philosophy. He had come to enjoy true *otium*, freedom of mind, "to have done with the uproar of transient things,"[22] for which he had so long yearned. In this freedom he was striving and longing for *deificari*, "to become like to God," which he understood and explained in Porphyry's sense.[23] In his letters Augustine mentions as characteristics of the truly wise man his familiarity with death (*cum morte familiaritas*), his purification from such faults as hardness of heart, temerity, vain ambition, and superstition (*duritia, audacia, cupiditas inanis gloriae, superstitiosa credulitas*), the dying away in him of earthly love (*amore corporeo mori*), and, as the fruit of all this, a life of spiritual joy and inviolable peace (*gaudium solidum, dulce vivere, securitas, tranquillitas, vita intrepida*).[24] From his own experience he reports that such peace of soul preserves its hours of prayer. And even if one must desert its inner sanctum to mingle in the business of the day, this calm will remain.[25] The variety of topics discussed in his collective work *On 83 Various Questions*, which, evidently, he had thrashed out at Tagaste,[26] give ample proof, for all their Neoplatonic coloring, of the extent to which Christian motifs were already beginning to penetrate Augustine's plans for an ascetic life; here, for example, we find him dealing with Christ's cross as the way to conquer one's fear of death[27] and offering a meditation on the verse in the Psalms (72:28) "But it is good for me to cling to God."[28] Augustine had long ago found in Christ Himself "the highest Truth and Wisdom, the archetype of all things," as he describes Him, God and Man, in another letter to Nebridius.[29]

Augustine's mind was still moving along Neoplatonic lines in other works of this period, for example, in *On Genesis Against the Manichaeans*, *The Teacher*, and *True Religion*.[30] And he was still working on the compendium on the liberal arts, which he had started in Milan, and of which he completed at Tagaste the six books of *On Music*. But even in these works there are superficial signs, such as the increasing frequency of Scriptural quotations, of how much his command of Christian ways of thinking had increased. *On Music* is, in fact, not a musicological textbook, but, particularly in the last book, an introduction to spiritual meditation. Augustine later states in the *Retractations* that he had hoped to show the reader "how God's invisible being can be scrutinized with the help of created things."[31]

The Tagaste foundation was not merely an association of learned men who were seeking to achieve a philosophical *anachoresis*, a withdrawal from public life and a turn to their interior selves.[32] But even if this ancient ideal of living did in many respects influence Augustine and his community, the foundation on which they built was different. It seems important in this connection to observe, as I have already done in one place, that Augustine saw no opposition between the *anachoresis* of Neoplatonic philosophy, now given his Christian interpretation, and the withdrawn life of Christian monasticism. Therefore when he gives philosophical justification in the letters and writings of this period for his longing for freedom of mind (*otium*) and for becoming like God (*deificari*), one cannot for all that exclude from him the efficacy of the monastic ideal of withdrawal. He himself testifies that at the time he perceived in the monk's withdrawal from the world the way to the life of happiness (*vita beata*) in the contemplation of the beauty of God.[33] And one can just as little deny the influence of Christian asceticism on him in those works in which he provides only philosophical support for his ascetical attitude, especially since in one of his works from this period he admires and extols the "perfect continence of Christian men" (*summa continentia hominum christianorum*).[34]

Furthermore, the Tagaste foundation already bore the clear marks of monastic life. "Loving God, serving Him, and clinging to Him"[35] was to be the true content of their communal life. Therefore, they were not to be together only from time to time, as had been the case at Cassiciacum. The friends who assembled at Tagaste were determined upon a life lived in constant community and totally dedicated to the service of God.[36] The fact that Augustine was searching for additional members for the community[37] clearly shows that he envisaged an institution that would last.

The Lord's counsel to the rich young man (Matt. 19:21) was the inspiration for the foundation: "If you wish to be perfect, go sell what you have, and give to the poor, and you will have treasure in heaven; and come, follow me."[38] Augustine came upon these words of the Saviour's after Pontitianus had told him about the life of St. Anthony.[39] In keeping with this divine counsel, Augustine completely renounced all his personal possessions when he began their common life at Tagaste. It is true that his family was not particularly well-to-do, especially in comparison with the senators' families and the great landowners of the time. His parents had had to endure considerable financial hardships to give their son an education.[40] Augustine may have exaggerated somewhat when he called himself "a poor man and the child of poor people,"[41] but in fact his patrimony consisted only of a house with some land.[42]

But if what he owned was not much, still he willingly surrendered what little he had to fulfill perfectly the Lord's counsels in his way of life.[43] How he achieved this renunciation is not clear from the various brief remarks he makes about it. In *Sermon 355* he seems to say that he sold his small estate for the benefit of the poor.[44] On the other hand he reports in a letter that he had turned over his land to the church in Tagaste.[45] Yet what Possidius relates permits us to suppose that Augustine simply surrendered his income—the greatest part, at least—to the community, and that their general maintenance was defrayed from this common source.[46] But it is possible that Augustine surrendered his entire income, including that for the house, to the church in Tagaste and relied upon it for the support of the community.[47] In the few sources we possess, nothing is said of how far Augustine's companions at that time followed his example. Perhaps the conduct of some in this respect left something to be desired. In any case, in later years it came to light that in their practice of personal poverty individual members of the Tagaste monastery had been found wanting. As late as 405, for example, it was not clear to outsiders that everything a brother of the house possessed belonged not to him personally but to the community.[48] And not all the brothers when they entered the community found that everyone made a final disposition of his means. Indeed, it emerged that one of them had indefinitely postponed doing this, without any apparent valid reason.[49] Nonetheless, most members must have renounced their personal possessions so completely that the economic existence of the foundation was assured. And the community may also have enjoyed much financial help from well-to-do friends and relatives.[50]

To sum up: we can say that the ideal which Augustine realized in Tagaste was still strongly influenced by the ancient Stoic and Neoplatonic aspirations to wisdom. Even the ascetic life of these years—notably their ideal of sexual continence—was determined and motivated by Neoplatonic ideas. Then, too, Stoic ideals of friendship and other ancient social and philosophical concepts also played a certain part in the formation of the life of the community.[51] And yet "serving God" (*Deo servire*), as Augustine and his friends sought to do, was more than the philosophers' freedom of mind (*otium*); it already manifested the essential characteristics of monastic life.[52]

Furthermore, in ancient Christian times a close connection had been established—among the Alexandrians, for example—between a philosopher's striving for wisdom and a Christian ascetic mode of life. Indeed, in those days it was not a strange idea that the life of the monk was a kind of philosophy, or, better expressed, was the true "pneumatic" philosophy.[53] Even if Augustine nowhere expresses himself in this sense, one may still say that the conduct of his ascetic and monastic life at the time corresponded in many respects with this concept of monasticism as a genuine philosophy.[54]

The years at Tagaste developed for Augustine into the most peaceful and withdrawn of his life. And yet the freedom of mind (*otium*) for which he had longed was not undisturbed. Certain undertakings that the confidence of his fellow-citizens imposed on him deprived him of considerable time and repose.[55]

What to his regret he had found to be true at Cassiciacum was in a certain fashion to be proved in his life at Tagaste: "Being quickly relieved of so many affairs did not bring me [the peace] I had dearly hoped for."[56]

But without a doubt Augustine's chief concern in these years was the young community over which he presided. With little direct experience of monastic life, he had the responsible task of educating the brethren for their lofty ideal. They all were too dependent, and could not, as Augustine once wrote, rely on themselves to live at peace with their souls.[57] So he was eager to use the opportunity to convey to them some of his own experiences and perceptions.[58] But with all the care and trouble this undertaking brought him, the good will of the brethren still allowed him to know considerable happiness. He thankfully acknowledged that they were making steady progress on the way toward God.[59]

Of the "brethren" who lived with Augustine at Tagaste we know only a few by name. Thus nothing certain can be said about the size of the community. Alypius, in his zeal and sense of community, was a shining example to everyone. He was to attain a bishop's dignity before Augustine, and preside over the diocese of his home town, Tagaste, for longer than a normal lifespan. Other companions too from these first years in the monastery were later numbered among the bishops of North Africa. Evodius, the one-time imperial official, became bishop at Uzali, and Severus, likewise a native of Tagaste, at Mileve.[60] Another monk of the monastery, Honoratus by name, was later active as a priest in Thiave, and died shortly before 405.[61] Augustine himself mentions in passing in a letter still two other brethren from the Tagaste monastery, Privatus and Emilianus.[62] Yet in the case of these two, as of Honoratus, we cannot show with certainty that they had entered the community in these first years.[63]

Above all it was in the life of the young Adeodatus that Augustine could not admire God's working enough. Then barely sixteen years old, "still he surpassed in intellect many mature and learned men." "I experienced so many wonderful things with him that I trembled at the powers of his mind." But during their time at Tagaste, God called the boy to Himself.[64]

How seriously Augustine and his companions undertook the fulfillment of their proposals and how true their service to God was is shown by the speed with which the report of their piety and learning spread.[65] But now there was growing in Augustine himself a dread of attaining ecclesiastical preferment. The responsibility of office, his awareness of his own weakness in the faith, and his preference for a retired life[66] made him zealously avoid every place where he knew that an episcopal see was vacant. He did not want, as he once said in a later sermon, to take the highest place for himself at the banquet of his Lord: "Yet then it pleased Him to command me: 'Come up higher.' "[67]

SUMMONS TO THE PRIESTHOOD

At the beginning of 391, when he was thirty-six years old, Augustine went to Hippo Regius. This city, called "Royal" to distinguish it from Hippo Diarrhytos, the modern Bizerta, was one of the most important commercial ports of Roman North Africa. Known today as Annaba (previously called Bône), it is still counted among the major cities of Algeria. Annaba, with its environs, is a well-endowed countryside. The city lies in the northern foothills of the Edoug Mountains, nestling by a wide bay of the Mediterranean, on both sides of the Seybouse, which flows into the sea there. Since the end of the last century, on a hill above the town, dominating the entire landscape, there has been a Christian basilica dedicated to the memory of St. Augustine.

Ancient Hippo was situated a little to the southwest of the present city. In recent decades a few important sites of the ancient city have been excavated. In addition to the forum, the amphitheater, and the baths, the most important finds are the ruins of two Christian basilicas, one of which, it is supposed, was the "Basilica of Peace" (*basilica pacis*), the Catholic episcopal church of ancient Hippo.[68] To be sure, all these ruins still give only a feeble impression of the beauty of the ancient city. The center of it was surrounded by an extensive protective wall dating from pre-Roman times. Christian basilicas and public monuments dominated the layout of the city itself. Between them stood the opulent houses of rich shipping magnates, senators, and merchants. There were also, it must be admitted, squalid slums, in which the greater number of the lower classes lived, fishermen, boathands, and artisans of every sort.[69]

The religious and moral conditions in Hippo were hardly the best. The city had been an episcopal see since the first half of the third century, and for that long the Christians had been in the majority. Even so, paganism still manifested itself in the daily life of the masses, and superstitions and the fear of evil spirits were deeply rooted among them.[70] For eighty years, the Donatist schism had exercised a fateful influence, splitting Christendom in Africa into two hostile camps. At that time, the Donatists in Hippo, under their bishop, Proculianus, had the upper hand and encountered no opposition. In addition, there were the customary evils of an ancient harbor city. Tirelessly Bishop Augustine, later, had to fight against "the ostentatious display of wealth, the inflated pride in honors, the gluttonies of taverns, the rival factions in the theaters, the filth of whorehouses, and the lewdness of the baths."[71]

This was the city which he visited early in the year 391. It probably took him three to four days to cover the more than one hundred kilometers —perhaps on horseback—which separated Tagaste from the northern harbor city. He came in complete poverty. Intending to make only a short visit to Hippo, he had nothing with him except the clothes on his back.[72]

Augustine himself gives two reasons for his journey.[73] First, he was planning a new foundation, and was looking for a suitable site for this monastery. In Hippo there was still nothing of the sort. Furthermore, the traveler was hoping to recruit one of his friends, an imperial official, for his community. But while this man was still hesitating over his decision, Augustine's life once again took a new turn.

The aged bishop of Hippo, Valerius, in preaching to the people, happened to say that their community could use another priest. He may have known that this visitor from Tagaste was present. Perhaps that was the occasion of his sermon. It became clear at once that Augustine's virtue and learning had also found their admirers in Hippo. While the bishop was still speaking, the eyes of those present turned to Augustine. According to the custom in the early Church, the people might express their wishes at the selection of a candidate for ordination. Thus, at the ordination of priests and bishops riotous scenes were no rarity. Augustine suddenly found himself, spontaneously and with little ceremony, seized by the bystanders. Despite his resistance, they led him to the bishop to be ordained. Valerius was in full agreement with the desires of the people, and without delay admitted Augustine to priestly orders.

Augustine was deeply shaken. This great responsibility, and the difficulties this new undertaking would present for his plans for a monastery, brought him to tears.[74] Still, weeks later, he could write of his reception of orders: "It happened to me because my sins were so great."[75]

This event in the church at Hippo was of great importance for Augustine, for his further spiritual growth, and for his hopes of a monastic life. First of all, he was conscious of the insufficiency of his religious knowledge. The fact that he must impart counsel and instruction to others made him apply himself with great zeal to the study of Sacred Scripture. Though he had been familiarizing himself with it since the day of his conversion, he had not yet succeeded in undertaking its systematic study, as he had planned to do by this time with his friends at Tagaste. So he now addressed an imploring letter to Bishop Valerius, begging him to allow him leave until the Easter feast, so that he could devote himself in complete peace to the study of Scripture. He also wanted to prepare himself for his priestly functions "with prayer, reading, and weeping."[76]

The hunger for God's word never thereafter left Augustine. He was to become such an "expert on and expositor of Holy Scripture"[77] as few were whom the ancient Church produced.[78] The more Augustine read and prayed himself into Scripture, the more he perceived its inexhaustible riches; after a life of most zealous searching into the Book of Books, he once had to confess, "When a man has finished, then let him begin" (*Cum consummaverit homo, tunc incipiet*).[79] He constantly recommended the reading of Holy Scripture to others.[80] The study of Scripture must also have found an important place in the daily regimen of his monasteries.[81] It was not to remain mere knowledge, which is why he required that study of the Scriptures be borne up and crowned by love.[82]

Augustine felt the tension between the priesthood and the monastic life to be great, and yet his determination to unite the one with the other was strong from the very beginning. Along with the responsibilities of the priesthood, though, it was chiefly the "business" side of his office—the onerous administrative tasks and the manifold obligations to settle worldly affairs—that he found a harsh contradiction of what he aspired to in his life. Later, as bishop, he would often spend the entire morning, and frequently the afternoon, in the settling of disputes.[83] The troubles of worldly matters pursued him even when he was praying.[84] No doubt, he tried to make his judicial activities profitable for the salvation of the litigants, through his admonitions and pastoral counsel; but all the same these tasks were and remained a cruel servitude for him.[85] These duties oppressed him so much that he would much rather have undertaken to perform manual labor, to which he was so unaccustomed, in the monastic community. His consolation was his hope for eternal life.[86]

These duties Augustine accepted with considerable self-denial; but what may have seemed a burden proved to be an enrichment for his aspirations to the monastic life. Until then, his only experience of Christian community was in the company of his brethren.[87] Now his thinking was permeated more and more with the idea of the Church as one great community of love and grace. Hitherto, he had regarded the Church almost exclusively as a divinely endowed institute for the education of mankind; but now her central place in God's plan of salvation was gradually revealed to him. Correspondingly, he now saw in her, with special love, the Bride of Christ and the Mystical Body of the Lord.[88]

Love of the Church was characteristic not only of Augustine's own attitude but also of the spirit which he fostered in his monasteries. He found sincere joy in everything good which happened in the Church, even in what he chanced to observe of virtue and piety in other monasteries.[89] His biographer Possidius writes in his praise: "He was always watchful and concerned for the profit of the entire Church. . . . Her profit always brought him joy; her losses, sorrow."[90]

Thus more and more he recognized that service to the Church was a task pleasing to the will of God, to which the comfortable tranquillity of monastic communities must always give place. His own monastic life acquired an increasingly apostolic character. Even if from time to time he longed for repose and reflection, still he accepted apostolic activity as a duty from which a monk might not retreat if it should be required of him. When Mother Church has need of monks to work, he once declared, we may neither take pride in this nor refuse our help on the pretext of monastic contemplation. Humble obedience can be our only response. If monks and clerics should refuse their service to the Church, who would assist her in the anguish of her spiritual labor?[91] Monastic life, as Augustine now understood it, finds its completion "in the service of Christ and of His members,"[92] and he took St. Paul's words (2 Cor. 5:15) as a signpost: "Christ died for all; that they also, who live, may not now live to themselves, but unto Him Who died for them, and rose again."[93]

This more intensive involvement with Holy Scripture and his acceptance of apostolic tasks brought to fulfillment in Augustine that spiritual development which in his writings betrays an ever stronger orientation toward what was specifically religious and Christian.[94] One can detect, as well, in his concept of monastic life that he is tilling new ground. Only in the years of his apostolic labors in Hippo is the development of his ideas of monasticism completed.

THE GARDEN MONASTERY

As soon as he undertook his priestly work in Hippo, Augustine informed old Bishop Valerius of his decision to continue as a priest the monastic common life. Valerius agreed to this plan, and indeed presented Augustine with a garden in the environs of the church as a site on which to build the monastery.[95] The community at Tagaste played its part, sending a few brothers.[96]

The monastery which was at once erected on the site included a kitchen and a dining room, which may also have served as a workroom, as well as storerooms for clothing and food.[97] Each of the monks probably had his own cell.[98] In any case, there was an oratory, which was to be used exclusively for prayer.[99] The monastery was even provided with a small library, and from it the monks could borrow books every day at specified times.[100]

Whoever wished to enter the community sold his possessions, as Augustine once did at Tagaste, and either distributed the proceeds to the poor or turned them over to the common funds.[101] But now a new distinguishing trait was added, to which Augustine's biographer Possidius bears specific witness in the sentences describing the foundation of the garden monastery: "He soon established a monastery within the church and began with the servants of God to live according to the manner and rule of the holy Apostles. Above all, no one in this community could possess anything of his own, but 'all things must be held in common, and there was given to everyone as he had need' " (Acts 4:32, 35).[102] What Possidius asserts here Augustine's sermons and writings confirm.[103] He seems to have given first clear expression to this notion of the monastic common life as modeled on the Christian communities of the early Church in the *Rule* which he composed, probably in the late 390s.[104] There he prefaces his comments with the very words from the narrative of the Apostles' story to which Possidius alludes: "The first object of our common life is to live together in unity, and to have 'one heart and one soul' [Acts 4:32] directed toward God."[105] From now on, this is what Augustine holds up before his brothers as the essential element of their monastic common life: they should hold earthly goods in common and possess one heart and one soul directed to God. Through this he strove to revive in his monasteries early Christianity's common life of property and love.

There is nothing unique to Augustine in establishing a monastic common life on these sentences from the Acts of the Apostles. Since the time of Pachomius the primitive Christian community had served as a model for monastic living, and one finds these sentences from Acts in the Coptic version of the Life of Pachomius,[106] the testament of Pachomius' pupil Orsisius,[107] and the so-called "Longer Rules" and "Shorter Rules" of St. Basil,[108] as well as in the writings of St. Jerome.[109] Yet however traditional this monastic principle he inherited, Augustine "applied it with greater force and carried it out with more severity" than did those who preceded him.[110] Indeed, we can say that it became an essential characteristic of his concept of monastic life.[111]

The men who gathered around Augustine were of differing ages. There were those who had achieved office and stature in the world, but they were soon joined by youths, still in need of education, who grew to maturity in the monastery.[112] The majority came from the lower classes: Augustine writes of slaves and freedmen, peasants, and manual laborers.[113] Yet there were also men from wealthy and distinguished families, and even senators and substantial landowners.[114] There were people who not only differed in temperament and character, but who also came from very different walks of life and different upbringing. They were not all from Hippo and its neighborhood; men from other dioceses were also accepted.[115] Augustine saw no objection, indeed, in particular cases, to sponsoring the admission to the monastery of catechumens.[116] From the very beginning, many clerics also joined the monastery, but the lay brothers were by far in the majority, and gave their stamp to the entire community. Illiterates would have been exceptional,[117] for whoever was still unable to read when he entered the monastery must have received instruction at once.[118] The daily Scripture readings and the communal use of the Psalms for prayer made an ability to read absolutely essential, even if it is true that the common prayer was learned by heart for recitation.[119]

Whether a probationary period preceded the official reception into the monastery is not known.[120] Nor is it evident from Augustine's writings whether, in the garden monastery and in the "monastery of clerics" (*monasterium clericorum*) founded a few years later, he required an explicit profession from newcomers when they were admitted to the community. Some passages seem to favor the interpretation that an entrant took a vow of poverty,[121] and made a binding promise to lead the common life.[122] But Augustine may have regarded entry to the monastery as itself a fully binding promise (*professio*) to lead the monastic life.[123] This would mean that when anyone had taken this step he professed himself, in Augustine's view, as "a poor man of Christ,"[124] and bound himself to renounce all personal possessions and to live an entirely communal life.[125] Certainly, in his monasteries there is no expressed promise of obedience. That was implicit when one gave oneself completely to God and to the community. Yet we may suppose that Augustine's monks—like the "continents" (*continentes*) and the consecrated virgins of that period—did take vows of chastity and of celibacy.[126]

In a letter to a young brother named Laetus,[127] who probably belonged to his monastery of clerics, Augustine expresses the profound significance of the monastic "profession" (*professio*). He calls the renunciation of the world and the taking up of Christ's cross the living heart of consecrated life in the monastery, as they were of cenobitic life in the East.[128] To develop his thought he alludes to the words of the Saviour: "If anyone comes to Me, but does not hate his father and his mother, his wife and child, his brother and sister, and even his own life, he cannot be My disciple. And if he does not carry his cross, he cannot be My disciple" (Luke 14:26–27). Becoming "a soldier of Christ" will mean a voluntary renunciation of possessions, of parents and relatives, and, in a certain sense, of one's own life. It will mean taking Christ's cross upon oneself and following the Saviour. Monastic life means a life in the sign of the cross.[129]

Augustine provides no evidence for an ecclesiastical blessing of the new entrant, in the manner of later monastic professions. But reception into the monastery may have been given external expression when the monastic clothing was bestowed.[130] Augustine testifies that in the African monasteries of his day monks wore distinctive habits,[131] though he does not describe them or specify how they differed from laymen's clothing.[132] We may probably correctly conjecture when we assume that they consisted of a close-fitting tunic, fastened by a linen belt or cincture, and a mantle of coarse cloth.[133] They wore footgear of the usual kind.[134] Their clothes were made of different materials according to the time of year.[135] They were regularly changed and washed. Laundering and storing were done for everyone, so that the monks would always have clean clothing, but not always what they had previously worn.[136]

Augustine's *Rule*, and what he wrote about manual labor in the monastery, give us fairly detailed information about the mode of life which he and his monks followed in the garden monastery. The order of the day for the community was governed by strict rules.[137] Time was divided into hours of prayer, Scripture reading, and physical labor.[138] They came together in the oratory and the dining room.[139] They all went outdoors together; they were together when they went into church, and, when reasons of health required it, to the public baths.[140]

And all their work was done for the benefit of the community. No one was to make anything for himself.[141] The care of the sick was entrusted to one of the monks, the administration of the kitchen to another, and still others looked after books, clothing, and shoes.[142] The majority of the monks must have been able to write. In Pachomius' monasteries, the copying of books had already been considered monastic labor.[143] In his early days at Hippo, Augustine established his own scriptorium and employed skilled stenographers and copyists.[144] We can hardly be mistaken in supposing that there were many monks among them who were not priests.

Undoubtedly, in the garden monastery there were also many brethren who had the training and talent necessary "to explain the readings from Holy Scripture and to discuss certain questions in a fruitful fashion."[145] Nonetheless, for the majority of the monks physical labor would be the usual day's chief occupation. Augustine recommended that they sing psalms as they worked, and thus consecrate their daily tasks "with divine consolation."[146] He regarded work in the monastery as above all else a most excellent means to personal salvation; it did not serve the individual, but was directed toward what Jesus Christ should be to him.[147] It was a duty incumbent upon everyone, the sick and crippled alone excepted. Even if a person was incapable of heavy manual labor, he should somehow make himself useful to the community.[148]

The monastery paid for its members' support out of its common income and from the proceeds of their manual labor. Only in exceptional cases would one have recourse to the charity of the faithful.[149] Poverty and simplicity were the rule, but a goodly sufficiency was also assured. Pressing want seemed to Augustine irreconcilable with the monastic ideal; outright worry over their daily bread would force the brethren to shorten their hours of prayer and reading, if it did not make those exercises altogether impossible.[150]

The relations of the new foundation with the monastery at Tagaste were close. Not only were they economically and financially allied,[151] but they formed one holy community of prayer, sharing one another's joys and sorrows, and encouraging one another in their zeal for virtue.[152]

Furthermore, Augustine probably quite soon handed over the direction of the monastery to someone chosen from among those monks who were not priests.[153] This "superior" (*praepositus*) was to act as a father, accepting the care of the needs of individual monks and of the community as a whole.[154] It was his task to distribute food and clothing,[155] to see to the prompt laundering of clothes,[156] to take charge of gifts and dispose of them,[157] and even to appoint those who were to accompany the monks on their walks.[158] He was to keep careful watch over the monastery's good order, to encourage and console, but also to correct and to punish whenever necessary.[159]

In this way, Augustine was better able to devote himself to his priestly duties and to the monks' pastoral needs.[160] In this period, he began to be active as a preacher in Hippo, and he launched a campaign, with what he said and wrote, against the Manichaeans and the Donatists.[161] It must be concluded that because of this circumstance the apostolic ideal came to exercise a certain influence on the monastic lifestyle of Augustine's foundations.[162] The cases soon multiplied in which monks from the garden monastery who were not priests were ordained or in which clerics asked for admission into the monastic community.[163] Indeed, this development spread to Tagaste, when, in 394 or 395, Alypius succeeded to the episcopal see there.[164]

THE CLERICS' MONASTERY

Augustine found himself faced with fresh problems and difficulties when he was consecrated auxiliary bishop of Hippo in 395 or 396.[165] A heavy responsibility lay ahead of him. "Manichaean heresy, burgeoning paganism, schism in the Church, social-revolutionary unrest in the land, political insecurity throughout the whole empire, . . . its frontiers hammered and shaken by Goths and Vandals, and, within, the Church's many troubles with the clergy and the people—those were the sad signs of the times" when Augustine became a bishop.[166]

Another care was added for him. What was to become of his hopes for his monasteries? He was even more aware of the conflicts between his pastoral duties and what he planned for his monasteries than he had been a few years earlier when he was ordained. When, shortly afterward, Valerius died, and he had to carry the weight of the bishop's office alone, he decided to leave the garden monastery in order not to endanger the peace of the community's existence; as bishop, he could not avoid receiving many visitors to his house.[167]

But he was firmly resolved to continue his own monastic life. So he gathered around him in the "house of the bishop" (*domus episcopi*) [168] clerics who were prepared to join him in a common life of voluntary poverty according to the example of the Apostolic Church.[169] He would have liked best to impose the common life upon all the clergy of Hippo.[170] He called for companions from the garden monastery, which in the days to come would also serve as a seminary for the clergy of the diocese. Augustine would choose only the best and most suited of the lay monks for this holy office.[171]

It corresponded with Augustine's aspirations to a life of apostolic poverty that, to be admitted, candidates must forsake all forms of private possession and accept a completely common life.[172] Therefore, admission was preceded by a final renunciation of money and goods. Whatever anyone possessed, he sold, and either put the proceeds to good use or turned them over to the community.[173] The only reasons Augustine would allow for postponing such testamentary dispositions were obligations to one's loved ones or legal minority.[174] As in the brothers' monastery, entry into this community meant promising oneself to a life, consecrated to God, of chastity, without marriage. The clerical state, too, of its members demanded that they live without marriage. Augustine specifically enjoined celibacy upon the African clergy. When a cleric received ordination, he was committted to forswear matrimony and to live in continence.[175]

On one occasion, during a sermon in the year 426, Augustine himself provided a list of the clerics who lived in his community.[176] Without indicating the order he had received, he named his nephew Patritius.[177] Valens, still very young, is called a subdeacon.[178] The deacons mentioned are Lazarus, who that day by command of the bishop read an excerpt from Acts before the sermon;[179] Faustinus, a former soldier, who had postponed receiving baptism and the diaconate until he had reached Hippo;[180] Severus, who was blind;[181] a deacon of Hippo not given any name, a man of poor circumstances;[182] and, finally, Heraclius, who soon afterward became a priest and later succeeded Augustine as bishop.[183] Augustine speaks, in conclusion, of the priests Leporius, a man from a highly respected family,[184] and Barnabas, who in the year in which he had served as provost had badly managed their affairs.[185] The business dealings of the priest Januarius, who had died not long before and who on his deathbed made a will, although "he had promised his life to the community,"[186] caused Augustine to investigate the conduct of these members—those whom he had just named—of his monastery of clerics toward the common life which they had undertaken. He was able to testify of them all: "I have found them all to be as I wished to find them."[187]

In the community of clerics, social differences were unimportant. What mattered was not how much money or land someone had brought into the monastery with him, but only the measure of his love for God and the brethren.[188] So, too, Augustine regarded it as quite unimportant how a brother disposed of his possessions and for whose benefit.[189]

Community life was organized as in the garden monastery, but with one essential difference: pastoral activity replaced manual labor.[190] The new foundation too was to be an independent monastery, built on the same fundamental ideas as the first. Augustine saw not the slightest objection to calling it the "clerics' monastery" (*monasterium clericorum*).[191] In establishing it, he had surrendered nothing of his plan of an ideal life; he had merely given greater stress to his concern for apostolic work.

Thus the bishop's monastery also combined the active and the contemplative life. Certainly, in the interests of spiritual direction, the daily regimen allowed greater freedom to a cleric than it had to lay monks in the garden monastery. All the same, Augustine's basic principle applied here too: "We should not be so wrapped up in our activities that we no longer want to contemplate God."[192]

They always ate their meals—the two daily repasts then customary, dinner and supper (*prandium* and *cena*)—in common.[193] On fast days, about the frequency of which in Augustine's monasteries we have no reliable information,[194] there was, for everyone who could observe them, only one meal, supper after None. Eating anything except at these mealtimes[195] and outside the house was forbidden. Augustine permitted only those who were sick or convalescent to take anything in the mornings; and he had no objection if the pious showed a special gift for abstinence.[196]

At these common meals, which were accompanied by religious readings or edifying conversation, their cultivation of the Christian common life was particularly evident. Augustine loved conversation. They talked about the events of the day, about their pastoral undertakings, or they discussed theological and religious questions.[197] Augustine took special care that such conversation should be free of uncharitable and slanderous stories about those who were absent. He had a distich carved on the table top to serve as a constant warning:

> If anyone feeds by biting at other men's backs,
> He will not find at this table the food that he lacks.

Possidius, his biographer, recounts an incident which he himself one day witnessed. A few bishops who were Augustine's close friends took part in the conventual meal. In the course of the conversation at table they forgot its inscription, and did not behave as it enjoined. Augustine reproved them strenuously. Very upset, he said that either the verses on the table would have to be erased or he would leave the meal and go to his room.[198]

He also took punitive measures against frivolous oaths, which in North Africa were a very bad habit. If anyone offended in this at the table, Augustine made him do penance by withholding one cup of wine from his daily allotment.[199]

There was considerable entertaining in the bishop's monastery, especially of visiting clerics and bishops. Strangers were also welcomed, despite the danger that one might be sheltering unworthy guests. Augustine would have preferred to receive an evil man in his house than once to deny some good man his hospitality.[200] That he kept this house open gave occasion to the legend that he was once privileged to shelter the Lord Himself in the guise of a poor pilgrim.[201] Women, on the other hand, never gained access to the monastery. By this prohibition, Augustine wanted to protect not only the virtue but the good name of his clerics.[202]

Usually the meals were simple. Green vegetables and cereals were plentifully served, and, to strengthen the sick and convalescents, meat as well. To please guests, more delicate foods and meat dishes were served. There was always wine; a fixed quantity was allotted to everyone. The vessels in which the food was served were of earthenware, wood, or alabaster. Only the spoons were silver. It was not want that dictated such simplicity; they had decided this by their own free will.[203]

The same simplicity was manifest in the way Augustine and his companions conducted their lives in other respects. Clothing, footwear, and bedclothes befitted their station, and was neither too fine nor slovenly.[204]

In cut and material their clothing was not essentially different from that of the laity. They wore a long-sleeved tunic of linen, and an overgarment, usually of wool, with a hood, called a byrrus, which reached to the knee.[205] All luxury in clothing was to be studiously avoided. Even Augustine, the bishop, was unwilling to wear a better byrrus than his priests and deacons.[206] As couches they would have, as was then usual, a bedstead resting on several feet, stretched with belts or straps. A blanket, probably of wool, was used as a coverlet.[207]

As far as provisions were concerned, the same rule of community prevailed. All were fed and clothed at the expense of the monastery.[208] Costs were borne by the income from ecclesiastical lands and gifts of the faithful. Augustine would have been glad to achieve an even more perfect evangelical poverty, and to be content solely with the faithful's alms. Had that been the case, no causes of envy would have remained, and the clergy would have been freed from dissipating administrative cares. But the faithful of Hippo could not be won over to this plan.[209]

Year by year Augustine appointed one of his clerics, usally a priest, "provost of the church house" (*praepositus domus ecclesiae*).[210] He was not provost (*praepositus*) of the monastery of clerics (*monasterium clericorum*),[211] but he was responsible for the care of the church buildings and all the other property of the church, and was to keep precise records of all income and expenses.[212] At the end of each year Augustine would review these records. He found these administrative chores a crushing burden, and usually tried to keep free of them. His biographer Possidius reports that he never had a key or a seal in his hand.[213]

Augustine was fundamentally opposed to the purchase of houses or parcels of land. The Church's income ought to increase only through the pious gifts of the faithful.[214] He showed great care for the poor and destitute. As monasticism in the East had done, he too, from the beginning, distinguished his monasteries by their corporal works of mercy. Augustine did not shrink from having the church plate melted down to purchase the release of prisoners and to support the many indigent in Hippo.[215]

Though he showed little personal interest in new buildings to serve pastoral and charitable ends, for he saw in them a heavy bond, he allowed considerable freedom to the wishes of the brethren.[216] With his permission the deacon Heraclius built a shrine to receive the relics of Stephen Protomartyr,[217] and the priest Leporius built a basilica dedicated to "the eight martyrs."[218] He also allowed the priest Barnabas to build a new monastery,[219] and, on his behalf, Leporius also built a hospice for strangers and pilgrims.[220]

The clerics in the monastery shared with Augustine the burden of apostolic works. His closest collaborators in divine service and in the care of souls were the priests and deacons. It was incumbent upon the priests occasionally, as his representatives and on his commission, to offer the Holy Sacrifice, preach, and administer the sacraments. The deacons were the bishop's assistants at the Mass, especially at the distribution of Holy Communion, which was given under both species; they might also assist in the instruction of catechumens. It would seem that, from the lower ranks of the clergy, only the lectors were prominent. They were responsible for the readings from Scripture and for leading the chants.[221]

From those who had received Holy Orders or who were to be promoted to a higher order, Augustine demanded not only the prescribed age but, more than anything else, good conduct and sufficient knowledge.[222] Candidates for orders had to possess adequate general education and, in particular, be well acquainted with Holy Scripture. The Bible was the proper school book and manual for future preachers and catechists. Furthermore, they could have had no better survey of homiletic material than Augustine's own sermons. In fact, among the African clergy of their day, Augustine's clerics were noteworthy for their education and their exemplary mode of life, as the efforts of neighboring dioceses to acquire from among them bishops and priests bear eloquent witness. In his bishop's monastery, Augustine had trained clergy who were well schooled and formed to acquit themselves well in the approaching times of persecution.[223]

Augustine's monastery of clerics was not the first attempt to unite monasticism and the priesthood in the West. St. Eusebius, bishop of Vercelli (d. 371), after his return from exile in the East, had established a similar monastic community of clerics (ca. 363) and, with the clergy of his cathedral church, lived a common life, dedicated to the praise of God, the care of souls, and study.[224] Whether Augustine knew of Eusebius and his foundation is not certain; but it is clear that he was to give this new institution a stronger basis.[225]

MONASTERIES FOR WOMEN

Augustine must have founded a first monastery for women in the 390s,[226] but exactly when the foundation occurred and where it was we do not know. There is specific mention, at any rate in later years, of a convent of women in Hippo itself.[227] The Augustinian houses of nuns were on the same economic and spiritual footing as the communities of brothers: a life according to the ideals of Acts, in total personal poverty, vowed to the common life. It was precisely in this that Augustine perceived the "better gifts" (1 Cor. 12:31) in this cloistered way of life, as contrasted with that of virgins in the world consecrated to God.[228]

The direction of the house was in the hands of the "mother" (*mater*), as Augustine called the superior. She relinquished only the spiritual direction of the nuns to a priest.[229] In important internal monastic matters, perhaps he sought her advice, as he would consult the lay superior of a men's community,[230] or perhaps he himself made the decision. Entering a women's convent was permitted to other clerics and monks only in extraordinary cases and with the special approval of the bishop.[231] Augustine himself avoided all unnecessary visiting, and reserved to himself only general supervision.[232]

Augustine mentions that cloistered women—he calls them "virgins of Christ" (*virgines Christi*)[233] or "nuns" (*sanctimoniales*)[234]—consecrated themselves to conventual life by a "profession" (*professio*).[235] We may presume that there was a liturgical celebration of the "veiling" (*velatio*) or "consecration" (*consecratio*), since by that time there was such a celebration whenever virgins consecrated themselves to God in the world;[236] there is, however, no certain evidence of this in Augustine's writings.[237]

Evidently the women in his convents wore a distinctive habit,[238] though Augustine does not describe it or indicate how it differed from customary feminine attire.[239] Like married women,[240] nuns wore a thick veil, which completely covered their hair and their hair nets and was held in place by a headband.[241]

Widows as well as virgins were admitted to Augustine's convents. In fact, at the time of her death, one of Augustine's widowed sisters was the superior of a convent; and some of his cousins and nieces lived as nuns.[242]

COMMUNAL PRAYER AND CELEBRATION OF THE EUCHARIST

The monasteries which Augustine founded in Hippo were places of prayer. Communal prayer formed a daily offering of the monks and nuns, but assisting at the Eucharistic sacrifice was the religious climax of each day in the monastery.

They assembled several times during the day for community prayers—the special prayers of the "hours" were intended to sanctify the various sections of the day[243]—and probably observed the times of prayer which by then were customary in the monasteries of Italy and the East.[244] They rose before dawn in order to carry out the "vigils," but whether these were observed every day in Augustine's monasteries cannot be clearly perceived from the sermon in which he mentions the matter.[245] The night office consisted of Scripture readings and prayers,[246] and began with the first cockcrow. Yet sometimes in their zeal for prayer, they began even sooner; indeed, on Easter Eve they and the faithful spent the entire night in prayer in the episcopal church.[247] The African Church had for a long time observed Terce, Sext, and None as the times of prayer during the day, as well as prayer in the morning and evening—"at the coming of the light and of the night" (*ingressu lucis et noctis*)[248]—and these hours of prayer would have been observed in Augustine's monasteries. Augustine himself specifically mentions in a letter written in 395, while he was still a priest, to Alypius in Tagaste, that the "brethren"—in this instance, probably the monks in the garden monastery—on the feast of St. Leontius, a bishop of Hippo, were present in the basilica at midday (*meridiano tempore*) or soon afterward (*postmeridiano die*) for "reading" and "the prayer of the psalms," and that a little while before darkness fell, as on every day (*vespertina, quae quotidie solent*), Vespers with the "hymn" were sung.[249]

In one of his sermons, Augustine also calls this last office, held in the late afternoon, the "service of the lamps" (*lucernarium*).[250]

Although in the letter just mentioned Augustine suggests that the brethren must have assembled for common prayer in the church, his *Rule* expressly states that they prayed to God "in psalms and hymns" at the fixed hours in the monastic oratory.[251] Thus, monks who were not priests cannot have followed the custom of the clerics' monastery, reciting their common hours in the basilica. On the contrary, the members of the clerics' monastery must from the beginning have performed their liturgical prayer together with the bishop in his church, in what was known as the "Basilica of Peace" (*basilica pacis*).[252] This was the biggest of the town's Christian holy places,[253] and therefore was also known as the "major basilica" (*basilica maior*).[254] Presumably it was located immediately alongside the bishop's residence.

During the excavations which in recent decades have unearthed important sectors of the town quarters of ancient Hippo Regius, the ruins of two ancient Christian basilicas have come to light. One of them, smaller in proportions, is divided into five naves, and has a rectangular choir. The second, close to it, is one of the largest church buildings which have been found in North Africa. It is twenty meters wide and, the presbytery included, forty-nine meters long. In the semicircular apse, raised above the level of the nave, there are still, on both sides, stone benches for the clergy, and in the center of the rear wall the base of the bishop's throne. The basilica is divided into three naves by two rows, each of six columns; the central nave is twice the width of those at the sides. The entire floor of the edifice was covered with mosaics, remnants of which are preserved; and in the side naves there is a series of gravestones. Beneath one especially richly decorated stone a grave was found, which subsequently must have been reopened and emptied. A chapel had been built onto the right-hand side nave, eighteen meters long and four wide, broadening into five meters at the rounded apse. Turning from here to the right, one enters the baptistry, in the middle of which, surrounded by four small columns, there is a marble font, three meters long, two wide, and one deep. To the left of the basilica, separated by a pair of smaller rooms, through which there may have run a corridor, there was a chapel, constructed from a row of three trefoil niches, the middle one five meters, the two others each four meters deep.[255]

Erwan Marec, the director of excavations at Hippo for many years, considers it very probable that this excavated basilica is Augustine's episcopal church, the so-called "Basilica of Peace,"[256] because of the dimensions of the building, which agree in remarkable fashion with one indication given by Augustine in a sermon,[257] and the finding of the episcopal throne, the baptistry, the subsequently opened grave, which might be considered Augustine's first burial place, and many other corresponding details. Marec supposes that in the chapel built to adjoin the church's east end there was the *consignatorium*, in which the bishop was accustomed to administer confirmation to the newly baptized, and in the small edifice with the three niches perhaps the *memoria* which was constructed by the deacon Heraclius, a member of Augustine's clerical community, in 424–425 to house the relics of Stephen Protomartyr.[258] Marec's hypothesis received strong support from an investigation, published by Othmar Perler in 1955, of the chief church and other Christian holy places in Hippo in the light of Augustine's writings.[259] Of course, no final determination will be reached until the entire area of the ancient town has been excavated.

Perler's investigations also provide some interesting details about the interior of Augustine's church. A few steps led down from the apse into the nave. That was where the altar stood, free of the apse, in the front part of the central nave. There was a lateral space about the altar, from which the people were excluded by the altar rails (*cancelli*). The ambo was probably placed inside them. The bishop and the assisting clergy stood here around the altar during the Eucharistic sacrifice; but during Easter Week the newly baptized also had their place in this hallowed area. The altar, shaped like a table, was probably made of wood. There were still no benches inside the church; the faithful were separated according to sex.[260] The lay monks and the nuns probably had their own places in the basilica.[261]

The faithful seem occasionally to have been present at the daily common prayer of the members of the clerics' monastery in the bishop's church and to have taken part in the singing of psalms.[262] Augustine considered the ordering and beauty of common prayer to be important. Various postures were used for prayer. When prayers of special solemnity were recited—during the Easter season and on Sundays—it was customary to stand, but during other prayers, expressive of penitence, to kneel. But the greater part of the psalms and Scripture readings were performed while people sat.[263] Often during prayer they lifted up their outspread hands. Many prayers were recited as they turned to the East. Often, and especially when they began their prayers and recited the creed, they signed themselves with the sign of the cross on their foreheads.[264] In performing liturgical prayer, too, certain rules were followed. This was not to be left to the pleasure and the mood of individuals: "Sing nothing but what the regulations prescribe."[265]

Augustine first became acquainted with liturgical chant as a recent convert in Milan. There, not only did he hear the older mode of responsorial singing, in which the psalm was sung by one or more singers, to which the people replied with a refrain, the "response" (*responsorium*), often repeated; but Ambrose was the first bishop in the West to introduce in his church the new, Eastern mode of performing the psalms by two alternating (antiphonal) choirs, in which the people could take a more active part. At this time the bishop had composed the first Latin hymns for liturgical use and had them presented in this new fashion.[266]

The introduction of responsorial and antiphonal chant into the liturgy found opponents in many places who considered it unseemly for liturgical use and who wished to forbid it in the Church. They preferred the mode of celebration St. Athanasius had once prescribed for Alexandria, which was more a sustained reading-tone than singing.[267]

We can find evidence for the use both of responsorial and antiphonal chant and of St. Ambrose's hymns in the episcopal church at Hippo.[268] And this mode was probably practiced by the Augustinian lay monks in their oratories.[269] Augustine had already countered the objections to it.[270] He too had seen that there was no little danger that someone might be captivated more by the chant than by the words chanted, more by a minister's fine voice and by delight in his singing than by the content of what was sung. Yet he considered it unduly strict if "one would therefore forbid to the Church all those sweet melodies to which David's psalms are sung." Recalling how deeply he had been moved by the chanting of the psalms and hymns in the episcopal church at Milan and how at the time he had experienced the Church's chant as a breath of God's grace, he reflected how even now as a bishop the psalms when they were chanted moved him far more to devotion than if they were not sung.[271] Moreover, chant was able "to move one's spirit to devotion and to enkindle the heart with divine love."[272] Thus he believed that singing in church should be approved so that the pleasure of the ears might lift the soul to more fervent devotion.[273] True, he cautions against chanting when "the voice rings out loud while the heart remains mute."[274] Devotion and fervor ought to inspire one's prayer, just as they do when one serves the monastic community and performs one's service in God's sight.[275]

The climax of the monastic divine service was the celebration of the ɛ, at which the monks were present every day in the episcopal [276] With the exception of Maundy Thursday and the Easter Vigil, ɔok place in the early morning.[277] Augustine's writings and sermons us a lively picture of this daily celebration. He informs us, down to smallest details, about the progress of the sacred ceremonies and the prayers.[278]

The service began with the solemn entry of the clergy. Augustine and his clerics wore what was customary in their time: a linen cassock-like tunic with long sleeves, and over it the byrrus, a woolen cloak with a hood. Special liturgical vestments were as yet unknown.[279] When he arrived at the throne, the bishop greeted the congregation with "The Lord be with you"; the clergy, in the meantime, had taken their places. The lector who was serving mounted the ambo and read the Epistle aloud. Then, with the lector leading, a psalm was sung; after every verse the clergy and the people answered with a brief response. With this, the climax of the Mass of the Catechumens had been reached: the lector chanted the Gospel of the day to a solemn tone.[280] Then Augustine customarily delivered a sermon either from his bishop's throne or from the ambo,[281] during which it would often happen that his lively audience would interrupt him with cries of applause or questions.[282] When the catechumens were dismissed, the service of readings ended.

After Augustine had again greeted the congregation with "The Lord be with you," he stepped down to the ambries to receive the gifts of the faithful. The people's offertory procession was accompanied by the choir singing the psalms. Afterward the bishop went to the altar. Loudly he pronounced the liturgical acclamations "The Lord be with you," "Lift up your hearts," "Let us give thanks to the Lord our God." The Eucharistic prayer of praise and thanks followed. Then once more the bishop spoke loudly, and began to use a solemn tone, in pronouncing the words of consecration. The clergy and the people answered with a powerful "Amen" ("So be it"). After the consecration there was a prayer for the entire Church of God, followed by the commemoration of the living and the dead. Priests who were present, bishops who had died, and consecrated virgins were mentioned by name; and at the end the bishop read out a list of the names of twenty African martyrs. Then the consecrated bread was distributed; and afterward Augustine recited the "Lord's Prayer." At the words "Forgive us our trespasses," the entire congregation struck their breasts as a sign of their contrition. Now the faithful exchanged the kiss of peace, saying to one another "Peace be with you"—"And also with you." Meanwhile the bishop and the clergy received Holy Communion. Then Augustine pronounced a prayer of blessing over the people, a fervent entreaty that the faithful be purified from evil and preserved in their love for one another. Then they advanced to the ambries. Augustine permitted not only the clergy, monks, and nuns daily access to Holy Communion, but also the laity. Before receiving the Eucharist, they followed the custom of the entire Church at that time by abstaining from food and drink, so that, as Augustine once expressed it, "in honor of so exalted a sacrament, the body of the Lord may enter the Christian's mouth before any other food."[283] Furthermore, Augustine stressed his demand that a necessary condition was to be free of heavy debt: "So pay heed, brother. If you will taste the heavenly bread, bring to the altar a clean conscience. If you have committed everyday sins, be free at least of those that are mortal."[284] The individual faithful received the sacred bread from the bishop in their hands placed one over the other, and a deacon gave them the chalice to drink from. The then customary formula of distribution seems most likely to have been "The Body of Christ" and "The Blood of Christ." In any case, the recipient attested his faith with the word "Amen."[285] The choir accompanied the distribution of the Holy Eucharist with the chanting of psalms. A prayer of thanksgiving followed; and then the bishop with the clergy left the church.

For Augustine and his monks and clerics, the daily communal celebration of the liturgy represented the firm bond uniting their souls and enclosing them in a holy community in God. Augustine saw in the Eucharist the mysterious and efficacious symbol of the unity of hearts among Christians. "Those who feast upon such bread," he wrote in one of his explanations of St. John's Gospel, "do not contend with one another, for all of us are one bread, one body. Through this bread God makes concord in the house."[286]

FRIENDS IN BETHLEHEM AND NOLA

After his return from Italy in 388, it would seem that Augustine did not again leave his native Africa. He was not fond of too much traveling. Sea voyages, in particular, must have been very difficult for him.[287]

And yet he was a man of catholic breadth. His care and attention were not confined to the narrow boundaries of Hippo's little see. Very early, he was counted as a champion of the Catholic cause throughout North Africa. And his pronouncements as bishop were respected overseas. During his lifetime he was a respected authority in the Church.

His ideals of monastic life, too, very soon manifested this impulse toward catholic breadth. This showed itself in his efforts to establish ties with monasticism outside North Africa.

In his early years as a priest Augustine had established a personal relationship, which he maintained during a long lifetime, with the learned Jerome, the hermit of Bethlehem, and with his monastic foundations. These contacts may have had stimulating effects even in his own monasteries.

About the year 393 Alypius, Augustine's friend and confrere, made a pilgrimage to the Holy Land and while he was in Bethlehem also visited the saintly Jerome. After his return he must have given detailed reports not only about Jerome's literary activities but also about the monasteries he had founded.[288] But the friendship so established between Jerome and Augustine was for a time overclouded, indeed much imperiled, through a mishap to Augustine when he sent his first letter to Jerome.[289] Yet by patience and moderation, Augustine succeeded little by little in overcoming to a degree the distrust of the aging and highly sensitive Jerome.

In the nineteen letters of considerable theological content Jerome and Augustine exchanged during the course of twenty-five years, Augustine's friendly relations with the Bethlehem monastery and with its founder were often mentioned. Only rarely does Jerome, who specifically calls himself the collaborator of Augustine and then of Alypius, fail to remember them in some special greeting.[290] Occasionally he gives Augustine news of events in the Bethlehem monastery. About the year 416 he informs him that Eustochium and the younger Paula, whom he calls Augustine's spiritual daughters, are living a life worthy of his exhortations. He sends him their greetings, and associates himself and the community of the brothers in this.[291] And in a letter to Augustine written two years later, there is a greeting from the "holy brethren" and the "holy, venerable daughters."[292] Shortly before his death Jerome wrote a final letter to both Augustine and Alypius. With great sorrow he tells them of Eustochium's death, and again sends the greetings of Paula, the dead woman's niece, who in her sorrow recommends herself to the bishops' prayers. The letter also contains greetings from the Roman widow Albina and her daughter, the young Melania, who about this time had settled in Bethlehem. Jerome calls them the "holy children" of the two African bishops since these Roman matrons had spent several years in North Africa and had received encouragement in their pursuit of an ascetic and religious life from Augustine, and especially from his friend Alypius.[293]

Paulinus, later the bishop of Nola, and his wife, Theresia, showed great admiration for the monastic life of Augustine and his monks.[294] This cultured man of senatorial rank had renounced all worldly honors after the early death of his son Celsus and with his wife had decided to live continently. In 394 he was ordained a priest at the insistence of the people of Barcelona; soon afterward he sold a great part of his possessions and left with his wife for Nola in Campania, where they settled. Here, he gathered monks around him, and with them practiced a "monklike brotherhood" (*fraternitas monacha*) in poverty and strict asceticism.[295]

Their common love for a life wholly dedicated to God[296] early established for Augustine and Paulinus an intimate and lasting friendship. When Augustine was still a priest, the young monastic community around him at Hippo found edification in the restrained courtesy of this onetime great statesman and in his zealous "seeking for the Lord."[297] Augustine was certainly speaking for his brethren when, after he was consecrated bishop, he invited Paulinus to come to take up residence in Africa.[298] Yet this wish was not fulfilled. It is likely that these two holy men never met, but messengers carrying letters between them often journeyed between Hippo and Nola. In 396 Paulinus sent two of his companions, Romanus and Agilis, to Hippo, and through them established the first personal relations.[299] Later, clerics from Augustine's monastery, or bishops on friendly terms with him who had to travel to Italy on Church business, consented to carry messages. So, in the year 405, Bishops Theasius and Evodius stayed with Paulinus in Nola,[300] as did Quintus the deacon in 408,[301] and, in that same year, Possidius, who by that time was bishop of Calama.[302] Alypius, too, as bishop of Tagaste must once have visited Nola.[303]

It was a joy for Augustine and his companions if someone should appear from Nola bringing letters or oral messages from Paulinus. The letters were read aloud to the community,[304] for there almost always were special greetings in them to Augustine's companions.[305] Likewise, Augustine never failed to send greetings in return to this friend of his clerics and monks.[306] Paulinus was also in personal communication with many of Augustine's companions, as he was after 395 with Alypius of Tagaste,[307] and with Profuturus, bishop of Cirta, and Severus, bishop of Mileve, all three of whom had come from Augustine's monasteries.[308] Thus this friendship was not restricted to St. Augustine and St. Paulinus, but included in its community of holy love those who shared with them the monastic life and their pastoral cares.

As in his friendship with Jerome, so too in his exchange of letters with Paulinus Augustine displayed in what he wrote of his monastic ideals a truly catholic breadth. He was unfeignedly devoted to everyone in the Church who was seeking to serve Christ "in His holy army."

AUGUSTINE AS "SERVANT OF GOD" IN THE COMMUNITY OF HIS BRETHREN

What Augustine required of others he realized in his own life. Possidius expressly testifies that in his life words and deeds were in harmony.[309]

Augustine joined the community of "God's poor men" voluntarily and unreservedly, and even as a bishop exercised a total personal poverty. Indeed, he owned literally nothing that he could have called his own. For that reason on his deathbed he declined to make a will.[310] What he received as personal gifts he accepted only as the property of the community, and allowed those to benefit from it who had need of it. He wanted nothing better than his brethren had.[311] His clothing, his couch, and his entire way of life were simple and modest.[312]

Even if, with his delicate physical constitution,[313] he was unable to undertake severe penances,[314] still he made vigorous war in the spirit of Christian asceticism upon our threefold concupiscence. From the day of his conversion he put away forever the evil of illicit sexual satisfaction.[315] His ideal form of living was unmarried chastity dedicated to God, and he sought to preserve it through wise precaution. He spoke to women only in the presence of witnesses, unless what had to be discussed was secret. He was absolutely opposed to the idea that women should live under the same roof as he or the brethren, even though they might be blood relatives.[316]

He tamed his greed with frequent fasts.[317] He had much opportunity to exercise asceticism in the custody of his eyes, which had brought him so much longing for "lovely and varying forms and gleaming, pleasing colors."[318] And he swore to do battle against the curiosity of his outer and inner senses.[319] He took great pains to preserve recollection, which was not made easy for him by the distracting cares of his office.[320] And he fought, as well, against the first stirrings of ambition.[321]

The daily demands of his bishop's office upon him were excessive, quite apart from his voluminous correspondence and the many friendly offices he willingly accepted. He had very little time for rest and relaxation,[322] and he usually spent what leisure time he did have in prayer or in spiritual exercise. "If he was at leisure," his biographer Possidius wrote, "he withdrew into the depths of his soul, or sought to fathom new depths of divine matters."[323] And his activities as a spiritual director, as the body of his letters which have survived allows us to see, were a daily occasion of earnest intercession for the sanctification and perseverance of his Christians and for the conversion of unbelievers and of those who had gone astray.[324]

As superior of the monastery, Augustine was a true father to his subjects. Even though, because of his episcopal duties, he could not give them his undivided time, still he was glad to sacrifice to them many of his free hours. It was a pleasant recreation for him if he could converse with them or instruct them on religious questions.[325] He bore their mistakes with patience,[326] and reprimanded breaches of the *Rule* with a loving seriousness, or deliberately passed them over, as circumstances required.[327] If he had to go as far as punishment, he was motivated in this, too, by love. Thus, in everything he realized what his monastic *Rule* required: he counted himself happy to be able to serve his subjects in love.[328] He was indeed in his life that "servant of Christ and of His members," as he so loved in his letters to describe himself.[329]

NOTES

1. *Confessions* 9.8.17.
2. *The City of God* 22.8.
3. Possidius 3.
4. See the interesting comparison of Augustine's *Rule* with those of Pachomius and Basil in Lorenz, "Anfänge, 46–59.
5. The treatise *The Teacher* originated in Augustine's conversations with his son, Adeodatus (*Retractations* 1.12 [11]; cf. also *Confessions* 9.6.14); *On 83 Various Questions*, in the brethren's queries (*Retractations* 1.26 [25]). Cf. also R. Flórez, "Sobre la mentalidad de Agustín en los primeros años de su monacato: El 'Libro de las ochenta y tres cuestiones,'" CD, 169 (1956), 464–77.
6. Flórez, "Sobre la mentalidad de Agustín," 473–77.
7. See, for instance, the "hymn" to the Church in *The Ways of the Catholic Church* 1.30.62f. Cf. J. Ratzinger, *Volk und Haus Gottes in Augustins Lehre von der Kirche* (Munich, 1954), pp. 24f.
8. 1.6.1.
9. *True Religion* 55.107.
10. 1.31.67.
11. 1.26ff.49ff.

12. Hendrikx, *Augustins Verhältnis*, p. 73, and Ratzinger, *Volk und Haus Gottes*, p. 39. Then one cannot justly reproach him that at this time he knew nothing of the true love of neighbor, which was in him "the expression of a badly disguised love of self" (Hofmann, *Kirchenbegriff*, p. 31).

13. Cf. *Letter 15* 2 and *Letter 18* 1f.

14. *Letter 18* 2.

15. *Letter* 20 2.

16. *Confessions* 9.3.6.

17. *Letter 10* 1.

18. *Letter* 9 1.

19. Gavigan dates it in the year 389 at the very latest ("St. Augustine's Friend Nebridius," 52).

20. 9.3.6.

21. *Letter* 6 (in the collection of Augustine's *Letters*) 1. *Letters 11* and *12* attempt a philosophical explanation of the truth of Christian doctrine concerning the Incarnation and the Trinity.

22. " . . . secessio a tumultu rerum labentium . . . " (*Letter 10* 2).

23. Ibid. Cf. G. Folliet, "'Deificari in otio': Augustin, Epistula 10, 2," in *Recherches Augustiniennes* II (Paris, 1962), pp. 225–36. For the present state of the debate on the influence of Porphyry on the young Augustine, see O'Meara, "Augustine and Neo-Platonism," pp. 95ff.

24. *Letter 10* 2f. Without a doubt, we can hear echoes of the Stoic ἀταραξία and ἀπάθεια then most strongly influencing Augustine.

25. *Letter 10* 3.

26. Cf. *Retractations* 1.26 (25).

27. *On 83 Various Questions*, question 25.

28. Ibid., question 54.

29. *Letter 14* 4.

30. For the date and occasions of these treatises, see *Retractations* 1.9–12.

31. 1.10. Cf. also Hofmann, *Kirchenbegriff*, pp. 49ff., and Hendrikx, *Augustins Verhältnis*, pp. 71–80. For his views on education in these years, see Marrou, *Saint Augustin et la fin de la culture antique*, pp. 159–327.

32. I agree in this estimate with Halliburton ("Inclination to Retirement," p. 339); see above, pp. 7–8.

33. *The Ways of the Catholic Church* 1.31.66.

34. Ibid. 1.31.65.

35. *Confessions* 9.8.17.

36. *Letter* 5.

37. *Sermon 355* 2 and Possidius 3. Cf. J. J. Gavigan, *De vita monastica in Africa Septentrionali inde a temporibus S. Augustini usque ad invasiones Arabum* (Rome & Turin, 1962), p. 34.

38. *Letter 157* 39 and Possidius 2.

39. *Confessions* 8.12.29.

40. Ibid. 2.3.5f.

41. *Sermon 356* 13.

42. Augustine is exaggerating the property's smallness somewhat when in

one place (*Letter 126* 7) he writes of "my father's little field" (*pauca agellula paterna*).

43. *Letter 157* 39.

44. *Sermon 355* 2.

45. *Letter 126* 7.

46. Possidius 5; *Sermon 355* 2.

47. This is the surmise of L. Bertrand (*Der heilige Augustin*, trans. M. E. Graf von Platen-Hallermund [Paderborn, 1927], pp. 203f.) and von Kienitz (*Augustinus*, p. 150), both of whom allude to pious bequests of this period with similar provisions. Founders wanted to be free both of the cares of administration and of oppressive taxation.

48. *Letter 83* 2.

49. *Letter 83* 2f.

50. Especially from Romanianus (cf. *Confessions* 6.14.24), with whom Augustine maintained close and friendly ties even though Romanianus still could not decide to enter the monastic community (cf. *Letter 15*). In addition to Romanianus, Nebridius mentions a certain Lucinianus, who also took a friendly interest in Augustine (cf. *Letter 5*).

51. Cf. also Lorenz, "Anfänge," 40f. In his note 21 Lorenz draws attention to the passage in *Against the Academics* (3.6.13) in which Augustine adopted Cicero's definition of friendship, in his *Laelius*, word for word.

52. G. Folliet has recently strongly contested this ("Aux Origines de l'ascéticisme et du cénobitisme africain," *Studia Anselmiana*, 46 [1961], 25–44): "Augustine's establishment resembled more a house of philosophers, of men of letters, than a monastery" (p. 38). He raises the following individual objections to the monastic character of the foundation at Tagaste: (*a*) The freedom of mind (*otium*) at Tagaste for which Augustine longed was that of the philosophers, as the content of the letters and other writings he composed testifies (pp. 36f.). (*b*) Only Augustine, apparently, renounced personal possessions and transferred them to the community (p. 38). (*c*) The Lord's counsel to the rich young man was impossible for Augustine to achieve before the end of the year at Tagaste; only then did Augustine, in fact, renounce his possessions (p. 40 and note 66). (*d*) Both Augustine and Possidius took pains to avoid describing the Tagaste community as a *monasterium* (p. 39). (*e*) In *Sermon 355* 2, Augustine, now an aged bishop, gives an explicit account of how, as a young man, he had gone to Hippo in search for a place "where I might institute a *monasterium* and live with my brethren"; this, Folliet asserts, was the first monastery he founded (pp. 41f.). Folliet is candid enough to concede, toward the end of the article, that at Tagaste Augustine, with a few friends, servants of God living in continence as he was, began to live a common life of great simplicity, a life of prayer, labor, and mutual help. But even then he considers that he must specifically deny the monastic character of this life. He writes: "But for Augustine this life was only a stage; his immersion in Christianity, his personal meditation on Sacred Scripture, his recollections of what Pontitianus had told him about the monks who inhabited the Egyptian wildernesses, as well as what he remembered of those houses of ascetics which

he had visited in Milan and Rome, were drawing him toward a more complete renunciation" (pp. 43f.). This evaluation of the facts of a truly cenobitic life, previously dispassionately recounted, is somewhat surprising. Why should this be a mere "recollection" of the reports of the lives of the monks when Augustine and his friends so clearly sought to put a common "serving God" (*Deo servire*) into practice, even if they did adapt this to their own circumstances? Or how can this be described as a "stage" when Augustine and his companions had decided to consecrate themselves forever to God's service when they renounced matrimony and earthly ambitions? Clearly these points are decisive when one seeks to answer the question whether the life at Tagaste did or did not manifest a monastic character. As far as Folliet's contrary arguments are concerned, I think that I have given a sufficient answer to his first three points in what I have demonstrated in this chapter. Furthermore, the question whether and to what extent the renunciation of personal possessions was in fact carried out at once by all the members of the community need not be decisive for the monastic character of their life together. Just as little can it be determined from the circumstance that neither Augustine nor Possidius employed the expression *monasterium* for the Tagaste community that they wished to deny that this common life had a monastic character. We can see, because they call the common life at Tagaste "serving God" (*Deo servire*) or "living for God" (*Deo vivere*), and the members the "servants of God" (*Dei servi*), that they took a clear stance on this question. What is more, I have already indicated that in *The Ways of the Catholic Church* as well Augustine nowhere employs the word *monasterium*, not even for the houses of Egyptian cenobites, whose monastic character he certainly does not wish to deny because of this. Folliet's final argument draws conclusions from *Sermon 355* 2 which cannot be made to follow. Augustine does not in any case maintain that in the plan which he formed then for a new monastic foundation there was any thought at all of the first monastery which he had established. That at that time the founding of additional monasteries was of concern to him, we can presume from *Letter 22* 9 in which a foundation in Carthage is mentioned. Finally, we must not forget that a letter of St. Paulinus to Alypius (*Letter 24* [in the collection of Augustine's *Letters*] 6) specifically testifies that as early as the year 394 there were *monasteria* in Hippo and Carthage as well as in Tagaste.

53. Cf. Lorenz, "Anfänge," p. 41, and the literature which he cites in note 31, especially G. Penco, "La vita ascetica come 'filosofia' nell'antica tradizione monastica," *Studia Monastica*, 2 (1960), 79–93.

54. Yet the generalizing formula of L. Cilleruelo ("Caratteri del monacato agostiniano," AVSM I, p. 45), "Monasticism is a philosophy for him," is hardly apt. See also J. Morán, "Filosofía y monacato en San Agustín," *Religión y Cultura*, 2 (1957), 625–54, who writes in a similar generalizing fashion: "The monasticism of St. Augustine is a department of his philosophy" (pp. 625, 641), asserting about his *Rule* that it "is the catechism of Augustinian philosophy" (p. 650).

55. Cf. *Letter 5* (in the collection of Augustine's *Letters*).

56. *Letter 4* 2.

57. *Letter 10* 1.

58. Possidius 3. Cf. *Retractations* 1.25.

59. *Letter 20* 2.

60. We may presume from *Letter 84* 1 that Evodius joined Augustine in these first years.

61. Cf. *Letter 83*.

62. Ibid. 4.

63. There are no proofs in Augustine's writings for the supposition of U. Domínguez-del Val ("Cultura y formación intelectual en los monasterios agustinianos de Tagaste, Cartago e Hipona," CD, 169 [1956], 428) that Augustine's brother Navigius was also in Tagaste.

64. *Confessions* 9.6.14.

65. Possidius 3.

66. *Letter 21*, *Sermon 355* 2, Possidius 3f.

67. *Sermon 355* 2.

68. See below, pp. 47–48.

69. On this, see F. van de Meer, *Augustinus de Zielzorger* (Utrecht & Brussels, 1947), pp. 27ff.

70. Cf. J. Zellinger, *Augustin und die Volksfrömmigkeit* (Munich, 1933), pp. 8ff.

71. *The Catechizing of the Uninstructed* 16.25.

72. *Sermon 355* 2.

73. Ibid. Cf. also Possidius 3.

74. Possidius 3f., *Letter 21* 2. Cf. W. Roetzer, *Des heiligen Augustinus Schriften als liturgiegeschichtliche Quelle* (Munich, 1930), pp. 199ff.

75. *Letter 21* 1.

76. Ibid. 3f.

77. *Christian Instruction* 4.4.6.

78. Cf. H. J. Vogels, "Die Heilige Schrift bei Augustinus," in *Aurelius Augustinus*, edd. M. Grabmann and J. Mausbach (Cologne, 1930), pp. 411ff.; and Marrou, *Saint Augustin et la fin de la culture antique*, pp. 391–430.

79. *Letter 137* 3. Cf. also *Letter 55* 38.

80. *Letter 55* 39, *Letter 132*.

81. Cf. *Letter 21* 3.

82. *Letter 55* 38f.

83. Possidius 19.

84. *Letter 48* 1.

85. Possidius 19.

86. *The Work of Monks* 29.37.

87. Some have wished to see in this a "certain spiritual egoism." Cf. Hendrikx, *Augustins Verhältnis*, p. 81.

88. Hofmann, *Kirchenbegriff*, pp. 74, 79ff. Cf. idem, "Wandlungen in der Frömmigkeit und Theologie des heiligen Augustinus," *Theologie und Glauben*, 22 (1930), 420; and T. Specht, *Die Lehre von der Kirche nach dem heiligen Augustin* (Paderborn, 1892).

89. Cf. *Letter 48* 1.

90. Possidius 18.

91. *Letter 48* 2.

92. Cf. *Letter 231*. Cf. also *Letter 130*, *Letter 147*, *Letter 217*.

93. Cf. *Confessions* 10.43.70.

94. Cf. Adam, *Die geistige Entwicklung*, p. 33. M. Wundt overstates the case, however, when he describes the effects of priestly ordination on Augustine's life as a "sharp break" with his previous spiritual orientation ("Ein Wendepunkt für Augustins Entwicklung," *Zeitschrift für neutestamentliche Wissenschaft*, 21 [1922], 60ff., and his "Nachtrag zu 'Augustins Konfessionen,'" ibid., 23 [1924], 154). H. Dörries, "Das Verhältnis des Neuplatonischen und Christlichen in Augustins *De vera religione*," ibid., 102; Mausbach, "Entwicklung," 6; and Hofmann, *Kirchenbegriff*, p. 79*n*8.

95. *Sermon 355* 2. Cf. Possidius 3: "within the church" (*intra ecclesiam*). O. Perler ("L'Eglise principale et les autres sanctuaires chrétiens d'Hippone-la-Royale d'après les textes de Saint Augustin," *Revue des Etudes Augustiniennes*, 1 [1955], 330ff.) thinks that this phrase means "the ecclesiastical district" of Hippo. E. Marec (*Monuments chrétiens d'Hippone, ville épiscopale de Saint Augustin* [Algiers, 1958], p. 230) conjectures that the garden monastery was close by the great basilica which has been excavated, and to its southwest, where the remains of a row of rectangular apartments have been uncovered, that they enjoyed a common entrance from the decumanus, and that they surrounded an inner court or garden.

96. From *Letter 31* and *Letter 33* 2, we know that Severus and Evodius were among them. Cf. also Manrique, *La vida monastica*, p. 88.

97. Cf. *Rule* 3ff. I consider it very probable that Augustine wrote the *Rule* for the garden monastery in his first years as bishop. See below, p. 285.

98. The rectangular apartments mentioned in note 95 seem to have been such monastic single cells. In any case, archaeological remains show that there were individual cells in numerous North African monasteries of the fifth to seventh centuries, as well as in Jerome's older monastery in Bethlehem (Gavigan, *De vita monastica*, p. 38). These differed from Benedict's foundations, where there were common dormitories (A. Wagner, "Der klösterliche Haushalt des heiligen Benedikt," in *Benedictus, der Vater des Abendlandes*, ed. H. S. Brechter [Munich, 1947], p. 80).

99. *Rule* 2.2.

100. Ibid. 5.10.

101. *Sermon 355* 2 and Possidius 11.

102. Possidius 5. That Possidius joined the community in the garden monastery may be assumed with certainty (ibid. 31; cf. *Letter 101* 1).

103. See below, pp. 148–49.

104. See below, p. 285.

105. *Rule* 1.2. Cf. also *The Work of Monks* 22.26 (written about 400) and *Holy Virginity* 45.46 (composed in 401). The quotation "one heart and one soul" (*cor unum et anima una*), glossed with the words "toward God" (*in Deum*), often appears in Augustine's monastic writings; see below, chap. 5, note 163. It exactly describes his ideal of monastic living.

106. Cf. L. T. Lefort, *Les Vies coptes de S. Pachôme* (Louvain, 1943), pp. 3, line 30, and 60, line 28.

107. Orsisius, *Doctrina de institutione monachorum* 50 (PL 103.473). Cf. H. Bacht, "Antonius und Pachomius: Von der Anachorese zum Zenobitentum," *Studia Anselmiana*, 38 (1956), 92f.

108. Basil, *Regulae fusius tractatae* ("Longer Rules") 7.19.34 (PG 31.933ff.) and *Regulae brevius tractatae* ("Shorter Rules") 85.93.131 (PG 31.1144ff.).

109. Jerome, *De viris illustribus* 11 (PL 23.657f.). Cf. also Sanchis, "Pauvreté monastique . . . : Le commentaire . . . des Actes 4, 32–35," 30.

110. Cf. Lorenz, "Anfänge," 45 and 57.

111. Cf. L. M. Verheijen, "Saint Augustin," in *Théologie de la vie monastique: Etudes sur la tradition patristique* (Paris, 1961), pp. 201–12. See also below, pp. 131–32 and 148–49.

112. Cf. *Letter* 209 3. Further evidence can be found in Manrique, *La vida monastica*, p. 84.

113. *The Work of Monks* 22.25 and 25.33. Cf. also *Exposition on Psalm 103* 3.16. For slaves to be accepted, a master's agreement was required. Generally, their reception into a monastic community would occur after they had been legally freed (*The Work of Monks* 22.25; cf. also Spreitzenhofer, *Entwicklung des alten Mönchtums*, p. 52, and A. Brucculeri, "Il pensiero sociale di S. Agostino: La schiavitù," *La civiltà cattolica*, 82, No. 2 [1931], 140.

114. *The Work of Monks* 25.33.

115. *Letter* 64 3.

116. Cf. *Sermon 356* 4.

117. As in the Italian and Eastern monasteries. Cf. Spreitzenhofer, *Entwicklung des alten Mönchtums*, pp. 90f., and S. Schiwietz, *Das morgenländische Mönchtum* I (Mainz, 1904), p. 206.

118. See the regulations to similar effect in Pachomius' *Rule* 77 (*Pachomii Regulae monasticae*, ed. P. B. Albers [Bonn, 1923], p. 41). Cf. O. Grützmacher, *Pachomius und das älteste Klosterleben* (Freiburg & Leipzig, 1896), pp. 128f.

119. Cf. *The Work of Monks* 17.20 and P. Wagner, "Über Psalmen und Psalmengesang im christlichen Altertum," *Römische Quartalschrift*, 12 (1898), 249f.

120. In the monasteries of the East and in Italy such probation was by now common (cf. Spreitzenhofer, *Entwicklung des alten Mönchtums*, pp. 53f.). Perhaps Augustine in *Letter 243* 1 means a probationary period as such by his term "apprenticeship" (*tirocinia*). In any case, *Exposition on Psalm 99* 11 is not definitive evidence against such probation.

121. "Another vows to give up all his possessions to be distributed to the poor, and to enter the life of a community, in the fellowship of holy men; this is a great vow. . . . So let no brother living in a monastery say 'I am leaving the monastery.' . . . This answer is given to him: 'But they did not make a vow; you did, and you have looked back" (*Exposition on Psalm 75* 16). It is not at all clear whether by this "vow" (*votum*) Augustine has in mind indi-

vidual cases which might occur or a practice common to all upon entry into the monastery.

122. " . . . Rightly I shall deprive him of his clerical status, because he broke the promise to live in a holy society and forsook the company which he had entered; . . . he has left the fellowship of the common life which he had accepted, he has fallen away from his vow and from his holy profession" (*Sermon 355* 6).

123. The expression "profession" (*professio*), and similarly "to profess" (*profiteri*), almost always have for him, particularly in *Sermon* 355f., this wider sense. The same applies to the meaning of the word "undertaking" (*propositum*) in *Letter 157* 39, *Letter 216* 6, *Sermon* 355f., and Possidius 4. On the other hand, "profession" in *Exposition on Psalm 75* 16 means a specific promise made by a vow.

124. Cf. *Sermon 355* 3.

125. Cf. ibid. 6 and *Sermon 356* 3.14.

126. There is no evidence of this in Augustine's writings.

127. *Letter 243.*

128. Cf. M. Rothenhäusler, "Die Anfänge der klösterlichen Profess," BMS, 4 (1922), 21–28; idem, "Der heilige Basilius der Grosse und die klösterliche Profess," ibid., 280–89; idem, "Unter dem Geheimnis des Kreuzes: Die klösterliche Profess bei Kassian," ibid., 5 (1923), 91–96.

129. *Letter 243* 2ff. and 11. Cf. Rothenhäusler, "Die Anfänge," 25f. and "Unter dem Geheimnis," 95f.

130. This exchange of garments, rich in symbolism, was a monastic custom since the most ancient of times. Cf. P. Oppenheim, *Symbolik und religiöse Wertung des Mönchskleides im christlichen Altertum* (Münster, 1932), p. 1.

131. *Habitus monachorum* (*The Work of Monks* 28.36).

132. P. Oppenheim (*Das Mönchskleid im christlichen Altertum* [Freiburg, 1931], pp. 17 and 73) supposes that the monks' clothing was black, and interprets in this sense the word *pullulare*, which Augustine uses in *The Work of Monks* 28.36. But in this context *pullulare* certainly has the more usual meaning "to sprout."

133. Augustine did know of the "shirt" often used in monastic establishments, a sacklike garment of goat or camel hair (*Letter 48* 4; cf. also *Sermon 216* 10 and Oppenheim, *Das Mönchskleid*, pp. 184ff., and idem, *Symbolik*, pp. 91f.). Yet it is improbable that this penitential garment was worn by his own monks, for he did not wish their clothing to be in any way remarkable or outlandish (see *Rule* 4.1).

134. *Rule* 5.11.

135. Ibid. 5.1.

136. Ibid. 5.4, 5.1.

137. *The Work of Monks* 18.21.

138. Ibid. 29.37 and *Exposition on Psalm 99* 12.

139. *Rule* 2.1, 3.2.

140. Ibid. 4.2, 5.7.

141. Ibid. 5.2.

142. Ibid. 5.8–9.
143. Cf. Spreitzenhofer, *Entwicklung des alten Mönchtums*, p. 90.
144. Cf. Possidius 18.24.28. See also Domínguez-del Val, "Cultura y formación," 437ff.
145. *The Work of Monks* 18.21.
146. Ibid. 17.20.
147. Ibid. 25.32
148. Ibid. 25.33.
149. Ibid. 16.19.
150. Ibid. 17.20.
151. *Letter 83* 6.
152. *Letter* 29 1f.
153. Cf. *Rule* 7.1.
154. Ibid.
155. Ibid. 1.3.
156. Ibid. 5.4.
157. Ibid. 5.3.
158. Ibid. 5.7.
159. Ibid. 7.2.
160. See, for example, *On 83 Various Questions*, question 71 (for the translation, see below, chap. 10), a "conference" which Augustine conducted in these years on mutual concerns of his brethren in the garden monastery.
161. Possidius 5ff. Cf. also A. Kunzelmann, "Augustins' Predigttätigkeit," in *Aurelius Augustinus*, edd. M. Grabmann and J. Mausbach (Cologne, 1930), pp. 155f.
162. Cf. F. M. Mellet, *L'Itinéraire et l'idéal monastiques de Saint Augustin* (Paris, 1934), p. 35.
163. Cf. Possidius 11.
164. Cf. *Letter 83*.
165. Possidius 8. On the problem of the date of his episcopal consecration, see Trapè, *S. Agostino*, p. 49, and, more recently, O. Perler, "Das Datum der Bishofsweihe des heiligen Augustinus," REA, 11 (1965), 25–37.
166. E. Krebs, *Sankt Augustin, der Mensch und Kirchenlehrer* (Cologne, 1930), p. 150.
167. *Sermon 355* 2.
168. This episcopal residence probably was situated close to the basilica, in its grounds, but not directly adjacent to it, because Augustine had to cross the street to reach the basilica from his residence (cf. *Sermon 61* 12, 13, and Perler, "L'Eglise principale," 340. Marec (*Monuments chrétiens*, pp. 230f.) assumes that this "bishop's house" (*domus episcopi*) was to the southwest of the great basilica which has now been excavated.
169. *Sermon 355* 2. Cf. *Sermon 356* 1.
170. *Sermon 355* 6 and *Sermon 356* 14.
171. *Letter* 60 1. Cf. Possidius 11.
172. *Sermon 355* 3, 6.
173. *Sermon 355* 6.

174. *Sermon 356* 3.
175. *Adulterous Marriages* 2.20.22.
176. In fact, this must have been the entire clergy of Hippo, because anyone who was not willing to live the common life with Augustine was immediately prohibited from receiving orders (*Sermon 355* 6); but if anyone had once vowed himself to this communal way of life and then broke his vow, he was threatened with exclusion (*Sermon 356* 14).
177. *Sermon 356* 3.
178. Ibid.
179. Ibid. 1.
180. Ibid. 4.
181. Ibid. 5.
182. Ibid. 6.
183. Ibid. 7. Cf. *Letter 213*.
184. *Sermon 356* 10.
185. Ibid. 15.
186. *Sermon 355* 3.
187. *Sermon 356* 3.
188. Ibid. 8f.
189. Ibid. 10. Cf. *The Work of Monks* 25.33.
190. *The Work of Monks* 27.35, 29.37.
191. *Sermon 355* 2.
192. *The City of God* 19.19.
193. *Sermon 356* 13.
194. See below pp. 227–28. According to a brief remark in what is called the *Ordo monasterii*, the Augustinian origin of which is uncertain, on weekdays the monks ate their chief meal of the day after the "ninth hour." Even Possidius (19) reports only an "hour of refreshment" in the clerics' monastery. But there is no clear proof that, Sundays excepted, they observed a constant fast.
195. Cf. *Rule* 3.1.
196. *Sermon 356* 13.
197. The exhortation and encouragement of his brethren in religion, which often must have meant the members of his episcopal monastery, frequently were a stimulus to Augustine in the composition of his writings (cf. B. Altaner, *Kleine patristische Schriften* [Berlin, 1967], p. 157 and note 2). See, for instance, *The Trinity* 3.1, *Against Faustus* 1.1, *Against an Adversary of the Law and the Prophets* 1.1, and *Retractations* 2.11 (this treats the lost work *Against Hilary*). Augustine specifically states that he was prompted by the "brethren" to compose all these works.
198. Possidius 22.
199. Ibid. 25. Cf. on this *Sermon 180*.
200. *Letter 38* 2. Cf. Mellet, *L'Itinéraire*, pp. 40f.
201. M. Rössler, "Augustinus-Legenden," in *St. Augustin* (Würzburg, 1930), p. 78.
202. Possidius 26.
203. Ibid. 22.

204. Ibid.

205. *Sermon 356* 13. Augustine himself gives this brief indication of the material of which their clothing was made: "The lower garments are of linen; the upper, of wool" (*Sermon 37* 6). Cf. Oppenheim, *Das Mönchskleid*, pp. 61, 64. For further information about the sleeved tunic (*tunica manicata*) and the byrrus, see ibid., pp. 98f., 161ff.

206. *Sermon 356* 13. Cf. Possidius 22.

207. AH 496 51. See also Wagner, "Der klösterliche Haushalt," pp. 80*n*11, and 91ff.

208. Possidius 25.

209. Ibid. 23. Cf. also *Letter 125* 2 and *Letter 126* 9 where Augustine indicates this preference.

210. Possidius 24 and 31. We may presume from *Sermon 356* 15, where there is mention of the priest Barnabas and of the "year of his provostship," (*annus praepositurae suae*) that a change was made each year.

211. Lorenz has produced convincing proof of this in "Anfänge," 59f.

212. Possidius 24.

213. Ibid.

214. Ibid.

215. Ibid.

216. Ibid.

217. *Sermon 356* 7.

218. Ibid. 10.

219. Ibid. 15.

220. Ibid. 10.

221. Cf. Roetzer, *Des heiligen Augustinus Schriften*, pp. 196ff., and D. Zähringer, *Das kirchliche Priestertum nach dem heiligen Augustinus* (Paderborn, 1931), pp. 110ff., 141ff.

222. Cf. Roetzer, *Des heiligen Augustinus Schriften*, pp. 198f.

223. Cf. J. Popp, *Sankt Augustinus als Erzieher des Klerus and Volkes, als Seelenführer* (Munich, 1910), pp. 8ff.

224. Ambrose, *Letter 63* and, especially, *Letter 66* and *Letter 71* (PL 16. 1258ff.). Cf. Spreitzenhofer, *Entwicklung des alten Mönchtums*, pp. 13ff., and Penco, *Storia*, p. 35.

225. See below, pp. 194–97.

226. Mention of a "monastery of virgins" (*monasterium virginum*) as an already existing institution appears for the first time in a decree of the North African provincial synod at Carthage in 397. J. M. del Estal ("Sobre los comienzos de la vida común entre las virgines de Africa," CD, 170 [1957], 335–60) assumes that Augustine was the spiritual director of this establishment. In any case, a few years later, in *Holy Virginity* 45.46, composed around 401, Augustine was calling for a monastic life for consecrated virgins.

227. *Sermon 355* 3 mentions a "monastery of women" (*monasterium feminarum*).

228. *Holy Virginity* 45.46

229. See the address of *Letter 210*, which Augustine wrote to a house of

women: "To our dearest and holiest mother Felicitas, and to Brother Rusticus and to the sisters who are with you, greetings in the Lord." For a translation of this text, see below, chap. 11. It is not clearly stated in this letter that this "Brother Rusticus" was a priest. He could be identical with the Rusticus who appears as *presbyter* among the other priests of Hippo in *Letter 213* 1.

230. *Rule* 4.9, 7.1.

231. This was decreed by the third North African provincial synod at Carthage (J. Hardouin, *Acta conciliorum et epistolae decretales ac constitutiones Summorum Pontificum ab anno 34 ad 1714*, 12 vols. (Paris, 1714ff.), 1 963f.

232. Possidius 27.

233. *Sermon 355* 3.

234. *Letter 254* 1. Cf. also *Exposition on Psalm 83* 4 and *Sermon 93* 1.1.

235. *Sermon 355* 3. That Augustine with the words "luster of avowal" (*fulgor professionis*) is alluding to an express commitment to the monastic life may also be conjectured from his use of the expression "guarantee of the one professing" (*sponsio profitentis*) in *Letter 254* 1.

236. Cf. Ambrose, *On Virginity* 7.39 (PL 16.289f.); Pseudo-Ambrose, *On the Lapse of a Consecrated Virgin* 5.19 (ibid. 388). Augustine himself uses the expression "to be consecrated among God's virgins" (*inter virgines Dei consecrari*) in *The Good of Marriage* 18.21, and testifies that at the consecration of Demetrias as a virgin, which was solemnized in 413–414 in Carthage by Bishop Aurelius, her relatives sent him a "veiling gift" (*velationis apophoretum*). See *Letter 150*.

237. *Letter 211* 4 specifically mentions the "veiling" (*velari*) of cloistered women, but since it is not completely certain that this letter is genuinely Augustinian, it cannot be used here as a source. For a translation of the letter, see below, chap. 11.

238. Augustine mentions once "the clothing of a nun" (*indumentum monachae*)—in *Letter 262* 9.

239. In the places cited he uses the expression "somber clothing" (*vestes nigellae*). In these contexts it could also mean the dress of widows. Augustine urges a fitting simplicity of clothing for virgins consecrated to God in *Holy Virginity* 34.34. Cf. Oppenheim, *Das Mönchskleid*, p. 73.

240. Oppenheim, *Das Mönchskleid*, pp. 165ff.

241. *Holy Virginity* 34.34.

242. Possidius 26.

243. "At the established hours and times" (*horis et temporibus constitutis*) —*Rule* 2.1.

244. A detailed order of prayer, comprising all the liturgical hours of prayer except Prime, is contained in the so-called *Ordo monasterii*. For a translation, see below, chap. 9. The Augustinian origin of this is still contested.

245. *Exposition on Psalm 118* 29.4.

246. Cf. *Sermon 219*.

247. *Exposition on Psalm 118* 29.4. For the Holy Saturday celebrations in Hippo, see Roetzer, *Des heiligen Augustinus Schriften*, pp. 15ff.

248. Tertullian, *On Prayer* 25 (CCL 1.272). Cyprian also mentions prayer at the hours of Terce, Sext, and None (*The Lord's Prayer* 34; CSEL 3.1.292).

249. *Letter* 29 10f. In *The City of God* 22.8, Augustine tells of the "Vespers hymns and prayers" (*vespertini hymni et orationes*) which the mistress of an estate some distance from Hippo used to sing with her maidservants and some nuns as a "memorial" (*memoria*) of the martyrs Protasius and Gervasius.

250. *Sermo Denis 11* 7, in Morin, p. 49.

251. *Rule* 2.3, 2.1.

252. The name is frequently attested in Augustine's writings.

253. Augustine mentions seven or eight churches and chapels in ancient Hippo. Cf. Perler, "L'Eglise principale," 299–343; see also Roetzer, *Des heiligen Augustinus Schriften*, pp. 72f.; and J. Sauer, "Der Kirchenbau Nordafrikas in den Tagen des heiligen Augustinus," in *Aurelius Augustinus*, edd. M. Grabmann and J. Mausbach (Cologne, 1930), p. 247.

254. *Sermon 325* 2 and *Sermon 258*. For this identification of the "Basilica of Peace" (*basilica pacis*) with the "major basilica" (*basilica maior*), see Perler, "L'Eglise principale," 313ff. To complete what he wrote there about the so-called Basilica Leontiana (ibid., 300–307), Perler not long afterward indicated the probability that this was identical with Augustine's episcopal church, the "Basilica of Peace" ("La 'Memoria des Vingt Martyrs' d'Hippone-la-Royale," REA, 2 [1956], 435–46. See also his "Hippo Regius," LThK, V^2, 376–78.

255. E. Marec, *Hippone la Royale, Antique Hippo Regius*, 2nd ed. (Algiers, 1954); idem, "Les Dernières Fouilles d'Hippo Regius," in AM I, pp. 1–18; idem, *Monuments chrétiens*.

256. "La dernier fouilles," pp. 14ff., and *Monuments chrétiens*, pp. 225ff. Because of the generally accepted theory that Augustine's episcopal church and that of the Donatists were adjacent, Marec presumed ("Les dernières fouilles," pp. 7 and 17) that the smaller church with five naves must have been the Donatists'. But Perler ("L'Eglise principale," 305) demonstrated that the basis for this theory, a passage from Augustine's *Letter 29*, is not conclusive. Marec in his last major investigation (*Monuments chrétiens*, pp. 219–22) made allowance for this. Today one assumes that this five-naved church is the "ancient church" (*ecclesia antiqua*) which Augustine mentions once in *Letter 99* 3.

257. *Homily on St. John's Epistle to the Parthi* 4 9.

258. *Sermon 356* 7; cf. also *The City of God* 22.8. See also Roetzer, *Des heiligen Augustinus Schriften*, pp. 72f.; Zellinger, *Augustin und die Volksfrömmigkeit*, pp. 54f.; Perler, "L'Eglise principale," 321ff.

259. Perler, "L'Eglise principale," 332ff.

260. Ibid.

261. Cf. Spreitzenhofer, *Entwicklung des alten Mönchtums*, p. 77.

262. Augustine tells us that his mother went to church twice a day, "morning and evening" (*mane et vespere*), to hear God's word and to pray (*Confessions* 5.9.17). Augustine as a priest related, in *Letter* 29 10f., how the people

of Hippo on a feast day joined in the singing of psalms. See also Roetzer, *Des heiligen Augustinus Schriften*, pp. 11f., and Wagner, "Über Psalmen and Psalmengesang," 248.

263. "For we pray not only standing, as it is written 'But the publican stood far off,' but kneeling too, as we read in the Acts of the Apostles, and sitting, as David and Elias did" (*On Various Questions to Simplicianus* 2.4). Cf. Roetzer, *Des heiligen Augustinus Schriften*, pp. 241f.

264. Roetzer, *Des heiligen Augustinus Schriften*, pp. 243ff.

265. *Rule* 2.4.

266. See Roetzer, *Des heiligen Augustinus Schriften*, pp. 227f. and L. Eisenhofer, *Handbuch der Liturgik*, 2nd ed., 2 vols. (Freiburg, 1941), I 208, 211, 223. Cf. *Confessions* 9.7.15.

267. *Confessions* 10.33.50, and Wagner, "Über Psalmen und Psalmengesang," 270f. Cf. also *Letter* 55 18.34, where Augustine says in so many words that not enough importance is attached in Africa to liturgical chant. The Donatists used this as propaganda against the Catholic Church. See also Zellinger, *Augustin und die Volksfrömmigkeit*, p. 85.

268. In countless places in his commentaries on the psalms, Augustine alludes to responsorial chant; cf. *Exposition on Psalm 46* 1: "Therefore in this psalm, which we have heard sung, and to which we have responded in our singing. . . ." He writes of antiphonal chant, in *Confessions* 9.7.15, that it had been accepted in almost every church throughout the world. From among the hymns of St. Ambrose he quotes that for the morning office, "Aeterne rerum conditor" (*Retractations* 1.21), the hymn for Terce, "Jam surgit hora tertia" (*Nature and Grace* 63.74), the evening hymn, "Deus creator omnium" (*Confessions* 9.12.32), and the Christmas hymn, "Intende, qui regis Israel" (*Sermon 372* 3). Cf. Eisenhofer, *Handbuch der Liturgik*, I 211.

269. According to the so-called *Ordo monasterii*, the Augustinian origin of which is not certain, the office in the early morning consisted of Psalms 62, 5, and 89. For Terce, Sext, and None, there were prescribed one psalm with a refrain, two psalms to be sung antiphonally, a Scripture reading, and a prayer; for Vespers, one psalm with a refrain, four antiphonal psalms, a second psalm with a refrain, a Scripture reading, and a prayer. In the evening familiar readings followed and "the customary psalms before going to bed." The regulations for night prayers took the seasons of the year into account. In wintertime twelve antiphonal psalms, six responsorial psalms, and three readings were prescribed; in the spring and fall, ten antiphonal psalms, five responsorial psalms, and three readings; but in the summer only eight antiphonal psalms, four responsorial psalms, and two readings. For a translation of the text, see below, chap. 9.

270. Cf. also Zellinger, *Augustin und die Volksfrömmigkeit*, pp. 82ff.

271. *Confessions* 10.33.50.

272. *Letter* 55 18.34.

273. *Confessions* 10.33.50. Cf. 9.6f.14ff.

274. *Sermon 198* 1.

275. Cf. *Rule* 2.3.

276. In Hippo the Sacrifice of the Mass was offered daily. Cf. Roetzer, *Des heiligen Augustinus Schriften*, pp. 97f.

277. Ibid., p. 97.

278. Cf. on my interpretation ibid., pp. 98ff.; Zähringer, *Das kirchliche Priestertum*, pp. 134ff.; and van der Meer, *Augustinus de Zielzorger*, pp. 342ff.

279. Roetzer, *Des heiligen Augustinus Schriften*, pp. 92ff.; Eisenhofer, *Handbuch der Liturgik*, I 408f.

280. Augustine recognized differences in the manner of chanting. On occasion he writes of "chanting solemnly" (*solemniter legere*); cf. Wagner, "Über Psalmen und Psalmengesang," 271.

281. Augustine also preached on weekdays. Cf. Roetzer, *Des heiligen Augustinus Schriften*, pp. 10, 112, and Kunzelmann, "Augustins Predigttätigkeit," pp. 156f.

282. Cf. Zellinger, *Augustin und die Volksfrömmigkeit*, pp. 89ff.

283. *Letter 54* 6.8. Cf. also Roetzer, *Des heiligen Augustinus Schriften*, pp. 173ff.; O. Blank, *Die Lehre des heiligen Augustin vom Sakrament der Eucharistie* (Paderborn, 1906), pp. 130ff. Daily communion was then commonly practiced, even if not general (Schiwietz, *Das morgenländische Mönchtum* I, pp. 316ff.

284. *Homily on St. John's Gospel 26* 11.

285. Roetzer, *Des heiligen Augustinus Schriften*, pp. 133ff.

286. *Homily on St. John's Gospel 26* 13f. See also below, pp. 132–33.

287. See *Letter 10* 2 and *Letter 122* 1. Cf. also O. Perler, "Les Voyages de Saint Augustin," *Recherches Augustiniennes* I (Paris, 1958), pp. 5–42.

288. *Letter 28* 1.

289. Augustine's first two letters (*Letter 28* and *Letter 40*), in which in a spirit of friendly openness he criticized Jerome's translation of the Bible and his explanation of Galatians 2:14, went astray and reached their intended recipient only years later. But in the interval the public, if without any blame to Augustine, had obtained copies of them. Cf. L. Schade, *Des heiligen Kirchenlehrers Eusebius Hieronymus ausgewählte Briefe* II (Munich, 1927), pp. 419ff.

290. Alypius is greeted by name in Jerome's *Letter 103*, *Letter 115*, and *Letter 142* (numbered 39, 81, and 123, respectively, in the collection of Augustine's *Letters*). In *Letter 142* Jerome asks Alypius to greet Evodius as well. *Letter 134* (numbered 172 in the collection of Augustine's *Letters*) asks Augustine to remember him to all his venerable co-workers.

291. Jerome's *Letter 134* (numbered 172 in the collection of Augustine's *Letters*). As early as Jerome's *Letter 103* (numbered 39 in the collection of Augustine's *Letters*), greetings are sent from the holy brethren who live in the monastery with him.

292. Jerome's *Letter 142* (numbered 123 in the collection of Augustine's *Letters*).

293. Jerome's *Letter 143* (numbered 202 in the collection of Augustine's *Letters*). Cf. on this below, pp. 87–88.

294. See Paulinus' *Letter 24* (in the collection of Augustine's *Letters*) 2.

295. F. Lagrange, *Geschichte des heiligen Paulinus von Nola* (Mainz,

1882). Cf. also Spreitzenhofer, *Entwicklung des alten Mönchtums*, pp. 21f.; O. Bardenhewer, *Geschichte der altkirchlichen Literatur* III, 2nd ed. (Freiburg, 1923), pp. 569ff.; and G. Bürke, "Paulinus," LThK, VIII^2, 208f.

296. Cf. *Letter 95* in which Augustine calls the couple his "fellow-pupils under our master, the Lord Jesus" (*condiscipuli sub magistro Domino Jesu*).

297. *Letter 27* 2.

298. *Letter 31* 4.

299. Paulinus' *Letter 30* (in the collection of Augustine's *Letters*) 3.

300. *Letter* 80 1. Evodius, a former friend and confrere of Augustine's in the monastery at Tagaste, had become bishop of Uzali.

301. Paulinus' *Letter 94* (in the collection of Augustine's *Letters*) 1 and 8.

302. *Letter 95* 1.

303. Cf. Lagrange, *Geschichte des heiligen Paulinus*, p. 469.

304. Cf. *Letter* 27 2 and Paulinus' *Letter 121* (in the collection of Augustine's *Letters*).

305. Paulinus' *Letter 24* (in the collection of Augustine's *Letters*) 6; Paulinus' *Letter 25* (in the collection of Augustine's *Letters*) 5; and Paulinus' *Letter 30* (in the collection of Augustine's *Letters*) 3.

306. *Letter* 27 6, *Letter 31* 9, and *Letter 42*. Cf. also P. Monceaux, "La Formule 'Qui mecum sunt fratres' dans la correspondance de S. Augustin," in *Mélanges Paul Thomas* (Bruges, 1930), pp. 529–37. Monceaux concludes that by "brothers" Augustine, before his episcopal consecration, meant the monks of the garden monastery, and thereafter, the members of the monastery of clerics.

307. Paulinus had written to Alypius before Augustine; see his *Letter 24* (in the collection of Augustine's *Letters*). Alypius, together with Augustine, wrote *Letter 45* and *Letter 186*.

308. Cf. Paulinus' *Letter 32* (in the collection of Augustine's *Letters*) 1.

309. Possidius 31.

310. Ibid.

311. *Sermon 356* 13.

312. Possidius 22.

313. Legewie, "Die körperliche Konstitution," pp. 5–21.

314. Cf. *Confessions* 9.6.14, where he admires the strict asceticism of his friend Alypius.

315. Ibid. 10.30.41.

316. Possidius 26.

317. *Confessions* 30.31.43ff.

318. Ibid. 10.34.51ff.

319. Cf. below, p. 228 and note 189.

320. *Confessions* 10.35.54ff.

321. Ibid. 10.37–39.60ff. Cf., on this paragraph, below, pp. 228–29.

322. *Letter 261* 1.

323. Possidius 24. Cf. *Confessions* 11.2.2.

324. Cf. C. Morel, "La Vie de prière de Saint Augustin d'après sa corre-

spondance," in *Saint Augustin parmi nous*, edd. H. Rondet, et al. (Le Puy & Paris, 1954), pp. 57–87.

325. Possidius 19. Cf. *Letter 73* 10.
326. Possidius 18.
327. Ibid. 25.
328. *Rule* 7.3.
329. *Letter 231*. Cf. also *Letter 130*, *Letter 157*, and *Letter 217*.

3

Dangers

IN THE REALIZATION OF HIS IDEALS for the monastic life, Augustine was not spared disappointment. He had to overcome great difficulties and considerable opposition: there were dangers from those of his confreres who fell away, threats from his personal adversaries, even among the faithful, open violence or underhand intrigues among pagans and non-Catholics, and undesirable tendencies in the life of monastic asceticism.

BACKSLIDERS

Augustine summarized his experiences as a monastic superior when he wrote: "I confess it openly before the Lord our God, who is the witness of my soul, that just as I have hardly ever, since I first began to serve God, found better men than those who perfected themselves in monasteries, so too I have never met worse than those who in monasteries went astray."[1] He experienced numerous disappointments in the forty years of his activity as a superior, and they left their traces in his writings.

The moral shortcomings of two members of the clerics' monastery caused Augustine considerable anguish. It was around the year 404 when Bonifatius, a priest of the community, accused a young brother named Spes of scandalous conduct. When called to account, the brother reproached his accuser with identical conduct, and declared himself completely innocent. Augustine was still endeavoring to determine who was guilty when the matter became public knowledge. It occasioned great scandal among the residents of Hippo, and threatened to destroy the monastery's good name. Thereupon the bishop, in a pastoral letter to the clergy and the faithful, described the state of affairs without ameliorating it. He wrote of his sorrow about what had happened, but, at the same time, he warned everyone against entertaining suspicion. If a bishop, a cleric, or a nun had fallen, there would surely always be evil tongues to assert that all religious were like that, even if it could not be proved against them all. And yet it would not occur to such accusers, should a married woman be discovered in adultery, to repudiate their own wives or to malign their mothers. "My house is no better than the abode of our Lord Christ Himself in which eleven good ones tolerated the treacherous and thieving Judas, and no better . . . than heaven, where even angels fell."[2]

A few years later there was an unhappy event that was to proceed so far that it reached the tribunal of the Holy See, and was to cause Augustine much vexation. There was a town called Fussala, forty miles distant from Hippo and belonging to its diocese. Augustine promoted its erection as an independent episcopal see, in the interests of the better pastoral care of its people. The primate of Numidia agreed, and, though he was old and frail, undertook the rigors of the long journey in order to give the new bishop episcopal consecration. Everything was prepared for the festivities when, at the last moment, the priest whom Augustine had had in view refused to accept the dignity. In this difficult situation, Augustine decided upon a young brother from his monastery of clerics, by the name of Antoninus, for bishop. Antoninus had grown up under Augustine's tutelage in the monastery, and at that time held the office of lector. The choice was a mistake, for Antoninus quite soon showed himself unworthy of the office. Though the hateful accusations made against him, including a charge of rape, proved to be unfounded, his thirst for power and his avarice were notorious and were the cause of considerable scandal among other diocesan bishops everywhere. Thus a conference of bishops ruled that he must restore the property he had unlawfully obtained, and reduced the area of his diocese. When Antoninus appealed the decision to Rome, and seemed to be succeeding in his appeal, Augustine felt compelled to set out the facts of the case in all candor in a letter to Pope Celestine and to petition for the decision to be reversed. The letter shows him full of zeal for God's cause, of love for the people of Fussala and for their bishop, his "son in Christ," who had caused him so much trouble. Augustine acknowledged his own share of responsibility for these misfortunes, since it was he who had proposed Antoninus for consecration. Indeed, he declared himself willing to resign his own episcopal office and to do penance for his blunder.[3]

In the year 425 Augustine experienced a bitter disappointment, caused by another member of his clerics' monastery, the priest Januarius, who had entered the community claiming that he had made a final disposition of his means. In fact, he still had money, but he maintained that it belonged to his daughter and would remain in his keeping until the daughter should come of age. But when Januarius felt death approaching, he made a will and disposed of the money as though it were his own. This event, as well, soon became public knowledge, and was used by the enemies of the bishop and his clerics against the community. When people began to hold the ideal of poverty up to scorn as nothing more than a cunning device to deceive ordinary men, Augustine made the case the occasion of a sermon. He repudiated with all severity these transactions of Januarius, who had died in the meantime. Not only had the priest broken his vow, but his entire life as a "poor man of God" had been nothing but one long hypocrisy. To this Augustine contrasted, as the first law of conventual life, what was written in the Acts of the Apostles: "No one called anything his own" (Acts 4:32). He ordered an inquiry into the financial status of his confreres, for under no circumstances was he prepared to tolerate other hypocrites around him. Falling short of one's profession (*professio*) to the full communal life (*vita communis*) was in his estimation so grave a fault that he considered himself justified as bishop in taking action against it with the full range of his ecclesiastical powers. He knew, certainly, that many of his fellow-bishops disagreed with him. It was no very grave matter, they maintained, if someone should withdraw from the community; it was merely that he could not endure living a common life with Augustine, preferring to live outside the bishop's residence and on his own means.[4] Augustine rejected this excuse. When, a few weeks later, he had completed his inquiry and could inform the people that the poverty of his clerics was unblemished, he resumed his attack upon hypocrisy. "Let him [an apostate] appeal against me to a thousand councils; let him sail against me where he will; indeed, let him live where he may. God will help me that where I am the bishop, he cannot be a cleric."[5]

With great emphasis Augustine warned his sons that they should look back on the way they had once chosen. A man who looks back should be judged differently from one who never made a decision for his ideals.[6] At times Augustine had to experience men who entered the monastery full of enthusiasm but later gave up the struggle and betrayed their chosen way of life.

When, about the year 400, the monk Donatus and his brother left the garden monastery, against Augustine's will, in order to receive clerical orders at the hands of Bishop Aurelius of Carthage, Augustine justifiably feared in this a disparagement of the status of religious. Soon, he thought, it would be said that a bad monk could still be a good cleric. He also regarded it as disadvantageous and dangerous for the lay monks if those who broke their vows were thereupon rewarded for their infidelity to the monastic ideal of life with ecclesiastical office. His thoughts on this matter, which he set out in a personal letter to Bishop Aurelius,[7] he had also presented not long before, at the provincial synod of the African Church at Carthage in the year 401. He had devised there a specific prohibition against accepting apostate or expelled monks into the diocesan clergy and against appointing them as superiors of monasteries.[8]

Letter 243 tells of Augustine's battle for the soul of a young brother by the name of Laetus, probably from the clerics' monastery, whose resolution in his undertaking threatened to waver because of the rhetorical persuasiveness of his mother. Quoting Holy Scripture, Augustine exhorted him to detach himself from the ties of this all too earthly familial love.[9] In many other instances as well, the occasion of men's leaving the monastery was a lack of the spirit of self-sacrifice and patience which life in such a small community demanded of each of its members.[10]

Then, too, there was no lack in Augustine's monasteries of those backsliders—he called them "grumblers" (*murmuratores*)—who had no community spirit or true brotherly love. Only their bodies lived in the monastery, and they were a real burden to the community.[11] Thus in *The Gift of Perseverance* Augustine mentions a monk who tried to excuse his failure by appealing to divine predestination. In spite of all admonition and brotherly correction he manifested no improvement, and in the end was expelled from the community.[12]

Throughout the decades, the thought impressed itself deeply upon Augustine that just as in the Church and among the clergy, so in monasteries, there would also always be good and bad.[13] Every way of life has its misfits.[14] It would be unjust to try to make them a cause of reproach either to monastic life or to its superiors. Some unsuitable candidates could not be prevented from entering communities. If one wanted to find out what they were like, one could not lock the doors against them.[15] True, the monastery was a peaceful haven in comparison with the world's stormy sea; but as every harbor has its outlet to the sea, through which storms can often penetrate, causing boats to collide and be damaged, so monasteries have their storms and shipwrecks.[16]

But in all this Augustine found comfort in the thought that in his monasteries there was but little dross and so many fine pearls.[17] Beyond a doubt and in spite of everything, a good spirit prevailed among his monks and nuns. And what he had once said, speaking generally of the Catholic Church in a sermon, applied to his monasteries: "Far be it from me to have doubts about the threshing-floor of so sublime a husbandman. It is true that anyone who views it only from afar presumes that there is nothing but chaff; but anyone who can see it for what it is will find the grain. The chaff may trouble you, but it is there that the abundance of grain is hidden."[18]

INTRIGUES

The resistance from outside against which Augustine had to defend his life's work, his monastic establishments, was also great. He encountered mockery and hostility from the Donatists,[19] who boasted of the abstinence and the religious zeal of those known as Circumcellions. Enthusiasts of a socialist bent in the Roman North Africa of those days, they had joined with the Donatists and were campaigning, and not shunning terrorism in doing so, for the abolition of class distinctions, the improvement of social conditions, and the promotion of the separatist Donatist Church.[20] In combating them, Augustine pointed to the exemplary lives of Christian monks.[21]

But throughout his life Augustine also had to do battle against both the open and the concealed hostility of the Catholic populace of his diocese. Even in those days it happened that parents, for selfish reasons, would oppose their children's wishes to enter a monastery.[22] Augustine would hardly have been greatly surprised by this. And yet, even among his fellow-bishops, there were many who received his aspirations for a monastic life with little understanding.[23] What is more, he and his monasteries were not spared attack from his own spiritual children. It is hardly surprising that early on he would make many personal enemies through his zeal as a bishop and his dauntless proceedings against abuses among the clergy and the people.[24] There were those in particular who had to see in the life of Augustine and his followers a reproach to their own way of living, so little Christian.[25] They took every opportunity to besmirch his good name and that of his clerics and monks, and were not above slandering them: now they would call Augustine avaricious and self-seeking;[26] now they would impute the failings of individual members of his entourage to everyone in his monasteries.[27] They even attempted to detect unworthy motives for his interventions, when these were impartial and obviously praiseworthy.[28]

Because of this, Augustine more than once realized that he must defend his own good name and the reputation of his clerics and monks by word and in his writings. His love for his neighbors, in this case the souls who had been entrusted to him, presented this to him as a duty. "For our sake," he said in a sermon, "a good conscience is sufficient. But for your sake our reputation must not be soiled but must be strong among you. . . . The man who, trusting in his conscience, neglects his reputation is unfeeling."[29] It was his intention never to weary in answering in speech and word his accusers and slanderers.[30] He made them see how disgraceful their behavior was when he reproached them with bearing, to an extent, the same yoke as unbelievers (cf. 2 Cor. 14).[31]

But Augustine was just as much on his guard against inordinate praise for himself and for his followers. He never assumed that everyone around him was perfect, and he knew that he, too, was human and could make mistakes.[32]

EXCRESCENCES

In the infant African monasteries of the late-fourth century, as in other great ascetic movements, there was no lack of men whose notions of monastic life became distorted. Things went so far that heretical movements attempted to exert their influence. Augustine also fought energetically against these dangers.

Around the year 400 some enthusiasts in the monasteries of Carthage rejected the principle of manual labor for monks, influenced probably by the heretical asceticism of the Euchites.[33] They wished to live only on alms, regarding themselves as Jesus' true disciples, and maintaining that they alone were realizing the ideal of Christian perfection. It is understandable that such excrescences of monastic living could win no sympathy among the faithful, and that in the monasteries themselves they could cause only confusion. So, in response to a request by Bishop Aurelius of Carthage and against their exaggerated notions, Augustine wrote his *The Work of Monks*, a brilliant defense of the manual labor of monks and of the dignity of such labor.[34] At the outset, he corrects such monks' misunderstanding of Scripture, and shows how the Apostle Paul was the model of monks at their work. Writing that such work should be held in esteem, Augustine attacks the opinion of pagan antiquity that those who work with their hands are to be despised. Rather, they are ennobled by the example of the Holy Family itself and of the Apostles. Work is the proper thing for rich and poor alike and, what is more, an excellent means for attaining perfection. Only those may consider themselves excused from it who are too weak or sick, or who have pastoral duties. These Carthage monks had set up a rule "Only pray and read," which Augustine countered with his own "Pray and work."[35] This basic law of Western monasticism—the form "To work is to pray" is not found before the Middle Ages—was a deeply held conviction expressed in his writings. Not only St. Benedict was influenced, in his esteem for the work to be performed in monasteries, by this oldest Christian treatise on manual labor,[36] but the entire ethical system of Christianity, in the Middle Ages and in modern times, as it concerns work, is indebted to this work of the Church Father.[37]

At the same time, Augustine had to oppose other erroneous developments in monastic ascetic thinking. Among the monks in Carthage there were some, whom Augustine greatly esteemed for their exemplary lives, who appealed to the authority of the Old Testament in refusing to have their hair cut. Evidently they considered that the essence of Christian asceticism consisted in such external matters. Augustine ridiculed them, saying that they were afraid that a barbered holiness would be of less worth to God and to men than the hirsute kind. Such scruffy monks were bringing monasticism into bad repute. Augustine vehemently rejected such asceticism, which defied the Church's received customs.[38] In his writings he quoted the Apostle Paul, who saw in long hair a form of veiling, suitable for women, indeed, but not for men. He regarded monks who behaved so as a stumbling-block, fit only to stir up strife and confusion.[39]

Finally, in *The Work of Monks* Augustine had severe things to say about the type of monks "who wander about the countryside, unauthorized and with no fixed place to live" and who do not belong to any monastery. He called them frauds in monks' clothing, the emissaries of the devil. Everywhere they were to be detected in their evil-doing. "They all seek, they all demand, either the expenses of their profitable poverty or the price of their pretended holiness."[40] In a letter he told of a scandal which two vagrant monks had occasioned. They had persuaded a rich woman called Ecdicia to give away her means to the poor without her husband's knowledge. The tricksters themselves would not have been the losers by this. The lady's husband had harsh things to say about the Church's asceticism in general, but Ecdicia made bitter complaints to Augustine about the two monks.[41]

Before this, St. Basil had fulminated in his "Longer Rules" (*Regulae fusius tractatae*) against the life of vagrant monks as a degeneration of the ascetic ideal of homelessness which had appeared in certain places.[42] Augustine, too, rejected this type of aberrant monasticism. For him, monastic life presupposed a cloistered community and, thus, a settled place of residence.

In the practice of fasting, Augustine stood for wisdom and moderation. Opposing the opinionated contentiousness of those who wished to introduce a Saturday fast into Africa, his first concern was that Christian love and unity should not suffer because of these secondary questions of external asceticism.[43] And he pointed to the saying of the Lord: "My yoke is easy and my burden light" (Matt. 11:30).[44] He proposed that in these questions the provinces of the Church should be given their freedom, but that individuals should conform to the practice of the diocese in which they then were residing.[45]

Augustine fought with energy against dualistic tendencies, motivated by the hatred of man's human nature, which here and there could then be seen to dominate those who would go beyond the Church's ordinances in their search for perfection.[46] During his youth, he too had allowed himself to be deceived for years by the ideals of continence, opposed to Christian matrimony, of the Manichaean "chosen ones." Now he was eager for the opportunity to contrast their dualistic notions with the Christian view, which does, indeed, esteem virginity more than matrimony, but without disparaging marriage or in any way condemning it.[47] He similarly rejected the foolishly motivated abstinence from wine which those so-called "chosen ones" also practiced. In his foundations he specifically permitted the monks to enjoy their wine, rejecting the ascetic practices of many Eastern monasteries,[48] for he wanted to emphasize that every creature of God is good, and that all creation springs from God.[49]

Throughout his monastic career, Augustine encountered movements that, resembling the Manichaeans and certain other sects,[50] far exceeded the prohibition of private possessions in their renunciation of personal ownership. He sharply denounced such extremes, for he saw in them as much sinfulness as in hugging worldly wealth to oneself. Highly though he esteemed and practiced evangelical poverty, he was still fully convinced of the lawfulness and allowability of private possessions.[51]

PERSECUTIONS

Augustine's monasteries were not even spared their own persecutions. In the early decades of his activities as a bishop, there were demonstrations by the Circumcellions, the followers of the Donatists I have already mentioned, from which many of the "servants of God" had to suffer.[52] In his final decades there came upon North Africa the affliction of the migrant hordes. According to Possidius' report, when the land was conquered by the

Vandals and the Alans, priests and clerics, virgins consecrated to God, and those vowed to a life of continence must have endured severe trials. Many fled, and others were killed. Of the fate of the many who were taken captive, Possidius writes: "Robbed of their spiritual and bodily integrity, and of their faith, they pay their enemies the hard and bitter tribute of their toil."[53]

This travail of the Church and of the cloisters touched Augustine very closely. He was able to comfort himself and his subjects in their bodily afflictions and sorrows with Christian fortitude and trust in God.[54] But he knew greater fears for the souls entrusted to him. Possidius reports that he entreated God to rescue Hippo from its enemies, or else to give his people strength to bear the affliction, and to take him to Himself.[55] In fact, Augustine did not live until the capture of the city by the Vandals. He died on August 28, 430, in the third month of the siege.[56]

NOTES

1. *Letter 78* 9.
2. Ibid. 6 and 8. For a translation of this letter, see below, chap. 11. In *Letter 65* 1, written at the beginning of 402, Augustine reports on a scandal of a similar nature involving a priest named Abundantius "of the manor at Strabonian" (*in fundo Strabonianensi*), a country estate belonging to Augustine's diocese (cf. A. Trapè, "San Agustín y el monacato occidental," CD, 169 [1956], 417). It cannot definitely be proved from this report whether Abundantius had belonged to the monastery of clerics or the garden monastery.
3. *Letter* 209.
4. *Sermon 355* 3 and 6.
5. *Sermon 356* 14. For translations of both *Sermon 355* and *Sermon 356*, see below, chap. 12.
6. *Exposition on Psalm 83* 4.
7. *Letter* 60. For a translation of this letter, see below, chap. 11.
9. For a translation of the letter, see below, chap. 11.
8. Hardouin, *Acta conciliorum*, I 988. Cf. *Letter 64* 3.
10. *Exposition on Psalm* 99 12.
11. *Exposition on Psalm 132* 12.
12. *The Gift of Perseverance* 15.38.
13. *Exposition on Psalm 132* 4.
14. *Exposition on Psalm* 99 13.
15. Ibid. 11.
16. Ibid. 10. For a translation, see below, chap. 12.
17. *Letter* 78 9.
18. *Sermon 311* 10.
19. Cf. *Against the Writings of Petilian* 3.12.13 and 3.40.48.

20. Cf. M. von Nathusius, *Zur Charakteristik der Circumcellionen des vierten and fünften Jahrhunderts in Afrika* (Greifswald, 1900); J. Ferron, "Circonncellions d'Afrique," *Dictionnaire d'Histoire et de Géographie Ecclésiastiques*, XII 837–39; G. Krüger, "Circumcellionen," LThK, II^2, 1206.

21. Cf. *A Letter to the Catholics against the Donatists, Commonly Called "The Unity of the Church"* 16.41 and *Exposition on Psalm 132* 3 and 6.

22. Cf. *Sermo Denis* 20 12, in Morin, p. 123, and *Letter 243*.

23. *Sermon 355* 6.

24. Cf. *Letter 124* 2 and *Sermon 356* 2.

25. *Sermon 356* 12.

26. *Letter 126* 7–9.

27. *Letter* 78 6.

28. *Sermon 355* 4 and *Sermon 356* 7.

29. *Sermon 355* 1.

30. *Sermon 356* 12.

31. *Letter* 78 5.

32. Ibid. 8 and *Exposition on Psalm* 99 12. Cf. *Sermon 356* 2.

33. Beyond a doubt, what Augustine reports about those Carthage monks in *The Work of Monks* provides such striking parallels to what is known of the notions of the Eastern Euchites that we can hardly question their influence, direct or indirect. It is true that from this we cannot deduce, as G. Folliet does ("Des moines euchites à Carthage en 400–401," *Studia Patristica* II, edd. Kurt Aland and F. L. Cross [Berlin, 1957], pp. 386–99), that in Carthage at this time there existed Euchite monasteries, founded by their monks from the East; for there is no supporting evidence in Augustine's writings or in other historical sources, particularly in the decisions of the synods of the African Church of the period (see Gavigan, *De vita monastica*, pp. 241–44; cf. also L. Cilleruelo, "Nota sobre el agustinismo de los monjes de Cartago," CD, 172 [1959], 365–69, and J. M. del Estal, "Desacertada opinión moderna sobre los monjes de Cartago," ibid., 596–616).

34. *Retractations* 2.21. For a translation of extracts from *The Work of Monks*, see below, chap. 10.

35. *The Work of Monks*, especially 1–3, 17–18, 25, and 29.

36. See Butler, p. 88, note; and C. Lambot, "L'Influence de Saint Augustin sur la règle de Saint Benoît," *Revue Liturgique et Monastique*, 14 (1929), 320–30. For St. Benedict's concepts of labor, see also H. Dedler, "Vom Sinn der Arbeit nach der Regel des heiligen Benedikt," in *Benedictus, der Vater des Abendlandes*, ed. H. S. Brechter (Munich, 1947), 103–18.

37. See below, pp. 188–92.

38. Manrique, *La vida monastica*, pp. 237f., note 359, shows, however, that there is evidence for a variety of hairstyles among the North African clergy in the course of the third and fourth centuries.

39. *The Work of Monks* 31–33. Cf. also Zellinger, *Augustin und die Volksfrömmigkeit*, pp. 28f.

40. *The Work of Monks* 28.36.

41. *Letter* 262.

42. Basil, *Regulae fusius tractatae* ("Longer Rules") 44 (PL 31.1031f.). Cf. also B. Bauerreiss, "Gyrovagen," LThK, IV^2, 1293f.

43. *Letter 54* 4.5.

44. Ibid. 1.1.

45. *Letter 36* 14.32 and *Letter 54* 2.2.

46. In addition to the Manichaeans, Augustine stigmatizes the Apostolics, the Hieracites, and the Aërians as enemies of human nature in *On Heresies* 40, 47, and 53.

47. *The Ways of the Catholic Church* 1.31 and 35, *Against Faustus* 5.9, *The Good of Marriage* 23.38, and *Holy Virginity* 1.1.

48. Cf. F. Mugnier, "Abstinence," *Dictionnaire de Spiritualité*, I 121f.

49. Possidius 22.

50. Cf. *The Ways of the Catholic Church* 1.35 and *On Heresies* 40 and 53.

51. *Letter 157* 39. Cf. A. Reul, *Die sittlichen Ideale des heiligen Augustinus* (Paderborn, 1928), pp. 116ff. For a translation of sections of this letter, see below, chap. 11.

52. Possidius 10 and *Letter 111*. Even if Possidius, in writing of the Circumcellions, exaggerates the frequency of such events (cf. H. J. Diesner, "Possidius und Augustinus," *Studia Patristica* VI, ed. F. L. Cross [Berlin, 1962], pp. 358–61), still we cannot doubt that they did occur. Nonetheless it is a question whether the "servants of God" whom he mentions were inhabitants of monasteries founded directly or indirectly by Augustine.

53. Possidius 28. The doubts C. Courtois expresses (*Les Vandales et l'Afrique* [Paris, 1955], pp. 165ff.) about the reliability of this report seem ill-founded and appear to give too little credence to the fact that it comes from a contemporary, a serious witness to what he himself had seen: the conquest of North Africa by the Vandals.

54. Cf. *Letter 111*.

55. Possidius 28f.

56. Ibid.

4

Development

MONASTERIES IN AFRICA

AUGUSTINE HAS BEEN CALLED the Father of North African monasticism, and, it seems, with a certain justice. He confessed once that it was his fervent desire to spread monastic life throughout Africa.[1] Though before his time there had been virgins and widows vowed to God,[2] who perhaps had occasionally lived in some sort of community,[3] and there was no lack of ascetics and hermits,[4] evidently it was Augustine's achievement to have founded the first monasteries of men in North Africa.[5]

From the beginning, his monastic community attracted attention. Thus it was important for the furtherance of his aspirations for religious living that after only a few years in isolated Tagaste he should transfer to Hippo Regius, an important shipping and trading center, where, soon to become its bishop, he was to acquire a position of influence in the African Church. Within a short time he created several monastic houses in his new sphere of activity—the garden monastery for monks who were not priests, the community of clerics, and at least one convent of women.[6] At almost the same time as the garden monastery was founded, another—also, it seems, for monks who were not priests—was established at Carthage, the North African metropolis, with the cooperation of Aurelius, the bishop there.[7]

But Augustine kept watch over the monasteries he had founded, and repeatedly showed them a fatherly care. While bishop of Hippo, he was occupied with some questions of inheritance concerning the house at Tagaste. At this time he was writing to Alypius about the business affairs of the garden monastery.[8] He was also concerned over two monks who had left the garden monastery and had applied for admittance among the clergy of Carthage.[9] When the monastic community at Carthage experienced its first internal crisis, around the year 400, he spent much time and trouble on these "sons and brothers" of his.[10]

In the course of the following years and decades, there were further monastic foundations, made for the most part by those monks and disciples of Augustine's who, because of their virtue and learning, had been promoted to African sees.[11] Possidius wrote of "some ten bishops" who had been promoted from the ranks of Augustine's monks.[12] From Augustine's own writings we know of Alypius, bishop of Tagaste, Evodius, bishop of Uzali, Severus, bishop of Mileve, Possidius, bishop of Calama, and Profuturus and his successor Fortunatus, bishops of Cirta.[13] As Augustine and his boyhood friend Alypius had done,[14] these men as their status changed remained faithful to their monastic ideals. At their episcopal sees they founded communities of clerics, and houses for lay monks and for virgins,[15] and through these houses many other monastic foundations may have been established or influenced.

Indeed, toward the end of Augustine's life Christian monasticism had begun to take root in many parts of Roman North Africa. Although the extant source material is sparse, J. J. Gavigan has determined that in fifth-century North Africa there were no fewer than thirty-eight houses of men and at least ten of women.[16] But the actual number may have been greater. In many instances there is no certain proof that these monasteries were founded under either the direct or the indirect influence of Augustine and his concept of monasticism. In fact, Ephrem Hendrikx has suggested that, in all of Africa, only the monasteries in the provinces of Numidia can properly be described as Augustinian; in those of Africa Proconsularis, he thought, a certain Augustinian influence had prevailed. In the monasteries of Bycacene, on the other hand, the prevailing influence, it would seem, was that, not of Augustine, but of an Eastern monasticism.[17] Andrés Manrique agrees, basing his opinion on certain texts, some of them Augustine's own, that as early as the beginning of the fifth century there existed in North Africa, alongside Augustinian-influenced monasticism, another of a more Eastern character, perhaps established by monks who had emigrated from Italy about the turn of the century or soon thereafter because of the Germanic invasions.[18]

In many cases, because we have so few sources, we shall never be able to answer the question of how much Augustine cooperated in the foundation of North African monasteries outside his own diocese. Yet, if we look at the whole picture, the answers may not be of great importance. As we estimate his influence on the monastic life of his own time and of successive centuries, what Augustine wrote about monasticism and asceticism is of far greater importance. Often, in his sermons and writings, he praised and defended what he himself, with his monks and his clerics, had tried to achieve. Thus, in fact, he became one of the great monastic teachers of the Western world.

Among his writings on monasticism, first place must be given to his *Rule*. It is the oldest monastic rule known in the West and even today it is one of the foundations of Catholic religious life.[19]

Sermon 355 and *Sermon 356*, which grew out of bitter experiences in his own monastery, allow us to see deeply into his own life and that of his clerics as monks; and as such they could not but influence the development of Western monasticism.[20]

But Augustine made contact with monasteries that were not his own. One fine proof of this is the letter to Eudoxius, a priest and the superior of monks on the island of Capraria.[21] In Augustine's first years as a bishop two monks from this monastery in the Mediterranean visited his own community. When this pair—they were called Eustasius and Andreas—talked with him, they reawakened in Augustine a longing for a life of retirement such as they could live on Capraria. In selfless joy he wrote to their superior, congratulating him and his subjects. Urgently he entreated their prayer, which surely must be far more recollected than his own, troubled as he was by the cares of his office. Yet in a spirit of brotherly love he added a word of admonition. In the years of his pastoral work he had very often seen that it was not only the self-chosen contemplation of the monastery which has merit in God's eyes. So he warns them not to be deaf to the cries of Mother Church if she appeals for the monks' help. Not even monastic solitude is any certain help against the evil snares of the enemy. There is only one thing of importance, the letter insists: that all things be accomplished to God's glory.[22]

In the company of his fellow-bishops and at the synods of the African Church as well, it was Augustine who served the interest of monasticism and who defended its rights.[23] His treatise *The Work of Monks* shows the esteem in which Augustine was held, as early as the beginning of the fifth century, as a respected authority in questions concerning monastic life. Bishop Aurelius of Carthage did not wish to make an independent ruling about confusions existing in the monks' houses in his diocese; rather, he turned for help to the bishop of Hippo, who himself had founded one of Carthage's monasteries. This was the occasion of Augustine's most comprehensive work about the concept of monasticism.[24] A second time, in the year 426 or 427, he had to guide with a firm hand the development of a far-distant monastery. This was during the tumults of the Pelagian controversy over grace. In the house at Hadrumetum in Bycacene, Augustine's letter to Sixtus had been misunderstood, and had caused great confusion among the monks, some of whom maintained that divine grace was so omnipotent that beneath it no independent act of the will could be made. Augustine learned about this from Cresconius and Felix, two young brothers of the monastery, who had come to Hippo to seek a decision in these difficult questions of faith. After the Easter days, Augustine sent the two monks back to Valentinus, their abbot, with a letter and with the treatise he had written especially for their needs, *Grace and Free Will*.[25] The abbot was glad to accede to Augustine's request, and sent the monk Florus, who had occasioned the dispute, to Hippo for Augustine's instruction. At the same time Valentinus asked him for directions in many questions concerning monastic life.[26] A little later, Augustine learned of a different dissension in the same monastery. One monk had denied that the superior had any right to correct him, and had appealed to the omnipotent operation of grace; under its influence, good works necessarily would follow. But where grace might be lacking, man must fall short. Once again, Augustine took up his pen, and wrote for Valentinus and his monks a short treatise, *Rebuke and Grace*.[27]

RESPONSE FROM THE LAITY

Augustine's efforts on behalf of a Christian ascetic life were directed not only to those men and women who imitated him in choosing monastic life. In various treatises[28] and in not a few of his sermons he appealed to wider circles among Christians, and sought to present to them the ideal of a life suitable to one's present station in life, consecrated to God. Without in any way questioning the moral excellence of marriage, he was zealous in recommending, in the sense of the Apostle Paul (1 Cor. 7 and 1 Tim. 5:5), a life undividedly devoted to God in continence and virginity. Many of his letters show, as they deal with these questions of Christian ascetic effort in the life of the laity, that he met with response from such Christians.[29]

As an experienced director of souls, Augustine did not work according to predetermined plans but took wise account of everyone's station, education, and circumstances. Above all, he took care not to create conflict for his Christian laypeople between a life of asceticism and their duties to their families and their callings. It was their task to sanctify themselves in the world and not to neglect their dependents, perhaps out of their vain longings for a withdrawn life.[30]

About the year 424, an interesting case arose. A high-ranking imperial officer called Bonifatius, who at that time was governor-general of Roman North Africa, was seriously occupied with plans, after his wife's early death, to forsake the world and become a monk. In a personal interview at Tubunae he outlined his proposal to Augustine and his friend Alypius. Yet both bishops were agreed in dissuading him, but not because they doubted the sincerity of his intentions. Certainly, they welcomed his proposal to live thenceforth unmarried and continently and enouraged him in this; but he was not to abandon his position in the state and his military service since, in so serving, he could be of much greater use to the Church of God.[31]

It was of special concern to Augustine to show any layman who had decided for the ideals of asceticism what the proper motives were for so acting. He directed his mind to the surpassing love of God, who surrendered His only-begotten Son to death for us. He showed him the transience of this world,[32] and reminded him of the imperishable reward that was to come,[33] of the "joy over Christ, in Christ, with Christ, following Christ, through Christ, where Christ dwells."[34] He depicted the exaltation of the joys of heaven, comparing with that our earthly existence, for the preservation of which men took so many dangers upon themselves, not even shrinking from grave offenses against God.[35]

And, too, he had to insist, again and again, that the promises made to God must be fulfilled. Make a vow, and keep it! A man who does not keep his vow will never become what he could have remained if he had made no vow. He will have broken faith with God Himself.[36] In a letter written in 427, Augustine is uncompromising in his reprimands even to the aforementioned Bonifatius, the governor-general, who disregarding the proposal he had once formed of dedicating his continent life to God, had married again, and must indeed have been leading a far from exemplary life as a married man.[37] On another occasion, Augustine took a noblewoman, Ecdicia, sharply to task; she had shamefully injured her husband, neglecting her duty of love and justice toward him out of a feigned zeal for the ascetic life. Without his knowledge, she had distributed her possessions to the poor and put on widow's attire. For this, Augustine demanded, gravely and severely, that she make full restitution to her husband.[38]

Through his celebrity as a man of religion and probably through his writings as well, Augustine exercised a considerable power of attraction among the women of the Roman aristocracy, where the enthusiasm for an ascetic life had not lessened since St. Jerome had been active among them.

The elder Melania, a Roman widow of the Antonian gens, was the first to cross over to Africa, in 404, to make Augustine's personal acquaintance. She brought a letter for him from his friend Paulinus, singing her praises and those of her son, the Roman senator Valerius Publicola. During the time she was in Hippo, the news of the death of her son reached her. Augustine in his reply to Paulinus praised her exemplary bearing when she received these sad tidings. He tells how she had lamented the son's early death most of all because it had prevented him from freeing himself even more completely from the things of this earth.[39]

A few years later, Melania's daughter-in-law Albina, Publicola's widow, and Melania's granddaughter, the young Melania, with her husband Pinianus, made their way to North Africa, driven out of Rome by the invasion of the Goths. At the beginning of the year 411 they arrived in Tagaste, to learn about Augustinian monastic life. Augustine regretted that, because of the winter cold and his impaired health, but most of all because of his pastoral duties, he could not undertake the journey to Tagaste.[40] So Melania and Pinianus came to Hippo, accompanied by Bishop Alypius. When these important visitors appeared in the church, a disagreeable contretemps occurred. The people created an uproar, demanding that Pinianus be ordained priest for them, as the young Augustine had once been. The tumult threatened to degenerate into violence, especially against Bishop Alypius, who opposed the people's demands. Calm was restored only when Pinianus bound himself by a forced oath to remain in Hippo, and to receive nowhere else—if he ever received it at all—priestly ordination. For a while this incident created disharmony between Augustine and Albina, Pinianus' mother-in-law, without, however, lastingly damaging the relations with the Roman visitors.[41] The younger Melania and her husband remained Augustine's faithful disciples all their lives. For many years they lived in Tagaste a life of continence dedicated to God, and, as they had already done in Italy,[42] founded in Tagaste two monasteries, one for men, another for women, and personally undertook their supervision. It was Augustine himself who counseled them to prudence in their endowments of the poor and of their houses. "The money which you are now distributing to monasteries," his advice ran, "will be gobbled up in a short time. But if you wish for a memorial that will not be forgotten, in heaven and on earth, then provide for each monastery a house with an assured income."[43] In the year 417, Melania and Pinianus went to Palestine, in order to continue living their ascetic life in Jerusalem.[44]

Three other distinguished Roman women, the widow Falconia Proba, her daughter-in-law Juliana, and her granddaughter Demetrias, from the

Anician gens, one of the richest Roman noble families, came to North Africa in 410, that year of upheaval, drawn there not least by the personality of the great bishop of Hippo.[45] For a number of years they found shelter in Carthage with other Roman women who had joined up with them. It was probably here, too, that Augustine made the personal acquaintance of Proba and her family, and was edified by her exemplary life.[46] He composed an instruction of some length on prayer at the request of this Roman matron.[47] He also recommended himself to her prayers.[48] Impressed by a sermon of his on virginity, Demetrias in 413 withdrew from the marriage that had been arranged for her, and, with the consent of her grandmother and her mother, received from Bishop Aurelius of Carthage the virgin's veil. Proba and Juliana lost no time in sending the news to Augustine, and to mark the occasion sent him a gift.[49] Shortly afterward, Augustine wrote for Juliana, the virgin's mother, who had been widowed at a young age, his treatise *On the Excellence of Widowhood.* He stresses that the circumstances that make widowhood Christian are "the preservation of love, piety, and the strength of the soul's union with God."[50] But his refutations of the Pelagian heresy which he had by then undertaken prompted Augustine to write in detail that the love of chastity and the joys of a heart lifted up to God are divine gifts, and that thanks for them are due to God.[51] A further letter to this distinguished widow, written in the year 417, has also been preserved. By chance Augustine had read the work of an unnamed author, treating of virginity, which bore a dedication to the virgin Demetrias. Augustine urgently warned Juliana and her daughter about the Pelagian errors represented in the treatise, and asked them to tell him the name of the author.[52]

DEVELOPMENT THROUGH THE CENTURIES

Severe blows were dealt to monasticism in North Africa by the Vandal invasion (429–435) and the persecutions of the Catholic Church which followed, under the Arian rulers Genseric (427–477), Hunneric (477–484), and Transimund (496–523). Many religious had to endure fierce hostility. During this period, there were many monks and nuns who did not keep faith with the Church and who, under the pressure exerted by the Arians, permitted themselves to be rebaptized. But the sources also tell of other monks and consecrated virgins who died as martyrs. Yet in spite of all this, monastic life in North Africa was not destroyed in this epoch of persecutions. A great number of houses of men and of women remained.

Moreover, in the peaceful era which the Church experienced after the victory (533–534) of Belisarius over the Vandals, in the sixth and seventh centuries, a series of new foundations followed, especially when monks and nuns arrived from the East, driven out of their monasteries in Palestine, Syria, and Egypt by Persian and Arab invasions. The end of monastic life in the region came only through its conquest by the Mohammedans in 709, and the general disintegration of Christendom, traces of which can still be found until the twelfth century.[53]

One important result of these persecutions was that North African monasticism became known in neighboring countries. African bishops, clergy, and monks, attacked by the Vandals or even banished from the land, sought new homes beyond the sea. These refugees and exiles made their way to Sardinia, Sicily, Spain, Gaul, and southern Italy. The facts that follow are derived from the few sources from which we can form conclusions.

St. Fulgentius, bishop of Ruspe (462–527), who as a young man had chosen the monastic life, founded in 502 at Cagliari on the island of Sardinia a kind of conventual community for a few clerics and monks who had come from Africa with him. When, ten or fifteen years later, after a brief sojourn in his native land, he again went into exile, a great company of monks accompanied him. Therefore he built a second house, specified as a cloister for monks, "away from the din of the town, beside the basilica of the holy martyr Saturninus."[54] Ferrandus, his contemporary, has an account of the inmates' way of life in which there are certain echoes of the prescriptions of Augustine's *Rule*. They followed, in particular, the directions in the Acts of the Apostles: "None of them called anything his own, but all was held by them in common."[55] J. J. Gavigan, who studied the sources in research for his history of North African monasticism after Augustine, considers it probable that this monastery survived for at least two hundred years.[56]

The African Rufinianus, a bishop from Bycacene, emigrated to Sicily, perhaps during the last years of Hunnerich's persecution. About the year 500 he was living as a monk on a small island off the Sicilian coast. We do not know if he entered an already existing monastery, if he himself founded such a house, or if he lived as a hermit. Nor can anything be determined about the sort of monastic life he followed.[57]

About 570, perhaps because of the persecution at the hands of the pagan Berbers, the African abbot Donatus, with about seventy monks, went to Spain, bringing with him a considerable quantity of manuscripts. He founded the Servitanum monastery, which was probably located in the diocese of Arcávica in New Castile.[58] His successor, Abbot Eutropius, perhaps an African as well, played an important part in the Third Synod of Toledo in 589 and soon afterward became bishop of Valencia. L. M. Verheijen has established that Eutropius in his *Letter About the Difficulties of Monks* seems to have used Augustine's *Rule*; this prompts the supposition that the *Rule* was known in the Servitanum monastery.[59] About the same time as Donatus arrived in Spain, another African abbot, Nunctus by name, is said to have settled with a number of monks in the diocese of Merida in southern Spain, but soon afterward was murdered by local inhabitants. The story comes from the partly legendary *Lives of the Holy Fathers of Merida*, and there are no other sources to confirm it.[60]

There is no evidence in the scanty sources available that African monks emigrated to Gaul, yet mention should be made of Julianus Pomerius, who came from Mauretania. Soon after the middle of the fifth century he came to southern Gaul, where, in Arles, around the year 497, he taught grammar and rhetoric to Caesarius, who was to become its archbishop. Shortly thereafter he became a priest, and died as abbot of a monastery, in which there probably were clerics. In his treatise, still preserved, *On the Contemplative Life*, he shows himself strongly influenced by Augustine, whose spiritual pupil he expressly calls himself.[61]

There is no incontrovertible evidence to show that during these centuries monasticism from North Africa also took root in Italy, but this is certainly highly probable. Reports from about the year 900 mention that the monastery at Naples dedicated to St. Gaudiosus was founded by an African bishop of that name who had fled from the Vandals.[62] And although Eugippius, the author of the copious *Excerpts from the Works of St. Augustine*, who died in 533 as abbot of the Lucullanum monastery near Naples, frequently asserts that he had come from North Africa, it seems more probable that he was of Styrian origin.[63] So, too, in the case of the younger Arnobius (died sometime after 455), who had lived as a monk in Rome from about 432 and who composed various theological works; his African birth is likely but not certain. Moreover, in his teaching about grace he opposes Augustine.[64]

Yet it is true that not one of the sources reports that in any of the foundations in Europe which have been mentioned, or in the then existing monasteries for men or women in North Africa, the religious lived according to the *Rule of St. Augustine*;[65] nor can it be proved beyond a doubt in any one case that we are concerned with truly Augustinian monasticism. Even when contacts are indicated, as with St. Fulgentius' house of monks at Cagliari, which suggest Augustinian influence, other such sources are not excluded. Yet we have one piece of evidence of the year 525 to show how highly Augustine was esteemed as an authority in questions concerning monastic life. An African abbot called Petrus brought a dispute in his monastery before the Council of Carthage, and made repeated and specific allusions to *Sermon 356*.[66] We must also assume that Augustine's works on monastic life, particularly *The Work of Monks*, *Holy Virginity*, *Sermon 355* and those following it, and perhaps also the *Rule*, were known in many North African monasteries, especially in those founded by bishops who came from his own houses.[67]

Even so, it is not merely a more or less well-founded supposition that Augustine's ideals for monasticism survived and exercised influence through the centuries. We possess important though indirect evidence of this in the *Rule of St. Augustine*.[68] We can observe how quickly this gained circulation from the influence—at times important—which it had on a number of the oldest monastic rules in Gaul, Italy, and Spain.[69] It was used as early as ca. 500 by St. Caesarius of Arles when he composed his monastic rule. When, later, between the years 512 and 534, Caesarius wrote a rule for nuns, he incorporated in it almost half of Augustine's text. Aurelian of Arles, in the rule for monks and nuns which he wrote ca. 540, borrows from Augustine by way of Caesarius; as does Donatus of Besançon in his rule for nuns, ca. 624, in which he quotes from the *Rule* of Augustine, naming him as its author.[70] In St. Benedict's *Rule*, too, there are six word-for-word quotations from Augustine.[71] In the *Regula Tarnatensis*, also written in the sixth century, for the Agaunum monastery on the Rhone, Chapters 14 to 32 of the second part show a most marked dependence on Augustine's *Rule*, almost the entire text of which is borrowed, albeit with frequent changes of word order and transposition of sentences.[72] In the sixth or seventh century Augustine's prescriptions concerning singing in monastic prayer (Chapter 2.1–4) were borrowed in a rule for monks which has come down to us as *The Rule of St. Paul and St. Stephen the Abbots* and is presumed to have originated in northern Spain.[73] Leander and Isidore, the archbishops of Seville, bear witness that Augustine's *Rule* was also known in the southern part of the Iberian peninsula. Leander, who died in 600 or 601, drew on it when composing his constitutions for nuns, *The Government of Virgins*; and in the *Rule of Monks* of his brother, Isidore, who died in 636, there is a series of quotations from Augustine's text.[74]

But the complete text of the *Rule* itself continued to be copied in manuscripts. Winfried Hümpfner during his decades of research on the *Rule* was able to establish a list of no fewer than twenty-six manuscripts from the period between 600 and 1100, which today are in libraries in Germany, France, Holland, Italy, Austria, Spain, and Switzerland, and which came mostly from former monastic libraries in these countries.[75] In addition, there are a number of manuscripts of the same period which contain the text of the *Rule* in a form composed for nuns.[76]

More recently, L. M. Verheijen has shown that the *Rule* in its oldest manuscripts is always found together with other monastic rules. His conclusion is that the *Rule* formed one component of the monastic "tradition of the Fathers," and was copied only as a component of this tradition.[77] Thus, when monasteries of this epoch knew of Augustine's *Rule* and were influenced by it, this influence could not have been single and predominant. According to Verheijen, therefore, it would be unhistorical to assume that certain monks from Augustine's monasteries in North Africa, after their exile across the Mediterranean, pursued a life lived according to his *Rule*, to the exclusion of all other monastic influences, and that the tradition of Augustinian monastic living, in this exclusive sense, had never been interrupted. But it would be just as exaggerated and unhistorical to maintain that in the monastic tradition between the fifth and ninth centuries there was no Augustinian element. Not only was Augustine's *Rule* copied in manuscripts there; it did in fact influence monastic life,[78] admittedly, along with other monastic rules within the many-sided monastic tradition of which it formed a part.[79]

As a single, binding rule of living, Augustine's *Rule*, it would seem, first reappeared in the setting of the reform of the canons regular, of whom the Third Lateran Council had demanded the strict practice of the common life. Among these reformed canons regular, the *Rule of St. Augustine* was first mentioned in the year 1067, in the province of Rheims. Alhough the *Rule* was never officially prescribed by Rome, fifty years later it had become generally circulated and recognized as the norm for the life of the canons regular throughout the Continent.[80] Most newly-constituted religious orders of the High and Late Middle Ages and many congregations in modern times followed the example of the canons regular. It is only more recently that Augustine's *Rule* lost its pre-eminence, when the Franciscan *Rule* exerted a comparably great influence.

Apart from the so-called "Augustinian Hermits," usually known simply as "Augustinians," with their ideals strongly marked by Augustine's spirit,[81] the following adopted his *Rule* in the High Middle Ages: orders that originated in the institution of the canons regular or were strongly influenced by them, such as the Premonstratensians (1120); the Bethlehemites (before 1169), and the Dominicans (1215); the knightly orders of Johannites (1118) and Teutonic Knights (1190) and other foundations of the times of the Crusades, such as the Hospitalers and Lazarites; the orders founded to redeem Christian slaves, the Trinitarians (1198) and Mercedarians (1235); and the Servites (1256). In the fourteenth century the *Rule* of St. Augustine became the rule of the confraternities of hermits, the Pauline Fathers, the Ambrosians and the "Apostle Brothers," and of confraternities of laymen, the Alexian Brothers, the Jesuates and the "Voluntary Poor." In the sixteenth century it was adopted by the Brothers of Mercy, and by teaching orders, the Fathers of Christian Doctrine and the Piarists, and, in more recent times, by the Augustinians of the Assumption of Mary, known as "Assumptionists."

In addition to the branches of these men's orders formed for sisters, there are also orders exclusively for women who follow Augustine's *Rule*, such as the Bridgettines (1344) [although St. Bridget planned monasteries that were two separate houses, one for women, the other for men], the various branches of the Annunciates (since 1500), the teaching orders of the Ursulines (1535), the Salesian Sisters, and the Poor Teaching Sisters of Our Blessed Lady (1833), the Magdalene Sisters of the Middle Ages (1224) and the more modern associations related to them, the Angelicals of St. Paul (1530), the Sisters of Our Lady of Charity of Refuge (1644), and the Daughters of the Good Shepherd (1692).

Through the Third Orders of the Dominicans, Augustinians, and Servites, the essentials of Augustine's *Rule* were conveyed to lay people. Concern for the concept of "third orders," in its turn, brought about the establishment of many congregations of tertiaries. Well over one hundred religious communities have in the course of the centuries accepted the Augustinian *Rule*.[82]

But for such associations to have taken over the *Rule* meant more than a mere commitment to one or two well-tried governing principles of the monastic life. Justly, Augustine's *Rule* has been called his legacy to those who would imitate him in that life.[83] In this treatise, he is using his personal and intimate thoughts. But because of this, he is in a certain sense to be regarded as the spiritual father of all religious communities who have ordered their lives in the spirit of his *Rule*. In these orders and congregations there still live today many of the monastic ideals which Augustine sought to realize in his monasteries.

NOTES

1. *The Work of Monks* 28.36.

2. Cf. Tertullian, *The Veiling of Virgins* (PL 2.935ff.) and Cyprian, *The Dress of Virgins* (PL 4.451ff.). See also J. M. del Estal, "Un cenobitismo preagustiniano en Africa? [Part I]," CD, 169 (1956), 377ff.; and idem, "El voto de virginidad en la primitiva iglesia de Africa," ibid., 175 (1962), 593–623 (also published separately, with a bibliography, in El Escorial in 1963).

3. J. Besse, "Règle de Saint Augustin," *Dictionnaire de Theologie Catholique*, I 2472. See also Spreitzenhofer, *Entwicklung des alten Mönchtums*, pp. 27f. Del Estal ("Sobre los comienzos," 335–60) cites two African synodal decisions for his opinion that the first evidence for a common life (*vita communis*) among consecrated virgins in the true sense of a convent for women is for the years between 393 and 397, and assumes that this cannot be attributed to anyone other than Augustine. But cf. on this Folliet, "Aux origines," 32*n*38.

4. J. M. del Estal, "Un cenobitismo preagustiniano en Africa? [Part II]," CD, 171 (1958), 162–95, esp. 167ff., and Folliet, "Aux origines," 27ff.

5. See Monceaux, "Saint Augustin et Saint Antoine," p. 65; del Estal, "Un cenobitismo [Part II]," 189ff., Manrique, *La vida monastica*, pp. 147f.; idem, "San Agustín y el monaquismo africano," CD, 173 (1960), 118–38, esp. 126f. (with, to be sure, certain reservations); L. Cilleruelo, *El monacato de San Agustín y su regla*, 2nd ed. (Valladolid, 1966), p. 129. Folliet's assumptions to the contrary lack proof; see his "Aux origines," 33f., 40.

6. Possidius' report (chap. 31) that at his death Augustine had bequeathed to the Church "monasteries filled with chaste men and women, with their superiors" seems to testify that he founded more than one convent of women in Hippo.

7. *Letter 22* 9 and *Letter 24* 6. See also L. Cilleruelo, "Los monjes de Cartago y San Agustín," CD, 169 (1956), 456–63, esp. 456ff.; Manrique, *La vida monastica*, pp. 91–100; Gavigan, *De vita monastica*, pp. 126f.; J. M. del Estal, "Institución monástica de San Agustín," CD, 178 (1965), 259ff.

8. *Letter 83*.

9. *Letter 60*.

10. Cf. *The Work of Monks* 1.1 and 28.36. It cannot be demonstrated with certainty, however, that the recipients of *The Work of Monks* were members of the "Augustinian" house at Carthage; cf. Lorenz, "Anfänge," p. 25 and note 21.

11. By this time it was the custom, both in the East and in Italy, to ordain monks as priests and bishops. Insofar as they possessed both moral firmness

and the necessary education, they were regarded as especially suitable candidates for Holy Orders. See Spreitzenhofer, *Entwicklung des alten Mönchtums*, pp. 125f.; and S. Schiwietz, *Das morgenländische Mönchtum* I, pp. 312ff., and idem, *Das morgenländische Mönchtum* III (Mödling, 1938), pp. 419f.

12. Possidius 11.

13. For the sources in Augustine's writings and for further information about the monasteries these bishops founded, see Manrique, *La vida monastica*, pp. 151ff., and Gavigan, *De vita monastica*, pp. 116ff., 128ff. It is probable that Urbanus, the bishop of Sicca Veneria, was also at one time a monk at Hippo, but there is no evidence that he founded a monastery. Antoninus, the bishop of Fussala, mentioned above, a cleric in Augustine's clerics' monastery, may be ignored; it is less than probable that he was a monastic founder. See Gavigan, *De vita monastica*, pp. 129 and 124, respectively.

14. *Letter 24* 2 specifically states that Alypius as bishop remained a faithful monk.

15. Possidius 11.

16. *De vita monastica*, pp. 95ff., 54ff.

17. Hendrikx' ideas were contained in a paper delivered at the "International Week of Augustinian Spirituality," sponsored by the Augustinian Order and held in Rome in October 1956, which dealt with the historical evolution of Augustinian monasticism from its beginnings until the Islamic invasions. The paper itself has not been published, but its results have been reported by L. Cilleruelo, "Un episodio en el primitivo monacato agustiniano," CD, 172 (1959), 357.

18. *La vita monastica*, pp. 131–46, and "San Agustín y el monaquismo africano," 128ff. There seems to me to be a lack of substantial evidence for his assumption that this monasticism of Eastern character came increasingly under Augustinian influence.

19. See below, chap. 9.

20. The Synod of Carthage in 525 made use of these sermons (Hardouin, *Acta conciliorum*, II 1087f.); they form a source for Chrodegang's *Rule* and the constitutions for canons regular of the Aachen Synod in 817; and, finally, they played an important part in the reform of the canons regular in the eleventh century. See below, chap. 12.

21. We cannot be absolutely sure which of the various "goat-islands" of the Mediterranean is meant. At that time there were at least three with the name "Capraria": the modern Capraja in the Ligurian Sea, the modern Caprera, to the northeast of Sardinia, and the modern Cabrera, south of Majorca. The pagan poet Rutilius testified in his *Itinerarium* that Christian monks lived on the Ligurian island (Spreitzenhofer, *Entwicklung des alten Mönchtums*, pp. 26, 63*n*8; Penco, *Storia*, p. 21). W. Hümpfner (AH, p. lxxxi) and J. Perez de Urbel ("Le monachisme en Espagne au temps de Saint Martin," *Studia Anselmiana*, 46 [1961], 49f., 56, 59) decided in favor of Cabrera, nearer to Africa; but when Perez assumed that perhaps Orosius had established the first connection between Augustine and this island monastery, he failed to observe

that *Letter 48* is to be dated a good decade earlier than Orosius' journey to Hippo.

22. *Letter 48*. See below, chap. 11.

23. *Letter 60* and *Letter 64* 3. Cf. *Sermon 356* 14.

24. *The Work of Monks*. See below, chap. 10; and *Retractations* 2.21.

25. *Retractations* 2.66.

26. Cf. *Letters 214–216*.

27. *Retractations* 2.67. The monastery at Hadrumetum survived for a long time (cf. Gavigan, *De vita monastica*, p. 201). For Augustine's treatment in *Rebuke and Grace* of the spirit and the justifiability of correction, see below, pp. 156–58ff.

28. Among Augustine's ascetic writings, the following, though directed beyond monastic circles, have had importance for them, both in Augustine's own day and in later centuries: *Continence* (a treatment of the fundamentals of Christian asceticism), *Christian Discipline* (a treatise on the whole of Christian teaching about right living), *The Usefulness of Fasting* and *Patience* (which show the significance of fasting and the blessings of patience), *Holy Virginity* and *The Excellence of Widowhood* (which treat of virginity consecrated to God and of Christian widowhood).

29. Cf. *Letter 127* 8; *Letter 150*; *Letter 188*; *Letter 208* 7; *Letter 212* 1; *Letter 218* 2.

30. Popp, *Sankt Augustinus als Erzieher*, pp. 25ff.

31. *Letter 220* 3.

32. *Letter 127* 1.

33. *Letter 208* 7.

34. *Holy Virginity* 27.27.

35. *Letter 127* 2ff.

36. Ibid. 8. Cf. also *Exposition on Pslam 75* 16 and *Exposition on Psalm 83* 4.

37. *Letter 220*.

38. *Letter 262*.

39. *Letter 94* 2f. See F. X. Murphy, "Melania die Ältere," LThK, VII², 249f.; see also idem, "Melania the Elder: A Biographical Note," *Traditio*, 5 (1947), 59–77.

40. *Letter 124*.

41. *Letters 125–126*. For these events in the basilica at Hippo, see Zellinger, *Augustin und die Volksfrömmigkeit*, pp. 94ff.

42. Cf. Spreitzenhofer, *Entwicklung des alten Mönchtums*, pp. 22, 25f., 34.

43. Cf. Zellinger, *Augustin und die Volksfrömmigkeit*, p. 30.

44. Cf. Gerontius, *Das Leben der heiligen Melania*, trans. S. Krottenthaler, Bibliothek der Kirchenväter 5 (Munich, 1912), pp. 445–98; and H. Leclercq, "Melaine (Sainte)," *Dictionnaire d'Archéologie Chrétienne et de Liturgie*, XI 206–30.

45. Cf. *Letter 188* 1.

46. Cf. ibid.

47. *Letter 130.*

48. *Letter 131.*

49. *Letter 150* and *Letter 188* 1. See also G. Bardy, "Démétriade (sainte)," *Dictionnaire de Spiritualité*, III 133–37; and A. P. Frutaz, "Demetrias," LThK, III², 215.

50. *The Excellence of Widowhood* 19.

51. *The Excellence of Widowhood* 16.20.

52. *Letter 188*. Cf. also G. de Plinval, *Pélage: Ses écrits, sa vie et sa réforme* (Lausanne, 1943), pp. 242–51. See also below, pp. 255–56.

53. Cf. Gavigan, *De vita monastica*. See also Gavigan's "Vita monastica in Africa septentrionali desiitne cum invasione Wandalorum?" *Augustinianum*, 1 (1961), 7–49.

54. Ferrandus gives a detailed report in his *Life of St. Fulgentius* 20, 43, and 27.51 (PL 65.138f. and 143). Cf. Gavigan, *De vita monastica*, pp. 149, 178f.

55. Gavigan, *De vita monastica*, pp. 149, 179f. I. Schuster has established that Ferrandus used Augustine's *Rule*, in combination with the so-called *Ordo monasterii*, in the composition of the *Life of St. Fulgentius* (cf. L. M. Verheijen, *La Règle de Saint Augustin*, 2 vols. [Paris, 1967], I 146).

56. Gavigan, *De vita monastica*, p. 180.

57. Ibid., pp. 175, 253.

58. Ibid., pp. 218f., 256. Ildefons of Toledo, in his *Of Illustrious Men* (PL 96.200), writes of Donatus: "This prior, as remarkable during his lifetime for the example of his virtue as he was famous after his death for the brightness of his reputation, is said to have introduced into Spain the practice and rule of monastic living." We must not understand this remark to mean that Donatus' foundation was the first in the Iberian peninsula, for it can be demonstrated that Spanish monasticism is much older. Cf. Perez, "Le monachisme en Espagne."

59. Gavigan, *De vita monastica*, p. 219. See also Verheijen, *La Règle*, I 249, 254, and U. Domínguez-del Val, "Eutropio de Valencia y sus fuentes de información," *Revista Española de Teología*, 14 (1954), 391–92.

60. Gavigan, *De vita monastica*, pp. 218, 256.

61. Ibid., p. 257; J. Quasten, "Julianus Pomerius," LThK, V², 1199; G. B. Ladner, *The Idea of Reform: Its Impact on Christian Thought and Action in the Age of the Fathers* (Cambridge, Mass., 1959), pp. 389f.

62. Gavigan, *De vita monastica*, p. 255. See also Spreitzenhofer, *Entwicklung des alten Mönchtums*, p. 20; and Penco, *Storia*, p. 41.

63. Gavigan, *De vita monastica*, p. 256; L. Lenzenweger, "Eugippius," LThK, III², 1179; Penco, *Storia*, pp. 25f.

64. Gavigan, *De vita monastica*, pp. 254f.; Altaner, *Patrologie*, p. 422.

65. Gavigan, *De vita monastica*, pp. 100f.

66. Ibid., pp. 103, 194.

67. See above, pp. 83–84. Even so, convincing proof is still lacking for Monceaux's assertion, in "Saint Augustin et Saint Antoine," p. 88, that a

century after his death Augustine was still "the legislator of monasticism" in North Africa.

68. For the problems presented by the *Rule*, see below, chap. 9.

69. A series of the following enumerated parallel texts is to be found in clearly arranged facing order in A. Casamassa, "Note sulla *Regula secunda sancti Augustini*," AVSM I, pp. 361ff., and Manrique, *La vida monastica*, pp. 432ff. Cf. P. Schroeder, "Die Augustinerchorherrenregel: Entstehung, kritischer Text und Einführung der Regel," *Archiv für Urkundenforschung*, 9 (1926), 293f.; K. Wirges, *Die Anfänge der Augustinerchorherren und die Gründung des Augustinerchorherrenstiftes Ravengiersburg* (Betzdorf, 1928), pp. 98ff.

70. C. Lambot, "La Règle de Saint Augustin et Saint Césaire," *Revue Bénédictine*, 41 (1929), 334f.

71. Butler, p. 187. Besides the six verbatim quotations, he indicates an additional number of parallels. Even if Benedict's quotations from Augustine are always limited to only a few lines (cf. Lambot, "L'Influence de Saint Augustin," 320–30), the few points on which there is agreement are, all of them, important. See also Steidle, pp. 13, 61.

72. For this *Rule*, see also M. Besson, *Monasterium Acaunense* (Fribourg, 1913), pp. 113–18. He denies that Acaunum is identical with the modern Saint Maurice in the Valais canton of Switzerland.

73. U. Berlière, "La Règle des SS. Etienne et Paul," in *Mélanges Paul Thomas* (Bruges, 1930), pp. 39–59; and Ladner, *Idea of Reform*, pp. 382f. For a critical edition of this rule, see J. E. M. Vilanova, *Regula sanctorum Pauli et Stephani abbatum* (Montserrat, 1959).

74. Verheijen, *La Règle*, II 209ff.

75. The catalogue of these manuscripts has been published in A. Zumkeller, "Zur handschriftlichen Überlieferung und ursprünglichen Textgestalt der Augustinusregel (aus dem Nachlass des P. Dr. Winfried Hümpfner OESA)," *Augustiniana*, 11 (1961), 427ff.

76. Verheijen, *La Règle*, II 210ff.

77. Ibid., 213ff.

78. Verheijen points out (ibid., 214, 215) the interesting fact that in one group of manuscripts, the oldest of which is MS Lambach 31 dating from the ninth century, there is a small addition to the text in the ninth chapter which can be explained only by the need to make the text of the *Rule* agree with conditions in some particular monastic environment.

79. Ibid., 213–15.

80. Schroeder, "Die Augustinerchorherrenregel," 295ff.; L. Hertling, "Kanoniker, Augustinerregel und Augustinerorden," *Zeitschrift für katholische Theologie*, 54 (1930), 343f.; C. Dereine, "Chanoines," *Dictionnaire d'Histoire et de Géographie Ecclésiastiques*, XII 387f.

81. The Augustinian Hermits were given their present formation by the bull *Licet ecclesiae*, issued by Pope Alexander IV on April 9, 1256. It dealt with the union of several already existing monastic communities: the Hermits of

St. William of Maleval, the Hermits of Monte Favali, the Friars of John Bonus, the Hermits of Brettino, and the Hermits of Tuscany; these last were designated in the bull as being "of the order of St. Augustine" (*ordinis sancti Augustini*), together with a few smaller, apparently relatively independent groups in Spain, Germany, France, and England. The number of already existing houses which this union comprised is estimated at about 180. The bull gives to this new institution the name "Order of the Hermits of St. Augustine" (*Ordo Eremitarum sancti Augustini*), which, in those days, was understood to signify a union under a form of living (*ordo*), of St. Augustine, in eremitical form (cf. A. de Meijer and R. Kuiters, "Licet Ecclesiae Catholicae," *Augustiniana*, 6 [1956], 15ff.). Furthermore, two of the groups which had united, the Hermits of St. William and those who had seceded from them at Monte Favali, had lived before 1256 according to the *Rule* of St. Benedict. The three other groups, on the other hand, had followed the *Rule* of St. Augustine for a considerable time, the followers of John Bonus since 1225, those of Brettino since 1228, and the Tuscan hermits since 1243 (F. Roth, "Cardinal Richard Annibaldi, First Protector of the Augustinian Order," ibid., 2 [1952] – 4 [1954], esp. 2 [1952], 108–44). The relevant bulls have been edited in B. Van Luijk, *Bullarium Ordinis Eremitarum S. Augustini: Periodus formationis, 1187–1256* (Würzburg, 1964), No. 102.12, 32. That some houses of the groups which have been mentioned, in Italy or elsewhere, had a direct descent from the monasticism of the old days, transplanted from North Africa, has not been proved.

82. More detailed information will be found in Besse, "Règle de Saint Augustin"; P. A. Rodriguez, "Catalogo de las ordenes y congregaciones religiosas, que militan o hon militado bajo la apostólica regla del eximio doctor de la iglesia N. P. Agustín," *Archivo Histórico Hispano-Agustiniano*, 25 (1926), 89–101; M. Heimbucher, *Die Orden und Kongregationen der katholischen Kirche*, 3rd ed., 2 vols. (Paderborn, 1933), I 392–655.

83. Monceaux, "Saint Augustin et Saint Antoine," p. 86.

II

The Essentials of Augustine's Thought Concerning His Aspirations for His Monks

Not only did St. Augustine found a number of monasteries and himself live for more than four decades in monastic communities, but in a certain sense he put the stamp of his own personality upon Christian thinking about monasticism and formed from the ideas current on the topic in the fourth century an image that was new and independent.

5

The Meaning and Object of Monastic Life

AUGUSTINE EMPLOYS VARIOUS PHRASES AND IMAGES from the language of the Bible and of ancient Christian literature to convey his notions of the object and meaning of monastic life. Choosing to live in the cloister means, according to him, abandoning everything, following Christ, and seeking the kingdom of God along a path that is both narrow and steep.[1] It means dedicating oneself to "God's combat" or, as well, volunteering as a "vassal of God" and surrendering oneself wholly to His service. Moreover, Augustine sees in the monastic life an anticipation of the "life of heaven and of the angels" (*vita caelestis et angelica*) and, above all, the realization of a perfect Christian community of possessions and of love, in imitation of the example of the first community in Jerusalem.

As he employs these various images and similes, it becomes clear that Augustine conceived of the ideal monastic life as a living expression of the striving for Christian fulfillment, and he often and expressly emphasizes the close connection between monasticism and evangelical perfection.

MONASTIC LIFE AND CHRISTIAN PERFECTION

The Nature of Christian Perfection

What, for Augustine, is the nature of Christian perfection? The answer to this question is closely allied to the question about the nature of the Christian life. The inner life of the Christian consists, according to Augustine, in the ever-progressing renewal of God's image in man. Man is created by God in His own image: that is, he is called to share God's wisdom and love through a growing knowledge of Him. Through man's fall into sin this image in him of God was deformed, but it has been restored through baptism. Now the image must grow toward its completion, as man with the help of God's grace gradually overcomes the weakness of concupiscence (*cupiditas*) remaining in him after baptism, and as he, rising from faith to understanding and leaving behind the old fleshly man, becomes more and more a spiritual man. Man's creation in God's image finds its earthly perfection, according to Augustine, in Christian wisdom, which consists not only in a knowledge of God which brings great happiness but also in a drawing closer to Him in love. He writes: "As you come close to this likeness [to God], you progress in love and begin to perceive Him."[2]

Thus, for Augustine, the perfection of Christian living in wisdom means a perfection in love. That *caritas*—that is, love of God and, in God, of one's neighbor—represents "the fulfillment of the law" and is the goal of all Christian life is a thought he repeatedly and explicitly emphasized in connection with Romans 13:10 and 1 Timothy 1:5. This interpretation is clearly sounded in an early work of Augustine's, *The Ways of the Catholic Church*, where he gives as the reason for the practice of Christian brotherly love in the Italian monasteries the fact that "they well know that Christ and His Apostles teach that everything is vain if love alone is lacking, but perfect if it is present."[3] The glosses to the Epistle to the Romans which Augustine wrote while still a priest, around the year 394, are clearly marked by this notion of *caritas–perfectio*.[4] Twenty years later in the treatise *Nature and Grace* he gave it the classical formulation: "Love in its beginnings is justice in its beginnings; love progressing is justice progressing; great love is great justice; love perfected is justice perfected."[5]

Augustine knew only this one final goal for all Christians. Shortly after his conversion, he firmly decided against the ambivalent morality of the Manichaeans which prescribed one law and object for their "chosen ones" (*electi*) and another for their so-called "hearers" (*auditores*) and permitted their "hearers" to do things deemed sinful according to Manichaean views.[6] Two decades later Augustine encountered similar moves toward division in the Christian moral code and ideals in the Pelagian contention that "Even if the rich who have been baptized appear to do something good, that good will not be imputed to them, and they will be able to attain the kingdom of God only if they renounce all their possessions."[7] Here as well Augustine defended the unity of a single Christian law of life and final goal for all men.[8]

The Christian's Earthly Imperfections

Another very characteristic feature of Augustine's teaching about Christian perfection, at least in the final two decades of his life, is the emphasis with which he insists that a Christian's righteousness will achieve its perfection only in the world to come. He developed his views on this in his controversy with Pelagius and his followers, who maintained as a central tenet—perhaps, indeed, the most important of all their erroneous teachings—that through his own powers man can achieve a life completely free of sin upon this earth. Through this teaching Pelagius wanted to incite Christians to the moral effort he advocated, but in fact his contentions denied the consequences of the Fall and of sin, imperiled the true significance of the work of man's redemption and of Christ's grace, and presented a distorted picture of the essence of Christian perfection.[9] From the year 412 onward, Augustine repeatedly and vigorously opposed the Pelagian doctrine of "sinlessness" (*impeccantia*) and its denial of the supernatural element of perfection. Among his other writings, one, *Man's Perfection in Righteousness*, composed about 415, treats in great detail and thoroughness the Christian's imperfection in this life.

Among his other propositions he maintains that, on the one hand, we are "born of God" (1 John 5:18), live in Christ, and renew ourselves in our inner selves day by day (2 Cor. 4:16). On the other hand, we cannot truly say that we may have no sin (1 John 1:8) because the whole of our "weakness" is not yet healed in us, "in which, from the first man on, we are born."[10] These "remnants" of Original Sin, "which diminish in those who are making progress from day to day,"[11] led him to think of the concupiscence (*concupiscentia*) that is still stirring, even in the justified; to be sure, without consent of the will, this is not sin, but it offers a constant incitement to sin.[12] Even if it does not lead a man into grave sin (*crimina damnabilia*), still, experience tells us, it does lead to many daily sins (*peccata venalia*) which are soon blotted out by good works and for which we daily seek forgiveness of our guilt in the Lord's Prayer.[13]

Therefore, Augustine considered that the Christian's perfection in this world consists, not in freedom from sin, but in the persistent striving for perfection. Quoting Philippians 3:12ff., where St. Paul says "Not as if I had already won or were already perfect. . . . Brothers, I do not believe that I have yet succeeded. But one thing I do do: I have forgotten what lies behind me, I am intent on what lies before me, and I press on toward the goal, the prize, God's supernal summons in Christ Jesus," Augustine draws this application: "Let however many of us who are running along the course of perfection realize that we are not yet perfect and that we shall reach our perfection along the same path we have been running up to now."[14] Augustine thus maintained that one of the most dangerous deceptions for the striving Christian lies in the belief that he is already perfect, that he has already reached the goal, as he explained in one of his sermons: "If you say that this is sufficient, then you have met your undoing. Press on, press forward, keep on going! Do not hang back on your journey, do not turn back, do not turn aside! Anyone who does not press on falls behind; anyone who turns back to what he has once freed himself from has retrogressed; every renegade has gone astray."[15] Here, in Augustine's conception of Christian perfection, there is a markedly eschatological trait. But he writes briefly and clearly of what constitutes that perfected justification which will be our portion in the vision of God, in the treatise I have mentioned, *Man's Perfection in Righteousness*: "Justification will be complete if our cure is complete; our cure will be complete if our love is complete; for 'the completion of the law is love' [Rom. 13:10]. But our love is then complete when 'we shall see Him as He is' [1 John 3:2]."[16]

The Various Gifts and Callings

There are numerous places, however, where Augustine writes of a perfection (*perfectio*) reserved for only certain Christians. What he has to say on this point he generally follows with that saying of the Lord's: "If you want to enter into life, keep the commandments. . . . If you want to be perfect, go, sell what you have, and give it to the poor, and you will have treasure in heaven; and come, follow me" (Matt. 19:17, 21). The "perfection" (*perfectio*) recommended here and, very similarly, the "holiness" of the consecrated virgins are a matter, according to Augustine's interpretation, of a "more exalted perfection" and a "higher degree of holiness" (*excellentior perfectio, gloriosissima perfectio, celsior sanctitatis gradus, excellentior sanctitas*),[17] which he occasionally likewise described as the "way of perfection" (*via perfectionis*).[18]

Does this mean that, for monks and consecrated virgins, Augustine prescribed a goal in life different from that of other Christians? He himself forestalled such a misunderstanding of what has just been quoted when he specifically said that the forsaking of possessions, the preservation of virginity, and any other such gifts (*dona*) are of no use to those who receive them if they lack love.[19] In a sermon, dealing with 1 Corinthians 13:1, he explained at length that even in achieving evangelical poverty, the true perfection that should be striven for consists in the imitation of Christ, and in the imitation of His love, in particular:

> "If I speak with the tongues of men and of angels, and have not charity, I am become as sounding brass or a tinkling cymbal" [1 Cor. 13.1]. What is more sublime than the gift of different languages? It is merely brass, it is only a tinkling cymbal, if you take love away. . . . And what does he [Paul] go on to say? "If I distribute all my goods to the poor" [1 Cor. 13:3]. What could be more perfect? This is precisely what the Lord once commended to a rich man for perfection's sake when He said: "If you want to be perfect, go, sell all that you have, and give it to the poor" [Matt. 19:21]. But is he then perfect because he has sold all his possessions and has given to the poor? No. That is why the Lord went on: "And come, follow me." "Sell everything," He says, "give it to the poor, and come, follow me." Why should I follow You? If I have sold everything and distributed it to the poor, am I not then perfect? Why should I follow You? "Follow me to learn that I am meek and humble of heart" [cf. Matt. 11:29]. But can anyone sell the whole of his possessions and give it to the poor if he is not yet meek, not yet humble of heart? Indeed he can. . . . "Learn of me, that I am meek and humble of heart!" For "if I distributed all my goods to the poor, and gave my body to be burned, but have not love, it would be of no profit to me" [1 Cor. 13:3]. Therefore it is just this love in which, my beloved, I encourage you.[20]

Furthermore, Augustine left no doubt that the ultimate goal of Christian living for all Christians, for monks and for consecrated virgins as well, consists in that same "reward of the just" in "eternal life" (*vita aeterna*), the "kingdom of heaven" (*regnum caelorum*).[21]

If on occasion Augustine did employ the expressions that have been quoted—"a more excellent perfection" (*excellentior perfectio*), "a higher degree of holiness" (*celsior sanctitatis gradus*), and the like—for certain groups of Christians, his intention in doing so was to show that on the way to the goal of eternal life, there are various "gifts" and many different callings, just as in the general joy of heaven there are "many mansions" (John 14:2)—that is, in proportion to "the different merits of the saints," there will be different degrees of blessedness.[22] He specifically states, in reference to 1 Corinthians 13:31, where Paul speaks of those that are "better" among the gifts of the Spirit (*dona meliora*), that there are many rewards (*munera*) of divine grace, of which one may be more sublime and excellent than another.[23] As examples he cites the continence of widows, chastity in marriage, virginity, martyrdom, evangelical poverty (in the sense of Matthew 19:21), and the monastic common life (*vita communis*).[24]

In the order of ascendancy Augustine gives martyrdom the highest place, and ranks virginity above the "good" of matrimony.[25] He justifies attributing a higher moral and religious value to the gift (*donum*) of virginity by saying, with Paul (1 Cor. 7:32), that it is a more complete surrender to the Lord.[26] Similarly, he prefers evangelical poverty because it makes a more perfect imitation of Christ possible,[27] and the monastic common life because in it the "law of Christ" finds its fulfillment in a peaceable living together in mutual tolerance.[28]

Furthermore, he emphasizes the free and prudent character of both holy virginity and evangelical poverty.[29] The Lord imposed the renunciation of our possessions on us, not as a strict duty, but only as "an excellent and sublime counsel."[30] He did not constrain us by command, but left us free to decide and to opt for the way of celibacy.[31] Here, according to Augustine, the Scripture saying applies: "Whoever can, let him do" (Matt. 19:12).[32] And in this connection he also liked to quote Paul's saying: "Every man has his own gift from God, this one after this manner, and another after that" (1 Cor. 7:7).[33]

But with all this Augustine warns those who have received the greatest treasure and the more sublime calling against considering themselves on this account more perfect than others, particularly because they do not know those others' hidden gifts, which will perhaps become visible only in the hour of trial.[34]

In a Pentecost sermon Augustine illustrates this theme of a variety of gifts and callings with Paul's teaching about the Mystical Body, and shows how the Holy Spirit, the one "soul" of the Church, acts through their multiplicity:

> You see how the soul acts in the body. It enlivens all its members. With its eyes the soul sees; with its ears it hears; with its nose it smells; with its tongue it speaks; with its hands it labors; with its feet it walks. The soul is at the same moment present in all the members, so that they live; it bestows life upon them all, but to each one its office. . . . The offices are various; the life is common to all. So it is too with the Church of God. In some saints, she performs miracles; in others, she makes the truth known. In some, she preserves virginity; in others, she preserves conjugal chastity. In this one, this thing; in another, that. Each saint has his

> own office, but all have life in the same fashion. What the soul is for man's body, so the Holy Spirit is for the body of Christ, which is the Church.[35]

According to Augustine, therefore, every member of the Mystical Body of Christ is called upon to use his own gift of grace to do his part in building up the whole, and in so doing to attain to that degree of perfection that God has ordained for him.

ECCLESIOLOGICAL ASPECTS OF THE MONASTIC LIFE

As has become evident by now, Augustine's concept of monasticism is closely tied to his teaching about the Church. But his ecclesiology is governed and marked by Paul's image of the Mystical Body, an image that from his first days as a priest Augustine made more and more his own.[36] His understanding of the Church finds its most striking expression in the formula which he was so fond of using: "the whole Christ, the head and the body" (*Christus totus, caput et corpus*).[37] With this he wanted to give expression to the deep and living community and the mysterious unity, founded on the Incarnation and the Redemption, between Christ and the Church. The Word of God became man to become the head of His Church. She is His body, extending over the entire world and embracing all the faithful, from the beginning of the world to its end. The head is now in heaven, interceding before the Father for His members upon earth. The head is the source of grace for the body, guiding her and remaining most closely bound to her in love. Christ and the Church are an organic whole, a single "I" to which one can reply with the name of Christ. Not only do all members of the body belong to Christ, they are also Christ, in that same certain sense as the head and the members together constitute the whole Christ.

With his formulation of "the whole Christ," Augustine thus sought to depict the deep, indissoluble union of Christ and the Church. He indicates that the Holy Spirit is the essence of this union, the Spirit whom he shows as the soul, the source of life of the Body of Christ. Through this "Spirit of Christ," who pours out the love of God into the hearts of the faithful (cf. Rom. 5:5), love rules in the body as its primary law—the love, that is, of the head for the members, of the members for the head and also for each other.

In this living organism of the Mystical Body, he sees a solidarity of union between head and members and between the members themselves. As the destiny of the head is to live, so is that of the body, and the body's destiny is that of the head. Whatever is done, whether good or evil, to the members is done as well to the head; and between the members it is true that "If one member suffer, all the members suffer with it; or if one member glory, all the members rejoice with it" (1 Cor. 12:26). The individual members have their own different tasks, to fulfill the body's whole being. So they complete and support one another in an exchange of action. Though the tasks vary, their love for one another is mutual.

Monasticism as the Predominant Member
*(*membrum honorabilius*) in the Mystical Body*

Augustine's ideal of the monastic life is not isolated in his thought; it is deeply rooted in his concept, already mentioned, of the nature of the Church, which was a strong emotional impetus for him.[38]

More than anywhere else, he offered his views about the place and significance of monasticism in the Church in his *Exposition on Psalm 132*. To the verse "Like oil poured out upon the head, running down into the beard, into the beard of Aaron," he gives this profoundly theological, allegorical interpretation: the whole figure of Aaron the priest "signifies Christ with the Church." The anointing oil, an image of the Holy Spirit, is said to have flowed down from the head, which is Christ, upon the beard, which is the Apostles.[39] What the Psalmist then goes on to say—namely, that the oil then trickles down "to the hem of his robe"—Augustine explains as follows: "If the oil had not flowed down from his beard, we should not now have monasteries." But then "the Church followed, and gave birth to the monasteries from the garment of the Lord," for Aaron's priestly robe is the "image of the Church." Augustine asks himself "What then is the hem of the robe? . . . Ought we to understand by the 'hem' 'completion' because a robe is completed by its hem, and those men are complete who know how to live together in unity?" Augustine decides in favor of this interpretation. Continuing in this playful allegorical vein, he then asks which seam on the robe of the Church the monastic communities were supposed to be. He replies: "The oil could trickle down from the beard only to that hem which is nearest the head and is the border of the neckline. Such are those who live in unity with one another." Then, in his summarizing conclusion, he gives full expression to his ecclesiological perception of monastic life: "As a man's head," he writes, "slips through the hem [the neckline's border] so that he can clothe himself," so Christ may find, when He, our head, puts on the Church as a robe, "entrance through the brotherly unity" of monks.[40]

How, then, does Augustine regard the relationship of monastic life to the Church? For him, the Church is the mother of monasteries; she has given life to them "from the garment of the Lord,"[41] by the power of the Holy Spirit, for whom he saw the oil as an image, flowing down from the head, Christ, onto the robe, the Church, and in so flowing, touching first the upper hem, the image of monastic communities. In other places Augustine stresses that Christ's Spirit, the Church's innermost source of life, is active in monasticism. Thus in the same homily he speaks of the Holy Spirit's call (*clamor Spiritus Sancti*) in the words of the psalm: "See how good and how pleasant it is for brothers to live together in unity" (Ps. 132:1), which monks have heard and which has brought them together in the community.[42]

Monasticism is thus a member—indeed, a more honored member (*membrum honorabilius*)[43]—of the Mystical Body. Its particular significance for the entire body Augustine recognizes first of all in the fact that monks express in their lives, as they live together in love and unity, the true fulfillment of the law of Christ (cf. Gal. 6:2).[44] In their brotherly unity he sees an image, particularly fine, of the unity of the Mystical Body: they might truly have only one heart and one soul. Their life together with their brethren might form "only one life, Christ's own."[45] Furthermore, Augustine thinks that in monasticism the poverty and the chastity of the Body of Christ, the Church, are made visible to all. In their voluntary poverty monks are the members of "the head of the poor," of the poor man Christ.[46] So "the poor of Christ" (*pauperes Christi*) is a title of honor for them.[47] But in their celibate life the Church is virgin, in body as well as in spirit,[48] whereas this chastity in the other members of the Mystical Body can find its expression only spiritually through "inviolate faith, unshakable hope, and unfailing love."[49]

The "Exchange of Love" between Monasticism and the Other Members of the Mystical Body

In Augustine's conception, there are "small and great" in the Body of Christ, who, "each in his own degree, fulfills the evangelical precepts and hopes for the evangelical promises."[50] But as members of this one Body they all are ranked one after another in their tasks.

Augustine is often drawn to write of the solidarity of this union between monks and all other members of the Body of Christ. If, for example, a Christian decides to distribute his possessions to the poor, so as to dedicate himself wholly to Christ's service, this good deed should be a reason for all Christians to rejoice, regardless of where it may have happened. For, as Augustine justifies this, "The unity of Christ is one; the Church is one."[51] Similarly, the contemplative peace of the monastic life may be of benefit to the entire Mystical Body. Indeed, as he contemplates the nature of the Church, he sees the peace as a mutual repose of the other members in Christ. He quotes St. Paul: "If one member suffer anything, all the members suffer with it; or if one member glory, all the members rejoice with it" (1 Cor. 12:26). Thus he knows himself to be so closely joined in the one Body of Christ to the far-off community of monks in Capraria that these monks share just as much in the troubles and sorrows of his bishop's office as he shares in their repose (*otium*).[52] And the love of monks, too, in his view is not limited to their other brethren and to their relatives, but embraces all the members of the Body of Christ. In this sense he contrasts, in a letter, the "private love" (*caritas privata*) for his mother of Laetus, a young member of the monastery, with the "public love in the house of God" (*publica in domo Dei caritas*), with which "public love" Laetus' mother is truly loved by him, Augustine himself, and the other members of the monastery as their "sister," who has God for her Father and the Church for her mother.[53]

This solidarity of monks with the whole Body of Christ is expressed in mutual concern and help. In one place Augustine wrote of "a kind of exchange of love" that takes place between the "front-line Christian troops" (*militia Christiana*) who fulfill the "more sublime evangelical commands" (*sublimiora praecepta evangelica*) and the other members who form the "tribute-paying multitude."[54] He reports in detail in one sermon about the many "distinguished, rich, and highly-placed of this world" who have shared "their incomes, their country estates, and their surplus" with the servants of God. Interpreting the words of Psalm 103:16 allegorically, he compares the wealthy laity with the "cedars of Lebanon" and monks with the "sparrows" who make their nests in the cedars. He uses this vivid image to depict for his listeners the many kinds of support monastic life was then receiving "throughout the whole earth" from well-endowed Christians.[55] And Augustine, prompted by the Lord's words in Matthew 10:40ff. and 25:35ff., saw in this service performed for the monks a service done for Christ Himself.[56]

On their side, monks distribute spiritual gifts to the other members of the Body of Christ. Even in his early treatise *The Ways of the Catholic Church* Augustine points out how much benefit the anchorites of the Egyptian desert are to other Christians. In writing this he was thinking how they influenced others by their example, in their disposition and their way of life.[57] And in a letter he wrote twenty-five years later, he called the monks' "holy way of life and sound instruction" a "spiritual harvest" (cf. 1 Cor. 9:11) they brought to the Church.[58] Thinking of this same good example which monasticism owes to the other members of the Mystical Body, Augustine is happy to apply to those who live in monasteries the Pauline image of the "sweet perfume of Christ" (2 Cor. 2:15): through their good name, which is gained by the way they live, they spread through the Church the "sweet perfume of Christ" (*bonus odor Christi*).[59] But the offenses monks give the Christian people dispel that good odor which they, as members of His Body, should diffuse.[60] Augustine goes on from this to teach that for monks it may become an imperative duty to dedicate themselves to apostolic work for the other members of the Church. He is convinced that those who live the monastic life are called before others to cooperate in working for the perfection of the entire Body of Christ.[61]

BIBLICAL AND EARLY CHRISTIAN THEMATIC IMAGES FOR MONASTIC LIFE

A number of religious themes of Biblical or early Christian origin have, each in its own way, influenced Augustine's ideal of the monastic life and the spirituality of his monasteries.

The Imitation of Christ

The theme of the imitation of Christ is based on the Lord's summons to follow him—*ἀκολουθεῖν* (cf. Mark 1:16–20, 2:14; Luke 9:59–61)—to become His disciples—*μαθητής* (cf. Luke 14:26–33)—and, as a prerequisite of this participation in His life and His station, to accept certain self-denials (cf. Mark 8:34; Luke 14:26–27, 33). In the course of the first Christian centuries this religious concept underwent a rich evolution and development. In the primitive Church, the idea of imitation was applied to all the faithful, and was interpreted as a willing acceptance of the work of salvation proffered to them, as a sharing with Christ of His destiny, or, also, as an imitation of His faith.

Very soon, a more ethical concept of the imitation of Christ was joined to this. This new concept understood the notion to signify, preponderately if not exclusively, the imitation of Jesus' exemplary conduct.[62]

Augustine made varied use of the concept of imitating and following Christ (*sequi*, "to follow," *imitatio*, "imitation," *imitari*, "to imitate") to show the nature of the Christian life.[63] He frequently does this while appealing to the Scriptural verses of Matthew 11:29—"Learn of me, that I am meek and humble of heart"—or 1 Peter 2:21—"Christ also suffered for us, leaving you an example that you should follow His footsteps." He is very specific about it: "What else does 'following' Him mean but imitating Him? . . . Everyone follows what He does who imitates what He is." Then, linking this with the Lord's Beatitudes (Matt. 5:3ff.), he goes on to show in how many different ways the imitation of Christ can, and should, be expressed.[64] It is precisely in this "imitation of Christ" (*imitatio Christi*), as he emphasizes in another place, that our love for Christ expresses itself: "If we truly love Him, let us imitate Him. For we can yield no better fruit of love than the example of our imitation."[65]

But Augustine knew well how to give this theme a solid foundation in Scripture and theology. Above all, he never ceases to view this teaching of the imitation of Christ in the light of the mystery of the Incarnation. In Christ's emptying and abasement of Himself as He became man and died on the cross (cf. Phil. 2:6ff.), Augustine recognizes that exemplary conduct of the Son of God, the imitation of which will bring to us a true "peace" (cf. Matt. 11:29).[66] Through the baseness and weakness He took upon Himself, Christ heals our pride, nourishes our love, and becomes our "way" (John 14:6).[67] Christ is also a teacher, who influences mankind not only from outside, but also from within, who speaks in man's heart and with His grace inwardly urges him on to follow Him.[68]

This religious theme of the following and imitation of Christ grew to be of great importance for Augustine, particularly as it concerned his ideal of monastic living. At the decisive turning point in his life, it was one of the Lord's sayings about following Him (Matt. 19:21) and the way in which the saying had been realized in Anthony of Egypt and the two young imperial officers in Trier which had greatly influenced him and made him, from the beginning, regard the monastic life as an aspect of "following Christ" (*sequi Christum*).[69] Therefore, he often used the saying about forsaking possessions and following

Christ in order to define what is essential in the monastic life.[70]

Augustine regarded monastic poverty, in the sense of Matthew 19:21, as a special following of Christ, and presented the Son of God, emptying, abasing, and impoverishing Himself as He became man as the model and the "head of the poor."[71] He also indicated to his monks that the following and imitating of Christ were the motives for all monastic asceticism if the freeing oneself of all earthly dependence on parents, relatives, and one's own life, or taking upon oneself the cross (cf. Luke 14:26) is to be of any value. But in such a following let the "champion of Christ" bear the image, not of the first Adam upon him, but of the second Adam who came down from heaven (cf. 1 Cor. 15:47).[72] Augustine in this way also motivates the virtue of humility, the predominant significance of which, for Christian life in general and for a life consecrated to God in particular, he presented as none of the Fathers of the Church before him had done, often connecting it with Matthew 11:29 and with the notion of the imitation of Christ.[73] Here, as well, he is expressly citing the example of the Son of God, emptying Himself as He became man, as he writes in *Holy Virginity*: "He exalts those who humbly follow Him who thought it no shame to descend to the fallen."[74] In the same work he interprets virginity consecrated to God as the imitation of Christ, "of the son of the Virgin and the bridegroom of virgins, born in the flesh from a virgin womb and wed in the spirit in a virginal marriage."[75] Alluding to the image in the Apocalypse (14:1–5) of the Lamb of God and His retinue, he urges virgins dedicated to God to hasten after the Lamb along the way of virginity: "hasten after Him . . . ; for the sake of this good alone, follow Him wherever He goes. . . . follow Him, keeping with perseverance the vow you have fervently made."[76]

In all his uses of the religious theme of the imitation of Christ, Augustine avoided a one-sided, moralizing interpretation, chiefly because he viewed the theme in the background of the Pauline teaching about life in Christ and about the Body of Christ. This is evident, for example, in the aforementioned ideas that the Christian through imitation of the poverty of Jesus becomes a "member of Christ the pauper" (*membrum pauperis Christi*), or in the thought that the imitation of Christ stamps man with the image of the new Adam, and finally in the concept that the virgin consecrated as member and likeness of the virgin Mother Church is betrothed in a spiritual marriage to Christ.[77] Augustine presented this theme of imitation as a growing into Christ at greater length when he glossed the verse in Galatians 4:19, "I suffer the pangs of childbirth again, until Christ be formed in you," with "Christ is formed in the one who receives Christ's form. But a man receives Christ's form when he depends upon Christ in spiritual love. And thus it comes about that through imitation he becomes what Christ is, insofar as that is granted to him in his present state. 'For whoever claims that he is dwelling in Christ,' says John, 'must himself walk even as He walked' [1 John 2:6]."[78]

In a sermon Augustine made a fine survey of the implications of the imitation of Christ as that is accomplished in the Church, in the "world redeemed" (*mundus salvatus*) and in the "body of all mankind" (*corpus universum*). It is constantly accomplished, through and in the individual members, and always in varying fashion:

> Yet in [the Church], this holy, good, reconciled, and redeemed, or, better, redeeming world—for it is now redeemed only in hope: "For through hope are we redeemed" [Rom. 8:24]—in this world, therefore, that is, in the Church, which as one body follows Christ, He has made known to all: "If any man will come after Me, let him deny himself" [Matt. 16:24; Luke 9:23]. It is not only virgins who must listen to this saying, or married women, or widows, not only married people or monks alone, not only husbands or clerics alone, and not only the lay people. No, the entire Church, the whole body, all its members, clearly divided though they are according to their various tasks, must follow Christ. They must follow Him undivided, this "only one" [cf. Ps. 21:20]; the "dove" [cf. Cant. 2:10, 14] must follow Him, the "bride" [cf. Cant. 4:8]; those who have been redeemed and given grace in the blood of the bridegroom must follow Him. . . . [And thus] these members, each of them taking his own place according to his nature, his rank, and his measure, must follow Christ. They must deny themselves: that is, they must not vaunt themselves. They must carry their cross: that is, they must endure for Christ's sake in the world what the world commits against them. They must love Him who alone does not turn back, in whom there is no deceit, who alone does not disappoint.[79]

Holy Warfare and Servitude before God

Two most ancient Christian concepts, closely allied in thought to the Scriptural teaching on the imitation of Christ, which also influenced Augustine's thinking about monasticism, were the notions of "Christian warfare" (*militia Christiana*) and "servitude before God" (*servitus Dei*).

Christian Warfare (militia Christiana) • The comparison of the life of a Christian with service in the military is fully explored by St. Paul, who thereby achieved the Christian transformation of a Stoic concept. In subsequent centuries the soldier of Christ (*miles Christi*) was recognized, above all, in martyrs and ascetics. Therefore from the beginning this idea was lavishly used and explored in monastic literature.[80]

By Augustine's day it had been a part of Christian ideology for a long time. Around the year 396 he himself had written a first monograph on the theme, under the title *The Christian Combat.* A Christian's principal battle, Augustine is convinced, is against Satan and his angels, and involves the mastering of man's own inner disordered appetites and the subjection of his will to God's. Fighting with spiritual weapons—above all, with the strength of faith and the exercise of the Christian virtues—he does battle and conquers through the power of Christ.[81]

Augustine often applies this theme of spiritual warfare and battle to Christian living in general. In a sermon for a martyr's feast day, for example, he showed how Christ, "the king of martyrs," "arms his cohorts with spiritual weapons, directs them in battle, offers them support, and promises them their reward."[82] But he preferred to compare monastic life with the service of a spiritual soldier, and he saw in such a life the realization of a "Christian army" (*militia Christiana*).[83] He called entering a monastery volunteering for a "holy military service,"[84] and made it signify "dedicating oneself to God's military service."[85]

In keeping with this concept of monks as serving in a spiritual army, Augustine repeatedly gives them the title "soldiers of Christ" (*milites Christi*),[86] or, in a letter to a young monk, "Christ's recruit" (*tiro Christi*).[87] In this letter to the young Laetus, after mentioning the pericope of Luke 14:26–33, he described in detail what he proposed this life of spiritual warfare should be for one close to him.[88] Christ, given the titles "king" (*rex*)[89] and "field commander" (*imperator*),[90] is said to have summoned monks into his camp (*castra*). There they are to build a "tower" (Luke 14:28ff.) to serve as both a lookout post and a rampart to enable them to spy out from it and repel "the enemy of everlasting life."[91] And it will be fitting for an army of ten thousand to be assembled against the enemy "king," who is advancing with twenty thousand troops (Luke 14:31–32).[92] Let it be the warrior's additional task to keep watch over the "standard" (*signum*) of Christ in the camp and at the resounding of his heavenly "trumpet" (*tuba*) to go forward into battle.[93] But, in the pericope already mentioned, the Lord has clearly said what the cost of building the tower and levying the force will be: forsaking everything one possesses, even to severing all earthly, "fleshly" ties to parents, relatives, and one's own life (Luke 14:26, 33).[94] As weapons for the fight, Augustine, alluding to St. Paul (Eph. 6:17), specified the spiritual sword of God's word (*arma Verbi Dei, spiritualis gladius Verbi Dei*).[95] The adversaries against whom the fight is directed are "the enemy of everlasting life"[96] or, as he wrote in another place in allusion to Ephesians 6:12, "the lordship, powers, and spirits of evil, who are Satan and his angels."[97]

Thus Augustine's monastic interpretation of the notion of Christian warfare led him to write that the monk has "broken asunder all the bonds of earthly hope" so that he may "dedicate his heart freely to the service of God."[98] In this sense, he also quoted in his treatise *The Work of Monks* the words of the Second Letter to Timothy (2:3–4): "Labor as a good soldier of Christ Jesus. No man, being a soldier to God, entangles himself with secular businesses; that he may please Him to whom he has dedicated himself."[99] Furthermore, Augustine showed, this image of military service implies that the monk is bound to follow his master loyally, and, because of his profession as "Christ's recruit," must not leave the camp in the lurch.[100]

What is distinctive in Augustine's development of this notion of a holy warfare is its stress on what is Christian and Biblical and its eschewing of the teachings about the virtues and vices, formed in Stoic thought, which characterize the treatment of this commonplace in the early monastic literature of the East.[101]

Servitude before God (servitus Dei) • The concept of servitude before God (*servitus Dei*) is related to the notion of military service, but it is a concept in which the idea of man's complete dependence on God is perhaps even more strongly expressed. By "servitude" the ancient world understood "a service that did not lie in the choice of those who served but must be performed by them, whether they liked it or not, because they were slaves, subject to the will of another, their owner."[102] This concept was taken over into the Old Testament and used to express man's relationship of total dependence on and servitude to God. The expression "servant of God" (*ebed Yahweh*) served not only as a designation of the people of Israel as a whole but also as a title of honor for their greatest religious leaders, and in particular for the anonymous "servant of God" of Isaiah's prophetic songs (chaps. 40–55). In the New Testament it is primarily Jesus who has the title "servant of God" (*δοῦλος θεοῦ, servus Dei*), while Christians appear for the most part as "servants" (δοῦλοι) of Jesus. In post-Apostolic times, however, the expression "servants of God" (δοῦλοι θεοῦ) very quickly became the term Christians used to describe themselves.[103]

Augustine, of course, was familiar with the concepts "servant of God" (*servus Dei*), "God's service" (*servitus Dei*), and "serving God" (*servire Deo*) in this general Christian sense. In *The Greatness of the Soul*, an early work, he described service (*servire, servitium*) to God as a perfected and genuine freedom.[104] It was, to be sure, a service "with a will whole, full, and ready."[105] By "servant of God," moreover, Augustine understood more than just the individual Christian; in his commentary on the Gospel of St. John, he wrote "The servant of God is the people of God, the Church of God."[106]

Nonetheless, he preferred to apply these concepts to monasticism. Shortly after his conversion, he referred to himself in the *Soliloquies* as the "servant of God" (*servus Dei*),[107] that is, a servant in the sense of serving a single master, to whose service he felt himself called. He wanted to be God's property and to depend totally on Him: "I long to be under your power" (*Tui iuris esse cupio*).[108] "Servant of God" gradually became his favorite appellation for monks and, used in this special sense, the expression is found some fifty times in his writings. The related expression "serving God' (*servire Deo*) is used about twenty-five times, and the substantives "service of God" (*servitus Dei*) and "servitude to God" (*servitium Dei*) likewise appear quite often.[109] For the residents of women's monasteries he used the corresponding term "handmaid of God" (*ancilla Dei*).[110] It followed that joining a monastery was termed "entering God's service"[111] and that the first decisive step in the monks' lives was "the profession of servitude to God" (*propositum* or *professio servitutis Dei*).[112]

Augustine uses this terminology not only for his own foundations, including the monastery of clerics,[113] but for the monks of Egypt[114] and Carthage,[115] as well. He was to use it throughout his life until he wrote the treatises, sermons, and letters of the final years of his life. Even when he was a bishop he included himself in the company of the "servants of God" when he spoke of his "fellow-servants" (*conservi*) in the monastery of clerics.[116] That Possidius also uses the same language in his biography of Augustine shows how deeply the notion of "serving God" (*servire Deo*) had impressed itself on Augustinian monastic thought.[117]

But what was it that Augustine meant to say through his concept of monastic life as "servitude"? Even more emphatically than in his use of the notion of "spiritual warfare," he is conveying here his idea that a monk's surrender of himself is unconditional and complete. In "serving God" (*servire Deo*) we can perceive the first and most important disposition of monks: "to hold [their] hearts in readiness to carry out the Lord's will in all the things He has destined His servants to accomplish, whether He may smite them or spare them."[118] What differentiates the monks' "servitude" (*servitium*) from the "service of God" (*servire Deo*) required of every Christian is their seeking to serve Him "unburdened of all worldly bonds."[119] Thus, as Augustine regarded it, monastic life offers a special way—and for those who are so called a very suitable way—to realize that "service of God" which is imposed as a duty on all Christians. But he was at pains to stress that it is a "free service" (*libera servitus*), that is, a servitude to which one commits oneself in complete freedom and which must be lived with a free heart.[120] The words "not as slaves under the law" in Augustine's *Rule* make a fundamental distinction between the service of monks and that subjection which St. Paul called a distinguishing mark of the Jewish service of the law and rejected (cf. Rom. 8:15, Gal. 2:4, 5:1).[121]

Eschatological Orientation of Monastic Life

The "Angelic Life" (vita angelica) · One influential religious image that from the second century on had left its mark on ancient Christian ways of piety, and on early monasticism in particular, is the notion of the so-called "life of the angels" (*βίος ἀγγελικός*). It was associated with the Lord's promise that after the resurrection of the dead marriage would no longer exist and the blessed will be "like the angels in heaven" (Matt. 22:30, Mark 12:25, Luke 20:35–36). Men hoped—perhaps because an interpretation in this sense of the text in Luke encouraged them to do so[122] —to realize this coming similarity to the angels while still here on earth, and thus in a certain way to anticipate their perfection beyond the grave. Christian eschatological expectations and longings for the eternal life to come (*vita caelestis*) were, therefore, compelling motives. In accordance with this saying of Christ's, people regarded human celibacy as the prime correlative between angels and men. Yet the content of this notion soon expanded, especially under the influence of the Alexandrians Clement and Origen, to encompass other aspects of the religious life and of Christian monastic asceticism. In the course of this development the early Christian eschatological direction of thought on such topics was undoubtedly influenced by Hellenistic, spiritualistic ideas.[123]

In Augustine's concept of the ascetic life this early Christian, not unproblematical, idea of the "angelic life" (*vita angelica*) also found a place. He may have encountered the notion for the first time in Ambrose[124] or Cyprian[125] and just as these two Church Fathers saw in the ideal of a life similar to that of the angels a particular basis for comparison in the celibacy of consecrated virgins and of ascetics,[126] so Augustine too prefers "holy virginity" (*sancta virginitas*) as their common characteristic. He praises it as "a sharing in the life of the angels and a striving for endless immortality here in this perishable flesh."[127] Practicing a continence dedicated to God is for him "imitating here in this flesh the life of the angels"[128] and it means "reflecting on the life of heaven and of the angels amid this earthly mortality."[129] Thus, whoever has taken a vow of celibate chastity, whether man or woman, must "live on earth the life of the angels," and begin to be on this side of the grave what other Christians "will be only after the resurrection."[130]

There is no justification for suspecting that these remarks of Augustine's express Neoplatonic or spiritualistic thinking. Hendrikx' characterization of many of Augustine's teachings—namely, that "despite his acknowledged Platonism, he did not remain in this philosophy, but lived in the theology . . . of Holy Scripture"[131]—appears to be valid in this connection as well. In the first place, the source of these remarks about the "angelic life" (*vita angelica*) is, not philosophical spiritualism, but, above all else, Augustine's deep roots in the spirituality of the primitive Church, of the Scriptures, and of eschatology. As he conceived of it, "the last hour" (1 John 2:18) was already at hand, even though it was a "long hour," the end of which could not yet be discerned.[132] The world was moving toward its end, and showing its advanced age in a general exhaustion.[133] But Christians are "a heavenly sowing" (*germen caeleste*); they are "strangers on the earth," and, unlike the "lovers of this world," do not wish to remain here below forever.[134] Therefore, like "good servants," they should wait, full of longing for the coming and the revelation of the Lord, keeping themselves prepared for Him, with loins girded and lamps aflame (cf. Luke 12:35–36).[135] Again and again Augustine wrote of the "eternal joy of the heavenly city"[136] and of that longing for the perfection of the City of God (*Civitas Dei*) which so filled him and which he endeavored to awaken in his hearers and readers.[137] As a deeper content of this eschatological expectation the wish appears that "God may be all in all" (1 Cor. 15:28).[138]

In keeping with this eschatological grounding of his thinking, Augustine, who never denied positive value to the service of the Christian,[139] employed the theme of the "angelic life" (βίος ἀγγελικός) as a model and guide for the Christian life in general.[140] Thus he describes Christians in the City of God as those who, here on earth, are entering into their fellow-citizenship with the angels: "For after we have been snatched from the powers of darkness, and have received the pledge of the Spirit, and been admitted into the kingdom of Christ, then we have begun to belong among the angels, with whom we shall at last possess the holy, above all, the lovable, City of God."[141] In particular, Augustine wished this angel-like life to be devoted to a constant striving for a true union with God: "As soon as you begin to be holy, you have started to imitate the life of the angels."[142] Without doubt, those who, without worrying, keep vigil "in chastity and innocence" are intent upon the "angelic life." For—such is Augustine's reasoning—"sleep is only for mortals. The angels know nothing of this kind of rest."[143]

To be sure, the kind of imitation that has just been described, just like the "angelic life" which is expressed in a continence dedicated to God, has much application to the monastic life. Yet we shall not find treatments of this early Christian ideal of the "angelic life" (βίος ἀγγελικός) in those writings, letters, and sermons in which Augustine is directly concerned with monasticism.

The "Heavenly Life" (vita caelestis) • As the passages quoted from *Holy Virginity* have shown,[144] Augustine at times joined the concept of the "angelic life" (*vita angelica*) to the related theme of the "heavenly life" (*vita caelestis*). But in his works on monasticism, this religious motif of the "heavenly life," treated on its own merits, is discussed repeatedly. Thus, in the profound exposition of Psalm 132, in which he writes at length about monastic life, Augustine appeals at the end to his hearers: "So depart now, and seek for yourself a dwelling place in heaven. But you reply, 'How should I be able to live in heaven, I, a man clothed in the flesh and delivered up to the flesh?' But hasten on ahead with your heart, where you cannot follow with your body. Do not be deaf when you hear 'Lift up your hearts.' Lift your heart up to the heights."[145] Above all, Augustine viewed monastic life as this kind of anticipation of the life of heaven.

To be sure, the whole of religious and ascetic life can serve the realization of a "heavenly life" (*vita caelestis*) in the sense in which it has just been described.[146] Yet Augustine has stressed certain points of comparison.

I have already discussed celibacy "for the kingdom of heaven" (Matt. 19:12). As evidence of the exemplary life that consecrated virgins lead, Augustine cites those "additional gifts of virginity" which "make known to men the life of angels, and to the earth the ways of heaven."[147]

Another point of comparison in which the "heavenly life" of monks becomes visible is, for Augustine, that "contemplation of God" (*contemplatio Dei*) which is practiced in the monastery. His thoughts on this subject underwent development. When in his early treatise *The Ways of the Catholic Church* he described the ideals of the Egyptian monks, he was greatly influenced both by Neoplatonic philosophy, which by that time he was interpreting in a Christian sense, and by the Stoic ideal of "freedom from passion" (ἀπάθεια), and he was filled with a longing for that happy life (*vita beata*) which he hoped to attain here upon earth through the contemplation of divine truth and beauty.[148] It was in the light of these spiritual insights that he then understood and interpreted the Egyptian anchorites' way of life, believed that they were sharing in a life of happiness while still in this world and had attained to the longed-for vision of God: they are "enjoying to the full their converse with God . . . and the contemplation of His most blessed beauty."[149] This object—namely, a heavenly life which one could anticipate here on earth—was still before Augustine during his Tagaste years, even if his hope that he might reach blessedness and the much-desired vision of God here in this life gradually receded.[150] Later, in his *Retractations*, he specifically withdrew what he had then thought about the happy life (*vita beata*) and declared that a perfect perception of God and the happiness that will accompany it are to be hoped for only beyond the grave.[151] But for the rest of his life this strong inclination toward divine contemplation (*contemplatio Dei*) remained with him.

Possidius, remembering this, wrote of Augustine: "He was an image of the Church in heaven, like Mary, that most devout woman, of whom it is written 'She sat at the feet of the Lord and listened attentively to His words' [cf. Luke 10:39]."[152] And Augustine himself had praised Mary of Bethany, "not busy" (*otiosa*), as a symbol of the life "to come . . . peaceful, . . . blessed, . . . everlasting."[153] The contemplative life for him was always a demonstration and a foretaste, as it were, of the life to come, in which this "holy idleness" (*otium sanctum*) would find its perfection.[154]

But in all this it was clear to him that thinking of anticipating the life of heaven nonetheless required us to limit and adapt ourselves according to the demands of life on this earth. He repeatedly protested against notions of monastic life which ignored this, and thus became exaggerated and distorted. Again and again he impressed it upon monks that, however great their inclination toward contemplative living might be, pure contemplation is reserved for the life that is to come and that one must be prepared to sacrifice the inactivity of monastic withdrawal (*otium*) when the obligations of love (*necessitas caritatis*) and, above all, one's apostolic ministry (*necessitates ecclesiae*) demand it.[155]

In one sermon he took to task those eulogists of monasticism who maintained that in monasteries there was to be found the dwelling place of an already perfect, in some way heavenly, joy, peace, and security. He said to them "Certainly there is joy here [on earth]." But "here we only taste of the hope of the life that is to come; it is there that we shall be satiated."[156] He conceded that monks do live "Far . . . from the noise of the great crowds [and] from the stormy waves of this world in a harbor, as it were," and that "in that harbor they are more fortunate than on the open sea." Yet even in a harbor there is no complete security; a storm can penetrate even there.[157] Augustine concluded his remarks with the declaration that in this life our security rests only on "our hope in God's promises. . . . But there, when we come to that goal, there is complete security. . . . There, in truth, full rejoicing and great joy will reign."[158]

Thus it cannot be disputed that Augustine was aware of the limitations of this religious and ascetic ideal of the "heavenly and angelic life" (*vita caelestis et angelica*). His own monastic life was certainly given its individual stamp, not by these notions, which were common in early Christian days, but by his aspirations for a Christian community built wholly in God and upon God, which would realize the motto which he took from the earliest Christian literature: "one heart and one soul toward God [*cor unum et anima una in Deum*]" (cf. Acts 4:32).

THE PRINCIPAL GOAL (*primum propter quod*) OF MONASTIC LIFE

A Community of Christian Love—"One Heart in God" (cor unum in Deum) *as Augustine's Basic Conception of Monasticism*

The program for Augustinian monastic life is expressed, briefly and forcefully, in Augustine's *Rule*: "You should live in unanimity in the house, with 'one heart and one soul' toward God."[159] He was concerned with achieving a community, founded in God,[160] in which all were to have a spiritual union, all were to form one entity, filled with life. Community is the cornerstone on which he built his form of monastic living. In one sermon he comments on the words of the psalm "See how good and how pleasant it is for brothers to live together in unity" (Ps. 132:1). He saw in this a "summons of the Holy Spirit" which mightily—like a trumpet blast—resounded over the whole earth, bringing monasteries to life everywhere.[161]

In Augustine's view monastic community is not based upon mere benevolence of a natural order; it is rooted directly in God. That is why he insisted so often that the communal living of his monks must be a community "toward God";[162] God must be the central point;[163] Christ, the "soul" of their community.[164] To gain a brother for the community is to gain him for God.[165] For him, the common life of a monastery is community with all the fullness not only of the Christian faith but also of a mutual and religious respect. This is defined in his *Rule*: "In one another honor God, whose temples you were made to be."[166]

This dominating conception, of a community of Christian love, dictates Augustine's ideal of monastic living down to the smallest details. It finds a many-sided realization in the community of feeding, clothing, dwelling, and possessions, and, in particular, in a peaceable common life.[167] The monks' oneness of heart expresses itself in the fervor of the common prayer and worship, and in their joining together around the monastic table as well.[168] In Augustine's *Rule*, the entire course of the day for his monks is directed toward their community.

Yet a proper balance between community and individuality is preserved. In contrast to the conceptions of community which prevailed in pagan antiquity,[169] the monastic life devised by Augustine represents no violation of the human personality. For him, the community of monks is a spiritual family, not a faceless crowd. He tries to bear in mind the peculiarities of each individual, his very weaknesses, and his special needs. "Not the same for everyone"[170] is his principle, not merely in the distribution of food and clothing but also in dealing with the different personalities. In his monasteries there was no compulsion; his monks were to live "not as slaves under the law but as free men under grace."[171] For him, a monastic community is a spiritual family, built on the love and the voluntary subordination of all its members. It has been said that the personal respect that a monastic community confers upon its members is greater by far even than that which it seeks to promote.[172] That is especially true of monastic life as Augustine sought to establish it.

Respect for the personalities and peculiarities of his brothers must, in Augustine's view, determine a monk's relationships with the others. He knew that a true community can exist only when a man is permitted to keep his personal distance from the others. Fraternal love must be free of all "carnal affection" (*carnalis dilectio*).[173] Even in the external forms of courtesy, his monks showed a religious respect for one another. The form of greeting in his monasteries was "Thanks be to God" (*Deo gratias*), for which Augustine provides this sound reason: "Consider whether a brother ought not to give thanks to God when he sees his brother. For is it not an occasion for thanksgiving when people who live together in Christ see each other?"[174]

In Augustine's view, true Christian love is found in a man's offering of himself to the community. A monk progresses through such love, on the way toward his perfection in conduct and belief.[175] Thus the community of love surpasses every joy the world has to bestow.[176]

But for Augustine the common life is more than just a means. It is in community that one may meet with God. He uses striking language: "Whoever is willing to live under one roof with me has God for his possession."[177] And he, the bishop, confesses that, weary with "the troubles of the world," he would gladly find refuge in the love of his brothers and confreres, to be able to find there an untroubled rest: "For I feel," he wrote, "that God is dwelling there, God in whom I find my safe refuge, in whom I take secure repose."[178]

It is precisely here that the distinctive element in his concept of monastic community is to be found: community for him was a goal to be pursued for its own sake, not merely to serve some other end. To be of one heart and one soul toward God is for Augustinian monasticism the "first thing for the sake of which" (*primum propter quod*), the chief object of the monastic common life.[179] It is true that there are forms of monastic living other than Augustine's which lay stress on living in common.[180] Yet one can find no other legislation in which the notion of community has so consciously and forcefully been made the central point of all monastic living, in which it has been declared the prime object for which men come together. To be a family of God, to be a community of love, and in that community to strive for the perfect realization of the ideals of Christian life—that is the thought at the heart of all that Augustine did in establishing his form of monastic life.[181] In this he had in mind the Lord's bidding "By this shall all men know that you are my disciples, if you have love one for another" (John 13:35).[182]

Now one can understand why Augustine attributed so much importance for the Church to his ideal of monastic communal life. It has already been shown how he conceived that it is through the monks' brotherly love that the head, who is Christ, finds entry, when He clothes Himself with the Church as if with His robe.[183]

The Biblical and Theological Foundation of the Monastic "Unity of Love" (unitas caritatis)[184]

Augustine provided a variety of motives, drawn from his wide reading and his theological speculation, for his community ideal of the monastic life. The Scriptural and theological justifications for it may be summarized as follows: he anchors his thoughts on Christian community, as he achieves an especially clear expression of it in his ideal of monastic life, in the teaching on love (*caritas*), and he explains it with the Pauline images of the Temple of God and the Body of Christ, and compares it with the mystery of the divine Trinity.

Monastic Community as the Field of Action for Christian Love · In his idealized report about the monasteries of men and women which he had visited in Rome soon after his baptism, Augustine wrote in admiration not only of the inhabitants' severe penances and of their industry, but also of the culture and finesse of their superiors. But even in those early days, he saw that the fundamental law of monastic life should be that of Christian love.[185] He wrote:

> Love is observed by everyone. Love is their guide as they eat, as they talk, in their conduct, in their demeanor. They are united in one love, and that love is the air they breathe. What injures that love is seen as an offense against God. What is hostile to love will be fought, will be rejected; what does harm to love must be suppressed that very day. For they well know that Christ and His Apostles teach that everything is vain if love alone is lacking, but that all is made perfect if love is present.[186]

Even if Augustine's understanding and justification of Christian brotherly love in this early work does leave something to be desired,[187] still this passage shows what a central position he had assigned to love in his earliest conception of monastic life. With the deepening in succeeding years and decades of his teaching on love, depth came as well to his understanding of monasticism as the field of action of Christian love.

Soon after his ordination to the priesthood, speaking, probably to his brethren in the garden monastery at Hippo, about mutual tolerance, Augustine calls brotherly love the "law of Christ,"[188] as Paul does (Gal. 6:2), and the essential sign by which the true disciples of the Lord may be recognized (cf. John 13:34–35).[189] His admonitions and appeals to these monks show us the conviction with which he is arguing that what he hopes for in a monastic community must be produced by love: "Christ so emphasized this prescription of the law that he said [John 13:34–35]: 'By this shall all men know that you are my disciples, if you have love one for another.' "[190]

Then, during his protracted disputes with the Donatists, his understanding of fraternal love reached depths best shown in his commentary on the First Epistle of Saint John and in *The Trinity.* In accordance with his theological teachings on man as the image of God,[191] Augustine now sees in human love, too, a likeness of the Trinity. He wrote:

> What then is this love or charity, which Holy Scripture so praises and esteems, if not our love for some good thing? But love presupposes someone who loves, and it directs itself toward something that is loved. There you may see a triad: the lover, the object of his love, and love itself. So what else is love but a vital force, joining or seeking to join two things together—the lover, that is, and the object of his love? This is the case even with outward, carnal love. But, to choose a purer, clearer example, let us forsake the flesh and mount to the spirit. What does the spirit love in a friend except his spirit? So here, too, is the triad: the lover, the object of love, and love.[192]

Thus he sees love among men "as a most happy image of, a very exact 'analogy' to, the Mystery of the Trinity."[193]

In the light of this, Augustine would henceforth understand human love as a participation (*participatio*) in the "incomprehensible" love of God Himself,[194] that love which has preceded all the love of His creatures and which has revealed itself in divine predestination, as well as in Christ's Incarnation and in His redemptive death.[195] So the saying of the Apostle that "God is Love" (1 John 4:8) becomes a central point in his teaching on love.[196] From this Augustine concludes that God's love and man's have an internal connection and that together they form only a single love. "Embrace God, who is love, embrace God through love," he wrote in *The Trinity*;

> He is that love which encloses all good angels and all God's servants by the bond of holiness, joining us and them together, joining us, beneath Him to Him. . . . My beloved ones, let us love one another; for love is from God. . . . He who does not love has not seen God; for God is love. Here Scripture shows us very clearly the supreme authority with which it has been revealed that this brotherly love . . . not only is from God but, indeed, is God. So, when we love a brother in love, we love him in God. And it is not possible for us not, above all, to love this very love with which we love our brother. So it comes that these two commands cannot exist one without the other. For because God is love, without doubt God loves whoever loves love; but of necessity whoever loves his brother must love love.[197]

Furthermore, Augustine concludes from Saint John's words "God is love" (*Deus est caritas*) that the Holy Spirit, the "supreme love" (*summa caritas*), who joins Father and Son together, joins us too, beneath them, to them.[198] Again and again he cites the words of Romans 5:5: "The love of God has been poured out in our hearts by the Holy Spirit, who is given to us."[199] From this he infers that his love cannot be in us without the Holy Spirit[200] and that in this love the Holy Spirit Himself is present in us;[201] without expressly saying so, Augustine identifies this love of ours with the Holy Spirit.[202]

In Augustine's theological speculations about love (*caritas*) as participation in the love of God or of the Holy Spirit, respectively, his thinking about monastic community received its solid foundation. It is through their love that the monks are "one heart and one soul toward God" (*cor unum et anima una in Deum*); for in their brotherly love they partake in the love of God Himself, which love, by the gift (*donum*) of the Holy Spirit, is poured into their hearts and over their community (cf. Rom. 5:5),[203] and then in this brotherly love they love the God who is love Himself.

The Christian and the Christian Community as the Temple of God · Augustine often quotes what Paul had written (1 Cor. 3:16f., 6:19; 2 Cor. 6:16 etc.) about God's gracious indwelling.[204] God summons men to his "most blessed temples" when in baptism He rescues them from the power of darkness and brings them into the kingdom of the Son of His love (Col. 1:13).[205] But for Augustine love is the sign of this divine indwelling; whoever possesses love has the Holy Spirit within him.[206] But it is not only the individual Christian whom he designates as the Temple of God; he repeatedly says this of the entire community of the faithful:

"We are all together His temple, as each one is by himself, for God deigns to dwell in the community of all men as He does in us one by one."[207] Augustine frequently applies the temple image to monastic communities of love as well as to their several members, and thus, in his *Rule*, he exhorts the monks to reverence in one another God Himself whose temple they are.[208] And when he writes there of their responsibilities toward one another for the faithful preservation of chastity, he observes: "God, who lives within you, will in this way protect you through yourselves."[209] And when monks bear a brother's weaknesses in patience, Augustine sees in this a deed of love by which they manifest Christ in him.[210]

Monastic Communities as Members of the Body of Christ · For Augustine the image of a spiritual Temple of God in the hearts of Christians and in the Christian community is closely allied to the teaching of the Mystical Body of Christ.[211] Yet in this image, which is so important for Paul's teaching on the nature of the Church, Augustine, as I have shown, found a strong basis for his ideal of monastic life. He has bestowed upon monasticism a place of honor in the Body of Christ.[212] The community and unity of monks in the whole Christ should be so deep that none of them should go on calling his life his own: "Your life is no longer your personal possession," he wrote to one of his monks; "it belongs to all the brethren, just as their lives belong to you, or, better expressed, their lives and yours no longer form a multiple of lives, but only one life, which is Christ's own."[213] He interpreted his Biblical motto "one heart and one soul" through this mysterious unity in Christ: the monks should live in such harmony that they form only one person, so that they might seem to have, as it was written, only one heart and one soul—many bodies, yet not many souls; many bodies, yet not many hearts.[214] For the sake of this mysterious unity, all the love they give to one another is related at once to Christ and to God.[215] Or, as Augustine wrote in his profound exposition of Saint John's First Epistle: "In the mutual love of His members, Christ, who is one, loves Himself."[216]

The Archetype of the Divine Trinity · The exalted archetype and the future perfection of all Christian and monastic unity and community Augustine found in the unfathomable unity and community of the triune God. Dealing with what is said in the Acts of the Apostles (4:32) about the "one heart" (*cor unum*) of the first Christians, he more than once represented the community of love among Christians as what he specifically called an analogy—imperfect, it is true—of the Trinity. "Only consider," he says in his commentary on Saint John's Gospel, "there were many thousands of them, and yet there was only one heart; think of it, they were many thousands, and yet there was only one soul. Yet where [did this happen]? In God! . . . So if many souls who are approaching God are in love one soul, if many hearts are one heart, what is it that the source of love itself achieves in the Father and the Son? There, are the three not, far more, the one God?"[217] There are other Scriptural texts that provide him with the opportunity to present God's union of three in one as the archetype of the unity of love among Christians. Thus, he refers to the words of Christ's prayer (John 17:22): "that they may be one as We also are one" and to His declaration to Martha of Bethany: "Only one thing is necessary" (Luke 10:42)—a saying that for Augustine, with his background in Platonic philosophy, is peculiarly dense with meaning. But for him it is the community of Christian fraternal love which will enable and bring us to share in this "one necessary thing" of the triune God; for, he reasons, "He leads us to this one only if we—the many—possess one single heart."[218]

The Example of Community in the Apostolic Church

Possidius described Augustine's ideal for monastic living as that of a life directed by the Apostles.[219] Indeed, the community of possessions and of love of the primitive Apostolic community had been, at least since the years of his priestly activities at Hippo, the example for his aspirations for monastic communal life. He saw in that first company of Christians the Psalmist's prophetic words "Behold how good and how pleasant it is for brothers to live together in unity" (Ps. 132:1) wonderfully realized.[220] Yet he stressed that this holy assembly did not come into being until the Holy Spirit descended upon the young Church.[221] It is through Him that love is poured into human hearts (cf. Rom. 5:5) and through Him man receives the strength to fulfill the law of the Lord, that is, the two-fold command of love.[222]

Augustine was strongly impressed by this ancient Apostolic example of Christian community, and it was his dearest desire to bring it to a new birth in his monasteries. Therefore, so that everyone would know where to find a description in writing of the life to which he and his monks were aspiring, Augustine had a deacon read aloud the narrative in the Acts of the Apostles before he preached that memorable sermon in which, in the presence of the entire populace, he gave an accounting of the life of the brethren in his clerics' monastery. When the deacon had finished, Augustine himself took the sacred text and turned to the people with the words "And I too wish to read it to you; for it gives me more joy to read these words than to say anything of my own to you." He ended his reading with the observation "You have heard what we wish for; pray that we be able to achieve it."[223]

Almost always, when he spoke of his hopes for monastic life, these words from Acts, "one heart and one soul," served as his motto.[224] They also offer a solution for his original and ingenious explanation of the word *monachus*, "monk." For him, a "monk is not an individual person, living for himself alone, or one who is striving for his own personal perfection and sanctification; . . . he is no solitary whom the community is serving in some subordinate means."[225] Rather, those men would be considered monks who through their harmonious living together have become, as it were, a *monos*, that is, a single being, and possess only one heart and soul toward God.[226]

The Eucharist as the Sign and Bond of Unity

The Acts of the Apostles (2:42) recounts how the first Christians continued the breaking of bread together. For Augustine, and for his monks and clerics too, the communal celebration of the Eucharist was a profound and efficacious symbol of their monastic common life. He saw in this Mystery "the sign of unity and the bond of love,"[227] "the mystery of peace and unity" (*mysterium pacis et unitatis*).[228]

It was Augustine's efforts in North Africa to restore the unity of the Church, broken for almost a century by the Donatist schism, which led him to develop his theology of Eucharistic community. He argued effectively against the Donatists and their particularism, confronting them with proofs that the very Eucharist they celebrated was a witness against them; for this mystery of salvation was nothing other than the sign of unity.[229]

For his concept of Eucharistic community, he appealed to the words of St. Paul in the First Letter to the Corinthians (10:16–17): "Is the bread which we break not the partaking of the body of the Lord? For we, being many, are one bread, one body, all that partake of the one bread." In this text he found combined the two ideas that formed his concept: it is on the Eucharist that our communion with Christ is founded, and it is through the Eucharist that we as Christians commune with one another.[230]

The "holy matter" (*res sancta*) of the Eucharist, of which Augustine often wrote, is, he shows, the body and blood of the Lord, who became man, suffered, and rose from the dead (*Christus incarnatus, passus et resuscitatus*).[231] Even if he did not clearly pronounce on the way in which Christ is present in the Eucharistic species, still his many brief allusions show that he presupposed an efficacious being-present of the Lord "in the sense of a real presence, actual and dynamic."[232]

In this connection and, indeed, much more often, Augustine wrote of another "matter" (*res*) of the Eucharist, which derives from the first. In the "individual unity of the Eucharistic body of Christ, the plurality of those partaking of it becomes a plurality–unity";[233] that is, as the faithful feed on Christ's flesh, they realize that they are members of Christ's one Body. Thus, the term "plurality–unity" conveys the idea that in the celebration of the Eucharist, individuals, without being deprived of their personal individualities, are absorbed in the union and unity, profound and not merely moral, of the "whole Christ, the head and the body" (*Christus totus, caput et corpus*).[234]

But because the Church in celebrating the Eucharist in this way constantly perfects and proves that unity, which comes to her from the glorified Christ, she accepts this mystery, in Augustine's view, not with any egoism or dissension, but to promote and establish fraternal charity among Christians. Therefore, he praises the Eucharist as that holy banquet by which God goes on making and strengthening the "unity within a house" (Ps. 67:7) and, especially, in monasteries.[235]

Community as a Burden on Earth and Perfection in Eternity

Augustine knew very well that the goals of monastic life as he envisaged them would be achieved perfectly only in the life to come, and he frequently expressed the thought that not even monasteries were places of untroubled peace. Thus, there is an entire chapter in his *Rule* devoted to "forgiveness."[236]

In his own foundations, the "burden of community" was probably felt much more keenly than it is in monasteries today, for social distinctions were sharper then, and thus differences in styles of living and conduct were more marked than they are now. It is true that Augustine compares a monastery with a quiet haven, away from the world's stormy sea, and one cannot doubt that ships are safer and happier in port than on the high seas. But sometimes storms do erupt in harbors, and although there are no cliffs there, still ships can dash against one another and shatter. By this perceptive metaphor Augustine showed that "one heart and one soul" cannot find its ideal realization in this world. He wrote, in the same context: "That joy will be complete and perfected 'when this corruptibility is clothed with incorruptibility, this mortality with immortality' [1 Cor. 15:54]. Then joy will be complete; then jubilation will be perfected. . . . Then love will rule without discord."[237] "After this pilgrimage," in that "commonwealth that is to come of those who have only one soul and one heart in God," there will be "the perfection of our unity."[238]

NOTES

1. Cf. *The Work of Monks* 28.36: ". . . to seek the kingdom of God [cf. Matt. 6:33] by the narrow and straitened way [cf. Matt. 7:14] of this undertaking" (cf. Matt. 6:33).

2. *Exposition on Psalm* 99 5. Compare this paragraph with pp. 172–74 below where Augustine's teaching on man's being made in the image of God and on wisdom is discussed in greater detail.

3. *The Ways of the Catholic Church* 1.33.73. In this early work of Augustine's there is as yet no explicit treatment of the theme of the inner unity of man's love of God and of his neighbor. See Ratzinger, *Volk und Haus Gottes*, pp. 38–40.

4. *An Exposition of Certain Propositions from the Epistle to the Romans* 75.

5. *Nature and Grace* 69f.83f. Cf. in addition *Sermon 142* 8f.9.; *Sermo Wilmart* 2 5 in Morin, pp. 677f.; *Man's Perfection in Righteousness* 3.8.

6. *Against Faustus* 30.5f. Cf. *The Ways of the Catholic Church* 1.35.78 and 80. See also Mausbach, *Die Ethik*, I 397ff.

7. *Letter* (in the collection of Augustine's *Letters*) *156*; *The Deeds of Pelagius* 11.23; *Letter 186* 9.32.

8. *Letter 157* 4.23ff. For a translation, see below, chap. 11. Cf. also Mausbach, *Die Ethik*, I 399ff.

9. Cf. also A. Sage, "Vie de perfection et conseils evangéliques dans les controverses pélagiennes," AVSM I, pp. 196ff.

10. *Man's Perfection in Righteousness* 18.39.

11. Ibid.

12. Ibid. 21.44.

13. Ibid. 9.20. Cf. also 6.15, 7.16, 8.18.

14. Ibid. 8.19.

15. *Sermon 169* 15.18.

16. *Man's Perfection in Righteousness* 3.8.

17. *Letter 157* 4.25 and 33; *The Work of Monks* 16.19; *Sermon 93* 1.1.

18. *Letter 157* 4.37.

19. Cf. *The Ways of the Catholic Church* 1.33.73: "If this [love] alone is lacking, all things . . . are in vain"; and *Holy Virginity* 47.47: "Lest [a virgin]

offend against that love which is supreme, and without which everything else she may have, be it few or many, be it great or small, is nothing."

20. *Sermon 142* 8f.9f.

21. *Against Faustus* 5.9; *Letter 157* 4.33; *Holy Virginity* 26ff.26ff.

22. *Holy Virginity* 26ff.26ff. Cf. *Homily on St. John's Gospel* 67 2.

23. "Divinae gratiae multa sunt munera, et est aliud alio maius ac melius" (*Holy Virginity* 46.46).

24. "Continentiam vidualem . . . coniugalis pudicitiae meritum . . . virginali gloriae . . . coronam martyrii . . . eorum cohabitationi sociari, in quibus nemo dicit aliquid proprium, sed sunt eis omnia communia" (ibid. 45.46).

25. Ibid.

26. Ibid. 22.22. Cf. also 8.8.

27. *Letter 157* 4.25.

28. *Exposition on Psalm 132* 9.

29. See also Mausbach, *Die Ethik*, I 396ff. and Sage, "Vie de perfection," pp. 212ff.

30. *Letter 157* 4.36.

31. *Holy Virginity* 14.14. See also 4.4 and 30.30.

32. Ibid. 30.30. Cf. also 9.9, 23.23, 36.37.

33. *Letter 157* 4.37; *Holy Virginity* 40.41.

34. Cf. *Holy Virginity* 44.45, 47.47.

35. *Sermon 267* 4.

36. Cf. J. Vetter, *Der heilige Augustinus und das Geheimnis des Leibes Christi* (Mainz, 1929); Hofmann, *Kirchenbegriff*; Ratzinger, *Volk und Haus Gottes*; A. Piolanti, "Il mistero del 'Cristo totale' in S. Agostino," AM III pp. 453–69; E. Franz, *Totus Christus: Studien über Christus und die Kirche bei Augustin* (Bonn, 1956); W. Gessel, *Eucharistische Gemeinschaft bei Augustinus* (Würzburg, 1966), primarily pp. 190ff. among others.

37. *Exposition on Psalm 17* 2; *Exposition on Psalm 58* 1.2; *Sermo Guelferbytanus 24* 2, in Morin, pp. 523f. It has been observed that what is peculiar to the Augustinian order is expressed in this concept of Christ. Benedict saw Him as the liturgical God–King; Francis, as the child of Bethlehem or as the Saviour on the cross; Ignatius, as the spiritual conqueror of the world (cf. A. Mager, "Zur Psychologie der Orden," BMS, 6 [1924], 373; and C. Schmid, "Das Gottesbild der Benediktinerregel," in *Benedictus, der Vater des Abendlandes*, ed. H. S. Brechter [Munich, 1947], pp. 16ff.). Augustine preferred to regard the God–Man as the intermediary and the head of all the redeemed, as Christ in us and beneath us, Christ, head and body, the one and entire Christ.

38. Cf. also L. M. Verheijen, "Saint Augustin," in *Théologie de la vie monastique: Etudes sur la tradition patristique* (Paris, 1961), pp. 205ff.; and A. Manrique, *Teologia Agustiniana de la vida religiosa* (El Escorial, 1964), pp. 93ff.

39. *Exposition on Psalm 132* 7.

40. Ibid. 9. Similarly, *Against the Writings of Petilian* 2.104.238f.

41. Cf. also *Letter 48* 2.

42. *Exposition on Psalm 132* 2. See also below, chap. 12.

43. Cf. *Homily on St. John's Gospel 13* 12.

44. *Exposition on Psalm 132* 9: "Those who fulfill the law are perfect. But how is the law of Christ fulfilled by those who live as brothers in unity? Listen to the Apostle: 'Bear one another's burdens, and thus you will fulfill the law of Christ' [Gal. 6:2]."

45. See below, p. 130.

46. See below, pp. 146–47: "See the head of the poor; . . . whoever is a member of this poor man is truly a poor man" (*Sermon 14* 7.9).

47. *Letter 157* 4.37.

48. See below, pp. 245–46.

49. *Homily on St. John's Gospel 13* 12.

50. *Against Faustus* 5.11.

51. "The unity of Christ is one; the Church is one. Wherever a man has done a good work, it belongs to us if we rejoice together in it" (*Sermon 356* 10).

52. "When we think of the peace that you have in Christ, then even we find rest in your love, however much we may be caught up in various and bitter toil. For we are one body under one head, so that in us you may be laboring and in you we may find rest" (*Letter 48* 1). For a very similar sentiment, see *Letter 145* 2.

53. "For since [your mother] is the sister of us all, whose father is God and whose mother is the Church, we are not prevented, you or I or all our brethren, from loving her, not with that private love which you had in your home, but with a public love in the house of God" (*Letter 243* 4).

54. "There is a tribute-paying multitude which is joined to these front-line Christian troops through a certain exchange, as it were, of love" (*Against Faustus* 5.9). There are similar thoughts in *Letter 157* 4.37.

55. *Exposition on Psalm 103* 3.16. Cf. also *Letter 157* 4.38.

56. *Against Faustus* 5.9f.

57. " . . . how much the fervor of their prayers and their life, by its example, benefits us" (*The Ways of the Catholic Church* 1.31.66).

58. " . . . so by living aright and teaching aright, they might well say to them: 'If we have sown a spiritual harvest for you, is it a great matter if we reap your material things?' [1 Cor. 9:11]" (*Letter 157* 4.38).

59. *Rule* 8.2 and *Letter 48* 4. Cf. also *Letter 27* 2.

60. *The Work of Monks* 28.36 and *Letter 83* 5.

61. See below, pp. 197–99.

62. A. Schulz and R. Hofmann, "Nachfolge Christi," LThK, VII², 758–62, and P. Nagel, *Die Motivierung der Askese in der alten Kirche und der Ursprung des Mönchtums* (Berlin, 1966), pp. 5–19. See also A. Schulz, *Nachfolgen und Nachahmen im Neuen Testament* (Munich, 1962) and H. J. Schoeps, "Von der *Imitatio Dei* zur Nachfolge Christi," in *Aus frühchristlicher Zeit* (Tübingen, 1950), pp. 286–301.

63. Cf. also Mausbach, *Die Ethik*, I 391–96.

64. *Holy Virginity* 27f.27f.

65. *Sermon 304* 2.2.
66. Cf. *Confessions* 7.9.14.
67. Ibid. 7.18.24. See also *The City of God* 10.29, 11.2; *Exposition on Psalm 90* 1.1; *Sermon 124* 3.3; *Sermon 142* 2.2 and 5.
68. *Sermon 134* 11; *Sermon 156* 12.13; *Homily on St. John's Gospel 3* 15; *Homily on St. John's Epistle to the Parthi 3* 13.
69. *Confessions* 8.6ff., 14f.29.
70. *Against Faustus* 5.9; *The Work of Monks* 25.32; *Holy Virginity* 45.46; *A Letter to the Catholics against the Donatists, Commonly Called "The Unity of the Church"* 16.41; *Exposition on Psalm 103* 3.16; *Letter 157* 4.39. See also Possidius 2.
71. *Sermon 14* 6f.9. See below, pp. 146–47.
72. *Letter 243* 2f. and 10. See below, pp. 224–25.
73. See below, pp. 232–40. See also O. Schaffner, *Christliche Demut: Des heiligen Augustinus Lehre von der Humilitas* (Würzburg, 1959), esp. pp. 83–135.
74. *Holy Virginity* 53.53.
75. Ibid. 2.2.
76. Ibid. 29.29.
77. Ibid. 2.2.
78. *Commentary on the Epistle to the Galatians* 37.
79. *Sermon 96* 7.9.
80. J. Auer, "Militia Christi: Zur Geschichte eines christlichen Grundbildes," *Geist und Leben*, 32 (1959), 340–51. Cf. also A. von Harnack, *Militia Christi: Die christliche Religion und der Soldatenstand in den ersten drei Jahrhunderten* (Tübingen, 1905); L. Hofmann, "Militia Christi: Ein Beitrag zur Lehre von den kirchlichen Ständen," *Trierer theologische Zeitschrift*, 63 (1954), 76–92; J. Auer, "Militia Christi," LThK, VII², 418f.
81. *The Christian Combat* 1ff.1ff. and 33.35. Cf. also A. d'Alès, "Le *De agone christiano*," *Gregorianum*, 11 (1930), 131–45.
82. *Sermon 276* 1. Cf. also the sermon *On the Cataclysm* 1f. (PL 40.693), the genuineness of which, it must be admitted, has been contested.
83. See also J. Morán, *El equilibrio: Ideal de la vida monastica en San Agustín* (Valladolid, 1964), pp. 349–53. The expression "Christian army" (*militia Christiana*) is to be found, in Augustine's writings on monasticism, in *The Work of Monks* 25.33 and 26.35 and in *Letter 243* 7. In a somewhat generalized sense, to designate all those who fulfill "the more sublime evangelical precepts" (*sublimiora praecepta evangelica*) by a celibacy dedicated to God, voluntary poverty, strict fasting, or also in the monastic community of possessions and love, the term is found in *Against Faustus* 5.9. One also finds the phrases "spiritual life and army" (*spiritalis vita militiaque*), "divine army" (*divina militia*), and "holy army" (*sancta militia*) in *The Work of Monks* 25.32, 16.19, and 22.26 respectively, and "your [i.e., God's] army" (*militia tua* [sc. *Dei*]) in *Confessions* 8.6.15, 9.2.4, and 9.8.17. In contrast, Augustine wrote of a "worldly army" (*militia saecularis*) or "army of the

world" (*militia saeculi*), that is, ordinary military service or service of any kind to an earthly ruler, in *Confessions* 8.6.15 and 9.8.17, and in *Sermon 356* 4.

84. *The Work of Monks* 22.26.

85. Ibid. 16.19.

86. Ibid. 28.36; *Letter 243* 6. The Donatists called their Circumcellions "soldiers of Christ" (*milites Christi*), which Augustine changed to "soldiers of the devil" (*milites diaboli*); see *Exposition on Psalm 132* 6.

87. *Letter* 243 1 and 7.

88. *Letter* 243.

89. "Consider too our Lord Jesus Christ, since He is our king" (*Letter 243* 1.) Cf. also Auer, *Militia Christi*, p. 346, who finds this monastic idea of Christ the King in Basil and again later in Benedict.

90. "Did not your field commander also have an earthly mother?" (*Letter 243* 9). This title for Christ is also found in *Letter 21* 1: " . . . nothing is more blessed in the eyes of God . . . than the office of a bishop or priest or deacon if he fights in the way our field commander orders."

91. *Letter 243* 1 and 6.

92. Ibid. 1f.

93. Ibid. 6.

94. Ibid. 3f.

95. Ibid. 1 and 5.

96. Ibid. 6.

97. *Letter* 220 12. Cf. also *Against the Writings of Petilian* 3.12.13.

98. *The Work of Monks* 16.19.

99. Ibid.

100. "Si te igitur tironem Christi profiteris, castra ne deseras" (*Letter 243* 1).

101. Cf. Auer, *Militia Christi*, pp. 345ff.

102. K. H. Rengstorf, "Δοῦλος, δουλεία, etc." *Theologisches Wörterbuch zum Neuen Testament* II (Stuttgart, 1935), p. 264.

103. Ibid. pp. 270ff. Cf. also F. Mussner, "Ebed Jahwe," LThK, III^2, 622–25.

104. *The Greatness of the Soul* 34.77.

105. *Exposition on Psalm* 70 1.2.

106. *Homily on St. John's Gospel* 10 7.

107. *Soliloquies* 1.15.30. In the same work (1.1.5) he also uses the more or less synonymous expression *famulus Dei.*

108. Ibid. 1.1.5.

109. Listing the individual occurrences of the concepts "servant of God" and "serving God" would occupy too much space. They are to be found in many letters and sermons, including the *Expositions on the Psalms*, and repeatedly in the *Confessions* and *The Work of Monks*, as well as here and there in others of his works. At times he also uses, with the same significance, the word *famulus*: see for instance *Rule* 3.5, 5.6. The terms "service of God"

and "servitude to God" are used in *Letter 126* 7, *Letter 179* 2, *Letter 220* 3, and *The Work of Monks* 22.25.

110. *Letter 111* 3. See also Possidius 26. Evodius too uses this expression in two letters: *Letter 158* (in the collection of Augustine's *Letters*) 3 and *Letter 163* (in the collection of Augustine's *Letters*).

111. *Letter 179* 2.

112. *The Work of Monks* 22.25. Cf. also Possidius 2.

113. The expression "servants of God" for the members of the monastery of clerics occurs in *Sermon 356* 15.

114. *A Letter to the Catholics against the Donatists, Commonly Called "The Unity of the Church"* 16.41.

115. *The Work of Monks* 29.37: *conservi.*

116. *Letter 149* 3.34.

117. Possidius 2, 5, 11, 23, 26.

118. *Letter 243* 12.

119. " . . . Deo sine saeculari compede expediti servire" (*Sermon 113* 1.1).

120. *Letter 126* 7.

121. See below, p. 262.

122. Cf. Nagel, *Die Motivierung der Askese*, pp. 35ff.

123. See S. Frank, ΑΓΓΕΛΙΚΟΣ ΒΙΟΣ: *Begriffsanalytische und begriffsgeschichtliche Untersuchung zum "engelgleichen Leben" im frühen Mönchtum* (Münster, 1964), and Nagel, *Die Motivierung der Askese*, pp. 34–38. Cf. also U. Ranke-Heinemann, "Zum Ideal der *Vita angelica* im frühen Mönchtum," *Geist und Leben*, 29 (1956), 347–57.

124. Cf. Ambrose's *A Rule for Virgins* 104 (PL 16.345). See also Frank, ΑΓΓΕΛΙΚΟΣ ΒΙΟΣ, pp. 173f., who indicates other contexts.

125. See his *The Dress of Virgins* 22 (CSEL 3.203). See Frank, ΑΓΓΕΛΙΚΟΣ ΒΙΟΣ, pp. 168f.

126. For places where Ambrose, dealing with the topic, enumerates similarities other than celibacy, see his *Letters 63, 71*, and *82* (PL 16.1261 and 1263). He speaks there of the "life of the angels" (*vita angelorum*) and "warfare of the angels" (*militia angelorum*) in Eusebius of Vercelli's communities of clerics. Cf. Frank, ΑΓΓΕΛΙΚΟΣ ΒΙΟΣ, pp. 175f.

127. " . . . angelica portio . . . incorruptionis perpetuae meditatio" (*Holy Virginity* 13.12). Cf. also ibid. 53.54: ". . . angelica vita . . . caeli mores."

128. " . . . in carne iam imitari vitam angelorum" (*Letter 150*).

129. " . . . caelestem et angelicam vitam in terrena mortalite meditantes" (*Holy Virginity* 24.24). Cf. also *The Good of Marriage* 8.8: " . . . angelica meditatio."

130. *Sermon 132* 3.

131. "Platonisches und biblisches Denken bei Augustin," AM I, p. 291.

132. *Homily on St. John's Epistle to the Parthi 3* 3; *Letter 199* 6.17.

133. *Letter 137* 4.16; *Sermon 81* 8.

134. *Sermon 81* 7.

135. *Letter 199* 1.1f.

136. *Letter 137* 4.16.

137. Cf. perhaps *Exposition on Psalm 136* 2.4ff.

138. *The City of God* 14.28 and *Letter 238* 2.13.

139. On this cf. Mausbach, *Die Ethik*, I 264ff., 434ff., II 410ff.

140. Frank, ΑΓΓΕΛΙΚΟΣ ΒΙΟΣ, p. 30*n*85, draws attention to seven places in which Augustine used the concept of the "angelic life" (*vita angelica*). But when I examined them, I found that only one (see below, note 142) deals with an imitation of the life of the angels and that all the others apply "the company of the angels" (*societias angelorum*), "being made an angel" (*angelus effici*), or "acting like an angel" (*angelus fieri*) to the life of the world to come.

141. *The City of God* 22.29.

142. *Sermo Casinensis* II *114* 1, in Morin, p. 416.

143. *Sermo Guelferbytanus 5* 3, in Morin, p. 458.

144. Cf. above notes 127 and 129.

145. *Exposition on Psalm 132* 13.

146. Cf. *Exposition on Psalm 26* 2.14 and *Exposition on Psalm 96* 10.

147. "Haec addita virginitati angelicam vitam hominibus et caeli mores exhibent terris" (*Holy Virginity* 53.54).

148. "The more the hope grows in me of looking upon that beauty for which I so violently long, the more all my love and my yearning are turned toward it" (*Soliloquies* 1.10.17). Cf. also *The Ways of the Catholic Church* 1.30.64. See also p. 10 above.

149. *The Ways of the Catholic Church* 1.31.66.

150. Cf. also above, pp. 27–28.

151. *Retractations* 1.2.

152. Possidius 24.

153. *Sermon 104* 3.4.

154. Cf. below, pp. 194–95.

155. See below, pp. 195–97.

156. *Exposition on Psalm 99* 8.

157. Ibid. 10.

158. Ibid. 11. Cf. also *Letter 48* 2.

159. *Rule* 1.1. To the word "soul" (*anima*) in this quotation, Augustine once gave the meaning "life" (*Letter 243* 4); *anima* signifies the vital force in man, the principle of life. We may compare this program with what he wrote of the object of their community at Cassiciacum: "So that we might together, as with one heart, search for our souls and for God" (*Soliloquies* 1.12.10).

160. Jordan of Saxony, an Augustinian in the Middle Ages, saw this very clearly when he wrote: "He [that is, the most holy father Augustine] founded his entire form of religious living upon community, or, better, upon communion" (AH, p. 7). This community upon which Augustine based his monasticism, after the example of the Apostles, was to be fourfold: (*a*) community of dwelling, as the *Rule* says: "You should live in unity in the house"; (*b*) community of heart: "with one heart and one soul toward

God"; (*c*) community of property: "You should not call anything your own, but everything you have should be common property"; and (*d*) community of use: "Your superior should distribute food and clothing to each of you, to each man as he may have need." All the regulations which may be contained in the *Rule* and in the order's constitutions can be traced back to this fourfold community. It is, therefore, the measure by which Jordan classifies Augustine's works.

161. *Exposition on Psalm 132* 2.

162. *Against Faustus* 5.9; *The Work of Monks* 25.32; *Exposition on Psalm 132* 2.8.12. Cf. also T. J. Van Bavel, "*Ante omnia* et *In Deum* dans la *Regula sancti Augustini*," *Vigiliae Christianae*, 12 (1958), 162ff.

163. *Sermon 355* 1 and 6; *Sermon 356* 10.

164. Cf. *Letter 243* 4.

165. Cf. *Sermon 355* 3.

166. *Rule* 2. Cf. *Homily on St. John's Gospel 65* 2.

167. Cf. *Rule* 1ff.

168. Ibid., 3.

169. Cf. A. Mager, "Religiöses Leben in und mit der Gemeinschaft," BMS, 2 (1920), 296.

170. "Non aequaliter omnibus" (*Rule* 1.3).

171. Ibid., 8.1. See also ibid. 7.1–4.

172. Z. Bucher, "Das Bild vom Menschen in der *Regula Benedicti*," in *Benedictus, der Vater des Abendlandes*, ed. H. S. Brechter (Munich, 1947), p. 45.

173. *Rule* 6.3.

174. *Exposition on Psalm 132* 6. E. Hendrikx ("Augustinus als Monnik," *Augustiniana*, 3 [1953], 346) tries to conclude from this that the form of greeting here was customary among the Catholics of Hippo; but the fact that Augustine specifically states that the greeting is to be given by the "brothers" (*fratres*), which, in the context, means the monks (*monachi*), leaves Hendrikx' argument unsupported.

175. Cf. *Rule* 5.2.

176. *Sermon 356* 8.

177. *Sermon 355* 6.

178. *Letter 73* 10.

179. *Rule* 1.2.

180. For the significance of community in Benedictine monasticism, cf. A. Schmitt, "Vom Wesen des benediktinischen Mönchtums," BMS, 9 (1927), 95f.; M. Frank, "Der Strafkodex in der Regel St. Benedikts," ibid., 17 (1935), 311ff.; S. Brechter, "Huldigung an den heiligen Vater Benedikt," in *Benedictus, der Vater des Abendlandes*, ed. H. S. Brechter (Munich, 1947), pp. 5f.; Bucher, "Das Bild vom Menschen," pp. 44ff.

181. It has, with justification, been suggested that the essential difference between the older and the newer religious orders in the Church is that the older orders were occasioned and formed for religious ends, the newer ones to perform apostolic or charitable functions (T. Graf, "Zur Wesensstruktur

des benediktinischen Geistes," BMS, 13 (1931), 11f. Cf. also P. Lippert, *Briefe in ein Kloster* (Munich, 1932), pp. 37f., 40ff., 45ff., 184f., and S. Brechter, "Die soziologische Gestalt des Benediktinertums," in *Benedictus, der Vater des Abendlandes*, ed. H. S. Brechter (Munich, 1947), pp. 67ff. In fact, Augustinian monastic life has as little need as the Benedictines have of external objects to justify its existence. Both these ancient institutions acquired their characters because they expressed great concepts of the way in which Christian aspirations to perfection might be realized. Benedict wishes to create a "school of holy servitude" (*schola divini servitii*); Augustine, a community of true Christian love: "one heart and one soul toward God" (*cor unum et anima una in Deum*).

182. *On 83 Various Questions*, question 71.1.

183. *Exposition on Psalm 132* 9. See above, pp. 109–11.

184. For this term, see *Sermon 356* 8 and *On Various Questions to Simplicianus* 2.1.10: " . . . love . . . does not divide unity, of which it is the strongest bond."

185. *The Ways of the Catholic Church* 1.33.70. On Augustine's teaching on love of our neighbors, cf. also M. Mellet, "Saint Augustin, prédicateur de la charité fraternelle dans ses commentaires sur saint Jean [I]," *La Vie Spirituelle*, 73 (1945), 304–25, 556–76, and "Saint Augustin, prédicateur de la charité fraternelle dans ses commentaires sur saint Jean [II]," ibid., 74 (1946), 69–91; L. Gallay, "La conscience de la charité fraternelle, d'après les *Tractatus in Primam Joannis* de saint Augustin," REA, 1 (1955), 1–20; S. J. Grabowski, "The Role of Charity in the Mystical Body of Christ According to Saint Augustine," ibid., 3 (1957), 29–63; A. Trapè, "Il principio fondamentale della spiritualità Agostiniana e la vita monastica," AVSM I, pp. 1–41. M. Huftier presents a systematic compilation of Augustine's texts on love (*caritas*) in *La Charité dans l'enseignement de saint Augustin* (Tournai, 1959).

186. *The Ways of the Catholic Church* 1.33.73.

187. Cf. Ratzinger, *Haus und Volk Gottes*, pp. 38–40.

188. *On 83 Various Questions*, question 71.1. Cf. also *Exposition on Psalm 132* 9.

189. *On 83 Various Questions*, question 71.1. Cf. also *Homily on St. John's Gospel* 65 3.

190. *On 83 Various Questions*, question 71.1.

191. On this, see below, pp. 172–77.

192. *The Trinity* 8.10.14.

193. Mellet, "Saint Augustin, prédicateur [II]," 87.

194. Cf. L. Bouyer, *La Spiritualité du Nouveau Testament et des Pères* (Paris, 1960), p. 581.

195. Cf. A. Nygren, *Eros und Agape*, 2nd ed. (Gütersloh, 1954), pp. 366ff., 437; Huftier, *La Charité*, pp. 18ff.; Grabowski, "The Role of Charity," 33ff.

196. See *Homily on St. John's Epistle to the Parthi* 7 4: " 'For God is love.' What more was to be said, brothers? If nothing were to be said in praise of love in all these pages of this epistle, if there were nothing in all the other

pages of the Scriptures, and if we were to hear only this one saying spoken by the Spirit of God—namely, 'For God is love'—we should not need to seek for more."

197. *The Trinity* 8.8.12. Cf. also *Homily on St. John's Epistle to the Parthi* 9 10f.

198. *The Trinity* 7.3.6.

199. Cf. A. M. La Bonnardière, "Le verset Paulinien Rom. V, 5 dans l'oeuvre de saint Augustin," AM II, pp. 657–65.

200. "Without the Spirit of God, there can be no love" (*Homily on St. John's Epistle to the Parthi* 6 10).

201. "Intelligamus in dilectione Spiritum Sanctum esse" (*Homily on St. John's Epistle to the Parthi* 7 6).

202. A. Turrado, "El platonismo de San Agustín y su doctrina acerca de la inhabitación del Espíritu Santo," *Augustiniana*, 5 (1955), 471–86, maintains and illustrates this against both older and more recent writers; his conclusion (p. 479): "But this Augustinian Platonism includes a fundamental distinction, as we have said: The realization in the creature of the concept of charity and the supreme concept which it verifies are like cause and effect. In reality, they are differentiated as Creator and created."

203. Cf. *Sermon 71* 12.18: "Through whatever is common to the Father and to the Son, They have wished us to share both among ourselves and with Them, and through that gift to gather us together in unity, because the two of Them are one, that is, through the Holy Spirit, God and gift of God."

204. Cf. Ratzinger, *Volk und Haus Gottes*, esp. pp. 169ff. and 240ff.; D. Sanchis, "Le Symbolisme communitaire du Temple chez saint Augustin," *Revue d'Ascétique et de Mystique*, 37 (1961), 3–30, 137–47; A. Turrado, "Eres templo de Dios: La inhabitación de la Sma. Trinidad en los justos según S. Augustín," RAE, 7 (1966), 21–55, 203–27.

205. *Letter 187* 12.35f.

206. *Homily on St. John's Epistle to the Parthi 8* 12.

207. *The City of God* 10.3. Cf. also *Letter 187* 13.38; *Sermon 336* 1.1; *Sermon 337* 1.1. Tertullian before him had known the image of God's temple as applicable to individuals as well as to the Church as a whole (Ratzinger, *Volk und Haus Gottes*, pp. 71f.).

208. Rule 1.8.

209. Ibid. 4.6.

210. *On 83 Various Questions*, question 71.7.

211. This union of the two images is evident, for example, in the following text: "So the Temple of God is the Body of Christ. What are our bodies? They are members of Christ. Hear the Apostle himself: 'Do you not know that your bodies are the members of Christ?' [I Cor. 6:15]. What is he showing when he says 'Your bodies are members of Christ' except that our bodies and our head, which is Christ, are at the same time the Temple of God?" (*Sermo Morin 3* 4, in Morin, pp. 598f.).

212. See above, pp. 110–11.

213. *Letter 243* 4.

214. *Exposition on Psalm 132* 6. Cf. also *The Creed for Catechumens* 2.4.

215. *Homily on St. John's Epistle to the Parthi 10* 3.

216. "Et erit unus Christus amans seipsum" (ibid.).

217. *Homily on St. John's Gospel 39* 5. See also *Homily on St. John's Gospel 14* 9 and *The Trinity* 8.10.14. On this cf. M. Nédoncelle, "L'Intersubjectivité humaine, est-elle pour saint Augustin une image de la Trinité?" AM I, pp. 595–602.

218. *Sermon 103* 3.4. Cf. *Letter 238* 2.16.

219. Possidius 5. Cf. also *The Work of Monks* 17ff.20, 25, 32, 38, where Augustine repeatedly refers to the "Apostolic precepts" (*praecepta apostolica*).

220. *Exposition on Psalm 132* 2.

221. Ibid. See also *Sermo Mai 158* 2 and *Sermo Guelferbytanus 11* 5, in Morin, pp. 382 and 477, respectively.

222. Cf. *The Catechizing of the Uninstructed* 23.41.

223. *Sermon 356* 1.

224. See above, note 162.

225. A. Wucherer-Huldenfeld, "Mönchtum und kirchlicher Dienst bei Augustinus nach dem Bild des Neubekehrten und des Bischofs," *Zeitschrift für katholische Theologie*, 82 (1960), 199f.

226. *Exposition on Psalm 132* 6.

227. *Homily on St. John's Gospel 26* 13. Cf. also Blank, *Lehre . . . vom Sakramente der Eucharistie*, pp. 93ff., and K. Adam, *Die Eucharistielehre des heiligen Augustin* (Paderborn, 1908), pp. 84f.

228. *Sermon 272* 1.

229. Gessel, *Eucharistische Gemeinschaft*, pp. 75ff.

230. Ibid., pp. 80ff.

231. Ibid., pp. 167ff.

232. Ibid., pp. 180f.

233. Ibid., p. 182.

234. Ibid., pp. 182f.

235. *Homily on St. John's Gospel 26* 14.

236. *Rule* 6.1–3.

237. *Exposition on Psalm 99* 8. Cf. also Mellet, *L'Itinéraire*, pp. 65ff.

238. *The Good of Marriage* 18.21.

6

The Monastic "Law of Life"

THE FOUNDATION ON WHICH AUGUSTINIAN MONASTIC LIFE IS BUILT is, in one respect, the obligation to live in community, and the many external manifestations of this. The common life, as Augustine and his companions lived it, meant more than a mere living together. It was a true community of life. They worked with one another and for one another; they prayed with one another; they ate and drank with one another. When they went into public places, they went together. Each man's own life was passed in the environment provided by the community.[1]

Augustine himself once summed up the law governing the life of his monastic communities in three great demands; the monk must be free of desires for personal possessions, he must contribute his manual labor toward the upkeep of the community, and he owed his superior willing obedience.[2]

POVERTY

The indispensable prerequisite of Augustine's ideal of the common life was the realization of complete personal poverty. He specifically calls this "the law of our life" (*lex vitae nostrae*), the life of the monastery.[3]

His ideal for this life of poverty was based entirely on Christian ways of thinking. It had nothing to do with a Cynical deprivation of the necessities of life, which might regard a neglected appearance as a mark of perfection, for he insists upon cleanliness of clothing and of the person.[4] Nor does it derive from heretical notions that private ownership is illicit; Augustine himself expressly defended human rights to personal possessions.[5]

Augustinian ideas about poverty do not constitute that contempt for the good things of this earth which the Stoic search for wisdom fostered, and they directed men toward more than a merely natural contentment. Though Augustine was fond of quoting outstanding examples of this sort from pagan antiquity—Scipio the conqueror, too poor to give his daughter even a marriage-portion; the consul Valerius, who had to be buried at the state's expense because of his indigence; Cincinnatus the general, just as unassuming after his victory as he had been before; the Roman-born Fabricius, who rejected the gifts and preferments proffered by Pyrrhus in order to lead a life of want in his native city[6]—he always insisted that one must practice Christian and monastic poverty for higher motives than these.[7]

Poverty as a Release from Earthly "Burdens" and an Enrichment in God

The object of Christian poverty, Augustine taught, is to free men from their dependence on earthly goods so that they might serve God in greater freedom.[8] For him poverty was, not an end in itself—he did not greatly love it because of its intrinsic excellence—but a means to something higher, which set us free from the many hindrances on our way toward our eternal goal. For him the obvious motive for voluntary poverty (*voluntaria paupertas*) was an eschatological longing for a heavenly homeland. He declared that men chose poverty "to travel less burdened on the pilgrimage of his life, on the road that leads to our native land, where God Himself is true riches."[9] And he knew that earthly goods cannot make men lastingly and truly happy. In one of his sermons he makes the human heart complain: "I cannot be satisfied by mortal creatures; I cannot be filled with the things of this transient world. Let God give me something that is immortal; let Him bestow on me something everlasting."[10]

Becoming poor for the love of God, according to Augustine, means entrusting one's money to faithful hands, laying it up in a safe account. Here the Lord's words are fulfilled: "Lay up to yourselves treasures in heaven: where neither the rust nor moth doth consume, and where thieves do not break through, nor steal" (Matt. 6:20).[11] Denying what is of the earth will make the heart open and receptive to God and to the things of God.[12] Through this one can prepare "a place for the Lord" (Ps. 131:5).[13] In their poverty the monks were rich; in their lack of all things they possessed what is worth more than earthly riches: they had the treasure beyond all treasures, God Himself, as their own.[14] "Listen to me, you poor men!" he cried; "What then do you not possess if you possess God? Listen to me, you rich men! What then do you possess if you do not possess God?"[15]

Poverty as Imitation of the Poor and Humble Christ

Augustine viewed monastic poverty as a close imitation of Christ, in the sense of His words: "If you will be perfect, go sell what you have, and give it to the poor, and you shall have treasure in heaven; and come, follow me" (Matt. 19:21). Without this imitation, poverty will have neither meaning nor value.[16]

But when Augustine presented Christ as the example for those who are truly poor (*veri pauperes*), he showed Him in His humility and self-abasement. For "true" poverty and humility, according to him, are deeply, inwardly connected. The "poor in spirit" whom Christ called blessed (Matt. 5:3) Augustine constantly identified with those who are humble.[17] In one sermon he expounded "What is the meaning of 'poor in spirit'? It is to be poor in one's disposition, not in one's possessions. For whoever is poor in the spirit is humble; he listens to the sighs of the humble, and does not despise their petitions."[18] In another sermon he makes the direct comparison "poor, that is, humble" (*pauper, id est humilis*), and says, correspondingly, that the "humble rich" (*divites humiles*) are the "rich poor" (*divites pauperes*).[19] In the same sermon he displays for his hearers, with the utmost vividness, Christ's self-abasement and His poverty in becoming man and in His passion as the example for those who are truly poor: "... that being rich He became poor, for your sakes" (2 Cor. 8:9). They must see Him in His riches: "All things were made by Him, and without Him was made nothing that was made" (John 1:3). They must see Him in His poverty:

> "The Word was made flesh and dwelt among us" [John 1:14]. . . . He is conceived in a woman's virginal womb, He let Himself be enclosed in His mother's womb. What deprivation! He came into this world in a mean little lodging; wrapped in swaddling clothes, He is placed in a manger . . . ; the Lord of heaven and earth, He who created the angels from nothing, He who called everything visible and invisible into being, feeds at His mother's breast; He whimpers and cries and lets Himself be tended like a babe. He grows up, He grows older, and He conceals His kingship. And in the end He is arrested, despised, scourged, mocked, spat upon, struck in the face, crowned with thorns, lifted up on a cross, and pierced with a lance. What dereliction! See there the head of all poor men, of which I would be one. Whoever is truly poor, in him we can see a member of Christ, this poor man.[20]

In this, above all, Augustine perceives the nobility of voluntary poverty, making visible in us a living likeness of the God–Man, who alone can bring about a closer union of the members with the head.

The Apostolic Community of Possessions and Love

Augustine's concept of monastic poverty received its characteristic stamp from his very conscious reliance on the example of the Christian community in the primitive Church (Acts 4:32–35). The thematic image of monastic poverty and common ownership of goods appears in his writings, to be sure, for the first time around the year 400.[21] The oldest pertinent text is his *Rule* which he seems to have written around the turn of the century for his garden monastery.[22] He wrote:

> First, because you have been gathered together as one body, you should live in unanimity in the house, with "one heart and one soul" [Acts 4:32] for God. And you should not call anything your own, but everything which you have should be common property, and your superior should distribute food and clothing to each of you, not the same to everyone, because you have not all the same strength, but rather to each man as he may have need. For this is what you read in the Acts of the Apostles [4:32, 35], that "all things were common to them, and distribution was made to everyone as he had need."[23]

In the same way, in his writings on monasticism, Augustine alluded to the primitive Church as a model of poverty and common property, founded on Christian brotherly love.[24] Certainly, the personal poverty Augustine advocated transcends what we read in Acts. What is described there as the free gifts made by individuals (cf. Acts 5:4) was accepted in his monasteries as an obligation incumbent on everyone; in the Apostolic Church, they were permitted to retain some portion of their property, but his monks fell short of their undertaking (*propositum*) for the common life (*vita communis*) if they did not renounce the whole of their personal possessions.[25]

In this respect, Augustine's ideal gained depth; and this was important. He ceased to regard poverty exclusively as simply a form of self-denial which would set men free for higher things and make the imitation of Christ possible, and came to view it instead, in keeping with the account in Acts, as a way to realize the consummate community of love in the monastic life. The renunciation of personal possessions would assist the monks in ridding themselves of all egoism and in giving themselves selflessly to the service of the brethren.[26] Possession and ownership, he said in a sermon, have always been at the root of all contention and warfare. In contrast, freely willed poverty as the primitive Christian community understood it was the source of peace and harmony.[27]

Basically, Augustine was concerned with only a single reality in considering this Apostolic community of possessions and of love; but the reality had two applications, one material and the other spiritual, which cannot be separated. In monastic poverty and common ownership he was henceforth to see a practical expression and an efficacious sign of spiritual love (*caritas*).[28] In the words of his *Rule*, it is that very "love, of which it was written that it 'is not self-seeking' " (1 Cor. 13:5).[29] This is precisely what he saw becoming real in the common life (*vita communis*) of the monasteries, where men no longer "have their own interests at heart, but Jesus Christ's" (Phil. 2:21).[30]

With the citing of this Biblical text, Augustine also brings the question of monastic poverty into the ecclesiastical perspective of the Mystical Body. Monks, he held, citizens of "the eternal, heavenly city of Jerusalem," give evidence through their common life (*vita communis*) that they esteem the shared interests of the monastic community and of the entire supernatural commonwealth (*res publica*) no less highly than so many a Roman leader, renowned for his selflessness, valued the general good of his earthly city.[31]

Realization of Personal Poverty and of the Common Life

Augustine's writings show us the energy and skill with which he set about achieving a complete realization in his own days of his aspirations for the life of poverty. So, for example, when it became known, about the year 405, that in the monastery of brothers at Tagaste a perfect poverty was not being observed because some of them had not surrendered all their possessions when they entered, he advised Alypius in the future not to admit anyone before the postulant had completely divested himself of all his property by selling it or by a notarial deed.[32]

This forsaking of one's possessions must allow, he said, no limitations, no exceptions. It must be carried out wholly, completely; and in his *Rule* he forbade the monks even to call anything their own.[33] The renunciation of private property which he demanded upon entry into the community was not to apply merely to present possessions; everything that a monk later received from outsiders belonged to the community as well. Augustine emphatically stated in his *Rule* that no one was to make any claim upon such gifts or to dispose of them as he pleased. They were not to be concealed but to be turned over to the superior to become, and to be used as, common property as he saw fit.[34] Gifts and presents that were intended, not for the community, but exclusively for one particular brother were out of the question as far as Augustine was concerned.[35] He was as strict in his own personal conduct. He said in a sermon to the people: "What I receive for myself is from the possessions of the community; for I know I may possess what I have only as common property. I do not want, my dear ones, for you to bring gifts that only I am supposed to enjoy, because you think that they are in some way more fitting for me."[36]

In spite of this resoluteness in his requirement of complete personal poverty, Augustine still proceeded intelligently and discreetly in his implementations of it. He made an exception to his monks' renunciation of possessions when their ties of affection toward near relatives were concerned and, for similar reasons, often mitigated the full effects of his *Rule*.[37]

He was insistent that this poverty must be practiced in the spirit as well. In his view, everything had not been achieved by a merely external renunciation; things had to be renounced promptly and gladly.[38] Whoever took a vow of poverty must kill his desire for personal possessions. "What use is it to you," he asked in a sermon, "if you stand there with empty hands, and yet with a heart full of greed?"[39]

How much someone might have renounced was of no consequence; but in his heart he should deprive himself of everything, whether in the world he had lived in riches or in poverty. If he had been rich, God would reward his good will and his outward act; if he had been poor, his good will alone would suffice.[40] Even if someone in his father's wretched hovel had had barely a bed and box to call his own, and now for the sake of Christ had vowed himself to poverty, one cannot maintain, Augustine says, that he has forsaken nothing. Peter and the other Apostles were only poor fishermen, and yet the Lord had promised them a great reward. For if someone renounces not only what he possesses but also what he would like to possess, then he has in both cases renounced much; it is as if with this he had renounced the entire world.[41]

According to Augustine, this disposition toward poverty manifests itself in the joyful willingness with which poverty is practiced. A monk should forgo his own possessions willingly, indeed joyfully.[42] The disposition toward poverty will also demand from him contentment with what is given to him, even if that be less than others receive.[43] Lack of contentment is, for Augustine, a sign of imperfection.[44] The disposition toward poverty must, in fact, lead us to a contentment that will characterize the conduct of our entire lives.[45] Those so disposed should beware of making demands in the monastery which could not be fulfilled outside.[46]

The personal poverty of individuals finds its completion in the full community of possessions. In his *Rule*, Augustine wrote: "everything which you have should be common property."[47] He was deeply engaged by the idea of a Christian community of ownership such as the primitive Church practiced, and he tried to realize it in its entirety in his monasteries. Even though he acknowledged men's fundamental right to private ownership, still he was convinced that possessions in themselves were the source of considerable evil: "Your love for one another," he said in a sermon, "should put you on guard against the things which each of us possesses as his own, because they engender among men quarreling, enmity, dissension, murder."[48] Community of possessions grew in his monasteries, not out of compulsion, but out of free choice and true love for the brethren; it sought, not the benefits of earth, but the everlasting salvation of one and all; and it was sought after, above all, not for the sake of men, but for the sake of God.[49]

Augustine achieved this community of possessions in the small details of daily life. Not only did his monks dine at a common table; even their wardrobe was held in common. The distribution, custody, and cleaning of clothing were not to be the concern of individuals, acting sometimes out of selfishness and pettiness, but were to be carried out according to some official's directions. He was to allocate garments that had been cleaned, which might not be those which the monks had given in. In this way, over-anxiety about material needs and neglect of one's spiritual well-being were to be avoided.[50]

Augustine did not deny that, by his commitment to the common life and his renunciation of his possessions, a monk had acquired a certain right to support, a claim to what he needed. Yet deciding what each man should receive was entrusted to the superior. In this, Augustine recommended to superiors and those with control over the community's property that they should exercise prudence and compassion in dealing with the weak.[51] No one should receive superfluities, yet no one should be in want. Everyone should receive what he might need.[52] Indeed, Augustine wished them to take the individual's special wants into account and, in particular, to show consideration to those who had had riches in abundance in the world, and to the sick and the convalescent.[53]

It was always his serious endeavor to suppress, as far as possible, the differences between the social classes in his monasteries. This was a much more urgent problem then than it is today. The huge gap between poor and rich, between slaves and free men, which characterized the social structures of ancient times still persisted. The disparities in wealth and the differences in styles of living were very great between one social level and another. Augustine, by what he said and what he wrote, did not weary in pressing for the easing of these tensions in society and for that easing to be based on Christian justice and love.[54]

Even in the monastic life of those days, there often were displeasing signs of social inequalities.[55] Here in fact Augustine did have much success in bridging the gaps and in raising the standards of monastic life by his philosophy of a Christian community of love. This was a singular achievement not only for the infant monasteries but also toward the solution of contemporary social problems.

He was successful in this difficult undertaking primarily because he tried to inculcate among his monks a Christian conception and evaluation of secular social relations. True riches consisted not in earthly possessions, but in frugality. True happiness lay not in a settled income but in possessing God. A Christian would find true joy of heart not as his goods accumulated but as he distributed what he had to the poor.[56]

Poverty of the Monastic Community

Augustine promoted the poverty of the communities alongside that of individuals. The poverty of his houses manifested itself, above all, in the spirit of simplicity, which inspired the common life. The meals that they ate together were simple; and their clothing was modest, as befitted their calling.[57]

Nonetheless, the poverty that Augustine demanded was not synonymous with want and deprivation. Well-ordered life in a monastic community, he felt, required a certain security of support since too much anxiety about earning one's daily bread, he once remarked, would be, not a kind of liberation for the community's religious life, but a burden.[58] In keeping with the example of the primitive Apostolic community, his monasteries held their possessions, movable and immovable goods, in common, which helped them toward a secure livelihood. Yet in this he tried to avoid everything that might give even the appearance of money-grubbing.[59] His basic principle was that it is better to forgo some right than in such a matter to sin against charity and give scandal to the laity.[60]

Augustine's view was that the community should obtain its living through the industry of its members. Of course, if monks were hindered from manual labor by their pastoral duties, or if the physical infirmity or sickness of individual brothers prevented them from working, then they were entitled to the alms of the faithful.[61]

For some time—this was about the year 411—Augustine toyed with the idea of organizing, within a smaller circle from his communities of clerics at Hippo and Tagaste, a life of even stricter poverty. He and these companions were to forgo the enjoyment of the income from their church property and to content themselves, on the pattern of the Levites and priests of the Old Law, with the gifts of the faithful. He could not help seeing that the Church's considerable wealth was a constant source of envious calumnies uttered by the laity against bishops and clergy. Then, too, he would have been glad to hand over his administrative problems to trustworthy laymen in order to devote himself and his clerics, undistracted, to their pastoral duties. But the people's opposition to this plan brought it to naught.[62]

But even this attempt, frustrated though it was, to make the support of his clerics' monastery wholly the responsibility of the faithful and of their charity shows how seriously Augustine regarded his striving toward Apostolic poverty.

BROTHERLY LOVE IN DAILY MONASTIC LIFE, AND CONCERN FOR THE COMMON GOOD (*res communis*)[63]

The extent to which Augustine's ideal for the monastic life is infused with Christian spiritual love (*caritas Christiana*) has already been demonstrated. But his conviction that in the daily monastic routine everything to do with "transient necessity" is irradiated by "an imperishable love"[64] is shown by his directions to his monks about working for the community, concern for the salvation of each other's souls, and mutual tolerance and forgiveness.

Work for the Community

Augustine speaks of various kinds of work and numerous undertakings in the monastery. Those who had tasks to perform he directed: "Those who are assigned to serve the brethren . . . should do so without complaining."[65] What they do should be marked, not by their lording it over the others, but by a loving service (*caritas serviens*).[66] And he required of all the monks that they put their working power at the disposition of the monastery, promptly and gladly: "make sure that no one is working for his own benefit, but that everything you do is for the common good, with more zeal and greater promptness than if each one of you were working for himself."[67]

He understood this statement to be a basic rule for daily living in the monastery which could free its individual members from narrow self-seeking and fill them with the love of Christ. For he was convinced that monks in their care for the community are seeking nothing other than the things that are Christ's (cf. Phil. 2:21).[68]

Thus he makes quite plain the significance he attaches to the fulfillment, as perfect as possible, of this precept of the *Rule*: "the more trouble you take over what you all have in common, and not over what is your own, the more progress people will see that you are making."[69] He saw in an individual's concern for the community, therefore, a clear sign and a reliable measure of his spiritual progress.

But to what extent does this show a monk's perfection? Augustine's argument is that unselfish care for the monastic community is true Christian love of one's neighbor. He says this in so many words: "love, of which it was written that it 'is not self-seeking' [1 Cor. 13.5] must be understood as putting the common good before private interests, and not the other way round."[70]

These words of St. Paul's about love—that "it is not self-seeking"—often appear in his writings.[71] He saw in them a statement of the essential characteristic of Christian spiritual love (*caritas Christiana*).[72] But because monastic life is entirely based upon this unselfish love, Augustine sees it as pre-eminently a "social life" (*vita socialis*).[73] The outward marks of its social character stand out as much through the selfless concern and effort of all for the community as for the reasons that no one in the monastery has private possessions (*proprium*) or supports himself by them (*de proprio*),[74] that everyone receives what he needs from a common fund (*de communi*), and that no one wishes to hold anything he may have except as common property.[75] But Augustine is concerned, beyond this common ownership of material goods, with a good of a higher kind: "we ought to have in common that great and richest possession which is God Himself."[76] So, in the social life of his monasteries, and in their brethren's concern for the common good, that eternal City of God is prefigured in which the blessed are united in their possession of that common good which is imperishable, God, into a society which is perfect and holy.[77]

Concern for the Brethren's Salvation, and the Duty of Correction

Care for the monastic community must, according to Augustine, also manifest itself in a genuine concern for the brethren's salvation and in watchfulness over one another and for one another.[78] For a monk fraternal correction is a duty, a grave obligation of conscience. If he were to keep silent, he would, through his negligence, share the responsibility for his brother's sin and ruin. Augustine remarked: "In such a case, the kind man is cruel."[79] "It is better for a man to be severe in his love than to let another go to hell through his tenderness."[80] In one sermon, to emphasize this duty, he describes a man in a torpor, and asks his hearers if it would not be true love to rouse the sick man out of the sleep that may prove fatal for him, even if one may hurt him as one strikes him and shakes him.[81]

He considered the fulfillment of this difficult duty so important, indeed so essential, to a Christian love of the brethren, that he devotes one detailed section to it in his *Rule.*[82] Closely following Christ's counsels in Matthew 18:15ff., he requires that an erring brother should first be admonished privately. But if this is of no use, one should tell the superior of his shortcomings so that he may reprimand him and, if necessary, condemn his fault and punish it in the presence of the entire monastic community. Such a declaration will have none of an informer's loveless meanness; it will be a duty of holy, fraternal love. There would be far more lovelessness if one allowed a brother, out of false compassion, to conceal some ailment from a surgeon who could treat it, however much his knife might hurt. But if the guilty one will not submit to the punishment imposed on him, the last step this Gospel passage envisages must be taken: he must be expelled from the community. This, too, will be done, not out of vindictiveness, but out of merciful concern for the entire body, so that others may not be infected and involved in ruin.

It was Augustine's opinion that fraternal correction would achieve its object, a culprit's reformation, only if it were undertaken in the proper spirit. That spirit would call for tact, gentleness, and self-command, and must always come from a truly loving heart. He wrote in his *Rule*: "this is to be done out of love for men and hatred for vices."[83] It is easy to delude oneself that one is acting out of love and concern for others when one's motives are, in fact, pride and egoism, and the real cause of offense may perhaps be that a man's misdeed was directed against us.[84] He also considered castigating private shortcomings in the presence of others unfitting, and deemed it, not benevolent correction, but betrayal.[85] Humbly he confesses how often he has erred, not knowing whether a man should be reprimanded publicly or privately, or whether, perhaps, the matter should be passed over in silence.[86] If whoever is doing the remonstrating and blaming wants to repay someone's fault with a fault of his own, Augustine thought him the wrong man to be correcting anyone; it would be far better for him to receive the correction.[87] Whoever does correct must remain aware of his own weaknesses, so that reproach and admonition may come not from hatred but from mercy.[88] Mindfulness of the danger he is in will give him proper understanding and compassion. Augustine makes it a fundamental rule: no one should undertake correction of another's sins unless he has first examined himself and can answer before God "I am doing it out of love." Using harsh words is permitted to love, and only to love. He insists: "Love, and then say what you wish. It will not be injurious, though it may sound injurious."[89]

If a culprit does improve through correction then this calls for a certain generosity in him, Augustine was convinced. He dealt with this point at some length in a letter to a convent of women.[90] He begins by insisting that no one enjoys being blamed. He wrote:

> it frequently happens that when someone is criticized he is saddened for the moment, and he resists and argues. Then later, in quiet, when God and he are alone together, he thinks it over. Now he is no longer afraid of man's displeasure and reprimands; his fear is that he may displease God because he does not do better. From then on he will not do what he was justly criticized for; and, indeed, he loves his brother, who he has now realized is the enemy only of his sin, as much as he detests his sin.[91]

From his own experience Augustine knew only too well how hard and irksome the duty of correction often can be. And yet he saw this as a task that a monk, and a superior[92] in particular, cannot escape, in the interests of a culprit and of the community. Furthermore, correction exercised in the right spirit seemed to him to be a suitable and necessary means to promote the community's growth and well-being, the object for which he was working in his monasteries. Yet with all this he was well aware that correction can be taken too far, so that brotherly peace and love can suffer. Therefore, at the end of this letter, he warns: "Put more of your effort into promoting harmony than you do in correcting one another." And he gives as his reason: "For just as vinegar rots the barrel if it is kept there too long, so anger rots the heart if it lingers overnight."[93] As he sees it, an ideal superior will be marked by the right balance between gentleness and severity: "Let him seek to be loved rather than feared by you."[94]

Toward the end of his life, in 426 or 427, Augustine once again explained and justified monastic correction, in a work entitled *Rebuke and Grace* and occasioned by the misinterpretation of his teaching on the relation between grace and the human will. Shortly before, in *Grace and Free Will*, he had written at length to the brothers of a North African monastery at Hadrumetum that the will of fallen man is incapable in itself of performing even the smallest deed that is truly good and that for a deed to be good God's grace, which man cannot merit and which will transform him inwardly and make him capable of good works, is required. But Augustine learned that someone in this house had drawn from his exposition the conclusion that "No one ought to be corrected because he does not fulfill God's commands; one should only pray that he may fulfill them." [95] What lay behind this quibbling was the opinion that correction cannot be justified since a culprit could not have avoided his fault because of his lack of grace and thus, ultimately, was not responsible for it.[96] In actual fact, the author of these objections was not interested in maintaining that correction is useless and unjustifiable; rather, he wanted to show that Augustine's doctrine of grace was untenable. In answer to this, Augustine, in *Rebuke and Grace*, began by reasserting his conception of divine grace, its absolute necessity, and the impossibility of meriting it, and then went on to demonstrate that, in this understanding of the grace of Christ, correction is both prudent and justified.

Augustine demonstrates that it is justified as, speculating deeply, he seeks to explain the relation of grace and human freedom and, using the doctrines of predestination and uncreated grace as his premisses, to show the nature of man's guilt and his responsibility.[97] Yet he perceives that correction has positive benefits: it shows a sinner what his duties are, makes him realize his own inadequacy and the hatefulness of his sin, rouses him to long to be set free, and drives him to pray for the grace he lacks.[98] This is why St. Paul, though he recognized that all his apostolic labors depended on grace, and entreated God for grace for his people, never abandoned his admonitions, instructions, commands, and reproofs.[99] In the same way, Augustine regarded his teaching on God's eternal, free predestination as fully guaranteeing the reason and benefit of monastic correction. He wrote:

> Therefore brothers who are subject should accept correction from their superiors, which should be given out of love and should differ in its severity according to the difference of a fault. . . . Because we do not know how to distinguish what is predestined from what is not, and ought therefore to wish that all may be saved, we must, as far as this is our concern, use with everyone serious correction as a medicine, so that they themselves do not go astray and do harm to others. But it is

> God's business to make this correction into a rod with which to beat into shape those who, in His foreknowledge and predestination, will be made into the same image as His Son [cf. Rom. 8:29].[100]

Patient and Pardoning Love

Augustine found another everyday practical application of fraternal love for the monks in mutual, patient long-suffering and in the pardoning of offenses and injuries. He often had occasion to write about this in dealing with the monastic life, and he was fond of quoting what St. Paul had written about mutual tolerance (Gal. 6:2 and Eph. 4:2). Earnestly he admonished in one of his sermons: "Keep watch over your love. The Apostle says 'Bear with one another in love, and take pains to preserve the unity of spirit through the bond of peace' [Eph. 4:2]. Bear with one another! Do you not have something about you that someone else has to bear with? I exhort you all—no, it is God's voice that is exhorting you all—bear with one another in love." If there is someone who is so advanced that he has no patience with others, he is showing precisely how little he has advanced.[101] Here the saying of the wise man Sirach is of worth: "Woe to them who have lost long-suffering" (Eccles. 2:16).[102] For what would anyone be capable of bearing who does not bear with his brother?[103] In an address to the "brethren" of the garden monastery, Augustine showed how serious the motives are for fulfilling this duty of mutual toleration when he reminded them of how much Christ bore for us.[104] And he saw in this patient love of the brethren a plain sign that the monks love Christ.[105]

Augustine demanded this patience from everyone, for everyone. Those who came from rich homes to the monastery must make allowances for their brethren from lower stations; instead of despising them, they should reckon community with them as an honor.[106] Conversely, the poor must not take it amiss if others, because of their former way of life, are given something better.[107] He required patience and forbearance for the sick and the infirm, whose weakened health required many exceptions to be made for them.[108] He specifically asked superiors to show long-suffering and patience toward their subjects. But in practicing obedience, subjects too must command some of this forbearance. They should have sympathy for the superior in the great responsibility to God that he carries.[109]

But if someone has offended another brother, he is obliged, openly and as quickly as possible, to ask for forgiveness; and the other must forgive him, glady with all his heart.[110] In his *Rule*, Augustine writes at length about this duty, giving two reasons why reconciliation must not be delayed. Otherwise, anger could take root in the soul and turn to hatred, a sin he judged quite differently from some sudden outburst of anger. He viewed the difference between anger and hatred as so great that he applied to them the Gospel image of the splinter and the beam (cf. Matt. 7:3ff., Luke 6:41f.), though, to be sure, Christ used it in a quite different connection. The anger that may turn into hatred can make a beam out of the splinter. He showed all the depths of the evil in hatred when, with St. John, he categorized hatred as a kind of murder: "Whoever hates his brother is a murderer" (1 John 3:15). By that he means that there is no essential difference between a disposition filled with hatred and that of a murderer.[111] But Augustine has another reason for insisting on a quick and full reconciliation: it is so that the prayers of the brethren may not be affected. A heart without love, or one filled with hatred, will rob prayer of all its worth and all its fruits.[112]

He closes his remarks about mutual forgiveness with the statement: "If there is anyone who will never ask forgiveness or who does so insincerely, he has no business in the monastery, even though you do not turn him out."[113] He did not consider that this observation needed further justification. In such conduct he saw the clear manifestations of a disposition that was no longer affirming or taking seriously the chief object of monastic life, the "one heart for God." In one decisive respect, he was lacking in brotherly love. But Augustine showed the ultimate significance of this lack when, alluding to the First Epistle of Saint John, he wrote: "Whoever does not love his brother is out of love; and whoever is out of love is away from God, for God is love."[114]

OBEDIENCE

According to Augustine, obedience is not the foundation of monastic life —without a doubt, in his eyes its foundation is love[115]—and yet for him obedience is an essential support for the communal life of the monastery.[116]

Obedience toward God

Augustine often writes of the great good of religious obedience in a broad sense. His understanding is of a submission to God and His commandments. Such obedience makes man like Jesus Christ. He, God and Man, gave us a unique example of obedience. He came, not at all to do His own will, but to serve the will of Him who had sent Him (John 6:38). In this respect he was quite different from that first man, who preferred his own willfulness to the will of Him who had created him.[117] So Augustine contrasts the disobedience of Adam, the first man, through whom many became sinners, with the obedience of the second Adam, who was obedient even unto death and thereby brought redemption and life to all.[118]

Obedience in this sense Augustine considered a virtue of exceeding value, well pleasing to God. To show that this is so, he wrote, God had forbidden to the first man something that in itself was not bad. Obedience alone should have gained the victor's crown, just as disobedience alone received the punishment.[119] Through his obedience, man might have risen, free from death, into the company of the angels, to a life of blessed immortality.[120]

Therefore, in Augustine's opinion, obedience to God and to His commandments is the way for the rational creature to true wisdom and freedom of heart.[121] Indeed, he makes the bold assertion that "Nothing is of such profit to the soul as obedience."[122] A single prayer from an obedient man is heard sooner than ten thousand from the recalcitrant.[123] Thus obedience is more highly to be esteemed than virginal chastity dedicated to God. However brightly such virginity may shine in God's eyes, without obedience it will remain barren. An obedient wife, he wrote in *The Good of Marriage*, is to be preferred to a virgin who cannot obey.[124] So obedience is the mother and guardian of all virtues,[125] the beginning and the perfection of all justice.[126] Obedience to God, seen for what it is, represents the one virtue of a reasonable creature, just as disobedience is the capital, the greatest, vice.[127] Indeed, doing God's will and obeying Him represents a task that will never end, not even beyond the grave. But only in that everlasting peace, obedience will be sweet and easy, and will bring no less joy to men than the eternal life of blessedness itself will.[128]

Significance and Justification of Monastic Obedience

Augustine did not write often about obedience in monastic life. And he certainly was no friend of a multitude of prescriptions and laws, as is shown by the brevity of his *Rule*, with its relatively few orders and prohibitions. And he was always concerned that the obligation in the monastery to obey should not become a heavy yoke. Yet it would undoubtedly be wrong to conclude from this that he paid little or no heed to his monks' obedience. The few passages in which he did write about monastic obedience, notably in his *Rule*, are quite unambiguous. And what he had to say, especially in his sermons, about the manifold obedience owed by men in every sector of human society is sufficient proof that he had a clear understanding of the need for authority in human endeavors of every kind, and that he saw all authority as deriving from God.[129] Monastic obedience, too, he valued above all for what it contributed to the life of the community.

Augustine considered the monastic community a spiritual family. The superior was to a certain extent the family's head, the community's father.[130] Augustine conceived of this fatherhood as a spiritual and ecclesial relationship, and the father for him was not just some charismatic, spirit-endowed, inspired teacher. He was the father because he had been given the office,[131] an office that comprised the power (*potestas*) and the authority to rule (*auctoritas regendi*).[132]

Augustine regarded this spiritual fatherhood as a commission from God for which the superior must render an accounting to God.[133] This attitude gave validity to the striking remark he once made in a sermon dealing with natural fatherhood: "A father's word must be listened to as God's word."[134] By that he wished to emphasize that all orders and commands coming from lawful authority have something in them of the authority of God Himself. God had sanctioned them when He commanded us to obey our parents. Even from the lips of an unworthy and bad superior, his subjects should hear the voice of God,[135] for God works as the light does. Light, even when it penetrates impurity, will not be rendered impure.[136] There is only one case in which a son is not permitted to obey his father: namely, if the father's command were to be contradicted by God's.[137]

The Ideal Portrait of a Monastic Superior (praepositus)

Drawing on his rich experience, Augustine vividly described the father-and-son relationship between superiors and their subjects. In this, he transformed the automatic obedience to any command demanded by Eastern monasteries[138] into a more human and personal intercourse between superiors and subordinates.[139]

His very earliest remarks about monastic obedience, in *The Ways of the Catholic Church*, indicate this concern. Here he gave an idealized description of the life of the Egyptian cenobites, which derives from Jerome's *Letter 22*.[140] But, ignoring what Jerome wrote and the actual situation in Pachomius' monasteries, where the sheer numbers of the monks made it barely possible for there to be any personal relations between superiors and subjects,[141] Augustine is captured by his notion of what an ideal monastic family should be, with everyone's yielding a willing obedience.[142] And in his own *Rule*, where he wrote in detail about monastic obedience, he began with the definitive sentence: "A superior should be obeyed as a father."[143] This may appear as the most important motive in the formation of his conception of obedience, and it shows how far he had progressed beyond the ideals of older monastic rules. Undoubtedly, from the beginning superiors had been called "Father," but to advance from that to the idea of obedience "as to a father" was to have come a long way. Basil himself, to illustrate monastic obedience, uses, not the father-and-son image, but the image of a master and his slaves.[144]

But Augustine's ideal portrait of a monastic superior has the essential characteristics clearly drawn. This is also the case with the Benedictine *Rule*, but that was composed a good hundred years later.[145] Precisely in this matter, Benedict could be guided by Augustine and borrow what was essential in his directions. Together, they indicated that a superior's office consists "not so much in being first as in being of use" (*Non tam praeesse quam prodesse*).[146] Augustine considered that a superior's attitude toward his monks should be marked not by dictatorial bearing but by loving concern. He would find joy in the selfless service of his subjects.[147] Here it is evident that he had the Saviour's words in mind: "Whoever among you wants to be great must be the servant of all" (Matt. 23:11).[148] A superior concerned only for his own honor and looking only toward his own profit would, as Augustine remarked, be serving no one but himself and would not be "feeding the sheep" entrusted to him.[149]

The superior's authority must, according to Augustine, be based less upon fear than on the love and confidence of his subjects, even though respect for the superior is necessary.[150] The superior must not be mistrustful or cold-hearted. Despite his many bitter experiences as superior, Augustine could say of himself "I think only well of my brethren, and I have complete trust in them."[151] Not only did he allow those in office great freedom in the performance of their duties, avoiding completely any kind of supervision,[152] but in all other respects, in all necessary legislation, a holy liberty prevailed in his monasteries.[153]

Above all else, Augustine demanded a good example from superiors. The superior himself ought to esteem and love good order in the monastery.[154] It is an absolute principle that only that man can require obedience from others who himself has learned to obey. Once he asked the question "Is there anything more scandalous than for someone to demand obedience from his subjects who will not obey those set in authority over him?"[155]

With great emphasis, Augustine in his *Rule* writes of the superior's great responsibility. He must always be mindful that one day he must account to God for his subjects.[156] That is why it would be folly for him to rejoice because he is a superior.[157] Even though it may appear that that office exalts him above his subjects, he should abase himself the more deeply before God.[158] Augustine himself very deeply felt this responsibility, the fear of the reckoning that was to come, and his knowledge of the dangers attaching to his bishop's office.[159]

His *Rule*, immediately after quoting a saying of St. Paul's (1 Thess. 5:14), describes a superior's varied duties toward his subjects: he must punish dissidents, encourage the timorous, protect the weak, and have patience with everyone.[160] Augustine found the hardest of these duties that of reprimanding and punishing. Yet this seemed necessary to him in the interests of good monastic order. Infractions could not be overlooked; they must be remedied through punishment.[161] For the superior, when he disciplines culprits, confers a benefit on them, for he does it for their improvement.[162] Even if a miscreant will not listen to him, the superior may not keep silence. Paul's admonition applies here: "Preach the word, welcome or unwelcome" (2 Tim. 4:2).[163] In his house of brothers, Augustine had given the superior an auxiliary, a priest with higher authority, precisely for this burdensome task. More serious shortcomings were to be made known, for him to punish.[164]

If the superior blamed and punished, that ought to be done, in the words of the *Rule*, "out of love for men and hatred for vices."[165] Augustine then asks whether a superior is obliged to ask his subjects for pardon if, in correcting them, he has out of human frailty gone too far. His answer to this difficult question is very prudent. One cannot and should not oblige the superior to make an apology as such. In this, Augustine is not attempting to spare the superior's pride; but "anyone having office who exceeds in humility may weaken his authority."[166] Experience can teach that such a humbling of a superior might only make his subjects proud and haughty. But still the superior has it as his duty to repair his fault. He should apologize to God, humble himself before the Lord, and impose punishment upon himself. And to his subject he must show the greater love; for a kindly word is also a sort of apology.[167]

*Subjects (*subditi*) in the Monastery*

Augustine held that respect and love should mark the subjects' bearing toward the superior. In what is called the *Ordo monasterii* there is the sentence that monks "should be loyally obedient, they should honor their 'father' next to God, they should treat their provost with deference, as is fitting to the saints."[168] Even if the Augustinian origin of these prescriptions is not assured, still they accord with Augustine's Scriptural thinking since in his sermons he sought to base obedience in every department of human life on divine authority, and to give it deeper religious and moral significance.[169]

From subjects' respectful and loving bearing toward their superior would grow that generous and happy obedience which Augustine recommended to his monks in his *Rule*.[170] They should obey their superior as sons obey their father; they should obey the monastery's statutes "not as slaves under the law but as free men established under grace."[171] In their obedience, something like compassion for their superior should be manifest. They ought to know how heavily his conscience was burdened, and seek to lighten his responsibilities before God.[172]

Augustine himself must have been an ideal superior to his brethren. It would seem that in his monasteries he hardly ever had cause to complain of serious cases of rebellion; and this must have been to a great extent because of his own fatherly concern and his courtesy. He paid high tribute to the members of the clerics' monastery in these words: "They all obey me gladly."[173] And he himself once testified that among the families in Hippo the fourth commandment was in general well observed.[174] Altogether, the psychological difficulties in obedience do not seem at that time to have created the great problems which they do nowadays. For it was a world in which a great part of humanity was accustomed to a lifelong social servitude, so that subjection to the power of fathers and the authority of the state, however much social unrest might occur, was accepted with less questioning and more as a matter of course than is now the case.

But what was the place of obedience in the ascetic life of Augustine's monasteries? It is plain that it did not have the importance that was attributed to it by later monastic ascetics. It is significant that Augustine nowhere employed the justification of monastic obedience which by that time had become popular in Eastern monastic ascetic writings, the Lord's command that we should "deny ourselves" (Matt. 16:24).[175] And we do not find in Augustine, as we do in Basil, for example, that sharp criticism of human self-will as a basis for demands for religious obedience.[176] Then, too, Augustine never recommends, never shows, as Cassian and Benedict do, for instance, monastic obedience as a means and support to the achievement of humility,[177] although he repeatedly impresses on those who strive for spiritual advancement the significance and necessity of the virtue. All in all, it would seem that he did not regard religious obedience as any special means counseled by Christ for the achievement of Christian perfection.[178] Thus one does not find in his monasteries any vow of obedience. A monk's duty of obedience grows out of his obligations to the community, which is, for Augustine, the chief importance of obedience for the monastic common life. "Ordered harmony among the dwellers in one house, in ordering and obeying"[179] was for him one of the important prerequisites for the realization in his monasteries of "one heart" (*cor unum*).

NOTES

1. *Rule* 2.1–4, 5.4–7; Possidius 22, 23, 25.
2. *The Work of Monks* 16.19.
3. *Sermon 355* 2.
4. *Rule* 5.4–5. Cf. *The Lord's Sermon on the Mount* 2.12.40f.
5. Cf. *Letter 157* 39.
6. *The Work of Monks* 25.32; *The City of God* 5.18.
7. Cf. *Sermon 355* 3, 6, *Rule* 1.7–8, *The City of God* 5.18.
8. *Sermon 113* 1.
9. *The City of God* 5.18.2.
10. *Exposition on Psalm 102* 10.
11. *Sermon 345* 3. Cf. *Sermon 36* 5.
12. *Sermon 177* 4. *Exposition on Psalm 94* 8: "by will, poor; from God, rich."
13. *Exposition on Psalm 131* 5f.
14. *Sermon 355* 2, 6.
15. *Sermon 311* 15.
16. Cf. *Sermon 85* 1 and *Letter 157* 25.
17. *The Lord's Sermon on the Mount* 1.1.3; *Holy Virginity* 32.32; *Sermon 53* 1.1. Cf. Schaffner, *Christliche Demut*, pp. 115–16, 216.
18. *Sermo Morin 11* 2, in Morin, pp. 627f.
19. *Sermon 14* 4.
20. Ibid. 9.
21. Sanchis ("Pauvreté monastique . . . : Le commentaire . . . des Actes 4:32–35," esp. 13ff.) traces a surprising change in Augustine's application and interpretation of Acts 4:32–35 as his notions of monastic poverty developed between 397 and 400. He bases this on an interesting analysis of some explanatory remarks, which can be dated, concerning this passage in Acts. Yet none of the five contexts—*Exposition on Psalm 4* 10; *Exposition on Psalm 94* 7f.; *Commentary on the Epistle to the Galatians* 26; *Sermon 252* 3; and *Christian Instruction* 3.6.10—in which, before 398, he cites the passage, refers to monasticism or attempts to apply the Scriptural passage to the monastic life.
22. See below, p. 285.
23. *Rule* 1.2–3. Sanchis ("Pauvreté monastique . . . : Le commentaire . . .

des Actes 4:32–35," 11) thought there was an earlier, hidden allusion to this account in Acts in *The Ways of the Catholic Church* 1.21.67.

24. *The Work of Monks* 16.17; *Holy Virginity* 45.46; *Against Faustus* 5.9; *Against the Writings of Petilian* 2.104.239; *Sermon 355* 2 and 6; *Sermon 356* 1. Cf. also Possidius 5. Even earlier, this passage had been important in the formation of concepts of poverty in Eastern monasteries (see above, pp. 36–37). It also appears later in Benedict's *Rule* (chaps. 33, 34, 35); see Linderbauer 60, 72; Butler 70, 103; and Steidle 132ff.

25. See, for instance, *Sermon 355* 2 and 6. P. Grech wrote, in his careful examination of the texts in Acts relevant to communal ownership in the primitive Church, "There was no 'vow of poverty' in the modern sense of the word, but an overflow of charity" ("The Augustinian Community and the Primitive Church," *Augustiniana*, 5 [1955], 465–66).

26. *Rule* 5.2.

27. *Exposition on Psalm 131* 5.

28. Cf. Sanchis, "Pauvreté monastique . . . : Le commentaire . . . des Actes 4:32–35," 19f.

29. *Rule* 5.2.

30. *The Work of Monks* 25.32.

31. Ibid. Cf. also Sanchis, "Pauvreté monastique . . . : Le commentaire . . . des Actes 4:32–35," 20f.

32. *Letter 83* 3f.

33. *Rule* 1.2.

34. Ibid. 5.3.

35. *Sermon 356* 13.

36. Ibid.

37. *Sermon 355* 3 and *Sermon 356* 3, 5, 7.

38. *Rule* 1.4.

39. *Exposition on Psalm 51* 14.

40. *Exposition on Psalm 85* 3.

41. *Exposition on Psalm 103* 3.16. Cf. *Letter 157* 39.

42. *Rule* 1.4.

43. Ibid. 3.3 and 5.1.

44. Ibid. 5.1.

45. Ibid. 3.1, 3.3, 5.1. Cf. *Sermon 85* 5.6: "Seek contentedness; see what will content, want nothing more. Anything else will weigh you down, not lift you up. It will burden, not honor, you"; and *Confessions* 10.31.45.

46. *Rule* 1.5.

47. Ibid. 1.3.

48. *Exposition on Psalm 131* 5.

49. Cf. also M. X. Deindl, "Klösterlicher Kommunismus," BMS, 6 (1924), 113–16.

50. *Rule* 5.1.

51. Ibid. 3.3.

52. Ibid. 1.2 and 5.1.

53. Ibid. 3.3–5.

54. Augustine's attitude toward slavery is most informative. Along with many other Fathers of the Church, he was in no doubt that slavery derived not from nature but from sin, not from reason but from tyranny, not from a divine but from a human ordinance. Nonetheless he recommended, as Paul had done earlier (see 1 Cor. 7:20ff. and elsewhere), that the institution should be tolerated, in the interests of peace and order in the state. Yet he was concerned in every way to form relations between masters and slaves in a Christian spirit; and he could only welcome and commend it when owners voluntarily freed their slaves. See *The City of God* 19.14ff. See also P. von Sokolowski, *Der heilige Augustin und die christliche Zivilisation*, Schriften der Königsberger Gelehrten Gesellschaft 4 (Halle, 1927), p. 137, and A. Brucculeri, "Il pensiero sociale di S. Agostino: La schiavitù," *La civiltà cattolica*, 82, No. 1 (1931), 119–33, and 82, No. 2 (1931), 130–41.

55. Spreitzenhofer, *Entwicklung des alten Mönchtums*, pp. 51ff.

56. *Rule* 1.4, 1.7, 3.3. Cf. also *The Work of Monks* 21.25.

57. Possidius 22.

58. *The Work of Monks* 17.20.

59. *Letter 83* 6. Cf. *Sermon 356* 10 and 15.

60. Cf. *Letter 126* 9.

61. *The Work of Monks* 16.19.

62. Possidius 23. Cf. *Letter 125* 2 and *Letter 126* 9, where Augustine indicates what he was proposing.

63. Augustine uses the expression "things in common" (*communia*) and "common good" (*res communis*) in *Rule* 5.2 and 5.3. In contrast, he uses the term *bonum commune* to mean "the highest good," which is God. Cf. Trapè, "Il principio fondamentale," p. 20.

64. *Rule* 5.2.

65. Ibid. 5.9.

66. Cf. ibid. 7.3.

67. Ibid. 5.2.

68. *The Work of Monks* 25.32.

69. *Rule* 5.2.

70. Ibid.

71. See also below, pp. 198–99.

72. Cf. Trapè, "Il principio fondamentale," pp. 21ff. The writer here differs from some of Nygren's analysis of Augustine's teachings about Christian love in *Eros und Agape*.

73. *Sermon 356* 14. In regard to life in his monastery of clerics, he uses here the expressions "our social life" (*socialis vita nostra*) and "this social life" (*socialis haec vita*).

74. Ibid.

75. *Sermon 356* 13.

76. *Sermon 355* 2.

77. *The City of God* 12.9. Cf. in addition also Trapè, "Il principio fondamentale," p. 39.

78. *Rule* 4.6.

79. *Sermon 13* 9.
80. *Letter 93* 4.
81. *The Usefulness of Fasting* 10.12.
82. *Rule* 5.7–11.
83. Ibid. 4.10.
84. *Sermon 82* 3.4.
85. Ibid. 7.10.
86. *Letter 95* 3.
87. *Letter 210* 2.
88. *The Lord's Sermon on the Mount* 2.19.64.
89. *Commentary on the Epistle to the Galatians* 57.
90. *Letter 210* 2. For a translation of this letter, see below, chap. 11.
91. Ibid.
92. Cf. *Rule* 6.3, 7.1–4.
93. *Letter 210* 2.
94. *Rule* 7.3.
95. *Retractations* 2.93 (67).
96. Cf. *Rebuke and Grace* 4.6.
97. Ibid. 6.9–13.42.
98. Ibid. 3.5, 5.7.
99. Ibid. 3.5.
100. Ibid. 15.46, 16.49.
101. *Exposition on Psalm 99* 9. For a complete translation, see below, chap. 12.
102. Ibid. 12.
103. *Letter 48* 3.
104. *On 83 Various Questions*, question 71 3.
105. Ibid., question 71 7.
106. *Rule* 1.7.
107. Ibid. 3.4.
108. *Rule* 3.3–5.
109. Ibid. 7.3–4.
110. Ibid. 6.1–2. Cf. also Possidius 25.
111. *Rule* 6.1–2. Cf. also *Homily on St. John's Epistle to the Parthi 5* 10.
112. *Rule* 6.1–2.
113. Ibid. 6.2.
114. *The Trinity* 8.12.
115. See above, pp. 124–34.
116. Cf. *The Work of Monks* 16.19. See in addition A. Zumkeller, "Der klösterliche Gehorsam beim heiligen Augustinus," AM I, pp. 265–76; B. Borghini, "L'obbedienza secondo S. Agostino," *Vita Cristiana*, 23 (1954), 453–78; A. Manrique, "Concepto monastico de obediencia en San Agustín," RAE, 2 (1961), 18–40; idem, "Obediencia agustiniana y voluntad de Dios," ibid., 6 (1965), 177–84. In my article of 1954 I believe that I pointed out, among other matters, that Hendrikx' assumption, in "Augustinus als Monnik," that in Augustine's writings practically nothing can be found about

obedience toward men is unjustified. And Hendrikx may have contrasted Augustine's notions of obedience and love far too sharply. The obedience which he required from his monks was one to be exercised from love and, therefore, ought not to prejudice "the freedom of the children of God." For Augustine, the dichotomy is to be found not in obedience/love, but in obedience under juridical compulsion/obedience out of free love.

117. *The Literal Meaning of Genesis* 8.14.32.

118. See also *The City of God* 13.20, 14.15.

119. *Exposition on Psalm* 70 2.7.

120. *The City of God* 12.22.

121. *Exposition on Psalm 118* 22.8 and *Exposition on Psalm* 70 1.2.

122. *Exposition on Psalm* 70 2.1.

123. *The Work of Monks* 17.20.

124. *The Good of Marriage* 23.30.

125. *The City of God* 14.12. Cf. *The Good of Marriage* 23.30.

126. *Exposition on Psalm 71* 6.

127. *The Literal Meaning of Genesis* 8.6.12.

128. *The City of God* 19.27.

129. See on this Zumkeller, "Der klösterliche Gehorsam," pp. 270ff. See also R. Melli, *Il concetto di autorità negli scritti di S. Agostino* (Lecce, 1948), pp. 15ff., although his proofs are concerned exclusively with obedience in civil life.

130. *Rule* 7.1. Cf. on this L. Dürr, "Heilige Vaterschaft im antiken Orient: Ein Beitrag zur Geschichte der Idee des 'Abbas,'" in *Heilige Überlieferung*, ed. Odo Casel, O.S.B. (Münster, 1938), pp. 1–19; H. Emonds, "Abt," LThK, I^2, 90–93.

131. He is the "superior" (*praepositus*), who is "first among you" (*qui . . . praeest*), and who "occupies a higher place among you" (*qui . . . loco superiore versatur*)—*Rule* 7.1, 3, 4.

132. Ibid. 5.3, 6.3.

133. Ibid. 7.3.

134. *Exposition on Psalm* 70 1.2.

135. Cf. *Letter* 208 5.

136. *Homily on St. John's Epistle to the Parthi* 5 15.

137. *Exposition on Psalm* 70 1.2.

138. Cf. Schiwietz, *Das morgenländische Mönchtum* I, p. 178, and J. Puniet, "Abbé," *Dictionnaire de Spiritualité* I, col. 51. The concept of obedience in Eastern monasteries is reflected in the numerous penalties provided for transgressions. See, for example, Pachomius' *Rule* 5f., 12, 15, 84, etc.; see also M. B. Biedermann, "Die Regel des Pachomius und die evangelischen Räte," *Ostkirchliche Studien*, 9 (1960), 243ff.

139. See above all *Rule* 7.1–4.

140. Cf. St. Jerome's *Letter* 22 33–36 (PL 22.419ff.).

141. Viller, *Aszese und Mystik*, pp. 92f.

142. "And indeed those fathers, who are not only most saintly in their ways but also most advanced in the holy teachings and distinguished in all

respects, without arrogance care for those whom they call their sons, giving orders with great authority and being obeyed with great good will" (*The Ways of the Catholic Church* 1.31.67).

143. *Rule* 7.1.

144. Basil, *Regulae brevius tractatae* ("Shorter Rules") 115 (PG 31. 1161f.).

145. Benedict, *Rule* 64 (Linderbauer 78f., Butler 117ff., Steidle 188ff.). In this chapter there are two word-for-word quotations from Augustine.

146. Ibid. This phrase appears in Augustine's *Sermon 340* 1. See also I. Herwegen, *Der heilige Benedikt*, 3rd ed. (Düsseldorf, 1926).

147. *Rule* 7.3.

148. Cf. also *The City of God* 19.14: "For those who rule serve those over whom they seem to rule. They do indeed rule not by their greed for domination but by their function of giving, not by lording it in pride but by caring in mercy."

149. *Sermon 46* 2.

150. *Rule* 7.3.

151. *Sermon 355* 2.

152. Cf. Possidius 24.

153. *Rule* 8.1. Cf. Mellet, *L'Itinéraire*, pp. 97f.

154. *Rule* 7.3.

155. *The Work of Monks* 31.39. Cf. *Exposition on Psalm 143* 6.

156. *Rule* 7.3.

157. *Sermon 46* 2.

158. *Rule* 7.3. and *Sermon 146* 1.

159. Cf. A. Zumkeller, "Das Charakterbild des Seelsorgers beim heiligen Kirchenvater Augustinus," *Anima*, 5 (1950), 63ff.

160. *Rule* 7.3.

161. Ibid.

162. *Faith, Hope, and Charity* 72.19.

163. Cf. *Sermon 46* 14.

164. *Rule* 4.9, 4.11, 7.1–2.

165. Ibid. 4.10.

166. Ibid. 6.3.

167. Ibid.

168. *Ordo monasterii* 6.

169. Cf. Zumkeller, "Der klösterliche Gehorsam," pp. 243f.

170. See also *The Ways of the Catholic Church* 1.31.67. Even a slave, Augustine wrote, should try to serve his master "not in calculating fear but in loyal good will" (*The City of God* 19.15).

171. *Rule* 7.1, 8.1.

172. Ibid. 7.4. Cf. *Sermon 46* 2.

173. *Sermon 355* 7.

174. *Sermon 9* 4.

175. Cf. R. Daeschler, "Abnégation," *Dictionnaire de Spiritualité* I, cols. 76–78.

176. Basil, *Regulae fusius tractatae* ("Longer Rules") 41 (PG 31.1021f.).

177. There are places in Augustine's writings in which he treats humility and obedience together, but these places are concerned, not with obedience to men, but with subjection to God and His domination. Cf. Schaffner, *Christliche Demut*, pp. 255ff.

178. Cf. also C. Boyer, "Saint Augustin," *Dictionnaire de Spiritualité* I, col. 1111.

179. This is the way in which he defined "domestic peace"; see *The City of God* 19.13.

7

The Monastic Way of Life

FROM THE DAYS OF PACHOMIUS, monastic life has been a life of strict order. Augustine in his first monasteries also instituted a daily regimen, by which the times of labor, prayer, reading, and eating were regulated. Its observation was to give to the life of his monks a tranquil harmony. He feared that otherwise the diversity of occupations and tasks might distract them.[1] The monastic routine, reflecting in its order a monastery's day-to-day existence, was marked by a wise admixture of contemplation and activity.

PRAYER

God was at the center of Augustine's thinking and living. His remark in the *Soliloquies* "All I ask is to know God and the soul . . . nothing else"[2] became something of a program for his future life. Accordingly, it was his conviction that prayer must be the most important element in the life of a Christian,[3] and he gave evidence of the importance he attached to it in the very many formal prayers and instructions on prayer in his writings and sermons—most notably in his most comprehensive treatment of Christian prayer, the letter to Proba.[4] The soul of prayer, he wrote, is "love's glowing fire"[5] or the "enduring longing" of man for God and the things that are everlasting,[6] a longing that should be expressed and nourished in daily Christian life by vocal and mental prayer, by private and common prayer. Still one gains a proper understanding of Augustine's concept of interior, contemplative prayer only if one situates his disquisitions on the subject within the framework of his teachings, formed by the early Church, about the spiritual life.

The Essence and Growth of the Spiritual Life

Augustine's conception of a Christian's spiritual life finds its most authoritative expression in his teaching about man as the image of God.[7]

All creatures, because they partake of God's being, necessarily resemble God. But man, the crown of visible creation, not only possesses resemblance to God, he is God's likeness. Augustine agrees with Plato and his followers in this teaching, which he formulated, soon after his baptism, in the spirit of Paul and of the early Christian Fathers, in terms of the Christian faith and of the Scriptures.[8] Alongside Paul's Christocentric justification "He has destined us from the first to be formed into the image of His Son" (Rom. 8:29),[9] he quoted, as other Church Fathers before him had done, Genesis 1:26, according to which God created man in His "image and likeness."[10] For all that, there is clearly here no question of an image similar in essence, as the Word was begotten of the Father, but of an image, through participation, yet dissimilar in essence (*impar imago*).[11] But, in addition to this likeness to Him, God has also given to man a participation (*participatio*) in His divine life: "For as the life of the whole body is the soul," Augustine wrote in *The Freedom of the Will*, "so the soul's life of blessedness is God."[12] Yet through this participation in God's being and life, the human soul in no way becomes God. Ever since his conversion, Augustine had emphatically opposed the teachings of Neoplatonic mysticism on deification, insisting that the human soul is created and remains a creature.[13]

What is Augustine's understanding of "the image of God in man"? He tells us: "The image of God is within us; it is not in the body. . . . Where our understanding is, where our spirit, where our reason for searching for the truth, where our faith, our hope, our love are, it is there that God possesses His image."[14] This is precisely why the human spirit "is created according to the image of God, so that it may employ reason and understanding to comprehend and contemplate Him."[15] But man, formed in God's likeness, possesses divine life to the extent that his soul participates in divine wisdom—that he has become receptive (*capax*) to God. He wrote: "As [men] through faith put on Christ, they all become sons [of God], not by nature, as was [God's] only Son, who is only His wisdom, . . . but through participation in wisdom" (*participatione sapientiae*).[16]

Augustine taught that it was through Adam's fall by sin and through the guilt which men have inherited from him that they lost the life of the soul—that is, their participation in God's life—and that their likeness to Him was, if not destroyed, at least distorted: man "lost through sin wisdom's justice and holiness. So the image became disfigured and deformed. He receives all this again if the image be restored and renewed."[17]

The foundation of this renewal begins at baptism, continues unceasingly in the Christian's religious and spiritual life, and will reach its perfection only beyond the grave. As he wrote in *The Trinity*: "Medical treatment begins when the cause of the infirmity is removed, and this removal is achieved [through baptism] through the remission of all sins. The second stage is reached when the infirmity itself is taken away, and this occurs as the image of God is gradually renewed. . . . Of this the Apostle spoke very clearly when he said 'Though our outward man is corrupted, yet the inward man is renewed day by day' [2 Cor. 4:16]."[18] In the same connection, and with close reference to Colossians 3:10, Augustine wrote about the nature of the renewal of man's likeness to God: "He will be renewed in a loving perception of God; that is

> in the justice and holiness of the truth [Eph. 4:24]. . . . Thus, in the loving perception of God and in the justice and holiness of the truth, man, progressing from day to day and being renewed, transfers his love from transient things to those that are eternal, from the visible to the invisible, from the carnal to the spiritual, and he labors to bridle and wear down his longings for what is transient, visible, carnal, and through love to cleave to the eternal, invisible, spiritual.[19]

Thus, the renewal of the image of God, deepening of one's perception of God, and growth of the love of God are closely connected. He said in one sermon: "As you come closer to likeness [with God], so you progress in love and begin to perceive Him."[20]

This renewal of likeness to God, which is perfected under the influence of the grace of God dwelling in a Christian, and which determines his spiritual life, will now enable him to progress more and more from a simple faith to a deeper perception of God and of the eternal verities, and thus to transform himself from a "fleshly" to a "spiritual" man.[21] This classification, which, like many other features of Augustine's spiritual teaching, bears a relationship to the Christian gnosis of Clement of Alexandria and to his division of man into the "hylic," the "psychic," and the "pneumatic,"[22] Augustine joins to a quotation of 1 Corinthians 3:1–2: "I, brethren, was unable to speak to you as people of the Spirit; I treated you as sensual men, still infants in Christ. What I fed you with was milk, not solid food, for you were not yet ready for it."[23] Similarly, he includes among the "fleshly" (*animales atque carnales*) those of the faithful who had indeed received the Holy Spirit through baptism, but who, unlike the "spiritual" men, "are not yet able to understand what they possess, that is, to know that it is there and to recognize it."[24] The "milk" with which the "fleshly" ones are nourished is the faith.[25]

In faith Augustine saw the necessary prerequisites and first stages.[26] He was fond of quoting in this connection Isaiah 7:9, in the Itala (Old Latin) translation: "If you have not believed, you will not understand" (*nisi credideritis, non intelligetis*). He was well aware that there are truths of the faith that always can be only believed, not understood.[27] Yet for him the ideal still was for reason, as far as possible, to attain with God's help to perception "as it mounts from visible things to the invisible, and from temporal things to the eternal."[28] Thus, in Augustine's theological system the watchword was "faith seeking understanding" (*fides quaerens intellectum*); his basic principle was "believe so that you may understand" (*crede, ut intelligas*).[29] Yet, in the light of John 6:29, he drew a distinction between "believing God" (*credere Deo*) and "believing in God" (*credere in Deum*). Only belief "in God" can lead to the understanding that brings blessedness. But this belief in God means "believing, to love Christ, believing, to come close to Him, and to be incorporated among His members": that is, what is intended is "not any belief, but 'the belief that finds expression in love'" (Gal. 5:6).[30] Elsewhere, he wrote that the prerequisites for this understanding which brings blessedness were prayer, ardent search, and a good life.[31] When difficulties in deeper understanding arise, a Christian must first in sincerity "keep himself more and more free from sin, perfect his good works, pray and entreat in holy intercession that thus with God's help he may love and understand always more."[32]

Although in Cassiciacum, under the tenacious influence of Neoplatonism, Augustine had been full of hope "lovingly and plainly to have sight of Him by whom you have been led into the truth and whom as truth you are tasting and possessing,"[33] in the course of the following years he recognized the limits to this which human reason imposes here on earth. Therefore his hopes were increasingly directed to that "vision of God, most pure, alive with love," of the other world.[34]

Motivated probably by the Neoplatonic teaching about the ascent of the soul by degrees to the world of the intelligible, Augustine repeatedly strove to establish in some set pattern the steps in the development of the spiritual life and in the gradual metamorphosis of the fleshly man into spiritual man, of faith into perception. He did not think of this gradation as any fixed sequence, but always supposed that these steps in progress might follow one upon the other and could occur more or less simultaneously in the soul.[35] In his very early writings there are several enumerations of such steps (*gradus* or *aetates spirituales*); they all are based on septenaries, though they strongly differ from one another in details.[36] Soon after his move to Hippo, Augustine granted a place of prominence in his teaching on the spiritual life of the Christian to the passage in Isaiah on the spiritual gifts of the Messiah (11:2f.), which had already played a role in the theologies of his patristic predecessors.[37] As the Holy Spirit rested upon Christ, so, according to Augustine, the Spirit fills the Body of Christ, the Church, and is imparted in baptism to the Church's individual members. Thus, he sees in the spiritual life of the Christian, first of all, the work of the Spirit. In one of his sermons he said: "It seems to me, as you too perceive and as we believe, that there is no true and divine sanctification apart from the Holy Spirit. . . . Yet Isaias says that the Spirit of God will descend upon him who believes, the Christian, the member of Christ—the Spirit of wisdom and of understanding, of counsel and of strength, of knowledge and of reverence, the Spirit of the fear of God."[38] So, in Augustine's teaching, it is the Holy Spirit who effects this transformation, little by little, of a fleshly into a spiritual man, by the love He pours into the hearts of the faithful (cf. Rom. 5:5) and with His sevenfold gifts. Thus the patterns evolved with which during the ensuing decades Augustine sought to represent the Christian's spiritual development, based almost invariably upon this division of the Spirit's gifts into sevens, which in broad outline resemble one another.[39] But he inverted the order in which he enumerated the gifts, appealing to the Psalmist's authority: "The fear of the Lord is the beginning of wisdom" (Ps. 110:10).[40] Furthermore, in his commentary on the Sermon on the Mount, he tried to enrich this design of the steps in the spiritual life even more, as he associated each individual gift of the Spirit with one of the Beatitudes and one of the petitions of the Lord's Prayer.[41]

If one collates these parallel presentations in the various schemes, something like the following sketch of Augustine's conception of the stages of spiritual life results: at the lowest stage, through fear (*timor*), man's pride is conquered, so that in fear of God's punishment he turns to repentance for his sins. At the second stage, devotion (*pietas*) leads him to a submission to God's will. The stage of knowledge (*scientia*) brings him, through the study of Scripture, to the perception not only of a Christ-like ideal but also of his own weakness and entanglement in transient affairs. At the stage of strength (*fortitudo*), he is filled with a longing for justice and a love for the eternal truths; and the light of divine truth has now begun to shine in him, though his inner purification is not yet complete. When he attains to the stage of counsel (*consilium misericordiae*), he devotes himself to the works of mercy, through which he is purified more and more. At the stage of understanding (*intellectus*), he has wholly died to the world, and becomes able to contemplate God, though only to a limited degree, as in a mirror and in riddles. His Christian spiritual life on earth is perfected at the stage of wisdom (*sapientia*), by which he savors eternity and rejoices in profound peace.[42]

Augustine's Conception of Wisdom and Contemplation

We have shown that in Augustine's spiritual teaching the attainment of wisdom is the goal of the Christian life in this world. Through wisdom, the life of the spirit comes to its fullest growth. In wisdom, too, the fleshly man passes over to become a spiritual man, and the renewal of his likeness to God reaches completion.

Striving after wisdom and finding happiness in its possession was Augustine's yearning ever since, at the age of nineteen, he had read Cicero's *Hortensius*.[43] At that time, by "wisdom," he, along with the Stoics, had understood "knowledge about things human and divine."[44] During the first decade after his baptism, he had continued deepening his conception of wisdom, Christianizing it, and making a place for it, as has been shown, at the very center of his teaching about the spiritual life.[45] He presents his teaching on wisdom, fully developed, especially in the final books of the *Confessions* and in Book XIV of *The Trinity.*

What is his mature understanding of the spiritual life, lived in wisdom? F. Cayré has formulated the results of his fundamental examination of this as follows: Wisdom is a conformity to God, deeply impressed upon the soul, in which God lives through the grace of Christ. This conformity presupposes an active and zealous search for God, as well as a certain religious experience of God's supernatural presence. But the search for God, rather than the religious experience, will be to the fore, a zealous searching which is at once loving, spontaneous, persisting, and efficacious.[46]

As Augustine demonstrates in Book XIV of *The Trinity*, the human soul through wisdom becomes an image of the Trinity, which is perfect wisdom itself. To be sure, this image will not achieve perfection here on earth—that the soul will attain when it reaches the glory of heaven—but the image even here possesses, darkly, through faith and hope, a true reality, produced in the searching, striving soul by wisdom and love. On this, Augustine teaches, the Christian's pious, loving intimacy with the three divine persons is founded, and he possesses a share in Their life by grace through wisdom.[47] His life is therefore wholly directed toward God, and a profound peace and complete harmony between the higher and the lower rule in him.[48] But the Stoic ideal of a freedom from feeling (ἀπάθεια) which Augustine in the first years after his baptism included in his ideal wisdom[49] no longer found room in his developed doctrine of Christian spiritual life.[50] According to him, wisdom's constant supports are faith, hope, and love. Indeed, in a certain sense his ideal of wisdom appears as a living synthesis of these God-given virtues.[51] He sees wisdom as the fruit of a living faith, which acts in love (Gal. 5:6);[52] wisdom signifies nothing other than "the love and knowledge of Him who is always present and who remains unchanged."[53]

Wisdom's proper activity, Augustine holds, is contemplation (*contemplatio*).[54] What does he understand by this? Contemplation is concerned with an inward vision—"seeing" (*videre*), "looking upon" (*conspicere*), "beholding" (*intueri*), "discerning" (*cernere*)—by which man finds God and rejoices in Him.[55] Augustine spoke once of a "beholding of the everlasting light of wisdom in a certain holy drunkenness of the spirit which has set itself free from things that are perishable and transient."[56] Undoubtedly, this inward, beatifying experience is concerned only with an indirect sight of God, a vision of Him through the ideas present in the human spirit.[57] He insists that such vision is imperfect: "Though it may be . . . that this light begins to glimmer and shine, still they say that it will be an enigma, seen darkly in a mirror [1 Cor. 13:12], because we walk more in faith than in sight [2 Cor. 5:7], even if we frequent heaven now" (Phil. 3:20).[58] Faith and hope are, therefore, the foundations of contemplation. Augustine stresses, too, that contemplation is not the work of the human spirit alone, but depends in its essence upon God's illumining grace. No one can achieve perception of divine things if God, "the good and only teacher," does not teach him.[59] Contemplation is a fruit of the Holy Spirit, who endows the soul with the gift of wisdom,[60] and the "surpassingly wonderful knowledge of the love of Christ" (cf. Eph. 3:19).[61] What is more, in Augustine's conception, true contemplation is always prayer.[62] Thus, our inward gaze is always directed toward God; as he said in a sermon: "Our very longing to achieve vision is a prayer to God."[63] Man in contemplation strives, praising and thanking, entreating and loving, to comprehend God ever more deeply, delight in Him ever more fully. Often Augustine wrote of the deep joy and happiness man experiences in this, which seems to him like a certain foretaste of eternal blessedness.[64] But he regarded it as an indispensable condition of contemplation that a man must be purified not only of all his sins and his perverse inclinations, but also of the sensual and sensuous projections of his imagination.[65]

In his writings and sermons Augustine often described the way upon which the soul enters as it seeks for God in contemplation. The soul mounts, away from the visible world, over the eternal truths into its own interior, to that God who dwells within the human spirit. This exposition of a gradual ascent to God, mounting on the human spirit, reveals, furthermore, a feature characteristic of Augustine's spiritual teaching: the principle of "inwardness."[66] The admonition "Return to your heart"—*Redi ad cor* (cf. Is. 46:8)—occurs repeatedly in his sermons and writings. Not only in his own inwardness—"in the core of his heart" (*in interiore hominis, in medulla cordis*)—does man encounter himself that he may recognize his weakness and sins;[67] but there, too, the "image of God,"[68] renewed in him, reveals itself to him, and there he finds the truth that gladdens him,[69] the teacher who instructs him,[70] his God who makes him happy.[71]

What has been said in this chapter about the characteristics of contemplation in Augustine may well conclude with a consideration of the description of the ascent of the soul in God which he gave in his exposition of Psalm 41:

> When day after day I had to hear "Where is your God?" [Ps. 41:4], 'my tears were my food every day' [Ps. 41:4], and I pondered day and night on what I had heard, "Where is your God?" And so I too sought for my God, so that if it were possible I might not only believe in Him but also catch some glimpse of Him. For though indeed I perceive what my God has made, yet I do not perceive my God Himself who made it. . . . What might I do to find my God? I will consider the earth, which was created, and which is of great beauty; yet it has a Creator. . . . I look up to the heavens and to the beauty of the stars. . . . Still my thirst is not yet slaked. I wonder at these things and I praise them, but I thirst for Him who made them. I come back to myself to inquire what even I myself am, I who ask these questions; and I know for certain that I possess a body and a soul. . . . Yet there is something which the spirit, ruling, leading, and inhabiting my body sees, something which it perceives with the body's eyes, not with its ears, not with its senses of smell and taste and touch, but of its own self. . . . Can it be that God is as my spirit is? . . . No, it cannot be. It is true that man can contemplate God only in the spirit, and yet not as man can contemplate the spirit. . . .
>
> Thus, I sought my God in what is visible and corporeal, and I did not find Him; I sought His substance in myself, just as if He were of my

own kind, and I did not find Him. So I discern that my God must be something superior to the soul. Therefore, in order that I might touch Him, "I have pondered these things, and I have poured forth my soul above myself" [Ps. 41:5]. . . . For there is only one whom I would touch, my God. For there is His dwelling place, above my soul. There He dwells; from there He looks down on me. . . . He who possesses this secret and exalted dwelling also has on earth a place in which to shelter. His shelter on earth is His Church, still on her pilgrim way. And it is here that we must seek Him, for in this shelter we find the way on which we shall come to His house. . . . "So I shall enter the courts of this glorious shelter, even into the house of God" [Ps. 41:5]. . . . God's shelter on earth is the men who believe in Him. . . . I pass over even their good works; however wondrous the shelter may be, still I shall lose my senses in amazement when I come, even to the house of God. . . .

So [the seeker] was led to God's house, as he pursued a certain sweetness, some inward and hidden delight, just as if from that house some instrument sounded sweetly. . . . In the house of God, the feasting is eternal. For nothing celebrated there comes to an end. An everlasting feast, the angels' choir, the face and presence of God, the joy without end! This is a feast day of the sort that has neither beginning nor ending. And from this everlasting, unending feast there sounds in the heart's ears some sweet melody, yet only, it is true, when the din of the world falls silent. . . .

Brethren, "as long as we live in this body, we stray far from the Lord" [2 Cor. 5:6]; "the corruptible body weighs down the soul, the earthly dwelling oppresses the spirit with its many thoughts" [Wis. 9:15]. Yet if we too, even though mists enshroud us, can sometimes come through our longing to that sound, so that we may catch some glimpse of the brightness of God's house, still we shall fall back under the burden of our weakness into our accustomed path, and we shall step back to our usual ways. . . . [Then one exclaims] "Why are you sad, O my soul, and why do you oppress me" [Ps. 41:6]? See, we do rejoice now in a certain inward sweetness; we can in our minds penetrate to what is unchangeable, even though it be only for brief instants. . . .[72] And it is as if his soul were to give him this wordless reply: Why do I oppress you? Only because I am not yet there, where I was carried only for a moment. Can I drink now of that brook, with nothing left to fear? Is there no further trouble before which I should quail? Am I safe, with all my longings overcome and defeated? Is the devil, my enemy, not on the prowl after me? . . . "Hope in God"—but what should I hope? "Because I shall confess to Him." What will you confess to Him? "The salvation of my countenance, my God" [Ps. 41:6f.]. Salvation cannot

> come to me from myself. This is what I shall say, this is what I shall confess: "The salvation of my countenance, my God."[73]

Thus, in Augustine's view, contemplation will accord the Christian who yearns for insight into faith and strives for a more profound perception of God a type of enrapturing experience which, to be sure, remains fixed in the system of faith and hope. This contemplation of God, Augustine contends, not only must be cultivated by monks and others dedicated to God in "holy leisure" (*otium sanctum*) but is the task and goal of every Christian.[74]

From ancient times, these and many other accounts of the contemplative process in Augustine's writings have often been interpreted in a strictly mystical sense, as describing the experience of God's indwelling, and, as a result, Augustine has been given the title of a "prince of mystics."[75]

Recently not a few scholars have questioned the validity of this, and some, indeed, have specifically denied that Augustine can be called a mystic or a mystical theologian in any exact sense. They have pointed to the markedly activist and intellectual character of Augustinian contemplation, which, they believe, can be regarded, in precise terms of mystical experience, only as a contemplation that is acquired, not infused.[76] Even now, the question is still disputed.[77] We may well agree with Hendrikx, who, in his article "Augustinus" in the *Lexikon für Theologie und Kirche*, has written that what Augustine in fact recorded about his own spiritual experiences and what we can observe from his teachings of his individual personality cannot easily be made to harmonize with the traditional accounts and categories of classical—that is, Spanish—mystics.[78]

Common and Private Prayer in the Monastery

Augustine considered the monk's life in community as a "holy leisure" (*otium sanctum*), as a life of withdrawal dedicated to God.[79] Communal and private pious exercises, hours of reading, and contemplation (*contemplatio*) constituted in all his monastic foundations an essential component of daily monastic life.

This was not the case in, for example, Pachomius' monasteries, where, during the day—in keeping with the anchorites' practice of so-called "perpetual prayer"—there were no hours of prayer as such, manual labor constituting this "perpetual prayer" (*oratio continua*).[80] But from the beginning Augustine prescribed fixed hours in the day which were to serve for the community's prayer. He wrote in so many words in his treatise on monastic manual work that it was an aberration for monks to become so engrossed in their labors that there was no time, or not enough time, left for prayer and reading.[81]

It is noteworthy that in his *Rule* the regulations governing common prayer follow immediately after the sentence "So all of you live with one soul and one heart, and honor in one another God, whose temples you were made to be."[82] Precisely at these times of common prayer, that supernatural community of love should establish and deepen itself, that community for which Augustine strove as the object of monastic life.[83] Voices and hearts should resound harmoniously, like the various instruments in an orchestra, and express the unity in God of each one. In one sermon he used this striking metaphor: "You are the trumpet, the harp, the zither, the kettle drum, the strings, the flute, the cymbal, of the song of praise, all sounding tunefully because they are in harmony."[84] Deeply convinced that the liturgy possesses a power to strengthen communities, he wrote, "Men will be able to coalesce as a religious family only if they unite in their sharing in the 'visible signs,' the sacraments."[85]

For him, liturgical prayer is the prayer of the Mystical Body, the Church. Christ Himself, he believed, prays in His members.[86] As their own voices resound, those who are praying should hear His voice, as He prays for them and in them.[87]

Augustine attached great importance to the seemliness and beauty of their common prayer. Especially in the holy ministrations they performed in God's presence, one man's preference and mood must not settle matters. "Do not recite anything unless you read that it is to be recited," he prescribed for his monks in the *Rule*.[88] He wanted to be sure that due propriety and due custom were being preserved, and that in his monasteries, there should be no deviation from what was usual. He repeated emphatically: "if it is not written down that it should be, it ought not to be, recited."[89]

But this care and esteem for the liturgy did not mean that private prayer was neglected at Hippo and Tagaste. Augustine performed a special service for monastic prayer when he directed that in the houses he founded there should be a separate place to be used exclusively for prayer. It would seem that until then in Western monasteries the oratory was also used as a workroom, following Eastern monastic custom.[90] But Augustine laid it down for his monks: "Let no one do anything in the oratory except what it was built for and from which it takes its name."[91] This passage in his *Rule* is the earliest evidence for the West of the existence of oratories inside monastic buildings; and this shows great progress. Plainly, through this regulation Augustine was the first to establish in the West oratories as such in the monasteries. We can see how long it took for this innovation to become commonplace, because Benedict, 120 years later, considered it important and timely to repeat Augustine's regulation word for word in his own *Rule.*[92]

The reason Augustine gives for it is noteworthy: "... if there are some who are at leisure and who may wish to pray outside the established times, no one who thinks that he has something else to do there should be a hindrance to them."[93] It was for the sake of his monks' private prayer that Augustine had instituted oratories. He could not have shown better the importance he attached to each monk's own piety.

The Right Way to Pray

The directions for prayer which Augustine gave in his *Rule* are contained in only a few, brief sentences, but they deal with what is essential. It may have seemed sufficient to him merely to recall these few important points for his monks, since he had so often given them detailed directions about the right way to pray in his sermons and instruction.[94]

He regarded devotion and inwardness as the soul of prayer. He knew that, just as in a community's praying, "the prayer of the lips" is a great danger. Therefore he asked from his subjects: "When you pray to God in psalms and hymns, turn over in your heart what your voice is uttering."[95] The lips must pronounce nothing in prayer that is not present in the heart.

Prayer full of willful distractions, however loud it may sound in a man's ears, is silent to God.[96] Indeed, every slovenly prayer is an affront to God. "If you are talking to me," Augustine said in a sermon, "and then suddenly turn round to your slaves and leave me standing there, am I not to consider that an insult? You ought to see that this is what you are doing to God every day."[97] Whoever is praying must keep careful watch over his senses. In prayer he must, as it were, shut his doors—that is, resist the enticements of the flesh and the senses.[98]

Beyond doubt, man on this earth, despite all his precautions, will not be able to avoid every distraction in prayer. Augustine said that with the best will in the world, his praying was a daily failure.[99] What he is praising is sublime, but the way that he praises is wretched.[100] "Look at that man over there," he once said; "he is singing long hymns of praise to God, and often as he sings his lips are moving. Yet his thoughts are straying around some heart's desire or other of his. How is it that you are chasing after other things? How is it that you are full of concern about earthly, perishable things?"[101] If a man is honest and recognizes himself in this unflattering picture, Augustine considered that he might well have self-doubts.[102] And yet he had honestly taken trouble; he had praised God as well as he could.[103]

Augustine considered these involuntary distractions as neither culpable nor sinful, but merely the consequences of human frailty. The body, with its sensuality and its ceaseless fantasies, oppresses the soul, making it direct its thoughts toward multiplicity, instead of turning them to Him who is one.[104] He is very honest in confessing how often his own prayer was invaded and maimed by the darkness and confusion of his worldly affairs.[105] Therefore he implored God: "Take away the body, which burdens my soul. . . . Take away from me this earthly dwelling, which oppresses my mind."[106] Not until eternity will man's prayer find its perfection. "When we have come to that heavenly city, when we are made equal with the angels," then we shall sing praises and not be found wanting.[107]

Yet while he is still on earth, a Christian must learn to sing that most perfect praise of God by practicing.[108] It would be folly for anyone to give up all or any of his praying because he cannot help it that his prayers are imperfect. For such pitiful prayer, Augustine said, is his only way to perfection.[109] The more praise he may give, the more power he will receive, and the more he will taste the sweetness of Him whom he praises.[110]

Ultimately, these unwished-for shortcomings in daily prayer are for man no more than God's testing, fostering his purification and his interior progress. Augustine put it very well: "It is better for you to fail in praising God than to pass in praising yourself."[111]

These shortcomings in prayer which are against our will are the best means of making us humble and diffident in God's presence. Augustine saw especially the great ascetic significance of this; for God wants humble prayer, and only humble prayer speaks the truth. Whoever, when he is praying, considers himself a fine fellow, and wants, as it were, to reward the Lord for this out of what he possesses, is a liar. He is praising himself, not God.[112] God does not bend his ear to the rich, to the sated, but only to him who will humble confess "I am needy and helpless."[113] Augustine tells us that humility and love are prayer's two wings, bearing it up into God's presence.[114]

Orationibus instate!—"Be constant in prayer! Devote yourself to it persistently, zealously," he bids his monks.[115] This constancy and persistence in their prayer, and enduring devotion that does not depend on mood and inclination, are what he required of them.

The beginner's zeal in prayer must not cool off. Augustine was able to see for himself, only too often, how soon men became halting and sluggish in praying. In one sermon he described their conduct with great perception: "In the beginning, after their conversion, they pray with great devotion, but later they are careless, then slothful, and in the end wholly indifferent, as if they were completely safe."[116]

According to Augustine, this steady, constant praying is something different from the prayer with many words which the Lord in the Gospel (Matt. 6:7) rejected. For the Saviour Himself admonished us: "One ought to pray continually, and never be discouraged" (cf. Luke 18:1). And we are told that He spent whole nights in prayer, and prayed with the greatest urgency. Augustine concluded that praying for long periods was not this "prayer with many words." There is nothing blameworthy in spending much time on prayer, if one is not prevented by obligations and duties. That is not garrulity in God's presence, but true devotion.[117]

In Augustine's opinion, the only useless talk was in that prayer that believes it has to use many words to instruct God and try to make Him change His mind. Long prayer is not needed for God's benefit, so as to weaken His purpose; it is we who need it, to make us attentive to what it is we are praying for, and to keep us always on the alert.[118] God is content with the entreaty of our heart.[119]

In prayer God looks above all else on our disposition; He listens to our words only as they reveal what our heart's true disposition is.[120] So Augustine admonished: "Do not let your well-sung praises be drowned by your ill-lived life."[121] God has no use for half shares; He demands the whole man: "If you are singing praise to God, sing to Him with everything you are. Your voice should praise Him, your life should praise Him, your deeds should praise Him."[122] Sometimes the praises of our lips must necessarily be silent, but the praises of the heart never should. Once in a sermon Augustine said: "You are praising God when you do your day's work; you are praising Him when you eat and drink; you are praising Him when you rest on your bed; you are praising Him when you are asleep. So when are you not praising Him?"[123]

Thus Augustine, like Eastern monasticism before him,[124] was at great pains to make the Scriptures' precept that we should pray unceasingly (Luke 18:1, 1 Thess. 5:17) a reality. Yet we must not ignore how differently it was realized. In the East, they pursued a more or less literal interpretation of "unceasing prayer"; but Augustine, from his perceptions of the innermost nature of Christian prayer, gave the Scriptural text a new, deeper meaning. "It is your very longings," he said in a sermon,

> that are your prayer; because you never cease to long, you never cease to pray. For it was not in vain that the Apostle said: "Pray without ceasing" [1 Thess. 5:17]. But would it be possible for us without ceasing to be on bent knees, to prostrate ourselves, to lift up our hands, because he said: "Pray without ceasing"? If we maintain that it is only so that we should pray, I do not see how we could do so without ceasing. But there is another inward prayer without ceasing, and that is longing. . . . Your unceasing longing is your unceasing entreaty; but you will be silent if you cease to love. . . . When love grows cold, the heart falls silent; but a burning love is the loud calling out of the heart.[125]

This constant prayer of the heart is, in Augustine's estimation, what gives to prayer its quality and value, which is reflected in the faithful Christian's whole life and his constant disposition of hope and of love. This could not be if vocal prayer were something extraneous. The Christian must pray with words many times in the day if the desires of his heart are to be fanned again into flames and not be extinguished.[126]

Augustine required sincerity from his monks as the final condition for the efficaciousness of their prayer. More than lack of devotion and firm purpose, an unforgiving heart can harm the one who prays. What we say is different from how we live; what the world sees us doing is different from what we feel in our hearts. So in his *Rule* Augustine insists that the more often prayer is offered, the more perfectly it will be offered. A heart without love or one filled with hatred can rob prayer of all value, and cannot hope to be heard: whoever is unwilling to forgive need not hope for his prayers to be heard.[127] Prayer like this is rotten to the core.

His monks ought to offer all their prayers in the spirit of the Lord's Prayer: forgive us our trespasses, as we forgive those who trespass against us. God has signed a kind of treaty with men, Augustine said in one sermon. Anyone who wants to pray "Forgive me my trespasses," and who wants his prayer to be efficacious, must first be able to say in all honesty "as we forgive those who trespass against us."[128] Augustine recommended to his monks, as an object for their life in the monastery, that they have one heart and one soul for God.[129] Anyone who rejects this object, nurturing anger in his heart, is living, as the *Rule* says, without any purpose in the monastery, and will find no hearing from God in his prayers.[130] For prayer like this is no praise of God. When we are divided in our hearts, we cannot praise God. Augustine says that if anyone has anger toward his brother, however much he may praise God with his words, he is reviling Him in his heart.[131]

READING

The way to contemplation which Augustine made his own from the beginnings of his quest for an ideal monastic life is manifest in his hours, every day, of spiritual reading. In this, he was an example to those in his charge. When he read the Epistle to the Romans—Romans 13:13, to be more precise—that had been to him, then in Milan, "light and safety," so that "every shadow of doubt disappeared." The admonition "Take and read," which he heard then,[132] he took to himself for the rest of his life.

In his monasteries, reading in common and in private was an important item in the order of each day. In the so-called, quasi-Augustinian *Ordo monasterii*, the period between Sext and None is assigned for reading, and then, after Vespers, some reading in common is assigned.[133] In *The Work of Monks* he demonstrated that in "well-ordered monasteries" there will be certain hours set for manual work, and that "the time left over" will be for "praying or for doing some work pertaining to Holy Scripture."[134] The *Rule*—that is, the *Praeceptum*—prescribes reading at table. Augustine saw this as a means of spiritualizing their common mealtimes: "It should be not only your jaws that are chewing food, but your ears that are thirsting for God's word."[135]

In his concern for the religious formation of his charges, Augustine instituted a library in each of his monasteries. Possidius left a precise record that they contained Augustine's own writings and sermons, as well as those of other divines.[136] But there can be no doubt that the books of the Old and New Testament were also available.

The reading that Augustine prescribed for his houses was primarily intended to promote spiritual perfection,[137] and it was this particular intention, he wrote, which was the essential difference between it and reading of the usual sort, making out of it a truly religious exercise. He valued it as much as prayer: "If you pray," he said in a sermon, "you are talking to God; if you read, God is talking to you."[138]

But evidently whoever reads will make more rapid progress in the good life, the more he strives to put what he has read into practice. It would be all topsy-turvy to devote oneself to reading but not to want to put that reading to any use.[139] Augustine was never interested in a merely intellectual formation; what he was aiming at was a religious and moral instruction of the heart, which would manifest itself in a love of God and of men. He wrote in one letter: "You ought to read and learn so that the truth of the words is fixed in your mind. 'Knowledge by itself puffs one up with pride; it is love which is constructive' " (1 Cor. 8:1).[140]

Augustine was deeply convinced of the profitability of regular religious reading;[141] for that had been his own experience, which he had not forgotten. Compared with other kinds of religious instruction, reading had the great advantage that one could employ it as often and as long as one pleased.[142]

The reading of Holy Scripture seems to have been given special importance in his monasteries.[143] All his life Augustine himself read and studied the Bible with a thirst for salvation and with deep reverence.[144] He praised the Bible as "the venerable stylus of God's Spirit,"[145] and, again, as "a letter from home," from the true, eternal Jerusalem.[146] He saw in it a source of "holy joy,"[147] an "instruction, uniquely fitted to bring life and renewal to souls,"[148] a "heavenly trumpet" that "rouses men from the somnolence of this mortal life, and urges them on to the victor's prize that awaits their heavenly calling,"[149] "a mirror" to show men themselves, as they are, without deceit or flattery.[150] Thus Augustine never wearied in commending the reading of the Bible to men concerned for spiritual things.[151] They should study in it with faithful devotion and with an earnest zeal to order their lives accordingly.[152] And he impressed on them that they should often pray for right understanding; for only God can give wisdom, knowledge, and true perception.[153]

MANUAL LABOR[154]

In the ordering of the day in his brothers' monastery, Augustine had carefully prescribed hours of reading and of prayer and, in addition, hours for working. In this, he could appeal to monastic usage.[155]

Work-shirking monks were repugnant to him. Soon after his conversion, he wrote an account, in *The Ways of the Catholic Church*, of the industry of the cenobites in the Egyptian houses of men and women who not only earned their own keep but also supported the poor on what their labors brought in.[156] And he commended the Roman communities of monks and nuns he visited at that time, because they supported themselves with the work of their hands.[157]

He composed one work especially to refute those who considered that monastic life and manual labor were irreconcilable.[158] They would quote Christ's words (Matt. 6:26ff.): "Behold the birds of the air! They neither sow; nor do they reap. . . . Your heavenly Father feeds them. . . . Consider the lilies of the field, how they grow! They labor not; neither do they spin." Augustine did not hesitate to use mockery and irony against these monks. "If they quote Scripture," he wrote,

> why do they not look at what follows? For it is not only this that is said [about the birds in the heavens], that they do not sow and do not reap; it goes on: "They do not gather into barns." So why do these people want to sit with idle hands, and even so have their storehouses full? . . . Why are they grinding corn and cooking? Birds do not do that. . . . They pump up water out of tanks or springs and then make it flow back again. Birds do not do that. . . . They should let us see people who are as good to the birds as they would like to be to themselves![159]

Thus Augustine points the finger at them, juggling the words of Scripture to dress up their laziness as piety. He wrote: "They all expect to be paid for their profitable poverty, to be rewarded for their counterfeit holiness."[160]

Their reprehensible conduct, giving scandal to the faithful and causing quarrels and dissension in the monasteries, he contrasts with his ideal, the industrious monk, following Paul's example, his "apostolic discipline,"[161] daily performing some manual labor. Idle monks justified themselves with their principle "Nothing but prayer and reading"; Augustine countered with his motto "Prayer and work."[162]

The Dignity and Duties of Labor

Throughout pagan antiquity, manual labor was little esteemed—indeed, was despised. The reason for this may be that it was primarily the concern of slaves. Nowhere do we find it regarded as morally estimable, if we except a certain romantic enthusiasm in imperial Roman times for the farmer's life, and a few attempts in Stoic literature to show it as possessing merit and dignity.[163]

In Augustine's view, every well-performed task that serves human progress, however mean, has its nobility and its honor. He vigorously attacked those in ancient times who had scorned it. They showed in their very dispraise of labor that they were lacking in "true honorableness." "Whatever task," he wrote, "men perform honestly and without deception is good." As guarantees of the moral value of manual labor, the Christian has the example of the Old Testament patriarchs, who were shepherds, and of the pagan philosophers, among whom were many craftsmen, but, still more, of the Son of God, who chose a carpenter for His guardian and fishermen for His apostles.[164]

Augustine's belief in the estimability of labor stems from his truly Christian conception of the goodness of creation and of the value of men's earthly activities. He knows and recognizes what the objects of human culture are. God Himself entrusted man with them when He entrusted Paradise to him, "to till it and to keep it" (Gen. 2:15).[165] Thus, in his opinion, total dedication to the service of God is in no way a prohibition to men from zealous cooperation to achieve the cultural goals of human progress. But the things of earth are given to them, not for their pleasure, but for their use. They should "obtain, with corporal and temporal things, those that are eternal and spiritual."[166]

He was convinced that God had imposed the duty of working as a condition of human life even before the Fall (Gen. 2:15). Without doubt, it had been a pleasurable and honorable duty for Adam, and represented not toil but refreshment.[167]

Through man's sin, this duty became a punishment,[168] and yet at the same time an excellent means for atoning for sins. Work has a power of expiation and can help man to attain his eternal goal. "We must toil along the way," Augustine wrote, "so as to rejoice when we come home."[169] He called the way steep and hard, but still a way leading out of this vale of tears to our everlasting rest.[170]

So, in sum, physical labor possessed a high ascetic value for the Christian, in Augustine's assessment. It was well suited to free him from pride and to train him in humility. It was especially in this that he saw its sanctifying power.[171]

The Monastic Work Ethic

Augustine discussed the monastic obligation to work in *The Work of Monks.* That it was such an obligation he demonstrated in detail, citing the teaching and example of St. Paul.[172] No one was to be excused because he wanted to occupy himself exclusively with prayer, psalmody, reading, and the word of God.[173] He did not exempt those who in the world had been so rich that they had no need to undertake any work. Obviously, no one would be able to compel them to perform tasks to which they were unaccustomed, and which would therefore be doubly arduous for them. One ought to give them work to do that would require, not great physical exertion, but careful attention. But not even they ought to eat without working.[174] Monks should be excused from the obligation of manual labor, in his opinion, only when they were prevented by feebleness and sickness or, as in his own case, when they were completely occupied with pastoral work.[175] The entire monastic community had the right to expect the help and alms of the faithful only when, for these or similar reasons, they were unable to be self-supporting, even though they worked industriously.[176]

To monks who do not want to work, even though they have the strength to do so, Augustine said with St. Paul: "If any man will not work, neither let him eat" (2 Thess. 3:10).[177] He was insistent in his warnings that monks must not become a nuisance to Christians out in the world: "show people that your concern is, not to live a life of ease and idleness, but only to reach the kingdom of God along the straight and narrow path of the life you have chosen."[178]

Augustine dealt with one criticism which, it would seem, was heard from those who held the monastic obligation to work in contempt. "What does it profit a servant of God," he makes them ask, "if he forsakes what he did in the world . . . to work like a laborer now?"[179] He took this opportunity to show that manual work in the monastery had its own special excellence. Even if a monk had to perform there the same work as he did in the outside world, the situations were different, even judged by outward appearances. In particular, he now was differently motivated, moved no longer by a desire for his own earthly profit, but by a selfless concern for others—and this for the love of Christ. He wrote: "He has freed himself from the longing to increase his own possessions, however small they be, and has given himself to the love of the common life, no longer thinking of his own benefit but of what will profit Christ" (Phil. 2:21).[180] It was in such self-abnegation, which model statesmen in ancient Rome had shown toward the secular state, that Augustine perceived the proper disposition for the "citizen of that eternal, heavenly city, Jerusalem, longing for his true home."[181]

Moreover, Augustine taught that a monk can sanctify the hours of his labor, and that he should do so. In one letter, he cited the example of "the brothers in Egypt" who were accustomed as they worked to utter brief ejaculations, so-called "arrows of prayer," to keep the devotion of their hearts alive as the day went on.[182] Here, writing about working in the monastery, he encourages the monks, as they occupy themselves with their manual labor, to sing holy songs, "so as to make their work sweet with heavenly melodies." If, as they work, men in the world often let their minds and their tongues stray in every kind of frivolity and indecency without interrupting what they are doing, why should the monk in his labors not direct his thoughts to God and be able to sing His praises?[183]

To sum up, Augustine was recommending to his monks, in the sense of St. Paul (1 Cor. 10:31, Col. 3:17), that they glorify God in whatever they did. He wrote about this in his letter to the monastery on the island of Capraria: Whatever may be occupying you—prayer and fasting, good works and penance, as well as the enduring of sufferings and temptations and of one another's faults and weaknesses—everything should be done for the glory of God. He said that this intention would influence a man's entire activity. It would mean that in everything he did "his eye would always be on the Lord" (Ps. 24:15), and he concluded: "disquiet will not disturb him, for he is always at peace. What he does is not impetuous, nor is it listless, not foolhardy or timorous, not reckless, not apathetic."[184]

Augustine's Assessment of the Religious and Moral Value of Manual Labor

One cannot easily overestimate the importance Augustine attributed to the moral and religious value of manual labor. It was he who, in *The Work of Monks*, established the work ethic of Western monasticism.[185] For him—unlike some of the Desert Fathers who used to destroy anything produced in the monasteries and not sold to support them[186]—such labor was more than merely a means to keep his monks occupied. Augustine and his monks knew well the destiny ordained by Divine Providence for man upon this earth. No one could reprove them, as people did the hermits of the East, for being useless members of human society.[187] As monasticism developed later in the West, it owed much of its great cultural achievement to Augustine and to his defense of the dignity of Christian and monastic labor.

But his influence in these respects was not confined to monastic life. *The Work of Monks* is the first systematic examination by any Father of the Church of the value and the obligations of manual labor. Though all the ideas in it are by no means new—much of what Augustine wrote about the ethics of working can be found in Ambrose, Tertullian, and John Chrysostom[188]—"no Christian writer of antiquity ever ordered the basic themes more clearly; no Father of the Church ever related with greater cogency what he wrote in praise of manual labor to everything theology and the Gospel have to give." In this way, Augustine was the true "pioneer in claiming for labor its dignity and its moral value," whose influence was to endure in the centuries to come,[189] and who in this way made his own great contribution to the Christian civilization of the West.[190]

APOSTOLIC WORK

Augustine's call to the priesthood deepened and broadened his entire concept of the monastic life. He had had no ambitions in this direction. On the contrary, he was positively frightened by the prospect of "the priestly office" (*officium*),[191] conscious as he was of its responsibilities and the deficiencies of his religious knowledge. Old Bishop Valerius bestowed Holy Orders upon him when the faithful of Hippo spontaneously made their will known.[192]

Yet this event came to be viewed as a disposition of divine grace. It soon became manifest that Augustine possessed the spiritual strength and breadth of vision to achieve a fundamental union between the ideals of life in a monastic community and those of the priesthood; and the union was to be fortunate and fruitful for the priesthood and monasticism alike.

His aspirations for the monastic life took on an increasingly apostolic character. Even if his own personal vocation was a contemplative one, so that he longed for a "holy leisure" (*otium sanctum*),[193] still he recognized the apostolic work was a duty a monk could not reject if it were asked of him.[194]

The "Burden" (sarcina) *of Spiritual Direction*

Augustine's exalted conception of the duties and responsibility of the priesthood deeply affected the way in which these apostolic ideals worked themselves out in practice. For him, a priest was "a dispenser of the word and the sacrament" (*dispensator verbi et sacramenti*).[195] This was not only his great undertaking, but also the measure of his responsibility before God. If one considers only the respect he enjoys from the people because of his office, it might seem as if there is nothing in this life easier, happier, more esteemed among men than the office of a bishop, a priest, or a deacon. But, seen for what it is, nothing can bring with it more difficulties, troubles, and dangers.[196]

Augustine wrote exhaustively about the burdens of the priesthood. The direction of the souls entrusted to him was hard for a priest,[197] and the many varied duties of his office were a great care: preaching, admonition, instruction, concerning oneself about everyone—these made a heavy load.[198] And Augustine thought that for men occupied in pastoral work the danger of falling short was not a small one. People expected a priest to be an example of good works to everyone (Titus 2:7);[199] surrounded by godlessness, he was supposed to live with a clean conscience.[200] And yet he was still a man, of flesh and blood, subject to every human need, even if they did regard him as an angel.[201] He too had to tread among temptation's snares. When he was still a layman, Augustine had seen for himself "how hard [it is for a man so placed] to preserve [his] high ideals of living and to guard [his] soul in peace and quiet."[202] And when he was an old man, he wrote in a similar vein to a younger bishop: "Do not imagine that no wrong impulses can arise in us, just because we are bishops. We shall do better to remind ourselves of the dangerous lives we lead, surrounded by the traps of temptations, because we are still men."[203] And in a sermon he admitted, with complete frankness and humility, "Certainly, because that is God's will, I am His priest; but even so, I am a sinner. I beat my breast as you do; I pray for forgiveness as you do; I hope, as you hope, in a merciful God."[204]

Thus, the office of priest was for Augustine one full of danger.[205] With deep conviction he wrote: "Those who hear God's word are happier than those who preach it."[206] Once he called God Himself to witness that he, in exercising his office, was filled with nothing but fear.[207] His consciousness of his responsibilities weighed heavily upon him. He recognized himself both in the servant of the Gospel story (Luke 19:20ff.) whom the master had entrusted with his money, only to ask for it back again with interest,[208] and in the watchman for God's people, as Ezechiel (33:2ff.) described him; only through faithful vigilance can he save his own life.[209] Perhaps God had promised him a richer reward for his heavier burden, but a crueller punishment threatened him if he did not keep faith.[210]

Apostolic Work and Monastic Contemplation

Business/Leisure (negotium/otium)
Action/Contemplation (actio/contemplatio)
Ministry of Love/Love of Truth (officium caritatis/amor veritatis)

It was because of his exalted conception of the tasks and responsibilities of the priest that Augustine was moved to combine, in a certain sense, the apostolic and the contemplative lives.[211]

He was convinced that for any spiritual director to withdraw, at least from time to time, for a period of "leisure" (*otium*) would bring rich fruits to the souls confided to him and to the Church.[212] He impresses two points in particular on a priest. Instruction of others, by word or in writing, must always be preceded by intercession for God's help and enlightenment. A director must pray first, then preach.[213] "Only if a preacher himself has caught fire," he said in a sermon, "will he be able to set light to his hearers."[214] His second point seemed to him as important: the way a director lived and what he taught must be in harmony. His weighty words are not so important as the way he lives.[215] In these two points Augustine saw the true secret of success for priestly activities.[216]

The monastery of clerics which Augustine and his charges created offered to its members, it is plain, rich opportunities for preparing themselves for their pastoral work and for continuing this formation through study. Pastoral work, in Augustine's opinion, imposed study on those who exercised it as a strict duty. A priest who was negligent in this respect would not, one day, before God's judgment seat, be able to make the excuse that his services to the Church had left him no time. Those who tried would surely hear their verdict: "You useless servant" (Matt. 18:32).[217]

Augustine wrote in detail about his basic plans for the education of the clergy in *Christian Instruction.*[218] He insisted that the foundation for all pastoral activity must be a sound knowledge of Holy Scripture, for a pastor will find there what will serve him and the souls put in his charge for their salvation.[219] But secular knowledge also had its place in this program of studies. Languages, natural sciences, history, geography, mathematics, astronomy, music, dialectic, rhetoric, and medicine were all to be called in to make proper understanding of the Bible possible.[220]

But he teaches that only that man will gain the full fruits of such studies who strives for knowledge in the right way and with the right intention. His motive must be love; knowledge without love is not merely superfluous, it is downright pernicious.[221] It would only lead to pride and intellectual confusion. St. Paul had warned men: "Knowledge puffs up" (1 Cor. 8:1). "So would you not do better," Augustine asked, "to flee from knowledge and to prefer to know nothing than to become puffed up?" But he refutes this: "On the contrary, love knowledge, but prefer loving to knowing. Knowledge puffs up where love does not build up. Where love is building that site is firmly founded. There there will be no idle pride, because you will have built on a rock."[222]

Augustine had before this prescribed hours of reading to his brothers' monasteries;[223] but it was only in the clerics' monastery at Hippo that adequate reading and study of Scripture were instituted. Like Basil and Jerome before him, Augustine made his contribution to the reconciling of the Church's asceticism and her scientific and literary activities.

So it was that what he envisaged as an ideally apostolic life did represent a certain combination of active and contemplative living.[224] He knew of the philosophers' distinctions in the contemplative, active, and mixed ways of life, and he declared unambiguously that one could live any of the three without prejudice to the faith, and thus attain one's eternal goal. Yet it was important to achieve a proper reconciliation between one's love for the truth and one's obligation to love. In *The City of God* he wrote: "We should not so surrender ourselves to the leisure of contemplation that we forget to help our neighbors; nor should we become so immersed in activity that we lose our longing to contemplate God in recollection."[225]

Beyond doubt, Augustine, in the spirit of ancient philosophy, gives preference to contemplation over action. It is that better part, that one thing necessary, that Christ once promised Mary of Bethany would not be taken away from her.[226] Augustine knew of nothing more delightful than to explore the treasures of the divine mysteries, far from all disturbance.[227] The life of contemplation, here on earth, offers a foretaste and a share in the life beyond the grave, in which it will be made perfect.[228] Yet we can detect how newer Christian modes of thought are undermining for Augustine the notions of contemplation and action which had been taken over from Greek philosophy. Contemplation is itself for him an act, the highest action man can perform in God's presence; and it is in activity that contemplation will persist. "This is how we must act if we are on the right way," he wrote in a letter, "keeping our eye always on the Lord. . . . Such action will not dissipate itself in restlessness; nor will it become rigid in repose."[229] In the life of every Christian there will be hours in which he resembles Mary. Withdrawn from his everyday concerns, freed from domestic cares, he will be wholly intent on listening for God's word. And yet his life here on earth will share much of Martha's industry and bustle. Pure contemplation is waiting, in another life.[230]

One sees how this form of living reflects Augustine's own life. In his biography Possidius wrote of Augustine that, in the midst of the many distractions of his activities as a bishop, his mind was "drawn up to the higher things of the spirit."[231] He always longed so much to build anew on the foundations God had laid that Possidius compared him with Mary of Bethany: "He was such an image of the Church in heaven, like Mary, that most devout woman, of whom it is written 'She sat at the feet of the Lord and listened attentively to His words.' "[232] And yet, in fact, Augustine was never permitted to enjoy this "holy leisure" (*otium sanctum*) undisturbed. Though true even of the years he lived in the retirement of Tagaste, it is all the truer of those he spent as a priest and bishop when, with sacrificial devotion, he performed the "Martha's service" of his weighty office.[233] As a bishop, he was filled with love for the Church and anxiety on behalf of the flock given to him; and he was a true father to the poor and the oppressed.[234]

His two monastic foundations at Hippo, the garden monastery and that of the clerics, reflected, each in its own fashion, his efforts to combine the contemplative and the apostolic lives. The brothers in their monastery had not withdrawn themselves from the world so much that they forgot, in their retirement, their neighbors' benefit; and the clerics at the episcopal residence were not so exclusively dedicated to apostolic work that they had forsaken every aspiration to a "holy leisure."[235]

Monasticism's Responsibility to the Mystical Body as the Motivation of the Apostolate

External circumstances compelled Augustine to combine apostolic activity with the contemplation of the monastic life; yet he was not content with this accidental and outward combination of the objects of the two ways. His aspirations for apostolic activity permeated his thinking about what monasticism should be, and found there a complete justification. But it was not only on this that all his hopes for what an active monasticism might achieve for the Church were allowed to rest. He may not have been the first to introduce the action needed for apostolic work into monastic living; but, even so, the religious and Scriptural motivation of these new ideals is due to him.

As Augustine's conception of the Church matured toward the Pauline notion of the Mystical Body of Christ, so his ideals for monastic life became more deeply rooted in the idea of this Mystical Body. More and more he came to see monasticism as closely, organically related to the Church's entirety, and he perceived it clearly to be a member—indeed, a vital member—of Christ's Body.[236] With this, he became more convinced that it was the vocation of monasticism to share in the labor of making the Body of Christ perfect.

Indeed, under certain circumstances that was its formal duty, he came to think. In his letter to the island community on Capraria he wrote: "If Mother Church requires some service from you, do not serve your own ambitions in performing it, or refuse to do it because you are more attracted by indolence. . . . No, do not put your own leisure before the needs of Mother Church. If there had not been good men to help her in her birth-pangs, you would find it hard to explain how you came to be born at all."[237] He had very similar notions when he admonished Laetus, a young brother, evidently from the clerics' monastery, who had the idea that he wanted to forsake the monastic life. Mother Church

> is troubled by so many different acts of hostility from the forces of error, that even her own premature children do not hesitate to fight her with unbridled hostility. And one of her sufferings is the apathy and idleness of so many whom she carries in her bosom, making her members everywhere grow cold, hardly able now to warm her own children. Where else can she with every right ask for help, where else than from among her other members, among whom you too are counted. Do you really want to leave her alone in her need? [238]

Augustine was able to assure the faithful of Hippo, speaking for himself and for his clerics: "We live with you here and we live for you; it is our dearest wish always to live here with you and with Christ."[239] Thus, his ideals for monastic living were influenced by his deep consciousness of their common responsibility for the Church.[240]

Indeed, Augustine viewed it as nothing but injustice if those who loved the contemplative life, but were fitted for the responsibilities of ecclesiastical administration, took refuge from that in contemplation.[241] For that reason he willingly accepted suitable members of the brothers' monastery into the ranks of his clerics.[242] And for him his monks' pastoral work was no "necessary evil, to be undertaken out of love."[243] Rather, he saw it as a service of love to Christ and to His members. It was, indeed, full of sorrows and care, but it conformed to the monastic ideal, and he wholeheartedly approved it, conscious as he was of the responsibility that he and his monks shared for the entire Church. Clearly, what Augustine said in a sermon, challenging Peter on the Mount of the Transfiguration to forsake the contemplative calm he had found with Christ, and to weary himself in a selfless love on earth for Christ, applied to Augustine and to his clerics:

> "Lord, it is good for us to be here," Peter said. He had had enough of the crowd, and he had found solitude on the mountain. There he was possessing Christ, the Bread of the spirit. Why should he withdraw, from where he had known a holy love for God and a life that was good, down again into labor and pain? . . . Come down, Peter! Do you want to rest in peace on the mountain? No, come down to preach the Gospel! . . . Labor, tire yourself out, bear your sorrows. "Love does not seek what is for itself" [1 Cor. 13:5], but gives away what it owns. . . . The Apostle says of himself: "I seek what is useful, not to me, but to the many, so that they may be saved" [1 Cor. 10:33]. Peter could not see the consequence of this when he asked to go on living with Christ on

> the mountain. Peter, he is keeping that for you until your death; now He is saying "Go down, to grow weary with labor on earth, to serve on earth, to be despised on earth, and to be nailed to the cross." Christ came down from life to suffer death; the Bread came down, to hunger; the Way came down, on the way to weariness; the Fount came down, to thirst. Do you refuse to take work upon yourself? You must not seek what is for yourself; preach the truth! That is how you will come to eternity, and there find security.[244]

Augustine in his *Rule* had shown his brethren that to be one heart and one soul for God is the goal of monastic life.[245] Individuals are to attain perfection in love through unselfish service to the community. The way to perfection of self which he showed to them was a caring, ready for any sacrifice, for the community.[246] Yet the life of apostolic activity is in some respects related to this way; for pastoral labors, for Augustine, meant self-surrender to a wider society, and he saw them as a service of love to the Church, to the Body of Christ.[247] It is very significant that Augustine appeals to the same words of St. Paul "Love does not seek what is for itself" (1 Cor. 13:5) both in his *Rule* and in this sermon about Peter on the Mount of the Transfiguration to justify the necessity of service to the monastic community and to the Church as well.[248]

From these Scriptural and theological proofs, it follows that in Augustinian monastic life working together for one's neighbor's salvation was viewed in a light different from that of many more recent religious communities of the Church. Unlike them, Augustine's foundation was not occasioned by any one determined apostolic or charitable purpose. His monastic ideals were, rather, marked and formed by his basic attitude toward religion. He was attempting to create communities in his monasteries in which the ideals of Christian life and Christian love might be realized, and the Lord's words "By this shall all men know that you are my disciples, if you have love one for another" (John 13:35) were always in his mind.[249] But the apostolic goals at which he aimed were, for him, not separated from his basic conceptions of the Christian faith; in a certain way, they had absorbed one another and supported one another.

NOTES

1. *The Work of Monks* 18.21. Cf. also 29.37.
2. *Soliloquies* 1.2.7.
3. "Peter prayed, Paul prayed, the rest of the Apostles prayed; the faithful

in those days prayed, the faithful in the following ages prayed; the faithful in the age of the martyrs prayed, the faithful in our own days pray, the faithful in the days to come will pray" (*Exposition on Psalm 101* 1.3). Cf. *Letter 130* 11.21; *The City of God* 19.19; *Forgiveness of Sin and Baptism* 2.2.2; *Man's Perfection in Righteousness* 21.44. See also Enrique del Sdo. Corazón, "Oración y contemplación en la teología espiritual de S. Agustín," *Revista de espiritualidad*, 14 (1955), 211ff.

4. *Letter 130*. See also M. Villegas, "La oración en San Agustín," CD, 175 (1962), 624–39.

5. ". . . flagrantia caritatis" (*Exposition on Psalm 37* 14).

6. ". . . continuatum desiderium" (*Letter 130* 9.18). See on this T. A. Hand, *Saint Augustine on Prayer* (Dublin, 1963), pp. 8f., and Enrique del Sdo. Corazón, "Oración y contemplación," 209f.

7. Hendrikx, *Augustins Verhältnis*, pp. 82ff.; E. Braem, "Augustinus' leer over de heiligmakende genade," *Augustiniana*, 1 (1951)ff., esp. 2 (1952), 201–204, 3 (1953), 5–20, 328–40. Cf. also T. Huijbers, "Het beeld van God in de ziel volgens Sint Augustinus' *De Trinitate*," ibid., 2 (1952), 88–107, 205–29; J. A. A. Stoop, *De deificatio hominis in de Sermones en Epistulae van Augustinus* (Leiden, 1952); H. Somers, "Image de Dieu et illumination divine," AM I, pp. 451–62.

8. Braem, "Augustinus' leer," *Augustiniana*, 2 (1952), 7ff.

9. *The Ways of the Catholic Church* 1.13.22.

10. *On Genesis Against the Manichaeans* 1.17.28; *On 83 Various Questions*, question 51; *The Incomplete Book on the Literal Meaning of Genesis* 16; *The Literal Meaning of Genesis* 3.19f.; *Sermon 52* 7.18, etc.

11. Cf. *Questions about the Heptateuch* 5.4; *On 83 Various Questions*, question 74; *The Trinity* 9.2.2.

12. *The Freedom of the Will* 2.16.41, and, similarly, *Exposition on Psalm 70* 2.3.

13. *The Ways of the Catholic Church* 1.11.18; *The Greatness of the Soul* 34.77. Cf. also *The Literal Meaning of Genesis* 7.2f., 7.28.43; *Letter 166* 3.7; *The Trinity* 9.11.16.

14. *Exposition on Psalm 48* 2.11.

15. *The Trinity* 14.4.6.

16. *Commentary on the Epistle to the Galatians* 27. Cf. also *The Trinity* 14.12.15: "Or, to say the same thing more briefly, let [the soul] worship God, who is not made, who made it capable of receiving Him and in whom it can partake; . . . not by its own light, but by participation in that supreme light will it be wise."

17. *The Trinity* 14.16.22. Cf. Hendrikx, *Augustins Verhältnis*, pp. 94ff.

18. *The Trinity* 14.17.23.

19. Ibid., and, similarly, 11.1.1, 12.7.12.

20. *Exposition on Psalm 99* 5.

21. Cf. Hendrikx, *Augustins Verhältnis*, pp. 99ff.

22. Ibid., pp. 186ff.

23. *Sermon 71* 18.30.

24. Ibid. 18.31 Cf. also *Homily on St. John's Gospel* 98 1ff.

25. *Homily on St. John's Gospel* 48 1.

26. See, for example, *True Religion* 24.25; "Authority demands faith and prepares men for reason." See also F. Cayré, *La Contemplation augustinienne: Principes de spiritualité et de théologie*, 2nd ed. (Paris, 1954), pp. 220ff.

27. "For some things are so believed that they can no longer be seen at all" (*The Trinity* 15.27.49). Cf. also *True Religion* 10.20. *On 83 Various Questions*, question 48.

28. *True Religion* 29.52.

29. *Sermon 43* 4 and 9. Cf. also *The Trinity* 15.2.2; *Letter 120* 1.2f.

30. *Homily on St. John's Gospel* 29 6.

31. ". . . orando et quaerendo et bene vivendo" (*The Trinity* 15.27.49).

32. Ibid. 4.21.31.

33. *The Happy Life* 4.35. Cf. also above, pp. 7–13.

34. *The Catechizing of the Uninstructed* 25.47. Cf. also Hendrikx, *Augustins Verhältnis*, p. 107, and the sources indicated there.

35. *The Greatness of the Soul* 35.79. Cf. also Hendrikx, *Augustins Verhältnis*, p. 111, and C. van Lierde, *Doctrina sancti Augustini circa dona Spiritus Sancti ex textu Isaiae XI, 2–3* (Würzburg, 1935), pp. 81ff.

36. Especially *The Greatness of the Soul* 33.70–76; *On Genesis Against the Manichaeans* 1.25.43; *True Religion* 26.49. For details, see van Lierde, *Doctrina*, pp. 20ff.; Hendrikx, *Augustins Verhältnis*, pp. 110ff.; see also Cayré, *La Contemplation*, pp. 69ff.; R. Hazelton, "The Devotional Life," in *A Companion to the Study of St. Augustine*, ed. R. W. Battenhouse (New York, 1955), pp. 398–414.

37. Van Lierde, *Doctrina*, pp. 39ff. Cf. also Cayré, *La Contemplation*, pp. 57ff.; Hendrikx, *Augustins Verhältnis*, pp. 185f.; Urbano de N. Jesús, "Ensayo sobre los dones del Espíritu Santo en la espiritualidad agustiniana," *Revista de espiritualidad*, 14 (1955), 227–50.

38. *Sermo Frangipane 1* 17, in Morin, pp. 184f. Similar thoughts appear not infrequently in Augustine's other works; for further references, see Hendrikx, *Augustins Verhältnis*, p. 117.

39. Such groupings are found in the following contexts: *The Lord's Sermon on the Mount* 1.4.11–2.11.38; *Christian Instruction* 2.7.9–11; *Sermon 347* 1f.1f.; *Letter 171A* (= *Fragment to Maximus*). Cf. Hendrikx, *Augustins Verhältnis*, pp. 119ff.

40. *Sermon 248* 5.4; *Sermon 270* 5.

41. *The Lord's Sermon on the Mount* 1.3ff.10–13, 2.11.38. Cf. also van Lierde, *Doctrina*, pp. 84ff.

42. Cf. van Lierde, *Doctrina*, p. 92, and Hendrikx, *Augustins Verhältnis*, pp. 120f.

43. *Confessions* 3.4.7.

44. *Against the Academics* 1.6.16. Cf. on this M. Meijer, *De Sapientia in de eerste geschriften van S. Augustinus* (Nijmegen, 1939), pp. 97ff.

45. Cf. J. Morán, *El hombre frente a Dios: El proceso humano de la ascensión a Dios según San Agustín* (Valladolid, 1963), pp. 149ff.

46. *La Contemplation*, pp. 7f.

47. F. Cayré, "Alta sapienza e vita cristiana," AVSM I, pp. 86f., 97ff. Cf. also *Christian Instruction* 1.8ff.8ff. where Augustine discusses the way in which divine wisdom became human in Jesus Christ in order to allow us a share in that wisdom.

48. *The Lord's Sermon on the Mount* 1.2.–4.9–11.

49. Cf. also above pp. 27–28 and note 24.

50. Cf. *Retractations* 1.19.2. See also Hendrikx, *Augustins Verhältnis*, pp. 127f.

51. *Christian Instruction* 1.39f.43f.; *The Trinity* 12.14.22 Cf. also Cayré, "Alta sapienza," pp. 95ff.

52. *Homily on St. John's Gospel 29* 6.

53. *Exposition on Psalm 135* 8.

54. *The Lord's Sermon on the Mount* 1.3.10: "Wisdom, that is, the contemplation of truth."

55. Cayré, *La Contemplation*, pp. 133ff.

56. *Against Faustus* 12.42.

57. Ibid. 163ff. Augustine denied the possibility, in general, of a direct vision of God's being for men upon earth, apart from fleeting, wavering moments (cf. Hendrikx, *Augustins Verhältnis*, pp. 178ff.).

58. *Christian Instruction* 2.7.11.

59. *Confessions* 11.8.10; *Exposition on Psalm 118* 17.3.

60. Cf. *Sermon 248* 5.4; *Sermon 270* 5. See also van Lierde, *Doctrina*, pp. 52ff.

61. *Confessions* 13.7.8.

62. Cayré, *La Contemplation*, pp. 189ff.

63. ". . . quia ipsum desiderium, quod vultis intelligere, oratio est ad Deum" (*Sermon 152* 1).

64. *On 83 Various Questions*, question 35 1f.; *Confessions* 10.40.65, 13.13f.14f.

65. *The Greatness of the Soul* 33.73–75; *Confessions* 10.7.11, 13.7.8; *Christian Instruction* 1.10.10, 2.7.11.

66. Cf. on this P. Blanchard, "L'Espace intérieur chez saint Augustin, d'après le livre X des *Confessions*," AM I, pp. 535–42, and Morán, *El hombre frente a Dios*, pp. 139–48.

67. *Exposition on Psalm 49* 28; *Exposition on Psalm 57* 2; *Exposition on Psalm 101* 1.10.

68. *Homily on St. John's Gospel 18* 10.

69. *Exposition on Psalm 50* 13; *True Religion* 39.72.

70. *Exposition on Psalm 50* 13; *Exposition on Psalm 139* 15.

71. *Confessions* 10.40.65.

72. The Latin of this important sentence is: "Ecce iam quadam interiore dulcedine laetati sumus, ecce acie mentis aliquid incommutabile, etsi perstrictim et raptim, perspicere potuimus."

73. *Exposition on Psalm 41* 7–11.

74. *The City of God* 19.19. Cf. also *Against Faustus* 22.52ff.

75. C. Butler, *Western Mysticism: The Teaching of SS. Augustine, Gregory, and Bernard on Contemplation and the Contemplative Life*, 2nd ed. (London, 1927), p. 24.
76. Particularly Hendrikx, *Augustins Verhältnis*, pp. 188–204, who gives a good survey of the problem as it then existed.
77. Cf. on this M. A. Madouze, "Où en est la question de la mystique augustinienne?" AM III, pp. 103–63.
78. LThK, I^2, 1099.
79. Cf. *Letter 10* 2f.; *Letter 48* 1; *Letter 213* 5f.; *Letter 220* 3; *Exposition on Psalm 54* 8.
80. Cf. Schiwietz, *Das morgenländische Mönchtum* I, pp. 192f., 197f., and Bacht, "Antonius und Pachomius," 82.
81. *The Work of Monks* 17.20.
82. *Rule* 2.1–2.
83. Cf. also *Against Faustus* 19.11, and *Confessions* 9.7.15.
84. *Exposition on Psalm 150* 8. This comparison of the faithful with musical instruments is found elsewhere in the Fathers. It is especially striking when one remembers that in Christian antiquity instrumental music was forbidden in worship. Cf. P. Wagner, "Über Psalmen und Psalmengesang," 253f.
85. *Against Faustus* 19.11.
86. *Exposition on Psalm 140* 3.
87. Cf. *Exposition on Psalm 85* 1 and *Exposition on Psalm 102* 1.
88. *Rule* 2.4.
89. Ibid.
90. On ancient Christian oratories, cf. Eisenhofer, *Handbuch der katholischen Liturgik*, I 322f., and H. Leclercq, "Oratoire," *Dictionnaire d'Archéologie Chrétienne et de Liturgie*, XLL 2357ff.
91. *Rule* 2.2.
92. Benedict, *Rule* 52; see Linderbauer 69f., Butler 95, Steidle 164. Cf. E. Drinkwelder, "St. Benedikt als Erbe urchristlichen Betens," in *Benedictus, der Vater des Abendlandes*, ed. H. S. Brechter (Munich, 1947), p 306.
93. *Rule* 2.2.
94. Cf. also A. M. Besnard, "Les Grandes Lois de la prière: St. Augustin, maître de prière," *La Vie Spirituelle*, 41 (1959), 237–80.
95. *Rule* 2.3. Cf *Letter 130* 21. Benedict also adopted this regulation of the *Rule* word for word; see his *Rule* 52.
96. *Exposition on Psalm 86* 1.
97. *Exposition on Psalm 140* 18.
98. *The Lord's Sermon on the Mount* 2.3.11.
99. *Exposition on Psalm 145* 4.
100. Ibid. 6.
101. Ibid.
102. *Exposition on Psalm 85* 7.
103. *Exposition on Psalm 145* 6.
104. "The body weighs down the soul" (ibid.).
105. *Letter 48* 1. Cf. also *Confessions* 10.35.57.

106. *Exposition on Psalm 145* 6. The somewhat negative attitude toward the human body which these remarks indicate is not tantamount to any Manichaean or Neoplatonic contempt for the body. Augustine gave full assent to the body's goodness and dignity, created by God; yet he recognized the consequences of sin and the Fall, always manifesting themselves in the body's revolt against the spirit, even though the body through the Redemption be destined for eternal glorification. See below, pp. 217–20.

107. *Exposition on Psalm 146* 2, and *Exposition on Psalm 148* 2.

108. *Exposition on Psalm 146* 2

109. *Exposition on Psalm 85* 7.

110. *Exposition on Psalm 99* 17. Cf. also *Exposition on Psalm 145* 1.

111. *Exposition on Psalm 145* 4.

112. *Exposition on Psalm 102* 4 and *Exposition on Psalm 112* 1.

113. *Exposition on Psalm 85* 2.

114. *Sermon 206* 3. Cf *Sermon 45* 7.

115. *Rule* 2.1.

116. *Exposition on Psalm 65* 24.

117. *Letter 130* 10ff.19ff.

118. Ibid. Cf. *Sermon 56* 3.4.

119 "We pray with words that we may rouse ourselves; we pray with the heart that we may be pleasing to Him" (*Exposition on Psalm 147* 5). Cf. *Exposition on Psalm 86* 1.

120. "He takes more heed of how you may be living than of how you may be sounding" (*Exposition on Psalm 146* 3). Cf. *Exposition on Psalm 91* 4f.

121. *Exposition on Psalm 146* 3.

122. *Exposition on Psalm 148* 2. Cf. *Exposition on Psalm 149* 8. See also J. Delamare, "La Prière à l'école de saint Augustin," *La Vie Spirituelle*, 34 (1952), 477–93.

123 *Exposition on Psalm 146* 2. Cf. *Exposition on Psalm 102* 2.

124. M. Marx's *Incessant Prayer in Ancient Monastic Literature* (Rome, 1946) is a detailed examination of the idea and the realization of "unceasing prayer" in the oldest Eastern monasticism.

125. *Exposition on Psalm 37* 14.

126. Cf. *Letter 130* 18.

127. *Rule* 6.1.

128. *Sermon 58* 7. Cf. also Augustine's commentaries on the Lord's Prayer in *Sermon 56* 11ff.; *Sermon 57* 8; *Sermon 59* 7.

129. *Rule* 1.2.

130. Ibid. 6.2.

131. *Exposition on Psalm 132* 13.

132. *Confessions* 8.12.29.

133. *Ordo monasterii* 2.2.

134. *The Work of Monks* 29.37. Cf. *Exposition on Psalm 99* 12.

135. *Rule* 3.2.

136. Possidius 31. Cf. *Ordo monasterii* 3 and *Rule* 5.9–10. See also Altaner, *Kleine patristische Schriften*, pp. 174–78.

137. "Apply yourself to prayer and reading to bring your soul good health" (*Letter 21* 3).

138. *Exposition on Psalm 85* 7.

139. *The Work of Monks* 17.20.

140. *Letter 55* 21.38f. Cf. *Christian Instruction* 1.35f.39f.

141. "It moves us much . . . ; it strikes great fear" (*Letter 132*).

142. Ibid.

143. Cf. *Letter 21* 3.

144. Cf. Vogels, "Die Heilige Schrift bei Augustinus," pp. 411–21; A. Penna, "Lo studio della Bibbia nella spiritualità di S. Agostino," AVSM I, pp. 147–68; see also Marrou, *Saint Augustin et la fin de la culture antique*, pp. 391–430 (on gaps and limits in Augustine's knowledge of Scripture). "Lo studio della Bibbia nella spiritualità di S. Agostino," AVSM I, pp. 147–68; see also Marrou, *Saint Augustin et la fin de la culture antique*, pp. 391–430 (on gaps and limits in Augustine's knowledge of Scripture).

145. *Confessions* 7.21.27.

146. *Exposition on Psalm 149* 5. Cf. also *Exposition on Psalm 90* 2.1.

147. *Exposition on Psalm 38* 2. Cf. also Penna, "Lo studio della Bibbia," pp. 152f.

148. *The Advantage of Believing* 6.13.

149. *Against Faustus* 13.18.

150. *Sermon 49* 5.5.

151. Cf. *Letter 55* 39; *Letter 132*.

152. Cf. *Letter 137* 3 and *Letter 55* 38.

153. *Christian Instruction* 3.37.56. Cf. Vogels, "Die Heilige Schrift bei Augustinus," p. 419.

154. Cf. on this section H. Weinand, *Antike und moderne Gedanken über die Arbeit, dargestellt am Problem der Arbeit beim heiligen Augustinus* (Mönchen-Gladbach, 1911), pp. 19ff.; von Sokolowski, *Der heilige Augustin und die christliche Zivilisation*, pp. 140ff.; L. Alvarez, "San Agustín y la ley del trabajo," *Religion y cultura*, 11 (1930), 224–38; A. Brucculeri, "Il pensiero sociale di S. Agostino: Il lavoro," *La civilità cattolica*, 81, No. 4 (1930), 303ff.; H. Holzapfel, *Die sittliche Wertung der körperlichen Arbeit im christlichen Altertum* (Würzburg, 1941), esp. pp. 122ff. Holzapfel's is the most comprehensive study of the theme and puts Augustine's importance in evaluating the Christian and moral value of manual labor in its proper light. But the author lacks much information about Augustine's attitude toward monasticism; he believes that Augustine himself never lived in a monastery and that *The Work of Monks* was a mere by-product of his pastoral care as a bishop (p. 135). This may explain why Holzapfel passes over in silence what Augustine wrote about the place of manual labor in the life of a monk.

155. *The Work of Monks* 29.37: "I should . . . prefer to do some work with my hands at fixed times each day (as much as has been established in well-ordered monasteries). . . ."

156. *The Ways of the Catholic Church* 1.31.67f.

157. Ibid. 1.31.70.

158. Namely, *The Work of Monks.* See, on this, pp. 77–78 above.
159. *The Work of Monks* 23.27.
160. Ibid. 28.36.
161. Ibid.
162. The motto of medieval monasticism "Pray and work" is not so formulated by Augustine in his writings, but it corresponds with his thinking and is one of the basic ideas of *The Work of Monks.*
163. Weinand, *Antike und moderne Gedanken über die Arbeit,* pp. 10–18, and Holzapfel, *Die sittliche Wertung der körperlichen Arbeit,* pp. 16–25.
164. *The Work of Monks* 13.14.
165. Cf. *The Literal Meaning of Genesis* 8.8ff.; and Mausbach, *Die Ethik,* I 314ff.
166. *Christian Instruction* 1.3f.3f. See below, pp. 211–12.
167. *The Literal Meaning of Genesis* 8.8.15 and 8.9.18.
168. *Exposition on Psalm 138* 1.
169. *Exposition on Psalm 102* 17. Cf. *Exposition on Psalm 90* 2.13 and *Exposition on Psalm 93* 23f.
170. *The Work of Monks* 29.37.
171. Ibid. 25.32.
172. Ibid. 3ff.4ff.
173. Ibid. 17.20.
174. Ibid. 25.33. If in this Augustine alleviates the obligation to manual labor for monks of a higher social standing, we should see in it, not the survival of ancient standards (as Weinand, *Antike und modern Gedanken über die Arbeit,* p. 56, maintains), but rather a consideration for their lack of strength and skills. Cf. Holzapfel, *Die sittliche Wertung der körperlichen Arbeit,* p. 134.
175. *The Work of Monks* 16.19. Cf. also J. Pintard, *Le Sacerdoce selon saint Augustin* (Paris, 1960), pp. 281–85. The reproach that Augustine showed himself lacking in true Catholic spirit in insisting on the general obligation of monks—and, indeed, of all Christians—to perform manual work is unjustified. Cf. Mausbach, *Die Ethik,* I 430ff.
176. *The Work of Monks* 16.19.
177. Ibid. 25.33.
178. Ibid. 28.36.
179. Ibid. 25.32.
180. Ibid.
181. Ibid.
182. *Letter 130* 20.
183. *The Work of Monks* 17.20.
184. *Letter 48* 3.
185. Benedict himself was strongly influenced by Augustine in his own monastic work ethic. He knew *The Work of Monks* and quoted it in his *Rule* 48. See Linderbauer 67, Butler 88, Steidle 156ff. See above, p. 78 and note 36.
186. Cf. Holzapfel, *Die sittliche Wertung der körperlichen Arbeit,* p. 146.

More recently, P. Nagel (*Die Motivierung der Askese*, pp. 98–101) has shown that the labor of the Egyptian monks was valued not only as an insurance against idleness and a means of self-improvement, but also because they would not be a burden on others and could support the poor with what they themselves did not require.

187. *The Ways of the Catholic Church* 1.31.66. But Augustine countered such criticism by showing the value of the Egyptian anchorites' example and prayers for society.

188. Holzapfel, *Die sittliche Wertung der körperlichen Arbeit*, pp. 134ff.

189. Ibid., p. 136. Cf. von Sokolowski, *Der heilige Augustin und die christliche Zivilisation*, p. 140.

190. Cf. on this entire section, Mausbach, *Die Ethik*, I 264ff., 427ff.; and P. Dessauer, "Geist des Abendlandes: *Regula Benedicti*," *Hochland*, 39 (1947), 508f.

191. Cf. *Letter 21*; *Sermon 355* 2; Possidius 3f.

192. *Letter 21* 1 and Possidus 4.

193. For sources, see above, note 79.

194. *The Work of Monks* 29.37. Cf. also *Exposition on Psalm 38* 4f. and *Against Faustus* 22.57f.

195. *Letter 21* 3. Cf. Zähringer, *Das kirchliche Priestertum*, pp. 121ff.; Pintard, *Le Sacerdoce*, pp. 239ff. See also van der Meer, *Augustinus de Zielzorger*, pp. 25f.; Zumkeller, "Das Charakterbild des Seelsorgers," 63–74; M. Pellegrino, *Verus sacerdos: Il sacerdozio nell'esperienza e nel pensiero di sant' Agostino* (Fossano, 1965).

196. *Letter 21* 1.

197. Cf. *Exposition on Psalm 106* 7.

198. *Sermon 339* 4.

199. Cf. *Questions about the Heptateuch* 2.119.

200. *Letter 21* 4. Cf. *The Ways of the Catholic Church* 1.32.69.

201. *Sermon 46* 6.

202. *The Ways of the Catholic Church* 1.32.69.

203. *Letter 250* 3.

204. Cf. *Sermon 135* 6f.

205. *Letter 21* 2.

206. *Exposition on Psalm 50* 13.

207. Ibid. Cf. also *The Eight Questions of Dulcitius* 3.6.

208. *Sermon 339* 4.

209. Ibid. 2.

210. Ibid. 1.

211. Manrique, *La vida monastica*, p. 363*n*, has pointed out that Augustine uses the expressions "contemplative life" (*vita contemplativa*) and "active life" (*vita activa*) in different senses. In this section I am using "contemplative life" to designate what Augustine understood as "a life of retreat, dedicated to God for study, prayer, and work" ("una vida de retiro consagrada a Dios por el estudio, la oración y el trabajo"). In contrast, "active life"

in this section means primarily the "total consecration of the person to souls" ("consagración total de la persona al bien espiritual de las almas").

212. Cf. *Letter 21* 6.

213. *Christian Instruction* 4.15.32 and 4.30.60.

214. *Exposition on Psalm 103* 2.4.

215. *Christian Instruction* 4.27.59f Cf. A. Brucculeri, "Il pensiero sociale di S. Agostino: La formazione sacerdotale," *La civiltà cattolica*, 83, No. 2 (1932), 448f.

216. Cf. also Popp, *Sankt Augustin als Erzieher*, p. 10.

217. Cf. *Letter 21* 5.

218. Cf. Brucculeri, "Il pensiero sociale di S. Agostino: La formazione sacerdotale," 437–51, and Kunzelmann, "Augustins Predigttätigkeit," pp. 158ff.

219. Cf. *Letter 21* 4.

220. *Christian Instruction* 2.16ff.23ff. Cf. Brucculeri, "Il pensiero sociale di S. Agostino: La formazione sacerdotale," pp. 440ff. Augustine counted the study of mathematics and arithmetic among "the sweets of life," and regretted that he did not have more time to give to it. He thought it well fitted to train the intellect and to lead to a deeper perception of truth (cf. A. Schmitt, "Mathematik und Zahlenmystik," in *Aurelius Augustinus*, edd. M. Grabmann and J. Mausbach [Cologne, 1930], pp. 353f.). He is not so enthusiastic about rhetoric. It is true that he had a regard for eloquence, with which to adorn sermons; but he did not demand from his clergy any extensive knowledge of the subtleties of classical rhetoric. He thought it better that teachers discourage over-eloquence in preachers than that the people not know what they were talking about (*Exposition on Psalm 138* 20, and Kunzelmann, "Augustins Predigttätigkeit," p. 159. Cf. also A. Schmitt, "Aus der Predigtwelt des heiligen Augustinus," BMS, 23 [1947], 210ff.). On the setbacks which Augustine's theological program encountered, despite his efforts, because of the general decline in culture standards in his time, see Marrou, *Saint Augustin et la fin de la culture antique*, pp. 398ff.

221. *Letter 55* 21.39.

222. *Sermon 354* 6.

223. *The Work of Monks* 29.37 and *Exposition on Psalm 99* 12.

224. The latest study of contemplation and action in Augustine is Morán's *El Equilibrio*, pp. 210–30. In a detailed analysis of the relevant texts from *The Trinity*, Morán presents Augustine's conception of the close inner connection between contemplation and action, as he formulated it, for example, in this sentence: "We have tried to achieve some reasonable union of contemplation and action in the mind of each individual man, since the functions are divided between the two, while the unity of the mind is preserved in both" (*The Trinity* 12.12.19).

225. *The City of God* 19.19. Cf. *Against Faustus* 22.57f. See also Wucherer-Huldenfeld, "Mönchtum und kirchlicher Dienst," 208f.

226. Cf. *Sermon 104* 3f.

227. *Sermon 339* 4.

228. Cf. *Sermon 103* 5f.; *Sermon 104* 3; *The Literal Meaning of Genesis* 4.14ff.25ff. See also Mausbach, *Die Ethik*, I 370f.

229. *Letter 48* 3 Cf. on this H. Urs von Balthasar, "Aktion und Kontemplation," *Geist und Leben*, 21 (1948), 361–70.

230. *Sermon 104* 4. In *Against Faustus* 22.56ff. Augustine typifies the two ways of life with Lia and Rachel, the two sisters in the Old Testament, as he does here with Martha and Mary.

231. Possidius 24.

232. Ibid.

233. Cf. *The Work of Monks* 29.37.

234. Possidius 19ff., 27.

235. Cf. Manrique, *Teologia agustiniana de la vida religiosa*, p. 361, and idem, "Orientación monastica de San Agustín: Acción o contemplación?" RAE, I (1960), 225–34.

236. Cf. *Exposition on Psalm 132* 9: "... Christ, who is our head, finds an entrance through brotherly unity, ... that the Church may cling to Him ..."; and *Homily on St. John's Gospel 13* 12: "... the holy integrity of men ... exists in the Church, and it is a more honorable member." See also above, pp. 110–11.

237. *Letter 48* 2.

238. *Letter 243* 8. Cf. also *Homily on St. John's Gospel 57* 3f.

239. *Sermon 355* 1.

240. See also above, p. 35 and the passages quoted in note 92. Cf., above all, *Confessions* 10.43.70.

241. *Against Faustus* 22.57.

242. "... we are not accustomed to admit to the clergy even those who remain in the monastery, unless they are more worthy and of better character" (*Letter 60* 1). Cf. also Possidius 11.

243. So Hendrikx, "Augustinus als Monnik," 346. For the entire passage, cf. A. Zumkeller, "Augustinus and das Mönchtum," *L'Année Théologique*, 14 (1954), 108ff.

244. *Sermon 78* 3 and 6. Cf. also Wucherer-Huldenfeld, "Mönchtum und kirchlicher Dienst," 211.

245. *Rule* 1.2. See above, pp. 124–27.

246. *Rule* 5.2. See above, pp. 153–54.

247. See, for example, *Letter 134* 1; *The Work of Monks* 29.37; *Against the Writings of Petilian* 3.1.2; *Homily on St. John's Epistle to the Parthi 5* 11; *Sermo Guelferbytanus 32* 2f., in Morin, pp. 564ff.; Possidius 18.

248. *Rule* 5.2 and *Sermon 78* 6.

249. *On 83 Various Questions*, question 71 1.

8

The Conduct of Monastic Life

To Augustine monastic profession (*professio*) meant a change in the conduct of one's life. It presupposed a sort of conversion (*conversio*)[1]—not that fundamental conversion through repentance and the reversal of the will which a man achieves when he turns away from serving false gods to serving "the true God."[2] In this case, Augustine was much more concerned with a new and special meaning of the word.[3] Its content is a decision to live a celibate life, the renunciation of "hope in this world,"[4] and a promising of oneself "in a freely chosen servitude to God"[5] in a monastic life of poverty and asceticism.[6] Mindful of St. Paul's words (1 Cor. 14:47ff.), Augustine demanded of his monks, as they did this, that they lay aside that image (*imago*) of the earthly Adam which they had borne until then, in order to carry the image of the second Adam, who had come down from heaven.[7]

The monastic way of life built on this conversion is characterized by renunciation of the "world," "denial of oneself," Christian humility, and a celibate chastity dedicated to God.

RENUNCIATION OF THE LOVE OF THE WORLD (*amor mundi*)

What St. John wrote in his First Epistle (2:15)—"Love not the world, nor the things of the world"—is very important for Augustine's spirituality. But to understand this renunciation of the love of the world (*amor mundi*), which Augustine required not only from "the servants of God but from every Christian, for what it is, one must observe carefully that Augustine uses the term "world" (*mundus* or *saeculum*) in many different senses, as Sacred Scripture did, which he has in mind. He wrote of the world as God's creation (*mundus, quem fecit Deus*) and again as the devil's empire (*mundus, quem regit diabolus*);[8] of the "good world" (*mundus bonus*) and the "evil world" (*mundus malus*);[9] and of the "world condemned" (*mundus damnatus, mundus hostilis*) and the "world redeemed" (*mundus redemptus, mundus reconciliatus*).[10] At times he contrasts the "world" with the "monastery."[11] In these various contraries he indicates the tension that he—always appealing to the New Testament—saw in a Christian's relationship to the world.[12]

Augustine's Esteem for the Created World (mundus creatus) *and for Man's Earthly Tasks*

The world—heaven, earth, sea, and all that is in them, beings endowed with reason not excepted—was for Augustine in the first place God's creation (*creatura, fabrica*).[13] He vigorously defended it as the good God's good work, and opposed the dualistic notions of the Manichaeans and the Priscillianists.[14] Again and again he returns to write of the goodness and beauty of this created world, in which the Creator God's greatness, beauty, and love are manifested.[15]

He held that no Christian could be apathetic or hostile in his attitude toward this created world (*mundus creatus*). Even in Paradise, God Himself had entrusted men with the world, "to till it and to keep it" (Gen. 2:15). Thus, he wrote, "what God had created should unfold itself, through the help of human labor, for man's happiness and profit."[16] And he described the knowledge which human civilization had since acquired as "magnificent, and all that is thoroughly suited to man."[17]

Without question, the created world, with all its benefits for man, cannot be his last home, but only his place of pilgrimage.[18] So, Augustine admonished, let us not reject these benefits, "as if they were not provisions of Divine Providence, lovely in their own fashion; yet let us not love them as if through their enjoyment alone we could be happy."[19] Augustine taught that what determines if a man's attitude toward the created world is in accordance with the divine will is whether man understands how to use it properly: "if we want to return to our native land, where we may be blessed, we must make use of this world, but not rejoice in it, . . . so that we, with the help of things that are bodily and temporal, may obtain for ourselves things that are eternal and of the spirit."[20]

Thus, his attitude toward the created world was in principle positive. He saw that world as a field of action, ordained by the Creator for man, for his physical and spiritual abilities, and the way God had willed for him to achieve his eternal destiny. He does not think that it was any inherent fault in the world that it could also be a source of dangers and errors for man; that, in his view, was rooted in man's sinful disposition.[21]

A World Opposed to God (mundus malus)
and Sinful Love of It (amor mundi)

To the world as God's creation, Augustine opposed the world as the devil's empire,[22] which he also described as the "wicked" and "rejected" world (*mundus malus, mundus damnatus*).[23] This world has not existed since the beginning of creation, but came into existence only with the Fall. By the "wicked world," Augustine understood, as does Holy Scripture (cf. John 1:10), "evil men," and by their "prince" (*rector*; cf. Eph. 6:12), the devil.[24] This world of evil appeared to him as a horrible travesty of the Mystical Body; for Satan, too, is closely united with all his damned, as are the Body's head and all His members.[25] This is the communion of evil spirits and of men who have rejected God which, as the "city of this world," the "city of the devil" (*civitas terrena, civitas huius mundi, civitas diaboli*), Augustine contrasts, in the twenty-two books of *The City of God*, with the City of God, the communion of all angels and of God-fearing men.

The distinguishing mark of the "evil world," that is, of "wicked men" (*homines mali, peccatores, iniqui, superbi infideles*), Augustine perceives in their "love of the world."[26] They have gone astray in their earthly desires, in their "gratification of the eyes, of the flesh, the empty pomp of living" (1 John 2:16).[27] They pay no heed to the "Lift up your hearts" (*Sursum corda*) of the Christian message. Thus, their life is not hidden with Christ in God (cf. Col. 3:3), but flowers only here in this world, because "all their longing and love are imprisoned here, wear themselves out, wander in a wilderness."[28]

Augustine often illustrated the essence of this false attitude toward the world with the aid of his typical contradistinctions "delighting in the world"/"using the world" (*frui mundo/uti mundo*), "desiring"/"loving" (*cupiditas/caritas*), "love of the world"/"love of God" (*amor mundi/amor Dei*).[29] To the concepts of "delighting" and "using" he attributes the following sense: "delighting" means surrendering onself in love to some object for its own sake; "using" means employing an object to achieve what one loves,[30] or loving the object only for the sake of some other object.[31] But those objects that are set apart for man to delight in would lead him to blessedness; but delighting in those he ought only to use would hinder him on his way to blessedness (*beatitudo*) or lead him astray entirely.[32]

In this given sense, the object of delight, in Augustine's view, can only be God for His own sake, and man's own self, and his fellow-man, for God's own sake. When man in this fashion turns to God, to himself, or to his neighbor, it is love (*caritas*) that is driving him, a well-ordered love (*ordinata dilectio*), a love of God (*amor Dei*). But when he is striving for delight in his own self, in his fellow-men, or in material possessions, and not for God's sake, then cupidity (*cupiditas*), the sinful love of the world (*amor mundi*), is ruling him.[33] For in this creatures are being sought as a final goal, whereas we, as far as they are at our disposal, ought to employ them only for the sake of God (*ad Deum*), and as far as they are our equals, ought to enjoy them only in God (*in Deo*).[34]

From this it follows that Augustine did not reject every kind of love for the world.[35] In his sermon on 1 John 2:12ff., he posed the question to himself: "So why may I not love what God has made?" His answer was "God does not order you not to love [*amare*] His creatures, just not to love them so that you find your blessedness in them [*diligere ad beatitudinem*]; what you may do is to know them and to praise them, so as to love the Creator."[36] To illustrate his point of view he makes a reflective comparison: "If a bridegroom had a ring made for his bride, and if she were to love the ring he gave her more than she loved him, would she not be considered, with regard to the bridegroom's gift, as unfaithful, even though all she loved was what the bridegroom had given her?" So, too, would the man be found guilty of infidelity (*amor adulterinus*) who loved the good things of the created world and neglected their Creator.[37]

In *The City of God* Augustine saw two different principles and laws of life in the two "states" that were represented by these two different kinds of love. "It was love of two sorts that founded these states: the state of this world was founded on a self-love that has grown into contempt for God; the heavenly state, on a love of God that led to contempt for oneself. The one boasts of itself; the other, of the Lord."[38] This "evil love of the world" (*malus amor mundi*),[39] which, he taught, inspires a world devoid of God (*mundus malus*), conforms to the principle of life of the earthly state (*civitas terrestris*) he described, turning away from God to itself and to the created world, and thus reaching a contempt for God. Augustine therefore shared with St. John (1 John 2:15) the conviction that this sort of love of the world cannot be reconciled with a love of God: "For how could such a love take root in such a jungle as earthly love is?"[40]

Augustine's writings and sermons show how his conception of an "evil world," turned away from God, dominated his cosmology. He thinks of it chiefly as a world that is "hostile," "persecuting," and "savage" (*mundus hostilis*, *mundus persequens*, *mundus saeviens*), and plotting against those who fear God and preparing persecutions for them;[41] it is a "deceitful world" (*mundus fallax*), trying with its lies and trickery to pry men loose from God;[42] it is the "seductive world," to whose temptations men so easily succumb.[43]

Therefore Augustine never wearied of warning men against this world's dangers and against love of it.[44] He compared it with the sea across which Peter walked (Matt. 14:24ff.), calling the cupidity in every man's heart the storm that threatened him. "If you love God, then you are walking on the waters. . . . If you love the world, it will swallow you. . . . But if your heart is thrown here and there by evil desires, call upon Christ's divinity, that you may conquer them."[45] In another sermon he recommended that we impose a constant fast upon ourselves, not by forgoing some dish or other, which will happen only occasionally, but by forgoing the love of the world, which ought to happen all the time. He justifies the necessity for this with arguments that are wholly eschatological. Man cannot love what is eternal until he stops loving what is of time. He appeals to St. Paul (1 Cor. 7:29): "Brethren, time is passing away. . . . Therefore those who make use of this world should live as if they did not, for the ways of the world will soon have an end." True, it is not everyone's duty and vocation to renounce all his possessions; but every Christian should "possess what he has in this world, not be possessed by it, be its master and not be mastered by it; be the lord of what he has, not its slave."[46]

Even if Augustine's view of the threats presented by this evil world to a Christian is a realistic one, still he describes how they must be combated in terms full of Christian hope and confidence. He understands how to encourage and console his children. "Is love of this world dragging you down? Hold fast to Christ! For your sake He came into the world, that you might come into eternity."[47] In another sermon he demonstrates that even if the world may threaten the Church, it cannot conquer or extinguish the Church. Undoubtedly "many fall, but the [Lord's] house is still standing; many are in great perturbation, but that house will not fall in ruins."[48] And he saw benefits to be gained from this hostility. He compared it with the goldsmith's oven, in which heat purifies the gold of its dross: "The world is the oven, the dross is evil men; the gold is the good, the fire is hostility; and the goldsmith is God." In His plan for man's salvation, the world with its troubles and temptations (*tribulatio*, *tentatio*) will in the end serve for good men's purification and perfection.[49]

The World Redeemed (mundus reconciliatus)*, Christian Love, and Contempt for the World*

There is a third conception of what "the world" is which occurs repeatedly in Augustine's writings and sermons: namely, the designation of "redeemed humanity," the Church. It was for him the "world reconciled" (*mundus reconciliatus*), in which he was alluding to 2 Corinthians 5:19: "God through Christ has reconciled the world to Himself"; or the "world rescued" (*mundus salvatus*), in the sense of John 3:16: "The Son of Man did not come into the world to reject it, but so that the world might be saved through Him"; and, finally, it was the "world purified" (*mundus mundatus*) of sin, following St. John, who called Jesus Christ the reconciliation for the sins of the entire world (1 John 2:1ff.).[50] And it was this world, reconciled, rescued, purified in Christ, that "had been chosen out of the rejected and besmirched world, which hates God."[51]

Augustine insisted that the choosing of this "world reconciled" was an operation wholly of grace. Its members "were chosen not for their merits, for they had not as yet performed any good works, and not for any natural causes, for the whole of nature, of its own free choice, had poisoned itself at its roots, but without consideration of merit—that is, out of true grace."[52] This, he thought, confirmed what St. Paul wrote (Rom. 9:21ff.) about the "vessels of mercy" and the "vessels of wrath," both fashioned from "the same lump," that lump "which is all men who had perished in Adam." By the "vessels of mercy" is meant the world made for reconciliation; whereas the "vessels of wrath" pertained to the world rejected, "made for destruction."[53] Augustine is treating of the unfathomable mystery of the election of divine grace, as an aspect of his doctrine of predestination, in the manner typical of his anti-Pelagian period, and forming his conception of the "world reconciled" and the "world rejected."[54]

Quoting John 15:18, he wrote at length of the true and false love of the world. With love and hatred of the rejected world, he contrasts love and hatred of the redeemed world. The world made for destruction "will say that it loves itself, because it loves that evil by which it itself is evil; and then it will say that it hates itself, because it loves what is harmful to it. Thus, it hates nature in itself and loves sickness; it hates what was created by God's goodness, and loves what was set in motion in it by its own free will."[55] The love and hatred of the redeemed world are quite differently manifested:

> For we too, if we understand it rightly, are both commanded to love the world and forbidden to love the world. We are forbidden where it says "Do not love the world" [1 John 2:15], but we are commanded where it says "Love your enemies" [Luke 6:27]. For our enemies are the world that hates us. Thus we are forbidden to love in the world what it loves in itself, and we are commanded to love in it what it hates in itself—that is, the work of God's creation and the various consolations of His goodness.[56]

So, for Augustine, it is the company of those redeemed in Christ which is this "holy, good, reconciled, and saved world." He recognizes, indeed, that, in St. Paul's words (Rom. 8:24), it is here only "saved in hope." He thinks it more cogent to speak, not of a "world that is saved" (*mundus salvatus*), but of "a world to be saved" (*mundus salvandus*)—that is, of that world whose salvation is only now being perfected in those elected by God's decree.[57]

The World and the Monastery (saeculum/monasterium)

Augustine once described his own decision to become a servant of God in the sentence "I set myself apart from those who love the world."[58] And in the same context he affirmed: "I had abandoned all hope in the world."[59] In the first affirmation he may have had in mind that sinful love of the world described in 1 John 2:15, but there is no doubt that by "hope in the world" he meant his coveted appointment as a rhetorician and the prospects it had offered of promotion to higher state offices. He had similar considerations in mind when in another place he called the monastic life "a retreat from worldly cares, so as to learn how to live."[60]

In the *Rule*, too, "world" (*saeculum*) and "monastery" (*monasterium*) are to some extent regarded as opposites, although *saeculum* is regularly used to mean only the dwelling places and activities of men "outside" the monastery.[61] There is an implied contradiction in this: for a portion of the monastery's inmates life in the *saeculum* had been one of worldly honors,[62] riches,[63] and opulence,[64] whereas, by entering the monastery, they had taken upon themselves a life of humility,[65] poverty,[66] and moderation.[67]

By this Augustine was in no way seeking to assert that life outside the monastery bore the marks of the "evil world," a world alienated from God. Nor did he think that Christians outside the monastery did not belong to the "redeemed world." In one sermon he had occasion to speak of the general obligation of Christians to keep themselves free of any sinful love of the world and, dealing with not becoming enslaved by earthly possessions, he expressly said: "If anyone can do this, and perfection requires it of him, let him renounce all his possessions. But if any necessity prevents him from doing this, he may well retain what he owns."[68] But there is one deciding condition: "he must be the lord of his possessions, and not their slave";[69] that is, the world and its riches may be for him only objects for use, not a final goal.

It is essential that we understand that the concepts "world" and "monastery" in Augustine's writings do not carry with them the same notion of contradiction we find in what he wrote of the "evil world" and the "reconciled world." He was more concerned with the different spheres of activity in which Christians' lives ought to develop, according to the different gifts God has given them.[70] There is no doubt that he was convinced that life in a monastery, with its voluntary renunciation of personal possessions and of marriage, "for the sake of the kingdom of heaven," was an especially suitable means not only of keeping the heart free of sinful love of the world and of cupidity, but also of making it grow in the love of God.[71]

MORTIFICATION AND SELF-DENIAL
(*mortificatio carnis* and *abnegatio sui*)

Arguing from Sacred Scripture (cf. Rom. 8:13, 2 Cor. 4:10, Col. 3:5, Matt. 16:24, Mark 8:34, Luke 9:23), Augustine maintained that mortification and self-denial were basic requirements for the Christian life in this world. To form a better judgment on his individual arguments for the necessity of ascetic renunciation and, especially, on his views on monastic self-denial, it will be useful to study them in their relation to his teachings about the body and its passions.

The Body's Worth

Augustine defined man as "a rational soul, which employs a mortal and earthly body."[72] Despite this Platonic-sounding formulation which Plato himself would have interpreted as implying a somewhat loose union between the body and the soul, Augustine considered them closely bound together. In his view, only body and soul together constitute the whole man.[73] And, unlike Plato, he regarded the union, not as a punishment, but as an expression of a wise Creator's will.[74] Furthermore, he saw the human soul, if not as the body's substantial form in the Aristotelian sense, still as its individual principle of life,[75] and he allied this thought with the quite un-Platonic idea that the soul is filled with a "natural longing" (*naturaliter velle*) for the body.[76]

Not only man's soul but his body as well is created by God and is therefore good.[77] In the hierarchical ordering of what is good and of value, the body, contrasted with the "great good" (*bonum magnum*) of the soul, possesses only a "lesser good" (*bonum infimum*), yet in truth it is a "good" (*bonum*)[78] that we may not despise. To be sure, St. Paul wrote: "The desires of the flesh are at war with the spirit, and the spirit's with the flesh" (Gal. 5:17), but he also wrote: "No man has ever hated his own flesh, but nourishes and cherishes it as Christ does His Church" (Eph. 5:29). Augustine reprimands the man who despises the body: "You should be afraid of what you are thinking! You consider that the body is a dungeon, but who loves his dungeon?"[79]

Thus he constantly opposed the Manichaean hatred of the body,[80] and attacked Porphyry for his contempt of it.[81] Nor in his criticisms did he spare Origen, who had subscribed to the Platonic notion of the body as the soul's "prison" (*ergastulum*).[82] Though Augustine himself, even later than this period, employs the inadequate Platonic images of "the soul's clothing" (*vestimentum animae*) and "the soul's conveyance" (*vehiculum animae*)[83] to describe the body, still he states: "There is a kind of marriage between spirit and flesh."[84] Such values show Augustine's basic agreement with St. Paul, which he makes very clear by citing Paul's metaphor of married love to signify Christ's love for His Church and man's proper care for his body (Eph. 5:25ff.), his frequent use of the image of the body and its members to illustrate the mystery of the Church, and his view of the risen body of the Lord as a pledge of the resurrection and glorification of our own mortal bodies (cf. Rom. 8:11).[85]

Augustine was convinced that in Paradise man's body and soul were in complete harmony with one another, and that then there was no conflict between the flesh and the spirit,[86] and that through the Fall that good order in man which God had willed for him was disturbed. He taught that this disorder in sinful man manifests itself above all in the destruction of the harmony between body and soul that had existed in Paradise, in the rebellion of the desires of the flesh against the spirit, in that concupiscence he saw manifesting itself "not exclusively, but preponderantly in the soul's sensory powers, and most especially in the sexual instincts."[87] And for him concupiscence was, "not the pleasures of the senses, in the physiological sense, pleasures of which man can make good use, but the disobedience of the flesh [*inobedientia carnis*], through which the lawful and good use of the senses in sexuality—as, for example, in eating and drinking—suffers a certain overshadowing or limitation of man's higher spiritual functioning."[88]

Augustine had come to believe that in a certain sense one might describe the body as the soul's "prison" (*carcer*), "not because what God has created is a prison, but because it has been surrendered to punishment and death."[89] The body has been made into the soul's "heaviest bond" (*vinculum*),[90] its grave (*sepulcrum*),[91] into an oppressive load (*pondus*; cf. Wis. 9:15), weighing the soul down and often refusing to obey it.[92] These, again, are terms borrowed from Platonism, which Augustine employs here for the body of fallen men, but in a wholly Christian sense and intention.[93] "In our bodies two things are to be seen," he said in a sermon,

> what God created, and the punishment we have deserved. Our whole formation, our walking, our standing, our well-ordered limbs, our endowment with senses, seeing, hearing, smelling, tasting, and touching, the complete coordination and the organization of our structure only God could have achieved, He who made everything, in Heaven and on the earth, what is highest and what is lowest, what can be seen and what is invisible. But what in this has merited that we be punished? This is because our flesh has been delivered over to corruptibility; it is frail, mortal, and indigent. . . . If thus your flesh is a prison, it is not your body that is the prison but your body's corruption.[94]

And through the mystery of the Incarnation man's body was redeemed and raised to a new dignity.[95] Augustine often used Pauline images to designate the Christian's body, calling it "a member of Christ," "the temple of the Holy Spirit," and stressing that it is a Christian's calling to glorify God in his own body (cf. 1 Cor. 6:20).[96] "The bodies of the faithful," he wrote, "are sacrificial offerings to God, members of Christ, and the temple of the Holy Spirit."[97] And yet "this easy harmony of the whole man, his body and his soul," is for Augustine an idealization to be achieved only at the resurrection of the dead.[98] "As long as the flesh is borne down by the weight of its mortal condition," he said in a sermon, "it cannot yet have that dignity that its glorified form in heaven will manifest."[99]

There is no doubt that Augustine continued both to refute Manichaean and Neoplatonic notions of a "natural antipathy between the spiritual and the fleshly-sensory," especially in his use of Scripture, and to acknowledge the importance of man's bodily nature. Nonetheless, the ethical "distinction between closeness to God and remoteness from Him, between the service of God and the service to the world, between life beyond the grave and life here and now," which is essential to the Biblical teaching about the Fall and Redemption, was expressed in Augustine's thought with growing authority, and at times harshly.[100] He laid great stress on the tension between body and spirit, especially after the beginnings of his controversies with Pelagius and his followers. He was fond of appealing to Scriptural passages, such as Galatians 5:17 on the "lusting of the flesh against the spirit," or Romans 7:14–25, one that in the last two decades of his life he understood as applying not merely to unredeemed man but also to the baptized.[101] Correspondingly, although he would admit to taking pleasure in earthly and sensory things as a principle,[102] he defined limits, often too narrow, to what was permissible.[103]

In considering the imbalance which in many respects is to be found in Augustine's conception of the relationship between body and soul, various writers have tended to believe that there was in it either an imperfectly healed Platonic dualism,[104] or else the remnants of Manichaean notions[105] he had not yet overcome. But in this perhaps they have failed to observe that his remarks about man's existence in body and soul—despite their occasional asperities[106]—closely correspond with the Bible's presentation, concrete and existential, of human nature,[107] and that even in the New Testament the tension between body and soul is emphasized, at times sharply.

Judgments on the Passions

Augustine's deep preoccupation with Scripture after his ordination to the priesthood also helped him to achieve a more positive attitude toward human affections and passions (*affectus et passiones*). At the beginning, after his baptism, when he was still under the influence of Stoic notions about apathy, "non-feeling," he had greatly distrusted them.[108] More and more the conviction grew in him that man's emotional life, since it is willed and created by God, is good in itself.[109] He dealt at length with this topic in *The City of God.* To designate perturbation of the emotions he used the Greek word πάθη (*passiones*) and the Latin terms *perturbationes, affectiones,* or *affectus* ("disturbances," "affections").[110] He made it very clear that in the soul there are not only affections of largely physical origin, but also those that are spiritual.[111] As philosophers of his day did, he called the four typical human affections "desire" (*cupiditas/concupiscentia*), "fear" (*timor*), "joy" (*laetitia*), and "sorrow" (*tristitia*).[112] His views developed as he moved away from the Stoic teaching that these affections (*passiones*) are sicknesses (*morbi*) with which the soul is afflicted through the members of the body[113] and from which, accordingly, a wise man should free himself.[114]

Against this, Augustine ruled that these affections and passions are morally indeterminate powers, becoming meritorious or culpable only through the exercise of a good or an evil will.[115] He wrote: "Both good men and bad are filled with desire, fear, or joy, some, indeed, to their own good, others to their harm, according to the just or perverted disposition of their will."[116] If the affections are to be well ordered, what will be decisive is that man should live "by the spirit and not by the flesh, that is, by God and not by himself."[117] Augustine proved by many quotations from both the Old and the New Testaments that the Christian can and should put these varied and powerful emotions to the service of the good.[118] Indeed, Holy Writ tells how strongly Christ Himself was moved by anger, joy, longing, and sorrow.[119] He concluded: "According to Sacred Scripture and sound doctrine, the citizens of the heavenly City of God, as they journey on the pilgrimage of this life, although they live for God, will be filled with fear and longing, will feel pain and joy. But because their love is a just love, all their affections are in proper order."[120]

To conclude: Augustine passed a clear judgment on "not-feeling" (ἀπάθεια, *impassibilitas*).[121] If by the term one is to understand that "man is living free from those affections that rebel against the reason and bewilder the spirit," Augustine thought that this was a noble ideal that could never be realized in this life, because 1 John 1:8 tells us that here on earth no one is free from sin.[122] But if one gives "not-feeling" its extreme Stoic interpretation, "that there is no affection at all which is able to stir in the soul," then he thought that one must call such "apathy" (*stupor*) vicious in the extreme. In that, not only did he see an opposition, impossible to gloss over, to the Christian conviction that man's perfect blessedness will partake of love and joy (*amor et gaudium*);[123] but he considered such a want of affection unnatural because without affection man is not "living rightly."[124] He mentions a third meaning of "not-feeling." One could also understand by the term a freedom from every fear and every pain. But that would be that ideal existence Christ has promised us not in this earthly life, but certainly for eternity.[125]

These essentially positive values given to the affections and passions—which to some extent contradict Ambrose's teaching—represent an important advance,[126] yet Augustine knew well that because of the Fall man's passions have become a source of danger. They rise up in him to fight against reason, they confuse him, they try to enslave him, and, seen as such, in Augustine's view, are a misfortune.[127] Thus, it must be a Christian's constant concern not to let himself be led astray by uncontrolled passions, to moderate them, to motify them, as St. Paul wrote in Galatians 5:24: "But those who belong to Jesus Christ have crucified their flesh with its passions and desires." Without this mortification of the passions, Augustine believed that something evil would remain (*perturbationes et libidines et concupiscentiae malae*).[128] Setting men free from the yoke of these disturbances was one of Augustine's chief concerns as a spiritual director.

Yet he was not intent on destroying the passions and affections. The "flesh" should not be hunted down as an enemy, but tended and bridled.[129] Wanting to exterminate the passons would be not only unnatural but impossible. One can suppress them; one cannot extinguish them.[130] In opposition to the Stoic ideal of "not-feeling," Augustine wanted to overcome and master the passions and desires. They must be tamed and checked, as a horseman tames and checks his steed.[131] And using the reins wisely, now slack, now tight, will be important.[132]

But there is more: in Augustine's view, even men's passions and affections can be made to serve justice.[133] He cited famous instances from the Old and New Testaments to show the sense in which he meant this. He points to the passionate way (*animi motus*) in which Moses struck at the Egyptians; later, as he led his people, this bore fruits of virtue. He wrote of the "savageness" (*saevitia*) with which Saul persecuted the Church in his zeal for the traditions of the fathers; but this was a portent of the rich harvest that as an apostle he brought home. Finally, he wrote of the "animosity" (*animositas*) with which Peter struck off Malchus' ear; this, too, later brought profits when Peter became the shepherd of the Church.[134]

Motives for Mortification

As we might expect, the marked influence that Neoplatonic and Stoic ideas about the body and the affections exerted on Augustine in the years immediately after his conversion found echoes in this early writing, as he reasoned over ascetic renunciation. Some of his arguments were typical of these schools of thought. For example, in the *Retractations* he blames himself for having written in 387, in *The Immortality of the Soul*, that it would be a great benefit for the soul "to be without a body,"[135] and for having defined, in the *Soliloquies*, written at the same time, that a "complete flight from things of the senses" would be a prerequisite for a perfect knowledge of God.[136] Later, he repeatedly and specifically rejected this basic tenet of Neoplatonic asceticism—in Porphyry's formulation, "everything corporeal is to be shunned"—and he sought to demonstrate that it was untenable.[137] It has also been indicated several times that in the early days after his conversion the Stoic ideal of "not-feeling" influenced his ascetic endeavors and his writing.[138]

As he delved further into Biblical thinking, he rejected more and more of these Neoplatonic and Stoic legacies. The mortification of the flesh (*mortificatio carnis*) and the denial of oneself (*abnegatio sui*), he came to see, were essentially Christ-like, deeply rooted in the teaching and the example of the Lord.

According to Augustine, mortification and self-denial in the life of a Christian have an entirely positive objective: to help him restore and strengthen in his own heart the proper order disturbed as a result of the Fall and sin.[139] He should destroy, "not the body, but its concupiscence," Augustine wrote in *Christian Instruction*; "that is, he should destroy his evil habits, completely master them, and make them as subject to the spirit as nature's good order requires. Thus, the spirit's contribution to this mastery of the flesh is that it frees men from reprehensible acquiescence in evil habits and enables the peace that good habits bring to make its way in."[140]

"But since," as he said once in a sermon, "it is hard to use what is permitted only to the extent that one does not go beyond moderation, even a little,"[141] Augustine therefore considered it necessary to forgo even what is permitted. For "anyone who cannot deny himself what he is allowed is coming very close to what is forbidden."[142]

Yet, with all this, ascetic self-denial has a higher aim. Fasting and other works of mortification, for Augustine, were expressions of man's longing for God, for the society of the angels, and for the joys of heaven.[143] When he was asked the reason for the Church's fasts, he replied: "If one renounces fleshly joy [*laetitia carnis*], one receives spiritual joy [*laetitia mentis*] in exchange."[144] And in his *Confessions* he wrote: "Through continence we become collected, and led back to the One from whom we fell away in fragments, down into the many."[145] He considered that ascetic renunciation ought to bring man back again, out of the dissipating multiplicity and transience of earthly things, to the "one thing that is necessary" (Luke 10:42), God, who will never pass away.[146] The teaching of the Scriptures on the mortification of the flesh is the true source of Augustine's thinking here, in spite of its formal resemblances to Neoplatonic concepts that "the One" is the perfect and true Being, while the many exist only through participation in it, and that the spiritual unites while the material divides.

He considered that Christ's example and teaching, above all else, attract Christians to the way of renunciation of the world and of mortification.[147] The Incarnation of God's Son and His entire earthly life do nothing but admonish man that he should deny himself. Augustine wrote: "Therefore He was despised in this life and was crucified, to teach us to despise more than to love the good things of this world."[148] "Therefore His obedience, therefore His passion; ... therefore His cross and His wounds.... We ought to learn, from His humanity so rich in mercy, from that form of a servant He took on, what we must despise in this life, what we must hope for in the next."[149]

Christ's teaching, too, is a message of self-denial and of the cross. Augustine made his monks see the deadly seriousness of what the Gospel asks of us: "Listen to what He said: 'If any man come to Me, and hate not his father, and mother, and wife, and children, brother, and sister, yea and his own life also, he cannot be My disciple' [Luke 14:26].... He also said 'So likewise every one of you that does not renounce all that he possesses cannot be My disciple' " (Luke 14:33).[150] What Christ has said about forsaking, even about "hating," parents and kin and one's own life demands of us, according to Augustine, that "with the spiritual sword of the word of God" we destroy in ourselves and in our families this all-too-earthly dependence.[151] For, he said, it was this dependence that "prevents us from gaining, not what we have, which is all temporal and perishable, but what we should all possess, which is eternal and does not pass away."[152] And once again he pointed to the example of Christ, who also had a mother:

> Yet when they told him that she had come, He who was concerned with heavenly things replied: "Who is My mother, and who are My brethren [Matt. 12:48]?" And then He gestured toward His disciples and said that His only kinsmen were those who fulfilled the will of His Father. Certainly He included among them Mary herself, full of love; for she too fulfilled the Father's will. So He, our best, our divine teacher, paid little heed when they spoke to Him of His "mother," which told of something He possessed and was of this earth, but He treasured instead a heavenly kinship.[153]

Augustine was writing wholly in the sense of Sacred Scripture when he demonstrated that the motives for mortification and self-denial are the same as those for that carrying of our cross the Lord has asked of us (cf. Matt. 10:38, 16:24; Mark 8:24; Luke 14:27). In the same letter, which he wrote to a young monk, there are these thoughts on Christian life, especially monastic life, as being that cross:

> Take up your cross upon yourself and follow the Lord. . . . The cross the Lord commands us to carry so that we may follow Him with no impediment signifies nothing other than the mortality of the flesh; for it is that which crucifies us, until death is swallowed up in victory [1 Cor. 15:54]. You must crucify this cross, piercing it with the nail of the fear of God; for otherwise you cannot carry it, for it will fight against your unbridled and unfettered members. But, indeed, you cannot follow the Lord at all unless you carry it. For how do you propose to follow Him if you do not belong to Him? "But those who are Christ's," the Apostle says, "have crucified their flesh with its passions and desires" [Gal. 5:24].[154]

In this letter to Laetus, Augustine also stresses another important aspect in the motivating and evaluating of monastic self-denial: the renunciation of an all-too-earthly attachment to parents, relatives, and even one's own self. This renunciation, which, in keeping with the Lord's words at Luke 14:26, he demanded of his monks, refers to things individuals may possess as their own (*propria*), "which often are snares and obstacles to achieving, not indeed these perishable and temporary possessions [*propria temporaliter transitura*], but rather our common treasure, which will last forever [*in aeternum mansura communia*]."[155] Similarly, when one denies oneself possessions, or, at least, the love of one's possessions,[156] as was the case in that first community in Jerusalem, one will rejoice in what one holds in common, "possessing one heart and one soul in God" (Acts 4:32), and thereby preparing "a single dwelling place in every man for the Lord."[157] One can see how in his hopes for monastic life Augustine was making ascetic renunciation in some fashion also serve toward his final goal, the "one heart in God" (*cor unum in Deum*).

Furthermore, he was familiar with the view that Christian mortification and self-denial are a form of sacrifice. By "sacrifice," he understood "every act that is so performed that in the company of the saints one may adhere to God."[158] It is a genuine sacrifice, to use the term in this sense, "if we hold our bodies in restraint by moderation; if we do it, as we should for the love of God, so that we use our limbs not as weapons of sinful wickedness but as the 'instruments of justice in the service of God' " (Rom. 6:13).[159] "God," he wrote, "does not want the sacrifice of a slaughtered beast, but of a heart brought low in contrition" (cf. Ps. 50:18–19).[160] A gift which one may offer and which can be seen is a *sacramentum*, a holy sign of this invisible sacrifice.[161] For a similar view of the mortification of the flesh as a sacrificial offering, Augustine instances St. Paul (Rom. 12:1): "Therefore, brothers, I entreat you by the merciful God to offer your bodies as a living, holy sacrifice to Him."[162] It seemed to him an even more precious sacrifice if "the soul turns to God, so that it may catch fire from His love, and laying aside the form of worldly desire, become like His unchangeable form and renew itself." Again, he cited the chapter in Romans: "Do not conform to this world, but be reformed in the newness of your heart, that you may find what is the good, and the acceptable, and the perfect will of God" (Rom. 12:2).[163]

In the ascetic self-sacrifice of individual Christians, he taught, the Church's universal sacrifice, that which was prefigured in Christ's sacrifice on the cross, is achieved. He wrote in *The City of God*: "So it is that this whole, redeemed state, which is the assembly or community of saints, is presented to God as a universal sacrifice by the High Priest, who sacrificed Himself as well for us as He suffered in His servant's form, so that we may be the body of this supreme head."[164] Moreover, he teaches that the universal sacrifice of the faithful, that is, the "many who have become one body in Christ" (cf. Rom. 12:5), is manifested to them in the celebration of the Eucharist. For this is what the Church perfects in "the mystery of the altar": "It is placed before the Church's eyes that in the gift [*res*] which she offers she herself is offered."[165] Christ, who in the Mass is at once high priest and sacrificial gift, wished this to be so, "that the mystery of this gift should be the Church's daily sacrifice, so that she, as the very body of this head, should learn through her head to sacrifice herself."[166] Thus, in Augustine's thought, a Christian's mortification and self-renunciation receive a final, profound basis and motivation in the ecclesiological–Eucharistic concept of the "whole Christ" (*totus Christus*).

The Exercise of Mortification in the Monastery

What were Augustine's views about the realization of the mortification of the flesh in Christian and monastic daily life? He had in mind, above all, an interior mortification and the habitual, daily mortification of the senses. There is no place in his asceticism for severe external mortifications and heavy physical penances. In this respect, as in countless other details, his spirituality is more humane and more moderate—even in his monastic life—than was customary in the ancient Church, and particularly in ancient monasticism. His anti-Manichaeanism, which impressed upon him the fundamental goodness of all creatures, together with his own natural disposition, may have pointed the way for him.[167]

As Augustine's *Rule* instructed his monks, their spirit of Christian mortification ought above all else to be expressed in the daily mastery of their senses. In the custody of the eyes, he saw a valuable means for the preservation of chastity. An unbridled eye betrays an unbridled heart. It may be said of such a man: "A fixed gaze is an abomination to the Lord."[168] In the same way, the governing of the tongue preserves the harmony of the community.[169] Augustine showed his monks how a well-ordered and seemly human conduct was a manifestation of Christian self-mastery: "Try to please by what you are. . . . Walking, standing, whatever movement you make, do nothing to offend anyone who sees you; let everything befit your holy way of life."[170] He is content to apply to them St. Paul's image of "the perfume of Christ" (2 Cor. 2:15); their outward self-mastery, modeled on the man Christ's, should spread a sweet smell.[171] In their "unremarkable clothing," too, he taught them that they should show their spirit of self-abnegation.[172] But there could be no question of a dirty and unkempt appearance, for he emphatically rejected the eccentric asceticism of certain monastic groups[173] which held that dirty clothes were the mark of a pure heart.[174]

He viewed fasting as a valuable means for restraining the body. "Tame your flesh by fasting, and abstaining from food and drink, as far as your health permits."[175] The qualification "as far as your health permits" (*quantum valetudo permittit*) shows his conviction that in this kind of mortification of the flesh particularly intelligence and prudence must be exercised. He, therefore, allowed a wide freedom to individual judgment. Yet it was always his wish that the monks practice a true abstinence in food and drink. "Let them think themselves better off," he wrote in the *Rule*, "when they become better able to endure scarcity."[176] Even those whose physical weakness does not permit them to fast in the real sense are not wholly dispensed from mortification in food and drink. Augustine forbade them to eat between meals: "Even when someone is unable to fast, still he should not take any nourishment between meals, unless he is unwell."[177]

He thought it important that the food in the monastery should be simple. "He ate simply and moderately," Possidius reports. There were green and shelled vegetables, but meat was served only occasionally.[178] And Augustine had forbidden the members of the clerics' monastery to eat outside, or to take part in public banquets, "in order to keep up their practice of moderation."[179] Apart from fasting during the forty-day Lenten season, which was then general,[180] and on Wednesdays and Fridays throughout the year apart from the Easter season,[181] many monks and nuns, as Augustine related, observed a perpetual fast, Saturdays and Sundays being the only exceptions.[182]

Augustine's own constitution was sound but delicate. "He had no great resistance, when exceptional exertion—mental, or, especially, physical—was required from him."[183] Since he was not robust, he could not demand any severe abstinences from his physique; yet because of this he did not consider himself in any way excused from the usual daily monastic mortifications of the flesh. In the tenth book of his *Confessions* he allowed readers to see much of his own efforts to achieve mastery of his senses.[184] But this same chapter also tells us that he often drew the limits of what was permissible in the enjoyment of material things too narrowly, especially when his own conscience was involved.[185] Like others of the Fathers, and in contrast with modern Catholic moral opinion, he thought that taking pleasure in eating and drinking, even in moderation, was not irreproachable. God had intended nourishment, not "for the service of pleasure," but "to preserve the body." Therefore it seemed to him that the ideal would be to use food and drink as medicine (*medicamenta*) for the body, that is, only for health's sake and according to its measure. Thus he often reproached himself because he could not be sure which he was serving, his concern for his body or his appetites.[186] Finding the proper mean was often difficult for men. "Where shall we find the man," he laments, "who never lets himself be enticed, not even by a little, beyond the bounds of what is needful?"[187] He shows a similar reservation, which smacks of rigorism, toward "delight of the ear" in music and song, toward "the pleasures of the body's eye" in "lovely and varied forms, in gleaming, charming hues."[188] Then, too, he considered it important to practice an external and internal mortification by restraining one's excessive curiosity.[189] Here, too, there is no doubt, he inclined toward rigorism, as, for example, he treated inquiries into the mysteries of the divine nature as a morally culpable "lust for experiencing and knowing" and "gratification of the eyes" (1 John 2:16), because this knowledge is of no profit to men and is sought only for the sake of the will.[190]

Augustine was convinced that the task of mortifying one's flesh would last one's entire life. The days of peace would not come here on earth; but until one's death, the words of the Apostle, "The flesh lusts against the spirit, and the spirit against the flesh . . . so that you do not the things that you would" (Gal. 5:17), will be proved true.[191] It was true, even for "valiant knights of Christ."[192] "We too," Augustine wrote of himself, "who have grown old in this warfare, have enemies who have weakened, but even so they are still our enemies."[193] "Of course, we should like no longer to be filled with desires; but this does not lie within our power; whether we want it or not, they lure us, flatter us, sting us, perturb us, and want to overcome us. One can suppress them; extinguish them, never."[194]

Once man has reached his perfection, the time of striving and renunciation should be over for him too. His nature should then be freed from all weakness, so that he no longer need fight for virtue.[195] "For when we have arrived there," he said in a sermon, "where we no longer have to fight at all against concupiscence, then there will be no more enmity we must fight."[196] There, a true and eternal peace will reign,[197] for man will no longer need asceticism, any more than angels need to exercise renunciation and self-denial.[198] Then his base desires will fall silent in him,[199] for even his flesh will have become spiritualized;[200] that is, the body, too, will have put on immortality and risen to eternal life.[201]

Consideration and Discretion

Beyond doubt, Augustine did not underestimate the importance of Christian asceticism for the monastic life, and he commended bodily mortifications to his monks within the limits that have been described. Yet he attached no special importance to the variety or frequency of ascetic exercises, as is obvious from a remark he once made concerning the succession of fast days in the Church: "In my view," he observed, "one would do better to relax fasting rather than increase its severity."[202]

Furthermore, he was emphatic in requiring that all ascetic effort, especially in monasteries, show consideration for one's fellow-men, and be subordinated to the main object of "one heart in God" and integrated with it. He was well aware how pride and self-will can conceal themselves under zeal for asceticism. In this, he had had to suffer many bitter experiences: "With sorrow and sighing I have often learned," he wrote in a letter, "that the contentious obstinacy of some of the brethren has brought great confusion to the weaker ones."[203]

Thus he was a severe opponent of ascetic exaggerations. In one piece he wrote, he made a wide-ranging attack on the arrogance of certain people who wanted at all costs to impose the Saturday fast on the Church.[204] What seemed fundamental to him, in regard to all these exercises of external asceticism, was the advice Ambrose in former days had given him and his mother: "Whatever church you may enter, follow its customs, if you want neither to take nor to give offense."[205]

Augustine thought that asceticism acquired its value, not from being practiced so that people could see, but from the intention with which it was practiced. Here, too, his basic rule was "Love above all else."[206] As a new convert, he had described the Italian monasteries—and, without a doubt, the same spirit he later fostered in his own houses is evident—"Love is their rule of life, in their eating and talking, in their deportment, in their conduct. . . . Whatever is hostile to love is opposed, is rejected."[207] Whoever gives scandal to others by his fasting is no enemy of the devil, but is giving him comfort.[208]

So, for example, he sees it as a duty of Christian fraternal charity, which does not need to be discussed, that those who by their own choice abstain wholly from wine should willingly make it available to any brother who needs it to build up his weakened physical condition.[209] And it is reported that, contrary to custom, Augustine permitted meat dishes to be served at his bishop's table so that guests and invalids might not be irked.[210] Thus, he was asking everyone to show understanding for others. That seemed to him true wisdom, not to despise those who fasted, even if one did not do so, and not to judge those who were eating, even if one did not eat.[211]

The same basic regard for charity is expressed in the discretion with which Augustine was accustomed to clothe the demands he did make for asceticism. They are clear and firm enough to give plain directions, and yet marked by a wise consideration for the needs of individuals and for the circumstances under which life is lived.

In what he established as rules, Augustine was gentle and considerate toward the average man. Instead of precise regulations on fasting, he gave only a general recommendation that his monks should practice abstinence from food and drink;[212] and in what sounds like a justification of this attitude he wrote in a letter that it was only fasting as such that was enjoined in the Gospels and in the Epistles, not prescribed days of fasting.[213]

He knew about the severity and chastisement of Eastern monks. They were said to be so far advanced in their self-mastery and abstemiousness that it seemed necessary to impose limits in order to call them back within the bounds of human nature.[214] He found the life of the anchorites in the Egyptian desert astonishing, but it is plain that he inclined to the opinion that such asceticism passed beyond what human nature can bear in the way of self-denial.[215] So, in his monasteries, the rule was what he had specifically written about those in Italy: no one there, he said, was forced to observe such severity. And no one was to be despised for admitting that he was too weak to do as others were doing.[216]

He recommended special consideration not only for the sick and the infirm, but also for those who had once lived in riches and luxury. He gladly allowed exceptions to be made in matters of food and clothing.[217] He permitted the sick and convalescents to be served meat to build up their strength. Indeed, he allowed them to receive some extra dish before the midday monastic meal, and for this to accept from outsiders whatever it pleased those outsiders to give.[218] Furthermore, he was prepared to mitigate the obligations of manual labor for the brethren of the upper classes, not through any sentimental regard for their former station in life, but out of sympathy for their physical weakness and lack of stamina.[219]

In this gentle "humaneness," Augustine was also attacking the un-Christian asceticism of the Manichaeans. To oppose their superstitious notions and to underscore what St. Paul had written in Titus 1:15 and 1 Timothy 4:4—that everything God has created is good[220]—he permitted a moderate enjoyment of wine in his monasteries. This was an innovation in monastic life. In Eastern monasteries, the conviction prevailed that wine was unsuitable for monks.[221]

Where monastic dress was concerned, too, Augustine deplored all exaggeration. He knew the peculiar point of view, prevalent in many monasteries of his day, that a slovenly appearance was the ideal to be cultivated.[222] By contrast, he expected his monks to be clean in their person and their clothing. His *Rule* deals with their visits to the public baths.[223] Their clothing was to be clean and suitable, not too fine, but also not neglected.[224] For him, looking uncared-for was not a mark of true holiness. On the contrary, dirtiness and self-neglect could often conceal ostentation and vanity just as much as dressing up and finery.[225] Yet experience had taught Augustine that care for one's appearance could easily go too far. A happy medium had to be struck.[226] Monastic poverty demands simple and modest attire.[227] His rule was that in such matters they should be satisfied with what were ordinary requirements.[228] Therefore, the regular laundering of clothes was not to be left until an individual thought fit, but was to be done at a superior's wise direction, "so that your souls do not become soiled by your craving for clean clothes."[229] His monks' chief concern should be "not for what you wear but for what you are."[230]

When Augustine, in his *Rule*, wrote of mortification of the eyes, what he required shows the same combination of firmness and moderation: it was not looking at women that he forbade, but staring at them with desirous gaze.[231]

Thus we can clearly see in his understanding of monastic asceticism how much consideration and discretion contributed to the formation of his ideals for monastic life. If we do not find the word *discretio*, used in the sense of Benedict's *Rule* and Cassian's *Conversations*[232] in his writings, still he is wholly familiar with the idea: a proper discrimination and the observance of moderation. It has been truly said that "looking out from Hippo, one can see Monte Cassino on the horizon"; that is, that the spirit of Western monasticism, moderate and discreet, was by then manifesting itself.[233]

But Augustine's discretion was rooted in *caritas*, Christian love, which, as I have already shown, had become the very soul of his monastic ideal. Rigid legalism will legislate uniformity in monasteries, but Augustine was attempting through the spirit of Christian love to help his monks to achieve their "holy enterprise," not by compulsion, "as slaves under the law, but as free men established under grace."[234]

Furthermore, in this discretion we can perceive how easily Augustine accepted the circumstances under which his fellow-men lived, how much he knew about life and about human nature, and how down-to-earth his thinking and aspirations were. Never bogged down in theorizing, he always understood how to measure what he saw as an ideal against realities, shrewdly, practically. That the form of monastic life to which he aspired evolved as something that would last and that could be practiced throughout the world was the result, to a great extent, of his calm good sense. This same good sense saved Augustinian monasticism from the bitter quarrels that marked the early history of the Franciscan Order, for example. Augustine's way of life possesses a spiritual generosity that has enabled it to acclimate itself easily to other times, other social circumstances, and to keep it close to life in every day and age.

HUMILITY

Augustine taught that all ascetic effort in the monastery must be made with consideration for the community. Self-will must not disguise itself as religious fervor; and pride and complacency can be just as harmful to a monk's endeavors. "What is the use," he asked in his *Rule*, "of a man's distributing his possessions by giving them to the poor, and making himself poor, too, if this contempt for wealth makes his miserable soul more proud than it was when he was wealthy?"[235]

In Augustine's view, humility is essential in deciding on and achieving the perfection of a servant of God.[236] Though he was convinced that love was of greater worth, he also knew that a true love of God cannot flourish unless it is planted in humility.[237] He recognized and argued with greater depth than any of the Fathers before him how uniquely important humility is for the Christian life.[238]

Christ's Humility

Pagan antiquity knew nothing of humility as a virtue, in the full sense of the word, even if, here and there, something of the intellectual notion can be seen—for example, in what is written about human subjection before the divinity, in the Greek ideal of "moderation" and self-control, or in what Socrates taught about "honorableness as a personal obligation."[239] The Old Testament teaches much about humility in the face of a high, exalted God, who accepts the poor and wretched but rejects the proud; and it recommends a modesty in dealing with one's fellow-men (Prov. 11:2, 29:33). Christ brought a deeper understanding of the nature of humility, before God and men, through His example and His teaching. He showed that it was important for the conduct of life in the new order of "the kingdom of heaven." And, in the New Testament's teaching about man's dependence upon God's actions through grace, and in the experience of a community of the faithful produced by the Spirit, the concept of humility was given a new value. In patristic times, particularly after Origen, teaching about it was greatly enriched.[240] Augustine may have received much inspiration here, especially from Ambrose; but the true source of his teaching is the New Testament.[241]

What is the principal characteristic of Augustine's teaching on humility? It is, above all, Christocentric. Its core is the figure of the "humiliated Christ." Indeed, this concept is so important for Augustine's Christology that it has been called its very center.[242] Only from Christ, the "model of humility," can man learn what humility truly is,[243] and only from Him will man receive "the grace of His humility."[244] Christ, the God–man, was "the teacher of humility in word and example."[245]

Augustine discovered the meaning of humility particularly in the mystery of the Incarnation. He was deeply impressed with the idea of *kenosis*, "self-exinanition," as it is presented in the words of the prologue to St. John's Gospel: "The Word was made flesh" (John 1:14).[246] "Although

He was the high exalted, He descended into abjection."[247] "So great was the humility of so great a God!"[248] By this "humility of the Incarnation" (*humilitas Incarnationis*) he understood "on the one hand, the abjectness of Christ's human existence, in comparison to the immeasurable exaltation of His divinity . . . and, on the other, the intention, expressed in this 'descent,' when the Creator humbled himself to become a creature in order to raise the creature up to Himself."[249]

Thus Augustine saw in Christ more than a mere teacher and example of humility. He wrote repeatedly of the "divine humility" that manifested itself to us in Christ,[250] and he employs the image of "the hand of God," stretched out to man through Christ's humility to rescue him from the misery of his sins.[251] Thus, he regarded that humility both as a moral example for human conduct and as the redeeming act of divine self-abnegation. Quoting Philippians 2:5–11, he shows that the divine humility (*humilitas Dei*) was established in God's coming down to be made flesh, flowered in the life, passion, and death of Christ, and bore the fruit of His exaltation to His divine glory, where all the redeemed will follow Him as their image.[252] According to Augustine, it was man's pride that caused the "humble God" to become man. This was the vice that "brought down the almighty physician from heaven and humbled Him, down to the form of a servant" so that such a wound might be healed through the power of so strong a medicine.[253] Repeatedly in this fashion he showed that Christ's humility is the great cure for human pride, which is the source of humanity's sinful misery.[254]

One often finds meditative descriptions of the God–man's humility at the various stages of His earthly life: at His birth, in the years of His hidden life, at His baptism, in His public ministry, and, above all, in His sufferings and death.[255]

> Christ was to come in the flesh. . . . But how was He to come? Born in mortal flesh, as a little child, lying in a crib, swaddled in bands, fed with milk. He was to grow in years and, in the end, to be carried off by death. All these are the marks of His humility, the lineaments of a humility great beyond measure. And whose was it? One high exalted. Which high exalted one? Do not seek for Him on earth; mount to the stars. Climb beyond all created things; . . . go on up to the Creator, and see there: "In the beginning was the Word" [John 1:1].[256]

And he never wearied in presenting Christ as the teacher of humility. Christ had made this virtue known by word and example; He had called man to imitate His humility, so that it might also become the way to glory.[257]

Essence and Justification of Christian Humility

For Augustine, as we have just seen, a Christian's distinguishing virtue was, above all else, the imitation of the humble Christ. Whoever wishes to share with Christ the joy of everlasting blessedness must follow Him along the way of suffering and shame; humiliation alone is the "stepladder" to the heights.[258]

What, more exactly, did Augustine understand by humility as a Christian virtue? One will find in his writings no exhaustive discussion of his ideas; and yet, in his frequent mentionings of the virtue, some of its separate characteristics are described in detail. For Augustine, humility is an attitude on the part of the Christian, essential for him, in which, in comparing himself with Christ, the pattern and teacher of humility, he perceives in himself what he ought to be and acknowledges to himself what he is.[259] This attitude is "as once abasement and exaltation: abasement, as opposed to an overweening pride, yet exaltation, for humility bestows on man true worth and wisdom."[260] In humility, as in every virtue, Augustine saw first and foremost a gift of the Holy Spirit.[261] Its essential qualities, according to him, are sincerity and inwardness.[262] "But humility will be sincere if it not only shows itself in words," but dwells within a man.[263] For Augustine, it was a question of a "humility of the heart."[264]

He taught that it is humility that determines man's essential disposition toward God.[265] He reasoned in this way from his Christian conception of what man is—a creature and a sinner, yet one redeemed and given grace.[266] "See yourself for what you are: weak, human, sinful. And see who it is who will justify you."[267] His teaching on man's total dependence on the grace of God plays an important part in his account of humility and its effect.

In a number of meditative passages, Augustine shows how humility manifests itself in the Christian's life in ways that correspond with various relationships between him and his God.[268] Since, in God's presence, he is His creature, humility makes him subject to God,[269] so that he no longer does his own will but God's.[270] It makes him care little for himself and his own honor, and makes him seek God's honor and be pleasing to Him. "Remember," he said in a sermon, "that you are a creature. Acknowledge your Creator! . . . Seek for His glory."[271] He made the faithful see the Son of God, who took on the form of a servant, and who "sought not His own honor but only that of His Father" as the example of such humility.[272]

Moreover, the fact that man is a sinner finds its proper expression in humility, according to Augustine. For humility would lead him to acknowledge and confess his guilt before God. Unlike the proud man who, "if he has sinned, considers it beneath his dignity to be convicted of it," and always has some excuse ready for his fault, the humble man "accepts accusation as a humiliation for his good."[273]

Above all, Augustine felt, humility is fostered by the awareness on the part of the Christian that he, who has been redeemed, depends wholly on God's grace. Thus he knows, as John 15:5 and 1 Corinthians 4:7 tell him, that "he can do nothing good, unless with His grace."[274] Everything that is good he has received from God who, indeed, in man's good works rewards "only the gifts of His own mercy."[275] Thus Augustine admonished men that in their striving after what is good, they should rely, not on their own powers, but on God: "Base your hope, not on yourself, but on your God! For if you base it on yourself, your soul will suffer a confusion beyond your powers; for it will have found nothing to make it trust in you. When 'my soul is cast down within me' [Ps. 42:6], what else remains for it except humility? . . . It should do nothing for itself, so that God may do for it what will be to its profit."[276] In this knowledge of his dependence on God, the humble man will not weary of asking for help and grace. He feels himself to be "a beggar in God's presence," which makes him "beg and seek and knock" (cf. Matt. 7:7, Luke 11:9).[277]

In accordance with Christ's teaching and example, humility determines what a Christian's relations with his fellow-men will be. One outstanding characteristic of this, which Augustine often calls attention to, is a "love that serves" (*caritas serviens*), a readiness to perform loving service for one another. He points to the example of the Lord in washing the feet of His Apostles: "Brothers, we have learned humility from Him who is the highest. Let us then humbly do what the highest one did in humility." But when such humble customs no longer exist, we should at least cultivate a humility of the heart.[278] It is not only, he taught, in monasteries that this law of the "love that serves" should prevail.[279] It exists throughout the entire City of God. All "serve one another in love: superiors, with a loyal care; subjects, by their obedience."[280]

Humility and a Life Dedicated to God

Even if Augustine did not set out for the "servants" and "handmaids" of God what the marks and the degrees of humility are, down to their smallest details, as, for instance, Cassian had done, and as Benedict, influenced by Cassian, was to do,[281] still he attributed supreme importance to the virtue for a life of ascetic effort.[282] "Do you want to be great?" he asked in a sermon. "Start with very small things. Do you plan to raise a great, towering building? Think first about its foundation, humility. . . . The higher you want to build, the deeper the foundation should be dug."[283] Thus, the measure of every man's humility is shown in the measure of his greatness.[284] He, therefore, was indefatigable in praising humility. "Where there is humility," he once wrote, constructing one of the antitheses he loved, "there is majesty; where there is weakness, there is might."[285] He even dared to affirm "That is our very perfection, our humility."[286] For this reason he warned his monks against pride and presumption. Pride is an insidious vice.[287] It can rob monastic life of all its merit, can, indeed, make it unpleasing to God. "Do not praise yourself, even if you are good," he said in a sermon, "for by taking pride in your goodness you will become bad."[288] And he ventured, "God is better pleased by humility in bad deeds than he is by pride in good works. The proud Pharisee and the humble tax-gatherer in the Lord's parable are His proof of that."[289]

He therefore insisted, time and again, on the words of Sirach the Preacher: "The greater you are, the humbler you must be, and the Lord will show you favor" (Eccli. 3:18).[290] He does understand what the psychological problems are for anyone, especially if his ideals are high, as he struggles to achieve Christian humility: pride can set greater snares for the more gifted.[291] The more anyone possesses in which he could take pleasure, the more he should fear that his self-satisfaction will dissatisfy Christ.[292] The tax-collector, the pagan centurion, the notorious adulteress, all of them, when they experienced conversion, attained humility without difficulty, mindful of their own vicious lives and of God's merciful pardon.[293] The great numbers of those who have vowed themselves to God are differently placed. They need not lament their former lives of sin; they can, on the contrary, say: "I have done more than was asked of me."[294]

Very many in their spiritual lives have been shipwrecked on this rock. "I am anxious," Augustine wrote, "that you do not do as that Pharisee did, boasting in pride about his merits. . . . I am afraid that you do not love much because you think that there is little in you to be forgotten."[295]

To put monks and nuns on their guard against this spiritual pride, Augustine knew no better antidote than Christ's words and example. Here, in particular, anyone whom God has richly endowed can find the proper incentives to humility. No one, however piously he may have lived, can be guiltless in the sight of God; no one can be Christ's equal in innocence and holiness. And yet He, the God–man, said of Himself: "Learn of Me, for I am . . . humble of heart" (Matt. 11:28).[296] Augustine continued: "So you do not need to have recourse to him who did not dare to lift his eyes to heaven for the burden of his sins; go to Him who came down from heaven, drawn by the burden of His love. You do not need to have recourse to her who washed the feet of her Lord with tears to gain pardon for her grievous sins; go to Him who as the redeemer of all sins washed the feet of His servants."[297]

Then he offered his charges some advice that reflects his rich experience of the religious life and his own ascetic endeavors. He did not ask them to ignore what was good in themselves or to deny that it was there, in a kind of spiritual hypocrisy; but they were not to take pride in it.[298] A religious must acknowledge God's gift in whatever good he possesses. It would be perverse if he were to love less the one from whom he had received more.[299]

The very vocation to the monastic life is, in Augustine's view, no merit in a religious but rather an unmerited gift from God. Anyone without a vocation can find no peace of soul in a monastery. He will constantly be tormented by temptations because his intentions were false in taking upon himself such a life, and he did not know what he was doing.[300] And no one on his own strength could live his profession suitably. It is God's grace—Augustine compared it with a life-saving dew—which enables the brethren to live together in holy community.[301] No one ought to give himself credit for having renounced his possessions[302] or having vowed himself to God in celibate chastity.[303] No one in his pride ought to think himself better than someone else who does not achieve the same good works as he.[304] If a monk faithfully carries out the precepts of monastic life, he ought rather to say thanks for this to God, "the giver of all good things."[305]

Moreover, Augustine recommended that his subjects often look on all the evil from which, through God's grace alone, they had been protected. And they could with every right consider the sins from which God had spared them as if in fact they had been forgiven them by God.[306] Such an attitude would be prudent, and entirely in keeping with the facts.[307] For those who have taken vows there is the special danger that, in their belief that they are better than others and that God has little to forgive them, they are in fact loving God less. And yet they should love him more fervently because it was God alone who preserved them from falling into those sins.[308]

Finally, Augustine's counsel to monks and nuns was: "Pay more attention to what you lack than to what you have acquired." For if anyone were to surrender to the thought that he had by now far surpassed others in his goodness, one would be justified in fearing pride in him. "But if you will think," Augustine said in a sermon, "how much is still wanting in you, you will sigh deeply; and, sighing, you will be cured; you will become humble; you will progress along the path that will take you out of pride and arrogance into safety."[309] Let no one dare to boast how virtuous and constant he has been so far; for no one can know whether he will in fact endure to the end. Far better, let him pray humbly that he be not tempted beyond resistance.[310] Let no one dare to look down upon others, despising them and saying with the Pharisee: I thank you, God, that I am not like that. It is very possible that there are many who in secret surpass him, though to the world he may seem better than they.[311] Therefore, in one allocution Augustine reminded his brethren in the garden monastery at Hippo of what St. Paul had written: "Have great humility of spirit, each of you thinking others better than yourself" (cf. Phil. 2:3). They were to take this very seriously, they were to believe it true that someone else, unknown to them, can possess something that far surpasses what they have, even though the good they possess, which makes them seem superior, is there for everyone to see.[312] And even if one is obliged to rate virginity dedicated to God higher than married life, still there is no monk or nun who has the right to consider himself or herself better than any other Christian in the world.[313]

As long as man remains on earth, he is still traveling, loaded down with imperfections. Augustine said that even monks are still stained with the dust of the earth. No one can assert that he has reached his journey's end. How he will end his days is still unknown.[314] It is very possible that there are Christians living in the world who far surpass professed religious in their love. Perhaps such religious, for all their zeal for the things of God, still do not have the strength to accept that martyrdom of which Christian lay people are capable, as they drink with Christ the cup of deepest humility.[315]

So, Augustine thought, a monk ought always to keep alive in his soul his dissatisfaction with himself, never falling into complacency. He said in a sermon: "When you have found some reason to be pleased with yourselves, you are losing ground. But if you have ever once said 'I have done enough,' then you are facing ruin."[316]

In the tenth book of his *Confessions*, when he gives an account of his struggles to achieve the ascetic life in religion, he constantly reverts to his striving for Christian humility. He is still so full of imperfections; there is so much uncertainty and hesitancy; he is still so conscious of his sinful poverty, his imprisonment in the impurity of his desires.[317] Again and again he repeats his prayer: "Give what you command, and then command what you will."[318] "There is only one single hope, one trust, one single certain promise, and that is your mercy."[319] Yet he has this conviction: "I can do all things in Him who gives me strength" (Phil. 4:13). And so he prays: "Then strengthen me so that I can do it. . . . Plainly it is you, O holy God, who are the giver, when that is done which you commanded to be done."[320]

"HOLY" VIRGINITY AND CELIBACY

From the very beginning, an essential mark of the monastic life has been a freely willed renunciation of marriage "for the sake of the kingdom of heaven" (Matt. 19:12). In Augustine's monasteries, too, "profession" included the obligation to live an unmarried life dedicated to God.[321] We do not know if a vow to this effect was taken, but this is not improbable since those in the outside world who were living lives dedicated to asceticism and virginity were familiar with such a vow.

When Augustine became a bishop, he demonstrated in many of his writings and sermons that the ideal of consecrating virginity and celibacy to God had its origins in the thought of the New Testament. It is generally recognized, of course, as the first part of this study has shown several times, that during the years Augustine spent in Milan, his ideas about sexual continence and its importance in the search for truth were formed and directed by Neoplatonism. What he wrote at Cassiciacum, especially the *Soliloquies*, make it clear that at that time he regarded his renunciation of marriage as an indispensable condition for achieving his goal, his Neoplatonic–Christian ideal of wisdom. He fancied that marriage was the enemy of a "freedom of the soul,"[322] and that everything "of the senses" should be fled if one wanted to take flight on high, "out of this darkness to that light."[323] Even in Tagaste, his ideals of sexual continence were still influenced by Neoplatonic spiritual notions.[324] But then the Platonic justifications of continence were being suppressed more and more and rectified by Christian spiritual thinking. What he wrote and preached as bishop of Hippo on the subjects of continence and virginity is formed by the teachings of Scripture and of Christian tradition.

The Christian ideal of a life of virginity had by that time a history of several centuries behind it. Augustine seems to have been influenced in his conceptions by Ambrose, Jerome, and Cyprian.[325] Yet here, too, it is to his credit that he took over this ideal and gave it a deeper theological reasoning and argumentation. His treatise *Holy Virginity*, written in 401, is beyond a doubt one of the best on the subject written during the patristic era, and it continued to exercise its influence during succeeding centuries. In particular, he viewed the ideal of a continent life dedicated to God as centered upon Christ and strongly supported by the arguments of eschatology and ecclesiology.

To be sure, *Holy Virginity* in its initial plan and in many of its chapters is exclusively concerned with the religious life of nuns. Yet what he wrote that is most fundamental to the theme of the celibate life as a religious ideal is also directed to those "youths . . . and men" who have vowed themselves to God in renouncing marriage.[326] Then, too, the many to whom he spoke who had dedicated themselves to God were divided into those living in the world and the others in religious communities who were achieving this religious ideal of a virginal continence.[327]

Holy Virginity as a Form of Living

We must first offer some brief explanation of Augustine's ideas. He uses two distinguishing terms: "virginity of the body" (*virginitas carnis*, *virginitas in carne*, *virginitas corporis*) and "virginity of the heart" (*virginitas cordis*, *virginitas in corde* [*in mente*], *virginitas mentis*, *virgo spiritu*).[328] When he wrote of the "holy virginity of virgins vowed to God," he was not, naturally, thinking of a physically inviolate state. Virginity in this purely physical sense possessed in his view no religious or moral value.[329] On the other hand, he did not regard the ideal of Christian virginity merely from the point of view of a purely spiritual virginity. He attributed a "virginity of the mind" (or "of the soul") to all Christians. By this he understood, as will in due course be shown, an integrity of faith, hope, and love, which, therefore, he designates a "virginity of faith" (*virginitas fidei*).[330]

For nuns' virginity, according to him, it is essential that the "virginity of the flesh" be preserved "by a pious offering of the spirit." But through this a physical virginity can to some extent become spiritualized.[331] Thus, the expression "holy virginity" ought to signify that those concerned are virgins in body as well as in spirit (*virgines et corpore et spiritu*).[332]

Dedication to God • In one place Augustine mentioned as a sort of parallel to Christian virgins the Vestal virgins of pagan Rome. The basic difference between them can be found in the answer to the question "To whom is this virginity vowed and for whom is it preserved?"[333] In Christian, sanctified virginity, as he expressed it, "the integrity of the flesh is vowed, is dedicated, is preserved, for the Creator of spirit and of flesh Himself."[334]

It has already been shown that the moral and religious ideal he set up was not sexual continence as such, but the full and undivided gift of oneself to God, made possible by the renunciation of marriage. "Virginity is honored, not because it is virginity, but because it is dedicated to God."[335]

Therefore, in Augustine's view, what determines the quality of anyone's chastity is a continence of the heart. No one possesses true chastity who has a lascivious eye, even if his body be untouched by sin; for "a shameless eye is the messenger of a shameless heart."[336] On the other hand, the body's chastity may not be injured, so long as the heart's purity is preserved intact, even if violence is offered to the body's members. Rape is not to be regarded as culpable and shameful, but as "a wound received as one suffers."[337]

The Life of the Angels (vita angelica) · We can better appreciate Augustine's understanding of virginity when we see how he, like Cyprian and Ambrose before him, loved to apply to it the ancient Christian concept of the "angelic life."[338] Living in a virginity vowed to God seemed to him as "a sharing in the life of the angels" (*portio angelica*),[339] and, as well, "an imitation of the life of heaven" (*caelestis vitae imitatio*).[340] He explained his reasoning in a sermon: "Angels do not marry; nor do they bring home any brides." At the Resurrection this will be the lot of all Christians, as the Lord has promised (cf. Matt. 22:30, Mark 12:25, Luke 30:35ff.). A celibate chastity, whether of men or of women, anticipates this way of life here and now upon earth.[341] He saw further resemblances to the angelic life in the way the continent, in this present life, direct their senses and their efforts "to what is eternal and immutable,"[342] and in their zeal for performing works of virtue, "so that they show to earth how life is lived in heaven."[343] I have already shown that these notions are derived, not from any high-blown "spiritism," but from Augustine's sound grounding in the eschatology of the early Christian Church.[344]

In *Holy Virginity* Augustine strenuously defended this eschatological concept of virginity against the views of the heresiarch Jovinian, who had flatly denied that the ideal of virginity could have any application to eternal values.[345] In support of his proposition "that perpetual continence is to be cherished not merely for its values in this present, earthly life, but also for what it gains of the promised life to come in heaven," Augustine cited the words of St. Paul: "He who is unmarried thinks of the Lord's business and the ways in which he can please Him. . . . The unmarried woman is concerned with the Lord's claim, that she be holy in body and soul" (1 Cor. 7:32, 34). Thus, it was in no way the Apostle's contention that the unmarried are intent on what can free their earthly lives of sorrows and hardships.[346] Then Augustine appeals to the classic passage in Matthew 19:12 in which Christ speaks of those who have made themselves eunuchs "for the love of the kingdom of heaven."[347] It was a cheap evasion for Jovinian to maintain that the "kingdom" of which Christ spoke here referred only to this present life. It is true that sometimes the Church on earth is called a heavenly kingdom, but only because "she will be the harvest of the everlasting life that is to come."[348] Augustine goes on to make special application of the Biblical metaphor of the servants with girt loins and burning lamps in their hands, waiting the return of their lord from the wedding feast (cf. Luke 12:35ff.), to men and women who have remained unmarried for the sake of the kingdom of heaven.[349] He comes to the conclusion: "Those who have formed the pious resolve to practice continence, to tame their bodies even to renouncing marriage, and who have castrated themselves, not in their bodies, but in the very roots of their concupiscence," are they who "in this present earthly mortality aspire to a heavenly, angelic life" (*caelestem et angelicam vitam*).[350]

Espousal and Imitation of Christ · Like the Fathers before him, Augustine regarded virginity vowed to God as a kind of espousal with Christ.[351] He called Christ no less than "the bridegroom of virgins" (*virginum sponsus*),[352] their "lover" (*amator*).[353] Accordingly, he compared the breaking of a vow of chastity with the misconduct of which married people are guilty if they do not keep faith with their spouses.[354] Sometimes he related this espousal to the spiritual marriage between Christ and His Church: "And those," he wrote, who have promised their virginity to God . . . are not unmarried. For they share with the entire Church that joining in marriage in which Christ is the bridegroom."[355]

In *Holy Virginity*, in particular, he had reflected on the loving relations between Christ and virgins, calling on those consecrated to Him to an ardent love for Him:

> You have despised espousal with the sons of men, so that you may with sons of men give life. So love with all your heart Him who is fair beyond all the sons of men [Ps. 44:3]. . . . See the beauty of your lover. . . . Regard

> how lovely in Him is that which proud men mock. With your heart's eyes, look on the wounds of the crucified one, on the scars of Him who has risen again, the blood of that dying one, treasure of the faithful, price of our redemption! Think of the great price of all this! Put it in the scales of love, and weigh against this whatever your renunciation of an earthly marriage has cost you. . . . Even if you owed your betrothed much love, how much must you love Him for whose sake you wanted no other betrothed. Wholly may He enclose you in His heart who let Himself be nailed to the cross for your sake. Wholly may He achieve in your soul what you would not permit to any earthly marriage. You may not love Him just a little for whose sake you have forsworn the love that you might have had.[356]

Once in a sermon Augustine expressed the view that the best fruit of a love for Christ is yielded in the imitation of Him.[357] He repeatedly justified virginity by showing its motivation as imitation of Christ; for manifestly one can find in Him "wonderful instruction and the ideal model of virginal integrity."[358] He developed this thought by referring to the prophetic vision in the Apocalypse (14:7ff.) of the Lamb and His retinue.[359] He encouraged unmarried men and women to follow the Lamb and reasoned: "For the flesh of the Lamb, too, is virginal; He always preserved in Himself still more wonderfully what He did not deprive His mother of by His conception and His birth."[360] Thus one can justly speak of following and imitating Christ "by the virginity of the heart and of the flesh."[361] It is true that this is a way of imitating Christ that is not enjoined upon all Christians, for whoever has once lost virginity cannot regain it.[362] He concludes his observations by commending men to follow Christ in whichever way is destined for them. "The rest of the faithful, who no longer have their virginity, may thus follow the Lamb, not 'wherever He goes' [Apoc. 14:4], but so far as they are able. . . . You, too, are following Him, for you follow, for the love of this sole good, 'wherever He goes.' "[363]

Models of Virginity Vowed to God

Augustine's eschatological and Christological contemplation on the significance of virginity as an ideal is mingled with powerful ecclesiological and Mariological motifs.

The Church, Virgin and Mother · Just as in the Old Testament Israel is often called "virgin," so St. Paul regarded the Christian community as a "chaste virgin" betrothed to Christ (2 Cor. 11:2). In this sense, and moved by the parable of the wise and foolish virgins (Matt. 25:1–13), Augustine lovingly calls the Church "the holy virgin, espoused to one husband alone, to be led in her chaste virginity to Christ."[364] Certainly, not all her members have physical virginity; but as parts of the whole body they are virgin in spirit.[365] When he considered in what this spiritual virginity of the Church and all the faithful consisted, his answer was: "in faith unblemished, in unshakable hope, and in sincere love."[366] In another place he explained that the Church as a body treasured her espousal with Christ "in faith."[367]

Thus, the significance of the metaphor is that the Church is virgin through her gift of herself to Christ in a living faith; and so Augustine regarded the virgin Church as the personification of the unity of all the faithful, to whom, too, as individuals he attributed a virginity of the soul, of the mind, of the heart, of faith (*virginitas mentis, virginitas cordis, virginitas fidei*).[368] As M. Agterberg has shown in his careful examination of the concept and of its theological background, in Augustine's thought, the Church's virginity and that of the faithful consist in their interior possession, in faith, hope, and love, through the grace of Christ, of knowledge and will that are no longer subject to the domination of concupiscence. This freedom is realized in the chastity (*pudicitia*) of the married state, widowhood and holy virginity, according to the different gifts of the Church's individual members.[369] Augustine knew well, of course, how many members of the Church do not preserve their chastity. How, then, can the proposition that the whole Church and all Christians possess this virginity of the heart be valid? It is plain that what was in Augustine's mind is that even if the Church is not yet virgin in all its believers, still it is her mission to become so; in one place he wrote: The whole "should" (*debet*) be virginal.[370]

Thus, in this metaphor of the Church's virginity, Augustine's fundamentally eschatological conception of her nature comes into play. In human time the virgin Church is on her way—that is, she has now been given her share in the work of our redemption, and in her living faith she is true to Christ, her bridegroom, but she is not yet fully without sin. "In an unblemished faith," Augustine wrote in *Holy Virginity*,

> a kind of virginal chastity is preserved, by which the Church, as a chaste virgin, is made ready for her one husband [cf. 2 Cor. 11:2]. But this one husband has taught not only those of the faithful who are virgin in spirit

> and flesh, but all Christians everywhere . . . that they should pray: . . . "Forgive us our trespasses, as we forgive those who trespass against us" [Matt. 6:12]; and by this petition He has shown us that we must not forget what we should be.[371]

The analogies Augustine saw between the Church's hierarchical ordering and the status of a continence dedicated to God become clear when we read how he assigned to it "a higher rank in honor and sanctity in the Church."[372] Those who preserve "their bodies holy and inviolate" form in the Body of Christ a "more honorable member" (*honorabilius membrum*) to which greater respect is due;[373] for even though the whole Church is holy in body and spirit, still in the untouched virginity of these, her dedicated members, her holiness and her gift of herself to her bridegroom, Christ, is seen with special clarity.[374] He found a further image with which to show the ecclesial meaning of Christian virginity: "This race of virgins," he wrote, "has borne in their bodies no fruit; nor are they children born according to the flesh. If you ask who is their mother, it is the Church. Only a holy virgin bears holy virgins, . . . virgins according to the flesh and according to the spirit."[375] Here he was taking care to emphasize the Christian and ecclesial origin of his idealization of holy virginity: the Church herself is the spiritual mother of virgins; and their bodily integrity, consecrated to God, is "as it were, a natural consequence of spiritual virginity," such as the whole Church possesses.[376]

Elsewhere, as well, in *Holy Virginity*, Augustine reverts to this theme of the Church's motherhood. The virgin Church is for him at the same time the mother Church. The Church is a mother, indeed, Christ's mother, "because she gives life to His members, that is, His faithful, by the power of God's grace."[377] The parallels between the Church, virgin and mother, and the virgin mother of Jesus, who, being such, appears as the type of the Church, are presented by him in these antitheses: "Mary bore in her body the head of this Body. The Church bears in spirit that Body's members. In neither one does fruitfulness blemish virginity."[378] Next, we must examine Augustine's teaching about the sense and the extent of the share of dedicated virgins in the Church's spiritual motherhood.

Mary, the Virgin Mother of the Lord · When, in *Holy Virginity*, Augustine contemplated Mary as a type of the Church, he passed on very easily to the idea of the virgin mother of God as the model of Christian virginity. He specifically called her the "example" for all consecrated virgins;[379] for she was the first who expressly and voluntarily "vowed her virginity to God,"[380] and, so, in her earthly mortal body, practiced "the imitation of a heavenly life."[381] In the will of God's Son to be born of a virgin Augustine saw that honor was paid to all virgins vowed to God.[382] Then, too, he alleged that Mary had consecrated herself to God as a virgin even before she knew that she had been chosen as the mother of Him who was both God and man. Even for her, the mother of the Lord, holy virginity was a matter, not of precept and duty, but of true choice. In that he saw divine approbation of every instance of the life of virginity.[383]

But Mary as the mother of God can also in some fashion be a pattern for virgins, in Augustine's view, not indeed by her bodily motherhood but rather as a spiritual mother.[384] This spiritual motherhood he understood in the sense of the Saviour's words: "Whoever does the will of My father in heaven is My brother, sister, and mother" (Matt. 12:50). Physical motherhood by itself would have been of no profit to Mary, he stated,[385] but by fulfilling God's will she "became the mother of Christ more gloriously, more blessedly,"[386] and this as she "through her love has cooperated in the birth of the faithful, the members of that head, in the Church."[387]

In the eighth book of his *Confessions*, in describing the internal conflict immediately before his conversion, Augustine presents a personified "ennobling, chaste continence" (*casta dignitas continentiae*), who invites him to look at the great numbers of the continent of both sexes and of every age. He then writes: "In them all, their continence is in no way unfruitful; rather, it is the mother of their children of joy, which they have borne to you, Lord, their bridegroom."[388] In *Holy Virginity*, which he wrote not long afterward, he treats this notion of the fruitfulness of Christian continence and virginity more fully. Consecrated virgins cannot, as Mary did, become mothers, "according to the flesh," but in terms of Christ's promise just quoted (Matt. 12:50), they can gain a share in her spiritual motherhood. "They are with Mary, the mother of Christ, as they do the will of His Father."[389] Augustine shows the nature of this motherhood to be a participation in the Church's motherhood, as she by the power of God's grace bestows life on the members of Christ.[390] But how does this participation in the Church's maternal services perfect itself? Augustine's answer is "Both faithful married women and virgins vowed to God are spiritual mothers of Christ, by the holy conduct of their lives, the love of their pure hearts, their clear consciences, and their unfeigned faith [cf. 1 Tim. 1:5] because they do the Father's will."[391]

Virginity as the Greater Good (bonum melius)

The ancient Church was unanimously convinced that a virginity dedicated to God was superior to marriage. Thus, when the ascetic Jovinian, about 385, argued in Rome for the view that marriage and virginity were of entirely equal value, thereby occasioning consternation among nuns and his fellow-ascetics,[392] two synods, held in Rome and Milan in 390, rejected his opinion, and Jerome felt himself called upon to attack him vigorously in his work of 393, *Against Jovinian*. Jovinian's teachings seem to have produced confusion even in North Africa.[393] Thus it was commonly held in certain Christian circles—perhaps because of Jerome's derogatory remarks on the subject of marriage[394]—that it was impossible to refute Jovinian without calling the value of marriage into question.[395] This was for Augustine the immediate occasion for the composition of his treatises on the two different states, *The Good of Marriage* and *Holy Virginity*: "Faithful spouses possess their own good," he wrote, "but they can go on, as until now has been their very proper custom, honoring in nuns a higher good."[396]

Virginity and Marriage • What did Augustine see as the "good," the value, of marriage? There are three "goods" which he constantly proposes: offspring, fidelity, and the mystery of salvation (*proles, fides, sacramentum*). "Fidelity takes care," he wrote,

> that there will be no commerce with this other woman or that other man outside the bond of matrimony; the good of offspring ensures that children are lovingly welcomed, kindly tended, and piously brought up; but the mystery of salvation provides that marriages are not dissolved, and that a man or woman who has been deserted does not marry again, not even for the sake of offspring.[397]

When Augustine wrote here of "mystery" (*sacramentum*), he was thinking, not of a sacrament instituted by Christ in a modern theological sense, but of marriage's mysterious, symbolical character (Eph. 5:31ff.), of its presenting an image of the union of Christ with His Church.[398] Besides these three benefits in marriage, which he often mentioned, he sometimes discussed other points which illustrate the excellence of marriage. For him, marriage is "the communion given by nature between opposite sexes";[399] and its determining characteristic is the love of the spouses for one another (*caritas coniugalis*).[400] What is more, marriage has not only the one object: to give life to children "honorably, lawfully, chastely, and for society's good";[401] it is also a means of salvation and an intended remedy against human weakness: in it "the weaknesses of both sexes, inclining them to a shameful fall, are given due support."[402] And parents' commerce in marriage is ennobled by the love that comes to them as parents (*affectus parentalis*) as long as man and wife in their dealings have the conscious intention of becoming father and mother.[403]

So Augustine stressed, again and again, the moral value of marriage, and in this he opposed, in particular, the Manichaeans, who regarded marriage as the work of an evil prince of darkness, and the production of offspring as a gravely sinful act insofar as it was the chaining of a soul to the flesh.[404] Nonetheless, his teachings on marriage are not free of a certain imbalance because they are based on his too negative attitude toward man's sexual instincts (*libido*). Usually he is concerned with their disordered nature, the "disobedience of the flesh" (*inobedientia carnis*).[405] Even when he does express the view that in marriage these instincts in man and wife can be put to good use in procreation, still they are evil in themselves, not in the sense of being sinful, but as a punishment for the sin of our first father.[406] For this reason the Pelagians later reproached Augustine with favoring the Manichaeans, a charge against which he defended himself with vigor and, beyond a doubt, with justice.[407]

From what has been said, it can be seen that the high esteem in which he held virginity in no way derives from any lack of esteem for marriage. Insistently he admonished all those who wish to choose a celibate life consecrated to God that in their love for a higher good they must not condemn those who have chosen something less. He considered that this would go against Holy Scripture (cf. 1 Cor. 7:28, 38). He saw the purity and sanity of the teachings of the Lord and of the Apostles, that men should "choose greater gifts, but not despise the lesser."[408] Esteem for virginity should never lead to a denial of divine truths, as they are expounded for Christians in Holy Scripture. Further, "the great good of unblemished virginity is in no way depreciated in acknowledging the good that is also in marriage."[409] Yet Augustine always saw in a consecrated virginity a more perfect way of life. Alluding to the pericope in Luke 10:38ff., narrating Christ's visit to Bethany, he wrote: "What Martha did, wholly occupied in her service of the saints, was good, but her sister's conduct, sitting at the Lord's feet and listening to His words, is to be reckoned better. We revere Susannah for the treasure of her chastity [cf. Dan. 3], yet we value the treasure of the widow Anna higher [cf. Luke 2:36ff.], and much higher still that of the Virgin Mary [cf. Luke 1:27]."[410] Augustine regarded this preference as justified, in the first instance, by what St. Paul wrote (1 Cor. 7:32ff.) about virginity's making possible an undivided gift of Christ.[411] Then, too, marriage possesses "no eternal status."[412] The begetting of offspring and the preservation of wedded chastity are "undertakings of a human order; but to guard an unblemished virginity . . . is to aspire, here in this perishable flesh, to what is everlasting and imperishable."[413]

So Augustine is convinced that "according to the law of God" continence and consecrated virginity rank before marriage.[414] Thus, when he applies, as others of the Fathers before him had done, the parable of the sower and the thirtyfold, sixtyfold, and hundredfold crop (Matt. 13:23) to the different states of Christian life, he places virginity immediately below martyrdom, and gives matrimony the lowest place.[415] Though here he did not make any firm identification of any one state of life with the different crops for, he wrote, the gifts of divine grace are too numerous "for one to group them in no more than three divisions,"[416] he considered that his ranking of virginity immediately below martyrdom was warranted by the Church's practice in the celebration of the Eucharist of reciting the names of those who had died in consecrated virginity after the commemoration of those who had shed their blood.[417]

Because he valued virginity so highly, Augustine never wearied in encouraging aspirations to this ideal. Quoting 1 Corinthians 7:7 and 29ff., he wrote: "If only everyone would live in such sincere love, from a pure heart, a good conscience, and unfeigned faith [cf. 1 Tim. 1:5], then the City of God would the sooner attain its perfection; the goal of all the ages of the earth would be reached more quickly."[418] The Scripture he quoted, and the allusion to the City of God, growing and maturing toward its eternal fulfillment, show clearly that this abrupt declaration is to be interpreted, not, as it might seem, in any Neoplatonic or spiritist sense, which he had once affirmed, but far more in the vision he now had of salvation history and of the last end of creation.[419]

Augustine viewed every historical event as it contributed to that salvation. The struggle between good and evil, between the redeemed world and the condemned world, between the City of God and the city of the ungodly, was the true content of human history. Christ is its central point. But in the ages before His coming, for the chosen people of God, "who were to make known and bring forth the prince and saviour of all peoples," their need for a great posterity had been their help.[420] With exaggerated idealism he offers it as his opinion that the patriarchs practiced polygamy only in obedience to the role they had been given in human salvation; "not conquered by the desires of the flesh, but led on by devotion of the spirit," they had made use of marriage when they might with joyfulness have led a life of continence, if at that time such counsels had been given to them.[421] He viewed the evolution of salvation history in the times after Christ quite differently. Because he regarded history from the point of view of man's final destiny, only one event is to be awaited which would be decisive for redeemed mankind, and that is the perfection of the City of God.[422] He wrote:

> The procreation of children was an imperative duty for the holy patriarchs if the people of God, in whom what was promised in Christ was to be fulfilled, were to be generated and preserved. Now this need no longer exists. A multitude of offspring from every nation presents itself to be reborn in the spirit, wherever they may have received life according to the flesh. What has been written "There is a time to embrace, and a time to refrain from embracing" [Eccles. 3:5] plainly should be applied to then and to now. For then was the time to embrace, but now is the time to refrain from embracing.[423]

Undoubtedly Augustine's hope that all should if possible renounce the use of marriage, so as to hasten the coming of the perfected City of God, must be understood in the light of his interpretation of the philosophy of history.

Yet it must be added that Augustine knew perfectly well that his hopes were illusory. Quoting the same words from St. Paul (1 Cor. 7:9), he himself can counsel those who are unable to practice continence to marry.[424] In another place, expressing the same wish that Christians should not marry, in the same context of eschatology and salvation history, he continues, in down-to-earth language: "But if we try to encourage everyone to lead a life of continence, there will be few with whom we shall succeed." This is what the Lord had said in so many words: "This cannot be accepted by everyone" (Matt. 19:11).[425] Similarly, he stressed in his commentary on St. John's Gospel that in fact the numbers of consecrated virgins and of those living continently in the Church are few.[426] But in this he sees no falling short of the ideal, and he explains the facts by alluding to the "various gifts" with which the individual members of the Church are blessed.[427] He frequently reverted to this concept of a divinely instituted diversity of gifts. He liked to quote what St. Paul had written about it: "Everyone has his own gift from God, this one after this manner, and another after that" (1 Cor. 7:7).[428] And he regarded all these members of the Body of Christ with their differing gifts and tasks as one organic whole.[429]

Virginity as a Counsel of Perfection • Augustine taught that consecrated virginity and celibacy are distinguished from the chastity of married people in another important way: virginity and celibacy are counsels of perfection, which are not imperative.[430] "One cannot say," he wrote, " 'You must not marry' as it is said 'You must not commit adultery.' One is a commandment; the other, a counsel. Whoever follows the counsel will be praised; whoever breaks the commandment will be condemned."[431] When he pointed to Mary as the model of Christian virgins, he was at pains to show that she dedicated herself to God as a virgin "because of a vow, not a command, through love and free choice, not through the constraint of a service that must be performed."[432]

To show virginity as voluntary and yet commendable, Augustine appealed to St. Paul's specific assurance: "Concerning virgins, I have received no command from the Lord; yet I offer you counsel as one who in God's mercy has been a faithful counselor" (1 Cor. 7:25).[433] And he often quoted what Christ Himself said: "This cannot be accepted by everyone, but only by those to whom it is given. . . . Whoever can adopt it, let him do so" (Matt. 19:11ff.) as evidence that the ideal of Christian virginity and continence was commended to us by Christ only as a counsel.[434] One should choose such a life, "not as a result of compulsion, but out of longing for a greater good."[435] But one's strongest motive should be a greater love for Christ. Once, preaching, he said: "Their greater love has laid a greater burden on virgins. They did not seek what was permitted, so as to please Him more to whom they have vowed themselves. . . . It is as if they were to say 'What is your command? What do you prescribe for us if we are not to become adulteresses? Because we love you, we shall do more than you command.' "[436]

Without a doubt, in Augustine's view, whoever has taken a vow of virginity or continence had made what previously could have been a free choice into a duty. He can no longer abandon it without making himself guilty in God's sight.[437] Whoever does not honor it will make the words applicable to him: "No one who sets his hand to the plow and looks back is worthy of the kingdom of God" (Luke 9:62) and "They incur the guilt of breaking the promise they have made" (1 Tim. 5:12).[438]

The Special Reward of Virginity

Augustine dealt with this subject at length in his short treatise *Holy Virginity*, the occasion of which was Jovinian's assertions that the lives of virginity, widowhood, and marriage would be rewarded exactly alike, and that for all the blessed in heaven there was only the same recompense.[439] In opposing him, Augustine quoted the words of Isaias about the "eunuchs" to whom God has promised a special place in His house, "better than sons and daughters" and, moreover, "an everlasting name" (Is. 56:4–5);[440] and those of St. Paul: "As one star differs from another in its brilliance, so will it be in the resurrection of the dead" (1 Cor. 15:41–42);[441] and, finally, the Lord's promise that in His Father's house there are "many mansions" (John 14:2).[442] He found further proof in the Apocalypse's vision of the Lamb and His followers. Augustine believed that among the 144,000 who are described there will be those Christians "who preserved an unblemished virginity of body and an unshaken fidelity of heart."[443] He saw what will be special in their reward in the "new song," which only they know how to sing (Apoc. 14:3) and in their following the Lamb "wherever He goes" (Apoc. 14:4). In these images of "the joy of Christ's virgins," he perceived one joy different from all the other joys of the blessed, which was "joy about Christ, in Christ, with Christ, for Christ, through Christ, because of Christ."[444] But that celibates vowed to God receive a special heavenly reward will mean no diminution for the rest of the blessed in their blessedness, no cause for envy. On the contrary, in this perfected communion of the saints, he wrote to his nuns, others "in their rejoicing with you will possess, with you and in you, what they do not have in themselves."[445]

Virginity as a Gift of God (donum Dei)

In the *Confessions* Augustine related how, in his youth, perhaps when he was reading Cicero's *Hortensius*, he had entreated God: "Give me chastity and continence," but had added: "but not yet" because he had feared that God would hear him at once and cure him of the "sickness of concupiscence," which, as he himself admitted, he would then have had gratified rather than taken away.[446] The idea that only God could give a man the strength to live chastely was at that time never completely absent from his mind, even though, as the years passed by, it recurred less and less.[447] But when in the summer of 386, at the time of his conversion in Milan, he decided to live a chaste and celibate life, he felt that the decision and its realization were the work of the divine "physician who works in utter secrecy," standing, healing, and helping, at his side.[448]

Many years before the beginnings of his controversies with Pelagius, Augustine had emphasized the gratuitous nature of a life of chastity, whether in marriage or in continence; and his own personal experiences in this must have been important. For when in 395 he composed his work

Continence, and in it contrasted the nature and significance of Christian continence with Manichaean dualism and its contempt for the body, he laid such stress on continence as a gift that critics have seen in this "the constant theme, guiding the whole treatise."[449] Indeed, in an introductory chapter he developed a detailed demonstration to justify his contention that "continence is a gift of God."[450] There are places in Scripture which in his later writings he repeatedly applied to the gratuitous nature of continence. As other Fathers had done, he attributed special weight to the words from the Book of Wisdom, "And as I knew that I could not otherwise be continent, except God gave it, and this also was a point of wisdom, to know whose gift it was, I went to the Lord and entreated Him" (Wis. 8:21).[451] In the Septuagint text, it is true, the context requires the word ἐγκρατής to be supplemented by σοφίας, and the passage is concerned, not at all with sexual continence, but with wisdom.[452] The passages he quotes from the New Testament are even stronger evidence. He saw continence clearly stated to be a divine gift in the assertion "for the sake of the kingdom of heaven" with which Christ introduced His commendation: "This cannot be accepted by everyone, but only by those to whom it is given" (Matt. 19:11).[453] St. Paul, considering the married and celibate lives, wrote specifically of this gift: "Every one has his proper gift from God, one after this manner, and another after that" (1 Cor. 7:7).[454]

In the brief work *Holy Virginity*, written in 401, Augustine stressed the gratuitous nature of virginity, using the same Scriptural texts.[455] He added to these proofs by quoting St. Paul and St. James: "What have you that you have not received?" (1 Cor. 4:7) and "Every best gift, and every perfect gift, is from above, coming down from the Father of lights" (James 1:17).[456] But he took special pains to set this teaching on virginity in the wider framework of what he taught on grace and predestination, as he had expounded it for the first time in his work, written about 396, *On Various Questions to Simplicianus.* He called virgins vowed to God not only a chosen race, but a race "specially chosen from among the chosen" (cf. 1 Peter 2:9). Yet their being chosen was not in consequence of their own works; it was, in St. Paul's words, a salvation by grace, a gift of God. They, too, were "images of God, made in Christ Jesus for the good works God has prepared" (Eph. 2:8ff.). It was God, St. Paul also taught, who "distributes to each one what He wills" (1 Cor. 12:11), and this with no injustice whatever (cf. Rom. 9:14), even if man cannot fathom "by what standards of equity He made some in this way, others in that."[457] So no man can attempt to assert his own justice before God (cf. Rom. 10:3). There can be no obedience to God's commands, no repentance for past sins, if this is not "begun by His grace and perfected with His help."[458]

Totally in keeping with this teaching about God's grace, which works in men's hearts "with inward, hidden, wonderful, and indescribable power,"[459] Augustine in his *Confessions*, published at more or less the same time as he wrote of continence as a grace, added the fervent prayer: "You command continence. Give what you command, and command what you will."[460]

This brief sentence in the *Confessions*, according to Augustine's own report, began the first clash with Pelagius, who was then still living in Rome, where he commanded great respect for his exemplary life and his ascetic teaching. But when an African bishop, in his presence, repeated this prayer of Augustine's, Pelagius "found it intolerable, repudiated it in some agitation, and almost fought with the one who had recounted it."[461] It is obvious that the real reason for this violent reaction is that Pelagius saw that his view of the unimpaired strength and autonomy of the human will was challenged by Augustine's words. For however earnestly Pelagius was striving for moral renewal in Christian life, he had no vision of the role of divine grace. It was not that he flatly denied that grace exists; but, rather, that, by the term, he understood, evidently to the exclusion of everything else, God's natural endowment of man with his freedom of will and the external help of the divine commandments and the teaching and example of Christ. This was made clear in a letter about consecrated virginity, which he wrote in the year 414 to Demetrias, a "virgin of Christ" of the upper classes.[462] Though Pelagius made various uses of the word "grace"—"the help of grace," "the grace of Christ," "the good of grace," "divine grace"—one must concede to Augustine's demonstration that in this letter Pelagius, "by using the word ambiguously and loosely," was attempting to conceal his wholly inadequate understanding of what grace is.[463]

Augustine first made his views about this letter known in what he wrote to Juliana, Demetrias' mother, probably toward the end of 417—before, indeed, he had discovered the name of the letter's author. He was especially moved to do this by the "no little error" of certain people who were maintaining that "what we possess in ourselves of justice, continence, piety, and chastity we have of ourselves."[464] The following formulation he found shocking; "Now you possess," Pelagius had written to Demetrias, "those riches for the sake of which you should rightly be preferred to others and, indeed, many more. One knows that your family has inherited nobility and wealth, which are not your personal merit; yet no one can obtain spiritual riches for you, save you alone. So we may justly praise you, see in you greater merit than others have, because you can possess this only from yourself and in yourself."[465] In the expression "from yourself" (*ex te*) Augustine saw an attack on the doctrine of divine grace,[466] and so he sought, using the Scriptural texts already mentioned, to prove that no one can possess "holy, virginal continence" from himself.[467]

At the same time Augustine took pains, as he had three years before in the brief treatise *The Excellence of Widowhood*, dedicated to the same Juliana, to show how divine grace and human freedom cooperate in the spirit for the preservation of continence.[468] He defined the relationship in his pregnant formula: Virginal continence constitutes "a divine gift, which, however, is bestowed on the man who believes and who wills."[469] It is at once given by God and belonging to man, without, however, deriving from man.[470]

Therefore in *Letter 188* Augustine called virginity that treasure of which St. Paul had written that we carry it "in earthen vessels, for its supreme power is given, not by ourselves, but by God" (2 Cor. 4:7).[471]

In this he was deeply convinced that the penetration of divine grace did not impede human freedom to make decisions. "In no way do we destroy the power of choice of the human will," he wrote to Juliana in *The Excellence of Widowhood*,

> when, knowing how God's grace comes to the aid of that power, we do not in our ungrateful pride deny that help, but acknowledge it in devotion and thanksgiving. It is we who do have the will; but our very will is admonished to rise up, is healed so that it may be strong, is extended so that it may comprehend, is filled so that it may possess. For if we did not have the will, we should certainly neither receive what is given nor possess it. Who would possess continence—to single it out from God's many other gifts, for it is of continence that I am speaking to you—who would, I say, call it his own if he had not the will to possess it?[472]

So he taught that God, inwardly penetrating the human will and yet preserving its freedom of choice, leads man to right decisions, makes him to be "of good will" (*bona voluntas*). But this does not merely refute Pelagius' opinion "that God gives us no more than the knowledge by which we know what we should do"; it affirms that "God also inspires the love by which, knowing, we learn, and loving, we act."[473]

Counsels for the Daily Preservation of Dedicated Chastity

Augustine knew well the difficulties and dangers that beset the realization of one's aspirations to a life of continence vowed to God. So he went on encouraging men and women who had promised themselves to God in persistence in fulfilling their vows.[474] Furthermore, he gave them, especially in his *Rule* and in the brief treatise *Holy Virginity*, a series of counsels for the conduct of their religious and ascetic lives drawn from his own rich experience. And it is beyond doubt that he was helped by similar advice other Fathers before him, especially Cyprian, Ambrose, and Jerome, had given to nuns.[475]

As with other questions, in the advice he gave on these topics, Augustine was both moderate and shrewd. His charges, in their care to preserve pure hearts, were not to become anxious and begin questioning. Far better, they were to behave naturally. "It is not that when you go out of doors you are forbidden to catch sight of women," he wrote for his monks in the *Rule*; but they were to guard against lustful and desirous glances.[476] And he had no qualms about permitting the brethren to visit the public baths.[477] His attitude in such matters differed not only from that of many ancient pagan philosophers, but also from that of certain circles of Christians practicing continence who thought that their asceticism prohibited them from using the baths.[478] He made such visits obligatory when this was advised on medical grounds.[479] But he made the wise provision that no one was to visit the baths alone.[480] This was to be a safeguard against the moral dangers which could attend going to the baths, especially now that the strict old Roman discipline had relaxed and the segregation of the sexes inside the buildings was no longer observed everywhere.[481]

Augustine recommended that those who had taken vows of chastity always "exercise prudence."[482] Once, preaching, he said: "Let no one persuade himself that the time of temptations is past. Whoever says this thinks that he will have peace; but whoever thinks that he will have peace will in his tranquillity be afflicted."[483] He knew too much about human weakness from his own experience; and he feared human suspicion, whether justified or not. He regarded it as a duty of a Christian's love of his neighbors, particularly for clerics and religious of both sexes, to do everything in his power to protect his own good name. "Whoever relies on his clear conscience," he said in a sermon, "and cares nothing for his reputation, is in great danger."[484] Thus he was not in favor of women having access to the brethren's living quarters, or living with them in one house. He wanted to prevent "weaker members taking offense or scandal by this" or "succumbing to the temptations that are our human lot."[485]

In particular, he recommended for the protection of the chastity of religious that they keep guard over their senses, and especially over their eyes. In his *Rule* he warns against the error of supposing that unchastity consists only in sins that are committed. "A shameless eye is the messenger of a shameless heart,"[486] which is the reason why Holy Scripture says: "A fixed gaze is an abomination to the Lord" (Wis. 27:20).[487] In the same chapter of his *Rule*, he enjoins a religious demeanor in one's whole conduct: "Walking, standing, whatever movement you make, do nothing to offend anyone who sees you; let everything befit your holy way of life."[488]

He also recommended to his charges, for a guard on their purity of heart, to remember the presence of the God who knows everything. In this connection he calls God "the witness who is on high, from whom nothing can remain concealed."[489] In one sermon he reflects on God's omnipresence, to bring it home to his hearers: "You go out, and He will see you; you come back, and He will see you. The lamp is burning, and He sees you; the lamp is out, and He sees you. You go into your bedchamber, and He sees you; you lock yourself in your private quarters, and He sees you. Fear Him whose concern it is to see you; and in this fear be chaste."[490] Here he did not mean that fear he had called "servile" (*timor servilis*) and regarded as the antithesis of the love of God, because in such a fear a man's proneness to sin remains.[491] It was of such fear that St. John wrote: "There is no fear in love, but perfect love drives out fear" (1 John 4:18).[492] He is much more concerned with the "chaste fear, enduring forever" (Ps. 18:10).[493] This will cause one who has taken vows to tremble "lest he gravely offend the one whom he loves and who, he knows, loves him."[494] For, Augustine wrote, "this chaste fear is united to a love from which it cannot be parted."[495]

As has been shown above, he always stressed the gratuitous nature, the gift, that is celibate chastity dedicated to God. But, accordingly, he was deeply convinced that all human self-reliance in striving for a consecrated chastity is bound to fail, and that, therefore, the most important aids for the preservation of this divine gift are humility and prayer. He called pride a "thief," making off with virginity.[496] Therefore, a basic rule for those with vows of chastity is "Take the path that leads to the heights, but walk with humble feet."[497] Thus, in *Holy Virginity* he wrote at length about the necessity and the practice of humility, saying that he was afraid that people might reproach him with having wandered from his subject and with writing, "not about virginity, but about humility."[498] Augustine countered this objection: "Only God, who has bestowed this treasure of virginity, is its protector, and 'God is love' " (1 John 4:8). Thus, virginity's protector is love, but the protector's workplace is humility. Therefore it was wholly practical for him in the short treatise to have sought "to make the workplace ready for this protector."[499]

Anyone who recognizes continence as God's gift, Augustine was convinced, will not count himself better than others because of it, but will thank God for it, and persist in prayer to Him to preserve what He has given. The Lord's admonition applies here: "Watch and pray, that you do not fall into temptation" (Matt. 26:41).[500] Often Augustine wrote of the urgent necessity of prayer for God's help in preserving this great treasure.[501] By such prayer one can turn "the burden of continence" into Christ's burden, for it will in a fashion be caused by Christ Himself, "if men have the faith that entreats from God, who commands, what he commands."[502] "Take all your support from Him, and do not be afraid," he wrote in the *Confessions*; "He will not weaken, and He will not let you fall."[503]

He was sure that "unmarried people who vow their purity to God" are more easily able to practice continence than, for instance, unmarried women who through special circumstances are compelled for years to forgo marital relations. Whereas such as these may still hope for their sexual desires to be satisfied, the concupiscence of the unmarried with vows is no longer fed upon expectation.[504] Then, too, it may happen that "in holy chastity the joys of the flesh are replaced by those of the spirit: reading, prayer, the chanting of psalms, mental aspirations, accumulation of good works, hope in the world to come, and a heart lifted up."[505]

Yet even so, for Augustine, continence dedicated to God in the monastery is not merely the personal concern of individuals, but a great good in the life of the community as well. Therefore, each one is responsible for his brethren and for the preservation of chastity in everything that is said and done. In his *Rule*, it is specified: "Guard each other's chastity."[506] But if someone becomes aware of folly or guilt in others, he should correct them in brotherly fashion, or bring the matter to the superior's notice, so that they can be put to rights in good time.[507] Above all else, the atmosphere of a monastery must breathe such a spirit as befits "lovers of spiritual beauty."[508] He counseled his monks: "The love between you should be, not fleshly, but spiritual."[509] So the community can and should become a powerful protection for its individual members, through the good example they set for one another and their watchfulness over one another. In one place Augustine mentioned the help in times of temptation offered by the knowledge that one is seen and observed by others.[510] But in this care for others he saw brotherly love at work, and, working through it, God's own fatherly love; as it is written in the *Rule*: "For God, who lives within you, will also in this way protect you through yourselves."[511]

SUMMARY: THE SPIRIT OF AUGUSTINE'S MONASTICISM

In recent decades, much thought has been given to the question of the real differences the separate characteristics of individual religious orders make. The fundamental variations in the spiritual formation of the Benedictines, the Franciscans, or the Jesuits have been described, and writers have asked what their origins are.[512]

The special features of a religious family are shared, naturally, by its members. Any community with an ordered formation will produce its own type of personality. It is not that this will be completely developed in every single member; but this type will represent the ideal toward which individuals should—must—strive if they want to be living members of the community.

Where do we look for the special stamp of Augustinian monasticism? It has been shown that what was new and significant in Augustine's moral code was his insistence that love is the basic element of the good life, and that he was the first to make love the cornerstone, uniting and supporting the entire structure of Christian morality.[513] The same is true of his ideals of monastic living. With clarity and logic he exalted love as the fundamental law of life in monasteries.[514]

Like a golden thread running through his *Rule* there is the watchword of Christian love: "Let love, which will not pass away, preside over everything."[515] Not continence or severe penances, not poverty or obedience, but love is the soul of the common life, the law of monastic perfection;[516] love ought to form a monk's whole life.[517] For him, love is the one fruit that life in his monasteries ought to bring to ripeness,[518] his monks' dearest treasure, which they should cherish more than all the wealth of the world.[519]

Therefore, there is at the beginning of the *Ordo*, as the theme for the whole *Rule*, the sentence: "Before all else, dearest brothers, God should be loved, and then your neighbor, for these are the chief commandments that were given to us."[520] One cannot, in fact, formulate better the essence of Augustine's monastic legislation than by this, the Gospel's chief command. He made no sharp distinction between love of God and love of one's neighbor. Usually he wrote simply of *caritas*, "Christian love," which is indivisible. The love of one's neighbor was for him only another kind of love of God. One cannot truly love one's neighbor without loving God,[521] just as one cannot truly love God and not one's neighbor.

Because love is the soul of Augustinian monasticism, his thinking about community occupies a central place. It is precisely in the community that a true, selfless love is preserved and goes on growing. It is here, according to Augustine, that true love is seen in the monastery, the love that seeks, not what is its own, but what will benefit the community.[522] And so for him monastic poverty is put to the service of love.

That love does preside over everything is shown by the individual traits of his ideal monk. He helped greatly toward the evolution of thought about what constitutes a real monastic family, where the superior is regarded as the father. Obedience in the monastery, in his view, presupposed a close personal relationship between superior and subjects, a relationship built on mutual confidence and mutual love. In all the formation and legislation which is needed, love must prevail.

The basic law of love is the source of the respect for persons and the moderation that characterize Augustine's monastic legislation. It was love that enabled him so willingly to make exceptions, to have regard for the weaknesses of some. It is love, he taught, that must determine the nature and the measure of monastic asceticism. And it is love in which his monks must bear with one another, forgiving shortcomings.

Because love inspires Augustinian monasticism, that way of life, by its essence, is an apostolic way. Love, he taught, cannot withdraw into itself, but is always striving to impart itself to others. Love for Augustine is a readiness to supply another's needs, and, above all, the need of Mother Church.

Augustine gave to his legislation clear ecclesial directions, which were expressed not only in its apostolic aims, but also in Augustinian monastic life growing out of the Mystical Body. But he taught that the importance of that life for the Body of Christ was principally because that basic law of love that governs "the whole Christ, head and body," was clearly visible in monastic communities.[523]

So it was that his monasticism received its character from his profoundest thinking about Christian love. It is this which gives it its true Augustinian nature. Augustine's own personality is reflected in it. The art of the Church could find no more striking attribute with which to endow him than a heart, the symbol of his love.

Another driving force that characterizes his monasticism and is very close in origin to his basic philosophy of Christian love is his teaching that monastic life is a life of Christian freedom. As early as his account of the Roman monasteries, in *The Ways of the Catholic Church*, he had written of the life of the monks in Rome as that of "Christian love, holiness, and freedom."[524] In a later letter, he insists upon the "free servitude before God" which is observed in the monastery.[525] And it is the same concept in St. Paul, of freedom from the "law," which he stressed when he wrote of the spirit in which the brethren of his own monasteries should observe the prescription of the *Rule*: "not as slaves under the law, but as free men established under grace" (cf. Rom. 6:14).[526]

In the concluding section of his *Rule*, that is how he describes the monks: "established under grace." In this, we must see a last typical feature of his ideal of monastic life. In other places, and even before he began to contend with Pelagius, he had stressed the concept we find here: that the life of complete surrender to God's service is God's gift and the work of grace.[527] In the religious vocation, he saw a special gift of God not offered to everyone.[528] But fulfilling one's vows and persisting to the end are possible only with the help of God's grace.[529] Therefore, if monks look back on their lives and are sure that they have faithfully observed the *Rule*'s prescriptions, they owe their thanks "to the Lord, the giver of all good things."[530] The object of all their works of piety, of their asceticism, and of their love of their neighbors must be nothing other than the honor of Him "who perfects everything in everything" (1 Cor. 12:6).[531] Therefore in *Holy Virginity* he admonished his nuns that they should not set themselves up as being righteous (cf. Rom. 10:3), but submit themselves to God, who justifies them.[532]

In a sermon, Augustine meditatively described how monks in their lives are directed by God and His grace. He quoted Psalm 132:3: "It is like the dew of Hermon, which falls on the mountains of Sion," and went on: "Dear brothers, he wanted to make us understand that it is God's grace that makes brothers dwell together in unity [Ps. 132:1], not their own strength, not their own merits, but His gift and His grace, like the dew of heaven."[533] So he appealed urgently to the monks: "All of you, who want to dwell together in unity, must long for this dew; let it be sprinkled upon you. If it is not, you will not be able to stand fast by what you profess before men. And you would not have dared to profess it, had God not made His voice resound. And you would not have been able to persevere, had He not spread His banquet lavishly before you."[534]

NOTES

1. Augustine writes of "conversion" (*conversio*) in this monastic sense in *Letter 83* 2 and *Letter 126* 7, and applies the term "converts" (*converti*) to those who had entered the monastery in *Letter 83* 3, *The Work of Monks* 21.25 and 25.32, and *Sermon 356* 3.

2. "Conversion to the true God . . . the penance of men and the conversion of the wills to God" (*The City of God* 7.33, 10.32).

3. For this sense, see H. Leclerq, "Conversion," *Dictionnaire d'Archéologie Chrétienne et de Liturgie*, III 2797ff.; A. D. Nock, "Bekehrung," *Reallexikon für Antike und Christentum*, II 105–18, esp. 117; M. Rothenhäusler, "Conversio morum," ibid., III 422–24.

4. Cf. on this what Augustine wrote of his own calling to a life of Christian asceticism: "For You converted me to Yourself, so that I never again sought either a wife or any other hope this world has to offer . . ." (*Confessions* 8.12.30).

5. "Ad Dei liberam servitutem conversus" (*Letter 126* 7).

6. See above, note 1.

7. *Letter 243* 10.

8. *Exposition on Psalm 141* 15.

9. *Sermon 81* 3.

10. *Homily on St. John's Gospel 110* 2 and *Homily on St. John's Gospel 111* 5; *Sermon* 96 7.8f.

11. *Rule* 1.4, 1.6–7, 3.4.

12. For recent literature, cf. R. Schneider, *Welt und Kirche bei Augustin: Ein Beitrag zur Frage des christlichen Existentialismus* (Munich, 1949); Ignacio M. de la Eucaristía, *Hombre, Mundo, Redención: Concepto agustiniano del hombre bajo el signo de Adán o de Cristo* (Valencia, 1954); S. Cuesta, "La concepción agustiniana del mundo a través del amor," AM I, pp. 347–56.

13. *Homily on St. John's Gospel 2* 10f.; *Exposition on Psalm 141* 14.

14. *On Heresies* 70; *Against Fortunatus* 1.

15. *Exposition on Psalm 145* 5 and 12; *Sermon 241* 2.2, etc. Cf. also Cuesta, "La concepción agustiniana del mundo," pp. 352ff.

16. *The Literal Meaning of Genesis* 8.8. Cf. Mausbach, *Die Ethik*, I 314ff.

17. ". . . magna . . . et omnino humana" (*The Greatness of the Soul* 33.72).

18. *Christian Instruction* 1.4.4., and frequently elsewhere.

19. *On Music* 6.14.46. Cf. Mausbach, *Die Ethik*, I 265ff.

20. ". . . utendum est hoc mundo, non fruendum" (*Christian Instruction* 1.4.4).

21. *Sermon 311* 11.12.

22. ". . . mundus, quem regit diabolus" (*Exposition on Psalm 141* 15). Cf. Schneider, *Welt und Kirche*, pp. 16ff.

23. *Homily on St. John's Gospel 111* 5, etc.

24. *Exposition on Psalm 141* 14f., etc.

25. *Sermon 144* 5.6.

26. *Exposition on Psalm 141* 15.
27. *Homily on St. John's Epistle to the Parthi* 2 10ff.
28. *Exposition on Psalm 141* 15.
29. Cf. on this Mausbach, *Die Ethik*, I 64ff., 222ff., etc.; Nygren, *Eros and Agape*, pp. 378ff., 395ff., Bouyer, *La Spiritualité du Nouveau Testament*, pp. 576ff.; Schaffner, *Christliche Demut*, pp. 154f.
30. *Christian Instruction* 1.4.4.
31. Ibid. 1.22.20.
32. Ibid. 1.3.3.
33. Ibid. 3.10.16. Cf. 1.27.28, and *Against Julian*, 4.3.33.
34. *The Trinity* 9.8.13.
35. Cf. Nygren, *Eros and Agape*, p. 400.
36. *Homily on St. John's Epistle to the Parthi* 2 11.
37. Ibid.
38. *The City of God* 14.28.
39. Augustine used this term in *Homily on St. John's Epistle to the Parthi* 2 9.
40. Ibid. Cf. also ibid. 14.
41. *Homily on St. John's Gospel 110* 2; *Sermon 96* 7.7; *Sermon 130* 4; *Sermon 335* 1.1, etc.
42. *Sermon 157* 1.1.
43. *Sermon 130* 4; *Sermon 335* 1.1.
44. Cf., for instance, *Exposition on Psalm 34* 2.15; *Exposition on Psalm 113* 1.3; *Homily on St. John's Epistle to the Parthi* 2 9ff.
45. *Sermon 76* 6.9.
46. *Sermon 125* 7.
47. *Homily on St. John's Epistle to the Parthi* 2 10.
48. *Exposition on Psalm 92* 8.
49. *Sermon 15* 4.4. Cf. Schneider, *Welt und Kirche*, pp. 81–82.
50. *Homily on St. John's Gospel 87* 2.
51. Ibid. 3.
52. Ibid.
53. Ibid.
54. Cf. A. Zumkeller, *Aurelius Augustinus: Schriften gegen die Pelagianer*, 2 vols. (Würzburg, 1964), II 491, and the literature cited there.
55. *Homily on St. John's Gospel 87* 4.
56. Ibid.
57. *Sermon 96* 7.9.
58. "Ab eis, qui diligunt saeculum, segregavi me" (*Sermon 355* 2).
59. "Spem quippe omnem saeculi reliqueram" (ibid.). Similarly, *Confessions* 8.12.30.
60. ". . . ad discendam vitam removeri a curis saecularibus" (*Letter 243* 6).
61. *Rule* 1.4, 1.7, 3.4, 3.5.
62. Ibid. 1.7.
63. Ibid. 3.4–5.
64. Ibid. 3.4.

65. Cf. ibid. 1.7, 3.4.
66. Cf. ibid. 1.7.
67. Cf. ibid. 3.5.
68. *Sermon 125* 7.
69. Ibid.
70. Cf. also above, pp. 107–109.
71. Cf. above, pp. 150–51 and below, pp. 248–51.
72. *The Ways of the Catholic Church* 1.27.52. Cf. also the similar definition in *Homily on St. John's Gospel 19* 15: "a rational soul which has a body."
73. "Bodies belong to that same human nature" (*The City of God* 1.13). Similarly, ibid. 19.3. Cf. also *Continence* 12.26. This is his correction of his original views, strongly colored by Platonism: "That for which I am called mortal is not mine" (*Of Order* 2.19.50).
74. Cf. *The City of God* 12.16.
75. R. Schwarz, "Die leib-seelische Existenz bei Augustinus," *Philosophisches Jahrbuch*, 63 (1955), 325–37. Although he cannot see in Augustine's teaching more than an "inwardly living, accidental unity" of body and soul, Hieronymus a Parisiis ("De unione animae cum corpore in doctrina S. Augustini," in *Acta Hebdomadae Augustinianae–Thomisticae* [Turin & Rome, 1931], pp. 271–311) asserted that Augustine was concerned with "a unity of nature, of substance, and of person."
76. *The Literal Meaning of Genesis* 7.27. Cf. also Hendrikx, "Platonisches und biblisches Denken bei Augustin," p. 291.
77. *Sermon 277* 3.3. Cf. also *The Literal Meaning of Genesis* 7.26.
78. *Continence* 7.18; *The City of God* 14.22.
79. *The Usefulness of Fasting* 4.4. On the questioned genuineness of this work, see R. Arbesmann, *Aurelius Augustinus: Der Nutzen des Fastens* (Würzburg, 1958), pp. viiff. Cf. also *Continence* 7ff.18ff.; *Christian Instruction* 1.24f.24–26; *Sermon 155* 15. See further Reul, *Die sittlichen Ideale*, pp. 76ff.
80. Cf. *On 83 Various Questions*, question 10; *The Two Souls* 3.2; *Against Faustus* 20.15 and 22; 21.7ff., 31.4.
81. *The City of God* 10.29, 22.26; *Sermon 241* 7.7; *Retractations* 1.4.3.
82. *The City of God* 11.23. Cf. *Sermon* 277 3.3. On Augustine's repudiation of all hatred of the body, cf. also Mausbach, *Die Ethik*, I 159ff.
83. *Exposition on Psalm 101* 2.14, and *Sermo Denis* 2, in Morin, p. 15.
84. *The Usefulness of Fasting* 4.5.
85. *Continence* 9ff.22ff.; *Against Faustus* 21.7f. and 24.2.
86. "There was peace [between body and soul] in our bodies, when we did not suffer the assaults and warfare of concupiscence in that life which was lost when, through the first man's sin, nature was violated" (*The Incomplete Work against Julian* 6.14).
87. Mausbach, *Die Ethik*, II 174.
88. Hendrikx, "Platonisches und biblisches Denken," p. 289.
89. *Exposition on Psalm 141* 18.
90. *The Ways of the Catholic Church* 1.22.40.
91. *Exposition on Psalm* 87 11.

92. *Sermon 277* 6.6; *The Usefulness of Fasting* 2.2.

93. Cf. *Sermon 241* 7.7.

94. *Exposition on Psalm 141* 18.

95. Cf. *The City of God* 10.29.

96. *Against Maximinus* 2.21.1. Cf. also *Against Faustus* 20.15, 22.27; *The City of God* 1.13.

97. *Against Maximinus* 2.21.1.

98. Schwarz, "Die leib-seelische Existenz," 359.

99. *The Usefulness of Fasting* 3.3. Cf. also Arbesmann, *Der Nutzen des Fastens*, p. 7.

100. Cf. Mausbach, *Die Ethik*, I 161f.

101. Cf. O. Bardenhewer, "Augustinus über Röm 7:14ff.," MA II, pp. 879–83; P. Platz, *Der Römerbrief in der Gnadenlehre Augustins* (Würzburg, 1938), pp. 146ff.; A. F. Lekkerkerker, *Römer 7 und Römer 9 bei Augustin* (Amsterdam 1942), pp. 15ff., 41ff.; Zumkeller, *Schriften gegen die Pelagianer*, II 517ff.

102. *Sermon 159* 2. Cf. Mausbach, *Die Ethik*, I 260ff.

103. Cf. *Confessions* 10.31ff.43ff., *Against Julian* 4.14.65ff. See also Mausbach, *Die Ethik*, I 244ff.

104. Schwarz, "Die leib-seelische Existenz," 332, 356; cf. also B. Stoeckle, *Die Lehre von der erbsündlichen Konkupiszenz in ihrer Bedeutung für das christliche Leibethos* (Ettal, 1954), p. 72. Schwarz's presentation occasionally lacks the necessary differentiation between the still strongly Platonic views on the value of the body of the young Augustine and those of the bishop and the theologian. See, for example, p. 353.

105. J. Bernhart, *Augustinus* (Munich, 1922), p. 22 (as cited in Schwarz, "Die leib-seelische Existenz," 357), and A. Adam, "Das Fortwirken des Manichäismus bei Augustin," *Zeitschrift für Kirchengeschichte*, 69 (1958), 20.

106. In the rigorism of Augustine's views, especially concerning the pleasure connected with the satisfaction of man's desires for food, drink, and sex, see Mausbach, *Die Ethik*, I 249ff. Part of the explanation may lie in the vicissitudes of his youth, when he was marked by uncontrolled impetuosity, especially in his sexual impulses. Cf. Zumkeller, *Schriften gegen die Pelagianer*, II 537.

107. Cf. Hendrikx, "Platonisches und biblisches Denken," pp. 289ff., and J. A. Beckaert, "Bases philosophiques de l'ascèse augustinienne," AM II, pp. 703–12.

108. "They are called merciful, even though they are so wise that now no sorrow of the mind can disturb them"—*The Ways of the Catholic Church* 1.27.53 (cf. on this also a latter correction of this statement in *Retractations* 1.7[6].4). "Therefore a wise man never fears either the death or the sufferings of the body"—*The Happy Life* 3.25.

109. With regard to the affections he wrote: "Therefore in our vices and sins we have no call to reproach the Creator of our flesh with injustice, for in its nature and order it is good" (*The City of God* 14.5).

110. Ibid. 9.4, 14.8.

111. "It is not only by the flesh that the spirit is stirred. . . . It can also be moved by itself" (ibid. 14.5).

112. Ibid. 14.5ff.

113. "For indeed some think that souls are affected through the limbs and members, so that their feelings of desire, fear, joy, or sorrow are sicknesses for them" (ibid. 14.5).

114. Ibid. 9.4.

115. Ibid. 14.6f.

116. Ibid. 14.8.

117. Ibid. 14.9.

118. Ibid. 14.7 and 9.

119. Ibid. 14.9.

120. Ibid.

121. Cf. also Secundo de Jesús, "Las pasiones en la concepción agustiniana de la vida espiritual," *Revista de Espiritualidad*, 14 (1955), 289f.

122. *The City of God* 14.9.

123. Ibid.

124. Ibid.

125. Ibid.

126. Cf. Reul, *Die sittlichen Ideale*, p. 152.

127. "Even if [the mind's affections and movements] do not consent, nonetheless if they are not governed with care, they pull the spirit asunder, weaken it, and make life most wretched" (*On Genesis Against the Manichaeans* 1.20.31). Cf. S. Cuesta, *El equilibrio pasional en la doctrina Estoica y en la de San Agustín* (Madrid, 1945), pp. 269ff.

128. *On Genesis Against the Manichaeans* 1.20.31.

129. *Continence* 12.26.

130. *Sermon 128* 11. Cf. *Continence* 8.20.

131. "My flesh is my beast. . . . I shall check it with fasting" (*The Usefulness of Fasting* 3.3). Cf. *Against Faustus* 30.5 and *Rule* 3.1.

132. *Confessions* 10.31.47.

133. *The City of God* 9.5.

134. *Against Faustus* 22.70. Cf. also Reul, *Die sittlichen Ideale*, pp. 153f.

135. *Retractations* 1.5.3. Cf. *The Immortality of the Soul* 13.22.

136. *Retractations* 1.4.3. Cf. *Soliloquies* 1.14.24.

137. *The City of God* 10.29, 22.26. Cf. Mausbach, *Die Ethik*, I 161ff.

138. Cf., for example, *Letter 10* 2f. What he was then longing for he describes here by the terms "security" (*securitas*), tranquillity (*tranquillitas*), and "a life free from fear" (*vita intrepida*).

139. Cf. *The Usefulness of Fasting* 4.5.

140. *Christian Instruction* 1.24.25. Cf. on this also *Continence* 12.26.

141. *Sermon 278* 10.10.

142. *The Usefulness of Fasting* 5.6. Cf. also *Sermon 206* 3; *Sermon 207* 2.

143. *The Usefulness of Fasting* 2.2.

144. Ibid. 5.6.

145. *Confessions* 10.29.40.

146. Cf. Mausbach, *Die Ethik*, I 364ff., 372ff.

147. Cf. ibid. 391ff.

148. *Letter* 220 1.

149. *Letter 140* 13f.

150. *Letter 243* 2.

151. Ibid. 5. See below, p. 375.

152. *Letter 243* 3.

153. Ibid. 9.

154. Ibid. 11. Even in the days of Pachomius it was customary to expound the whole cycle of monastic duties as symbolized by the cross. See Rothenhäusler, "Die Anfänge," 25f., and idem, "Unter dem Geheimnis," 95f.

155. *Letter 243* 3.

156. *Exposition on Psalm 131* 6.

157. Ibid. 5.

158. *The City of God* 10.6. Cf. on this paragraph also A. F. Krueger, *Synthesis of Sacrifice According to Saint Augustine* (Mundelein, 1950), pp. 127ff., and J. Lécuyer, "Le Sacrifice selon saint Augustin," AM II, pp. 905–14.

159. *The City of God* 10.6. Cf. also *The Usefulness of Fasting* 3.3, where Augustine treats the mortification of the body under the image of "victim."

160. *The City of God* 10.5.

161. Ibid.

162. Ibid. 10.6.

163. Ibid.

164. Ibid.

165. Ibid. Cf. also Krueger, *Synthesis of Sacrifice*, pp. 128 and 131, as well as Gessel, *Eucharistische Gemeinschaft*, p. 207.

166. *The City of God* 10.20.

167. E. Hendrikx, "Augustinus," *Theologisch Woordenboek* I (Roermond & Maaseik, 1952), p. 329. Cf. also M. M. Steggink, *Studie over de zelfverloochening en de versterving* (Utrecht, 1955), pp. 33–37.

168. This is the Septuagint version of Proverbs 27:20, quoted in *Rule* 4.4.

169. *Rule* 3.1.

170. Ibid. 4.1.

171. Ibid. 8.1.

172. Ibid. 4.1.

173. Oppenheim, *Das Mönchskleid*, pp. 32ff.

174. *The Lord's Sermon on the Mount* 2.12.41. Cf. also Possidius 22.

175. *Rule* 3.1.

176. Ibid. 3.5. Cf. A. Vermeersch, "Le Concept de la vie religieuse dans saint Augustin," *Gregorianum*, 11 (1930), 120f.

177. *Rule* 3.1.

178. Possidius 22.

179. Ibid. 27.

180. Cf. *Against Faustus* 30.5.

181. In Rome and elsewhere fasting was observed on Saturdays. Cf. *Letter 36* 7f.

182. Cf. ibid. 8 and *The Ways of the Catholic Church* 1.33.70.

183. Legewie, "Die körperliche Konstitution," p. 21.

184. *Confessions* 10.31.43ff.
185. Cf. Mausbach, *Die Ethik*, I 244ff.
186. *Confessions* 10.31.44.
187. Ibid. 10.31.47.
188. Ibid. 10.33f.49–53.
189. Ibid. 10.35.54ff. Cf. H. Blumenberg, "Augustins Anteil an der Geschichte des Begriffs der theoretischen Neugierde," REA, 7 (1961), 34–70; idem, "*Curiositas* und *veritas*: Zur Ideengeschichte von Augustin, *Confessiones* X 35," in *Studia Patristica* VI, ed. F. L. Cross (Berlin, 1962), pp. 294–302.
190. *Confessions* 10.35.55. There seems to me to be no evidence for the claim that Augustine's conception of curiosity evinces an "inexpugnable dualism" (Blumenberg, "Augustins Anteil," 49; see also his "*Curiositas* und *veritas*," p. 298). This kind of Neoplatonic concept in the early writings (*The Ways of the Catholic Church* 1.20.37: "everything sensory is to be condemned") Augustine would later retract and correct.
191. *Sermon 128* 8.10.
192. Ibid. 9.11.
193. Ibid.
194. Ibid.
195. Cf. *Retractations* 1.10.2 and *Continence* 8.19ff.
196. *Sermon 128* 10.
197. *Exposition on Psalm 35* 6.
198. Cf. *The Usefulness of Fasting* 1f.
199. *Sermon 154* 8.
200. *Continence* 11.25.
201. *The Usefulness of Fasting* 3.
202. *Letter 36* 11.25.
203. *Letter 54* 2.3.
204. *Letter 36*.
205. Ibid. 14.32 and *Letter 54* 2.3.
206. Cf. *Rule* 5.2.
207. *The Ways of the Catholic Church* 1.33.73.
208. *Letter 36* 9.21.
209. *The Ways of the Catholic Church* 1.33.72.
210. Possidius 22.
211. *Letter 36* 9.26. Cf. also 8.20, and *Rule* 3.3–5.
212. *Rule* 3.1.
213. *Letter 36* 11.25.
214. *The Ways of the Catholic Church* 1.31.66.
215. Ibid. 1.31.67.
216. Ibid. 1.33.71. Cf. *Rule* 3.1–2.
217. *Rule* 1.3, 3.4–5.
218. *Sermon 356* 13.
219. *The Work of Monks* 25.33.
220. Possidius 22. Cf. *The Ways of the Catholic Church* 1.33.71f.; *Letter 55* 20.36; *Against Faustus* 30.5; *Confessions* 10.31.46.

221. Cf. *The Lives of the Fathers* 5.5.31 (PL 73.868).

222. Cf. *The Lord's Sermon on the Mount* 2.12.41, and Oppenheim, *Das Mönchkleid*, pp. 32ff.

223. *Rule* 5.5, 5.7.

224. Possidius 22.

225. *The Lord's Sermon on the Mount* 2.12.41.

226. Possidius 22.

227. *Rule* 4.1. Cf. *Sermon 356* 13.

228. *Rule* 5.1.

229. Ibid. 4.5.4.

230. Ibid. 4.3.

231. Ibid. 4.4.

232. Cf. D. Feuling, "Discretio," BMS, 7 (1925), 241–58, 349–66; H. Walter, "Die benediktinische Discretio," in *Benedictus, der Vater des Abendlandes*, ed. H. S. Brechter (Munich, 1947), pp. 195–212; R. Schlund, "Diskretion," LThK, III[2], 418f.

233. Meller, *L'Itinéraire*, p. 108.

234. *Rule* 8.1.

235. Ibid. 1.7.

236. Cf. Vermeersch, "Le Concept," 100.

237. *The Trinity* 4.1.2.

238. Reul, *Die sittlichen Ideale*, pp. 99f.; Schaffner, *Christliche Demut*, pp. 37ff.

239. Schaffner, *Christliche Demut*, pp. 37ff.

240. Ibid., pp. 45ff., and J. Gewiess, "Demut (biblisch)," LThK, III[2], 223f.

241. Schaffner, *Christliche Demut*, p. 295.

242. A. von Harnack, *Lehrbuch der Dogmengeschichte* III, 5th ed. (Tübingen, 1932), p. 130, as cited in Schaffner, *Christliche Demut*, p. 87.

243. *Sermo Mai 126* 11, in Morin, p. 365.

244. *Homily on St. John's Gospel 3* 15.

245. *Sermon 62* 1.1.

246. Cf., for example, *Sermo Mai 127* 2, in Morin, p. 369.

247. *Exposition on Psalm 31* 2.18.

248. *Faith and the Creed* 4.8.

249. Schaffner, *Christliche Demut*, p. 104.

250. For the sources, see ibid., p. 102*n*56.

251. *The Creed for Catechumens* 3.6.

252. Schaffner, *Christliche Demut*, pp. 104f. Cf. for instance *Confessions* 7.9.14 and *Homily on St. John's Gospel 104* 3.

253. *Exposition on Psalm 18* 2.15. On this image of Christ the physician, a favorite of Augustine's, see R. Arbesmann, "Christ the *Medicus humilis* in Saint Augustine," AM II, pp. 623–29, and idem, "The Concept of *Christus medicus* in St. Augustine," *Traditio*, 10 (1954), 1–28.

254. For further sources, see Schaffner, *Christliche Demut*, p. 129*n*142.

255. Ibid., pp. 107ff., 117ff.

256. *Sermon 293* 5.

257. Schaffner, *Christliche Demut*, pp. 113ff., 129ff.
258. *Sermon 96* 3.3. Cf. also *Sermon 206* 1.1.
259. Cf. Schaffner, *Christliche Demut*, pp. 211f.
260. Ibid., p. 216.
261. *Commentary on the Epistle to the Galatians* 45.
262. Cf. Schaffner, *Christliche Demut*, pp. 212ff.
263. *Exposition on Psalm 118* 2.1.
264. *Sermon 32* 13.
265. Schaffner, *Christliche Demut*, pp. 251ff.
266. Ibid., pp. 139ff.
267. *Sermon 137* 4.4.
268. Schaffner, *Christliche Demut*, pp. 251ff.
269. *The City of God* 14.13.
270. *Homily on St. John's Gospel 25* 16.
271. *Homily on St. John's Gospel 29* 8.
272. Ibid.
273. *Continence* 5.13.
274. *Exposition on Psalm 93* 15; *The Spirit and the Letter* 7.11; and frequently elsewhere.
275. *Homily on St. John's Gospel 3* 10.
276. *Exposition on Psalm 41* 12.
277. *Sermon 61* 4.4.
278. *Homily on St. John's Gospel 58* 4.
279. *Rule* 7.3. Cf. 5.9.
280. *The City of God* 14.28.
281. Cf. L. Bopp, "Die Demutsstufen der Benediktinerregel," in *Benedictus, der Vater des Abendlandes*, ed. H. S. Brechter (Munich, 1947), pp. 241–62.
282. Cf. M. Viller, *Aszese und Mystik*, pp. 251ff.
283. *Sermon 69* 2.
284. *Holy Virginity* 31.31.
285. *Sermon 160* 4.
286. *Exposition on Psalm 130* 14.
287. See AH 495, note on line 27. The origin of this expression is uncertain.
288. *Exposition on Psalm 25* 2.11.
289. *Exposition on Psalm 93* 15.
290. Cf. *Holy Virginity* 31.31, 33.33, 43.44.
291. Ibid. 31.31.
292. Ibid. 34.34.
293. Ibid. 36.36.
294. Ibid. 36.37.
295. Ibid. 37.38.
296. Ibid. 37.37. Cf. also 49ff.49ff.
297. Ibid. 37.38.
298. Cf. Reul, *Die sittlichen Ideale*, pp. 101f.
299. *Holy Virginity* 40.41. Cf. also 42.43.
300. *Against Faustus* 5.9.

301. *Exposition on Psalm 132* 10f.
302. *Rule* 1.7.
303. *Holy Virginity* 35ff.35ff.
304. *Exposition on Psalm 93* 15.
305. *Rule* 8.2.
306. *Holy Virginity* 40.41. Cf. also 52.53.
307. Ibid. 41.42.
308. Ibid. 40.41. Cf. also 52.53.
309. *Sermon 354* 5.
310. *Holy Virginity* 52.53.
311. Ibid.
312. *On 83 Various Questions*, question 71 5.
313. *Holy Virginity* 44.45.
314. *Exposition on Psalm 36* 2.11; *Exposition on Psalm 83* 4. See above, pp. 105–106. See also Mausbach, *Die Ethik*, 1 402ff., and Viller, *Aszese und Mystik*, p. 255.
315. *Holy Virginity* 44.45. Cf. also 47.47.
316. *Sermon 169* 18.
317. *Confessions* 10.30f.
318. Ibid. 10.29.31, 37.
319. Ibid. 10.32.48.
320. Ibid. 10.31.45. Cf. also Hofmann, "Wandlungen," 413ff.
321. Once, in writing about the lives of monks, Augustine specifically called it "serving God in celibacy" (*in coelibatu servire Deo*). See *Exposition on Psalm 132* 5.
322. "I feel that there is nothing which can so undermine the defenses of a manly spirit as the blandishments of women and that contact with their bodies without which no wife can be contented. . . . For this reason I fully believe it proper and useful for the freedom of my soul that I have commanded myself not to wish for, not to look for, not to marry, a wife" (*Soliloquies* 1.10.17).
323. "It is of the highest importance to flee these things of the senses and to be wary, as long as we live, lest our wings, which we need sound and unimpeded if we are to fly out of this darkness into that light, be hindered by the limestone of sensual things" (ibid. 1.14.24).
324. "Nothing is a greater obstacle to perceiving that truth than a life given over to carnal pleasures and deceitful images of sensible things, which, pressed on us by the sensible world through our bodies, generate various opinions and errors" (*True Religion* 3.3).
325. He knew and used Ambrose's *Of Virgins* and Cyprian's *The Dress of Virgins*. See *Christian Instruction* 4.21. See also I. Dietz's *Aurelius Augustinus: Heilige Jungfräulichkeit* (Würzburg, 1952), p. xi, which establishes that these works are echoed in Augustine's *Holy Virginity*. In his *Forgiveness of Sins and Baptism* 3.7.13 and *Letter 166* 3.6, both of which are late compositions, Augustine himself shows that he knew Jerome's *Against Jovinian*, written in 393.
326. "Therefore, you saints of God, persevere, you boys and girls, you men and women, celibate and unmarried, persevere zealously to the end" (*Holy

Virginity 27.27). In *Sermon 132* 3.3, he alludes to those of both sexes—"whether men or women" (*sive mares sive feminae*)—who have taken vows of chastity. See also *Homily on St. John's Gospel 13* 12: "Few women have physical virginity and, if one can speak of virginity in men, there are few men in the Church who have this holy bodily integrity."

327. "We know that there are many men and women who preserve their virginal continence to such an extent that . . . they would not dare to join themselves in a habitation of those in which no one calls anything his own, but all things are held in common" (*Holy Virginity* 45.46).

328. Ibid. 2.2; *Exposition on Psalm 147* 10; *Homily on St. John's Gospel 13* 12; *Sermon 341* 4.5. For the significance of this distinction, see below, pp. 244–46.

329. Cf. *Holy Virginity* 11.11. See also D. Riccardi, *Verginità nella vita religiosa* (Rome, 1961), pp. 113ff.

330. *Exposition on Psalm* 90 2.9 and *Sermon 93* 3.4. In *Sermon 213* 7, he calls the Church "virgin in faith." See on this also M. Agterberg, *Ecclesia–Virgo: Etude sur la virginité de l'Eglise et des fidèles chez saint Augustin* (Héverlé & Louvain, 1960), pp. 25ff., and R. Hesbert, "Saint Augustin et la virginité de la foi," AM II, pp. 645–55.

331. *Holy Virginity* 8.8.

332. Ibid. 12.11.

333. *Against Faustus* 20.21.

334. *Holy Virginity* 8.8.

335. Ibid.

336. *Rule* 4.4. Cf. *Continence* 2.5; *Holy Virginity* 11.11.

337. *Letter 111* 9. Cf. *Lying* 19f.40f. *The City of God* 1.16ff. See also Riccardi, *Verginità*, pp. 137–41.

338. See also above, pp. 120–22.

339. *Holy Virginity* 13.12.

340. Ibid. 4.4. Cf. also *Letter 150*.

341. *Sermon 132* 3.3.

342. *Holy Virginity* 13.12.

343. Ibid. 53.54.

344. See above, pp. 120–22.

345. Cf. *Retractations* 2.48 (22), and Dietz, *Heilige Jungfräulichkeit*, pp. viiif.

346. *Holy Virginity* 22.22.

347. Ibid. 23.23.

348. Ibid. 24.24.

349. Ibid. 27.27.

350. Ibid. 24.24.

351. He called virginity "a marriage that has no end" (*Letter 150*).

352. *Holy Virginity* 2.2 Cf. also *Homily on St. John's Gospel 13* 13: "Let us see, if they love the bridegroom, that they preserve their virginity." *Letter 188* 2.6: "Let the virgin hear Him, who is not only her bridegroom but the bridegroom of the entire Church, speaking of such chastity and integrity."

353. *Holy Virginity* 54.55.

354. *The Excellence of Widowhood* 11.14. Cf. *Exposition on Psalm 83* 4: "For a nun to marry is regarded as adultery against Christ."

355. *Homily on St. John's Gospel 9* 2.

356. *Holy Virginity* 54f.55f. Cf. also 27.27: "Love Him more ardently whom you please more attentively"; and ibid. 40.41: "Therefore will you love Him so much less in proportion to the richness of the gifts He has bestowed on you? . . . May you love Him most fervently, by loving whom you have been freed from the chains of marriage." Cf. also *The Excellence of Widowhood* 19.23.

357. *Sermon 304* 2.2.

358. *Holy Virginity* 35.35.

359. Cf. also above, p. 115.

360. *Holy Virginity* 27.27.

361. Ibid.

362. Ibid.

363. Ibid. 28f.28f.

364. Ibid. 12.11. Cf. also 2.2 and 48.48. See above all Agterberg, *Ecclesia–Virgo*, pp. 9–25. The places where Augustine writes about the virginity of the Church are very numerous; see ibid., nn. 15 and 58.

365. *Holy Virginity* 12.11.

366. Ibid. And similarly *The Excellence of Widowhood* 10.13; *Sermon 188* 3.4.

367. *Holy Virginity* 2.2.

368. Agterberg, *Ecclesia–Virgo*, p. 25ff.

369. Ibid., pp. 35ff., 94ff.

370. *Exposition on Psalm 49* 9. Cf. Agterberg, *Ecclesia–Virgo*, pp. 97ff.

371. *Holy Virginity* 48.48. Cf. also Agterberg, *Ecclesia–Virgo*, pp. 104ff.

372. *Homily on St. John's Gospel 9* 2.

373. *Homily on St. John's Gospel 13* 12. Cf. also *Holy Virginity* 2.2.

374. *Holy Virginity* 2.2.

375. Ibid. 12.11.

376. Agterberg, *Ecclesia–Virgo*, p. 33.

377. *Holy Virginity* 5.5, and, similarly, *Faith, Hope, and Charity* 34.10.

378. *Holy Virginity* 2.2.

379. Ibid. 4.4.

380. Ibid. Augustine's view of Mary's vow of virginity, which is based on Luke 1:34, is rejected today as untenable by many exegetes.

381. *Holy Virginity* 4.4.

382. Ibid. 5.5. Similarly *Sermon 51* 16.

383. *Holy Virginity* 4.4.

384. Augustine writes of her as "bodily a mother, spiritually a mother" (ibid. 5.5) and "a mother both in spirit and in body" (ibid. 6.6).

385. Ibid. 3.3.

386. Ibid. 5.5.

387. Ibid. 6.6.
388. *Confessions* 8.11.27.
389. *Holy Virginity* 5.5.
390. Ibid.
391. Ibid. 6.6. Similarly, 7.7.
392. Cf. *Forgiveness of Sin and Baptism* 3.7.13 and *Retractations* 2.48 (22). See also *On Heresies* 82.
393. Dietz, *Heilige Jungfräulichkeit*, p. viii.
394. Cf. Riccardi, *Verginità*, pp. 33f.
395. *Retractations* 2.48 (22).
396. *Holy Virginity* 10.9.
397. *The Literal Meaning of Genesis* 9.7.
398. *Marriage and Concupiscence* 1.10.11. Cf. A. Reuter, *Sancti Aurelii Augustini doctrina de bonis matrimonii* (Rome, 1942), pp. 250ff., and N. Ladomérszky, *Saint Augustin, docteur du mariage chrétien* (Rome, 1942), pp. 110ff.
399. *The Good of Marriage* 3.3.
400. *Sermon* 51 13.21.
401. *Holy Virginity* 12.12.
402. *The Literal Meaning of Genesis* 9.7.
403. *The Good of Marriage* 3.3.
404. *The Ways of the Catholic Church* 1.35.77f., 2.18.65ff.; *Continence* 9.22; *In Reply to Two Letters of the Pelagians* 1.24.42, 3.9.25, 4.5.9. Cf. also Riccardi, *Verginità*, pp. 224ff.
405. Cf. also above, pp. 218–20.
406. See for example *The Grace of Christ and Original Sin* 33f.38f. Cf. also Zumkeller, *Schriften gegen die Pelagianer*, II 536f.
407. *The Incomplete Work against Julian* 5.24f.
408. *Holy Virginity* 18.18.
409. Ibid.
410. *The Good of Marriage* 8.8. See the translation of A. Maxsein, *Aurelius Augustinus: Das Gut der Ehe* (Würzburg, 1949), p. 13.
411. *Holy Virginity* 22.22.
412. Ibid. 13.12.
413. Ibid.
414. Ibid. 1.1.
415. Ibid. 45.46; *Problems in the Gospels* 1.9.
416. *Holy Virginity* 45.46.
417. Ibid.
418. *The Good of Marriage* 10.10. Cf. 9.9; *Holy Virginity* 9.9; *The Excellence of Widowhood* 23.28.
419. Cf. also Maxsein, *Das Gut der Ehe*, p. 50, and P. Keseling, "Askese II (christlich)," *Reallexikon für Antike und Christentum* I (Stuttgart, 1950), 778.
420. *The Good of Marriage* 9.9.
421. Ibid. 13.15.

422. See above, pp. 121–22.

423. *Marriage and Concupiscence* 1.13.14. Cf. also *The Good of Marriage* 13.15; *The Excellence of Widowhood* 8.11.

424. *The Good of Marriage* 10.10.

425. *The Excellence of Widowhood* 23.28.

426. *Homily on St. John's Gospel 13* 12.

427. Ibid.

428. Cf. above, chap. 5 at note 33.

429. Cf. above, pp. 110–11. If the notions which have just been described, and which are very important for Augustine's thinking, are taken into account, the answer of T. J. Bigham and A. T. Mollegen ("The Christian Ethic," in *A Companion to the Study of St. Augustine*, ed. R. W. Battenhouse [New York, 1955], pp. 382ff.) to the question of the extent to which Augustine's teaching on marriage and virginity was influenced by Neoplatonism is particularly one-sided and unsatisfactory. Laying great stress on Augustine's impractical hopes, Bigham and Mollegen assert that his concept of marriage and continence is based on the "basic principles and presuppositions" (p. 382) of Neoplatonism and that his higher regard for continence is conditioned by "a Neoplatonic reading of the Bible" (p. 384). In fact, Augustine's ideals of married and celibate life are much more deeply rooted in the Christian and Biblical tradition than these writers will allow. Cf. also G. Armas, "La continencia perfecta en la ética agustiniana," *Augustinus*, 1 (1956), 559–71.

430. Cf. also above, p. 108.

431. *Holy Virginity* 30.30.

432. Ibid. 4.4.

433. Ibid. 14.14. Cf. *Sermon 161* 11.11.

434. *Holy Virginity* 23.23, 30.30, 36.37; *Adulterous Marriages* 2.18.19; *Grace and Free Will* 4.7.

435. *Adulterous Marriages* 2.18.19.

436. *Sermon 161* 11.11.

437. *Adulterous Marriages* 2.19.20. Cf. also *Letter 127* 8; *Sermon 148* 2.2; *The Excellence of Widowhood* 9.12; *Sermon 355* 6. See also Manrique, *Teología agustiniana*, pp. 167f.

438. *Exposition on Psalm 75* 16.

439. Cf. Jerome's *Against Jovinian* 1.3 (PL 23.224). See also Riccardi, *Verginità*, pp. 203f.

440. *Holy Virginity* 24f.24f.

441. Ibid. 26.26. Cf. also *Sermon 132* 3.3.

442. *Holy Virginity* 26.26.

443. Ibid. 27.27.

444. Ibid.

445. Ibid.

446. *Confessions* 8.7.17.

447. Ibid. 6.11.20.

448. In the *Soliloquies* (1.14.25) Augustine has Reason say, with respect to his nightly sexual temptations: ". . . so that He, the physician who works in

utter secrecy, might make you see both how you had fled from His healing and what remained to be healed."

449. P. Keseling, *Aurelius Augustinus: Die Enthaltsamkeit* (Würzburg, 1949), p. 48.

450. *Continence* 1.1. He reverts to this theme in 5.12 and 14.32.

451. Quoted in *Confessions* 6.11.20 and 10.29.40; *Holy Virginity* 41.43; *The Excellence of Widowhood* 17.21; *Letter 188* 2.8; *Grace and Free Will* 4.8.

452. Cf. Keseling, *Die Enthaltsamkeit*, p. 45.

453. Also quoted in *Letter 188* 2.6; *Grace and Free Will* 4.7.

454. Also quoted in *Holy Virginity* 40.41; *Letter 188* 2.6; *Grace and Free Will* 4.8.

455. *Holy Virginity* 40ff.41–43.

456. Ibid. 40f.41f. Augustine also used 1 Corinthians 4:7 as proof of continence as a gift in *The Excellence of Widowhood* 16.20 and *Letter 188* 2.7.

457. *Holy Virginity* 40.41.

458. Ibid. 41.42.

459. *The Grace of Christ and Original Sin* 1.24.25.

460. *Confessions* 10.29.40. The work repeats this prayer twice: 10.31.45 and 10.37.60, where Augustine is dealing with wantonness of the eye and with overweening ambition.

461. *The Gift of Perseverance* 20.53.

462. PL 33.1099–1120. See also de Plinval, *Pélage*, pp. 242–51. See also above, p. 189.

463. *The Grace of Christ and Original Sin* 1.37.40–1.40.44. Cf. also *Letter 188* 3.12f. On Pelagius' concept of grace, see Zumkeller, *Schriften gegen die Pelagianer*, II 79ff.

464. *Letter 188* 1.3.

465. Pelagius, *Letter to Demetrias* 11 (PL 33.1107).

466. *Letter 188* 2.5.

467. Ibid. 2.6ff.

468. Cf. on this *Grace and Free Will* 4.7: "Therefore, it is a gift of God and man's free choice that this verse [Matt. 19:11], which is not understood by all, is understood by some."

469. *Letter 188* 2.6.

470. "These are God's gifts, and they are yours, but they are not from you" (ibid.).

471. Ibid. Cf. also 2.5.

472. *The Excellence of Widowhood* 17.21. Cf. Maxsein, *Das Gut der Witwenschaft*, p. 24.

473. *Letter 188* 2.7.

474. Cf. *Holy Virginity* 27ff.27ff.; *Letter 127* 8.

475. Cf. Riccardi, *Verginità*, pp. 28–34.

476. *Rule* 4.4.

477. Ibid. 5.5–7.

478. J. Jüthner, "Bad," *Reallexikon für Antike und Christentum*, I 1136, 1141f.

479. *Rule* 5.5. At that time it was normal medical procedure to prescribe baths, especially the popular heated and steam baths, for a variety of physical ailments (Jüthner, "Bad," 1136).
480. *Rule* 5.7.
481. Jüthner, "Bad," 1138, 1140.
482. *The Excellence of Widowhood* 22.27.
483. *Second Exposition on Psalm 30* 1.10.
484. *Sermon 355* 1. Similarly, *The Excellence of Widowhood* 22.27.
485. Possidius 26.
486. *Rule* 4.4.
487. Ibid. 4.5.
488. Ibid. 4.3.
489. Ibid. 4.5.
490. *Sermon 132* 2.
491. Mausbach, *Die Ethik*, I 185ff.
492. *Holy Virginity* 38.39.
493. Ibid.
494. Ibid.
495. Ibid.
496. Ibid. 51.52.
497. Ibid. 52.53.
498. Ibid. 51.52.
499. Ibid.
500. Cf. *The Excellence of Widowhood* 16f.20f.
501. Ibid.; *Continence* 5.12, 14.32; *Confessions* 6.11.20; *Letter 188* 2.7f.
502. *Adulterous Marriages* 2.19.20.
503. *Confessions* 8.11.27.
504. *The Excellence of Widowhood* 20.25.
505. Ibid. 21.26.
506. *Rule* 4.6.
507. Ibid. 4.7–9.
508. Ibid. 8.1.
509. Ibid. 7.3.
510. Ibid. 4.5.
511. Ibid. 4.6.
512. Graf, "Zur Wesensstruktur," 10ff. Cf. Schmitt, "Vom Wesen," 91f.
513. Reul, *Die sittlichen Ideale*, pp. 33, 147ff.
514. Cf. also H. J. Seller, "Augustinus und seine Regel," in *St. Augustin, Festgabe der deutschen Provinz der Augustinereremiten* (Würzburg, 1930), pp. 89ff.
515. *Rule* 5.2.
516. Mellet, *L'Itinéraire*, pp. 63ff. Cf. also *Sermon 356* 8.
517. *The Ways of the Catholic Church* 1.33.73. See above, pp. 127–29.
518. See also *Homily on St. John's Gospel 87* 1.
519. *Sermon 356* 8f.

520. *Ordo monasterii* 1. For discussion of the authenticity of this text, see below, pp. 285–86.

521. Cf. *Homily on St. John's Gospel 65* 2.

522. *Rule* 5.2.

523. See above, pp. 110–11.

524. *The Ways of the Catholic Church* 1.33.70.

525. *Letter 126* 7.

526. *Rule* 8.1.

527. See above, pp. 238–39 and note 310. In his article "Vie de perfection" Sage deals with Pelagius' erroneous notions about Christian perfection and the evangelical counsels and with Augustine's refutation of them.

528. See, for example, *Letter 157* 4, *Sermon 343* 4, *Holy Virginity* 52.53.

529. See, for example, *Exposition on Psalm 75* 16, *Letter 48* 3, *Letter 157* 4.39, *Letter 215* 8, *Continence* 1.1, *Holy Virginity* 40.41.

530. *Rule* 8.2.

531. *Letter 48* 3.

532. *Holy Virginity* 52.53; see also 40.41.

533. *Exposition on Psalm 132* 10.

534. Ibid. 11.

III

Augustine's Monastic Ideals in His Writings

Only a short time after his conversion, Augustine began to write in favor of the monastic life. His activities as an author promoting monasticism made him the teacher of the monasteries of his day and of later centuries. Even now we can discern in these writings what his ideals for monasticism were, in their first beauty and allure.

We must put his *Rule* first. It is not, indeed, the first of Augustine's works to express his views about monastic life, but no other of his writings can equal its influence upon monasticism. Even though we cannot determine with certainty when it was written, there is no doubt that it is genuine. The rest of his works echo, again and again, the sentences in which he outlines his program. One can truly say that the spirit of the *Rule* is the spirit of everything he wrote about monasticism.

9

The *Rule* of St. Augustine

Augustine's *Rule* is of no less significance than those of St. Benedict and St. Francis. It has been described, with every justification, as "a foundation-stone of monasticism."[1] Even so, its origins, like those of Benedict's *Rule*,[2] are shrouded in a certain darkness that is only slowly clearing. The acknowledged expert in these questions, Luc Verheijen, published in Paris in 1964 a good survey of the present state of research.[3]

What are the problems concerning the *Rule*? Its text, composed in Latin, has been transmitted in one form for men (called by Verheijen the *Praeceptum*) and in another for women (called by Verheijen the *Regularis informatio*). In many ancient manuscripts, in addition, a shorter text (called by Verheijen the *Ordo monasterii*) is prefaced to the *Praeceptum*, and this, too, is found, although very rarely, in a form for women.[4] Moreover, the *Regularis informatio* commonly appears in the manuscripts as an appendage to an admonitory letter, which passes for Augustine's (*Letter 211*, called by Verheijen the *Obiurgatio*). The form of the *Rule* used most often by orders of men and women today, and, indeed, since the High Middle Ages, is composed of the introductory sentence of the *Ordo monasterii* ("Before all things . . . given to us") and the *Praeceptum*.[5]

The various texts that have been handed down present the following questions concerning the *Rule*:

1. Are the text of the *Praeceptum*, and that of the *Regularis informatio*, for the most part identical,[6] in fact by Augustine?
2. Did Augustine write this text for men (the *Praeceptum*) or for women (the *Regularis informatio*)?
3. Where, when, and for whom did Augustine write the *Praeceptum*?
4. Who is the author of the *Ordo monasterii*?
5. Is the *Obiurgatio* of *Letter 211* really to be attributed to Augustine, and who wrote the *Regularis informatio*?

1. The first question, that of the authenticity of the text of the *Rule*, in whatever form, had been answered affirmatively by all researchers

until very recently. In 1956, F. Châtillon, in his still unpublished dissertation at Strasbourg, for the first time called Augustine's authorship of the text into question. He believed that there are strong influences of Eastern monasticism to be found in the *Rule*, and associated its origins with the personality of St. John Cassian (who died between 430 and 435).[7] This attack on the authenticity of the *Rule* has now finally been refuted by Tarcisius Van Bavel's outstanding study of the sources.[8] In more than sixty printed pages, he has indicated, for almost every sentence of the *Rule*, many literal parallels from Augustine's other writings, and has shown that the *Rule*'s vocabulary, Biblical quotations, and trains of thought wholly correspond with what Augustine has written elsewhere.[9]

2. So, if the text of the *Rule* is in fact Augustine's, did he then write it for men or for women? This second question—which is the original text, the *Praeceptum* or the *Regularis informatio?*—has not until now been completely answered.[10] To be sure, in the specialized literature one finds fewer and fewer experts who pronounce in favor of the women's *Rule*, although only twenty years ago that theory was regarded as the traditional, classic solution.[11] More recent research, however, has shown beyond a doubt that the priority of the *Praeceptum* is the better solution.[12]

But what facts in favor of the men's *Rule* has this modern research produced? As early as 1929, Cyrille Lambot demonstrated that St. Caesarius of Arles (d. 542) used the *Praeceptum*, not the *Regularis informatio*, in composing his *Rule for Virgins* around the year 520.[13] The *Praeceptum*, therefore, was already known in southern Gaul at that time. As additional certain fact, Verheijen pointed out that in the oldest manuscript of the women's *Rule* (= *Letter 211*) there is an explicit, a formula of conclusion, between the *Obiurgatio*, used as a preface, and the *Regularis informatio*.[14] This shows, once again, that the connection between the two texts of the so-called *Letter 211* is by no means as close as those who would defend the priority of the women's *Rule* have assumed up to now; nor is it at all certain that the two texts, the *Obiurgatio* and the *Regularis informatio*, originally formed a single entity. Finally, Verheijen has recently established another interesting fact. The sequence of verses (32b + 32c + 35), in which Possidius, reporting on the garden monastery of Hippo and the form of life there "according to the way and rule established under the holy Apostles" (*secundum modum et regulam sub sanctis apostolis constitutam*), cites the well-known words from the fourth chapter of the Acts of the Apostles (4:32–35)[15]—

> No one in that community possessed anything of his own,
> as everything was held in common;
> it was then distributed to each one as he had need

—is to be found in this form only in Augustine's *Rule*, although the pericope as such is often mentioned by Augustine and in patristic literature overall. Clearly, these striking linguistic parallels, placing the text of the *Rule* squarely in the times and locality of the Augustinian monastery at Hippo, are a strong argument for the priority of the *Praeceptum*.[16]

3. The answer to the third question—"Where, when, and for whom did Augustine write the *Praeceptum*?" —cannot at present take us further than this, apart from some more or less well-founded suppositions. Pierre Mandonnet, who died in 1936, and Winfried Hümpfner believed that Augustine wrote the *Rule* for his monks in the garden monastery, before his consecration as bishop in 395.[17] N. Merlin, Lope Cilleruelo, Luc Verheijen, and Tarsisius Van Bavel generally agreed with him, but assumed that the date of composition was somewhat later—that is, in Augustine's early years as bishop (396–400).[18] Recently, Cilleruelo has come to consider that the *Praeceptum* was addressed, not to the monks in the garden monastery, but to those at Carthage, for whom at that same time (ca. 400) Augustine also wrote *The Work of Monks*, a treatise in which a number of striking parallels to the text of the *Rule* is to be found.[19] The latest hypothesis is that Augustine wrote the *Rule* in 426 or 427 for the monks at Hadrumetum. The first to advance this idea was Andrés Manrique; later it was adopted by A. Sage, and most recently it has been defended in detail by A. C. Vega.[20] In the meantime, it has met with well-argued opposition from many sides. Above all, the arguments for so late a date are not considered convincing.[21]

It seems to me that the assumption that Augustine wrote the *Rule* for his garden monastery in the years after his consecration as bishop still possesses the great probability. And this assumption could receive strong support from the striking similarity of the quotation from the Acts of the Apostles in the *Rule* and in Possidius' account of the garden monastery.

4. Inquiries about the identity of the author of the *Ordo monasterii* have not yet been answered; but two facts are certain. The *Ordo* is very old. Caesarius of Arles knew it, and in the greater number of the ancient manuscripts of the *Rule*, the *Ordo* is prefaced to the *Praeceptum*. Yet there is another circumstance: in a smaller number of the oldest manuscripts, one of which dates from the ninth century, the *Praeceptum* appears without the *Ordo*. When all this is considered, two possibilities emerge: either the *Ordo* was originally joined to the *Praeceptum*, but was lost in the second group of manuscripts, for reasons which we do not know; or perhaps Augustine's *Rule* originally consisted only of the *Praeceptum*, and was later amplified by the addition of the *Ordo*.[22] L. M. Verheijen mentions the following fact, which seems to favor the first

possibility, even though it is not conclusive proof: Isidore of Seville (d. 636) uses the *Praeceptum* in his monastic rule, with the textual characteristics of the smaller group of ancient manuscripts just described. Elsewhere, however, Isidore has also made use of the *Ordo*. The supposition is that he owned a manuscript with a *Praeceptum*-text of the smaller group of manuscripts, but which, unlike the manuscripts of the group which are known to us, also contained a text of the *Ordo monasterii*.[23] Yet Verheijen goes on to mention another circumstance permitting one to suppose that the *Ordo* was only later joined to the *Praeceptum*: an Old Latin translation of the Acts of the Apostles, circulating in Italy, as is shown by a sermon of St. Maximus of Turin (d. ca. 420), had a unique reading of Acts 4:32: "No one might make a claim on anything as his own" (*nemo proprium aliquid vindicaret*); but this reading is also found in the *Ordo*, which seems to indicate an Italian origin for this text of the *Rule*.[24]

But even if one chooses to assume that the *Ordo monasterii* was joined onto Augustine's *Praeceptum* from the beginning, that still does not guarantee the *Ordo*'s Augustinian origin. Particularly because of the style of this brief work, it has been supposed that the *Ordo* was not written by Augustine himself. Verheijen believes that the language of the *Ordo* more closely resembles Alypius'.[25]

5. The final question as well—who is the author of the *Obiurgatio* of *Letter 211*, and what is the origin of the *Regularis informatio* appended to this letter?—cannot at the present time be answered with certainty. Guided chiefly by consideration of its contents, Winfried Hümpfner was the first to reject Augustine's authorship of *Letter 211*. His supposition was that St. Fructuosus (d. 665), archbishop of Braga, wrote the *Obiurgatio* and also edited the *Praeceptum* in a form to be used by conventual women.[26] Against this, Verheijen points out that the reading "your understanding of me should have sprouted again" (*repullulastis sapere*) instead of "your feeling for me should have blossomed afresh" (*refloruistis sentire*) in the quotation of Philippians 4:10 found in the *Obiurgatio* is an Augustine characteristic. Thus, Verheijen considers it wholly probable that Augustine himself wrote the *Obiurgatio* for that convent of women in Hippo where his own sister was the superior and that the re-edition of the *Praeceptum* in a form for nuns was undertaken in that very house.[27]

Thus far, the researches of recent decades have yielded these results: experts are certain that the *Praeceptum* was written by Augustine. It is highly probable that he composed it for men, though the possibility that he originally wrote this *Rule* for a house of women cannot yet be completely ruled out. I have prefaced the following translation of the *Praeceptum* with the so-called *Ordo monasterii*; but I cannot emphasize enough that Augustine's authorship of this monastic statute has yet to be determined.

The *Rule* of St. Augustine could be the oldest surviving monastic rule in the West.[28] It is more than 1500 years old, and it was born in the early days of Christian monasticism. It is older than St. Benedict's *Rule*, itself immensely ancient. Yet above all it is its deeply religious content that gives Augustine's *Rule* a supreme significance. In it, he expresses his ideals for the monastic life in all their beauty. In a certain sense, it contains his plans for his own life as a monk. In it are reflected the deepest trains of thought of his being.[29]

All this explains the great influence that Augustine's *Rule* has had on the monastic life of the Church. There have been founders of monasteries and promoters of orders from every nation and every age who have found in it the ideal introduction to monastic life. It has proved itself practical for men and for women, for priests and the laity, for monks and canons, for contemplative houses and for those living the active life, for orders founded during the Middle Ages as well as those of modern times.

Knowledge of human nature and discretion, philosophical depth and a firm grasp of Holy Scripture, and, not the least, the clear direction of monastic living toward the highest goal of all Christian life, which is love, give to this oldest *Rule* of the West its significance, which is timeless.[30]

ORDO MONASTERII

1. Before all else, dearest brothers, God should be loved, and then your neighbor, for these are the chief commandments which have been given to us.

2. I shall describe how we should pray or recite the psalms: that is, for Matins,[31] three psalms should be said, the sixty-second, the fifth, and the eighty-ninth. At Terce, one psalm should be said as far as its response, then two psalms recited antiphonally, a reading and the closing prayer; and so ought Sext and None to be said. But at Vespers say one psalm to its response, then four psalms antiphonally, and then another psalm to its response, a reading and the closing prayer. At a suitable hour after Vespers, when all are seated, the lessons should be read; and after that there should be said the psalms customary before sleeping.[32] The night prayers, during

the months of November, December, January, and February, should consist of twelve antiphonal psalms, six psalms to their responses, and three lessons; in the months of March, April, September, and October, of ten antiphonal psalms, five to their responses, and three lessons; in the months of May, June, July, and August, of eight antiphonal psalms, four psalms to their responses, and two lessons.

3. The brothers[33] should work in the mornings until Sext. From Sext until None they should devote to reading; and at None they should return the books. Then, after they have eaten, they should do their work, either in the garden or wherever it is needed, until the time for Vespers.

4. No one should claim anything as his own, whether clothing or anything else. It is our choice to live the Apostolic life.

5. No one should do anything grudgingly, lest he perish as God condemned grumblers to do.[34]

6. They should be loyally obedient; they should honor their "father"[35] next to God; they should treat their "provost" with deference, as is fitting to the saints.

7. While they are seated at table, let them keep silence and listen to what is being read. But if something is needed, let their provost look after it. On Saturdays and Sundays, let those who wish for it receive wine, as is the custom.

8. If something is needed for the monastery and they must be sent out of doors, let them go two by two. No one must eat or drink outside the monastery without permission, for this is contrary to the monastery's discipline. If brothers are sent out to sell the monastery's produce, they should take care that nothing is done against the rules, realizing that if they offend God's servants they offend Him. And if they must buy something the monastery needs, let them act carefully and loyally, as servants of God.

9. Let there be no idle words among them. From early morning on, let them sit at their work. After the prayers at Terce, let them go back to their work. They should not stand about making up stories, unless it be for the profit of their souls. When they sit at their work, let them keep silence, unless what they are doing requires someone to speak.

10. But if someone does not try with all his might and with the help of God's mercy to fulfill these orders, but rather despises them with a stubborn heart, let him be warned once, and a second time, and if he then does not improve, he should know that he is liable for fitting punishment from the monastery. If he is young enough for this, let him even be beaten.[36]

11. But when these things are faithfully and devoutly carried out in the

name of Christ, not only will you prosper, but we shall rejoice greatly over your well-being. Amen.

PRAECEPTUM

1.1. We enjoin you who are established in the monastery to keep these rules.

2. First, because you have been gathered together as one body, you should live in unanimity in the house, with "one heart and one soul" [Acts 4:32] for God.

3. And you should not call anything your own, but everything which you have should be common property, and your superior should distribute food and clothing [cf. 1 Tim. 6:8] to each of you, not the same to everyone, because you have not all the same strength, but rather to each man as he may have need [Acts 4:35]. For this is what you read in the Acts of the Apostles, that "all things were in common to them, and distribution was made to everyone as he had need" [Acts 4:32, 35].

4. Those who owned anything in the world should be willing without begrudging for it to be common property after they have entered the monastery.

5. But those who had nothing ought not to be seeking in the monastery for what they could not have outside. All the same, they should be given what they need when they are weak, even if their poverty, when they were outside, denied them even the bare necessities. Nonetheless, do not let them congratulate themselves because they have found food and clothing such as they never found outside.

6. Nor should they give themselves airs because they are mixing with others whom they never dared to approach outside; rather, let them lift their hearts up to God, and not be seeking after worldly vanities, lest monasteries become profitable to the rich but not to the poor, if the rich are to become humble there and the poor puffed up with pride.

7. Yet, in the same way, those who seemed to be something in the world should not despise their brothers because they were poor before they joined this holy company. They ought rather to strive to take pride, not in the prominence of their rich families, but in the companionship of their poor brethren. Nor should they boast if they have contributed something to the common life out of their means, or take more glory in their wealth because they are sharing it with the monastery than if they were enjoying it in the world. Every other kind of wickedness works in wicked deeds, so that

they may be committed, but pride creeps into even good deeds, so that they may come to nothing. What is the use of man's distributing his possessions by giving them to the poor, and making himself poor too, when this contempt for wealth makes his miserable soul more proud than it was when he was wealthy?

8. So all of you live with one soul and one heart, and honor in one another God, whose temples you were made to be [2 Cor. 6:16].

2.1. Assemble for prayers at the established hours and times.

2. Let no one do anything in the oratory except what it was built for and from which it takes it name; so that if by chance there are some who are at leisure and may wish to pray outside the established times, no one who thinks that he has something else to do there should be a hindrance to them.

3. When you pray to God in psalms and hymns, turn over in your heart what your voice is uttering.

4. And do not recite anything unless you read that it is to be recited; if it is not written down that it should be, it ought not to be, recited.

3.1. Tame your flesh by fasting and abstaining from food and drink, as far as your health permits. But even when someone is unable to fast, still he should not take any nourishment between meals, unless he is unwell.

2. When you come to the table and until you rise, listen to what is being read aloud to you according to custom, making no noise or disturbance; [for] it should be not only your jaws that are chewing food but your ears that are thirsting for God's word.

3. If there are invalids of long standing who are given special diets, that ought not to be a grievance or appear unjust to others whose constitutions are different and who are stronger. Nor should they think those others better off because they are eating differently; rather, let them rejoice because they have good health which the others do not.

4. And if some food, clothing, rug, or coverlet is given to those who came to the monastery from more comfortable homes, and such is not given to those who are more hardened and therefore happier, those who do not receive these things ought to think how much the others' living standards have declined since they were in the world, even though they have not been able to achieve the frugality of those who are more robust. Nor should anyone want the more he sees a few receiving, not out of favor but out of sufferance, lest there should develop that hateful corruption whereby in a monastery where, insofar as possible, the rich become laborers, the poor would be pampered.

5. Clearly, in the same way as the sick are given lighter tasks lest they become overburdened, so after their illness they should be treated in such a way that they recover more quickly, even though they come from the humblest walks of life in the world, as though more recent illness had bestowed upon them what former custom had given the rich. But when they have regained their former strength, let them return to that happier way of life, which is so much more fitting to God's servants insofar as they require less. The fit should not allow anything to become a pleasurable indulgence which was a sustaining necessity while they were ill. Let them deem themselves better off when they become better able to endure scarcity; for it is better to need a little than to have too much.

4.1. Do not let your clothing be remarkable; and do not seek to please by what you wear, but by what you are.

2. When you go out of doors, walk together; when you arrive at your destination, stay together.

3. Walking, standing, whatever movement you make, do nothing to offend anyone who sees you; but let everything befit your holy way of life.

4. Even if your eyes do fall upon some women, fix them on none. It is not that when you go out of doors you are forbidden to catch sight of women; but to desire them, or to want to be desired by them, is a grave sin. The desire for women is stirred, and stirs, not only by touching and by inviting glances, but even by looking. You cannot say that you have shamefast minds if you have shameless eyes, for a shameless eye is the messenger of a shameless heart. And if people, even when their tongues are silent, exchange glances that tell of their shameless hearts, and with their ardor give each other pleasure as the flesh desires, though they may never touch each other's bodies impurely, true chastity has gone from their lives.

5. Nor should anyone, fixing his eyes on a woman and enjoying hers fixed on him, imagine that others do not see what he is doing. Those he thinks are not noticing can see well enough. But even if this activity is concealed and seen by no man, what of Him who looks down from on high, from whom nothing can be concealed? Are we to suppose that He does not see, just because His patience is as great as His knowledge? Thus a holy man should fear to displease God [Prov. 24:18]; nor should he wish to please a woman wrongfully. Let him reflect that God sees everything, and he will not wish to sin by looking at women. For in this matter the fear of God was commended, when it was written: "A fixed gaze is an abomination to the Lord."[37]

6. So when you are together in church, and anywhere else where women are also present, guard each other's chastity; for God, who lives within you, will in this way protect you through yourselves.

7. And if you become aware of what I am talking about, this roving eye, in anyone else among you, warn him at once, so that he does not go from bad to worse, but is corrected by his neighbor.

8. But if after a second warning or on some later occasion you see him doing the same thing, whoever finds this out should treat him as a man already injured who must be healed; but first it should be made known to one or two others, so that what two or three have to say to him may convince him, when they warn him with suitable severity. And do not think yourselves ill-disposed when you point this out. You would be doing more harm if you let your brothers go to ruin by your silence, when you could rescue them through speaking to them. If your brother had a wound in his body which he wanted to hide because he is afraid of the surgeon's knife,[38] would it not be cruel if you said nothing, merciful if you told about it? Then how much more should you make it known, in case a more perilous gangrene should grow in his heart?

9. But before making this known to others, by whom he would be condemned if he denies it, you should first tell your superior, if your brother has been warned and has failed to mend his ways, so that he may perhaps be privately admonished and his fault not be made known to anyone else. But if he rejects this, the foolish man must be confronted with others, so that he may now in front of everyone be shown to be guilty by two or three persons, and not accused merely by a single witness. When he has been condemned, the superior, or the priest who has charge of these matters, should impose a corrective punishment; and if he refuses to perform it, he should be expelled from your community, if he has not left of his own accord. This is to be done, not out of vindictiveness, but in mercy, lest he destroy others with his contagion.

10. And what I have said about not letting your eyes rove should be diligently and faithfully applied to other sins, which should be uncovered, prohibited, made known, condemned, and punished; and this is to be done out of love for men and hatred for vices.

11. But if anyone is so far gone in his evil ways that he is secretly receiving letters or tokens from some woman, let him be spared and prayed for if he confesses it freely; but if, however, he is caught in the act and found guilty, the superior or the priest should decide on some heavy punishment.

5.1. Keep your clothes in a common wardrobe, with one or two brothers in charge, or as many as are needed to ensure that there is no damage from moths. Accept your clothing from one wardrobe-keeper, just as you have your food from one cellarer. If this has been arranged, you ought not to be concerned with what you are given to wear, according to the season of the year, or whether each of you receives back the clothes he turned in or others someone else has worn, provided always that no one is refused what he needs. But if arguments and complaints start among you because someone is grumbling that what he has been given is inferior to what he had, and that it is an indignity for him to be dressed in what another brother has worn, learn from this how meanly your spirit is clothed, when you are quarreling about what you put on your bodies. But even if they indulge you in your weakness, and give you back the clothes you turned in, still everything you are not wearing is to be kept in one place by the same keepers.

2. And make sure that no one is working for his own benefit, but that everything you do is for the common good, with more zeal and greater promptness than if each one of you were working for himself. For love, of which it was written that it "is not self-seeking" [1 Cor. 13:5], must be understood as putting the common good before private interests, and not the other way round. And, therefore, the more trouble you take over what you all have in common, and not over what is your own, the more progress people will see that you are making. Let love, which will not pass away, preside over everything our passing needs demand.

3. And so it follows that if someone brings even to his sons or to anyone bound to him by any close tie in the monastery clothes, or anything considered a necessity, it is not to be received in secret, but is to be put at the superior's disposal, so that it belongs to the common property, and can be given to whoever may need it.

4. Your clothing should be washed as the superior decides, whether by you or by the launderers, so that your souls do not become soiled by your craving for clean clothes.

5. Your bodies, too, need to be washed as their infirmity requires, and this should not be refused, but done without complaint according to medical advice, so that everyone, though unwillingly, does as his superior orders for the sake of his health. But if he wants to wash and doing so is bad for him, he ought not to give in to his own wishes, for sometimes he will think that what is pleasing is good, even if it may be harmful.

6. Furthermore, if some servant of God has a bodily infirmity that

cannot be seen, when he says what is afflicting him he must be believed without question; but if it is not certain that what he would prefer to take for his sickness will cure it, a doctor should be consulted.

7. No fewer than two or three should go together to the public bath houses or anywhere it is necessary to go. Nor is anyone who needs to go out to be accompanied by companions of his own choosing, but by those the superior directs.

8. The care of the sick, or of those recuperating, or of anyone enfeebled, even if he has no medical symptoms, ought to be entrusted to one particular brother, so that he may ask the cellarer for whatever he may see someone needing.

9. Those who are assigned to serve the brethren as cellarers or wardrobe-keepers or librarians should do so without complaining.

10. Books are to be asked for every day at a fixed time; they should not be given to anyone outside the proper time.

11. Those who are in charge of clothing and footwear should not delay in giving them to those who need them and ask for them.

6.1. You should either refrain from disputes, or settle them as fast as you can, lest anger grow into hatred, a mountain be made out of a molehill, and your soul turn into a murderer. For this is what you read: "Anyone who hates his brother is a murderer" (1 John 3:15).

2. If anyone injures another by insulting or cursing or even attacking him, he must remember to make amends and put this right as soon as possible, and the injured party must forgive him without further ado. If they have injured one another, they must pardon one another because you have asked them to do so; and the more often you do this the more beneficial it will be. It is better for a man to be much tempted by anger and yet to be quick to acknowledge that he has wronged another and to ask for his forgiveness than to be slow to anger and slower still to submit to asking for pardon. If there is anyone who will never ask forgiveness or who does so insincerely, he has no business in the monastery, even though you do not turn him out. Thus, do not use harsh words; but if your tongue has uttered them, that same tongue ought not to gag over offering words to heal the wound it has made.

3. But when you are controlling your juniors and the needs of discipline require you to say hard things, even if you feel that you are going too far, you do not need to ask pardon from those who must be subject to you; for anyone having office who exceeds in humility may weaken his authority. Still you should ask pardon from the Lord of all, who knows with what

kindness you love those whom you correct perhaps even more than is fair. For the love between you should be, not fleshly, but spiritual.

7.1. A superior should be obeyed as a father, and due respect shown, for in offending him you offend God; and this respect is owed all the more to the priest who has charge overall.

2. It is the special concern of the superior that all these matters be observed, and that whatever has not been observed not be carelessly passed over but carefully amended and corrected; and should matters outside his competence arise, they should be referred to the priest, who among you is the major superior.

3. And he who is first among you should count himself happy, not because he has the power to lord it over you, but because he is serving you in love. Let his prelacy among you be the honor you pay him, and let him be prostrate at your feet in his fear of God. In all things, let him offer himself as a pattern of good works, correcting the unruly, cheering the fainthearted, supporting the weak, patient with everyone. Let him be ready to wield discipline and impose fear; and yet, though either may be necessary, let him seek to be loved rather than feared by you, always remembering that he must give an account of you to God.

4. So, through your greater obedience, have mercy not only on yourselves but also on him; for the greater is his authority among you, the more are the dangers in which he is placed.

8.1. May the Lord grant that you observe all these things in love, like lovers of spiritual beauty, burning with Christ's sweet perfume from your good way of life, "not as slaves under the law but as free men established under grace" [Rom. 8:14–22].

2. And so that you may look into this little book as though into a mirror, and neglect nothing through forgetfulness, it should be read aloud to you once a week. And when you find yourselves doing what is written here, give thanks to the Lord, the giver of all good things. But if anyone among you sees something wanting, let him mourn for what is past, and let him beware for the future, praying that his trespasses be forgiven and that he not be led into temptation.

NOTES

1. T. F. Gilligan, "Die Augustiner—Schrittmacher des Mönchswesens," *Katholischer Digest*, 1 (1947), 55.

2. Cf. A. Mundó, "Regula magistri," LThK, VIII^2, 1103f., and Steidle, pp. 14–32.

3. "La Règle de S. Augustin," *Augustinianum*, 4 (1964), 109–22. (The author continues with a provisional notice of Verheijen's two volumes of the same title, published in the same year as *Das Mönchtum*. As stated in the Preface, wherever necessary, the author's references have been brought up to date in the light of Verheijen's 1967 volumes.—Translators.) For older surveys, see U. Domínguez-del Val, "La Regla de San Augustín y los ultimos estudios sobre la misma," *Revista Española de Teologia*, 17 (1957), 481–529; H. Vissers, *Vie canoniale* (Vorau, 1957), pp. 100–24; Manrique, *La vida monastica*, pp. 413–76.

4. All previous studies of the manuscript tradition and critical editions have now been superseded by Verheijen's *La Règle*, though, naturally, not all his opinions or readings have found universal acceptance.—Translators.

5. There was yet a third rule which for a long time was called Augustine's, the so-called *Regula consensoria*. As early as the fourteenth century, the Augustinian Jordan of Saxony rejected its authenticity because of its style (see AH lxxvii). I. Herwegen (*Das Pactum des hl. Fructuosus von Braga* [Stuttgart, 1907], pp. 71ff.) indicated that this brief work is of Spanish origin. D. de Bruyne ("La Première Règle de Saint Benoît," *Revue Bénédictine*, 42 [1930], 318ff.) put forward the opinion that this rule originated in the fifth century in Priscillianist monastic circles in northwest Spain; Hümpfner (AH lxxviff.) considers its author to be St. Fructuosus of Braga.

6. For the differences in text between the *Rule* for women and the *Rule* for men, see the critical apparatus for Hümpfner's edition of the *Rule* (AH 489–504). The principal variants are found in lines 69 (the beginning of Chapter 6), 135 (the middle of Chapter 8), 150 (prohibition of the baths in Chapter 9), 171 (the beginning of Chapter 10). They are places where the women's *Rule* contrasted with that for men offers a somewhat expanded text.

7. "La Règle de Saint Augustin: Etude historique et critique," Diss. University of Strasbourg, 1956. See also idem, "Quelques remarques sur 'Ante omnia,'" REA, 2 (1956), 365–69. On this, see as well Van Bavel, "'*Ante omnia*' et '*In Deum.*'" (Verheijen, *La Règle*, II 195, wrote: "[Châtillon's] study has never been published, nor, if our information is correct, will it be."—Translators)

8. "Parallèles: Vocabulaire et citations bibliques de la *Regula sancti Augustini*," *Augustiniana*, 9 (1959), 12–77.

9. The latest hypothesis about the *Rule*'s origins, presented by R. Lorenz in his article "Die Anfänge," therefore concedes without reservations that it "derives, in its essential ideas and in their formulation, from Augustine." Yet Lorenz hesitates to ascribe its composition to Augustine himself because of defects in its style and construction. He sees in it, rather, "the echo of Augustine's verbal monastic instructions" and supposes that it "was assembled, not by Augustine himself, but by someone from his circle—perhaps even after his death." Yet what Lorenz produces as examples of digressions in thought, non sequiturs, lack of construction, and so on can be demonstrated in other of his works (cf. Marrou, *Saint Augustin et la fin de la culture antique*, pp.

665–72). So, too, with regard to the "monotonous repetition of the same verb," adduced by Lorenz as evidence of Augustine's "awkardness of expression," parallels elsewhere in his writings can be found. See, for instance, *Letter* 217 5.16, where the verb *dare* ("to give") is repeated ten times in a short passage, and *Man's Perfection in Righteousness* 11.28, where Augustine in a single sentence uses the verb *facere* ("to do") seven times; *The Grace of Christ and Original Sin* 2.25.29, where in quick succession the verb *dicere* ("to say") appears five times. Clearly he was fond of such parallelisms. But Lorenz's suggestion that the Latinity of the *Rule* should for the first time be given close philological examination merits attention.

10. Verheijen in *La Règle* is fully satisfied that it was the *Praeceptum*.—Translators.

11. The priority of the women's *Rule*, which Erasmus (*Opera divi Augustini* I [Basle, 1529], p. 591) maintained, arguing from internal criteria, has recently been supported by Besse, "Règle de Saint Augustin"; Schroeder, "Die Augustinerchorherrenregel"; Wirges, "Über den Ursprung der Augustinerregel" and *Die Anfänge der Augustinerchorherren und die Gründung des Augustinerchorherrenstiftes Ravengiersburg* (Betzdorf, 1928), pp. 88–117; W. Hümpfner, "Augustinusregel," LThK, I[1], 824f., I[2], 1104f.; Lambot, "L'Influence de Saint Augustin"; idem, "Un code monastique précurseur de la Règle bénédictine," *Revue Liturgique et Monastique*, 14 (1929), 331–37; idem, "La Règle de Saint Augustin et Saint Césaire"; idem, "Saint Augustine et la vie monastique," *Revue Liturgique et Monastique*, 15 (1930), 292–304; idem, "Un 'Ordo officii' du ve siècle," *Revue Bénédictine*, 42 (1930), 77–80; idem, "La Règle de Saint Augustin, ses origines, et son histoire jusqu'au XIIe siècle," *Les Echos de Saint Maurice*, 29 (1930), 129–37; idem, "Règle de saint Augustin," *Dictionnaire de Droit Canonique*, I, 1412–16; idem, "Saint Augustine a-t-il rédigé la règle pour moines qui porte son nom?" *Revue Bénédictine*, 53 (1941), 41–58; idem, "Le Monachisme de Saint Augustin," AM III, pp. 64–68; Hertling, "Kanoniker, Augustinerregel, und Augustinerorden"; de Bruyne, "La Première Règle de Saint Benoît"; G. Morin, "L'Ordre des heures canoniales dans les monastères de Cassiodore," *Revue Bénédictine*, 43 (1931), 145–52; J. Chapman, "The Origin of the Rules of St. Augustine," *The Downside Review*, 49 (1931), 395–407; S. Salaville, "Une version grecque de la Règle de Saint Augustin," ΕΛΛΗΝΙΚΑ, 4 (1931), 84ff.; Monceaux, "Saint Augustin et Saint Antoine"; Vega, *La regla de San Agustín*, pp. 12ff.; Mellet, *L'Itinéraire*, pp. 53–60; C. Boyer, "Règle de Saint Augustin," *Dictionnaire de Spiritualité*, I, 1126–30; idem, "Agostino Aurelio," *Enciclopedia cattolica*, I, 563f.; P. I. Fernández, *De figura iuridica ordinis recollectorum S. Augustini* (Rome, 1938), pp. 35–80; I. Schuster, *Storia di San Benedetto e dei suoi tempi* (Milan, 1946), pp. 217–24; C. Dereine, "Vie commune: Règle de Saint Augustin et chanoines réguliers sur au XIe siècle," *Revue d'Histoire Ecclésiastique*, 41 (1946), 365–406; idem, "Enquête sur la Règle de Saint Augustin," *Scriptorium*, 2 (1948), 28–36; J. C. Dickinson, *The Origins of the Austin Canons and Their Introduction into England* (London, 1950), pp. 225–72; A. M. dal Pino, "Autenticità della Regola di Sant' Agostino," *Studi storici dell'*

Ordine dei Servi di Maria, 5 (1953), 5–36. Hümpfner and Vega, after further research, changed their viewpoints and supported the priority of the men's *Rule* (see the next note).

12. In recent times the priority of the *Praeceptum* has been defended by E. Bellandi, "La Regola agostiniana," *Bollettino Storico Agostiniano*, 5, No. 2 (1929), 39–47; T. Disdier, "Augustin (Ordre dit de Saint-)," *Dictionnaire d'Histoire et de Géographie Ecclésiastiques*, V, 498f.; B. Garnelo, "Datos históricos acerca de la Regla de San Agustín," ArA, 38 (1932), 364–97; N. Merlin, *Saint Augustin et la vie monastique: Etude historique et critique* (Albi, 1933); idem, "Exemple typique d'un préjugé littéraire," *Analecta Praemonstratensia*, 24 (1948), 5–19; P. Mandonnet, *Saint Dominique* II (Paris, 1938), 103–42; Hümpfner, in AH lxxviii–lxxx; A. Zumkeller and W. Hümpfner, "Die Regeln des heiligen Augustinus," in *Die grossen Ordensregeln*, ed. H. U. von Balthasar, 2nd ed. (Einsideln, Zürich, & Cologne, 1961), pp. 135–71; W. Hümpfner, "Die Mönchsregel des heiligen Augustinus," AM I, pp. 241–54; idem, "Das Problem der Augustinus-Regel," in *Augustinus: Bij het zestiende eeuwfeest van zijn begoorte* (Averbode, 1954), pp. 64–80; idem, "Augustinusregel," I², 1104f.; Cilleruelo, *El monacato de San Agustín*, pp. 39ff.; idem, "Nuevas dudas sobre la *Regula ad Servos Dei* de San Agustín," ArA, 44 (1950), 85–88; L. M. Verheijen, "Autour de la *Règle de S. Augustin*," *L'Année Théologique*, 11 (1951), 345–48; idem, "La *Regula Sancti Augustini*," *Vigiliae Christianae*, 7 (1953), 27–56; idem, "Les Sermons 355–356 de Saint Augustin et *Regula Sancti Augustini*," *Recherches de Science Religieuse*, 41 (1953), 231–40; idem, "La *Regula Puellarum* et la *Regula Sancti Augustini*," in *Augustiniana—sexto decimo exacto saeculo a die natali S. Aurelii Augustini* (Louvain, 1954), pp. 42–52; idem, "La Vie de Saint Augustin par Possidius et la *Regula Sancti Augustini*," in *Mélanges offerts à Mademoiselle Christine Mohrmann* (Utrecht & Antwerp, 1963), pp. 270–79; idem, "La Règle de S. Augustin"; W. Nigg, "Augustin und das gemeinsame Leben der Kleriker," in *Vom Geheimnis der Mönche*, ed. W. Nigg (Zürich & Stuttgart, 1953), pp. 137ff.: M. Melchior (Beyenka), "Who Wrote the *Rule* of St. Augustine?" *Cross and Crown*, 8 (1956), 162–79; Dominguez-del Val, "La Regla de San Agustín"; D. Sanchis, "Pauvreté monastique et charité fraternelle chez Saint Augustin: Note sur le plan de la *Regula*," *Augustiniana*, 8 (1958), 5–21; Van Bavel, "Parallèles," 75ff.; Manrique, *La vida monastica*, pp. 447–53; Ladner, *Idea of Reform*, pp. 356–59; Sage, *La Règle de Saint Augustin*, p. 259; A. Mundó, "Mönchsregeln," LThK, VII², 540–42; A. C. Vega, "Notas histórico-críticas en torno a los orígines de la *Regla de San Agustín*," *Boletín de la Real Academia de la Historia*, 152 (1963), 13–94; E. Boularand, "Expérience et conception de la vie monastique chez S. Augustin," *Bulletin de Littérature Ecclésiastique*, 64 (1963), 172ff.

13. Lambot, "La Règle de Saint Augustin et Saint Césaire." Verheijen points out that savants of the seventeenth century, such as the canon regular Alain le Large and the French Augustinian Ange le Proust, were aware of this (*La Règle*, II 63*n*4). Furthermore, Casamassa ("Note sulla *Regula*," 362–70) has shown that it was, not the *Regularis informatio*, but the *Praeceptum* which

was used as a source in the "Tarnatensis Rule" (where "Tarnoto" may have been, no one knows; see the learned note to that effect in PL 66.977.—Translators) of the sixth century, and in the *Rule* of St. Benedict, ca. 529.

14. "Les manuscrits de la "Lettre CCXI de saint Augustin"; see also his *La Règle*, I 107.

15. Possidius 5.

16. Verheijen, "La Vie de saint Augustin"; see also chap. 4 of the second volume of *La Règle.*

17. Mandonnet, *Saint Dominique*, II 126ff.; Hümpfner, in AH lxxvii; idem, "Die Mönchsregel," 250; idem, "Das Problem der Augustinus-Regel," p. 69.

18. Merlin, "Exemple typique," 14; Cilleruelo, *El monacato de San Agustín*, pp. 73–74; idem, "Nuevas dudas," 88; Verheijen, *La Règle* II, chap. 4; Van Bavel, "Parallèles," 75.

19. "Los destinatarios de la *Regula Augustini*," ArA, 54 (1960), 87–114.

20. Manrique, *La vida monastica*, pp. 454–64; Sage, *La Règle de Saint Augustin*, pp. 260–63; Vega, "Notas histórico-criticas," 65–89.

21. Cilleruelo, "Los destinatarios"; Verheijen, *La Règle* II, chap. 4; J. Morán, "Notas sobre el monacato agustiniano," CD, 175 (1962), 535–47.

22. Verheijen, *La Règle* II, chap. 4. Recently, the Augustinian origin of the *Ordo* has been defended by Mandonnet, *Saint Dominique* II; Hümpfner, in AH lxxviiif.; idem, "Die Mönchsregel," pp. 242ff.; idem, "Das Problem der Augustinus-Regel," pp. 65ff.; Cilleruelo, *El monacato de San Agustín*, pp. 65f.; A. Zumkeller, *Das Mönchtum des heiligen Augustinus*, 1st ed. (Würzburg, 1950), pp. 215f.; Domínguez-del Val, "La Regla de San Agustín," 506ff.; M. B. Hackett, "The *Rule* of St. Augustine and Recent Criticism," *The Tagastan*, 20 (1958), 43–50.

23. Verheijen, *La Règle* II, chap. 4.

24. Ibid., pp. 93–94.

25. Ibid., pp. 164ff. Although Casamassa ("Il più antico codice" and "Note," pp. 377ff.) judged differently from Verheijen, not by stylistic criteria but by the contents, he too refused to accept Augustine's authorship for the *Ordo.* Cf. U. Mariani, "A New Critical Study on the *Rule* of St. Augustine," *The Tagastan*, 19 (1956), 44–47; idem, *Gli Agostiniani e la grande Unione del 1256* (Rome, 1957), pp. 17–28; idem, "The *Regula Secunda Ordo Monasterii*," *The Tagastan*, 21 (1959), 38–40. But see also, most recently, Lorenz, "Die Anfänge," 43f.

26. "Die Regeln des heiligen Augustinus," esp. pp. 145–50; "Die Mönchsregel," pp. 250–54; "Das Problem der Augustinus-Regel," pp. 77–79.

27. *La Règle*, II 203–204.

28. We possess no other Western rule which goes back to the late fourth century, for the rule of the monk and deacon Vigilius (PL 50.373ff.), which is unimportant and dependent on Pachomius, was written around 420 (Heimbucher, *Die Orden und Kongregationen*, I 131); and St. John Cassian's treatise "Rules for Cenobites" (CSEL 17.1–231), out of which, very early, a "Rule of Cassian" was compiled (H. Plenkers, *Untersuchungen zur Überlieferungsgeschichte der ältesten lateinischen Mönchsregeln* [Munich, 1906], pp. 70–76)

was begun only in 419 and completed in 426 (Altaner, *Patrologie*, p. 416).

29. The following more recent commentaries, which have appeared since the publication of the first edition of this book, provide discussions of the contents of Augustine's *Rule*: C. Vaca, *La vida religiosa en San Agustín*, 4 vols. (Madrid, 1955, 1964); A. Zumkeller, *Die Regel des heiligen Augustinus, mit Einführung und Erklärung*, 2nd ed. (Würzburg, 1962); H. Vissers, "L'Esprit de la *Règle de Saint Augustin*," in *Canonicorum Regularium Sodalitates XVI revoluto saeculo ab ortu S. Augustini* (Vorau, 1954), pp. 19ff.; A. Ceyssens, *De geest van de Regel van Sint Augustinus* (Diest, 1957); Sanchis, "Pauvreté monastique" (a commentary on the first two chapters of the *Rule*, with remarks on its general plan); Sage, *La Règle*. These newer works, which are more weighty than those of F. Weninger (*Die Regeln des heiligen Augustinus* [Innsbruck, 1929]) and E. Wallbrecht (*St. Augustins Regel in Wort und Sinn* [Würzburg, 1933]), attempt to explain the *Rule* in the light of Augustine's own spirit and writings. Valuable information concerning the traditions of the Augustinian order as illustrative of the *Rule* is furnished in A. Turrado's "El ideal monástico agustiniano en Santo Tomás de Villanueva," RAE 1–6 (1960–1965), and in the *Traicte de la Regle de Saint Augustin* of the French Augustinian Ange le Proust (d. 1697), which was published for the first time in Paris in 1963 in a sumptuous edition of 410 pages.

30. The German translation of the *Rule* which followed was that of Winfried Hümpfner, in H. U. von Balthasar's *Die grossen Ordensregeln*. These English translations have been prepared from Luc Verheijen's critical Latin texts in his 1967 volumes, although not all his new readings have been adopted. As in Hümpfner and in Zumkeller, the *Ordo monasterii* is prefixed to the *Praeceptum*.—Translators.

31. This corresponds with the modern canonical hour of Lauds.

32. This corresponds with the modern Compline.

33. "The brothers" (that is, not the priests) is an addition in many manuscripts which Hümpfner translates; but it does not appear to be what Augustine wrote, though, plainly, that is what he meant.

34. The allusion here is to the Israelites in the desert (Num. 14:2ff.; cf. 1 Cor. 10:10).

35. The "father" in the garden monastery was its spiritual head, a priest; and the "provost" was his second-in-command. Pachomius, too, had organized the management of his monasteries in a similar fashion (cf. B. Steidle, "'Der Zweite' im Pachomiuskloster," BMS, 24 [1948], 97ff.).

36. Such monastic measures were not regarded as any disgrace; in ancient times corporal punishment, inflicted even upon grown men, was not extraordinary, and was no cause for offense. Pachomius' *Rule* and that of Benedict contain similar directions.

37. The Septuagint version of Prov. 27:20.

38. This is the reading, *secari*, of many manuscripts; but Verheijen has found an alternative, *sanari*, "to be treated," which he follows in his text and which, he assures us, he is convinced is what Augustine wrote.—Translators.

10

Thematic Writings

FROM THE *Soliloquies* (WRITTEN EARLY IN 387)

Augustine's Ideal of Living on the Eve of His Baptism[1]

The *Soliloquies*, the youthful work Augustine wrote at the country estate of Cassiciacum near Milan, even before his baptism, shows him filled with a spirit of asceticism and with a zeal for a life of virtue. By this time he had dedicated himself to "God's service." It is true that in this fictitious dialogue between Augustine and his reason the renunciation of possessions, honors, marriage, and the pleasures of the table is viewed from the standpoint of ancient ideals of wisdom and is founded on Neoplatonic ideas; yet we cannot miss its strongly religious, Christian undertones.[2]

Book I

5. [My God and Lord, my king and Father!] Now I love You alone; You alone do I follow; You alone do I seek. I am ready to serve only You, because only You rule justly; I long to be possessed by You. Order, I beg You, and command whatever You wish, but heal and open my ears, so that I may hear Your words. Heal and open my eyes, that I may see Your nod. Drive the madness out of me, that I may come to know You. Tell me where to look that I may gaze upon You, and I trust that I shall do all that You command. Receive Your fugitive, I beg, Lord, most merciful Father. Let me have been sufficiently punished; let me have served Your enemies, whom You trample under Your feet, long enough; let me have been sufficiently the sport of their deceits. Receive me, your servant, fleeing from these people, because even they received me, the property of another, when I was fleeing from You. I feel that I must return to You. Let Your door be open to me when I knock; teach me how to come to You. I have nothing other than my will. I know nothing except that transient and perishable things should be despised; sure and eternal things, sought. I do this, Father, because I know only this; but I do not know how to come to You. Suggest

to me, show me, and furnish the provisions for the journey. If those who flee to You find You through faith, give me faith; if through virtue, give me virtue; if through knowledge, give me knowledge. Increase my faith, my hope, my love. Oh how wondrous and singular Your goodness is! . . .

17. REASON: Do you not see that these bodily eyes, even in health, are often driven back by the light of this sun and turned away, and flee to their own darkness? Moreover, you consider what you have accomplished; you do not consider what you would like to see. Nevertheless, I shall discuss this very thing with you: namely, what you think we have accomplished. Do you long for riches?

AUGUSTINE: No, indeed, and not from this time only. Now that I am thirty-three years old, it is almost fourteen years since I stopped longing for riches; nor have I thought of anything of this sort, even if it chanced to be offered to me, beyond the necessary food and a generous livelihood. A single book of Cicero persuaded me completely and with the greatest of ease that wealth should not be sought after at all, but if it comes, it should be very wisely and carefully managed.

REASON: What about the honors of office?

AUGUSTINE: I confess, I have just recently, almost within the last few days, ceased to long for honors.

REASON: What about a wife? Doesn't a beautiful, modest, obedient, educated woman, or one whom you could easily educate, occasionally charm you? A woman who brings you enough of a dowry (since you scorn wealth) to make her no burden at all to your leisure—especially if you hope and are certain that she would not be an annoyance to you?

AUGUSTINE: However much you may want to adorn her and to gather together in her every good trait, I have decided that I must avoid nothing so much as sexual relations. I feel that nothing casts a man's mind down from its citadel more than the allurements of women and that joining of bodies necessary to marriage. Therefore, if it is part of the duty of a wise man—and I have not yet learned that this is the case—to give his attention to raising a family, whoever marries for the sake of this alone seems to me worthy of admiration, but not at all worthy of imitation. For there is more danger in attempting this than there is happiness in accomplishing it. So, I think, I have fairly and usefully enough, for the sake of my own freedom of mind, ordered myself not to desire, seek, or take a wife.

REASON: I now ask not what you have decided, but whether you are still struggling, or have not truly overcome desire itself. Indeed, this is a question of the health of your eyes.

AUGUSTINE: I seek absolutely nothing of the sort; I desire nothing. I even remember such things with horror and contempt. What more do you want? And this good increases in me from day to day. The more the hope grows in me of looking upon that beauty for which I so violently long, the more all my love and my yearning are turned toward it.
REASON: What of the enjoyment of food? How much does it concern you?
AUGUSTINE: The things I have decided not to eat do not in the least concern me. Moreover, I admit that I take pleasure in the presence of those things that I have not eliminated, but in such a way that the sight or taste of them could be withdrawn from me without any disturbance to my spirit. Furthermore, when they are not present, the appetite for them does not dare to introduce itself as an impediment to my thoughts. But ask nothing at all about either food or drink, or baths, or other bodily pleasures; I seek to have only what can be granted for the good of my health.

FROM *The Ways of the Catholic Church* (COMPOSED AT THE BEGINNING OF 388)

Christian Monasticism in the Fourth Century

This work, *The Ways of the Catholic Church*, drafted in Rome at the beginning of the year 388, but not completed until a considerable time later in Africa, shows how much Augustine had been preoccupied with thoughts of the life of Christian monks since his Milan days. He depends on similar descriptions by Jerome; and he brusquely rejects the un-Christian asceticism of the Manichaean "chosen ones," as he tells of the life of the anchorites and cenobites of the East. This idealizing report witnesses to his unbroken confidence in the power of man's free will. Yet Augustine believes that there are many like the desert hermits who may have achieved complete blessedness here upon earth.[3] The chapters in which he tells of the life of monastic communities in Milan and Rome show that even then his knowledge of monasticism was not derived merely from books.

Book I

64. . . . [O Catholic Church, true mother of Christians,] many [of your children] so steadfastly burn with the love of God that they take pleasure even in solitude, living in perfect continence and in remarkable scorn for this world.

65. What is it, I ask, that those people see, who cannot live without loving man and yet can live without seeing him? Clearly, whatever it is

which enables man as he contemplates it to live without other men is superior to human affairs. Now, indeed, Manichaeans, hear about the ways and the remarkable continence of perfect Christians, to whom perfect chastity has seemed worthy not only of praise but of practice. Do not, if you have any shame, dare to boast rashly about yourselves before the minds of the unlearned, as if abstinence were the most difficult of things. And I will not speak of things unknown to you but of things that you conceal from us. For who does not know that the multitude of Christian men of perfect continence is daily spreading farther and farther, throughout the entire world, and especially in the East and in Egypt—a fact which can in no way be unknown to you.

66. I shall say nothing of those whom I mentioned a little before, who in the most remote places, away from all sight of men, inhabit the most deserted of lands, content with only bread, which is brought to them at certain times, and water. Enjoying to the full their converse with God, they adhere to Him with pure minds, and are most blessed in the contemplation of His beauty, which can be perceived only with the understanding of the blessed. I shall not speak at all, I say, of them. For, indeed, to some who do not realize how much the spirit of these men in prayer benefits us and how much the life of those whose bodies we are not allowed to see serves as an example to us, these men seem to have withdrawn from human affairs more than might be fitting. But I think that discussion of that point would be protracted and unnecessary; for how can my words make this outstanding peak of saintliness seem admirable and honorable to anyone to whom it does not so appear of its own accord? Only those people who make empty boasts about themselves must be reminded that the self-restraint and temperance of the most saintly Christians of the Catholic faith have progressed so far that they seem to need to be checked and, as it were, called back within limits; for the souls of these men are judged, even by those who disapprove, to have gone beyond human endurance.

67. But if this far surpasses our endurance, who would not admire and praise those who, having scorned and abandoned the allurements of this world, and come together in a most pure and holy common life, spend their time in prayers, reading, and discussion; and who, not puffed up with any arrogance, not troublesome with any inflexibility, not spiteful out of jealousy, but meek, modest, and peaceful, offer a most pleasing gift to God, from Whom they have gained the ability to do these things: namely, a life lived in the greatest harmony and fully directed toward Him? No one possesses anything of his own; no one is a burden to anyone. They make with

their own hands things that can nourish the body but cannot keep the mind from God. Moreover, they hand over the product of their labor to those whom they call deacons—because they are put in charge of the tithes—so that the care of his own body is a concern to no one, either in the matter of food or clothing or in anything else required either for daily usage or, as often happens, in the case of sickness. And these deacons, arranging everything very carefully and carrying out promptly whatever demands that way of life makes upon the weakness of the body, nevertheless give an accounting to one man, whom they call "father." And, indeed, those fathers, who are not only most saintly in their ways but also most advanced in the holy teachings and distinguished in all respects, without arrogance care for those whom they call their sons, giving orders with great authority and being obeyed with great good will. Moreover, at the end of the day they come together, each from his own dwelling, while they are still fasting, to listen to their father; and there assemble before each father at least three thousand men. Indeed, even a much greater number at times assembles before a single father. Then in complete silence they listen with incredible eagerness, revealing the effect upon their souls either by groans, or by tears, or by quiet joy free from all outcry, depending on how the words of the speaker have moved them. They eat next, just as much as is sufficient for their health and well-being, with each one keeping a check on his appetite lest he go to excess even in the spare and inexpensive food that is before him. To curb the desires of the body, therefore, they abstain not only from meat and wine but also from those foods which, to the extent that they more quickly whet the appetite and tease the tastebuds, appear to some more elegant, so to speak; under this name a base desire for exotic foods, other than meat, is foolishly and basely defended. Indeed, what is left over after their essential nourishment (for a great deal remains from the work of their hands and the restrictions imposed by their diet) is distributed to the needy with greater care than was taken in the growing of it. For though they in no way plant to guarantee an abundance, still they make every attempt to see that they retain none of what is left over—even to the extent of sending heavily laden ships into the areas the poor inhabit. But there is no need for me to say anything more about such a well-known fact.[4]

68. This is also the life of women who serve God zealously and chastely, living in separate dwellings as far removed from the men as is proper and joined to them only by their pious love and the imitation of virtue. Young men have no access to these women; nor do even older men, no matter how respectable and upright, except to place at the entrance door whatever

necessities the women lack. For the women spend their time and support themselves by spinning wool, and they give cloth to the brothers, accepting in return whatever food they need. If I should wish to praise these customs, this way of life, this arrangement, these practices, I would not be able to do justice to the subject, and I fear that if I decide that I must add the lofty style of the panegyrist to the simplicity of the narrator, it may seem that I consider this way of life, merely described as it is, incapable of pleasing anyone. Find fault with these things, Manichaeans, if you can. Do not point out our tares [Matt. 13:25–26] to those who are blind and unable to discriminate.

69. Nonetheless, the excellent customs of the Catholic Church are not so narrowly observed that I consider praiseworthy only the lives of those people whom I have mentioned. For how many bishops have I known to be excellent and most saintly men, how many priests, deacons, and ministers of the divine sacraments, of whatever rank, whose virtue seems to me all the more marvelous and worthy of fuller description as it is the more difficult to preserve among the manifold race of men and in this too troubled life! For they have the care of those who need to be healed no less than of those who have been healed. The vices of the multitude must be tolerated in order to be cured, and a pestilence must be endured before it can be checked. Here it is very difficult to preserve [one's] high ideals of living and guard [one's] soul in peace and quiet. Indeed, to put it briefly, the latter dwell among people who are learning to live; the former, among those who are living.

60. Nor would I on this account scorn a praiseworthy class of Christians: namely, those who live in cities but far removed from the ordinary life. I have seen in Milan a dwelling place of holy men, in no small number, which was presided over by a priest, a holy and most learned man. I have known even more places in Rome in which individuals outstanding in dignity and wisdom and holy knowledge preside over the others living with them, dwelling in Christian love, saintliness, and freedom; not even these people are a burden to anyone, for in the custom of the East and by the authority of the Apostle Paul, they live by the work of their own hands. I have also learned that many of them fast to a quite incredible degree: they do not fast daily, eating once in the evening, which is a common method everywhere; rather they spend three entire days, and often much longer, without food or drink. And this is the custom, not of the men only, but of the women as well. In every single instance those who preside over the many widows and virgins living together in the same way as the men and earning their

livelihood by wool-making and spinning are most respectable and upright women, skilled and experienced not only in establishing and directing the conduct of their charges but also in forming their minds.

"QUESTION 71," FROM *On 83 Various Questions* (COMPOSED BETWEEN 391 AND 395)

"Let Us Carry One Another's Burdens" (Gal. 6:2)

As Augustine reported in his *Retractations*, *On 83 Various Questions* is not concerned with a single theme; nor was it written for one particular occasion or at one time. It is, rather, an anthology of discussions of topics, none of them major, some minimal, which arose during the period between his return to Africa and his consecration as bishop (388–395). The discussions arose out of questions put to him by the brethren, when he did not seem to them to be occupied. He had become a bishop before he had these notes written up as a book and gave them consecutive numbers.[5]

Though it may not be so with every question, still in many of them the "brethren" who ask the questions were members of his monastic communities in Tagaste or, later, Hippo. This is certainly the case with Question 71, which deals with what is a real concern to those living a communal, monastic life. We may presume, not only from the arrangement of the discussions in the last quarter of the book but also from the extensive knowledge of Scripture Augustine can now display, that this Question was written, not in Tagaste, but in the garden monastery at Hippo. It is, indeed, nothing less than a religious discourse, presented when he was a priest in Hippo, to his confreres, dealing with the theme of a mutual tolerance. We can discern from it that at times there may have been great tensions in this new community, caused, not least, by the wide social and cultural differences in the classes from which the brethren came.[6] In his presentation, Augustine shows his perception of their mentalities and his great experience, as well as the skill and vigor with which he was seeking, in spite of all difficulties and resistance, to attain the "one heart for God" in his monasteries.

71. On that which is written: "Carry one another's burdens, and thus you will fulfill the Law of Christ" (Gal. 6:2).

1. Because the guardianship of the Old Testament involved fear, it could not be stated more openly that the gift of the New Testament is love than in this passage in which the Apostle says "Carry one another's burdens, and thus you will fulfill the law of Christ." For he is understood to speak of that

law of Christ's in which the Lord Himself ordered us to love one another, placing the weight of a command in that sentence in which He said: " 'By this shall all men know that you are My disciples, if you have love one for another' " [John 13:34–35]. Moreover, the duty of this love is to bear one another's burdens. But this duty, although it is not eternal, surely leads to eternal blessedness, in which there will be no burdens that we are ordered to bear for one another. Now, indeed, since we are in this life, that is, on this path, let us bear one another's burdens, in order to arrive at that life that is without any burden. For just as some who are learned in such lore have written that deer, when they cross a channel to an island in search of food, so arrange themselves that they share the mutual burdens of their heads (which they always carry, in the shape of the antlers on their heads), with the one behind bending his neck down and placing his head on the one in front. And because there must be one in front who has none upon whom to place his head, they are said to take turns at this, so that the first one, when he has been tired out by the weight of his head, takes his place behind the others and is replaced by the one whose head he bore when he was in front. Thus bearing each other's burdens in turn, they cross the channel until they come to solid land. Perhaps Solomon had this habit of deer in mind when he said "Let the stag of friendship and the dove of your graces speak with you."[7] For nothing is so great a proof of friendship as the carrying of a friend's burden.

2. And yet we would not carry each other's burdens if we who bear them should both be weak at the same time, or with the same type of weakness; but varying times and types of weakness render us capable of bearing each other's burdens. For instance, you will bear the anger of your brother at a time when you are not angry with him, so that in return, when anger has seized you, he will bear you with kindness and tranquillity. This example applies to the case in which, although the weakness itself is the same, the people bear it at differing times; for in both cases anger is borne in turn. But another example must be considered in which the type of weakness varies: when, for example, one man has overcome loquacity but has not yet conquered stubbornness, and another is still talkative but no longer stubborn, then the former must bear the latter's loquacity, and the latter must in charity bear the stubbornness of the former until this vice be cured in the one and that in the other. To be sure, if the same weakness should befall two men at the same time, they cannot tolerate each other, since their attention is directed against one another. Against some third person two angry men both agree with and tolerate each other, although they

should be said not to endure but to console each other. So, too, those who are unhappy for the same reason bear each other and almost depend upon each other more than if one were sad and the other rejoicing. If, however, they should be unhappy because of one another, they cannot endure each other at all. And, likewise, a sickness from which you wish another to be released through your help must to some degree be approached with feelings of this sort, and the approach must be so made that it serves as a relief of suffering, not a sharing of it, just as he who stretches out his hand to the sick person leans over. For he does not stretch out, so that both of them are lying down; he merely bends over so that he may lift up the one lying down.

3. And nothing makes this necessary task of bearing the burdens of others more gladly borne than considering how much the Lord has borne for us. Indeed, the Apostle, admonishing us about this, says: "Perceive this in yourselves, which was also in Jesus Christ, Who, being in the form of God, did not consider that an equality with God was something to be grasped; but He emptied Himself, taking on the form of a servant, being made in the likeness of men, and in habit was found as a man. He humbled Himself, becoming obedient unto death, even to death on a cross" [Phil. 2:5–8]. For he had said earlier "Each one considering not the things that are his own, but those that are other men's" [Phil. 2:4]. To this he added what was just quoted: "Perceive this in yourselves, which was also in Christ Jesus." With regard to this, He considered not His own burdens but ours, to the extent that the Word became Flesh and dwelt among us [John 1:14] and, although He was without sin, bore our sins; thus, in imitation of Him, let us likewise bear each other's burdens willingly.

4. To this thought is added another: that He took on the appearance of man. We, moreover, are men and ought to consider that we, too, either could have had, or can have, the sickness of mind or body that we perceive in another. Therefore let us show him whose weakness we wish to bear what we would wish him to show to us if, by chance, we were in that state and he were not. To this the words of the Apostle apply: "I become all things to all men, that I might save all" [1 Cor. 9:22], that is, by considering that he too might have had that vice from which he wished to free another. Indeed, he did this by being compassionate, not by lying, as some suspect, especially those who, in defense of their own lies, which they cannot deny, seek the protection of someone of great worth.

5. Then this, too, should be considered: every man can have some good quality, even if hidden, which you do not yet have and in which he, without

a doubt, can be superior to you. This thought is good for blunting and taming arrogance, lest you think that, since your own good points are conspicuous and apparent, someone else on that account has no hidden good points, good points perhaps of great weight, by which he might surpass you in your ignorance. For the Apostle does not order us to be deceived or, rather, to make use of flattery when he says "Let nothing be done in competition or in vain conceit, but in humility of spirit, each one thinking the other to be superior" [Phil. 2:3]. We ought to believe this, not in such a way that, though imagining ourselves to believe it, we do not do so; but let us really believe that there may be something hidden in another which makes him superior to us, even if our own good point, by which we seem to be superior to him, is not hidden. These thoughts, which check arrogance and sharpen our feelings of love, allow us to bear our brothers' burdens not only with equanimity but also with the greatest pleasure. Moreover, the opinion that no one is known except through friendship must not be held concerning any stranger. And, therefore, we endure more firmly the bad qualities of our friends because their good qualities delight us and hold us fast.

6. Thus, no one offering himself in friendship should be scorned as a friend; let him not be accepted immediately, but let him be chosen as one who is to be accepted, and let him be treated in such a way that he will be accepted. For we can say that we have accepted as a friend that man to whom we dare to pour forth all our plans. And if there is anyone who does not dare to offer himself as a friend, since he is held back by some temporal honor or office of ours, we must go to him and, with a certain friendliness and humility of spirit, offer him what he does not dare to seek on his own. Indeed, no matter how seldom, it nonetheless sometimes happens that the faults of one whom we wish to accept as a friend become known to us before his good qualities, and, offended and somehow repelled by those faults, we abandon him and do not arrive at an investigation of his good points, which are perhaps more hidden. Therefore, our Lord Jesus Christ, Who wishes us to become His imitators, warns us to bear the weakness of that man in order to be led through the tolerance of love to certain strengths, in the enjoyment of which we find rest. For He says " 'It is not the healthy who need a doctor, but the sick' " [Matt. 9:12]. And on this account if, for the sake of Christ's love, we ought not to drive from our minds even that man who may be sick in every part, since he can be healed by the Word of God, how much less should we drive out that man who

may seem to us completely sick, because in the first stages of friendship we could not endure certain of his weaknesses? And, what is more serious, along with the offense of the spirit, we have dared to pass a rash sentence of prejudice on the entire man, without fear of what was said: " 'Judge not, lest you be judged' " and " 'The measure you mete out is the measure that will be meted out to you' " [Matt. 7:1, 2]. Often, however, the good qualities appear first; in these cases, too, precautions should be taken against rash judgment, lest, when you have thought the whole to be good, the bad qualities which appear later find you unaware and unprepared and offend you more seriously, with the result that you hate him all the more bitterly whom you had rashly loved—a wicked thing. For even if none of his good points came first and those bad points that later appeared had been apparent from the beginning, they should nevertheless have been tolerated while together you tried every means by which such faults are often cured. How much more should they be tolerated when those good qualities that, like pledges, should constrain us to bear what comes later have come first?

7. That, then, is the law of Christ: that we should bear one another's burdens. Moreover, by loving Christ we easily endure the infirmity of another, even one whom we do not yet love for the sake of his own good qualities. For we consider that the Lord, Whom we love, died for the sake of that man. The Apostle Paul enjoined that love on us when he said "And through your knowledge the weak brother will perish, for whose sake Christ died" [1 Cor. 8:11]! So that if we love the weak man less because of the vice by which he is weak, let us consider in him the One Who died for his sake. For failure to love Christ is, not weakness, but death. Therefore, having sought the mercy of God, we must take thought very carefully lest we neglect Christ for the sake of the weak man when we ought to be loving the weak man for the sake of Christ.

FROM THE *Confessions* (COMPOSED CA. 400)

Augustine's Vocation

Augustine, looking back on the days of his youth, describes with psychological subtlety his interior development. Doing this, he sheds considerable light on the events and the decisions of those times, which had become important for his later Christian monastic ideals.

Book III

Awakening of the Love for Philosophy

7. . . . and now, following the customary order of study, I had come to a book of a certain Cicero, whose language is almost universally admired, but not his heart. But that book of his contains an exhortation to philosophy and is called the *Hortensius.* Truly it changed my attitudes and turned my prayer toward You Yourself, Lord, and changed my hopes and redirected my desires. Suddenly, all my vain ambition counted for naught, and with an immeasurable fervor in my heart, I yearned for the immortality of Wisdom, and I started to rise, that I might return to You. For I was using that book, not to increase my facility with language—which I seemed to be buying with my mother's money, since I was then nineteen years old and my father had died two years before—not, therefore, to increase my facility with language or to improve my style, but because the content of the book had captivated me.

8. How I burned, my God, how I burned to fly from earthly things back to You! . . .

Book VI

Longing of the Thirty-Year-Old Augustine for "Retirement"

20. When I was saying these things, and these currents were flowing in different directions, driving my heart now one way, now another, the time passed, and I was slow to be turned toward God; I put off from day to day living in You [Eccli. 5:8], and yet I did not daily put off dying in myself. Though loving the happy life, I feared it in its own abode, and, though fleeing from it, I sought it. For I thought that I would be too miserable if I should be deprived of the embraces of a woman, and I did not consider the medicine of Your mercy, which would cure that same sickness, because I had not tried it. I thought that continence was due to our own strength, which I knew I did not have, since I was so foolish that I did not know that, as it is written, no one is able to be continent unless You have granted it [Wis. 8:21]. And surely You would have granted it if I had struck Your ears with my inner moaning and in unwavering faith had cast my cares upon You [cf. Ps. 54:23]. . . .

24. And many of us who were friends had taken thought and, discussing and abhorring the troublesome annoyances of human life, we had by then almost decided to live at leisure, far from the crowd. We planned to achieve that leisure in such a way that anything we might have we would contribute to the common property, and we would make one household from all, so

that through the sincerity of friendship one thing might not belong to this man and another to that, but one possession might be made from all. The whole thing would belong to each individual, and everything would belong to all of us. It seemed to us that there could be about ten men in this society, some of whom were very rich men—especially Romanianus, our fellow-townsman and a very close friend of mine from childhood, who had been brought to the imperial court at that time by serious business matters. He was especially enthusiastic about the project, and wielded great authority in the discussion because his large fortune far surpassed that of the others. And we had decided that two men, chosen like magistrates for a term of one year, would make all necessary arrangements, while the rest of us would be without responsibilities. But after we began to consider whether the wives whom some of us already had and others wished to have would allow this, the entire plan, which we were successfully shaping, fell apart in our hands, and was broken and tossed aside. From there [we returned] to sighing and moaning, and to steps along the broad and well-worn paths of the world [cf. Matt. 7:13]. . . .

Book VIII

His Encounter with Monasticism, and His "Conversion"

14. For, on a certain day (I forget the reason for Nebridius' absence), behold, one Ponticianus, a fellow-citizen—to the extent that he was from Africa—who was prominent in the palace guard, came to the house to visit us, Alypius and me; he wanted something or other from us, and we sat down to talk. By chance he noticed a book on the table before us, which was used for games; he picked it up, opened it, and, contrary to his expectation, found it to be a text of the Apostle Paul. For he had thought it was one of the texts I wear myself out in teaching. Then, indeed, looking at me and smiling, he offered me congratulations, and marveled that he had suddenly found that text and that text alone before my eyes. For he was a Christian and a faithful one, who often prostrated himself before You, our God, in church in frequent and daily prayer. When I told him that I was taking great pains with that text, he began to tell the story of Anthony, a monk of Egypt, whose name was very well known among Your servants but was until that time unknown to us. When he learned this, he expanded upon that story, recommending to us, who were ignorant of him, that very great man, and marveling at that very ignorance of ours. For we were astonished upon hearing about those miracles of Yours, which were so widely witnessed and which took place in such recent memory and almost

in our own time, done in true faith and in the Catholic Church. All three of us were astonished: we because the miracles were so great, and he because we had not heard of them.

15. Then his conversation turned to the companies of monasteries and the ways of your sweetness and the fertile deserts of the wilderness, of which we knew nothing. There was also a monastery in Milan, outside the walls of the city, which was full of good brothers under the nourishing care of Ambrose, and we did not know about it. He continued to speak, and we listened in silence. Then it happened that he told us that once he and three other of his fellow-soldiers had gone out for a walk in the gardens near the city walls (at Trier, in fact, when the emperor was busy for the afternoon at the Circus). There, as they chanced to be strolling along in pairs, one walked away with him, and the other two likewise walked off together; the second pair, wandering along, came upon a certain house where some of Your servants lived, poor in spirit, of whom such is the kingdom of heaven [cf. Matt. 5:3]. And there they found a book that contained the life of Anthony. One of them began to read it and to be amazed at and excited by it; as he continued to read, he began to think about taking up such a life and, giving up the service of the world, about serving You. For they were of the group which is called "Agents for Public Affairs." Then suddenly, filled with holy love and a sober sense of shame, and angry with himself, he looked at his friend and said to him, "Tell me, I beg you, what goal are we trying to reach with all this effort of ours? What are we looking for? Why are we soldiers? Can we hope for any more in the palace than to be friends of the emperor? And what is not fragile and dangerous there? Through how many dangers do we arrive at a greater danger? And when will that be? But if I wish to become a friend of God's, behold, I now become one." He said this, and, troubled by the pains of bringing forth a new life, turned his gaze again to the book; and he read and was changed within, where You saw, and his mind put off the cares of this world, as was soon apparent. For as he read and as the surging of his heart continued, he moaned at times, and he came to a realization of and decided upon better actions; and then, having become Yours, he said to his friend, "I have just now torn myself away from that ambition of ours and have decided to serve God, and I enter upon this from this hour and in this place. If you are reluctant to imitate me, do not oppose me." The other answered that he would accompany him as a partner in such a great service and for so great a reward. And then they both, Your servants, built a tower at the appropriate cost [Luke 14:28], leaving behind all their possessions

[Matt. 19:27] and following you [Luke 5:11, 28]. Then Ponticianus and the one who was walking with him in other parts of the garden arrived in search of their friends and, on finding them, told them to go back, because the day had already begun drawing to a close. But these two servants of Yours, having announced their decision and their resolve, and related how such a wish had arisen and was strengthened in them, asked Ponticianus and his companion not to be angry if they refused to join them. These two, though they had not changed at all from their former ways, nonetheless wept (so he said) and piously congratulated their friends, commending themselves to their prayers. Then, turning their attention toward earthly matters, departed for the palace. But the other pair, fixing their gaze on heaven, remained in the cottage. Each of these men had a fiancée, and, when these women heard what had happened, they too dedicated their virginity to You.

16. As Ponticianus told this story, You, Lord, in the midst of his words, were turning me back toward myself, taking me away from behind my back, where I had placed myself, as long as I did not want to consider myself. But You placed me before my own eyes [Ps. 49:21] so that I might see how shameful, how deformed and befouled, how bespotted and ulcerous, I was. And I saw and shuddered, but there was no place I might flee from myself [Ps. 138:7]. And if I tried to turn my gaze from myself, Ponticianus went on telling his story, and once again You placed me before myself and thrust me before my own eyes, so that I might discover and hate my wickedness [cf. Ps. 35:3]. I knew it, but pretended not to; I forced myself not to think about it, and forgot it.

17. Then, indeed, the more ardently I loved those men, whose wholesome passions I heard about, because they had given themselves totally to You to be cured, the more bitterly I hated myself in comparison with them. For many years of my life—perhaps twelve—had passed since, in my nineteenth year, I had been stirred to the zeal for Wisdom after reading the *Hortensius* of Cicero. Yet I was putting off scorning earthly happiness and finding the free time to investigate Wisdom, not the discovery of which but the mere search for which should have been placed before the treasures and kingdoms of the world, even if already discovered, and the physical pleasures which were mine at a nod. But I, truly a wretched young man, wretched at the very beginning of my adolescence, had even sought chastity from You, saying "Give me chastity and continence, but not yet." For I was afraid that You might soon hear me and quickly cure me of the disease of lust, which I wanted satisfied rather than extinguished. . . .

19. Then in that great conflict of my inner house, a conflict that I had strongly stirred up against my soul in the chamber of my heart, I went to Alypius, troubled in expression as well as in my mind, and I cried out, "What is wrong with us? What have you heard? The unlearned rise up and seize heaven, and, behold, we with our learning are wallowing in flesh and blood! Are we ashamed to follow because they have gone before? Are we not at least ashamed not to follow?" ...

26. The very trifles of trifles and vanities of vanities, my former mistresses, held me back, and kept plucking at my fleshly garments and murmuring, "Are you sending us away?" and ""From now on we will never be with you again" and "From now on you will never be allowed this and that." And what did they suggest with the phrase "this and that"? What did they suggest, my God? May Your mercy turn it away from the soul of Your servant! What foulness, what shamelessness, they suggested! But now I much less than half heard them, not as if they were freely contradicting me face to face, but as if murmuring behind my back and furtively plucking at me as I was leaving them, so that I would look back. And yet they delayed me as I was hesitating to rescue myself, shake myself free of them, and leap across to where I was being called; for my violent habit would say to me "Do you think that you will be able to live without them?"

27. But already it was saying this very faintly. For from that direction where I had turned my face and where I was hesitating to go, the chaste dignity of continence, cheerful but not dissolutely joyous, was revealed, honestly coaxing me to come and to have no doubts, and stretching forth devout hands full of multitudes of good examples to receive and embrace me. There were so many young men and maidens, such a band of youth and of every age, and sober widows, and aged virgins, and in all of them there was continence herself, by no means barren, but the fruitful mother of children, joys from You, her husband, Lord. And she smiled at me in mocking encouragement, as if to say, "Will you be unable to do what these men and women have done? Indeed, are they able to do this by themselves, and not through the Lord their God? The Lord their God has given me to them. Why do you stand in yourself, and thus not stand at all? Cast yourself upon Him; do not be afraid. He will not withdraw so that you will fall. Cast yourself upon Him free of care; He will receive and heal you." And I was blushing excessively because I still heard the murmuring of those trifles, and full of hesitation I hung back. And again she seemed to speak, as if saying, "Become deaf to those unclean members of yours of earth, so they will be mortified. They speak to you of delights, but not as the law of

the Lord your God" [cf. Ps. 118:85]. This argument in my heart was nothing but myself against myself. . . .

29. . . . And, behold, from a nearby house, I heard the voice of someone—whether a boy or a girl I don't know—chanting and repeating over and over "Take and read, take and read." My expression changed immediately, and I began to consider very seriously whether children usually chant any such phrase in any type of game; and it occurred to me that I had never heard this anywhere. I checked the flood of my tears and stood up, interpreting that I was being divinely ordered to do nothing other than open the book and read the first chapter I happened upon. For I had heard about Anthony that he had been admonished by a Gospel reading, which he had chanced upon, as if what was being read were being said to him: " 'Go, sell what you have, and give it to the poor, and you will have treasure in heaven. And come, follow Me' " [Matt. 19:21]. And through such a sign he had been converted to You immediately. So I returned quickly to the place where Alypius was sitting, for when I had arisen I had left the book of the Apostle there. I snatched it up, opened it, and read in silence the first chapter my eyes fell upon: "Not in rioting and drunkenness, not in debauchery and wantonness, not in strife and jealousy, but put on the Lord Jesus Christ and make no provision for the concupiscence of your flesh" [Rom. 13:13–14]. I did not want to read any further; nor did I need to. Indeed, immediately after I finished this sentence, all the shadows of my hesitation fled, as if the light of security had been poured into my heart.

30. . . . Then we went into my mother and told her; she rejoiced. We told her how it happened; she exulted and triumphed and gave thanks to You, Who have the power to do more than we ask or understand [Eph. 3:20], because she saw that You had granted her so much more for me than she used to ask for in her pitiful and mournful groaning. For You converted me to Yourself, so that I never again sought either a wife or any other hope this world has to offer, standing in that rule of faith in which You had shown me to her so many years before; and You converted her grief into a joy [Ps. 29:12] much richer than she had wished for, and much dearer and chaster than she used to seek from the offspring of my flesh.

Book IX
"Holy Enterprise"

17. You "Who make those of like mind live in one house" [Ps. 67:7] also gave us a companion Evodius, a young man from our town, who, when

he was serving as an Agent for Public affairs, was converted to You before we were and was baptized. Leaving the warfare of this world, he took up arms in Your service. We were together, intending to live together in our holy enterprise. We asked what place had more use for us as Your servants: together we were returning to Africa. . . .

Augustine's Ascetic Endeavors

The tenth book of the *Confessions* gives deep insights into Augustine's ascetic endeavors at the time he was examining his own dispositions and way of life. Man's inclination to evil appeared to him, in conjunction with the well-known words "What does the world offer? Only the gratification of corrupt nature and of the eye, the empty pomp of living" (1 John 2:16), as a threefold concupiscence: delight of the flesh and of the eye and of the pride of life. Still he knew that he was weak and vulnerable, and therefore he never wearied in praying "Lord, give me what You want of me, and want what You will." In this way, his attitude toward human sensory activity and the pleasure inseparable from it, as in his judgments of eating and drinking, are not free of rigorism. The limits he defines for what is permitted in the enjoyment of earthly pleasures are often too narrow.[9]

Book X

41. Surely you order me to hold myself back from the lust of the flesh and lust of the eyes and a striving after the world's honors [1 John 2:16]. You have ordered me to abstain from sexual relations, and concerning marriage itself You have ordered something better than You have allowed. And since You granted it, it was done, even before I became a dispenser of Your sacrament. But there still live in my memory, of which I have spoken so much, the images of such things, which my habits have fixed there, and though lacking in strength, they rush in upon me when I am awake. When I am asleep, however, they come not only to the point of pleasure, but even to the point of consent and most similar to the actual deed. . . .

42. All powerful God, is Your hand not able to heal all the diseases of my soul and by Your abundant grace to quench the lascivious motions even of my sleep? You will increase Your gifts in me more and more, Lord, so that my soul, freed from the birdlime of lust, follows me to You. . . .

43. There is another evil of the day; would that it were sufficient unto it [Matt. 6:34]! For we repair the daily decay of the body by eating and drinking, until you destroy food and stomach [1 Cor. 6:13] when You kill my want with wondrous satiety and clothe this corruptible [body] with

eternal incorruptibility [1 Cor. 15:53]. But now necessity is sweet to me, and I fight against that sweetness so as not to be caught, and I wage a daily war by fasting. . . .

44. You have taught me this, to approach taking food as if it were medicine. But until I pass from the discomfort of need to the pleasure of sufficiency, the snares of lust are set for me in the very act of passing. For the passage itself is a pleasure, and there is no other way to cross than the path necessity forces us to use. And although the reason for eating and drinking is health, a dangerous pleasure adds itself like an attendant, and often tries to go ahead, that it may become the cause of what I say I am doing or want to do for the sake of health. Nor do both have the same limit, for what is enough for health is too little for pleasure, and often it is uncertain whether the necessary care of the body still seeks nourishment or whether the sensual deceit of greed offers its service. My unhappy soul finds joy in this uncertainty, and prepares from it the defense of an excuse, rejoicing that what is sufficient for the moderation of health is not apparent, so that the activity of pleasure may be concealed under the guise of health. I try every day to resist these tempations, and I call upon Your right hand and refer my troubles to You because I do not yet have a fixed plan in this matter.

45. I hear the voice of my God commanding: " 'Let not your hearts be weighed down in surfeiting and drunkenness' " [Luke 21:34]. Drunkenness is far from me; have pity on me, lest it approach me. But surfeiting has sometimes crept up upon Your servant; have pity on me, that it may be far from me. For no one is able to be continent unless You grant it [Wis. 8:21]. . . .

47. So, placed among these temptations, I struggle daily against the desires of eating and drinking; for it is not a thing that I may decide to cut off once for all and not touch again, as I was able to do with sexual relations. And so the reins of the throat must be held with a measured slackening and tightening. And who is there, Lord, who is not to some degree carried beyond the limits of necessity? Whoever he is, he is a great man; let him magnify Your name. But I am not he, for I am a sinful man. . . .

48. I am not overly concerned with the enticements of aromas; when they are absent, I do not seek them, but when they are present, I do not refuse them. I am even prepared to be without them forever. So I seem to myself, but perhaps I am mistaken. . . .

49. The pleasures of sounds had more stubbornly enslaved me and enfolded me, but You untied and freed me. Now I confess I find some rest to

a degree in the songs to which Your eloquence gives life, when they are sung by a sweet and trained voice; yet not indeed so that I cling to them but so that I arise when I wish. Nevertheless, these sounds, along with the words which give them life so that they may gain entrance to me, seek a place of some dignity in my heart, and scarcely do I furnish them a suitable one. Indeed, at times I think I give them more honor than is fitting, while I perceive that our spirits are stirred to the flame of piety more religiously and ardently by those same holy songs when they are sung in such a way than if they are not sung that way. And all the emotions of our spirit have, by reason of their own diversity, their appropriate measures in voice and song, which are aroused by some hidden familiarity with these measures. But this delight of my flesh (to which the mind ought not to be given over to be weakened) often deceives me; and the sense does not so accompany reason as follow behind patiently, but, since it has deserved to gain admission for the sake of reason, even tries to run ahead and to lead the way. Thus in these matters I sin without being aware of it, and afterward I realize it.

51. The pleasure of these bodily eyes of mine remains, about which I confess that the ears of Your temple hear, brotherly and devout ears, so that we may conclude discussion of the temptations of the lust of the flesh, which still strike me, groaning and desiring to put on my dwelling that is from heaven [2 Cor. 5:2]. The eyes love beautiful and varied shapes, bright and pleasant colors. Let these things not hold my soul; let the Lord hold it, Who has made these things very good [Gen. 1:31] indeed. He is my good, not they. They touch me every day while I am awake; nor am I given any rest from them, as rest is sometimes given from the voices of song and sometimes from all sounds, in silence. For the very queen of the colors, that light flooding everything we see, soothes me wherever I have been during the day as it glides past in many forms while I am engaged in some task and am not noticing it. For it so strongly insinuates itself that if it should suddenly be withdrawn, it would be longingly sought again; and if it should be long absent, it saddens the mind.

53. How countless are the things that by different skills and manufactures men have added as enticements for the eyes, in the form of clothing, shoes, vessels, and products of every sort, as well as paintings and various images, all far exceeding necessary and moderate use and holy signification! Following outwardly what they have created, men desert inwardly Him by Whom they were created, and destroy what they themselves were created.

But I, my God and my glory, even on this account sing a hymn to You and make a sacrifice of praise to my Sanctifier, since the beautiful patterns come through the souls of men into their skillful hands from that beauty which is above our souls for which my soul sighs day and night. But the makers and followers of external beauties draw from that source a means of approving, but not a means of using, them. Although they do not see Him, He is there, so that they do not wander too far, and so that they may preserve their strength for You and not scatter it upon delightful weariness. But I who say and discern these things entangle my steps in these beauties; but You, Lord, rescue me, You rescue me, since Your mercy is before my eyes [Ps. 25:3]. For I am wretchedly captured, and You mercifully rescue me, sometimes not perceiving it because I had come upon these beauties with hesitation, and sometimes sorrowful because I had already been held fast by them.

54. To this is added another form of temptation, and a much more dangerous one. For besides the lust of the flesh, which is present in the gratification of all the senses and pleasures (in the service of which those people who go far from You perish), there is present in the soul through the same senses of the body a certain empty and curious desire, cloaked in the name of knowledge and learning, not to take pleasure in the flesh but to make experiments through it. Since this desire consists in the appetite for knowledge and since the eyes, moreover, lead the senses in acquiring knowledge, it is called in Holy Scripture "the lust of the eyes" [1 John 2:16]. . . .

56. In so huge a forest full of ambushes and dangers, behold, I have cut off many things and driven them from my heart, as You have enabled me to do, God of my salvation [Ps. 17:47]. And yet when do I dare to say, since so many things of this sort buzz around our daily lives on all sides, that nothing of this sort makes me eager for the sight of it, and that no vain care makes me eager to possess it. Truly the theaters do not captivate me; nor do I care to know the courses of the stars. My soul has never sought responses from the dead; I despise all sacrilegious oaths. . . .

57. Nevertheless, who can truly count how many infinitesimal and contemptible things daily tempt our curiosity, and how often we fall? How many times do we at first tolerate, as it were, those telling foolish tales so as not to offend the weak, and then gradually hear them with pleasure? . . . And my life is full of such things; my sole hope is Your truly great mercy. For when our heart becomes a receptacle of this sort of thing and carries crowds of abundant vanity, then on this account our prayers are often

broken off and disturbed, and while before Your eyes we direct the voice of our heart to Your ears, so great a matter is cut off by trifling thoughts rushing in from somewhere.

59. But Lord, You Who alone rule without pride because You are the only true Lord, Who have no lord—has this third type of temptation left me, or can it ever leave me through my whole life: that is, the wish to be respected and loved by men for no other reason than that from this there may come a joy which is not joy? This life is wretched, and this boasting is empty. . . . And, therefore, since on account of certain responsibilities of human society it is necessary to be loved and respected by men, the enemy of our true happiness presses upon us everywhere, scattering "well done, well done" among his snares, so that while we eagerly collect them, we may be caught unaware and separate our joy from Your truth, placing that joy in the lying deceit of men and finding pleasure in being loved and respected not for Your sake, but in Your place. . . .

62. Behold, Truth, in You I see that I should be moved by praise of myself not for my own sake but for the good of my neighbor. And I do not know whether I am this way. In this connection I am less known to myself than You are. . . .

64. . . . In all these things and in dangers and troubles of this sort, You see the trembling of my heart, and I feel that my wounds are often healed by You rather than not inflicted on me.

66. And in this way I have considered the weariness of my sins in my threefold lust, and I have invoked Your right hand for my salvation. . . .

FROM THE TREATISE *Against Faustus* (COMPOSED CA. 400)

Christian Striving for Perfection

Faustus the Manichaean, in a controversy with Augustine, had boasted of his own literal obedience to the commands of the Gospel: "I have forsaken father and mother, wife and child. I have despised gold and silver, and no longer carry money in my purse, content with my daily maintenance, and with no care for tomorrow." These are the injunctions of Christ which he, the Manichaean, fulfills, but which the Christians despise. Augustine contrasts Christian striving for perfection with the ostentation of this man, who demands from others what he only makes a show of carrying out himself.

Book V

9. Yet how many there are in our community who truly obey those more sublime evangelical commands, while you deceive the unlearned by appearing to obey them! How many, both men and women, are pure and free from all sexual contact! How many, having experienced it, are continent afterward! How many there are who have shared or given up their own possessions, and how many who subject their bodies to servitude by fasting, whether frequently, or daily, or—incredible as it is—continuously! How many congregations of brethren there are who have no possessions of their own but hold everything in common (and then only what is necessary for food and clothing) melding together, in the fire of love, one mind and one heart in God [cf. Acts 4:32]! And among all these professions, how many deceitful and corrupt people are discovered, how many still lie hidden, and how many who at first walked the straight path quickly fall away from it through misdirected desire! How many are found out in times of temptation because they undertook such a life with an intention other than the reason they falsely professed, and how many persevere right to the end and are saved, guarding their holy undertaking humbly and faithfully! . . . Nor do only those who in order to be perfect sell or put aside their possessions and follow the Lord reach the kingdom of heaven; there is a tribute-paying multitude that is joined to these front-line Christian troops through a certain exchange of love, as it were. And to this band it will be said at the end, " 'I was hungry, and you gave me to eat,' " and so forth [Matt. 25:35].

FROM THE TREATISE *The Work of Monks* (COMPOSED CA. 400)

Work and Pray

At the request of Bishop Aurelius of Carthage, Augustine took part in a controversy that had arisen among the monks of his diocese. Some of them practiced manual labor according to ancient monastic traditions, appealing to the example of St. Paul; others considered that such work could not be reconciled with evangelical perfection, basing their views on the words of Scripture: " 'Behold the birds of the air, for they neither sow, nor do they reap, nor gather into barns; and your heavenly father feeds them. . . . Consider the lilies of the fields, how they grow; they labor not, neither do they spin' " (Matt. 6:26, 28). With great concern for the good name and the future of monasticism, Augustine opposes the Carthage monks who do not want to work.

14. At this point perhaps someone might say "If the Apostle was doing physical work to sustain this life, what was that work and when was he free both to work and to preach the Gospel?" To him I answer: Assume that I do not know. . . . I do know one thing: that he was not a thief, not a burglar, not a bandit, not a charioteer, not a hunter, not an actor, not any base seeker of wealth; yet he worked blamelessly and honorably at tasks suitable for human employment, such as the work of carpenters, builders, cobblers, peasants, and others of this sort. Nor indeed does this very respectability find fault with the tasks that are criticized by the arrogance of those who love to be called, but not to be, honorable. Therefore, the Apostle would not have scorned either to undertake some peasant's work or to busy himself at labor of workmen; for in this matter I do not know of whom he could have stood in awe, he who says, "Be without offense to the Jews and the Greeks, and to the Church of God" [1 Cor. 10:32]. If, they say, of the Jews, the patriarchs drove cattle; if of the Greeks (whom we also call pagans), they too had philosophers whom they held in high esteem who were cobblers; if of the Church of God, that man who was just and chosen to bear witness to an everlasting conjugal chastity, the man to whom the Virgin Mary, the mother of Christ, was betrothed—that man was a carpenter. Therefore, whatever of these tasks men perform honestly and without deception is good. . . .

19. For just as the Apostle—or, rather, the Spirit of God possessing and filling and compelling his heart—never ceased to exhort the faithful, who possessed this sort of goods, to sever every bond of secular ambition and to dedicate their freed minds to divine service so that nothing would be lacking to the servants of God who wished to maintain a higher level of sanctity in the Church; so, too, the same servants of God ought to obey the Apostle's precepts that they have compassion on the weak, and, since they are not bound by a love of private possessions, to labor with their own hands toward the common good, and obey without murmur those placed in charge, in order that what they think is lacking to them, as they do manual labor or work at some task to earn a living, because of the bodily weakness of some and ecclesiastical duties or learning of the doctrine of salvation, may be supplied from the offerings of the faithful.

20. I should like to know what, indeed, those men who do not want to do physical labor should do and for what task they should have free time. For prayer, they say, and psalms, and reading, and the word of God. Clearly, a holy life, and one praiseworthy with the sweetness of Christ. But if we are not to be called away from these things, then neither ought we to eat;

nor can our daily food be prepared, so that it may be placed before us and eaten. But if the demands of our weakness compel the servants of God to be free for these matters at certain fixed intervals of time, why do we not also allot some portions of time for observing the commands of the Apostle? For a single prayer of an obedient man is heard more quickly than ten thousand of a scornful man. Indeed, even men working with their hands can easily sing sacred songs and can lighten that labor by a sacred rowing-song, so to speak. Or are we unaware to what frivolous and oftentimes scurrilous stories all workers give their hearts and their tongues, although their hands do not stray from their work? What, then, prevents the servant of God working with his hands from meditating on the law of the Lord [Ps. 1:2] and singing to the name of the Lord most high [Ps. 12:6]? Certainly he may do this, provided he has times set aside for learning the things that he may practice by memory. To this end, the good works of the faithful should serve as an additional source for supplying what is necessary, so that the time the brethren devote to instructing their minds, and during which they would not be engaged in their manual labor, would not result in their wanting for anything. Moreover, do not those who say that they spend their time in reading find in that reading what the Apostle has instructed? Then what is this wrongheadedness, to refuse to obey one's reading at the same time as one wants to be free to engage in it, and to refuse to do what one reads in order to spend more time reading what is good? For who could be unaware that after one reads about good actions, the sooner one does as one reads the sooner one profits?

25. If they at least had possessed some assets in this world, by which they supported themselves easily and without manual labor and which, when they turned to God, they distributed among the needy, then we should believe in their weakness and tolerate it. For such men, who have been brought up, not in a better fashion, but, in fact, less practically, often are not able to endure the toil of physical labor. . . .

Moreover, men now are coming to this profession of service to God even from the condition of servitude, being either freedmen or those who for this purpose have been or are about to be freed by their masters, or from the peasant class or from among the craftsmen and the common laborers, with a training all the more suitable insofar as it was strenuous. It is a grave mistake not to admit them, for many from this number were truly great men and worthy of imitation. On this account "God chose the weak of the world, so that He might confound the brave; and He chose the foolish of the world so that He might confound the wise; and He chose the base things of the world, and those that are not, as though they were, so that those things which are not base may be brought to naught and no flesh glory in His sight" [1 Cor. 1:27–29]. Therefore, this pious and holy thought brings it to pass that even such men are admitted who bear no proof of a life that has been changed for the better. For, indeed, it is not apparent whether they have come out of resolution for the service of God or whether, at loose ends and fleeing a life of want and hardship, they wished to be fed and clothed and, what is more, esteemed by those who had been accustomed to scorn and criticize them. Therefore, . . . such men cannot make excuses for themselves on the grounds of bodily weakness in order to work less—to be sure, they are convicted by the habit of their former lives. . . .

26. . . . And there are among them those who came to the holy military service with this intent: to serve Him to Whom they have proved themselves [cf. 2 Tim. 4]. Though vigorous enough in bodily strength and so sound of health that they are able not only to be educated but also (following the Apostle) to work, they have been seduced through the idle and corrupt conversations of those they are unable to judge correctly because of their inexperience, and, afflicted through that disease-bringing contagion with that same sickness, not only are failing to imitate the obedience of the holy men who work quietly and in the most beneficial discipline of other monasteries live according to the Apostle's dictum, but also are insulting their superiors, preaching laziness as though it were the preserver of the Gospel and indicting compassion as its partner in collusion. Indeed, the man who takes thought for the good reputation of the servants of God does far more merciful work for the souls of the weak than the man who breaks bread for the hungry does for the bodies of the needy. Would that those who want to be exempt from manual labor would also want to be totally exempt from speaking, for they would not encourage so many others to imitate them if they set before them an example not only of laziness but of silence as well!

32. Some will say "What, then, does converting to the spiritual life and service profit a servant of God if it is still necessary for him to work actively just like a common laborer?" As if, in truth, it could easily be explained in words how much profit there was in what the Lord told the rich man seeking a plan for attaining eternal life to do if he wished to be perfect: that, having sold what he had and distributed it for the needs of the poor, he should follow Him [Matt. 19:21]. Or who has followed the Lord in so prompt a course as that man who said "I have not run in vain; nor have I

labored in vain" [Phil. 2:16]? He nonetheless both commanded and performed these works. Such a great authority as this should have sufficed for us who are learned and educated [as an example] both of giving up our former property and of working with our hands. But even we, aided by the Lord Himself, can perhaps in some way learn what good it does the servants of God still working in this fashion to have left behind their former tasks. For if someone is converted from a life of wealth to this life and is not prevented by any bodily weakness, are we so without understanding of the savor of Christ that we do not realize what a great swelling of that man's former pride is healed when, once the superfluous things that fatally inflated his mind before have been cut away, he does not at all refuse even the humble station of a workman in order to obtain the trifles that remain naturally necessary for this life? If, however, he is converted to this life from a life of poverty, he should not think that he is doing what he used to do if, no longer seeking things that are his own out of a love of increasing even what little private wealth he has, but seeking the things that are Jesus Christ's [cf. Phil. 2:21], he has turned himself to the love of the common life, with the intention of living in the society of those who have one soul and one heart in God, so that no one calls anything his own but all hold things in common [Acts 4:32]. For if the ancient rulers of this earthly commonwealth are often praised in the splendid eloquence of their own writers because they were so accustomed to placing the welfare of the entire populace of their state before their own concerns that after the conquest of Africa a certain triumphant general would have had nothing to give to his daughter, who was being married, if through the action of the senate she had not been voted a dowry from the public treasury, what spirit ought a citizen of that eternal city, the heavenly Jerusalem, to manifest toward his own commonwealth except that in which he shares with his brother whatever he makes with his own hands and if he needs anything he receives it from the common stock, saying with the one whose command and example he has followed: "having almost nothing, and yet possessing everything" [2 Cor. 6:10].

33. Therefore, if even those who, after giving up or distributing their wealth (whether ample or such as it was), have chosen in their pious and salutific humility to be numbered among the paupers for Christ, and are physically strong enough and free from ecclesiastical occupations—though the community itself and brotherly love owe them in exchange the maintenance of their lives since they brought with them such great proof of their purpose and contributed either very much or no small amount of the prop-

erty they possessed to the support of this same society—nonetheless work with their hands in order to take away any excuse from those lazy men coming from a more humble and, for this reason, more demanding life, they act far more mercifully than when they divided all their goods among the poor. But if they should be unwilling to do so, who would dare to force them? Still, tasks must be found in the monastery for these men to do, even if the tasks should require less physical exertion and demand careful supervision by a watchful administrator, so that not even they can eat their bread without charge, though it has now become common property. Nor should it matter in which monastery or where each one has shared what he possessed with the needy brethren. For there is a single commonwealth of all Christians. For this reason, whoever has supplied the necessities to Christians anywhere, wherever he likewise receives what he needs, he receives it from Christ. For wherever he too has given to such people, who but Christ has been the recipient? But if those men who even outside this holy society spent their lives in physical labor (from which number come the majority of those who enter monasteries, since they are the majority of mankind as well) do not want to work, they should not eat [2 Thess. 3:10]. For in the service of Christ the rich are not humbled to piety that the poor may be raised up to arrogance. Indeed, it is not at all fitting that in this way of life where senators become laborers, workmen should become men of leisure, and that where men of property relinquish their possessions on entering, peasants should be pampered.

36. Therefore, allow me, holy brother—for the Lord gives me great courage through you—to address briefly those very sons and brothers of ours. I know with what great love you labor with us over them until the apostolic discipline should be shaped in them. O servants of God, soldiers of Christ, do you so pretend not to see the plots of our most crafty enemy, who, wishing to obscure completely by his own foul odor your good reputation, the sweet fragrance of Christ, lest good souls may say "We shall run after the fragrance of your perfumes" [Cant. 1:3] and thus avoid his snares, has scattered everywhere so many hypocrites in the attire of monks, traveling about the provinces, sent nowhere, fixed nowhere, standing nowhere, sitting nowhere? Some traffic in the relics of martyrs (if indeed they are of martyrs); others make much of their tassels and phylacteries [cf. Matt. 23:5]; others falsely claim that they have heard that their parents or relatives are living in this or that country and that they are traveling to them. And they all seek, they all demand, either to be paid for their profitable poverty or to be rewarded for their counterfeit holiness. Meanwhile,

when they have been found out in their evil deeds somewhere, or have somehow become known, your enterprise, which is so good and so holy, and which in the name of Christ we wish to propagate throughout all Africa and in other lands as well, is blasphemed under the general name of "monks." Then are you not enflamed with zeal for God? Does your heart not grow warm within you, and is a fire not kindled as you meditate [cf. Ps. 38:4], that you should follow the evil works of these men with good works, in order to cut them off from the opportunity for the base trafficking by which your reputation is damaged and a stumbling block placed before the weak? Have pity, then, and feel compassion, and show people that your concern is, not to have a life of ease and idleness, but only to reach the kingdom of God, along the straight and narrow life of this enterprise [cf. Matt. 6:33, 7:14]. Your cause is the same as the Apostle's: to cut off the opportunity from those who seek an opportunity [2 Cor. 11:12]—so that those who are suffocated by the stench of those people may be refreshed by your sweet fragrance.

37. We do not tie up and place on your shoulders heavy burdens which we are unwilling to touch with a finger [cf. Matt. 23:4]. Seek out and recognize the hardships of our occupations and, in the case of some of us, the weaknesses of our bodies and the custom of the churches we serve, which is now such as not to allow us to be free for those works to which we exhort you. For although we are able to say "Who ever serves in the army at his own expense? Who plants a vineyard and does not eat of its fruit? Who grazes a flock and does not partake of the milk of the flock?" [1 Cor. 9:7], nevertheless I call to witness upon my soul the Lord Jesus, in Whose name I say these things without fear, that insofar as my own convenience is concerned, I should prefer to do some work with my hands at fixed times each day (as much as it has been established in well-ordered monasteries) and to have other hours free for reading and praying or doing some work pertaining to Holy Scripture than to endure the exceedingly confusing complications of other people's involvements in secular affairs which we must either break off by adjudication or cut short through intervention. The same Apostle has bound us to these troubles, not by his own decision, but by the decision of Him who spoke through him. Still, we do not read that he himself was bothered with such chores; for the nature of his apostolate did not permit it. He did not say "Therefore, if you have lawsuits over things of this world, bring them to us or appoint us to adjudicate them" but rather "The people who are not respected in the Church, those people do you appoint? To your shame, I say to you. Is it so, then, that

there is not a wise man among you who can judge a case between his brethren? But brother goes to court against brother, and this before the unbelievers" [1 Cor. 6:4, 6]. Therefore he wished the wise faithful and the holy men who were settled in their places to be the examiners in such matters, not those who were traveling for the sake of spreading the Gospel. For this reason it is not written anywhere of him that on any occasion he gave his time to such matters, from which we cannot excuse ourselves, even if we are without respect in the Church. For he wished even such people to be appointed if there should be a lack of wise men rather than for the business of Christians to be brought into the civil courts. Nevertheless, we undertake this labor not without the consolation of the Lord, in the hope of eternal life, in order that with patience we may bear fruit. For we are servants to His Church and especially to the weaker members, for whatever sort of member we are, we are still members of the same body. I make no mention of countless other ecclesiastical cares which, perhaps, no one would believe unless he has experienced them. Therefore we do not tie up and place on your shoulders heavy burdens we are unwilling to touch with a finger, for we should prefer to do what we urge you to do if we could without jeopardizing the interests of our office (He sees, Who examines our heart) rather than what we are forced to do. Truly for all, both for you and for ourselves, who toil according to our rank and office, the way is narrow in both hardship and tribulation, and yet for those rejoicing in hope, the yoke is easy and the burden light [cf. Matt. 11:30] of Him Who has called us to rest, Who first made the crossing from the vale of tears, where not even He Himself was without afflictions. If you are our brothers and our sons, if we are your fellow-servants, or rather your servants in Christ, hear what we admonish, acknowledge what we command, take what we dispense. But if we are Pharisees, tying up heavy burdens and placing them on your shoulders, do what we say, even if you disapprove of what we do.

FROM THE TREATISE *Holy Virginity*
(COMPOSED CA. 401)
"Let Him Who Can Achieve This Do So" (Matt. 19:12)

In his discourse on *Holy Virginity* Augustine first of all appeals to the status in the ancient Church of virgins consecrated to God, but then he goes further, calling upon all who deny themselves marriage and families "for the love of the kingdom of Heaven." This treatise shows the significance and beauty of Christian virginity, defends it against Jovinian's attacks, and offers ascetic counsels for its preservation. In this Augustine has a Christocentric ideal of virginity consecrated to God and of continence, and he supports it with ecclesiological and eschatological arguments.

Throughout, Augustine avoids all exaggeration. As much as he esteems virginity above marriage, and appeals in this to Holy Scripture, he still stresses and emphasizes the moral excellences of married life. And even if he sees the Church's holiness manifested more splendidly in the state of virginity, still with great earnestness he warns continent souls against every kind of pride. In the *Retractations* Augustine himself admits that the object of this little book was to show that holy virginity is "a great gift from God" and that it can, therefore, be preserved only by deep humility.[10]

1. . . . Moreover, the people to whom it has been said " 'Let him who is able to accept this, accept it' " [Matt. 19:12] should be encouraged not to be frightened, and should be frightened lest they become puffed up. For the state of virginity should not only be preached about so that it becomes loved, but also be admonished lest it become puffed up with pride.

2. This is the task we have undertaken in this treatise. May Christ help us, Who is the son of a virgin and the bridegroom of virgins, born in the flesh from a virgin womb, and wed in the spirit in a virginal marriage [cf. 2 Cor. 11:2]. Therefore, since the entire virgin Church itself has been betrothed to one husband, Christ, as the Apostle says, of what great honor are its members worthy who guard even in the flesh what the entire Church guards in faith, imitating the mother of her husband and Lord! For the Church too is both mother and virgin. Indeed, if she is not a virgin, for whose purity do we take thought? If she is not a mother, whose offspring do we address? Mary bore in the flesh the head of this body; the Church bears in the spirit the members of that head. In each case, virginity does not prevent fruitfulness; in each case, fruitfulness does not destroy virginity. Therefore, since the entire Church is holy both in body and in spirit, and yet the entire Church is a virgin not in body but in spirit, how much holier is the Church with respect to those members in which she is a virgin both in body and in spirit!

3. It is written in the Gospel that when the mother and brothers of Christ—that is, His relatives according to the flesh—had been announced to Him and were waiting outside, because they could not approach Him on account of the crowd, He answered " 'Who is My mother and who are My brothers?' Stretching His hand out over His disciples, He said: 'These are My brothers; and whoever does the will of My Father, he is My brother and

My mother and My sister' " [Matt. 12:48–50]. What else was He teaching us but to place our spiritual family before kinship of the flesh and that men are blessed not because they are joined to just and holy men by a blood relationship but because they cling to the doctrine and custom of those men in obedience and imitation. Mary, then, was more blessed in perceiving the faith of Christ than in conceiving the flesh of Christ. For when someone said " 'Blessed is the womb that bore you,' " He Himself answered " 'Blessed rather are those who hear the word of God and keep it' " [Luke 11:27, 28]. Finally, for those brothers—that is, His relatives according to the flesh—who did not believe in Him, what did the blood relationship profit them? So even the maternal relationship would have been of no benefit to Mary if she had not borne Christ more fruitfully in her heart than in her flesh.

4. Her very virginity, too, on that account is more pleasing and acceptable, not because Christ, once He was conceived, rescued it in order to preserve it from a husband who would violate it, but because before He was conceived, He chose a virginity already dedicated to God from which He would be born. This is indicated by the words Mary said to the angel announcing her offspring to her: " 'How will this come about, since I know not man?' " [Luke 1:34]. She clearly could not have said this if she had not previously promised herself as a virgin to God. But because the custom of the Israelites at this time prohibited this, she was betrothed to a just man who would not take away by violence what she had already vowed, but would guard it against the violent. And yet even if she had said only " 'How will this come about?' " and had not added " 'since I know not man,' " she would certainly not have asked how a woman would bear the son promised to her if she had married with the intention of having sexual relations. She could also have been ordered to remain a virgin, in whom the Son of God might by a fitting miracle take on the form of a servant; but as an example to holy virgins, so that she who had merited to conceive a child even without intercourse would not be thought the only one who must remain a virgin, she dedicated her virginity to God. And she did this when she did not yet know what she would conceive, so that in her earthly and mortal body there might be an imitation of heavenly life, in accordance with a vow, not a command, and from the love of choice, not the necessity of service. So Christ, being born from a virgin who, before she knew who would be born from her, had decided to remain a virgin, preferred to approve of holy virginity rather than command it. And so even in the very woman in whom He took on the form of a servant, He wished virginity to be freely chosen.

5. Therefore, there is no reason why the virgins of God should be sad-

dened that if they preserve their virginity they cannot also be mothers in the flesh. For only virginity could fittingly give birth to Him who could have no equal in His birth. Nevertheless, that offspring of the one holy virgin is the glory of all holy virgins, and they with Mary are the mothers of Christ if they do the will of His Father. For this reason Mary, too, is the mother of Christ in a manner more worthy of praise and more blessed, according to the words repeated above: " 'Whoever has done the will of My Father in heaven is My brother and My sister and My mother' " [Matt. 12:50].

8. Therefore, no fruitfulness of the flesh can be compared with holy virginity, even of the flesh. For even the latter is honored, not because it is virginity, but because it has been dedicated to God, and although it is preserved in the flesh, it nonetheless is preserved by the reverence and devotion of the spirit. And through this the virginity of the body, which the continence of piety vows and preserves, is also spiritual. For just as no one uses his body immodestly unless wickedness has been conceived in his soul beforehand, so no one preserves modesty in his body unless chastity has first been planted in his soul. And, furthermore, if conjugal modesty, although it is guarded in the flesh, is attributed not to the flesh but to the soul, under whose direction and guidance the flesh itself has intercourse with no one outside its own married state, how much more and in how much greater honor must that continence by which the purity of the flesh is vowed, consecrated, and preserved for the very Creator of the soul and the flesh be numbered among the goods of the soul!

11. . . . Therefore, that virgin deservedly takes precedence over a married woman, who neither puts herself forward to be loved by the multitude when she is seeking the love of one from among it, nor, having the one man, unites herself to him, thinking on "the things of this world, how she may please her husband" [1 Cor. 7:34], but who so loved Him "beautiful in appearance beyond the sons of men" [Ps. 44:3] that, because she could not conceive Him in the flesh as Mary did, she still guarded her flesh in a state of purity for Him who was conceived in her heart.

No bodily fruitfulness brought forth this type of virgin; this is not the offspring of flesh and blood. If you seek the mother of these virgins, she is the Church. No one brings forth consecrated virgins except a consecrated virgin, who has been betrothed to be presented chaste to one spouse, Christ [cf. 2 Cor. 11:2]. From her, a virgin not wholly in body but wholly in spirit, there are born virgins holy both in body and in spirit.

12. Let marriages have their own good, not because they bring forth

children, but because they do so honorably, lawfully, modestly, and for society, and because they bring up their offspring fairly, wholesomely, and earnestly, because they mutually keep the promises of the marriage bed, because they do not violate the sacrament of marriage.

But all these things are the duties of a human office; virginal purity and the abstention from all carnal intercourse through holy continence, on the other hand, are a sharing in the life of the angels and a striving for endless immortality here in this perishable flesh. Let all fruitfulness of the flesh and all the chastity of marriage yield to this. The first is not in our power; the second, not in eternity. Free choice does not control the fruitfulness of the flesh; heaven does not contain the chastity of marriage. Indeed, those who already have in the flesh something not of the flesh will have something great beyond others in that shared immortality.

18. Therefore, I admonish the followers, both men and women, of perpetual continence and holy virginity to prefer their own good to marriage in such a way that they do not judge marriage an evil, and that they know that the Apostle spoke, not deceitfully, but entirely truthfully when he said "He who gives his daughter to be married does well; and he who does not give his daughter to be married does better" [1 Cor. 7:28], and "If you take a wife, you do not sin, and if a virgin marries, she does not sin" (1 Cor. 7:28], and a little further on, "But, in my opinion, she will be happier if she stays as she is" [1 Cor. 7:40]. And let his verdict be thought that only of a man, he adds "I too have the spirit of God, I think" [1 Cor. 7:40]. It is the teaching of the Lord and of the Apostle, and it is a true and wise teaching, to choose the greater gifts in such a way that the lesser gifts are not condemned. The truth of God in the Scriptures of God is better than virginity in the mind or the flesh of any man. Let what is chaste be loved in such a way that what is true is not denied. . . . Therefore let those who have chosen to remain unmarried not flee marriage as the pitfall of sin, but let them pass over it as the hill of a lesser good, so that they may find rest upon the mountain of a greater good, continence.

27. Go forth, therefore, holy people of God, boys and girls, male and female, unmarried men and women, go forth in perseverance to the end. Praise the Lord more sweetly upon Whom you meditate more fruitfully; hope more happily in Him Whom you serve more eagerly; love Him more ardently Whom you please more attentively; await the Lord " 'with loins girt and lamps lit' " [Luke 12:35] when He comes from the wedding. You will bring to the wedding of the Lamb a new song, which you will sing to the accompaniment of your harps. To be sure, it will not be such a song as

the whole earth sings, to which it is said "Sing to the Lord a new song: sing to the Lord all the earth" [Ps. 95:1], but such a song as no one but you can sing. For thus did a certain man who was loved above others by the Lamb, and who was accustomed to lie on His breast, and who drank in and repeated the word of God about heavenly wonders, see you in the Apocalypse [cf. 14:1ff.]. He saw twelve times twelve thousand of you, holy harpists, of undefiled virginity in the body and inviolate truth in the heart, and he wrote of you because you follow the Lamb wherever He goes. Where do we think this Lamb is going, where no one but you either dares to or can follow? Where do we think He is going? Into what forests and meadows? Where, I believe, the grasses are joys, not the empty joys of the world, deceitful madnesses, nor such joys as there will be in the kingdom of God for others who are not virgins, but joys apart from everyone else's share of joys, the joys of the virgins of Christ, from Christ, in Christ, with Christ, after Christ, through Christ, on account of Christ. The joys proper to the virgins of Christ are not the same as the joys of those who, although of Christ, are not virgins; for some have some joys and others have others, but none have such joys as these. Go forth into these joys; follow the Lamb, because the flesh of the Lamb, too, is certainly virginal. For when He had grown, He kept in Himself that which His conception and birth did not take away from His mother.

29. . . . Therefore, hasten after Him, you, His virgins; hasten after Him even to that place where for the sake of this good alone you follow Him wherever He goes. For, indeed, we are able to exhort married people to follow Him to any other gift of holiness by which they can follow Him except this one, which they have irretrievably lost. You, therefore, follow Him, keeping with perseverance the vow you have fervently made. See to it while you can that you do not lose the gift of virginity, for you can do nothing to reclaim it. The remaining multitude of the faithful who cannot follow the Lamb to this point will see you, and they will not be envious; and by rejoicing with you, they will have in you what they do not have in themselves. For they will not be able to sing that new song which is properly yours; but they will be able to hear it and to take pleasure in your so outstanding gift. But you, who will both sing and hear because you will also hear from yourselves what you are singing, will rejoice more happily and will rule more joyously. Yet those who lack this will have no sorrow because of your greater joy. To be sure, the Lamb Whom you follow wherever He goes will not desert those who cannot follow where you can. We are speaking of the all-powerful Lamb. He will go before you, yet He

will not go away from them, since God will be "all things to all men" [1 Cor. 15:28]. And those who will have less will not shrink away from you. For where there is no envy, differences are shared. Therefore, be confident, trust, be strong, remain firm, you who vow and offer to the Lord your God [cf. Ps. 75:12] your vows of perpetual continence, not for the sake of the present world, but for the sake of the kingdom of Heaven.

30. And you who have not yet made this vow and who can accept it, do so [cf. Matt. 19:12]; run in perseverance "that you may gain the prize" [1 Cor. 9:24]. Each one of you "raise up your sacrifices and enter into the courtyard of the Lord" [Ps. 95:8], not out of necessity, but voluntarily. For it cannot be said "You shall not marry" in the same way as it can be said "You shall not commit adultery; you shall not kill" [Ex. 20:13, 14]. The latter are commanded; the former, offered. If the former offerings are made, they are praised; if the latter commands are not followed, they are condemned. In the latter the Lord enjoins a command upon you; but in the former, if you have paid out anything in excess, He will repay you. Think about a place, whatever it is, within His walls deemed much better than that of sons and daughters [cf. Is. 56:5]. Think about an eternal name there. Who will explain what sort of name it will be? Yet whatever it is, it will be eternal. By believing in and hoping for and loving it, you will be able, not to avoid marriages that have been prohibited, but to transcend those that have been allowed.

53. Therefore, do this, virgins of God, do this: follow the Lamb of God wherever He goes. But first come to Him Whom you follow and learn that He is "meek and humble of heart" [Matt. 11:29]. If you love Him, come in humility to Him Who is humble, and do not depart from Him lest you fall. For he who fears to depart from Him pleads and says "Let not the foot of arrogance come to me" [Ps. 35:12]. Go forth, with the foot of humility, on the path of sublimity. He Who thought it no shame to descend to the fallen exalts those who humbly follow Him. Entrust His gift to Him for safekeeping; guard your strength of heart for Him. Consider whatever evil you do not do while He is watching over you as having been forgiven by Him, lest thinking that little has been forgiven you, you love Him moderately and with a ruinous pride despise the publicans striking their breasts [Luke 18:13]. Beware of your tested strength lest you become puffed up with pride because you have been able to endure something; but pray about the untested strength lest you be tempted beyond your power. Consider that there are some people who are your betters, though this is not apparent,

and whose superiors you seem to be. When you credit the good points of others, which are by chance unknown to you, your own good points, which you do know, are not diminished in the comparison but strengthened in love. And those that you perhaps are still lacking will be given to you so much more readily insofar as they are longed for more humbly. Let those in your number who persevere provide an example to you; but let those who fall away increase your fear. Love the first, that you may imitate them; love the others, that you may not become proud. Do not establish your own righteousness, but submit it to God [Rom. 10:3]. Grant forgiveness for the sins of others, and pray for your own; avoid future sins by being vigilant, and blot out your past sins by confessing them.

54. Behold, you are already such that in your other habits you are suited to the virginity that you have professed and preserved. Behold, not only do you now abstain from homicide, diabolical sacrifices and abominations, theft, robbery, fraud, perjury, drunkenness and all luxury and avarice, jealousy, rivalry, impiety and cruelty [cf. Gal. 5:19ff., 1 Cor. 5ff.], but even those things that either are or are thought to be frivolous are not found and do not arise among you: not a shameless face, not wandering eyes, not an unbridled tongue, not impudent laughter, not scurrilous jests, not unsuitable attire, not an arrogant or a dissolute walk. You already do not "render evil for evil, or curse for curse" [1 Peter 3:9]; lastly, you already fulfill the measure of love: that you would lay down your life for your brothers [cf. John 3:16]. Behold, you are already so because even so you must be. These [qualities] added to your virginity manifest the angelic life to men and the ways of heaven to earth. But whoever among you is great, by as much as you are great, by so much humble yourselves in all things so that you may find favor before God [James 4:6] lest He resist the proud, humble those who exalt themselves, and not lead those puffed up with pride through the narrow places. And yet all this concern may be unnecessary, for where there is the warmth of love, there is no lack of humility.

55. If, therefore, you have scorned marriages with the sons of men from whom you might bear the sons of men, love with all your heart Him "beautiful in appearance beyond the sons of men" [Ps. 44:3]; you have the opportunity; your heart is free from the bonds of marriage. Look upon the beauty of your beloved; think of Him, the equal of His Father, yet subject to His mother, ruling even in heaven and serving on earth, creating all things and created among all things. See how beautiful is that very thing that the arrogant mock in Him; with the eyes of your heart contemplate

the wounds of the Crucified One, the scars of the Risen One, the blood of the Dying One, the ransom of the believer, the price paid by the Redeemer.

Think how much these things are worth; weigh them in the scales of Christ's love, and whatever love you had to be measured out in your marriages, weigh out to Him.

56. It is well that He seeks your beauty within, where He has given you the power to become children of God [John 1:12]. He seeks from you, not a beautiful body, but beautiful habits, by which you may bridle also the flesh. He is not one to whom anyone may lie about you and make Him rage with jealousy. Know that you may love Him in great security since He cannot be displeased because of false suspicions. A man and his wife love each other, since they see one another, and they are afraid of whatever they do not see in each other. Nor do they rejoice in the certainty of what is apparent, while often they secretly suspect what does not exist. In Him Whom you are unable to see with your eyes and know only through faith, there is no real defect with which to find fault; nor should you be afraid that you might offend Him with an imagined fault. If, then, you would have owed great love to your spouses, how much more ought you to love Him for Whose sake you have refused to have spouses! Let Him who was fixed upon the cross be fixed in your whole heart; and let Him hold everything in your heart—whatever you did not want to be taken up by marriage. It is not permitted to you to love too little Him for Whom you have not loved what is permitted.

FROM *The City of God*
(COMPOSED BETWEEN 413 AND 426)

Contemplative or Active Life

Leisure and activity, the contemplative and the active life—these are complementary notions Christianity did not originate. Pagan philosophy had concerned itself with the question of which was the better way of life. From the point of view of the Gospel, either way of life can lead to an everlasting goal. Augustine's personal disposition led him toward a contemplative existence, but since he had not been permitted to enjoy an undisturbed "holy leisure," he still had felt in himself that "driving love" which burdened him with the cares of a bishop's office. In this it was his recommendation that one should achieve a just admixture between the love of truth (*amor veritatis*) and the duties of charity (*officium caritatis*).

Book XIX

19. Indeed, although a man can lead a life of any of the three types—contemplative, active, or a combination of the two—and gain an eternal reward, provided he preserves his faith, nevertheless what he keeps out of a love of truth and what he spends out of the duty of charity does make a difference. A man ought neither to lead such a contemplative life that in his leisure he does not consider the welfare of his neighbors, nor to lead so active a life that he does not seek the contemplation of God. . . . Therefore the love of truth seeks holy leisure; the demands of love takes up the proper task. If no one imposes this burden on us, we have the time free to perceive and contemplate the truth; but if this burden is placed on us, we must take it up as charity demands. But not even under these circumstances must we completely abandon our pleasure in the truth, lest its sweetness be withdrawn and the demands of love overwhelm us.

NOTES

1. To give readers a quick indication of the questions discussed, each text will be given a subtitle.
2. Hofmann, *Kirchenbegriff*, pp. 23ff.
3. See below, chap. 66. Cf. Hofmann, *Kirchenbegriff*, pp. 54, 66ff.
4. This description of the cenobites' life is taken, in places word for word, from Jerome's *Letter 384*, addressed to the virgin Eustochium.
5. *Retractations* 1.25.
6. See also Hendrikx, "Augustinus als Monnik," 342.
7. Augustine uses the Old Latin translation of a Proverbs reading to the Septuagint. The legend of the swimming stags is found in Pliny's *Natural History* 8.32.114.
8. The CSEL text has "a holy house," "God's house," but "nearby" is supported by other editions.
9. Cf. Mausbach, *Die Ethik*, II 241ff.
10. *Retractations* 2.49 (23).

11

Letters

LETTER 5
(WRITTEN IN 388)
The Dearest Wish of the Newly Baptized Augustine

Nebridius was an African compatriot of Augustine's, on terms of intimate friendship with him. He had learned with regret in his parents' home at Carthage that Augustine in Tagaste was being burdened by his neighbors with many business anxieties. So he invited Augustine to come to his estate, that he might find there the peace he was longing for.

Nebridius to Augustine.

Is it really so, my Augustine? Do you show resolution and endurance in the affairs of your fellow-citizens, and is that inactivity you have longed for not yet granted to you? Tell me, who are the men who refuse you such a good? Those, I suppose, who do not know what you love, what you are longing for. Is there no friend of yours who could tell them of your wants? Would neither Rominianus nor Lucinianus do so? Surely they would listen to me. I will cry out; I will bear witness that you love God, that you long to serve Him and cleave to Him. I should like to invite you to my country place, to find rest there. For I am not afraid that people will say that I have seduced you away from your fellow-citizens, whom you love too much and by whom you are too much loved.

LETTER 48
(WRITTEN PERHAPS IN 398)
Monastic Contemplation or Apostolic Activity

In Augustine's first years as bishop, two monks, named Eustace and Andrew, came from Capraria,[1] an island in the Mediterranean inhabited by monks, and received a friendly welcome in the bishop's monastery at Hippo. Eustace died very soon, and Augustine considered himself obliged to write to Eudoxius, the monastery's superior. He made use of the opportunity to tell these unknown souls of his own experiences of the monastic life. He congratulated them on the peace in which in their convent they spent their lives; yet he was insistent in warning them, even if they were caring for one another, not to be oblivious to the needs of their mother, the Church.

Augustine and the brothers who are with him send greetings in the Lord to his beloved lord and most-longed-for brother and fellow-priest Eudoxius and the brothers who are with him.

1. When we think of the peace that you have in Christ, then even we find rest in your love, however much we may be caught up in various and bitter toil. For we are one body under one head, so that in us you are laboring and we in you find rest. For "if one member suffer, all members suffer together, and if one member is honored, all the members rejoice with it" [1 Cor. 12:26]. So we admonish and we ask and we beseech you, through the deepest humility of Christ and through His most merciful exaltation, to remember us in your holy praying, which we believe you do more vigilantly and soberly than we. For the cloud and uproar of secular concerns often wound and weaken our prayers. Even if we have no worldly concerns of our own, nevertheless the concerns of those who compel us [to walk] a mile and with whom we are ordered to go two more [cf. Matt. 5:41] weigh us down so much that we are scarcely able to breathe. Nevertheless, we are confident that, through the intercession of your prayers, He, in Whose presence the sighing of prisoners is heard [Ps. 78:11], will free us from all shortwindedness, as we continue in that ministry in which He, with His promise of reward, has deigned to place us.

2. We exhort you in the Lord, brothers, to keep watch over your resolution and persevere to the end, and if Mother Church has any need of your assistance, not to offer it with eager pride nor refuse it with fawning slothfulness, but with a meek heart to obey God, carrying in gentleness Him Who rules you, Who "guides the mild in judgment, Who will teach the meek His ways" [Ps. 24:9]. Nor should you place your leisure before the needs of the Church, for if there were no good men to assist her, you would not find a way to be born. For just as a man must make his way between fire and water in such a way that he neither is burned nor drowns, so we must steer a path between the peak of pride and the whirlpool of sloth, "turning," as it is written, "neither to the right nor to the left" [Deut. 17:11; Prov. 4:27]. For there are some who, while they are so afraid that they will be carried up on the right, fall and drown on the left; and others, who, though they draw back too much from the left, lest they be overwhelmed

by the numbing luxury of leisure, are corrupted and destroyed by the boasting on the other side, and fade away into smoke and ashes. Therefore, dearly beloved, love your leisure in such a way that you curb your delight in all earthly things and remember that there is no place where he whom we judge the enemy of all good men, and whose captives we have been, cannot lay traps for us, fearing that we shall fly back to God; and consider that there is no perfect rest for us "until iniquity pass away" [Ps. 56:2] and "justice be turned into judgment" [Ps. 93:15].

3. Similarly, when you do anything energetically and eagerly, and when you work readily, whether in praying, or in fasting, or in almsgiving, or in donating anything to the needy, or in forgiving injuries, "even as God has forgiven us in Christ" [Eph. 4:32]; or when you are overcoming harmful habits and "castigating the flesh and bringing it into subjection" [1 Cor. 9:27], or bearing tribulation and above all else bearing one another in love—for what can he endure who does not endure his brother?—or being on the watch for the cleverness and snares of the tempter and repelling and "extinguishing his burning arrows with the shield of faith" [Eph. 6:16], or "singing and chanting to the Lord in your hearts" [Eph. 5:19], or with voice in harmony with your hearts; when you do these things, "do everything for the glory of God" [1 Cor. 10:31], "Who works all in all" [1 Cor. 12:6], and be so "earnest in spirit" [Rom. 12:11] "that your soul is praised in the Lord" [Ps. 33:3]. For this is the activity [of those] on the straight path who "have their eyes always on the Lord, for He will pluck their feet from the snare" [Ps. 24:15]. Such activity is neither parched by business nor chilled by leisure; nor is it weak or rash or fleeting or precipitate or lazy. "Do these things, and the God of peace will be with you" [Phil. 4:9, 2 Cor. 13:11].

4. In your Christian love, do not consider me a burden because I wanted to speak with you even through a letter. For I have not warned you about these things because I do not think you are doing them; rather I believed that if, with the memory of our letter, you should do those things you perform with God's grace, I would then be commended by you to Him in no small degree. For even before, your reputation, and now the brothers Eustace and Andrew, who have come from you, have brought us the sweet fragrance of Christ from your holy way of life. Of these two Eustace has gone ahead to that resting place that is not beaten by waves, as islands are, and he does not long for Capraria, for he no longer seeks to be clothed in goat's hair.

LETTER 60
(WRITTEN IN 401)

A Bad Monk Can Never Become a Good Cleric

The monk Donatus, along with his brother, whose name is unknown, had abandoned the garden monastery in order to be accepted into the clergy in his native diocese of Carthage. In reply to inquiries from Bishop Aurelius of Carthage, Augustine wrote that both men had acted without his permission. But an African episcopal synod of September 13, 401, had provided—evidently at Augustine's insistence—that apostate monks might not receive clerical ordination. Augustine requests that this prohibition apply especially in the case of Donatus' brother, chiefly responsible for their flight from the monastery. He asks the synod to take action against these apostates because only in this way can loyal monks be spared difficulties and their spiritual good standing remain unassailed.

Augustine sends greetings in the Lord to his most blessed lord and duly revered and sincerely loved brother and fellow-priest Bishop Aurelius.

1. I received no letters from Your Holiness since we parted from one another. Now, indeed, I have just read a letter from Your Grace about Donatus and his brother, and for a long time I have been in doubt as to what I should reply. But, as I considered again and again what would benefit the welfare of those for whose upbringing in Christ we are responsible, nothing else could come to mind but that this course must not be offered to the servants of God lest they think they are more easily elected to some better position if they have become worse. And, indeed, we make defections easy for them and do a most undeserved injury to the rank of the clergy if we select for service in the clergy those who desert the monasteries. For we are not accustomed to admit to the clergy even those who remain in the monastery, unless they are more worthy and of better character, lest it come about that, just as the common crowd says, "a bad singer is a good choirboy," so this same common crowd will say of us jokingly "a bad monk is a good cleric." It is a pity if we raise monks up to such destructive arrogance, and if we think that the clergy, of whose number we are, deserve so great an insult, since sometimes even a good monk barely makes a good clergyman if he has sufficient self-control but lacks the necessary instruction or the personal integrity that comes from the *Rule.*

2. But concerning those men, I think, Your Holiness may have judged that they had left the monastery with our blessing, in order to be of service

instead to those in their district. But this is untrue. They went away of their own will; they deserted us of their own will, though we resisted as much as we could for their own welfare. And, indeed, with regard to Donatus, let your wisdom do what it will, if by chance he has been corrected from the stubbornness of his pride. For it had already come about that he was ordained before we could make any decision on this matter in the council. With regard to his brother, for whose sake in particular Donatus too left the monastery, since you know what I feel, I do not know what to answer. I do not presume to contradict your wisdom and your rank and your love, and I truly hope that you will do what you consider beneficial to the members of the Church. Amen.

LETTER 78

(PROBABLY WRITTEN IN JUNE 404)

Troubles in the Monastery

> Boniface, a priest in the bishop's monastery, had denounced the young monk Spes to Augustine for a grave moral lapse. But the accused man alleged that the priest was guilty of the same offense, and asserted his own innocence. The affair came to public knowledge, and created considerable disturbance among the people, threatening, indeed, to destroy the monastery's good name and the good standing of all the clergy. It would seem that at this time Augustine was absent on his travels. He therefore attempted through Felix and Hilary, two outstanding members of the community, and especially through this pastoral letter, to calm the general perturbation. After some initial hesitation, and with heavy misgivings, he agrees to the community's request that the priest's name be struck from the roll and no longer read aloud during their services. Insistently he warns the faithful that this regrettable case should not make them less zealous for good, and should not encourage them to believe ill of all clerics and monks.

Augustine sends greetings in the Lord to his most beloved brothers, to the clergy, the elders, and all the people of the church of Hippo, whom he serves in the love of Christ.

1. I wish that, following the Scriptures of God with careful thought, you would have no need of our instruction in any stumbling block and that you would be consoled rather by Him Who consoles us as well. For in the past He predicted and took care to have written down not only the good that He would repay to all His holy and faithful people, but also the evil in which this world would abound, so that we would in greater certainty

await the good that is to come after the end of this world than we would feel the evils, similarly foretold, coming before the end of this world. Thus the Apostle says: "Whatever was written was written for our instruction, so that through patience and the consolation of the Scriptures we would have hope in God" [Rom. 15:4]. Moreover, what need was there for the Lord Jesus Himself not only to say "Then shall the just shine like the sun in the kingdom of their Father" [Matt. 13:43], which will be after the end of this world, but also to exclaim "Woe to the world because of scandals" [Matt. 18:7], except so that we would not flatter ourselves that we can come to the seat of eternal happiness unless, tried by temporal evils, we are not found wanting? What need was there for Him to say "Because wickedness has abounded, love in most men grows cold" [Matt. 24:12] except so that those people of whom He spoke next, adding "He who perseveres right to the end will be saved" [Matt. 24:13], would not be disturbed or frightened when they saw love growing cold in this abundance of wickedness and, saddened as if by unhoped-for and unexpected conditions, they would not be found wanting; but rather, seeing that what is happening is what was predicted to take place before the end of the world, they would persevere in patience up to the end, so that without fear they would deserve to rule after the end in that life that has no end.

2. Accordingly, beloved friends, in this present problem involving Boniface the priest, which is disturbing to some, I do not tell you not to grieve—for they who do not grieve at such things do not have the love of Christ in them; moreover, those who rejoice even at such things have in abundance the malice of the devil—not because there has come to light in the aforementioned priest something that might be judged worthy of condemnation, but because two people from our household are in such a situation that one of them is considered ruined beyond doubt, and the reputation of the other is bad among some people and dubious among many others, even if his conscience is without a stain. Mourn for these circumstances, since they ought to be mourned, yet not in such a way that your Christian love, which begins from living well, grows cold. Rather let your love be kindled to pray to the Lord that, if your priest is innocent (as I prefer to believe, because when he had perceived the immodest and unchaste conduct of the other, he wished neither to consent to it nor to keep silent), the Lord in His own service will quickly reveal him as innocent, made manifest by His own divine judgment. But if, having a sense of his own guilt (which I do not venture to suspect), he wanted to injure the good name of another, since he could not corrupt his chastity (as the man with whom he has the

dispute claims), pray that the Lord does not allow him to hide his wickedness, so that what men are not able to discover may be revealed by a divine judgment regarding one or the other of them.

3. Indeed, since this case had tormented me for a long time, and I did not find a way to prove one of the two guilty, although I had believed more in the priest, I at first had considered leaving them to God until something should be revealed in the one whom I suspected which might provide a just and clear reason to cast him out of our dwelling place. But when he attempted most earnestly to advance in the clergy, either there with my help or elsewhere with the help of a letter from me, and when I was in no way persuaded to place the hands of ordination upon that man of whom I believed such evil, or through a personal recommendation to introduce him to any of my brothers, then he began to cause more trouble, so that, if he himself could not advance in the clergy, the priest Boniface would not be allowed to remain at his own rank. While he made his accusation, I saw that Boniface was unwilling to offer any opportunity for error about the doubtful nature of his own life to certain people who were weak and prone to suspicion. Moreover, I saw that he was prepared to suffer the loss of his own honor before men rather than to proceed in vain and to the disturbance of the Church in an argument in which he would not be able to reveal his own clear conscience to the ignorant and doubtful or to those more inclined to suspect the worst. Then I chose some middle course, that by a fixed agreement they both would swear to go to a holy place where the awesome works of God might far more easily reveal the guilty conscience of one of them and force his confession either by punishment or by fear. For God is everywhere, and He Who created all things is not contained or enclosed in any place; and "it is fitting for Him to be worshipped in spirit and truth by true worshippers" [John 4:23–24], so that, listening in secret, He may in secret also vindicate and crown. And yet, with regard to the things that are visibly known to man, who can fathom His plan, why miracles occur in some places and not in others? For the holiness of the place where the body of the blessed Felix of Nola is buried is well known to many. I wanted them to go there, because whatever was divinely revealed about one of them could then more easily and more faithfully be written down for us. For we too know of a certain thief at the monument of the saints in Milan, where evil spirits make confession in wondrous and awesome ways. Although the thief had come to that place intending to cheat by swearing a false oath, he was compelled to confess his theft and to return what he had stolen. And is Africa as well not full of the bodies of holy martyrs? And yet we do not

know of such occurrences anywhere in Africa. Indeed, according to the Apostle [cf. 1 Cor. 12:30], just as not all the saints have the gift of healing or the gift of the discernment of spirits, so He "Who distributes His gifts to different people as He wishes" [1 Cor. 12:11] did not want these miracles to be performed at all the monuments of the saints.

4. Therefore, although I did not want to bring to your attention this very grave sorrow of my heart, lest I upset you by cruelly and vainly causing you grief, perhaps God was not willing to conceal it so that you will diligently join us in prayer that He may deign to reveal to us too what He knows in this matter but we cannot know. Yet I did not dare either to suppress or to delete the priest's name from the number of his colleagues for this reason: that I should not seem to interfere with the divine power under whose consideration the case still lies, if I wished to anticipate His judgment by my prejudgment. Even judges in secular affairs, when they refer a doubtful case to a higher power, do not act in this way, daring to change anything while a case is still pending. And in the council of bishops[2] it was decided that no cleric who has not yet been proved guilty should be suspended from the community unless he has not presented himself for the examination of the case. Nevertheless Boniface took on such humility that he did not accept even a letter by which he could request the respect due to him on his pilgrimage, so that impartiality could be observed toward both men in that place where both are unknown. And now, if you think it best that his name not be read in the number of his colleagues so that, as the Apostle says, we do not give "opportunity to those seeking opportunity" [2 Cor. 11:12], that is, to those unwilling to come to the church, this will not be our doing but theirs, for whose sake it has been done. For what harm is done to a man if human ignorance does not want his name to be read from that list, as long as a guilty conscience does not blot his name from the book of the living [cf. Apoc. 3:5]?

5. Therefore, my brothers, those of you who fear God, remember the words of the Apostle Peter: "For your enemy, the devil, goes around like a roaring lion, seeking someone to devour" [1 Peter 5:8]. He tries to defile the reputation of the man whom he cannot seduce to wickedness and devour so that, if it is possible, this man may through the taunts of men and the slanders of wicked tongues be found wanting, and in this way fall into the open jaws of the enemy. But if he cannot stain the reputation of an innocent man, he tries to persuade him to make a judgment in malicious suspicion about his own brother and, once entangled in this way, to be swallowed up by him. And who would be able either to describe or to

enumerate all his deceptions and frauds? Yet against them there are three things that pertain to the present situation. First, do not be led astray to wickedness by imitating bad examples. So God addresses you through the Apostle: "Do not be pulling the yoke with the unbelievers; for what share has righteousness with wickedness, or what association has light with shadows" [2 Cor. 6:14]? Likewise, in another place He says: "Be not seduced. Evil communications corrupt good habits. Be sober, just, and do not sin" [1 Cor. 15:33–34]. Moreover, so that you may not falter before the words of your critics, He speaks through the prophet in these words: "Hear me, you who know my judgment, my people, in whose hearts my law is written. Do not fear the taunts of men; do not be overcome by their insults; and do not consider it important that they scorn you. For just like clothing, they will be worn away by time, and just like wool they will be devoured by the worm; yet my justice remains forever" [Is. 51:7–8]. Now indeed, so that you do not come to ruin by maliciously suspecting false things about the servants of God, remember that passage of the Apostle in which he says "Do not judge anything before its time, until the Lord comes and shines light upon the hidden places of the shadows; and He will reveal the thoughts of men's hearts, and then there will be praise for each one from God" [1 Cor. 4:5]. And, likewise, in another passage, it is written "the things that are revealed belong to you, but the things that are hidden belong to the Lord your God" [Deut. 29:29].

6. Indeed, it is clear that this sort of thing does not happen in the Church without great distress to the saints and the faithful. Nevertheless, let Him console us, who has predicted all things and warned us not to lose strength because of the abundance of wickedness but to persevere to the end in order to be saved. Indeed, for my part, if I have within me to some small degree the love of Christ, "who of you is sick, and I am not sick? Who is scandalized, and I am not on fire?" [2 Cor. 11:29]. Therefore do not increase my torments by faltering either because of unfounded suspicions or because of the sins of others; I beg you, do not do this, lest I say of you "they have added to the pains of my wounds" [Ps. 68:27]. For truly those people who rejoice at these wounds of ours are endured with great tolerance. Concerning them, it was said long ago in the person of the body of Christ: "they who sat at the city gate mocked me, and they who were drinking wine sang songs about me" [Ps. 68:13]. Yet we have learned to pray even for them and to wish good things for them. For what other purpose do they sit, and what else do they seek, but that, whenever a bishop or a cleric or a monk or a religious has fallen, they may believe, boast, and argue that all are of

this sort, although not all can be revealed to be so? And yet even these people, when some married woman is found in adultery, neither cast out their own wives nor accuse their own mothers; but when either some false charge has been rumored or some accusation has been revealed about anyone who professes a holy name, they are zealous, they are busy, and they rush around, trying to make this charge believed concerning all. So it is that we easily compare people seeking sweetness for their evil tongues from our sorrow to dogs, if by chance those dogs are to be understood as evil that licked the wounds of the poor man lying before the gate of the rich man and enduring all hardships and indignities until he came to rest in the bosom of Abraham [Luke 16:20–22].

7. Do not torment me further, you who have some hope in God. Do not increase those wounds that they lick, you on whose behalf we are in danger at every hour, having "quarrels without and fears within, in danger in town, in danger in the open country, in danger from the pagans, in danger from false brothers" [2 Cor. 7:5, 11:26]. I know that you grieve, but do you grieve more bitterly than I? I know that you are troubled, but I fear that "the weak men, for whose sake Christ died" [1 Cor. 8:11] may falter amidst the tongues of the slanderers and come to ruin. Do not let our sorrow increase on your account, because your sorrow was not caused by any fault of ours. For it is this that I have tried to guard against, so that, if possible, this evil would be neither neglected as something to be avoided nor brought to your notice, to torment the strong to no purpose and to confound the weak dangerously. But may He Who has allowed you to be tempted with the knowledge of this give you the power to endure, and may He instruct you according to His own law; may He teach you and "give you rest from the evil days, till a pit be dug for the wicked" [Ps. 93:12–13].

8. I hear that some of you are further troubled on this account, concerning the lapse of those two deacons who had come to us from the Donatists, and some of you have scoffed at the discipline of Proculianus,[3] as if to boast that no such thing had ever happened among the clerics under our discipline. Whoever of you has done this, I say to you, you have not done well. Behold, God has taught you that "he who boasts may boast in the Lord" [1 Cor. 1:31, 2 Cor. 10:17]. Nor should you reproach the heretics for anything, except that they are not Catholics, lest you be like them. For, not having any defense in the matter of their separation, they are eager to collect nothing but accusations against men, and they very dishonestly claim that these accusations are more numerous than they are, so that, since they cannot denounce and obscure the truth of Holy Scripture, by which the

Church of Christ has spread everywhere and is praised, they may make the preachers of the truth hated. And they can fabricate whatever comes to mind about these preachers. "But you have not so learned Christ, if indeed you heard Him and were taught in Him" [Eph. 4:20–21]. To be sure, He made his faithful free from fear of even the bad stewards who do their own evil deeds and speak of His good deeds, when He says: " 'Do as they say, not as they do; for they say a thing and do not do it' " [Matt. 23:3]. Indeed, pray for me, so that "while preaching to others, I may not be found to be false" [1 Cor. 9:27]. Yet when you boast, boast not of me but of the Lord. However watchful the discipline of my house may be, I am a man and I live among men, and I do not dare to claim that my house is better than Noah's ark, where among eight men, only one wicked man was found [Gen. 7:13, 9:22–27]; or better than the house of Abraham, where it was said: "Cast out this bondwoman and her son" [Gen. 21:10]; or better than the house of Isaac, of whose two sons it was said "I loved Jacob, but hated Esau" [Mal. 1:2–3]; or better than the house of that same Jacob, where the son defiled the bed of his father [Gen. 49:4]; or better than the house of David, where one son lay with his sister and another rebelled against his father's holy clemency [2 Kings 13:14, 15:12]; or better than the abode of the Apostle Paul, who, if he lived among men who were all good, would not say (as I quoted earlier) "quarrels without and fears within" [2 Cor. 7:5], or in speaking of the holiness and faith of Timothy, "I have no one else here who is truly concerned for you; they all seek their own interests, not those of Jesus Christ" [Phil. 2:20–21]; or better than the abode of the Lord Jesus Christ Himself, in which eleven good men tolerated the traitor and thief, Judas; or, finally, better than heaven, from which even angels have fallen.

9. I confess frankly to your Christian love in the presence of our God, Who is witness over my soul from the time I began to serve Him, that just as with difficulty I have found better men than those who have advanced in monasteries, so I have not found worse men than those who have failed in monasteries. Thus from this I may judge what has been written in the Apocalypse: "He who is just, let him be justified still, and he who is filthy, let him be filthy still" [Apoc. 22:11]. So even if we are saddened by some punishments, still we are also consoled by more honors. Therefore, do not, because of the dregs that are offensive to your eyes, hate the presses that fill the Lord's storehouses with the fruit of a clearer oil. Beloved brothers, may the mercy of the Lord our God guard you in His peace against all the treachery of the enemy.

LETTER 83
(WRITTEN CA. 405)

Love Before Justice

Honoratus, a monk of the Tagaste monastery, was called as a priest to the Church at Thiave. At the time of his entry into the monastery, he did not immediately put into effect the renunciation of his property, but, with Augustine's knowledge and permission, had postponed doing so to a future occasion. This in no way affected his priestly ordination. Consequently, it must have seemed to outsiders that he was still the full owner of his possessions. Now, at his death, the monastery asserted its rights through Augustine and Alypius, and claimed these possessions for themselves; but the Thiave Catholics resisted this strongly. Therefore Alypius, the former jurist, proposed a compromise: half the property should come to the Church at Thiave, and Augustine should decide concerning the other half.

This letter contains Augustine's views on this proposal. After he had consulted with Samsucius, the elderly and experienced bishop of Turres, he rejected it for weighty reasons: it would necessarily bring him and the monastery under suspicion of avarice; the monks would see reasons for putting off any final renunciation of their possessions; and it would create discord among the Thiave Catholics, most of whom had only recently returned from the Donatists to the Church. Therefore Augustine wishes to act on the principle "Love before justice," and he earnestly begs his friends to implement this decision and to cede the whole of Honoratus' goods to the Church at Thiave.

Augustine and the brothers who are with him send greetings in the Lord to the most blessed lord and most reverently cherished and longed-for brother and fellow-bishop Alypius and the brothers who are with him.

1. The sad state of affairs of the Church at Thiave does not allow my heart to find rest until I hear that the members have been restored to their former good feeling toward you, which must come about quickly. For if the Apostle takes so much trouble over one man when he says "lest he who is of this sort be swallowed up by greater sorrow" [2 Cor. 2:7], and also when he says "in order not to be captured by Satan, we are not ignorant of his devices" [2 Cor. 2:11], then how much more vigilantly ought we to act not to lament this situation throughout our flock, and especially among those who have just recently entered the peace of the Catholic Church and whom I cannot in any way abandon? But since the shortness of our time together did not permit us to formulate a carefully planned opinion on

this matter, may Your Holiness hear what seemed right to me as I considered the question at length since we parted. If it also seems right to you, then let the letter that I have written to them in our common name be sent without delay.

2. You have said that the monks should have half and that I should provide the other half for them from some source. But I think that if the whole were taken from them, we might be said to have concerned ourselves not so much with the money as with justice. Indeed, when we yield half to them and thereby come to an agreement with them at some time, it will seem sufficiently clear that our concern was nothing else but monetary, and you will see what harm would follow. For we shall seem to them to have brought half of someone else's property, and they will seem to us to have dishonorably and unfairly allowed themselves to be helped by the half that belonged completely to the poor. For your statement that "We must be careful that, in our desire to improve an uncertain situation, we do not cause greater wounds" will be just as valid if half should be yielded to them. For because of this same half, those people whose conversion we wish to accomplish will put off the sale of their goods through excuses and delays, so that their own cases may be treated according to this precedent. Is it any wonder, then, that there is such a scandal throughout the community over this disputed property, when they think that their bishops, whom they hold in great esteem, are tainted with base avarice as long as the appearance of evil is not avoided?

3. For when someone is converted to monastic life, if he is converted with a true heart, he does not think about keeping his worldly goods, especially since he has been warned how great an evil doing so is. But if he is deceitful and "seeks his own interests, not those of Jesus Christ" [Phil. 2:21], he has no Christian love at all, and then "what does it profit him if he distributes all his goods to the poor and hands over his own body to be burned" [1 Cor. 13:3]? Moreover, as we have already said, the problem can be avoided in the future, and can be solved with the one who is being converted if he cannot be admitted to the society of the brethren until he has divested himself of all these impediments and is directed to the monastic life from a life of leisure, since his property has already ceased to belong to him. But this death to the weak and this great stumbling block to the salvation of those we are toiling so diligently to win to the peace of the Catholic Church cannot be avoided on any other condition than that they understand most clearly that we are not at all concerned with money in such cases. And they will not understand this in any way unless we re-

linquish for their use the property which they have always considered the priest's; for if it was not his, they should have known that from the beginning.

4. Therefore, it seems to me that in matters of this sort this rule should be followed: whatever according to the laws governing possession belonged to a man who is ordained a cleric, no matter where he is ordained, should belong to the church where he was ordained. Moreover, that property of Honoratus' which is in question must be dealt with under the same law, to the extent that if he had died not only after being ordained elsewhere but also while still established in the monastery at Tagaste, and if he had died without selling or transferring his property to anyone by outright gift, no one but his heirs would inherit, just as Brother Aemilianus inherited the thirty gold pieces of Brother Privatus'. Thus we should take precautions against such eventualities. But if we have not taken precautions, we ought to follow in these matters the laws that have been established in civil society for possessing or not possessing such things, in order to refrain as far as possible not only from all evil deeds but also from all appearance of evil, and to guard the good reputation most essential to our office of stewardship. Let your Holy Wisdom observe how evil the appearance really is. Their sadness (which we have shared) aside, lest I somehow deceive myself, as can happen when I have not yet decided but am more inclined to my own opinion, I told our brother and colleague Samsucius about the matter, not mentioning at first what seemed best to me, but adding instead what seemed best to both of us when we are arguing with them. He was greatly taken aback and astonished that this course seemed best to us, and he was disturbed by nothing but the very appearance of baseness, which is most unfit not only for our life and character but for anyone's.

5. Accordingly, I beg you not to put off signing the letter I have written to them in both our names, and sending it. And if by chance in carefully reading this letter you perceive that this course is just, let the weak not be forced to learn now what I do not yet understand, that, in this case, the words of the Lord may be applied to them: " 'I have many things to say to you, but you are not able to bear them now' " [John 16:12]. Indeed, sparing such weakness, He also said, about paying the tribute, that " 'Behold the children are free; but that we may not scandalize them,' " etc. [Matt. 17:26–27], when He sent Peter to pay the didrachmas that were demanded then. For He knew another law under which He did not owe any such amount; but Peter paid the tribute for Him under that law by which we claim that the heir of the priest Honoratus would have inherited if Hon-

oratus had died before either giving his property away or selling it. Although according to the law of the Church the Apostle Paul spares the weak and does not exact the owed payment, certain in his own mind that he could rightfully collect it [1 Cor. 9:1–15], he avoided even the suspicion of anything disturbing the pleasing fragrance of Christ, and he held himself back from the appearance of evil in those districts in which he knew that such conduct was proper, perhaps even before he had experienced the sad condition of man. But let us, though we are slower and have experienced it, correct what we should have foreseen.

6. Finally, because I fear everything and I remember what you suggested when we parted, namely, that the brothers at Tagaste hold me responsible for half the amount, if you really think that this is fair, I do not refuse. I make only one condition: that I shall pay the money when I have it—that is, when such a sum comes to the monastery at Hippo that this can be done without difficulty—and that after an equal share in proportion to the number of residents in that monastery has been subtracted, it will come to the brothers in ours.

LETTER 111
(WRITTEN AT THE END OF 409)

Assaults upon Monasticism

> Moved by the afflictions which the migrations of peoples throughout the Roman cultural world had brought, in 409 a priest, otherwise unknown, "Victorianus," had put to Augustine the question why at least God's Church and His monasteries had not been spared His chastening rod. The letter is the answer to his questions: No one, however holy he may be, can be so completely free from sin that he deserves no chastisement. The chief reproach of dying paganism, that the Empire in ancient times never experienced what it must now endure in the Christian era, is briefly dismissed by Augustine, and answered with the words of Scripture (Luke 12:47–48): " 'The servant ignorant of his master's will and doing things that merit a beating will be beaten less; but the servant who knows his master's will and does things that merit a beating will be beaten more.' " In his *City of God*, Augustine had already encountered this approach and totally rejected it.

Augustine sends greetings in the Lord to his most beloved and longed-for brother and fellow-priest Victorianus.

1. The letter in which you asked me to answer certain questions at some

length filled my heart with great sorrow, since what is due such evils are protracted groans and weeping rather than lengthy books. Indeed, the whole world is afflicted with such great disasters that there is almost no part of the earth where such events as you described do not occur and are not lamented. For a short time ago even in the wilderness of Egypt, where monasteries exist almost free from fear, since they are cut off from all worldly troubles, the brothers were killed by barbarians. And I think that the abominable crimes committed these days in the districts of Italy and in Gaul are known even to you; and similar reports are beginning to be made as well about so many of the Spanish provinces, which for a long time seemed untouched by these evils. But why do we go far afield? Behold, in our own district of Hippo, since the barbarians have not yet reached it, the brigandage of the Donatist and Circumcellion clergy has laid waste the churches to such an extent that the deeds of the barbarians are perhaps milder by comparison. For what barbarian could have contrived as they did to put lime and vinegar in the eyes of our clergymen, after having injured other parts of their bodies as well with dreadful beatings and wounds? They even raid and set fire to some homes, pull down the dry crops, and pour away the liquid harvests, and by threatening such actions against others also force many people to be rebaptized. The day before I dictated these words to you, I heard a report that in one place some forty-eight souls were rebaptized through terrors of this sort.

2. We should lament these things, not wonder at them, and cry out to God to free us from such great evils, not according to our merits, but according to His own mercy. For what then could the human race have hoped for, since these events were predicted so long ago in both the prophets and the Gospel? Therefore, we ought not to be in such conflict with ourselves that we believe these things when we read them, and complain when they come to pass. But rather, even those people who were incredulous when they read or heard of these things written in the holy books now at least ought to believe, when they see that these things are already coming to pass, so that from such great pressings, as it were, in the oil press of the Lord our God, just as the dregs of the murmuring and blasphemous unbelievers flow forth, so too the oil of the faithful who confess and pray may continue to be pressed and made liquid. Indeed, it is easy to respond from the Gospel to those people who continue to put forth wicked charges against the Christian faith, claiming that before this doctrine was preached throughout the world the human race did not suffer so many evils. For the Lord said, " 'The servant ignorant of his master's will and doing things that

merit a beating will be beaten less; but the servant who knows his master's will and does things that merit a beating will be beaten more' " [Luke 12:48, 47]. What wonder is it, then, if in Christian times this world, like a servant already "knowing his master's will and doing things that merit a beating, is beaten more"? These men notice how energetically the Gospel is preached, but they do not notice how stubbornly it is scorned. But the humble and holy servants of God, who suffer temporal evils doubly since they suffer both because of these weaker people and along with them, have their own consolation and hope of the world to come, of which the Apostle says, "the sufferings of these times are not comparable to the glory to come, which will be revealed in us" [Rom. 8:18].

3. And so, my dear Victorianus, when those whose words you say you cannot endure say "If we sinners have deserved this, why have the servants of God also died by the swords of the barbarians, and why have the handmaidens of God been led away as captives," reply to them humbly and truthfully and piously: indeed, however much we preserve righteousness, however much obedience we show to the Lord, can we be better than those three men who were cast into a furnace of burning fire for keeping the law of God [Dan. 3:13–23]? And yet read what Azarias, one of the three, said

> opening his mouth in the midst of the flames: "Blessed are You, Lord God of our fathers, and Your name is praiseworthy and glorious forever, since You are just in all that You have done for us. And all Your works are true, Your ways straight, and all Your judgments true. You have made true judgments in all the things that You have brought down upon us and upon Jerusalem, the holy city of our fathers; for according to truth and judgment You have brought down all these things upon us for our sins. For we have sinned, and have not obeyed your laws or listened to your commands, that it might go well with us; and all that You have brought down upon us You have done in true judgment. And You have delivered us into the hands of our wicked and most hostile enemy, and You have delivered us to a king unjust and most wicked beyond all that are upon the earth. And now we cannot open our mouths; truly we are become a shame and a reproach to Your servants and to those who worship You. Do not abandon us forever, Lord, for Your name's sake, and do not abolish Your covenant. And do not take away Your mercy from us for the sake of Abraham, who was loved by You, and for the sake of Isaac, Your servant, and Israel, Your holy one. You declared to them that You would multiply their seed as the stars of heaven and the sands along the shore. For, Lord, we have become the least among all the nations and are brought low in all the earth this day because of our sins" [Dan. 3:25–37].

Surely you see, brother, what sort of men they were, how holy they were, and how bravely in the midst of tribulation, when the flame itself yet spared them and was afraid to burn them, they confessed their sins. They knew that they were deservedly and rightly being humbled for their sins, and they did not keep silent.

4. Can we be better than Daniel himself, about whom, through the prophet Ezechiel, the Lord spoke to the ruler of Tyre, saying " 'Are you wiser than Daniel' " [Ez. 28:3]? For Daniel was placed among three just men, and the Lord said that He would free only them, revealing that in them there were indeed three certain types of just men. The Lord said that He would free them in such a way that they would not be able to free their own sons, but they alone, Noah, Daniel, and Job, would be freed [Ez. 14:14]. Yet read Daniel's prayer too, and see how in captivity he confessed not only the sins of his people but also his own sins, and declared that because of these sins, through the justice of God, he had come to the punishment and disgrace of captivity. For it is written:

> And I turned my face to the Lord God, to pray and make supplications, with fasting and sackcloth. And I prayed to the Lord my God and I confessed, saying "Lord God, great and awesome, Who keep Your covenant and have mercy on those who love You and keep Your commandments, we have sinned, we have acted against the law, we have acted wickedly, and we have turned aside and departed from Your commandments and Your judgments. We have not listened to Your servants, the prophets, who spoke in Your name to our kings and to all the people of the earth. Righteousness is yours, Lord, and the shame upon our faces is ours, just as this day is shame upon the people of Judah and the inhabitants of Jerusalem and all Israel, those who are near and those who are far in every land to which You have scattered them on account of their arrogance, because they have not honored You, O Lord. The look of shame belongs to us, our kings, our princes, and our fathers, for we have sinned. To the Lord our God belong mercy and pardon, for we have departed from Him and have not listened to the voice of the Lord our God, that we might follow the commandments of His law, which He gave into the hands of His servants, the prophets before our eyes. The whole of Israel has sinned against Your law and turned away so as not to hear Your voice, and the curse and oath that are written in the law of Moses, the servant of God, have come upon us because we have sinned. And He has carried out the words that He spoke against us and against our judges who judged us that He would bring down upon us great evils, greater evils than ever took place in the whole world, according to the evils

> which befell Jerusalem. And just as it is written in the law of Moses, all these evils have come upon us, and yet we have not begged the Lord our God to turn our sins away from us and to make us understand all His truth. And the Lord God has kept watch over each of His holy ones, and He has brought down upon us the things that He has because He is just in all the world, which He created, and we have not listened to His voice. And now, O Lord our God, who by Your mighty hand has led Your people forth from the land of Egypt and made a name for Yourself which still endures today, we have sinned against Your law. Lord, by all Your acts of mercy, let Your anger and Your wrath be turned away from Your city, Jerusalem, and Your holy mountain. For, on account of our sins and the iniquity of our fathers, Jerusalem and Your people are scorned by all around us. And now hear, O God, hear the prayers of Your servant and hear his plea; show Your face again to Your sanctuary, which is deserted. For Your own sake, Lord my God, turn Your ear to us and hear; open Your eyes and look upon our ruin and upon the ruin of your city of Jerusalem, which is called by Your name. For we offer our prayer in Your sight, relying not upon our own righteousness but upon Your mercy, which is great. Hear, Lord; forgive, Lord; act, Lord, and, for Your own sake, my God, do not be slow, since this city of Yours and this, Your people, are called by Your name." And as I was still speaking and praying and enumerating my sins and the sins of my people . . . [Dan. 9:3–20]

—see how he spoke first of his own sins and then of the sins of his people. He both commends the justice of God and sings the praises of God because He scourges even His saints, not unjustly, for their sins. So, if they, in the most outstanding holiness, were surrounded by flames and by lions without being harmed, and say this, what ought we, who are so far unequal to them, to say in our humility, however much we may seem to preserve righteousness?

5. But so no one may think that those servants of God who according to you were killed by barbarians ought to have escaped this death in the same way as those three men were freed from the flames and Daniel was freed from the lions, let him know that those miracles were done on this account, that the kings who handed these men over to such torments might believe that they worshipped the true God. For this was done by the hidden judgment and mercy of God, so that in this way He might take thought for the salvation of those kings. Yet He did not wish to take thought in this way for King Antiochus, who killed the Maccabees by cruel tortures; but He punished the heart of this harsh king more severely through the most

glorious sufferings of the Maccabees. For read what one of them, who was the sixth to suffer, says; for thus it is written: "And after him, they brought the sixth. He, ready to die, said, 'Do not delude yourselves; we are suffering these things through our own fault, having sinned against our God, and we deserve what has happened. But do not think that you, who wanted to fight against God and against His laws with your own laws, will be unpunished' " [2 Macc. 7:18–19]. And you see how humbly and truly wise are those who confess that they are scourged for their sins by God. On this point it is written: "For the Lord chastises the one He loves, and He scourges every son whom He acknowledges" [Hebr. 12:6; Prov. 3:12]. The Apostle also says of this: "For if we would judge ourselves, we should not be judged by the Lord; but since we are judged by the Lord, we are corrected, lest we be condemned with this world" [1 Cor. 11:31–32].

6. Read these things faithfully, preach them faithfully, and be as careful as you can and teach others to be careful not to murmur against God in these temptations and tribulations. You say that good and faithful and holy servants of God have died at the swords of the barbarians. Yet what difference does it make whether fever or a sword freed them from the body? Except that a lengthy illness brings more punishment than a very swift death, God notices, not the circumstances under which His servants go forth to Him, but their condition. And yet we also read of such long and dreadful illnesses, such as Job suffered, to whose righteousness, indeed, God Himself, who cannot be deceived, bears witness.

7. The captivity of chaste and holy women is certainly a very serious matter, and one greatly to be lamented. But their God is not a captive; nor does He desert His captives if He knows them to be His. For even those saints whose sufferings and confessions I have related from Holy Scripture, when they were led away into captivity by their enemies, said these things so that they might be written down and read by us and that we might learn that the servants of God are not deserted by their Lord. Yet how do we know what miracles the all-powerful and all-merciful God wishes to be accomplished in this barbaric land, even through these women? May you only continue to lament to God on their behalf and to seek, as much as you can and as much as He will permit, since He has given you the time and the ability, [to learn] what has become of them and what consolations you can give them. For a few years ago a nun, the niece of Severus, the bishop [of Sitif], was taken captive by barbarians, and by the wondrous mercy of God was restored to her parents with great honor. For the barbarian household where she was held captive began to be troubled by the

sudden illness of its masters, to such an extent that all the barbarians—three or more brothers, if I am not mistaken—were suffering from a most dangerous disease. When their mother realized that the girl was dedicated to God and believed that the girl's prayers might free her sons from the imminent danger of death, she asked the girl to pray for her sons, promising that if they were saved, she would be returned to her parents. The girl fasted and prayed, and was heard immediately; indeed, as the outcome shows, it was for this purpose that the incident had taken place. So the brothers, astonished that they had recovered their health by so sudden a gift from God, respected and fulfilled the promise their mother had made.

8. Therefore, pray to the Lord for these women and ask Him to teach them too to speak as the holy man Azarias, whom I mentioned before, did, pouring forth his prayer and confession to God. For these women in the land of their captivity are just as those men were in that land where they could not sacrifice to the Lord according to their own customs. So, too, these women can neither bring an offering to the altar of God nor find there a priest to make an offering to God for them. Therefore may the Lord grant them to say what Azarias said at the end of his prayers:

> There is at this time no prince, no prophet, no leader, no holocaust, no oblation, no supplication, no place to sacrifice in Your sight and to find Your mercy. But let us be accepted with a contrite heart and in a spirit of humility. As in holocausts of rams and bulls, and as in a multitude of fat lambs, so let our sacrifice be made in Your sight today, to perfect those who follow You, since those who trust in You will not be confounded. And now we follow You with our whole heart, and we fear You, and we seek Your face. Do not cast us into confusion, but deal with us according to your kindness and according to the multitude of Your mercies, and free us according to Your wonderful works, and give glory to Your name, O Lord. And let all who show evil to your servants fear, and let them be cast into confusion by all Your might and let their strength be broken; let them know that You are the Lord, the only God, and that You are glorious over all the earth [Dan. 3:38–45].

9. He who is accustomed to hear His people will surely hear them speaking and lamenting to God in these words, and either He will permit no violence to be perpetrated against their chaste limbs by the enemy's lust or, if He allows it, as long as their minds are not tainted by any base consent, He will defend even their flesh against accusations. And whatever the lust of the victim has neither committed nor allowed to be worked upon the flesh will be the sin of the perpetrator alone, and all that violence will be

considered not the baseness of corruption but the wound of suffering. For the strength of the chastity of the spirit is so strong that, if it is inviolate, the chastity of the body, though the limbs may have been overcome, cannot be violated either. This letter, though too brief for your wishes, is yet too long for my duties, and is too quickly written because of the bearer's haste. May it be sufficient for your Christian love. The Lord will console you much more richly if you read His Scriptures very carefully.

LETTER 157
(WRITTEN IN 414 OR EARLY 415)
The Evangelical Counsel of Poverty

Even in the Christian community of Syracuse, the erroneous teachings of Pelagius had found their adherents. Hilary, a leading member of the community, perhaps its priest, submitted to Augustine the disputed theses of such people for a decision (*Letter 156*). Augustine gives a comprehensive answer, and, among other matters, deals with the question whether Matthew 19:21—" 'sell what you have, and give to the poor' "—is to be considered a counsel or a binding command.[4] He uses the opportunity to shed Biblical and Christian light on questions concerning poverty and riches.[5]

Augustine, bishop and servant of Christ and of His Church, sends greetings in the Lord to his most beloved son Hilary.

23. Now listen to a few words about the wealthy; this is the next point in your letter which must be investigated. For in this matter you claimed that those people say that a rich man who continues in his wealth cannot enter the kingdom of God unless he has sold all his possessions; nor can it be of any advantage to him if he chances to have fulfilled the Lord's commands from his own riches. Our fathers Abraham and Isaac and Jacob, who left this life so long ago, avoided the arguments of such people. To be sure, they all had great wealth, as Scripture most truthfully testifies; for He Himself, who "although He was rich, was made a pauper for our sake" [2 Cor. 9:9], predicted and truly promised that many men would come from the East and from the West and would take their places at the banquet in the kingdom of Heaven [Matt. 8:11], not above them or without them, but alongside them. And although the proud rich man who "used to dress in purple and in linen and to feast magnificently every day" is tormented in Hell after death, yet if he had taken pity on the poor man covered with sores who lay despised before his gate, he too would deserve mercy. And if

the pauper had merited not through his righteousness but through his poverty, he would certainly not have been carried by angels into the bosom of Abraham, who was a rich man on earth [Luke 16:19–24]. But the fires of torment received the godless wealthy man just as the wealthy Abraham received the pious pauper to his bosom, so that it might be revealed to us, not that the poverty of one man was divinely honored for its sake and the other man's wealth condemned, but rather that the former's piety and the latter's godlessness each had its own result. Clearly when Abraham lived here on earth as a rich man, he thought of his wealth in such a way and, in keeping with the precepts of God, placed so little value on it that he was willing to please God Who commanded him, even to sacrificing the very person who he hoped and wished would inherit his wealth [Gen. 22:1–10].

24. At this point, to be sure, they say that our ancient fathers did not sell all that they had and give to the poor because the Lord had not ordered them to do so. For the New Testament had not yet been revealed, and it would not be except in the fullness of time [Gal. 4:4, Eph. 1:10]. Nor was the virtue of these ancients yet revealed; but because of their virtue God in their hearts knew that they could easily forgo their possessions. For He gave them such a splendid testimony when, although He is God of all the holy and the just, He nevertheless saw fit to say of these particular friends of His " 'I am the God of Abraham and the God of Isaac and the God of Jacob; this is My name for all time' " [Ex. 3:15]. Later, to be sure, "the great mystery of our religion was made manifest in the flesh" [1 Tim. 3:16], and the coming of Christ, in Whom even these fathers had believed, illumined all the nations who were to be called; but these same fathers protected at the root, as it were, of that tree, of which the Apostle speaks [Rom. 11:17], the fruit of that faith which was to be manifested in its own time. For it was said to the rich man, " 'Sell what you have, and give to the poor, and you will have treasure in Heaven; and come, follow Me' " [Matt. 19:21].

25. When they say this, they appear to be speaking reasonably. But let them hear the whole thing, and let them pay attention; let them not open their ears in part and in part become deaf. For to whom did the Lord give this command? To that rich man, to be sure, who was trying to find a way to gain eternal life; for he had asked the Lord, " 'What should I do to gain eternal life?' " In answer, the Lord did not say to him, " 'If you wish to enter into life, go, sell what you have,' " but rather " 'If you wish to enter into life, keep the commandments' " [Matt. 19:16–17]. When the young man responded that he had kept God's commandments as they had been

handed down to him in the law, and asked what he was still lacking, he received this reply: " 'If you wish to be perfect, go, sell what you have, and give to the poor.' " And lest the young man think that he would thereby lose what he greatly prized, He added, " 'and you will have treasure in Heaven.' " Then He continued: " 'and come, follow Me,' " lest anyone think that, when he had done these things, it would be to his advantage even if he did not follow Christ. But, indeed, when he saw how he had kept the commandments of the law, the young man "went away sad"; for I think that he had responded more in arrogance than in truth that he had kept the commandments. Yet the Good Master made a distinction between [keeping the] commandments and that more outstanding state of perfection when He said " 'If you wish to enter into life, keep the commandments' " and then added " 'If you wish to be perfect, go, sell all that you have' " etc. Why, therefore, do we deny that rich men, although they are not in that state of perfection, nevertheless come to eternal life if they have kept the commandments, and have given that it may be given to them, and have pardoned that they may be pardoned [Luke 6:38, 37]?

26. For we believe that the Apostle Paul was the servant of the New Testament when he said, in writing to Timothy, "Warn the rich of this world not to be wise in arrogance and to put their hope, not in the uncertainty of riches, but in the living God, Who offers us all things in abundance for our enjoyment. Tell them to do good, to be rich in good works, to give willingly, to share, to store up a good foundation for their future, so that they may attain true life" [1 Tim. 6:17–19]. The Lord also said to the young man, " 'if you wish to enter into life. . . .' " I think, when he gave this advice, the Apostle was counseling the rich. He did not say "command the rich of this world to sell what they have, give to the poor, and follow the Lord," but rather "warn them not to be wise in arrogance and not to put their hope in the uncertainty of riches." It was that pride, and that hope in the uncertainty of riches, by which he counted himself fortunate in his purple and linen and splendid feasting, not the riches themselves, which led the rich man, who scorned the righteous pauper lying outside his gate, to the torments of Hell.

27. Or do these people think perhaps that because the Lord went on to say " 'Amen, I say to you, with difficulty will a rich man enter the kingdom of Heaven; and again I say to you, a camel will more easily pass through the eye of a needle than a rich man enter the kingdom of Heaven' " [Matt. 19:33–34] a rich man cannot enter the kingdom of Heaven even if he does the things the Apostle counsels the rich to do? What, then, is this? Is the

Apostle contradicting the Lord, or do these people fail to understand what he is saying? Let the Christian decide which of these things he should believe. I believe it is better for us to believe that they do not understand his words than to believe that Paul is contradicting the Lord. Why, then, do they not listen to the Lord Himself when immediately afterward He says to His disciples who are saddened by the misfortune of the rich: " 'What is impossible for men is easy for God' " [Matt. 19:25–26]?

28. But, they claim, this was said for this reason only: that, after hearing the Gospel, rich men who had sold their patrimony and given to the poor would follow the Lord and enter the kingdom of Heaven. And this would come about (which seems difficult) in such a way, not that, retaining their wealth, they would gain true life by obeying the command of the Apostle—that is, by not being wise in arrogance and putting their hope, not in the uncertainty of riches, but in the living God, doing good, giving willingly, sharing with the needy—but by selling all their goods they would fulfill even that command of the Apostle.

29. If they make these claims—and, indeed, I know that they do—they do not notice in the first place how the Lord has preached His own grace against their doctrine. For He does not say "What seems impossible for men is easy for them if they will it," but " 'What is impossible for men is easy for God' "; and He points out that when these things actually come about, they come about, not through the power of men, but through the grace of God. So let these people take notice of this and, if they censure those who boast of their own wealth, let them in turn beware of trusting in their own virtue. For both are censured alike in the psalm: "they who trust in their virtue and who boast of the abundance of their wealth" [Ps. 48:7]. Therefore let rich men hear, " 'What is impossible for men is easy for God,' " and either retaining their wealth and using it for good work, or having sold their possessions and distributed the proceeds among the needy poor, let them enter the kingdom of Heaven, and let them attribute their good fortune, not to their own power, but to the grace of God. For what is impossible for men is easy, not for men, but for God. Let them also hear this, and if they have either sold their belongings and given to the poor or are still doing so and arranging things and preparing in this way to enter the kingdom of Heaven, let them attribute this, not to their own power, but to that same divine grace. For what is impossible to men is easy, not for men—for they too are men—but for God. For the Apostle also has this to say to them: "With fear and trembling, work out your salvation; for it is God Who works in you, both to will and to accomplish, according to His

good will" [Phil. 2:12–13]. Certainly they say that they have taken from the Lord their plan to achieve perfection by selling their possessions, so that they may follow Him, since it is added, " 'and come, follow Me.' " Why, then, in these good works that they are performing, do they presume so much concerning their own will and not hear the Lord, Whom they claim to be following, reproaching them and calling out to them, " 'Without Me you can do nothing' " [John 15:5]?

30. But if the Apostle has said "Warn the rich of this world not to be wise in arrogance and not to put their hope in the uncertainty of riches," so that they will sell all that they have and, distributing the income to the poor, they will do what follows: "give willingly, share, and store up a good foundation for their future" [1 Tim. 6:17–19], and if he believes that they cannot otherwise enter the kingdom of Heaven, then he deceives those whose homes he so diligently sets aright with the benefit of his teaching. For he admonishes and instructs them on how they are to behave—wives to husbands, husbands to wives, children to parents, parents to children, servants to masters, masters to servants. Yet how can these instructions be carried out, unless one has a home and some financial assets?

31. Or are they moved by these words of the Lord's: " 'Whoever has put aside his possessions for My sake will be repaid one hundredfold in this world and in the world to come will possess eternal life' " [Matt. 19:29]? To "put aside" is one thing; to "sell" is another. For among the things He has said are to be put aside, wives as well are mentioned; but no law of man permits the sale of wives. Moreover, the laws of Christ do not permit wives to be put aside, except in cases of adultery [Matt. 5:32]. What, then, do these commands mean—for they cannot contradict each other—except that sometimes a choice must be made, and either a wife or Christ must be put aside. To omit other examples: what if a Christian husband has not pleased his wife and it is suggested to him that he divorce either her or Christ? In this case, what should this man choose except Christ? And for the sake of Christ is he to put aside his wife and be praised for doing so? Indeed, when both are Christians, the Lord has commanded that no one may put aside his wife, except in cases of adultery. But when either of them is an unbeliever, the advice of the Apostle is followed: that if an unbeliever agrees to live with a Christian husband, the husband may not put aside his wife; likewise, a Christian wife may not put aside her husband if he has agreed to live with her [1 Cor. 7:12–13]. But, he says, "if the unbeliever departs, let him depart; for a brother or sister is not under servitude in such cases" [1 Cor. 7:15]. That is, if an unbeliever does not wish to be with a Christian

spouse, in this case let the Christian recognize that he is free; let him not consider himself so bound to servitude that he puts aside his faith itself in order not to lose an unbelieving spouse.

32. This is understood also with respect to children and parents, with brothers and sisters. All are to be put aside for the sake of Christ if it is suggested that a person wishing to have these people with him should put Christ aside. These instructions are likewise to be followed with respect to house and field and those possessions that come under the pecuniary laws. At the same time He does not say of these people "Whoever has sold for My sake the things that is permitted everywhere to sell . . ." but " 'Whoever has put aside. . . .' " For it may happen that someone in power says to a Christian "Either you will not remain a Christian or, if you wish to remain in your faith, you will not have a house and possessions." Then truly let even those rich men who had decided to keep their wealth in such a way as to merit God by the good works done with it put it aside for Christ's sake rather than put Christ aside so that in this world they may receive one hundredfold—all things are signified by the perfection of this number; for the whole world of riches belongs to the faithful, and in this way they become as people "having nothing, yet possessing everything" [2 Cor. 6:10]—and let them possess eternal life in the world to come, lest, on account of these things, having cast Christ aside, they be cast headlong into eternal death.

33. This law and condition embrace not only those who in the excellence of their mind undertake this plan for achieving perfection by distributing the income from the sale of their goods to the poor and bearing the light burden of Christ on shoulders made free of every worldly burden, but also whoever, though weaker and less suited to that most glorious perfection, yet remembers that he is truly a Christian and, when it is suggested to him that unless he has put aside all worldly possessions and ties, he must put aside Christ, chooses rather the "tower of strength in the face of the enemy" [Ps. 60:4]; for, when he was building that tower in his faith, he reckoned the cost to complete it [Luke 14:28]—that is, he approached his faith with the intention of renouncing the world not only in words, so that even if he bought something it was as if he did not possess it, and if he used this world, it was as if he did not use it [1 Cor. 7:30–31], placing his hope, not in the uncertainty of riches, but in the living God.

34. Therefore since everyone who renounces this world without a doubt renounces all that he has in order to be a disciple of Christ—for Christ

Himself, following the metaphors about the money needed to build a tower and about the king preparing to go to war against another king, went on to say, " 'Whoever does not renounce all that he has cannot be My disciple' "—he, to be sure, also renounces his fortune, if he has any, in one of two ways: either he does not love his wealth at all, and by giving it to the poor he is stripped of his unnecessary burdens; or because he loves Christ more than his wealth, he transfers his hope from riches to Him, and thus uses it so that he, giving willingly and sharing, stores up treasure for himself in Heaven and is prepared to give up even his wealth, just as he would give up his parents and sons and brothers and wife, if it should be suggested to him that he could not have them unless he put aside Christ. For if he should renounce the world in any other way, when he comes to the sacrament of faith, he does precisely what the Blessed Cyprian laments about lapsed Catholics, saying that they "renounce this world in word alone, not in fact" [*Ep.* XI.1]. Indeed, it is said of this sort of man who in times of temptation is more afraid of losing his worldly goods than of denying Christ, " 'Behold the man who began to build and was not able to finish' " [Luke 14:30]. He is also the man who sends his envoys to sue for peace when his enemy is still far off—that is, when temptation is not yet afflicting him but is now threatening and impending, he agrees to abandon and deny Christ in order to retain the things that he loves more. And there are many men of this sort who even think that the Christian faith ought to help them increase their wealth and multiply their earthly pleasures.

35. But the rich Christians who, although they possess earthly goods, are nevertheless not so possessed by them that they place them before Christ are not like this. For they have renounced this world with a truthful heart, and they place no hope in its possessions. By sound teaching these men educate their wives and children and entire households to keep the Christian faith; in their houses, warm with hospitality, they receive the righteous man in the name of righteousness, so that they may receive the reward of the righteous [Matt. 10:41]. They break their own bread for the hungry, they clothe the naked, they ransom the captive [Is. 58:7, Matt. 25:35–36], they "store up a good foundation for the future, so that they may attain true life" [1 Tim. 6:19]. And if by chance they must suffer monetary losses for the sake of the Christian faith, they despise their wealth. If this world threatens bereavements or separations for Christ's sake, they despise their parents, brothers, children, wives. Finally, if they must make an agreement with the enemy regarding their life in the body, then they despise even life

itself, lest Christ, once deserted, desert them. Indeed, concerning all these things they have heard the command that they cannot in any other way be disciples of Christ.

36. And yet they ought not to consider that their lives should be sold or poured forth by their own hand because they have been commanded to despise even their lives for Christ's sake. But they are prepared to lose their lives, dying for Christ's name, lest they live in death by denying Christ. In the same way they should be prepared to lose for Christ's sake their riches too, which they were not willing to sell when He commanded it, lest having lost Christ, they perish with their wealth. For this reason we have rich and famous people, both men and women, who have been exalted in the glory of martyrdom. In this way many who had hesitated to be made perfect by selling their possessions have suddenly been made perfect by imitating the suffering of Christ; and many who had spared their riches because of some weakness of their flesh and blood have suddenly fought for their faith against sin, even to the point of bloodshed. There are, moreover, those who have not attained the crown of martyrdom and have not taken that excellent and sublime counsel about selling their possessions to reach perfection and yet, free from more condemnable offenses, have fed Christ when He was hungry, given Him drink when He was thirsty, clothed Him when He was naked, and taken Him in when He was a stranger [Matt. 25:34–40]. These people will not sit on high and give judgment with Christ, but will stand at His right to be judged in mercy; since " 'Blessed are the merciful, for they shall obtain mercy' " [Matt. 5:7]. "And there will be judgment without mercy for him who has not shown mercy, but mercy will exult in its judgment" [James 2:13].

37. Therefore let these people stop speaking against the Scriptures, and in their exhortations let them stir up others to greater things in such a way that they do not condemn the lesser. For in their exhortations they are not able to suggest even holy virginity except by condemning the bonds of marriage, although the Apostle in his teachings says, "Every man has his own gift from God, this one after this manner, and another after that" [1 Cor. 7:7]. And therefore let them walk the way of perfection when they have sold all their goods and given to the poor in mercy. But if they are truly paupers of Christ, and if they gather not for themselves but for Christ, why would they punish His weaker members before they have taken the seats of judgment? For if it is they to whom the Lord says " 'You will sit upon the twelve thrones to judge the twelve tribes of Israel' " [Matt. 19:28] and of whom the Apostle says "Do you not know that we will judge the

angels?" [1 Cor. 6:3], then let them prepare themselves to receive "into everlasting dwellings," not the godless, but the God-fearing, rich, with whom they "have made friends of the mammon of iniquity" [Luke 16:9]. For I think that certain of these people who impudently and imprudently chatter about these things are sustained in their needs by rich and devout Christians. For in a certain sense the Church has its own soldiers and its own provincials; in this connection the Apostle asks: "Whoever serves in the army at his own expense?" [1 Cor. 9:7]. It has its own vineyard and its own vinegrowers; it has its own flock and its own shepherds, as the Apostle goes on to say: "Who plants a vineyard and does not eat of its fruit? Who grazes a flock and does not partake of milk of the flock?" [1 Cor. 9:7]. But to argue as these people do would be not to serve but to rebel. It would not be to plant a vineyard but to destroy it; it would not be to gather the sheep for grazing, but to separate them from the flock to be lost.

38. Moreover, just as those who are fed and clothed by the merciful services of the rich—for they do not accept anything for their own needs except from those who sell their possessions—are nevertheless not judged and condemned by the more outstanding members of Christ who live more virtuously by the work of their own hands, as the Apostle often commends [1 Thess. 4:11, Acts 20:34], so they ought not to condemn the Christians of lesser merit, by whose resources they are supported. But, by living aright and teaching aright, they might well say to them, "If we have sown a spiritual harvest for you, is it a great matter if we reap your material things?" [1 Cor. 9:11]. For the servants of God who live by selling the respectable products of their own manual labor with much less impudence condemn those who give them nothing than those people who are unable to do manual labor because of some bodily weakness condemn the very ones by whose energies they are supported.

39. I, who write these words, have greatly loved that state of perfection of which the Lord spoke in telling the rich young man, " 'Go, sell what you have, and give to the poor, and you will have treasure in Heaven; and come, follow Me' " [Matt. 19:21], and I have done this not by my own strength but with the help of His grace. And indeed this will not be considered any less an accomplishment on my part because I was not a rich man, for neither were the Apostles, who were the first to do this, rich men. But he who puts aside both what he has and what he has wished for puts aside the whole world. I know more than any other man how far I have progressed on this path to perfection; yet God knows more than I. And to the best of my ability I exhort others to this undertaking, and I have allies

in the Lord's name whom I have so persuaded through my ministry that they keep to a particularly healthful doctrine. Nor do we rashly judge those who do not keep to this doctrine, claiming that they will not profit by living chastely in the married state, by managing their homes and families in a Christian manner, by storing up treasure for their future through works of mercy, lest by arguing in such a way we might be found to be, not interpreters, but critics, of the Holy Scriptures. I have mentioned this because these people, when prevented from saying such things by those who have not taken the Lord's advice, reply that their opponents are unwilling to argue about matters that are favorable to their own vices and that detract from the fulfillment of the Lord's commands. It is as if (I make no mention of those who, though comparatively weak, yet use their wealth to serve religion) even those greedy and avaricious people who abuse their wealth and fix their hearts of clay upon earthly treasure, whom the Church must carry along right up to the end, just as the fisherman's net drags the bad fish in to the shore [Matt. 13:47–48]—even those people, I say, are not to be tolerated in the Church any more than those who, preaching and spreading such beliefs, so wish to appear great, because, following the precept of the Lord, they have sold their wealth or whatever patrimony they have, that they undertake to upset and overturn by their unsound doctrine our inheritance from Him, which is spread and diffused to the ends of the earth.

41. You have read what seems best to me. Let better men explain these things better, not men whose opinions I already know deserve criticism, but others who can explain truthfully. For I am more ready to learn than to teach, and you will do me a great service if you do not keep me in ignorance of what the holy brothers in your monastery are saying about the foolish chatter of those people. May you live rightly and happily in the Lord, most beloved son.

LETTER 210
(DATE OF COMPOSITION UNKNOWN)

Monastic Correction

This short letter was sent to a community of women. Their superior was called Felicity. She had as her support a certain Rusticus, evidently a priest and the nuns' spiritual director. It seems that the atmosphere of the community was unhappy. So the letter begins with reminders of God's love for His creatures. He is good, and He confers benefits, even though

He may conceal them as afflictions. But the true occasion of the letter is to inquire of the sisters how improvements in the convent might be achieved. Augustine gives directions and, in particular, rejects the implied reproach that anyone making necessary correction seems to be reproving affection which he regards as unworthy.

Augustine and those who are with him send greetings in the Lord to our beloved and holy Mother Felicity and to Brother Rusticus and to the sisters who are with them.

1. "The Lord is good" [Lam. 3:25], and His mercy that consoles us with the love in His heart for you is everywhere. For He shows especially how much He loves those who believe and hope in Him and who love Him and one another, and what He saves for them for the future, when He threatens with eternal fire and the devil [Matt. 25:41] the unfaithful and those without hope and those who have turned away and persevere to the end in their wickedness. Yet He generously bestows so many blessings upon this world; for He "makes His sun rise upon the good and the bad, and the rain to fall on the just and the unjust" [Matt. 5:45]. This is expressed in only a few words, so that we may think about it all the more. For who can count all the unearned gifts the wicked have in life from Him Whom they scorn? Among these gifts is an especially great one: for He has warned them, if they are willing to pay attention, by the examples of the tribulations which He, like a good physician, blends in with the sweetness of this world, to flee from the wrath that is to come [Matt. 3:7, Luke 3:7], and, while they are on the path—that is, while they are in this life—to be in harmony with the word of God, Whom they have made their enemy by living in wickedness. What, then, is not offered to men by the mercy of the Lord God, from Whom even tribulation is a favor? For prosperous circumstances are the gift of a God Who consoles; adverse circumstances are the gift of a God Who warns. And if, as I said, He offers these things even to the wicked, what does He prepare for those who uphold Him? Rejoice that by His grace you are gathered in that number, "bearing with one another in love, eager to preserve the unity of the Spirit in the bond of peace" [Eph. 4:2–3]. For there will be no lack of burdens that you may bear for one another until "death has been swallowed up in victory" [1 Cor. 15:54], and the Lord bears you in such a way that "God may be all in all" [1 Cor. 15:28].

2. Moreover, we ought never to take pleasure in discord. But sometimes either it arises out of Christian love, or it tests that love. For who can easily be found who would wish to be criticized? And where is that wise man of

whom it was said "Rebuke a wise man and he will love you" [Prov. 9:8]? And yet should we not criticize and rebuke our brother so that he does not heedlessly go forth to his death? For it is not unusual, indeed it frequently happens, that when someone is criticized, he is saddened for the moment, and he resists and argues. Then later, in quiet, when God and he are alone together, he thinks it over. Now he is no longer afraid of man's displeasure and reprimands; his fear is that he may displease God because he does not do better. From then on, he will not do what he was justly criticized for; and indeed he loves his brother, who, he has now realized, is the enemy only of his sin, as much as he detests his sin. But if he is one of those of whom it has been said "Rebuke the foolish man, and in return he will hate you" [Prov. 9:8], the discord is not born from his love. Nevertheless it tries and tests the love of his critic since the foolish man is repaid not with hatred but with love, which compels the correction and remains undisturbed, even when he who has been criticized repays with hatred. But if he who criticizes wishes to return evil for evil to the man who becomes angry with his critic, then he was not fit to criticize, but clearly was one to be criticized. Act in such a way either that provocations to anger do not exist among you or if they have flared up they may be extinguished by a quickly made peace. Put more of your effort into promoting harmony than in correcting one another; for just as vinegar rots the barrel if it is kept there too long, so anger rots the heart if it lasts overnight. "So do these things, and the God of peace will be with you" [Phil. 4:9]. And at the same time pray for us that we may cheerfully follow the good advice that we give you.

LETTER 211

(DATE OF COMPOSITION UNKNOWN[6])

Endangering Monastic Harmony and Love

The recipients of this letter were a community of women, with many members, which, the writer indicates, had been founded many years ago and was situated close to his own house. The superior (the "mother," the "provost") had been in office for a long time, and had had among her predecessors the writer's own sister, and had enjoyed great esteem in the community. As in the convent to which the previous letter, no. 210, was sent, this superior had a male official to help her in its direction, a cleric presumably, who had the masculine form of the title "provost."

The occasion of this letter was some uproar among the sisters, who were demanding, with violence, the appointment of a new superior. We cannot see clearly from the letter why they were no longer satisfied with the present one. One circumstance may have been that not long before they had received a new man as provost, with whom the nuns were greatly taken. The letter is a serious call for the restoration of harmony and love among the sisters, and it reminds the recipients of the grace that God has given them of wishing to live "in one mind together in a single house," to be there only "one soul and one heart toward God." As a conclusion to this letter, there follows, without any preface, the text of Augustine's *Rule*, the so-called *Praeceptum*, in the form composed for nuns.

That this letter, based entirely on Biblical conceptions, and, despite a certain sternness, completely humane in its expression, was written by Augustine has in recent times been strongly contested by Winfried Hümpfner.[7] But his arguments are not so compelling that his point of view can be maintained.[8] As a proof of the Augustinian origin of the letter, still contested, the entire text is offered here.

1. Just as severity is prepared to punish the sins that it has found, so Christian love does not wish to find sins to punish. This is the reason why I did not come to you, when you sought my presence not to enjoy your peace but to increase your discord. For how would I have considered it unimportant and left it unpunished if as great an uproar had existed even in my presence as assaulted my ears with your outcry, even if it escaped my notice while I was absent? And perhaps your quarrel would have been still greater in my presence, which had to be denied you; for you were seeking something that is not expedient to you, as a most harmful precedent against sound teaching. And so I would not have found you to be such as I wish, and you would have found me to be such as you do not wish.

2. Therefore, since the Apostle says in his Epistle to the Corinthians: "I call God to witness upon my soul that, to spare you, I did not after all come to Corinth, not because we are dictating your faith to you, but working with you for your happiness" [2 Cor. 1:23–24], I too say this to you, because, to spare you, I did not come to you. I also spared myself "that I might not have sorrow upon sorrow" [Phil. 2:27, 2 Cor. 2:3]. And I chose not to show my face to you but to pour forth my heart to God for you and to plead your dangerous cause, not before you in words, but before God in tears, lest He convert to grief the joy with which I am accustomed to rejoice in you and sometimes to find consolation among the great stumbling blocks abundant everywhere in this world; for I reflect upon your large congregation, and your chaste love, and your holy way of life, and the more

abundant grace God has given you, so that you not only scorned marriages of the flesh but also chose the fellowship of living with one mind in the same household, so that there would be one soul and one heart toward God [Acts 4:32].

3. When I consider these good qualities of yours and these gifts of God, my heart often finds rest among the many storms and other evils by which it is tossed. "You were running well. Who was it who hindered you? Whatever persuasion he used did not come from God Who has called you. A little leaven . . ." [Gal. 5:7–9, 3:1; 1 Cor. 5:6]—I do not want to quote the rest. Indeed, I wish and pray and urge this rather: that this yeast would change back for the better, so that all the dough would not be changed for the worst, as has already almost happened. So if you have blossomed again to sound mind, " 'pray that you not enter into temptation' " [Matt. 26:41, Mark 14:38, Luke 22:46] nor again into "contention, rivalry, jealousy, discord, quarrels, strife, sedition, and whispering" [2 Cor. 12:20]. For we have not so planted and watered the Lord's garden in you to reap these thorns from you [1 Cor. 3:6–8, Jer. 12:13]. But if you are weak and still confused, pray to be rescued from temptation. Yet if those sisters who trouble you continue to do so, whoever they may be, if they do not correct themselves, they will bear their judgment.

4. Think how unfortunate it is that while we rejoice about the Donatists' return to unity we lament the internal dissension in your monastery. Persevere in your good undertaking, and you will not want to change your superior. While she, who was like a mother and conceived you, not in the womb but in the soul, has persevered in that monastery for so many years, you have grown both in number and in age. For all of you who came to that monastery found her there, either serving and pleasing her holy superior, my sister, or acting as a superior herself. Under her you were educated, under her you took the veil, under her you increased in number. And now you clamor that she should be replaced, when you ought to lament if we wanted to replace her. It is she whom you know, it is she to whom you came, it is she under whose leadership you have grown for so many years. You have received no new official except a priest superior; if for his sake you seek a change and if through jealousy for him you have rebelled against your mother in this way, why do you not ask to have him replaced instead? But if you shrink from this proposal—since I know how reverently you love him in Christ—why do you not shrink all the more from the first proposal? For his attempts to rule you are confounded to such a degree that

he would rather desert you than endure the hateful rumor that if you had not begun to have him as a priest superior, you would not have asked for another mother superior. Therefore, let God calm and compose your spirit; do not let the work of the Devil prevail in you, but "let the peace of Christ be victorious in your hearts" [Col. 3:15]. Do not rush to death in your grief of spirit because your wish is not fulfilled, or in your embarrassment at having wished for what you should not have wanted. Instead, renew your virtue through repentance—not the repentance of Judas the betrayer, but the tears of Peter the shepherd. . . .

LETTER 243
(WRITTEN PROBABLY CA. 400[9])
On the Meaning of the Monastic Dedication

Laetus, a young Christian from a wealthy family, had joined the community of the brethren in the clerics' monastery. Having returned home to set his finances in complete order, he allowed his decision to falter, weakened by his mother's tears and his relatives' demeanor. So Augustine warns him of this foolish dependence and of a too great regard for his family, and encourages him to persist bravely in the way of life which he had chosen.

In the Scriptural quotation "'If any one comes to me, and does not despise his father and mother, wife and children, brothers and sisters, and even his own life, he cannot be My disciple'" (Luke 14:26), Augustine sees a condemnation of a too earthly dependence on one's blood relatives and on one's own life. Even if he does not deal in detail with the purely natural love of a son for his mother and hers for him, still, plainly, he has now freed himself of that rejection of every earthly family love which he often expressed in the writings of his first years as a priest when he quoted this Scripture text.[10] Furthermore, in the *Retractations* he revoked specifically these harsh expressions,[11] and laid down that in only one instance was a relative to be hated as an enemy: "that is, if he holds us back from the kingdom of God."[12]

What Augustine writes to this young "soldier for Christ" in many ways reminds us of the instructions that were then commonly given to new entrants into the monasteries of the East.[13] Here, too, we see consecration to the religious life as a renunciation "of all things" (Luke 14:26ff.), and an unconditional acceptance of Christ's cross: "Take up your cross and follow the Lord." For Augustine, monastic life means a likeness to the crucified Christ.

A number of literary parallels that have recently been established prove that Augustine, composing this work, was in many ways inspired by Jerome's Letter No. 21, to Heliodorus.[14]

Augustine sends greetings in the Lord to his most beloved and longed-for lord and brother Laetus.

1. I have read the letter that you sent to the brothers and wanted to console you, because your first campaigns in spiritual warfare are shaken by many temptations. And in the letter you made it clear that you longed to hear from me. I sympathized, brother, and I did not delay writing, so as to fulfill my own wish along with yours. For I saw that I owed this act to the duty of Christian love. Therefore, if you declare yourself a recruit of Christ, do not desert the camp in which you too must build that tower mentioned by the Lord in the Gospel [Luke 14:28]. Indeed, no temptations from any quarter are strong enough to pierce the man who stands fast in this tower and serves under the protection of the word of God. The weapons hurled against the enemy from that tower fall heavily, and those perceived from that strong fortress are turned aside. Consider, too, that our Lord Jesus Christ, although He is our king [Luke 14:31], nevertheless in that company in which He deigned to be a brother has ordered kings to call forth their soldiers. And He has ordered every king to be prepared to lead an army of ten thousand against a king who has twenty thousand.

2. But listen to what He said shortly before setting forth the encouraging comparisons about the tower and the king: " 'If anyone comes to me, and does not despise his father and mother, wife and children, brothers and sisters, and even his own life, he cannot be My disciple' " [Luke 14:26]. Then He adds: "Who of you, wishing to build a tower, does not first sit down to reckon whether he has enough money to complete it, lest, having laid the foundations, he be unable to build, and lest all who pass by and see begin to say 'This man began to build, and was not able to finish'? Or what king going forth to battle against another king does not first sit down to reckon whether with ten thousand men he can go against the king who comes forth to meet him with twenty thousand? If not, while he is still far off, he sends an envoy asking for peace" [Luke 14:28–32]. It is patently clear from the conclusion what these comparisons refer to, for He says: "So therefore each of you who does not renounce all that he has cannot be My disciple" [Luke 14:33].

3. And, so, both the cost of building the tower and the strength of ten thousand pitted against the king who has twenty thousand mean nothing

other than that each person should renounce all that he has. For the foreword above agrees with the conclusion. The idea of the conclusion that each one "should renounce all that he has" is already included in the idea of the foreword that he should despise "his father and mother, wife and children, brothers and sisters, and even his own life." For all these are his own ties, and they often entwine him and prevent him from attaining, not his particular and transitory possessions, but possessions everlasting and common to all. Now, because a certain woman is your mother, she is not on that account mine. Therefore, this is a temporal and transitory tie, just as you see that it has already come to pass that she conceived you, that she carried you in her womb, that she bore you, that she nourished you with her milk. But because she is a sister in Christ, she is a sister to you and to me and to all those for whom one heavenly inheritance and God as father and Christ as brother are promised in the same fellowship of Christian love [Rom. 8:16–17]. These ties are eternal; they are not worn away by the passage of time. Just as one hopes that these things will be kept more firmly, so one preaches that they will be obtained less by private than by common right.

4. You can recognize this fact very easily in the case of your own mother. Why else did she entwine you as you are now ensnared, and why else, after she had slowed your progress, did she turn you away and deflect you from the course you had undertaken, if not because she is your mother? For since she is a sister of us all who have God as father and the Church as mother, we are not prevented, you or I or any of the brethren, from loving her, not with that private love which you had in your home, but with a public love in the house of God. That you are bound to her by ties of blood as well ought to help to provide an opportunity for more private conversation and for more open consultation, so that the very thing for which she loves you privately may be killed in her, lest she consider it of greater importance that she bore you in her own womb than that she, along with you, was born from the womb of the Church. Moreover, what I have said about your mother is also to be understood about other such close relationships. Therefore let everyone so consider even his own life that he hates in it even the private affection that is, without doubt, a temporal thing but loves in it the communion and fellowship, of which it has been said: "They had but one heart and one soul in God" [Acts 4:32]. So, indeed, your life is not your own; it belongs to all the brethren—just as their lives belong to you, or, better expressed, their lives and yours no longer form a multiple of lives, but only one life, which is Christ's own, and which, as the Psalmist says,

may be snatched "from the paw of the dog" [Ps. 21:21]. From this state it is very easy to arrive at a contempt for death.

5. Nor should parents become angry because the Lord commands us to despise them, since He orders us to despise our own life. For just as we are now ordered to despise our life and our parents for Christ's sake, so the Lord's words about life in another passage can most appropriately also apply to parents. He says: " 'He who loves his life will lose it' " [John 12:25]. I shall also say with confidence: "He who loves his parents will lose them." Indeed, in the first passage [Luke 14:26], He said "let him despise" life; in this passage [John 12:25], He says "he will lose" it. However, just as the command that directs us to lose our life does not mean that everyone should kill himself, which would be an unatonable crime, so it means that everyone should kill in himself the earthly attachment to life; for the present life delights us, with impediments to the life to come—this is the meaning of the words "let him despise his own life" and "he will lose it." This happens through love, for in the same command He speaks very plainly of the fruit of this same life which we must seek, saying " 'He who has lost his life in this world will find it in eternal life' " [John 12:25]. So it is rightly said that he who loves his parents will lose them, not by killing them as parricides do, but by killing, with the spiritual sword of the word of God [cf. Eph. 6:17], the earthly attachment to them which they use to bond both themselves and those whom they have begotten to the entanglements of this world. By devoutly and faithfully striking down and killing this attachment, a man brings to life in his parents that which makes them his brothers and causes them, along with their temporal sons, to recognize God and the Church as their eternal parents.

6. Behold, you are seized by an eagerness for the truth and for recognizing and understanding God's will in Holy Scripture, and by the duty of preaching the Gospel. The Lord gives the signal for us to be watchful in our camp, to build a tower from which we will be able both to look out for and to repel the enemy of everlasting life. The heavenly trumpet calls the soldier of Christ to battle, and his mother, who is not at all like the mother of the Maccabees or the mothers of Sparta, holds him back. For it has been handed down to posterity that these mothers stirred their sons to pour out their blood for an earthly fatherland in the struggles of war much more generously and passionately than the sound of the signals did. Indeed, a mother who does not allow you to retreat from worldly cares in order to learn about life clearly reveals how little she would allow you to re-

nounce the world completely in order to go forth to death, should it prove necessary.

7. But what does she say or what claim does she make? Those ten months she carried you beneath her heart, perhaps, and the pains of childbirth, and the hardships of raising a child? Kill this with the word of salvation; destroy this in your mother so that you may find her in eternal life. Remember to hate this in her if you love her, if you are a recruit of Christ, if you have laid the foundation of your tower, so that those who pass by may not say "This man began to build and was not able to finish." For this is an earthly attachment and still sounds like your former self [Eph. 4:22, Col. 3:9, Rom. 6:6]. Christian service encourages us to destroy this earthly attachment both in ourselves and in our loved ones, yet not in such a way that anyone is ungrateful to his parents and mocks the many kindnesses with which he was born, brought up, and nourished. Let him rather preserve filial love everywhere; these emotions have their place, as long as they do not call forth stronger ones.

8. Mother Church is also your mother's mother. She has conceived you both in Christ; she has carried you in the blood of the martyrs; she has brought you forth into the eternal light; she has nursed and now nurses you with the milk of faith. She shrinks from preparing solid food for you, since you are still toothless children who want only to cry. This Mother Church that has spread throughout the entire world is disturbed by such diverse and manifold infestations of errors that even her premature children do not hesitate to wage war against her with unbridled hostility. She grieves that because of the laziness and inactivity of certain people whom she holds in her embrace her limbs are growing cold in many places and she is becoming less capable of warming her young. From whom can she rightly and deservedly seek aid if not from her other sons, her other members, among whom you are counted? Are you deserting her in her need and turning to the words of the flesh? Are her grave sorrows not ringing in your ears? Is she not offering a more loving heart and a heavenly embrace? Add to this the fact that Jesus Christ took on the flesh so that you might not cleave to the things of the flesh, and that all that your mother holds before you was taken from the Eternal Word so that you might not be ensnared in the things of the flesh; add to this the insults, scourgings, and death—even death on the cross.

9. Do you, who were conceived from such seed and in such a marriage begotten for a new life, languish and waste away to your former self? Did

not your field commander also have an earthly mother? Yet when she was announced to Him as He was doing heavenly works, He replied: " 'Who is my mother and who are my brothers?' And stretching forth His hands toward His disciples," He said that no one was related to Him who did not do His Father's will [Matt. 12:47–50]. To be sure, He beneficently included as well Mary herself; for she was doing the will of His Father. In this way, the best and divine teacher put aside even the name of mother, which had been privately and personally announced to Him, because, in comparison with the heavenly relationship, it was of this world. And speaking with His disciples about this same heavenly relationship, He revealed in what fellowship of birth that holy virgin, along with the other saints, was bound to Him. And in order that the mistake of denying that He had a mother might not receive any support from His most beneficial instruction that earthly attachment to parents is to be scorned, in another place He admonished His disciples not to say that they had fathers here on earth [Matt. 23:9]. In this way He made it clear that He had a mother, just as it was clear that they had fathers. Yet by scorning His earthly relationship to her, He offered His disciples an example of how such relationships are to be scorned.

10. Are these words then interrupted by the words of your mother, and in the midst of them does the story of her pregnancy and nursing find a place, so that you are another Adam, born and nourished by Adam and Eve? Reflect, then, reflect upon the second Adam who came down from heaven, and bear now the image of the heavenly Adam, just as you bore the image of the earthly one [1 Cor. 15:47–49]. To be sure, even here let those earthly services of your mother, which she enumerates until you are weak at heart, have a place; by all means let them have a place. Do not be ungrateful; return thanks to your mother; return spiritual services for bodily ones, eternal services for temporal ones. She does not want to follow? Then let her not hinder you. She does not want to change for the better? Then take care that she does not corrupt and overwhelm you for the worse. What difference is there whether a man is on guard against Eve in a wife or in a mother, as long as he is on guard against Eve in any woman? For the shade of filial devotion comes from the leaves of that same tree with which our parents first covered themselves in their damnable nakedness. And whatever she shows to you in her intimations as the duty of Christian love, so that she may turn you away from the true and pure love of the Gospel, is part of the cleverness of the serpent and the duplicity of that king who has twenty thousand men. We are taught to overcome that duplicity by the

simplicity of the ten thousand, that is, the simplicity of our heart, through which we seek God.

11. Pay attention to these words above all, dearest brother, and take up your cross and follow the Lord. For when I myself noticed, when we were together, that you were kept from divine study by the concerns of your household, I felt that you were carried and led by your cross, rather than carrying and leading it. For what else does the Lord mean by the cross that He commands us to carry in order to follow Him without hindrance, but the mortality of this flesh? For it crucifies us until death is swallowed up in victory [1 Cor. 15:54]. Therefore we must crucify this cross itself, and we must transfix it with the nail of the fear of God [Ps. 118:120], so that as it resists we can carry it with free and unfettered limbs. For you cannot follow the Lord at all unless you carry this cross. For how can you follow Him if you are not His? "Those who belong to Christ Jesus," the Apostle says, "have crucified their flesh, with its passions and desires" [Gal. 5:24].

12. If your family fortune consists of any wealth, it should be divided between your mother and your household, since it is neither proper nor fitting for you to be involved in its administration. To be sure, if you have decided to distribute your goods to the poor in order to become perfect, the needs of your household must come first. For the Apostle says, "Anyone who does not provide for his own relations, and especially members of his own household, has denied his faith and is worse than an unbeliever" [1 Tim. 5:8]. If in the management of these affairs you have set out from us in order to expose your neck to clothe it in the bonds of wisdom, how can such things as your mother's tears moistening her flesh, or a slave's flight, or a maidservant's death, or a brother's ill-health harm you or tear you away? What harm can these things do if you have in you Christian love that has been properly put in order and knows how to place greater concerns before lesser ones, and how to be moved by mercy to preach to the poor and not leave the Lord's abundant harvest lying as plunder for the birds through lack of workers? What harm can they do if you have Christian love that knows how to hold a heart in readiness to carry out the Lord's will in what He has destined His servants to accomplish, whether He smite them or spare them? "Think about these things, be active in these things, so that your progress may be clear to all" [1 Tim. 4:15]. I beg you, take care not to give greater concern to your brothers by your inactivity than the joy that you have already given them by your eagerness. But I considered that commending you in a letter, as you wished, was as superfluous as if someone had wanted to commend you to me in one.

NOTES

1. It is uncertain which of the various "goat-islands" in the Mediterranean is intended. See above, p. 96*n*21.

2. This synod was held at Carthage in 397; cf. Hardouin, *Acta conciliorum*, I 961f.

3. Proculianus was the Donatist bishop of Hippo.

4. See also Zumkeller, *Schriften gegen die Pelagianer*, II 23–26.

5. On this problem, see H. Rondet, "Richesse et pauvreté dans le prédication de saint Augustin," *Saint Augustin parmi nous*, edd. H. Rondet et al. (Le Puy & Paris, 1954), pp. 111–48.

6. The Maurist editors date it about 423. They and CSEL regard it as genuine.

7. First in H. U. von Balthasar, *Die grossen Ordensregeln* (Einsiedeln & Zürich, 1948), pp. 108ff.

8. See above, pp. 283–87, esp. p. 286.

9. This hypothetical dating is based on Augustine's use of the key image of "Christian warfare," so evident here, in *The Work of Monks*, also composed ca. 400, and on a few relevant chapters of the *Confessions*. It is evident that the letter cannot have been written later, since his ideas about "contempt for death" (*contemptus mortis*), influenced by the Stoic ideal of "apatheia," still find expression here.

10. *True Religion* 46.88 and *The Lord's Sermon on the Mount* 1.15.41. See also Mausbach, *Die Ethik*, I 257ff.

11. *Retractations* 1.12.8 and 1.18.5.

12. Ibid. 1.18.5.

13. Rothenhäusler, "Die Anfänge," 21–28; idem, "Der heilige Basilius," 280–89; and idem, "Unter dem Geheimnis," 91–96. We may well suppose that in Augustine's monasteries too the notion of surrender to Christ's cross was important in early monastic instruction. Perhaps Augustine intended by this letter to remind the hesitant Laetus of what he had been taught.

14. Celleruelo, *El monacato*, pp. 179ff.

12

Sermons

EXPOSITION OF PSALM 75

"Make a Vow and Keep It" (Ps. 75:12)

Quoting these words of the Psalmist's, Augustine declares his views on the religious vow. He writes first of those vows that every Christian takes and is required to fulfill: that is, the vow to believe in Christ, to hope for everlasting life from Him, and to live a good life, as prescribed by the general Christian commandments. "This vow simply signifies man's response to God's command and ordinance, not merely the renunciation of the devil, but also his assent to God."[1]

Then Augustine goes on to write of those vows that are special to individual men: the vow of conjugal chastity, the vow of virginity, the vow of practicing Christian hospitality, the vow of the renunciation of personal possessions and of the common life in monastic communities. He stresses the binding nature of these special vows. No one is obliged to take such vows; but if he has done so, he is compelled to keep them. He warns such men of "looking back" (Luke 9:62). A man with such vows should, rather, look to God and love Him with Whose help he will keep them.

16. "Make a vow to the Lord our God and keep it" [Ps. 75:12]. Let each man vow what he can and let him keep his vow. Do not vow without keeping it; rather let each man vow what he can and let him keep his vow. Do not be slow to make a vow, for it is not through your own power that you will keep it. You will be found wanting if you trust in yourselves, but if you trust in Him to whom you make your vow, then make a vow and you will keep it safely.

"Make a vow to the Lord your God and keep it." What ought we all to vow in common? To believe in Him, to hope for eternal life from Him, to live well according to the common measure. For there is a certain measure common to all. The commandment not to steal is not given just to women vowed to chastity and not to married women; the commandment not to commit adultery is given to all; the commandment not to love drunkenness, with which the soul is gorged and corrupts in itself the temple of God, is given equally to all; the commandment not to be proud is given equally to all; the commandments not to kill, not to hate one's brother, not to do harm to anyone are given to all in common. Each of us ought to vow all of this.

There are also vows that are proper for individual people. One man vows to God chastity in marriage, promising that he will not know any woman but his wife; so, too, his wife vows that she will not know any man but her husband. Some men also vow, even if they have known such a marriage, not to experience any such thing in the future, and neither to desire nor to allow it; the latter have made a greater vow than the former. Others pledge their virginity from an early age; they vow not even to experience what the others have experienced and left behind. They have made the greatest vow. Others vow that their own homes will be open to all the holy people who approach; theirs is a great vow. Another vows to give up all his possessions to be distributed to the poor, and to enter the life of a community, in the fellowship of holy men; this is a great vow.

"Make a vow to the Lord our God and keep it." Let each one vow what he has wished to vow; let him take care to keep his vow. If anyone "looks back" [Luke 9:62] at what he vows to God, this is an evil. A consecrated virgin wants to marry? What does she want? What every virgin wants. And what does she want? What her mother wanted. Has she wished for some evil? Certainly. Why? Because she has already made a vow to the Lord her God. For what did the Apostle Paul say about such matters? Although he says that young widows can remarry [1 Tim. 5:14], yet in one place he says, "But she will be happier if she stays as she is, in my opinion" [1 Cor. 7:40]. He points out that she will be happier if she stays as she is, yet she is not to be condemned if she wishes to marry. But what does he say of women who have made a vow and have not kept it? [They are] "condemned because they have broken their original promise" [1 Tim. 5:12]. What does "because they have broken their original promise" mean? They have made a vow, and they have not kept it. So let no brother living in a monastery say, "I am leaving the monastery, for not only those living in a monastery will come to the kingdom of Heaven; nor do those outside the monasteries not belong to God." This is the answer for him: "But they did not make a vow; you did, and you have looked back." . . . Do not be slow, those of you who are able and who are inspired by God to attain the higher levels. For we say this not so that you do not make a vow, but so that you make a vow and keep it.

"Make a vow to the Lord our God and keep it." Now, because we have discussed this question, perhaps you were willing to make a vow earlier, and now you are no longer willing. But listen to what the Psalm says to you. For it does not say "Do not make a vow," but "Make a vow and keep it." Are you now hesitant to make a vow because you have heard the words "keep it"? Were you, then, willing to make a vow and not keep it? On the contrary, do both. Let the first be accomplished through your profession, and the second through God's help. Look upon Him Who leads you, and you will not look back at the place from which He leads you. He Who leads you walks before you; the place from which He leads you is behind you. Love Him Who leads you, and He will not condemn you if you look back. "Make a vow to the Lord our God and keep it."

EXPOSITION OF PSALM 83

" 'Whoever Sets His Hand to the Plow' " (Luke 9:62)

Sometimes it had to be Augustine's experience that men undertook the ideals of monastic life in the first enthusiasm, but soon wearied and betrayed their undertaking. Therefore, he utters warnings that in this, as in every other walk of life, those who lapse are to be judged differently from those who have never decided upon such ideals of life.

3. . . . Those people of Israel who made haste were condemned; the eagerness of people making haste is constantly criticized in Scripture. Who, then, are those who hasten? Those who have turned to God as people wearied by a journey, since they have not found here on earth the rest they had sought and the joys promised to them. They think that they have a long time left until this world or this life is finished, and they seek some rest here; but even if they find it, it is false. Therefore, they look back and fall away from their undertaking. And they do not heed the fear with which " 'Remember Lot's wife' " [Luke 17:32] was said. For why else was she made a pillar of salt [Gen. 19:26] if not to season men so that they might taste wisdom? Thus her bad example becomes a good example to you if you take heed. " 'Remember Lot's wife,' " He said; for she looked back to Sodom, from which she had been freed, and she remained fixed in the place where she stood and looked back. She will remain in that place, and she

will season those who pass by. Therefore, when we have been freed from the Sodom of our past life, let us not look back. For to look back is to make haste and not to pay attention to God's promise because it is still far off; and to look back is to look back at what is nearest, from which you have already been freed. . . .

4. Moreover, each man, beloved brothers, looks back from the place that he has reached by setting out on his own journey and that he has vowed to God upon leaving it behind. For example, a man has decided to keep chastity in marriage (for righteousness begins with this); he has withdrawn from fornication and all other unlawful unchastity. When he turns to fornication, he has looked back. With God's help another man makes a greater vow and decides not to experience marriage. If this man, who would not be condemned if he had taken a wife, marries after making this vow to God, he will be condemned, although he does the same as the man who had not made this vow. And yet one is condemned and the other is not. Why, unless because one of them has looked back? For he was already ahead, at a point the other man had not yet reached.

So if a virgin were to marry, she would not sin [1 Cor. 7:28], but if a woman vowed to chastity marries, she will be considered an adulteress of Christ. For she has looked back from the place that she had reached. So it is, too, for those who think it good, when they have left behind all worldly ambition and all earthly activity, to enter the fellowship of holy men and the shared life in which no one calls anything his own but they hold all things in common and they have one heart and one soul toward God [Acts 4:32]. Whoever wishes to leave this place will not be considered in the same way as one who has not entered. For the latter has not reached this place, and the former has looked back. Therefore, beloved brothers, let each of you to the best of his ability vow and fulfill to the Lord your God [Ps. 75:12] whatever he can. Let no one look back; let no one take delight in his past; let no one turn away from what is before him to what is behind him. Let him run until he reaches his goal; for we run, not on foot, but in our desire. Yet let no one say that he has reached his goal in this life. For who can be as perfect as Paul? And yet he said, "Brothers, I do not think that I have reached my goal. All I can say is this: forgetting what is behind me, and reaching out for what lies ahead, I press toward the goal to win the prize which is God's call to the life above, in Christ Jesus" [Phil. 3:13–14]. You see that Paul is still running, and you think that you have already reached your goal?

EXPOSITION OF PSALM 99

"As a Lily Among Thorns" (Cant. 2:2)

In a sermon preached to the people Augustine speaks of troubles in the Church. What he says is neither overly optimistic nor confused by pessimism. Bitter experience had led him to the conviction that here on earth—and also in the Church—there will always be troubles. So long as kingdoms contend with one another, there can be no rest and security. Lilies must grow among thorns, and the wheat will be hidden in the chaff. Even among the clergy and in monasteries, bad men will always be found.

8. "Serve the Lord in gladness" [Ps. 99:2]. That gladness will be complete and perfected when "this corruption will put on incorruptibility and this mortal state will put on immortality" [1 Cor. 15:54]. Then joy will be complete, then jubilation will be perfected; then there will be praise without defect, love without discord, enjoyment without fear, life without death. What is here? Is there no joy here? If there is no joy or rejoicing, then how is it written "Sing joyfully to the Lord, all the earth" [Ps. 99:2]? Certainly there is joy here too. But here we only taste the hope of the life that is to come; there we will be satiated.

But it is necessary for the wheat to suffer much among the tares; there are seeds among the chaff [Matt. 3:12], and there is a lily among the thorns [Matt. 13:30]. For what does the Church hear? "Just as the lily among the thorns, so is my love among the daughters" [Cant. 2:2]. These words were not "among the strangers," but "among the daughters." Oh Lord, how You console, how You comfort, how You terrify! What are You saying? As the lily among what kind of thorns? So is my love among what kind of daughters? Are you calling the very daughters thorns? He replies: "They are thorns because of their ways; they are daughters because of my sacraments." Would that there would be lamenting amidst the groans of strangers! There would be less lamenting. This is the greater lament: that "If my enemy had insulted me, I would have endured it; and if one who hated me had spoken great things against me, I would perhaps have hidden myself from him" [Ps. 54:13]. These are the words of the Psalm. He who knows our Scriptures can follow them. Let him who does not know them learn them so that he can follow. "If one who hated me had spoken great things against me, I would perhaps have hidden myself from him. But you are a man of one mind with me, my leader and my friend, who used to take sweet food with me" [Ps. 54:13–15]. What sweet food do those people who will not always be with us take with us? What sweet food, unless "Taste and see that the Lord is sweet" [Ps. 33:9]. Living among these people, we can do nothing else but lament.

9. But where will the Christian retreat not to lament among false brothers? Where will he go? What will he do? Is he to seek solitude? Scandals follow him. Will he who makes good progress retreat so that he permits no human company at all? What if before he made progress no one wished to suffer him either? If he does not want to suffer any human company because he makes progress, then the very fact that he does not want any human company convinces him that he has not made progress. Let your love then pay attention. The Apostle says "bearing with each other in love, eager to preserve the unity of the Spirit in the bond of peace" [Eph. 4:2–3]. "Bearing with each other"—do you not have some fault in you for another to bear? I am amazed if you do not. Then, because you already have no fault in you for another to bear, you are all the stronger to bear others. You are not borne by others; so bear others. I cannot, you say. Therefore, you do have some fault for others to bear. "Bearing with each other in love." You leave behind human affairs and segregate yourself so that no one sees you. Whom do you help? Would you have reached this point if no one had helped you? Or because you think your feet are swift enough to make the crossing, will you then cut away the bridge? I exhort you all; the word of God exhorts you all: "Bearing with each other in love."

10. Someone says, "I shall withdraw with a few good men; in their company all will go well for me. For it is cruel and wicked to be of help to no one. The Lord my God has not taught me to do this. For He condemned the servant, not because he embezzled what he received, but because he did not spend it. The punishment for embezzling may be learned from the punishment of the lazy man. 'Wicked and lazy servant' [Matt. 25:26], the Lord says in condemnation. He does not say 'You have embezzled my money'; He does not say 'I gave it to you and you did not return to me all that I gave.' He says 'Because it did not increase, because you did not spend it, I shall punish you.' God is greedy for our salvation. Therefore I shall withdraw with a few good men. What is it to me to have dealings with the crowds?" Fine. But from what crowds have these few good men been sifted? Yet if they are few, they are all good men. It is yet a good intention of man and a praiseworthy one to be with those who have chosen a quiet life. Far from the roar of the people, from the noise of the great crowds, from the stormy waves, they are in a harbor, as it were. Then is that joy

already here? Is that promised rejoicing already here? Not yet. There are still laments and worry over temptations. For even a harbor has an entrance somewhere—if a harbor had no entrance on any side, then no ship could enter it. So it must of necessity lie open on one side. Yet sometimes the wind rushes in from that open side. And even where there are no rocks, the ships are dashed against each other and are shattered. Then, where can that security be found, if not in a harbor? And yet we must confess, we must grant (for it is true), that those in the harbor are still much more fortunate than those on the open sea. Let them love one another; let the ships in port be bound to each other by good; let them not be dashed against each other. Let impartial equality and constant love be preserved there, and if by chance the wind rushes in from the open side, let there be careful piloting.

11. Now what will someone who chances to be in charge of such a place, or rather who serves his brothers in those places called monasteries, say to me? What will he say? "I will be careful; I will not admit an evil man." How will you not admit an evil man? "I will allow no evil man, and no evil brother, to enter; in the company of a few good men, all will go well for me." How do you recognize the man whom you may want to exclude? To recognize a man as evil, you must first test him within the monastery. So how do you shut out the man who is about to enter and who is to be tested afterward, but cannot be tested unless he has entered? Will you send all the wicked men away?

You say so, and you know how to examine them. Do they all come to you with their hearts bared? Those who are about to enter do not know themselves; how much less do you know them? For many have promised themselves that they would fulfill that holy life that holds all things in common, where no one calls anything his own, and where they have one soul and one heart toward God [Acts 4:32]. They have been put into the furnace and they have cracked. How, then, do you recognize a man who is still unknown to himself? Will you shut out the wicked brothers from the assembly of the good? Whoever says this, shut out all evil intentions from your own heart if you can. Do not let even the suggestion of evil come into your heart. I do not agree, you say. But it comes in nonetheless. For we all want our hearts to be fortified, so that nothing prompted by evil may enter. But who knows how it enters? And we fight daily in our own individual hearts; each man struggles against the crowd in his own heart. Avarice prompts us; lust prompts us; greed prompts up; the happiness of the common crowd prompts us. Everything prompts us, and each man holds himself back from everything. It is difficult not to be struck by some temptation.

Where, then, is security? Here it is nowhere. In this life it is nowhere, except in the hope of God's promises. But there, when we come to that goal, is complete security, when the gates are closed, when the bars of the gates of Jerusalem are made fast [Ps. 147:13]. There, in truth, full rejoicing and great joy will reign. Only do not rashly praise any life, and do not praise any man before his death [cf. Eccli. 11:30].

12. Yet in this men are deceived, so that either they do not undertake a better life or they rashly attack it. Even when they want to praise, they praise without speaking of the evils that are mixed in; and those who want to criticize do so with such envy and perversity of spirit that they close their eyes to the good things and exaggerate only the bad, either real or imagined. So it is that when any profession wrongly, that is, rashly, praised has by being praised invited men to that life, those who come find there some men such as they did not think were there. And offended by the evil men, they shrink from the good. Brothers, apply this teaching to your life, and listen in such a way that you may live.

The Church of God, to speak in general terms, is praised; Christian men—only Christian men—are great, and the Catholic Church is great. They all love one another, and they each make whatever effort they can for each other. They devote themselves to prayer, fasting, and hymns throughout the entire world, and they praise God in the harmony of peace. Perhaps a man who does not know that they keep quiet about the wicked men mingled among them hears of them. He comes invited by praise of that life; he finds, mingled with the good, wicked men who were not mentioned to him before his arrival; and he is offended by false Christians, and he flees from true Christians. Again, hateful and slanderous men rush to find fault. What kind of people are these Christians? Who are the Christians? The greedy; the profiteers. Are not the very people who fill the theaters and the amphitheaters for the games and other spectacles the same ones who fill the churches on feast days? They are drunken, gluttonous, envious slanderers of one another. There are Christians of this sort, but not of this sort alone. The man who finds fault blindly is silent about the good Christians, and the man who praises rashly is silent about the wicked ones.

But if the Church of God is praised like this in these days, how do His Scriptures praise it? "Just as the lily among the thorns, so is my love among the daughters" [Cant. 2:2]. A man hears this and considers it. The lily pleases him, he enters, he cleaves to the lily and tolerates the thorns. He who says "just as the lily among the thorns, so is my love among the daughters" deserves the praise and kisses of his betrothed.

So it is, too, among the clergy. The praisers of the clergy here refer to the good servants, the faithful stewards, tolerant of all and devoting their hearts to those who want to make progress, seeking "not their own interests but those of Jesus Christ" [Phil. 2:21]. They praise these things and forget that they are mingled with evils. In return, those who chastise the avarice of the clergy, their wickedness, and their quarrelsomeness claim that they seek the possessions of others and that they are drunkards and gluttons. You, on the one hand, slander invidiously, and you, on the other, praise rashly. You who praise, say too that there are wicked men mingled with the good; you who slander, see that there are good men there too.

So it is, as well, in that common life of the brothers in the monastery. Great men, holy men, live there in daily hymns, prayers, and praise of God. They occupy themselves in reading, and support themselves by manual labor. They do not seek anything greedily, but use in contentment and love whatever their pious brothers bring to them. No one takes anything for his own that another does not have; they all love one another, and bear with each other [cf. Phil. 2:21]. You have praised them; you have praised them. But the man who does not know what happens within the monastery, and who does not know how even ships in a harbor are dashed against each other when the wind enters, goes into the monastery as if he hopes for security and as if he will have no one there to tolerate. He finds there evil brothers, who could not be found out as evil if they were not admitted (for they must first be tolerated, just in case they may be corrected, and they cannot easily be excluded, unless they have first been tolerated). And then this same man becomes intolerably impatient. Who asked me to come to this place? I thought that Christian love existed here. And irritated by a few bothersome men, while he has not persevered in fulfilling his vow, he becomes a deserter of so holy an undertaking and is charged with not fulfilling a vow. And then when he has left that place, he, too, becomes a critic and a slanderer; he tells only of those things that he swore he could hardly have endured. And sometimes they are real. But he should tolerate the real actions of the wicked for the sake of the fellowship of the good. Scripture says to him, "Woe to those who have lost their will to endure" [Eccli. 2:16]. What is more, he belches forth the bad odor of his indignation, and frightens away those intending to enter the monastery, since, when he himself had entered, he could not persevere. What sort of people are those brothers? They are envious, quarrelsome, completely intolerant, greedy. This one did this there, and that one did that. Wicked man, why do you keep quiet about the good brothers? You shout of those whom you could not tolerate, but you keep quiet about those who tolerated you in your wickedness.

3. Rightly, dearest brothers, the Lord in His Gospel said " 'There are two men in the field, one will be taken, and the other will be left. There are two women grinding at the mill; one will be taken, and the other will be left. There are two men in their beds; one will be taken, and the other left" [Matt. 24:40–41, Luke 17:34–35].[2] Who are the two men in the field? The Apostle tells us, "I planted, Apollo watered, but God made things grow. . . . You are God's husbandry" [1 Cor. 3:6, 9]. We labor in the field. The "two men in the field" are clerics; "one will be taken, and the other will be left"; the good cleric will be taken, and the wicked one will be left.

The "two women grinding at the mill" refers to the laity. Why "grinding at the mill"? Because they are bound to this world, to the revolution of temporal affairs, as if held by a millstone. And "one will be taken and the other will be left." Which one of them will be taken? The one doing good works and being attentive to the needy poor, the one faithful in confession, sure in the gladness of hope, watchful before God, willing evil to no one, loving not only friends but enemies as much as possible, knowing no woman but his own wife, knowing no man but her own husband. This one will be taken from grinding at the mill. The one who has acted otherwise will be left.

But some people say, "We want quiet, we do not want to endure anyone, we are withdrawing from crowds; in a certain security, all will go well for us." If you seek quiet, it is as if you seek your bed, so that you may rest free from all anxiety. And from there, too, "one will be taken and the other left." Let no one deceive you, brothers. If you do not want to be deceived, and if you want to love your brothers, know that every profession in the Church has its pretenders. I have not said that every man is a pretender, but that every profession has its pretenders. There are bad Christians, but there are good ones, too. You see more bad ones because they are the chaff and they do not allow you to reach the grain. But there is grain there too. Approach, try, investigate, and make your judgment. You will find women vowed to chastity who are undisciplined. Is chastity to be deplored on this account? Many women do not stay in their own homes but "go around to other people's homes, acting inquisitively, speaking when they should not"

[1 Tim. 5:13]. They are arrogant, garrulous, and drunk. Even if they are virgins, what good is an undefiled body if the mind has been corrupted? A humble marriage is better than arrogant virginity. For if a woman married, she would not have the name of virginity to boast of, and she would have a bridle to hold her in check. But because of the bad virgins, will we condemn the ones who are holy in both body and spirit [1 Cor. 7:34]? Or because of these praiseworthy virgins, are we compelled to praise even those reprehensible ones? In every case, one will be taken and the other will be left.

EXPOSITION OF PSALM 103

"As those who have nothing and yet possess everything" (2 Cor. 6:10)

As an aged bishop in Carthage, Augustine in four sermons gave an allegorical exposition of the Psalter's hymn to creation. Even in this, he is able to praise Christian monasticism.

The Psalmist's sparrows, for him, are his monks. Like sparrows, they are held in little esteem, for with few exceptions they had come from the humbler walks of life. But, like sparrows, they are not weighed down to the earth, and they can fly high above the great ones of this world. They have freely renounced all that is earthly, and thus have become spiritual.

16. "There the sparrows will make their nests . . ." [Ps. 103:17]. Where will the sparrows build their nests? In the cedars of Lebanon. We have already heard what the cedars of Lebanon are; they are the celebrated of this world, prominent in birth, wealth, and office. . . . Indeed, sparrows are birds, flying things of the sky, but insignificant birds are often called sparrows. Therefore, there are certain spiritual ones building their nests in the cedars of Lebanon; that is, there are certain servants of God hearing the words of the Gospel: " 'Put aside all your possessions,' " or " 'sell what you have, and give to the poor, and you will have your treasure in heaven; and come, follow Me' " [Matt. 19:21]. And not only the great have heard this command, but the lowly as well have wished to do this and to be spiritual—not to be bound to wives, not to be distressed by cares for their children, not to be tied to their own abodes but to enter some shared life.

But what have these sparrows put aside? For the sparrows seem to be the insignificant people of this world. What have they put aside? What that is great have they put aside? One man has been converted; he has put aside the poor hut of his father, scarcely one bed and one chest. Yet he has been converted; he has become a sparrow, he has sought spiritual things. Good, excellent. Let us not mock him and say "You have put aside nothing." He who has put aside many things should not be proud. We know that Peter was a fisherman. What could he have put aside to follow the Lord? Or what did his brother, Andrew, or James and John, the sons of Zebedee, who were also fishermen, put aside? And, nevertheless, what did they say? " 'Behold we have put aside everything and followed You' " [Matt. 19:27]. The Lord did not say in reply "You have forgotten your poverty. What have you put aside that you should receive the whole world?" He has put aside much, my brothers, he has put aside much, who has put aside not only whatever he has but also whatever he had hoped to have. For what pauper does not swell with the hopes of this world? Who does not long daily to increase what he has? It was approaching vastness, but it took on a limit; and was nothing put aside? Certainly Peter put aside the whole world, and Peter received the whole world. "As though having nothing, yet possessing all things" [2 Cor. 6:10]. Many people do the same. They who have little do it and come, and they become useful sparrows. They seem insignificant because they do not have the lofty status of high rank in this world.

They build their nests in the cedars of Lebanon. Indeed, even the cedars of Lebanon, the celebrated and rich and exalted of this world, who hear with fear the words "Blessed is he who takes thought for the poor and the weak" [Ps. 40:2], tend to their possessions, their villas, and all the unnecessary wealth by which they appear exalted, and they offer them to the servants of God. They give fields; they give gardens. They build churches, monasteries; they gather sparrows so that the sparrows can build their nests in the cedars of Lebanon. So "the cedars of Lebanon the Lord has planted" are filled, and "there the sparrows will build their nests" [Ps. 103:16–17]. Observe whether it is not so throughout the world. I did not merely believe these things, so that I might talk this way; I actually saw them. Experience itself has given me knowledge. You who know the farthest lands, make inquiries, and see in how many cedars of Lebanon those sparrows mentioned build their nests.

17. Nonetheless, my brothers, although those sparrows, if they are spiritual, will build their nests in the cedars of Lebanon, they should not consider the cedars of Lebanon to be of great value. And the sparrows should not think that the cedars that supply their needs are superior to them. For they are sparrows, but the others are merely cedars of Lebanon. . . . And if, by chance, the cedars of Lebanon have become angry and have stirred up

any trouble or difficulty for the servants of God in their branches, the sparrows, to be sure, will fly away. But woe to the cedar that remains without sparrows' nests. For the sparrows will not be shipwrecked; they will not come to harm. . . .

EXPOSITION OF PSALM 131

"Blessed Are the Poor in Spirit" (Matt. 5:3)

Augustine esteems those Christians as blessed who fulfill the evangelical precept of poverty and "no longer seek their joy in their possessions." In them he sees the saying of the Psalm fulfilled: they have "prepared a place for the Lord" (Ps. 131:5). For it is precisely apostolic poverty that will make the heart free for God and set aside all hindrances that would oppose a harmonious living together.

4. . . . In his meekness [David] vowed that there should be a house of God. "I will not enter into the tabernacle of my house, I will not climb upon my bed, I will not grant sleep to my eyes" [Ps. 131:3–4]. This seemed insufficient to him, so he added: "I will not grant sleep to my eyes nor slumber to my eyelids, nor rest to my temples, until I find a place for the Lord, a tabernacle for the God of Jacob" [Ps. 131:5]. Where did he seek a place for the Lord? If he was meek, he sought it in himself. How is a man a place for the Lord? Hear the words of the prophet: "Upon whom will my spirit find rest? Upon the humble man and the peaceful, and the man trembling at my words" [Is. 66:2]. Do you wish to be a place for the Lord? Be humble and peaceful and tremble at the words of God, and you will become what you seek. For if what you seek is not accomplished in you, what good does it do you in another? . . . But he who teaches does good, and so he teaches and becomes a place for the Lord along with the one whom he teaches. All who believe make a single place for the Lord. For the Lord has His place within our heart, and there is one heart belonging to all those joined in Christian love.

5. How many thousands, my brothers, believed when they placed the price of their possessions at the Apostles' feet! But what does Scripture say about them? Surely they have become a temple of God; not only has each become a temple of God, but they have all together become a temple of God. Therefore, they have become a place for the Lord. And so that you may know that one place for God has been made in all of them, Scripture says: "they had one soul and one heart toward God" [Acts 4:32].

But in order not to make a place for God, many people seek their own possessions, and love their own possessions, and rejoice in their own power, and strive in their own private interests. But he who wishes to make a place for the Lord ought to rejoice, not about his own interests, but about the common interest. That is what these people have done with their own private possessions; they have made them possessions held in common. Have they lost what they possessed as their own? If they as individuals had possessions, and each one had his own possessions, then each one would have only what he possessed as his own. But when he made his own possessions common, then the possessions of others also became his own.

Therefore, let your Christian love consider that because of our private possessions there exist lawsuits, hostilities, quarrels, wars between men, uproars, disturbances against one another, offenses, sins, wickedness, and murders. For what? For the sake of our private possessions. Do we quarrel over the things we hold in common? We consider that the air is shared; we all see that the sun is shared. Therefore, blessed are those who make a place for the Lord in such a way that they do not rejoice in their own possessions. For such a person was described by him who said "I will not enter into the tabernacle of my house" [Ps. 131:3]. For this was his own. He knew that his own possessions prevented him from making a place for the Lord, and he said what referred to himself: I will not enter "into the tabernacle of my house until I find." What? When you find a place for the Lord, will you enter into your tabernacle? Or when you find a place for the Lord, will that be your tabernacle? Why? Because you yourself will be the place for the Lord, and you will be one with those who have been the place for the Lord.

6. Therefore, brothers, let us abstain from possessing private property, or, if we cannot abstain from possessing it, let us abstain from loving it. And so we make a place for the Lord.

EXPOSITION OF PSALM 132

"How Blessed It Is When Brothers Live Together in Harmony"

In Augustine's mystical and allegorical exposition, this psalm becomes a hymn of praise to Christian monasticism. For it is in monasteries that the harmonious community the psalm praises as a great joy of life finds its realization. The significance which the preacher gives here to the name of "monk" is deeply reflective and truly Augustinian: we call a man a *monachus* who by his single-minded presence has become *monos*—

that is, has become a single being, has acquired one heart and one soul for God. We can see how close and essential Augustine knows the connection between monasticism and the Mystical Body of Christ to be, as he calls it the collar of the Church's lordly robe; for it is the brotherly love of the monks which permits the head, Christ, to emerge, as he adorns Himself with the Church, His vesture. The more exalted Augustine's ideal of monastic life is, the more he stresses the gratuitous nature of that life, and, yet, the more painfully he is aware of the rift between the ideal and reality.

Augustine preached this sermon about the year 410 to the Catholics of his see. In fact, this allegorical exposition of the brief psalm represents a declaration of his own monastic life. His only good in his monasteries had been the realization of a Christian community of love, and, by that, to bring Christ more deeply into the Church and the world.

1. This psalm is short, but it is well known and celebrated. "Behold how good and how pleasant it is for brothers to dwell together in unity" [Ps. 132:1]. This sound is so sweet that even those who do not know the Psalter sing this verse. It is as sweet as the Christian love that makes the brothers live in unity. And, indeed, brothers, "how good and how pleasant it is to live in unity" needs no interpretation or explanation, but the words that follow have some meaning that may be opened to those who knock. And yet, so that our understanding may flow down from this verse to the whole construction of the psalm, let us first consider over and over whether "how good and how pleasant it is to live in unity" is said of all Christians, or whether there are certain perfect Christians who live in unity, and the blessing pertains, not to all, but to certain ones, and may flow from them down to the others.

2. For these words of the Psalter, this sweet sound, and this pleasing melody (as pleasing in the song as in our understanding) have also given birth to monasteries. By this sound brothers who wanted to live in unity were stirred up; this verse was their trumpet. It sounded throughout the entire world, and those who had been divided were assembled together. The cry of God, the cry of the Holy Spirit, the cry of the prophets was not heard in Judea, and yet it was heard in all the world. Those among whom that sound was sung were deaf against it, and those of whom it is said "those who were not told of him shall see, and those who have not heard will understand" [Is. 65:2]. And yet, dearest brothers, if we consider, this blessing was first born from that wall of circumcision. For all the Jews did not perish, did they? Then, whence the Apostles, the sons of the prophets,

the "sons of those who were shaken" [Ps. 126:4]? We speak as if to people who already know. Whence those five hundred people who saw the Lord after His resurrection and who are mentioned by the Apostle Paul [1 Cor. 15:6]? Whence those one hundred and twenty people who were together in one place after the resurrection of the Lord and His ascension into Heaven, and upon whom, as they were assembled there, the Holy Spirit came down from Heaven on the day of Pentecost, sent down from Heaven just as promised? They were all from among the Jews. And they first lived in unity who sold all that they had and laid the price of their belongings at the Apostles' feet, as is written in the Acts of the Apostles: "and it was shared out to each one, according to his need"; "and no one called anything his own, but they held everything in common" [Acts 2:45, 4:35]. And what does "in unity" mean? He says "and they had one soul and one heart toward God" [Acts 4:32].

Therefore they were the first to hear the words "Behold how good and how pleasant it is for brothers to live in unity." They were the first to hear, but they were not the only ones. For that brotherly love and unity did not reach only as far as them. Indeed, this exultation in Christian love and this vow to God also came to later generations. For one vows something to God, as it was written "Make a vow to the Lord your God and keep it" [Ps. 75:12]. But it is better not to make a vow than to make a vow without keeping it. The soul must be quick, so that it both makes a vow and keeps it; otherwise if it consider itself less able to keep a vow, it may be slow to make one. Certainly it will never keep a vow if it believes that it will do so by its own power.

3. Monks have also taken their name from the words of this psalm, lest anyone reproach you Catholics for the name. Because you rightly began to reproach the heretics about the Circellions, so that they might be saved by their shame, they reproach you about monks. First, see whether the two should be compared; if there is need for you to speak, then you already labor. There is no need for you to speak except to admonish each one to pay attention—let each one pay attention and compare. What need is there for you to speak? Let the drunken be compared with the sober; let the rash be compared with the circumspect, the raging with the honest, the wandering with the settled. And yet they have been accustomed to ask "What does the word 'monk' mean?" How much better for us to ask "What does the word 'Circellion' mean?" "But," they say, "we are not called Circellions." Perhaps we call them that through some corruption of the sound. We will tell you their full name. Perhaps they are called Circumcellions,

not Circellions. Then, if they are called this, let them explain what they are. For they have been called "Circumcellions" because they wander "around" the monastic "cells." Indeed, they are accustomed to go here and there, having no fixed abodes anywhere, and to act as you know they do—and as they know too, whether they wish to or not.

4. And yet, dearest brothers, there are also false monks; we even know men of this sort. But devout brotherhood does not die because of those who profess to be what they are not. Indeed, there are false monks as well as false clergy and false faithful. All three types of life, my brothers, which we have at times—and not just once, I think—commended to you, have their own good and bad members. For of these three types it was said: " 'There are two men in the field; one will be taken, and the other will be left. . . . There are two men in their beds; one will be taken, and the other will be left. There are two women grinding at the mill; one will be taken, and the other will be left' " [Matt. 24:40–41, Luke 17:34–35]. The men in the field are those who pilot the Church. Thus the Apostle said (and see whether he was not in the field), "I planted, Apollo watered, but God made things grow" [1 Cor. 3:6]. By those in bed he meant to indicate those who love quiet, for by bed he meant quiet—people who do not mingle with crowds amid the bustle of the human race, but who serve God in leisure. And yet one of them will be taken, and the other will be left. There are good men there, and there are bad. Do not tremble when bad men are found there, for some also lie hidden and are found out only at the end. Likewise he names the two grinding at the mill as women, for he wanted to indicate the laity. Why grinding at the mill? Because they are living in this world, which is indicated by the mill, since this world revolves like a millstone. Woe to those whom the stone grinds down! The good faithful live there in such a way that one of them is used up and the other is taken up. For the lovers and deceivers and pretenders of this world carry out certain earthly activities. But others are present in this world just as the Apostle says: "And let those who use this world be as if people not using it. For the fashion of this world is passing away. I want you to be without care" [1 Cor. 7:31–32]. . . .

6. What, then, do those who reproach us for the name of monks say? Perhaps they are going to say "Our people are not called Circumcellions. It is you who call them by that insulting name; we do not." Let them say what they call them, and you will hear. They call them "Agonists." And we confess that this is an honorable name, if the facts agree with it. In the meantime, let your holiness consider this: let those who say to us "Show

us where the name monks has been written" show us in turn where the name "Agonists" has been written. "We call them this because of their struggle," they say. To be sure, they fight; and the Apostle says, "I have fought the good fight" [2 Tim. 4:7]. Because they are people who fight against the devil and prevail, the soldiers of Christ are called "Agonists." Would that those people, whose cry of "Praise be to God" is more feared than the roar of the lion, were soldiers of Christ and not of the devil. These men even dare to reproach us because when the brothers see people they say "Thanks be to God." They ask "What does 'Thanks be to God' mean?" Are you so without understanding that you do not know what "Thanks be to God" means? One who says "Thanks be to God" is giving thanks to God. Consider whether a brother ought not to give thanks to God when he sees his brother. For is it not an occasion for thanksgiving when people who live in Christ see each other? And yet you laugh at our "Thanks be to God"; men weep at your "Praise be to God." But certainly you have given a reason why you call them "Agonists." So be it, call them that; so be it, we are entirely in favor of it. May the Lord grant them to fight against the devil, and not against Christ, Whose Church they persecute.

Yet because they fight, you call them "Agonists," and you have found a reason to call them this, since the Apostle said "I have fought the good fight" [2 Tim. 4:7]. Why, then, should we not also use the name "monks," since the psalm says "Behold how good and how pleasant it is for brothers to live in unity"? For *monos* means "one," and not just "one" in any sense. For even in a crowd a man is alone, and he can be called one in the company of many. But he cannot be called *monos*, that is, "alone," because *monos* means "one alone." They therefore live in unity so as to make up one man, so that they really have what has been written "one soul and one heart" [Acts 4:32]. They have many bodies, but not many souls; they have many bodies, but not many hearts. They are rightly called *monos*, that is, "one alone." For this reason, too, that one man was healed in the pool [John 5:7]. Let those who reproach the name of monks respond to us and explain why that man, who was found to have been ill for thirty-eight years, said to the Lord: " 'When the water is disturbed, I have no one to put me into the pool; another climbs in before me' " [John 5:7]. One man has climbed in; now the other was not climbing in. One man alone was healed; he signified the oneness of the Church. With good reason do those who have cut themselves off from oneness reproach the name of oneness. With good reason do those who do not want to live in unity with their brothers but who, following Donatus, have put Christ aside, dislike the name of monks.

Your Christian love has heard my words on the subject of "one" and "one alone." Now let us take delight in the psalm, so that we may see what follows. The psalm is brief; we can make as much haste as the Lord allows. Indeed, I think from what I have said what follows may be obvious, although it might seem to be unclear.

7. "Behold how good and how pleasant it is for brothers to live in unity." He who said "Behold" revealed this. We see it, too, brothers, and we praise God, and pray that we, too, may say "Behold."

And let the psalm tell us what they are like: "like oil poured out upon the head, running down into the beard, into the beard of Aaron; that flows down to the hem of his robe" [Ps. 132:2]. What was Aaron? A priest. Who is a priest, but that one priest who entered into the holy of holies? Who is that priest, but the one who was both sacrifice and priest? He Who, when He did not find in the world anything clean that He might offer, offered Himself. The oil is on His head because Christ is a whole with the Church, but the oil comes from the head. Christ is our head Who, crucified, buried, and risen, ascended into Heaven; and the Holy Spirit comes from the head. Where does it go? To the beard. The beard signifies the strong; the beard signifies the young, the energetic, the active, the vigorous. For this reason, when we describe men like this, we say "He is a bearded man." Therefore, that oil flowed down first upon the Apostles; it flowed down upon those who endured the first attacks of this world. Therefore the Holy Spirit flowed down upon them. For those who were the first to begin to live in unity also suffered persecution, yet because the oil had flowed down upon the beard, they suffered but were not conquered. For the head from which the oil flowed had already suffered and had gone before them, and with the precedent of such an example, who could have conquered the beard?

8. From that beard came Saint Stephen. And not to be conquered means namely this: that Christian love is not conquered by its enemies. For the persecutors of the holy thought that they had conquered. They slaughtered, the holy were slaughtered; they killed, the holy were killed. Who would not have thought that they were conquering and that the holy were being conquered? But because Christian love was not conquered, the oil flowed down upon the beard. Consider Stephen. Christian love raged in him. He raged against them when they heard him, and he prayed for them when

they stoned him. For what was he saying when they heard him? " 'You stiff-necked and uncircumcised in heart and ears, you always resist the Holy Spirit' " [Acts 7:51]. See the beard. Did he flatter them? Did he fear them? When they heard the words that he spoke against them, Stephen was indeed like one in a rage; he raged in his speech, but in his heart he loved. And that love in him was not conquered, for they, shrinking from his words like shadows fleeing the light, began to run for stones, to stone him. Just as earlier Stephen's words stoned them, so afterward their stones stoned him. When should Stephen have become more angry—when they were stoning him, or when they were listening to him? Behold, he became calm while they stoned him, and he raged when they listened. Why did he rage when they listened? Because he wanted to change those who listened. Christian love was not conquered by the stones that fell upon it, because the oil had flowed from the head to the beard, and the beard had heard what the head had to say: " 'Love your enemies, and pray for those who persecute you' " [Matt. 5:44]. It had heard the head as He hung on the cross and said, " 'Father, forgive them, for they know not what they do' " [Luke 23:34]. So, in this way, the oil had flowed down upon the beard from the head, because Stephen, too, as he was being stoned, knelt and said " 'Lord, do not count this sin against them' " [Acts 7:60].

9. So these people were like the beard. For many of them were strong and endured many persecutions. But if the oil had not flowed down from his beard, we should not now have monasteries. Yet because it flowed down even to the edge of this robe—for so it says, "that flows down to the hem of his robe" [Ps. 132:2]—the Church followed and gave birth to the monasteries from the garment of the Lord. For the priestly garment is the image of the Church. It is this garment of which the Apostle says, "so that He might take to Himself a glorious Church, having neither stain nor wrinkle" [Eph. 5:27]. It is cleaned, so that it has no stain; it is spread out, so that it has no wrinkle. Where does the fuller spread it out, but on the wood of the cross? Every day we see that clothing is, in a sense, crucified by fullers; it is crucified, so that it has no wrinkles.

What then is the hem of the robe? What are we to understand, brothers, by the hem of the robe? The hem is the end of the robe. Is it that at the end of time the Church is to have brothers living in unity? Or ought we to understand by the "hem" "completion" because a robe is completed by its hem, and those men are complete who know how to live together in unity? Those who fulfill the law are perfect. But how is the law of Christ fulfilled by men who live as brothers in unity? Listen to the Apostle: "Bear one another's burdens, and thus you will fulfill the law of Christ" [Gal. 6:2]. This is the hem of the robe.

Brothers, how do we understand which hem he means, and to which hem the oil could flow? I do not think that he intended the edge of the robe to mean the sides, though there are edges at the sides. But the oil could trickle down from the beard only to the hem which is nearest the head and is the border of the neckline. Such are those who live in unity with one another; as a man's head slips through the hem [the neckline's border] so that he can clothe himself, so Christ, who is our head, can find an entrance through the brotherly unity, so that He may be clothed, that is, so that the Church may cling to Him.

10. What else does the psalmist say? "Like the dew of Hermon, which flows down over the mountains of Zion" [Ps. 132:3]. Brothers, by this he meant that the brothers dwell in unity by the grace of God—not by their own power, not of their own merits, but by His gift, by His grace, like the dew from heaven. For the earth does not rain upon itself, and whatever the earth has brought forth would dry up if the rain does not flow down from above. Somewhere in the psalms it says: "You will set aside a rain of your own will for your people, O Lord" [Ps. 67:10]. Why does it say "of your own will"? Because it is not by our merits but by His will. For what good have we sinners merited? What good have we wicked ones deserved? From Adam is born another Adam, and on the first Adam many sins are born. Whoever is born is born another Adam, a condemned man born from the condemned, and he increases the sins upon Adam by living in wickedness. For what good did Adam merit? And yet the merciful one loved him, and the bridegroom loved the bride, not because she was beautiful, but so that he might make her beautiful. So the Psalmist called God's grace the dew of Hermon.

11. . . . But whoever of you wish to live in unity, choose the dew of righteousness, and let it rain down upon you. Otherwise you will not be able to keep to what you profess; nor will you be able to dare to profess unless He has sounded. Nor will you be able to remain steadfast if you are without His nourishment. For that nourishment flows down upon the mountains of Sion.

12. Now, the "mountains of Sion" are the great of Sion. What is Sion? The Church. And who are the mountains there? The great. The mountains signify the same people as the beard and the hem of the robe. The beard is understood to mean only the perfect. So those in whom the love of Christ has not been made perfect do not live in unity. Those in whom the love of

Christ has not been made perfect, even though they may be in the same place, are hateful, troublesome, and quarrelsome. By their own restlessness they disturb others, just as the restless beast in the yoke not only does not pull but also breaks with his hooves whatever is yoked to him. But if a man has the dew of Hermon "that flows down over the mountains of Sion," he is quiet, peaceful, humble, and tolerant, and he pours forth his prayer instead of murmuring. For all the murmurers are splendidly described in a certain passage in Scripture: "the feelings of a fool are like a cartwheel" [Eccli. 33:5]. What does "the feeling of a fool are like a cartwheel" mean? A cartwheel carries hay, and it murmurs. For it cannot find rest from murmuring. Many brothers are like this; they do not live in unity, except in the body. But who are they who live in unity? Those of whom it has been said "And they had one soul and one heart toward God; and no one called anything his own, but they held everything in common" [Acts 4:32]. The ones who belong to the beard, those who belong to the edge of the robe, and those who are numbered among the mountains of Sion have been pointed out and described. And if there are other murmurers there, let them remember the word of God: " 'one will be taken, and the other will be left' " [Matt. 24:40].

13. "For there the Lord has ordered His blessing" [Ps. 132:3]. Where has He ordered His blessing? Upon the brothers who live in unity. There He has ordered His blessing; there those who live in harmony praise the Lord. For in discord you do not praise the Lord. You wrongly claim that your tongue sounds praise of the Lord if you do not sound it in your heart. You praise with your lips, and you curse Him in your heart. "They praised with their lips, and they cursed in their hearts" [Ps. 61:5]. Are these words my own? Certain people are meant by them. You praise the Lord when you pray; and right on the heels of your prayer, you curse your enemy. Is that what you have heard from the Lord Himself, Who said " 'Love your enemies' " [Matt. 5:44]? But if you should do as He says and love your enemy and pray for him, "there the Lord has ordered His blessing"; there you will have "everlasting life" [Ps. 132:3], that is, eternal life. For many men who love this life curse their enemies. Why do they do this, if not for this life and for earthly profit? Where has your enemy constrained you so that you are compelled to curse him? Are you constrained on earth? Depart now, and seek for yourself a dwelling place in Heaven. But, you reply, "How should I be able to live in Heaven, I, a man clothed in the flesh and delivered up to the flesh?" But hasten on ahead with your heart where you cannot follow with your body. Do not be deaf when you

hear "Lift up your hearts." Lift up your hearts to the heights, and no one will constrain you in Heaven. . . .

SERMONS 132 AND 343

"How Fair Is a Chaste Generation" (Wis. 4:1)

Augustine in his sermons often refers to individual classes in the Church, especially when he has an opportunity to demonstrate their special virtues. He always speaks with a holy enthusiasm when he reflects on those men and women who serve God in an unwedded chastity. Without detracting from the moral worth of marriage, he depicts the excellence and the rewards of an unmarried life consecrated to God.

Sermon 132

3. You who have already taken vows of chastity, discipline your bodies strictly. Be on your guard lest you slacken the bridle on your desires, even for what is permitted. Not only must you abstain from forbidden commerce; you must reject even what you are permitted to glimpse. Men and women alike, remember that you are living the life of the angels here on earth. For angels are not given in marriage; they choose no spouses for themselves.

That is how we all shall be when we have risen from the dead [Matt. 22:30]. How much better is your lot, you who even before death have begun to be what others will be only after the resurrection. Guard your calling well; for God will ensure that you adorn it. The resurrection of the dead has been compared to the stars in the heavens; "For one star differs from another in its brightness," the Apostle says; "and so it will be too with the resurrection of the dead" [1 Cor. 15:41–42]. For there virginity will shine out in one way; married chastity in another; holy virginity still differently. They will not be equally bright, but Heaven is for them all.

Sermon 343

4. Just as married women have known joy in Susanna, so virgins should rejoice in Mary. Both should preserve their chaste living, the one in marriage, the other in virginity, for each chasteness will have its reward from God. Even if virginity is the more excellent and marriage less so, still both are pleasing to Him, for both are His gifts. All will attain everlasting life. Yet in eternal life not all will receive equal honor, equal worth, equal reward. In everlasting life and in God's kingdom, it will be the same, to use a comparison, as it is now with what we call the heavens. Every con-

stellation is found there, just as every good and faithful soul will be in the kingdom of God. Eternal life will be the same for everyone; no one will have more than another, for we shall all live forever. For that is the penny the laborers will receive, whether they have toiled in the vineyard from early morning or did not arrive until the eleventh hour [Matt. 20:9–16]. That penny is eternal life, which is the same for everyone. But contemplate the heavens, and remember what the Apostle says: "Heavenly bodies are of one kind; earthly bodies of another. The sun shines in one way, but the moon differently, and the stars differently again. For one star differs from another in its brightness, and so it will be too with the resurrection of the dead" [1 Cor. 15:40–42]. Therefore, dear brethren, let everyone struggle in this world, in proportion to the gift which he has received, so that he may rejoice in the world to come.

SERMONS 355 AND 356
(PREACHED WINTER 425/426[3])

The Perfect Common Life

The occasion of these sermons was a sad one for Augustine. A priest from the clerics' monastery had made a will on his deathbed, and so had betrayed the esteemed common life. The ideal which Augustine had striven to realize with his brethren for longer than a normal lifespan, and, even more, the community's good name, could be seen to have been gravely endangered. Therefore Augustine chose to preach two public sermons on this event, in order to reprehend severely the priest's breach of faith, protect the community's reputation, and avoid such happenings in the future. He makes an earnest profession of his life's ideals, based on that perfect common way of living, modeled on what we read in the Acts of the Apostles, as this is shown to be the very soul of all men's communion of hearts in God.

Bitter disappointment has made Augustine cautious. Until then he had always opposed the notion that any of his clerics should withdraw himself from the common life and live on his own earnings. Anyone in Hippo who wished to become a cleric was obliged to enter their monastery. But now, in order not to create any cause for total alienation, he was prepared for the future to permit a life lived outside the monastery. In only one matter did he remain implacable: whoever had once vowed himself to a community and had withdrawn from it was to have no hope of being considered still one of its members.

Sermon 355

1. My wish and request of yesterday was that you assemble in great numbers today because of what I am about to say. We live here with you, and we live for you, and it is our intention and our vow to live with you without end in Christ's presence. I think that our way of life is well known to you, so that perhaps we too might dare to speak the Apostle's words, though we are greatly inferior to him: "Be imitators of me, just as I am of Christ" [1 Cor. 4:16]. And for this reason I do not want anyone to find in us an excuse for living badly. "For we are taking thought for what is good, not only in the sight of God but also in the sight of men," as the same Apostle says [2 Cor. 8:21]. For our sake a good conscience is sufficient, but for your sake our reputation must not be soiled, but must be strong among you. Pay attention to what I have said and note the difference. Conscience and reputation are two different things. Conscience concerns you; reputation concerns your neighbor. The man who, trusting in his conscience, neglects his reputation is unfeeling, especially in that situation of which the Apostle writes to his disciple: "show yourself as an example of good works before others" [Tit. 2:7].

2. I will not keep you long, especially since I am speaking seated, but you suffer standing. All of you, or almost all, know that we live in the house called the Bishop's House in such a way as to imitate to the best of our ability the saints of whom the Acts of the Apostles says: "No one called anything his own, but they held everything in common" [Acts 4:32]. Since perhaps some of you are not such careful examiners of our life that you know this as I wish you to, I will explain what I have briefly said. I, whom you see here by God's will as your bishop, came to this community as a young man, as many of you know. I was looking for a place to establish a monastery and live with my brothers. To be sure, I had left behind all worldly ambition, and I did not want to be what I might have been; and yet I did not seek to be what I am. "I chose to be cast down in the house of my God rather than to live in the tabernacles of sinners" [Ps. 83:11]. I separated myself from those who love this world, but I did not make myself equal to those who are in charge of nations. And at the banquet of my Lord, I chose, not the better place, but the lowly and humble place, and it has please Him to say to me " 'Move up' " [Luke 14:10].

Yet I so feared the bishopric that when my reputation had already begun to be of some importance among the servants of God, I did not go to any place where I knew there was no bishop. I was avoiding this position, and I was doing whatever I could to remain safe in a humble station and not to be in danger in an exalted one. But, as I have said, a servant ought not to contradict his lord. I came to this city to see a friend whom I thought I could win for God, and who would live with us in the monastery. I was relatively safe because this community had a bishop. I was seized, I was made a priest, and through this rank I came to the rank of bishop. I did not bring anything with me; I came to this church with only the clothing I was then wearing. And because I had been planning to live in a monastery with my brothers, when old Valerius of blessed memory learned of my plan and my wish, he gave me the garden in which the monastery now stands. I began to assemble brothers to be my companions in this holy undertaking, men possessing nothing just as I possessed nothing and imitating me. Just as I sold my tiny bit of property and gave the proceeds to the poor, so they too who wished to be with me did the same, that we might live from our shared resources; but what we shared would be a great and very rich estate: God Himself.

I achieved the episcopacy, and I saw that a bishop had to show constant courtesy to all those who came or went. For if a bishop did not do so, he would be called rude. Yet if this practice should be allowed in a monastery, it would not be fitting. On this account I wanted to have a monastery of clerics in my Bishop's House.

See how we live: No one in our fellowship is allowed to have any property of his own. But perhaps some people do. No one is allowed to; if some do, they are doing what is not permitted. Yet I think well of my brothers, and, trusting them, I have never given any attention to this sort of inquiry. For even to ask such questions seemed to me to be thinking ill of them. For I knew, and I know now, that all who live with us know our undertaking and the rule of our life.

3. The priest Januarius also came to us. By sharing generously he disposed of almost all he seemed to own, but not everything. He still had some money left, in silver, which he said belonged to his daughter. His daughter is by God's will in a convent, and there is great hope for her. May the Lord guide her so that she fulfills our hopes for her, not through her own merits, but through His mercy. And because she was under age and could take no action concerning her own money—indeed, although we saw the splendor of her profession, we still feared the instability of her youth—we arranged that the silver be held as if for a girl. When she came of age legally, then, she might do with it as befitted a virgin of Christ, since

she would then be able to act in the best way. While we were awaiting this, her father began to approach death. At length, he made a will, as though the money were his own, and he swore that it was his property, not his daughter's.

He made a will, I say, our priest and companion, staying with us, supported by the Church, professing a common life. He made a will and named heirs. A bitter sorrow for this fellowship! A fruit not borne of the tree that the Lord had planted. But he designated the Church as his heir. I do not want this gift; I do not love the fruit of bitterness. I sought him for God. He professed himself to our fellowship; he should have held to it; he should have carried it out. Did he own nothing? He would not have made a will. Did he own something? Then he should not have pretended to be our companion, as if he were a pauper of God. This is a great sorrow for me, brothers. I speak to your Christian love: because of this sorrow I have decided not to accept his legacy to the Church. Let what he has left belong to his children; let them do as they wish with it. For it seems to me that if I accept it, by the fact of my displeasure and my sorrow, I will be taking a share in it.

I did not want this to be kept from your Christian love. His daughter is in a convent; his son is in a monastery. He disinherited both of them: her in words of praise; him in a clause of disinheritance, that is, with censure. Moreover, I advised the Church not to accept those portions belonging to the disinherited until they have come of age legally. The Church is holding the money for them. In this way she has put an end to a dispute between her children in which I have been involved. The daughter claims "It belongs to me. You know my father always said so." The son says "You should believe my father because he could not have lied on his deathbed." What an evil this dispute is! But if these are servants of God, we will soon put an end to the quarrel between them. I will listen to them as a father, and perhaps better than their own father. I will see what the law is, and as God has willed, with a few faithful and respected brothers of your number, that is, of the laity, God willing, I will hear the case between them and put an end to it as God grants.

4. Nevertheless, I ask you, let no one criticize me because I do not want the Church to accept his legacy. First, I deplore his action; secondly, this is my decision. Many people will praise what I am about to say; but there are also those who will condemn it. It is truly difficult to satisfy both sides.

You have just heard the reading of the Gospel. " 'We played for you, and you did not dance; we sang dirges, and you did not mourn. John [the Baptist] came, neither eating nor drinking, and they say "He has a devil." The Son of Man came eating and drinking, and they say "Behold the glutton, the drinker of wine, and the friend of the tax collectors" ' " [Matt. 11:17–19]. What am I to do among those who are ready to criticize me and to bare their teeth against me if I accept the legacies of people who in anger have disinherited their children? Again, what am I to do for those for whom I play and who do not wish to dance? Those who say "See, this is why no one gives anything to the church at Hippo; this is why people on their deathbeds make no legacies to the Church: because the Bishop Augustine in his goodness"—for they bite by praising; they caress with their lips and then sink their teeth—"gives everything away and accepts nothing." Indeed, I do accept gifts. I declare that I do accept good offerings, holy offerings. But if a man is angry with his son and on his deathbed disinherits him, would I not placate him if he lived? Would I not have to reconcile him with his son? In what way, then, do I want him whose legacy I am seeking to be at peace with his own son? But clearly if he should do as I have always urged, that is, if he has one son, let him consider Christ a second; if he has two sons, let him consider Christ a third; if he has ten sons, let him make Christ the eleventh—then I accept his legacy. So because I have done this under certain circumstances, they now want to twist my goodness or the praise of my reputation into something else so that they may criticize me in another way because I do not want to accept the offerings of devout men. Let them consider how many I have accepted. What need is there to list them? Here, I name one. I accepted the legacy of the son of Julian. Why? Because he died without children.

5. I was unwilling to accept a legacy from Boniface, that is, Fatus, not out of compassion but out of fear. I did not want the Church of Christ to become a shipping line. There are many indeed who make money out of shipping. Yet there might be a storm, ships might have gone out and been wrecked. Were we to give men over to be tortured so that as is customary an inquiry could be held into the sinking of the ship, and so that men who had been rescued from the waves might be tormented by a judge? But would we have given them over? It is not at all fitting for the Church to do so. Should the Church have paid back the financial losses? From what sources would we have paid? It is not fitting for us to have a treasury. For it is not a bishop's task to hold gold in reserve and to brush aside the hand of a man who begs from him. Every day so many ask, so many groan, so many needy beseech us, that we must leave a great number of them in sadness because we have not enough to give to them all. And we should

have a treasury in case of a shipwreck? Thus, I have taken action by avoiding, not by giving. No one should praise me in this; but neither should anyone censure me. Clearly, when I gave the son what his angry father took away on his deathbed, I acted rightly. Let those who want to praise me do so; let those who do not, spare me. What more, my brothers? Let whoever has disinherited his son and wants to make the Church his heir look for someone else to accept the legacy, not Augustine; but, God willing, he will find no one. How praiseworthy was the action of the holy and venerable Bishop Aurelius of Carthage, how he filled the mouths of all who knew about it with the praise of God! A certain man who had no children and no hope of any gave all his possessions to the Church, having reserved the usufruct to himself. When children were born to him, the bishop returned what he had been given, though the man did not expect it. It was in the bishop's power not to return the property, but by the law of the court, not the law of Heaven.

6. Indeed, your Christian love should know that I have also said to the brothers who live with me that whoever has any property should either sell it and give away the profits or make it a gift and a common possession. Let the Church have it, through whom God nourishes us. And I gave them until Epiphany, for the sake of those who either have not divided with their brothers and shared what they have among their brothers, or have not yet done anything with their property because they are waiting to come of age. Let them do as they want with it, as long as they are paupers along with me, awaiting God's mercy together. But if they are not willing, as far as those who may be unwilling are concerned, certainly I am one who had decided, as you know, not to ordain any cleric who did not want to remain with me. If someone wanted to depart from our undertaking, I would be right in taking away his clerical office because he would be deserting his promise of holy fellowship and the common life he had undertaken. Behold, in your sight and in God's, I change my mind. Let those who want to have some property of their own, those for whom God and His Church are not enough, remain where they want to and where they can; I will not take away their clerical status. I do want not to have hypocrites. For who does not know that that is a bad thing? It is bad to fall away from one's undertaking, but it is worse to pretend to it. Behold, I say, he falls who deserts the fellowship of the common life, once he has undertaken it, that common life praised in the Acts of the Apostles; he falls away from his vows and from his holy profession. Let him pay heed to his judge, not me, but God! I will not take away his clerical status. I have made it clear

to him how great a danger it is; let him do what he wants. For I know that if I want to demote someone for doing this, he will not lack patrons; he will not lack support both here and among the bishops, who will say "What has he done wrong? He is not able to endure this life with you. He wants to live away from the bishop and to support himself. And for this he must lose his clerical status?" I know how wrong it is to take a solemn vow and not to fulfill it. The Scriptures say "Make a vow to the Lord your God and keep it" [Ps. 75:12] and "It is better not to make a vow than to make one and not keep it" [Eccli. 5:4]. A young woman who is a holy virgin is not permitted to marry, even if she has never been in a convent, although she is not compelled to live in a convent. But if she began to live in a convent and has deserted it, she is half ruined, even if she is still a virgin. So, too, a cleric has made two professions: to live a life of purity and to fulfill his clerical office. Inwardly he has professed a life of purity—for God has placed the clerical office on his shoulders for the sake of His own people, and it is more a burden than an honor; but "who is wise and will understand these things" [Ps. 106:43]? Therefore he has professed a life of purity, he has professed the fellowship of living in a community, he has professed "how good and how pleasant it is for brothers to live in unity" [Ps. 132:1]. If he falls away from this undertaking and, though living outside, remains a cleric, then he too has half fallen. What has this to do with me? I do not judge him. If he preserves his life of purity outside, he has half fallen; but if he makes a pretense within, he has totally fallen. I do not want him to find it necessary to pretend. I know how men love the clerical offices; I will not take an office away from anyone who does not want to live in a community with me. He who is willing to remain with me has God. If he is ready to be nourished by God through His Church, to have no possessions of his own, but either to give them to the poor or to put them into the common stock, let him remain with me. Let whoever is not willing to do this have his freedom; but let him see whether he is able to have eternal happiness.

7. For the time being let these words suffice for your Christian love. When my brothers and I have acted, I shall announce our decision to you. I hope that it will be a good one, because they all obey me gladly; nor will I find that any of them has anything, unless on the grounds of some religious necessity, not through an opportunity for greed. So by God's will I shall announce to you after Epiphany what I have done, and I shall not keep from you the way in which I have settled the dispute between a brother and a sister, the children of the priest Januarius. I have spoken at length; give

indulgence to my talkative old age or, rather, to my trembling and weakness. As you see, in years I have just recently grown old, but in bodily weakness I have been an old man for a long time. And yet, if what I have just said pleases God, may He Himself give me strength, and I will not desert you. Pray for me, that, as long as there is breath in this body and with whatever strength I have, I may serve you in the word of God.

Sermon 356

1. Today we ourselves will be the subject of the sermon given to your Christian love. For the Apostle says: "We have been made a spectacle to the world, for angels and for men" [1 Cor. 4:9]. Those who love us look for something to praise in us, but those who hate us criticize us. We are placed in the middle, and with the help of the Lord our God must so guard both our life and our reputation that our critics do not embarrass our praisers. Although many of you know from the Holy Scriptures how we wish to live, how, God willing, we are already living, nevertheless a reading from the Acts of the Apostles will be given to remind you, so that you may see where the form of life we want to fulfill has been described. And while it is being read, I want you to pay very close attention so that after the reading, if God grants it, I may tell you what I have decided.

[And Lazarus the deacon read:]

> When they prayed, the place in which they had assembled moved, and they were all filled with the Holy Spirit, and they proclaimed the word of God with all willing faith. Moreover, the multitude of believers had one soul and one heart, and no one called any of the things that he possessed his own, but they held everything in common. And with great power the Apostles gave testimony to the resurrection of our Lord Jesus, and His grace was great upon them all. And no one among them was in need, for those of them who owned property or houses sold them and brought the money from them and placed it at the feet of the Apostles. And it was shared out among them, to each according to his need [Acts 4:31–35].

[And when Lazarus the deacon had read and had given the book to the bishop, Augustine the bishop said:] And I too wish to read it to you. For it gives me more joy to read these words than to say anything of my own to you.

> When they prayed, the place in which they had assembled moved, and they were all filled with the Holy Spirit, and they proclaimed the word

of God with all willing faith. Moreover, the multitude of believers had one soul and one heart, and no one called any of the things that he possessed his own, but they held everything in common. And with great power the Apostles gave testimony to the resurrection of our Lord Jesus, and His grace was great upon them all. And no one among them was in need, for those of them who owned property or houses sold them and brought the money from them and placed it at the feet of the Apostles. And it was shared out among them, to each according to his need [Acts 4:31–35].

[And when the bishop had finished reading, he said:] You have heard what we wish for; pray that we be able to achieve it. But there is some need for me to treat this matter more fully. As you already know, there was a priest in our fellowship—the reading that you have just heard us give testifies to the sort of fellowship it is—who on his deathbed made a will since he had some possessions to bequeath. There was property that he called his own, in spite of the fact that he lived in that fellowship where no one is permitted to call anything his own, but they hold everything in common. If someone who loves and praises us were to commend our fellowship before one of our critics and were to say "All those who dwell with Bishop Augustine live with him as it is written in the Acts of the Apostles," right away that critic would shake his head, gnash his teeth, and say "Do they really live there as you say they do? Why are you lying? Why are you honoring the unworthy with false praise? Didn't a priest in their fellowship just recently make a will, and didn't he dispose of what he had and leave it as he wished? Is everything there really held in common? Does no one really call anything his own?" In the face of such words, what would the man who praises me do? Wouldn't that critic seal his lips as if with lead? Wouldn't he be sorry that he had praised us? Filled with shame and confused by the other's words, wouldn't he curse either us or the man who had made that will? This is what made it necessary for us to be so careful.

3. So I will announce a reason for you all to rejoice. I have found all the brothers and clerics who live with me, the priests, the deacons, the subdeacons, and my nephew Patricius to be such as I wished. But there are two of them, Valens the deacon and my nephew the subdeacon whom I just mentioned, who have not yet done as they had decided to do with whatever small means they possess. The support of Patricius' mother was preventing him from doing so, since she was living from his means. In the case of Valens, we were also waiting for him to come of age legally, so that whatever action he took might be permanently binding. But he has not yet

done anything because he holds those plots of ground in common with his brother, in an equal partnership. But if they should be divided, Valens wants to give them to the Church, for the support of those who have undertaken a holy life, as long as they remain in this life. For it is written, and the Apostle says "Anyone who does not provide for his own relations, and especially for members of his own household, has denied his faith and is worse than an unbeliever" [1 Tim. 5:8]. Moreover, Valens still owns some slaves in common with his brother. He plans to set them free, but he cannot do so until the property has been divided. For he does not know yet what belongs to each of them. The division of the property is for the elder, and the choice for the younger. His brother is also a servant of God; he is a subdeacon with my brother and fellow-bishop Severus in the church at Mileve. This is being taken care of; he must see to it without delay that the slaves are divided between them and set free and that he gives to the Church so that she may receive support from her brothers. But my nephew, since he was converted and began to live with me, was prevented from doing anything with his plots of land because his mother, who had the usufruct of them, was unwilling. She died this year. There are now some matters to be settled between him and his sisters quickly with the help of Christ, so that he too may do as is fitting for a servant of God and as his profession and this reading demand.

4. Faustus the deacon, as almost all of you know, converted to our monastery from the warfare of this world. Here he was baptized and then ordained a deacon. But because what he seemed to possess was small, he had left it, as the legal scholars say, in fact and not in law,[4] and it was held by his brothers. He never thought about the life from which he converted, and he did not ask anything of his brothers nor they of him. Now, at this critical time, he has divided his property according to my advice: he has given half to his brothers and half to the needy church of this place.

5. You know how Severus the deacon lives under the discipline and scourge of God, and yet he has not lost the light of his intellect. He bought a house here for his mother and sister, whom he wanted to bring here from his homeland. Moreover, he did not buy it with his own money, since he had none, but with a donation from worshippers, whom he identified by name at my request. I cannot say what he has done with that house, or what he now plans to do, except that he has placed it entirely at my disposal, so that whatever I might wish could be done with it. But he has certain legal matters with his mother, over which he has made me a judge. As soon as these matters have been settled, let what I have decided about the house

be done. Yet if God directs me, what can I wish, except what righteousness orders and piety demands? He also owns some plots of land in his homeland; he plans to distribute them in such a way that in this as well he may bestow a gift upon the poor of the church there.

6. The deacon of Hippo is a poor man and has nothing to give to anyone. Nevertheless, before he became a cleric, he had bought through his own labor some slaves, whom he is going to set free today in your sight, as will be registered in the Acts of the Bishop.

7. The life of the deacon Heraclius lies before you, and his works shine before your eyes. From his work and at his expense we have the shrine of the holy martyr.[5] From his own funds he also, following my advice, bought an estate, for he wanted his money to be dispensed through my hands and according to my wish. If I were greedy for money or cared more in this instance for my own needs, which I have because of the poor, I would accept the money. "Why?" someone asks. Because the estate that he bought and gave to the Church does not yet bring the Church any income. For he had less than the purchase price and, because he had borrowed, he is still paying back the amount from the income. I am an old man; how much income from that estate can come to me? Am I to promise that I will live for so many years, until it repays its purchase price? If I had wanted to take it, at this moment I could have the entire amount, which will hardly come in by installments over a long period of time. I did not do so; I had something else in mind. For I confess to you that I mistrusted his youth and was afraid that, as is man's nature, he might be displeasing his mother in this matter; and she might say that I exerted influence on a young man in order to spend his patrimony and leave him in need. Thus I wanted his money to be kept in that estate, so that if something turned out other than we wished—God forbid!—the estate could be returned and the bishop's reputation would not be faulted. For I know how essential my good reputation is to you; for me, my good conscience is enough.

As you know, he also bought a plot of land with money he later received from the Church, and he built a house with his own money. You know this too. A few days before I was to give you a sermon on this subject, he gave the house to the Church. This, again, you know. For he was waiting until he could complete it and give it in a finished state. Moreover, he had no need to build a house unless he thought that his mother would come here. If she had come before, she would have been living from her son's property; if she comes now, she will live in his house. I testify on his behalf that he has remained a pauper; yet he has remained in an estate of Christian love. He has had a few servants remaining and living in the monastery, and today he will set them free, recording the action in the Acts of the Bishop. Let no one say then that he is rich; let no one think it; let no one speak evil of him, or rend himself or his soul with his teeth. The man has no money. And he has no money set aside. I hope that he will be able to pay back what he owes!

8. The others, that is, the deacons, are paupers and, God willing, they await His mercy. They have nothing to give away, and, having no means, they have finished with worldly desires. They live in shared fellowship with us, and no one distinguishes them from the people who have contributed something. The unity of Christian love is to be placed before the advantage of earthly legacies.

9. There remain the priests. For I wanted to climb step by step to them, like this. Let me say immediately that they are paupers of God. They have brought nothing to the house of our fellowship but Christian love, and there is not anything more valuable than that. And yet, since I know that rumors have arisen about their wealth, I must justify them to you through my words.

10. I will tell those of you who perhaps do not know (for most of you know), although the priest Leporius is of distinguished ancestry in the world and was born into a family of very high rank, I nevertheless received him as a pauper when he was already serving God and had left all his possessions behind. I accepted him not because he possessed nothing, but because he had already done what this reading suggests. He did not do it here, but we know where he did do it. The unity of Christ is one; the Church is one. Wherever a man has done a good work, it belongs to us if we rejoice together in it. There is a garden well known to you; there he established a monastery for his brothers, because they too serve God. That garden does not belong to the Church; nor does it belong to him. "And to whom does it belong?" some might ask. It belongs to the monastery that is there. And it is a fact that right up until today he took so much care of them that he kept by him the small sums by which they live and paid out the money himself as he thought best. But so that men who gnaw at their suspicions and fail to fill their stomachs with them might not find an opportunity for criticism on this account, both he and I agreed that the brothers should live as if he had already departed from this world. For when he has died, is he going to distribute anything to them? It is better that he should see them living a holy life there and living in such a way under God's rule and Christ's teaching that he may only rejoice over them

and not concern himself with their needs. Therefore he too has no money which we can or dare to call his own. He had to build a guest house, and you see now that it has been built. I enjoined this upon him; I ordered it. He obeyed me most willingly and, as you see, he has been active, just as, following my orders, he also built the basilica to the eight martyrs from the means God gave us through you. For he began from the money given to the Church for the guest house, and when he had begun to build, since there are worshipers who want their good works to be noted down in Heaven, they helped him, each one as much as he wanted, and the building was finished. We have his work before our eyes; each man sees what has been accomplished. Let them believe me about the money: he did not have it. Let them not gnash their teeth lest they break. From the money for the guest house he had bought a certain house in Carraria, which he thought would be useful to him because of its stone. But the stones from this house were not needed for building the other, since stones were supplied from some other source. So that house remained as it was, and it provides a rent—but to the Church, not to the priest. Let no one continue saying "into the priest's house," "before the priest's house," "to the priest's house." Look—see where the priest's house is. Where my house is, there the priest's house is. He has no house anywhere else, but he has God everywhere.

11. What more do you seek? Only this: for me to remember that I also promised to report to you what I did in the case of those two, the brother and sister, children of the priest Januarius, since a quarrel had arisen between them (but, as happens between brothers and sisters, without diminishing their Christian love, God willing). Thus, I had promised to listen to them in order, by giving a judgment, to put an end to whatever was between them. I had prepared myself to adjudicate, but before I could do so, they themselves put an end to the matter I was to decide. I found a cause, not for adjudication, but for rejoicing. In complete harmony they acquiesced in my will and my advice: that they share equally in the money their father had left and that the Church refuse it.

12. After this sermon of mine, men are going to talk, but whatever they may say, some of it will reach my ears on whatever wind is blowing. But if their talk is such that we must again justify ourselves, I shall respond to the critics, I shall respond to the slanderers, I shall respond to the unbelievers, to those who do not put credence in what their superiors say, I shall respond to the best of my ability, as God grants me to do it. For the time being, it is not necessary to respond, because perhaps they are not

going to say anything. Those who love us will rejoice freely; those who hate us will grieve quietly. Yet if they exercise their tongues, they will hear in your presence, God willing, my defense, not my accusation. For I am not going to name people and say: This one said this, this one made this criticism, when perhaps even false reports are brought to me, since this too can happen. And yet I will speak to your Christian love of whatever may be reported, if it seems necessary. I want our life to be before your eyes. I know that the people who seek a license to do evil seek the example of those who live in evil, and they speak ill of many so that they may seem to have found companions. For this reason we have done what is in our power; there is nothing more we can do. We are before your eyes. We desire nothing from anyone except your good works.

13. And I urge you, my brothers, if you want to give anything to the clerics, to be aware lest you foster their vices, as it were, against me. Offer what you will to all; offer of your own accord. What is held in common will be distributed to each according to his need. Place it in the Church's treasury, and we will all share it. It gives me great pleasure if this is our manger, so that we can be God's draft oxen and you His field. Let no one give a byrrus or a linen tunic[6] unless he gives it to the community. Let each one receive what he receives from the community. I accept things from the community for myself also, since I know that I want to hold whatever I hold in common. I do not want your holiness to offer the sort of gifts that only I may fittingly use. Someone offers, for example, a valuable byrrus. Perhaps it is fitting for a bishop, but it is not fitting for Augustine—that is, for a poor man born of poor parents. Some people will say that I have found expensive clothing that I could not have had either in my father's house or in my worldly profession. It is not fitting; I ought to have the sort of clothing that I can give to my brother if he has none. I am willing to accept such clothing as a priest may have, or a deacon and a subdeacon may fittingly have, because I accept it for the community. If someone gives something better, I sell it, and I do so often so that when a garment cannot be shared, its price may be. I sell it, and give the money to the poor. If it pleases someone for me to have a garment, then let him give me one that does not embarrass me. For, I confess to you, I am embarrassed by expensive clothing, because it is not fitting for this profession, for this instruction, for these limbs, for these white hairs.

I say this too: if someone in our house or in our fellowship happens to be ill, or is recovering from an illness, so that it is necessary for him to eat before lunchtime, I do not prevent faithful men and women from sending whatever they think it good to send. Yet no one will take his luncheon or his dinner outside.

14. Behold, I say, you have heard, and they have heard. If someone wants to have his own property and to live from it and to act contrary to our orders, it is not enough for me to say "He will not remain with me"; "he will also no longer be a cleric." Indeed, I had said, and I know that I said it, that if they were not willing to undertake our life of fellowship, I would not take away their clerical office, but they would remain apart and live apart, and they would live for God insofar as they knew how. And yet I have made it clear to them what a great evil it is to fall away from their undertaking. For I prefer to have even lame men with me than to weep for dead men—for the man who is a hypocrite is dead. So just as I would not take away a clerical office from whoever had wished to remain outside the community and to live from his own property, so too, God willing, I do not allow whoever has lived in hypocrisy, whoever has been found to have property, to make a will concerning it just because this life of fellowship has pleased him. Rather I will delete his name from the list of the clergy. Let him invoke a thousand councils against me, let him sail against me wherever he may wish, indeed let him live where he may, God will help me so that where I am bishop he cannot be a cleric. You have heard, and they have heard. But I have hope in our God and in His mercy that just as they have received this instruction of mine gladly, so they will keep it truly and faithfully.

15. I have said that the priests who live with me, including the priest Barnabas, do not have any property of their own. But I have heard certain rumors about him, above all that he has bought an estate from my beloved and respected son Eleusinus. This is untrue. Eleusinus did not sell it; he gave it to the monastery. I am a witness. I do not know what more you ask. I am a witness: he did not sell it; he gave it. Though no one believes that he could have given it, every one believes that he sold it. He is a happy man who has done such a good work that no one believes it. At least believe it now and stop listening with pleasure to his critics. As I have already said, I am a witness. It has been said of him that in his year as superior, he contracted debts on purpose, so that when I wanted the debts to be repaid, I would give him the estate at Victorianum at his request, as if he had said to me "Give me the estate at Victorianum for ten years, so that I may pay back my debts." This too is untrue. But this is how the rumor started. He did contract debts that had to be repaid. We have repaid them in part, as

much as we could. The monastery that God had founded through him had something left that was owed. Since there was something left, we began to ask how we could repay the debt. No one who came forward to rent the estate offered more than forty gold pieces. But we saw that the estate could bring in more so that the debt might be repaid more quickly. And I entrusted it to him to see to it that the brothers would not seek any profit from the lease, but whatever the estate brought in, they would put toward repaying the debt. And this is being done faithfully. The priest is ready for me to choose someone else to repay the brothers from the profits. Let the person to whom I entrust this matter be someone from your number, someone from among the people who brought these reports to us. For there are among you worshipers who grieved that he had been criticized falsely, and yet believed that he had done what was rumored. So let someone of these people come to us; let him take possession of the land; let him faithfully sell all its products at his own price, so that the debt can be repaid more easily. And the priest's concern on this account will vanish today. That place where my respected son Eleusinus, mentioned earlier, established a monastery was given to the priest Barnabas before he was ordained to the priesthood. And there he established a monastery. But now, because the place had been given to him in his own name, he has changed the deed so that it may be held in the monastery's name.

As far as the estate at Victorianum is concerned, I ask, I urge, I request, that if anyone is a worshiper, he will act faithfully and render this service to the Church so that I may quickly repay the debt. But if no one is found from among the laity, I will propose someone else. The same man who has been there will not return. What more do you wish? Let no one torment the servants of God, because it does not do the tormentors any good. The reward of God's servants increases through false criticism, but the punishment for the critics increases as well. Not without reason was it said " 'Rejoice and be glad, when they revile you, speaking all that is evil, because your reward is very great in Heaven' " [Matt. 5:11–12]. Let us have less there, and yet let us rule there with you.

NOTES

1. B. Lohse, *Mönchtum und Reformation: Luthers Auseinandersetzung mit dem Mönchsideal des Mittelalters* (Göttingen, 1963), pp. 70f.

2. Cf. on this G. Folliet, "Les trois catégories de chrétiens a partie de Luc (17:34–36), Matthieu (24:40–41), et Ezéchiel (14:14): Etude de ce thème augustinien," AM II, pp. 631–44.

3. On this dating, see A. Kunzelmann, "Die Chronologie der Sermones des hl. Augustinus," MA II, pp. 417–520 at 509.

4. *Corpore non iure*: on the meaning of this technical term in the Roman law of the late classical period, see E. Albertario, "Di alcuni riferimenti al matrimonio e al possesso in Sant'Agostino," *S. Agostino* (Milan, 1931), pp. 374–76.

5. Augustine refers here to the chapel which was added on to the "Basilica of Peace" in 424 as a fitting repository for the relics of St. Stephen. Cf. *City of God* 22.8.17–22; Roetzger, *Des heiligen Augustinus Schriften*, pp. 72f., and Zellinger, *Augustin und die Volksfrömmigkeit*, pp. 54ff., 73. It is believed that the ruins of this *memoria* have been rediscovered in the excavated ecclesiastical quarter of ancient Hippo. See above, p. 48.

6. The byrrus and the tunic were the two principal pieces of clothing current in North Africa at that time. The byrrus was a hooded cloak, made primarily of wool, which was worn, like a mantle, over the tunic, a long-sleeved undergarment.

13

Possidius' Life of Augustine

(WRITTEN BETWEEN 431 AND 439)

St. Augustine's Monastic Life

This is an account by one of Augustine's contemporaries, who could say of himself: "By God's grace I was permitted to live with such a man for almost forty years as an intimate and dear friend; and now with all my powers I am trying to live as he did."[1] Possidius was a somewhat younger African contemporary of Augustine's, and had been his companion in the early days of the garden monastery at Hippo. In 397 he became bishop of Calama in Numidia. Even if he did not succeed in drawing a true portrait of Augustine's personality,[2] yet his account is important, especially for Augustine's monastic life, many details of which only he recorded.

2. And soon Augustine gave up all his worldly ambitions from the innermost depths of his heart. No longer seeking a wife, or sons of his flesh, or riches, or worldly honors, he decided rather to serve God with his brothers, eager to be both in and of that little flock the Lord addressed with the words " 'Fear not, little flock, for it has pleased your Father to give you a kingdom. Sell what you possess and give alms. Get for yourselves purses that do not wear out, a treasure in Heaven that will not fail you' " [Luke 12:32–33], and so forth. And this same holy man wanted to do as the Lord said: " 'Sell what you have. If you wish to be perfect, go and give to the poor, and you will have treasure in Heaven; and come, follow Me' " [Matt. 19:21].

And he wanted to build on the foundation of faith, not "in wood, hay, and straw, but in gold, silver, and precious stones" [1 Cor. 3:12]. At that time he was over thirty years of age, and only his mother was still alive—she lived with him and rejoiced more in the plan he had undertaken for serving God than in grandchildren from his body—for his father was already dead. He also announced to his students, whom he instructed in rhetoric, that they should find themselves another teacher because he had decided to serve God.

3. And when he had received the grace [of baptism], he decided to return to Africa and his own home and lands in the company of some countrymen and friends who were serving God in the same way. Upon arriving and settling there, he abandoned all worldly cares and lived nearly three years for God, in the company of the people who were close to him, in fasting, prayers, and good works, "meditating on the law of the Lord day and night" [Ps. 1:2]. And through his sermons and his books he instructed people both near and far in the things that God made known to him in contemplation and prayer. . . .

5. So, having become a priest, he soon established a monastery within the church, and began with the servants of God to live according to the manner and the rule of the holy Apostles. Above all, no one in this community was to have anything of his own; everything was to be held in common, and there was given to everyone according to his need [Acts 4:32–35]. He himself had lived in this way earlier, when he had returned to his homeland from Italy. . . .

11. As the sacred teaching spread, those who served God in the monastery under the holy Augustine's leadership and in his company began to be ordained as clerics for the church at Hippo. And, then, as the truth of the Catholic Church's preaching, and the holy life, continence, and complete poverty of God's holy servants grew in reputation and daily became more famous, the peace and unity of the Church began to seek bishops and clerics from the monastery which owed both its existence and its growth to this remarkable man; and these requests were later honored. For the blessed Augustine gave some ten holy and venerable men, continent and of the greatest learning, who were known to me personally, to various churches, even some of the better known ones. And likewise these ten, coming out of that community of holy men, increased the number of churches and founded monasteries. And as the zeal to teach God's word increased, they presented to other churches brothers as candidates for the priesthood.

22. Augustine's clothing and shoes and even his bedclothes were of moderate and suitable appearance, neither too splendid nor too lowly. For often men either pay too much attention to these things or ignore them completely, and in both instances they are seeking, not Jesus' interests, but their own. But he, as I have said, held to the middle course, turning neither to the right nor to the left. He kept a frugal and simple table, which, along

with greens and legumes, also occasionally offered meat for guests or for the sick; but he always served wine. For he knew and taught the words of the Apostle, that "every creature of God is good, and nothing is to be rejected that is received with thanksgiving; for it is sanctified by the word of God and prayer" [1 Tim. 4:4–5]. . . . His only silver utensils were spoons; the other vessels in which food was placed on his table were of earthenware, wood, or alabaster. This was done through voluntary choice not because of poverty. Yet he always provided hospitality. At the table he preferred reading or conversation to eating and drinking, and to counteract a contagious habit of men he had these words inscribed on his table:

If anyone feeds by biting at other men's backs,
He will not find at this table the food that he lacks.

In this way he warned every guest to refrain from unnecessary and malicious tales and from criticism. Indeed, at one time he severely reprimanded even some fellow-bishops, very close friends of his, who had forgotten about the inscription, saying in great agitation that either those lines had to be erased from the table or that he himself would get up in the middle of the meal and go to his room. I myself heard this, as did others who were present at that meal.

23. He was always mindful of those living in poverty, and he gave to them out of the same source from which he provided for himself and all those living with him—that is, either from the income from the estates of the Church or from the offerings of the faithful. And whenever envy of the clergy happened to arise because of the Church's estates, as it often did, he addressed the people of God, saying that he preferred to live from their offerings rather than be bothered with the care and management of those estates. And he claimed that he was prepared to yield the lands to the laity, so that all God's servants and ministers might live as the Old Testament says: "each one who serves the altar taking a share from it" [Deut. 18:1; cf. 1 Cor. 9:13].

24. He delegated the management of the church's house and all its property to the more qualified clergymen in turns. He himself had no key and wore no signet ring on his finger. These same superiors kept a record of everything brought in or paid out, and at the end of the year, the receipts and expenditures were read to him so that he would know how much had been taken in, how much had been paid out, and what remained. In many official matters he relied on the trustworthiness of the overseers instead of investigating the evidence and the proof. He never had any desire to purchase a house, land, or estate. Yet if anyone of his own free will gave any-

thing to the Church or left any legacy, he would not refuse it, but would order the Church to accept it. . . . Not passionately interested or involved in the Church's holdings and possessions, he was dedicated and devoted instead to higher, more spiritual matters. It was with difficulty that at times he tore himself away from the contemplation of the eternal things and turned toward temporal affairs. As soon as these temporal matters had been put in proper order, he redirected his mind, as if away from gnawing and troublesome problems, toward the inner and higher concerns of the intellect, so that he might contemplate the discovery of divine knowledge, dictate something that he had already discovered, or emend something that had already been dictated and transcribed. And he did this, working by day and toiling by lamplight at night. He was an image of the Church in Heaven, like Mary, that most devout woman, of whom it is written that she sat at the feet of the Lord and listened attentively to His words. And when her sister complained that Mary did not help her, although she was busy with many tasks, she heard this answer: " 'Martha, Martha, Mary has chosen the better part, which will not be taken away from her' " [Luke 10:39–41].

He had no interest at all in new buildings, and avoided involving his mind in these matters; for he always wanted to keep it free from all worldly annoyances. Nevertheless, he did not prevent those who wanted to construct new buildings from doing so, except those who were extravagant. From time to time when the Church was without money he announced to the Christian people that he had nothing to share out among the poor. Indeed, he even ordered some of the holy vessels to be broken and melted down and [the proceeds] distributed among the poor, to help prisoners and as many of the needy as possible. . . .

25. The clerics always lived with him, even in the same house, and they were fed at the same table and clothed at common expense. And lest anyone should sink through swearing oaths easily to swearing oaths falsely, he both preached to the people in the church and instructed the members of his own household not to swear, not even at the table. But if one of them slipped, that one would forfeit one drink from his ration; for the people living and eating with him had a fixed number of drinks. He rebuked infractions of discipline and transgressions against the propriety of the *Rule* and good morals, yet he tolerated them as much as was fit and proper. . . .

26. No women ever lived in his house, and none ever stayed there—not even his widowed sister, who lived for a long time in the service of God, right up to the day of her death, as a superior of His handmaidens; or his

cousins and nieces, who also served God. And the councils of the holy bishops have made these people exceptions! Indeed, he used to say that even if no suspicion of evil could arise concerning his sister and his nieces if they lived with him, nonetheless since they required other women to stay with them as attendants, and because still other women would be coming in from the outside to visit them, some temptation or stumbling block to the weak could arise; and with all these women living there with them or visiting, the men who lived with the bishop or perhaps with some cleric might either come to ruin through human temptation or be seriously slandered by people's wicked suspicions. For this reason, then, he used to say that women ought never to remain in the same house with the servants of God, not even with the purest of men, lest, as has been said, some stumbling block or temptation be placed before the weak by such an example. And if, by chance, some women asked to see him or to greet him, they could never enter his presence without a cleric as a witness; nor did he ever speak in private with unaccompanied women, even if it was a question of some confidential matter.

31. Augustine lived seventy-six years, and was a cleric or a bishop for about forty years. . . . He was whole in all his limbs, and his sight and hearing were unimpaired. As we stood by, looking on and praying with him, he, as the saying goes, "went to sleep with his fathers" [3 Kings 2:10], "advanced in happy old age" [1 Chron. 29:28]. And in our presence a Mass was offered to God to commemorate the burial of his body, and he was laid to rest. He made no will because, as a pauper of God, he had no property to leave. He always used to instruct that the church's library and all its books were to be maintained carefully for later generations. But if the church possessed any money or valuables, he left them in the trust of the priest who under his leadership had the care of the church's house. And in life and death he did not treat his relatives, whether in religious life or outside it, as people generally do. While he was still alive, if they needed anything, he gave to them as to others, not so that they would be rich, but so that they would be either less needy or not needy at all. To the Church he left a large number of clergy, and monastic communities of men and women, filled with chaste brothers and sisters and their superiors, along with libraries containing books and treatises which he and other holy men had written. From these books by God's gift we can learn what sort of man he was, what a great man he was in the Church. And in these books the faithful can find him living forever. . . .

NOTES

1. Possidius 31.

2. For this, see Diesner, "Possidius und Augustinus," pp. 355f., and Gessel, *Eucharistische Gemeinschaft*, p. 52*n*18. I agree with Gessel in considering Diesner's attitude too negative.

CONCLUSION

Augustine's Significance for Christian Monasticism

AUGUSTINE HAS BEEN DESCRIBED as the greatest philosopher of the patristic period and without doubt the Church's most influential theologian. He "combined Tertullian's creative powers and Origen's breadth of spirit with Cyprian's feeling for the Church, Aristotle's dialectical acuity with Plato's idealizing brio and deep speculation, a Latin's practicality with a Greek's spiritual vivacity."[1] Nor is it easy to overestimate his significance for the history of Christian monasticism.

Augustine presided over the cradle of Western monastic life. Well over a hundred years before Benedict, he formulated the oldest Western monastic rule. From its beginnings his *Rule* exercised important influence on monastic life in the West. Indeed, once the great orders founded during the High Middle Ages took it over as their rule, it entered on a triumphal progress through the centuries.

Nor is Augustine's importance in Christian monastic history confined merely to his having been the first to attempt to impose regular dimensions on the life in monasteries through written norms. His principal achievement is the philosophical form and the theological depth he gave to the monastic ideal. In this, as in so many other theological and religious questions, he proved himself to be "prodigal of genius and of thought."[2]

Christian monasticism received its earliest form from the holy man Anthony; it was an anchoritic life spent in severe penance. Practical reasons, and even dissensions among the hermits, prompted Pachomius, around the year 320, to establish the first monastery and thus lead the anchorites out of the wilderness back into human society. By imposing wise restraints, obedience, and monastic order on the independence of individual religious, Pachomius gave a new direction to Christian monastic ideals.[3]

Basil (d. 379) some decades later decisively determined that the cenobitic, not the eremitical, way of life represented the more perfect realization of the Christian life; for only in community could all the Lord's commands find fulfillment and all virtues be practiced.[4] Basil was especially concerned to direct the lives of his monks according to Holy Scripture and to base the individual prescriptions of his monastery on the Bible. And he made a break with the Egyptian cenobites, who had by now become culturally alienated. His monasteries became places for a native training.[5]

Augustine learned of the cenobitic way of life of the East as a new convert, and was inspired by it.[6] But he was far more than a mere conduit of Eastern ascetic ideals to the West, as his contemporaries Jerome and Cassian in the main were. Augustine, who has been called the greatest of the Church Fathers, placed the stamp of his own personality on Christian monastic thinking. His ideals of monastic living were a new and independent creation.

Augustine shifted the notion of community to the center of monastic life. The chief thought behind his ideal of life was to form a community of Christian love and in that community to do everything possible to represent in its perfection the Christian ethic of living. This, above all, is the uniqueness of his monasticism.

He contributed much to inspire and deepen the life of religious. In the early years of monasticism, works dealing with external ascetic practices were too much in evidence. But after Augustine there was no longer any question of how numerous and how difficult such ascetic exercises should be. The difference, thenceforth, was always one of inner intention. A prayer devoid of interior content was always an affront to God. What the lips might say must have its echo in the heart. Similarly, merely external observance of the evangelical precepts would remain fruitless. Augustine sought to promote poverty of the spirit and continence of the heart. In his view, the whole of monastic life should be an unforced service of God, a service of "free men," that is, of the free children of God.

In yet another respect, Augustine gave powerful support to monastic ideals. Christian monasticism had developed in the East, and in its views of life and its external forms manifested much that had no appeal to men in the West. This lack of balance had to be overcome if the monastic way of life was to take hold in the West. In *The Ways of the Catholic Church*, an early work, Augustine reports the twofold reproach the people of his day were making against the hermits of the Egyptian desert: they had gone too far in their penitential practices and they were non-productive members of society.[7] Making essential corrections in these two areas, Augustine set the human measure and apostolic direction of monastic life, and thereby created a monasticism with a Western spirit.

Benedict has been praised for his genius in introducing the concept of discretion into monastic life, and for masterfully combining, in his *Rule*, all the fertile elements of monastic existence into a balanced totality: severity and meekness, solitariness and community, prayer and work.[8] But Augustine had preceded him in this. His ideal monk is marked especially by compassion and discretion. Augustine had a rich experience of life and a knowledge of humanity, but, more than that, he had a loving and understanding heart. Whenever he stresses what is essential in his monastic legislation, he shows himself to be gentle and compassionate. He condemns ascetic excesses and obsessions; he abhors the severities of Eastern monasticism. He encourages prudence in all dealings with the sick and the weak, as well as with those who had once lived in better circumstances. He is ready to make exceptions in his monasteries. The whole idea of perfection which he draws for his subjects is governed by a prudent moderation, to answer to the special needs and weaknesses of individuals and to the circumstances of their lives.

Moreover, the Western stamp of Augustinian monasticism manifests itself in its ecclesial and specifically apostolic character. It was not just that Augustine urged his monks to participate with all their powers in the life of the Church. Through his foundation of the clerics' monastery, he sent his clergy to serve in pastoral work, and encouraged this in other North African clerics' monasteries. Here he was observing a basic precept: if Mother Church asks one to serve, one cannot refuse. The needs of the Church demand that we forgo our own peace and contemplation.[9] This union of the two lives, the sacerdotal and the monastic, was more to him than a solution imposed by necessity, for he sought to harmonize what he had found in cenobitic monastic ideals with the goals of the sacerdotal life.

From its beginning, Augustine's monastic life was rooted in the Mystical Body of Christ. He viewed his community as a precious limb of the Body of the Lord, manifesting the vitality of the Church itself. For the Church "gave birth to monasteries from the garment of the Lord."[10] Monasticism is, therefore, a call from God to collaborate in the perfection of the Body of Christ. Thus Augustine saw in apostolic activity a service of love—sacrificial, to be sure, and yet consonant with the monastic ideal of life—to be performed for Christ and His members which, out of his awareness of monasticism's joint responsibility for the entire Church, he thoroughly endorsed as a life's work.

And on this rests Augustine's importance for the subsequent life of religious orders in the Church. Even if he was not the first to have founded a monastic community of pastoral workers, still he gave to this new way of life a spiritual foundation, formed from the concept of the Mystical Body of Christ. In this, he released for the apostolic and charitable work of the Church the religious and moral powers that monasticism possessed.

Augustine's formation of Christian monastic thought is, in comparison with the cenobitic ideals of the East, a new and independent creation. And even when compared with later Western monastic institutions, such as the Benedictine or the Franciscan, his still possesses its own characteristics, which can be discerned today, with varying degrees of clarity, in Augustinian communities.

As far as influence on and importance for later monastic living in the Catholic Church is concerned, Augustine and Benedict have been ranked alongside one another, and justifiably so.[11] Benedict's importance consists primarily in his achievements as an organizer. He codified the monastic legislation of his times. In this, he created no new ideas; but he extracted his material with skill from the traditions of the Church.[12] His *Rule* contains much derived from Augustine's thought.[13]

Augustine, on the other hand, stands at the beginning of Western monastic life as one of its great instructors. By the power of his spirit, he illumined and deepened the monastic ideals which had migrated from the East, and with the zeal of his heart he won for himself friends and disciples. In this way "he had achieved the most, in tending and forming that life dedicated to God,"[14] and still today much of his ascetic and monastic thinking lives on in the religious life of the Catholic Church.

NOTES

1. Altaner, *Patrologie*, p. 378.
2. Reul, *Die sittlichen Ideale*, p. 160.
3. Grützmacher, *Pachomius und das älteste Klosterleben*, pp. 115ff.; H. Bacht, "Pakhôme—der grosse 'Adler,'" *Geist und Leben*, 22 (1949), 367–82; idem, "Antonius und Pachomius"; Biedermann, "Die Regel des Pachomius und die evangelischen Räte."
4. Basil, *Regulae fusius tractatae* ("Longer Rules") 7 and 35 (PG 31.928ff., 1004ff.).

5. M. G. Murphy, *St. Basil and Monasticism* (Washington, 1930), pp. 68, 94ff.; D. Amand, *L'Ascèse monastique de Saint Basile* (Maredsous, 1949), pp. 118ff., 341ff.

6. Whether Augustine knew the *Rule* of Pachomius and the two by Basil cannot be determined. His knowledge of Greek was so defective he could scarcely have read the original texts (see Altaner, *Kleine patristische Schriften*, pp. 129–63). At about this time Basil's monastic rules received treatment in Latin by Rufinus, and this version soon became known in the West (cf. Spreitzenhofer, *Entwicklung des alten Mönchtums*, pp. 41ff.). Pachomius' *Rule* was not translated until the year 404, when Jerome produced an amplified version of a Greek text.

7. "For they appeared to some to have abandoned human affairs more completely than they should, . . . to have promoted the temperance and continence to be observed by the Catholic Church's greatest saints to such an extent that it seemed to certain men that they should be restrained and, as it were, recalled to a realization of what is humanly possible" (*The Ways of the Catholic Church* 1.31.65).

8. Dessauer, "Geist des Abendlandes," 505ff. Cf. Graf, "Zur Wesensstruktur des benediktinischen Geistes," 13ff.; F. Zoepfl, "Regula sancta—Zum Benediktusjahr," *Geist und Leben*, 20 (1947), 307f. By contrast, Walter, "Die benediktinische Discretio," begins by conceding that *discretio* is not exclusively Benedictine.

9. *Letter 48* 2.

10. *Exposition of Psalm 132* 9.

11. Cf. Mausbach, *Die Ethik*, I 46f.: "His actions and monastic legislation, like those of Benedict, influenced later developments of conventual life in the most decisive fashion."

12. Cf. Herwegen, *Der heilige Benedikt*, passim. For the close relationship between the Benedictine *Rule* and the so-called "Rule of the Master" (*Regula Magistri*), see Steidle, pp. 14–32.

13. See above, chap. 4, note 71.

14. Mausbach, *Die Ethik*, I 353.

BIBLIOGRAPHY

Adam, A. "Das Fortwirken des Manichäismus bei Augustin." *Zeitschrift für Kirchengeschichte*, 69 (1958), 1–25.

Adam, K. *Die Eucharistielehre des heiligen Augustin.* Paderborn, 1908.

——. *Die geistige Entwicklung des heiligen Augustinus.* Augsburg, 1931.

Agterberg, M. *Ecclesia–Virgo: Etude sur la virginité de l'Eglise et des fidèles chez Saint Augustin.* Héverlé & Louvain, 1960.

Albertario, E. "Di alcuni riferimenti al matrimonio e al possesso in Sant' Agostino." *S. Agostino.* Milan, 1931. Pp. 361–76.

Alès, A. d'. "Le *De agone christiano.*" *Gregorianum*, 11 (1930), 131–45.

Alfaric, P. *L'Evolution intellectuelle de Saint Augustin.* Paris, 1918.

Altaner, B. *Patrologie.* 6th ed. Freiburg, 1960.

——. *Kleine patristische Schriften.* Berlin, 1967.

Alvarez, L. "San Agustín y la ley del trabajo." *Religion y Cultura*, 11 (1930), 224–38.

Alvarez Turienzo, S. "San Agustín y la soledad." *Giornale di Metafisica*, 9 (1954), 377–406.

Amand, D. *L'Ascèse monastique de Saint Basile.* Maredsous, 1948.

Antolín, G. "Historia y descripción de un 'Codex regularum' del siglo IX." CD, 75 (1908), 23–33, 460–71, 637–49; 76 (1908), 310–23, 457–70; 77 (1908), 48–56, 130–36.

Arbesmann, R. "Christ the *Medicus humilis* in St. Augustine." AM II. Pp. 623–29.

——. "The Concept of *Christus medicus* in St. Augustine." *Traditio*, 10 (1954), 1–28.

——. *Aurelius Augustinus: Der Nutzen des Fastens.* Würzburg, 1958.

——, and Hümpfner, W. *Jordani de Saxonia Liber Vistasfratrum.* New York, 1943.

Armas, G. "La continencia perfecta en la ética agustiniana." *Augustinus*, 1 (1956), 559–71.

Auer, J. "Militia Christi: Zur Geschichte eines christlichen Grundbildes. *Geist und Leben*, 32 (1959), 340–51.

——. "Militia Christi." LThK. VII^2, 418f.

Bacht, H. "Pakhôme—der grosse 'Adler.'" *Geist und Leben*, 22 (1949), 367–82.

——. "Antonius und Pachomius: Von der Anachorese zum Zönobitentum." *Studia Anselmiana*, 38 (1956), 66–107.

Balthasar, H. U. von. "Aktion und Kontemplation." *Geist und Leben*, 21 (1948), 361–70.

Bardenhewer, O. *Geschichte der altkirchlichen Literatur* III. 2nd ed. Freiburg, 1923.

——. *Geschichte der altkirchlichen Literatur* IV. Freiburg, 1924.

——. "Augustinus über Röm 7:14ff." MA II. Pp. 879–83.

Bardy, G. "Démétriade (sainte)." *Dictionnaire de Spiritualité.* III, 133–37.

Barion, J. *Plotin und Augustinus: Untersuchungen zum Gottesproblem.* Berlin, 1935.

Bauerreiss, B. "Gyrovagen." LThK. IV², 1293f.

Beckaert, J. A. "Bases philosophiques de l'ascèse augustinienne." AM II. Pp. 703–12.

Beckmann, T. "Das Leben des heiligen Augustin von St. Possidius—Übertragung." *St. Augustin: Festgabe der deutschen Provinz der Augustinereremiten.* Würzburg, 1930. Pp. 9–26.

Bellandi, E. "La Regola agostiniana." *Bolletino Storico Agostiniano*, 5, No. 2 (1929), 39–47.

Berlière, U. "La Règle des SS. Etienne et Paul." In *Mélanges Paul Thomas.* Bruges, 1930. Pp. 39–59.

Bernhart, J. *Augustinus.* Munich, 1922.

Bertrand, L. *Der heilige Augustin.* Trans. M. E. Graf von Platen–Hallermund. Paderborn, 1927.

Besnard, A. M. "Les Grandes Lois de la prière: St. Augustin, maître de prière." *La Vie Spirituelle*, 41 (1959), 237–80.

Besse, J. "Règle de Saint Augustin." *Dictionnaire de Théologie Catholique.* I, 2472–83.

Besson, M. *Monasterium Acaunense.* Fribourg, 1913.

Biedermann, H. M. "Die Regel des Pachomius und die evangelischen Räte." *Ostkirchliche Studien*, 9 (1960), 241–53.

Bigham, T. J., and Mollegen, A. T. "The Christian Ethic." In *A Companion to the Study of St. Augustine.* Ed. R. W. Battenhouse. New York, 1955. Pp. 371–97.

Billicsich, F. *Studien zu den Bekenntnissen des heiligen Augustinus.* Vienna, 1929.

Blanchard, P. "L'Espace intérieur chez Saint Augustin, d'après de livre X des *Confessions*." AM I. Pp. 535–42.

Blank, O. *Die Lehre des heiligen Augustin vom Sakrament der Eucharistie.* Paderborn, 1906.

Blumenberg, H. "Augustins Anteil an der Geschichte des Begriffs der theoretischen Neugierde." REA, 7 (1961), 34–70.

——. "*Curiositas* und *veritas*: Zur Ideengeschichte von Augustin, *Confessiones* X.35." In *Studia Patristica* VI. Ed. F. L. Cross. Berlin, 1962. Pp. 294–304.

La Bonnardière, A. M. "Le verset paulinien Rom. V, 5 dans l'oeuvre de Saint Augustin." AM II. Pp. 657–65.

Bopp, L. "Die Demutsstufen der Benediktinerregel." In *Benedictus, der Vater des Abendlandes.* Ed. H. S. Brechter. Munich, 1947. Pp. 241–62.

Borghini, B. "L'obbedienza secondo S. Agostino." *Vita cristiana,* 23 (1954), 453–78.

Boularand, E. "Expérience et conception de la vie monastique chez S. Augustin." *Bulletin de Littérature Ecclésiastique,* 64 (1963), 81–116, 172–94.

Bouyer, L. *La Spiritualité du Nouveau Testament et des Pères.* Paris, 1960.

Boyer, C. *Christianisme et Néo-Platonisme dans la formation de Saint Augustin.* Paris, 1920. 2nd ed. Rome, 1953.

——. "Saint Augustin." *Dictionnaire de Spiritualité.* I, 1101ff.

——. "Règle de Saint Augustin." *Dictionnaire de Spiritualité.* I, 1126–30.

——. "Agostino Aurelio." *Enciclopedia cattolica.* I, 519–67.

Braem, E. "Augustinus' leer over de heiligmakende genade." *Augustiniana,* 1 (1951) ff.

Brechter, S. "Huldigung an den heiligen Vater Benedikt." In *Benedictus, der Vater des Abendlandes.* Ed. H. S. Brechter. Munich, 1947. Pp. 1–10.

——. "Die soziologische Gestalt des Benediktinertums." In *Benedictus, der Vater des Abendlandes.* Ed. H. S. Brechter. Munich, 1947. Pp. 57–76.

Brucculeri, A. "Il pensiero sociale di S. Agostino: Il lavoro." *La civiltà cattolica,* 81, No. 4 (1930), 20–30, 303–16.

——. "Il pensiero sociale di S. Agostino: La schiavitù." *La civiltà cattolica,* 82, No. 1 (1931), 119–33; No. 2, 130–41.

——. "Il pensiero sociale di S. Agostino: La formazione sacerdotale." *La civiltà cattolica,* 83, No. 2 (1932), 437–51.

Bruyne, D. de. "La Première Règle de Saint Benoît." *Revue Bénédictine,* 42 (1930), 316–42.

——. "La regula consensoria: Une règle des moines priscillianistes." *Revue Bénédictine*, 25 (1908), 83–88.

Bucher, Z. "Das Bild vom Menschen in der *Regula Benedicti*." In *Benedictus, der Vater des Abendlandes*. Ed. H. S. Brechter. Munich, 1947. Pp. 23–56.

Bürke, G. "Paulinus." LThK. VIII², 208f.

Butler, C. *Western Mysticism: The Teaching of Saints Augustine, Gregory, and Bernard on Contemplation and Contemplative Life*. 2nd ed. London, 1927.

——. *Sancti Benedicti Regula monasteriorum*. 3rd ed. Freiburg, 1935.

Capelle, B. "L'Epitre 211ᵉ e la règle de Saint Augustin." *Analecta Praemonstratensia*, 3 (1927), 369–78.

Casamassa, A. "Il più antico codice della regola monastica di Sant' Agostino." *Rendiconti, Atti della Pontificia Accademia Romana di Archeologia* I. Rome, 1923. Pp. 95–105.

——. "Note sulla *Regula secunda sancti Augustini*." AVSM I. Pp. 357–89.

Cayré, F. *La Contemplation augustinienne: Principes de spiritualité et de théologie*. 2nd ed. Paris, 1954.

——. "Alta sapienza e vita cristiana." AVSM I. Pp. 77–101.

Ceyssens, A. *De geest van de Regel van Sint Augustinus*. Diest, 1957.

Chapman, J. "The Origin of the Rules of St. Augustine." *The Downside Review*, 49 (1931), 395–407.

Châtillon, F. "La Règle de Saint Augustin: Etude historique et critique." Diss. University of Strasbourg, 1956.

——. "Quelques remarques sur '*Ante omnia*.' " REA, 2 (1956), 365–69.

Cilleruelo, L. *El monacato de San Agustín y su regla*. 2nd ed. Valladolid, 1966.

——. "Nuevas dudas sobre la *Regula ad Servos Dei* de San Agustín." ArA, 44 (1950), 85–88.

——. "Los monjes de Cartago y San Agustín." CD, 169 (1956), 456–63.

——. "Caratteri del monacato agostiniano." AVSM I. Pp. 43–75.

——. "Un episodio en el primitivo monacato agustiniano." CD, 172 (1959), 357–64.

——. "Nota sobre el agustinismo de los monjes de Cartago." CD, 172 (1959), 365–69.

——. "Los destinatarios de la *Regula Augustini*." ArA, 54 (1960), 87–114.

——. "Concepto agustiniano del apostolado." *Religión y Cultura*, 5 (1960), 57–76.

Courcelle, P. *Recherches sur les Confessions de Saint Augustin.* Paris, 1950.
——. "Litiges sur la lecture des *Libri Platonicorum* par Saint Augustin." *Augustiniana,* 4 (1954), 225–39.
——. *Les Confessions de Saint Augustin dans la tradition littéraire.* Paris, 1963.
Courtois, C. *Les Vandales et l'Afrique.* Paris, 1955.
Cuesta, S. *El equilibrio pasional en la doctrina estoica y en la de San Agustín.* Madrid, 1945.
——. "La concepción agustiniana del mundo a través del amor." AM I. Pp. 347–56.
Daeschler, R. "Abnégation." *Dictionnaire de Spiritualité.* I, 67ff.
Dedler, H. "Vom Sinn der Arbeit nach der Regel des heiligen Benedikt." In *Benedictus, der Vater des Abendlandes.* Ed. H. S. Brechter. Munich, 1947. Pp. 103–18.
Deindl, M. X. "Klösterlicher Kommunismus." BMS, 6 (1924), 113–16.
Delamare, J. "La Prière a l'école de Saint Augustin." *La Vie Spirituelle,* 34 (1952), 477–93.
Dereine, C. "Vie commune, Règle de Saint Augustin et chanoines réguliers au XIe siècle." *Revue d'Histoire Ecclésiastique,* 41 (1946), 365–406.
——. "Enquête sur la Règle de Saint Augustin." *Scriptorium,* 2 (1948), 28–36.
——. "Chanoines." *Dictionnaire d'Histoire et de Géographie Ecclésiastiques.* XII, 353–405.
Dessauer, P. "Geist des Abendlandes: *Regula Benedicti.*" *Hochland,* 39 (1947), 501–13.
Dickinson, J. C. *The Origins of the Austin Canons and Their Introduction into England.* London, 1950.
Diesner, H. J. "Possidius und Augustinus." In *Studia Patristica* VI. Ed. F. L. Cross. Berlin, 1962. Pp. 350–65.
Dietz, I. *Aurelius Augustinus: Heilige Jungfräulichkeit.* Würzburg, 1952.
Disdier, T. "Augustin (Ordre dit de Saint-)." *Dictionnaire d'Histoire et de Géographie Ecclésiastiques.* V, 498–628.
Domínguez-del Val, U. "Eutropio de Valencia y sus fuentes de información." *Revista Española de Teología,* 14 (1954), 369–92.
——. "Cultura y formación intelectual en los monasterios agustinianos de Tagaste, Cartago, e Hipona." CD, 169 (1956), 425–55.
——. "La Regla de San Agustín y los ultimos estudios sobre la misma." *Revista Española de Teología,* 17 (1957), 481–529.

Dörries, H. "Das Verhältnis des Neuplatonischen und Christlichen in Augustins *De vera religione.*" *Zeitschrift für neutestamentliche Wissenschaft*, 23 (1924), 64–102.

Drinkwelder, E. "St. Benedikt als Erbe urchristlichen Betens." In *Benedictus, der Vater des Abendlandes.* Ed. H. S. Brechter. Munich, 1947. Pp. 281–316.

Dürr, L. "Heilige Vaterschaft im antiken Orient: Ein Beitrag zur Geschichte der Idee des 'Abbas.' " In *Heilige Überlieferung.* Ed. Odo Casel, O.S.B. Münster, 1938. Pp. 1–19.

Eisenhofer, L. *Handbuch der Liturgik.* 2nd ed. 2 vols. Freiburg, 1941.

Emonds, H. "Abt." LThK. I², 90–93.

Enrique del Sdo. Corazón. "Oración y contemplación en la teología espiritual de S. Agustín." *Revista de Espiritualidad*, 14 (1955), 205–26.

Erasmus of Rotterdam. *Opera divi Augustini* I. Basel, 1529.

Estal, J. M. del. "Un cenobitismo preagustiniano en Africa?" CD, 169 (1956), 375–403; 171 (1958), 162–95.

——. "Sobre los comienzos de la vida común entre las virgines de Africa." CD, 170 (1957), 335–60.

——. "Desacertada opinión moderna sobre los monjes de Cartago." CD, 172 (1959), 596–616.

——. "El voto de virginidad en la primitiva iglesia de Africa." CD, 175 (1962), 593–623.

——. "Institución monástica de San Agustín." CD, 178 (1965), 201–69.

Fernández, P. I. *De figura iuridica ordinis recollectorum S. Augustini.* Rome, 1938.

Fernández-González, J. "Teología de la virginidad en San Agustín," RAE, 7 (1966), 231–50.

Ferron, J. "Circoncellions d'Afrique." *Dictionnaire d'Histoire et de Géographie Ecclésiastiques.* XII, 837–39.

Feuling, D. "Discretio." BMS, 7 (1925), 241–58, 349–66.

Fingerle, A. *Aurelius Augustinus: Die Vollendung der menschlichen Gerechtigkeit.* Würzburg, 1964.

Flórez, R. "Sobre la mentalidad de Agustín en los primeros años de su monacato: El 'Libro de las ochenta y tres cuestiones." CD, 169 (1956), 464–77.

Folliet, G. "Les trois catégories de chrétiens à partie de Luc (17:34–36), Matthieu (24:40–41), et Ezéchiel (14:14): Etude de ce thème augustinien." AM II. Pp. 631–44.

———. "Des moines euchites à Carthage en 400–411." In *Studia Patristica* II. Edd. Kurt Aland and F. L. Cross. Berlin, 1957. Pp. 389–99.

———. "Aux origines de l'ascétisme et du cénobitisme africain." *Studia Anselmiana,* 46 (1961), 25–44.

———. " 'Deificari in otio': Augustin, Epistula 10, 2." In *Recherches Augustiniennes* II. Paris, 1962. Pp. 225–36.

Foray, J. M. C. *Le Milieu monastique autour de S. Augustin.* Paris, 1948.

Frank, M. "Der Strafkodex in der Regel St. Benedikts." BMS, 17 (1935), 310–18, 380–88, 465–73.

Frank, S. ΑΓΓΕΛΙΚΟΣ ΒΙΟΣ: *Begriffsanalytische und begriffsgeschichtliche Untersuchung zum "engelgleichen Leben" im frühen Mönchtum.* Münster, 1964.

Franz, E. *Totus Christus: Studien über Christus und die Kirche bei Augustin.* Bonn, 1956.

Frutaz, A. P. "Demetrias." LThK. III^2, 215.

Gallay, L. "La conscience de la charité fraternelle, d'après les *Tractatus in Primam Joannis* de Saint Augustin." REA, 1 (1955), 1–20.

Garnelo, B. "Datos históricos acerca de la Regla de San Agustín." ArA, 38 (1932), 364–97.

Gavigan, J. J. "St. Augustine's Friend Nebridius." *The Catholic Historical Review,* 32 (1946), 47–58.

———. "The Mother of St. Augustine." *The American Ecclesiastical Review,* 119 (1948), 254–80.

———. "Vita monastica in Africa septentrionali desiitne cum invasione Wandalorum?" *Augustinianum,* 1 (1961), 7–49.

———. *De vita monastica in Africa septentrionali inde a temporibus S. Augustini usque ad invasiones Arabum.* Rome & Turin, 1962.

Gerontius. *Das Leben der heiligen Melania.* Trans. S. Krottenthaler. Bibliothek der Kirchenväter 5. Munich 1912. Pp. 445–98.

Gessel, W. *Eucharistische Gemeinschaft bei Augustinus.* Würzburg, 1966.

Geweiss, J. "Demut (biblisch)." LThK. III^2, 223f.

Gialdini, H. *Ideale monastico di Sant' Agostino: Insegnamenti dell' esperienza e fondamentali dottrinali.* Vatican City, 1954.

Gilligan, T. F. "Die Augustiner—Schrittmacher des Mönchswesens." *Katholischer Digest,* 1 (1947), 53–57.

Gordini, G. D. "Origine e sviluppo del monachesimo a Roma." *Gregorianum,* 37 (1956), 220–60.

Grabowski, S. J. "The Role of Charity in the Mystical Body of Christ According to Saint Augustine." REA, 3 (1957), 29–63.
Graf, T. "Zur Wesensstruktur des benediktinischen Geistes." BMS, 13 (1931), 9–23.
Grech, P. "The Augustinian Community and the Primitive Church." *Augustiniana*, 5 (1955), 457–70.
Grützmacher, O. *Pachomius und das älteste Klosterleben.* Freiburg & Leipzig, 1896.
Guardini, R. *Die Bekehrung des Aurelius Augustinus.* Leipzig, 1935.
Habitzky, A., and Zumkeller, A. *Aurelius Augustinus: Der christliche Kampf.* Würzburg, 1961.
Hackett, M. B. "The Rule of St. Augustine and Recent Criticism." *The Tagastan*, 20 (1958), 43–50.
Halliburton, R. J. "The Inclination to Retirement—The Retreat of Cassiciacum and the 'Monastery' of Tagaste." In *Studia Patristica* V. Ed. F. L. Cross. Berlin, 1962. Pp. 329–40.
Hand, T. A. *Saint Augustine on Prayer.* Dublin, 1963.
Hardouin, J. *Acta conciliorum et epistolae decretales ac constitutiones Summorum Pontificum ab anno 34 ad 1714.* 12 vols. Paris, 1714ff.
Harnack, A. von. *Augustins Konfessionen.* Giessen, 1887.
——. *Militia Christi: Die christliche Religion und der Soldatenstand in den ersten drei Jahrhunderten.* Tübingen, 1905.
——. *Augustin: Reflexionen und Maximen.* Tübingen, 1922.
——. *Lehrbuch der Dogmengeschichte* III. 5th ed. Tübingen, 1932.
Hazelton, R. "The Devotional Life." In *A Companion to the Study of St. Augustine.* Ed. R. W. Battenhouse. New York, 1955. Pp. 398–414.
Hefele, H. *Des heiligen Augustinus Bekenntnisse.* Jena, 1928.
Heimbucher, M. *Die Orden und Kongregationen der katholischen Kirche.* 3rd ed. 2 vols. Paderborn, 1933.
Hendrikx, E. *Augustins Verhältnis zur Mystik.* Würzburg, 1936.
——. "Augustinus." *Theologisch Woordenboek* I. Roermond & Maaseik, 1952. Pp. 289–333.
——. "Augustinus als Monnik." *Augustiniana*, 3 (1953), 341–53.
——. "Platonisches und biblisches Denken bei Augustin." AM I. Pp. 285–91.
——. "Augustinus." LThK. I^2, 1094–1101.
Hertling, G. von. *Die Bekenntnisse des heiligen Augustinus.* 27–28th ed. Freiburg, 1936.

Hertling, L. "Kanoniker, Augustinerregel und Augustinerorden." *Zeitschrift für katholische Theologie*, 54 (1930), 335–59.

Herwegen, I. *Das Pactum des hl. Fructuosus von Braga.* Stuttgart, 1907.

——. *Der heilige Benedikt.* 3rd ed. Düsseldorf, 1926.

Hesbert, R. "Saint Augustin et la virginité de la foi." AM II. Pp. 645–55.

Hieronymus a Parisiis, "De unione animae cum corpore in doctrina S. Augustini." In *Acta Hebdomadae Augustinianae–Thomisticae.* Turin & Rome, 1931. Pp. 271–311.

Hofmann, F. "Wandlungen in der Frömmigkeit und Theologie des heiligen Augustinus." *Theologie und Glauben*, 22 (1930), 409–31.

——. *Der Kirchenbegriff des heiligen Augustinus.* Munich, 1933.

Hofmann, L. "Militia Christi: Ein Beitrag zur Lehre von den kirchlichen Ständen." *Trierer theologische Zeitschrift*, 63 (1954), 76–92.

Holl, K. "Augustins innere Entwicklung." In *Gesammelte Aufsätze zur Kirchengeschichte* III. Ed. K. Holl. Tübingen, 1928. Pp. 54–116.

Holzapfel, H. *Die sittliche Wertung der körperlichen Arbeit im christlichen Altertum.* Würzburg, 1941.

Huftier, M. *La Charité dans l'enseignement de Saint Augustin.* Tournai, 1959.

Huijbers, T. "Het beeld van God in de ziel volgens Sint Augustinus' *De Trinitate.*" *Augustiniana*, 2 (1952), 88–107, 205–29.

Hümpfner, W. "Die Regeln des heiligen Augustinus." In *Die grossen Ordensregeln.* Ed. H. U. van Balthasar. 2nd ed. Einsiedeln, Zürich, & Cologne, 1961. Pp. 135–71.

——. "Die Mönchsregel des heiligen Augustinus." AM I. Pp. 241–54.

——. "Das Problem der Augustinus-Regel." In *Augustinus—Bij het zestiende eeuwfeest van zijn geboorte.* Averbode, 1954. Pp. 64–80.

——. "Augustinusregel." LThK. I^1, 824f.; I^2, 1104f.

Ignacio M. de la Eucaristía. *Hombre, Mundo, Redención: Concepto agustiniano del hombre bajo el signo de Adán o de Cristo.* Valencia, 1954.

Jüthner, J. "Bad." *Reallexikon für Antike und Christentum.* I, 1134–43.

Keseling, P. *Gottes Weltregiment: Des Aurelius Augustinus "Zwei Bücher von der Ordnung."* Münster, 1939.

——. *Das Ethos der Christen: Des Aurelius Augustinus Buch "Von den Sitten der katholischen Kirche."* Münster, 1948.

——. *Aurelius Augustinus: Die Enthaltsamkeit.* Würzburg, 1949.

——. "Askese II (christlich)." *Reallexikon für Antike und Christentum.* I, 758–95.

Kienitz, E. R. von. *Augustinus: Genius des Abendlandes.* Wuppertal, 1947.

Kopp, S., and Zumkeller, A. *Aurelius Augustinus: Schriften gegen die Semipelagianer.* Würzburg, 1955.

Krebs, E. *Sankt Augustin, der Mensch und Kirchenlehrer.* Cologne, 1930.

Krueger, A. F. *Synthesis of Sacrifice According to Saint Augustine.* Mundelein, 1950.

Krüger, G. "Circumcellionen." LThK. II^2, 1206.

Kunzelmann, A. "Augustins Predigttätigkeit." In *Aurelius Augustinus.* Edd. M. Grabmann and J. Mausbach. Cologne, 1930. Pp. 155–68.

——. "Die Chronologie der Sermones des heiligen Augustinus." MA II. Pp. 417–520.

Ladner, G. B. *The Idea of Reform: Its Impact on Christian Thought and Action in the Age of the Fathers.* Cambridge, Mass., 1959.

Ladomérszky, N. *Saint Augustin, docteur du mariage chrétien.* Rome, 1942.

Lagrange, F. *Geschichte des heiligen Paulinus von Nola.* Mainz, 1882.

Lambot, C. "L'Influence de Saint Augustin sur la Règle de Saint Benoît." *Revue Liturgique et Monastique,* 14 (1929), 320–30.

——. "La règle de Saint Augustin et Saint Césaire." *Revue Bénédictine,* 41 (1929), 333–41.

——. "Un code monastique précurseur de la Règle bénédictine." *Revue Liturgique et Monastique,* 14 (1929), 331–37.

——. "Saint Augustin et la vie monastique." *Revue Liturgique et Monastique,* 15 (1930), 292–304.

——. "Un 'ordo officii' du ve siècle." *Revue Bénédictine,* 42 (1930), 77–80.

——. "La Règle de Saint Augustin, ses origines, et son histoire jusqu'au XIIe siècle." *Les Echos de Saint Maurice,* 29 (1930), 129–37.

——. "Règle de Saint Augustin." *Dictionnaire de Droit Canonique.* I, 1412–16.

——. "Saint Augustin a-t-il rédigé la règle pour moines qui porte son nom?" *Revue Bénédictine,* 53 (1941), 41–58.

——. "Le monachisme de Saint Augustin." AM III. Pp. 64–68.

——. *Sancti Augustini sermones selecti duodeviginti.* Utrecht & Brussels, 1950.

Lang, F. "Des heiligen Augustinus Jugendfreundschaften." *Der Fels,* 24 (1929–1930), 250–64.

Leclerq, H. "Conversion." *Dictionnaire d'Archéologie Chrétienne et de Liturgie.* III, 2797ff.

——. "Melaine (Sainte)." *Dictionnaire d'Archéologie Chrétienne et de Liturgie.* XI, 206–30.

——. "Oratoire." *Dictionnaire d'Archéologie Chrétienne et de Liturgie.* XII, 2346–72.

Lécuyer, J. "Le sacrifice selon Saint Augustin." AM II. Pp. 905–14.

Lefort, L. T. *Les Vies coptes de S. Pachôme.* Louvain, 1943.

Legewie, B. *Augustinus: Eine Psychographie.* Bonn, 1925.

——. "Die körperliche Konstitution und die Krankheiten Augustins." MA II. Pp. 5–21.

Lekkerkerker, A. F. *Römer 7 und Römer 9 bei Augustin.* Amsterdam, 1942.

Lenzenweger, J. "Eugippius." LThK. III², 1179.

Leonet, J. M. "Situación de la virginidad en la espiritualidad agustiniana." RAE, 6 (1965), 215–49.

Lesaar, H. H. "Alypius." *Miscellanea Augustiniana.* Rotterdam, 1930. Pp. 220–32.

Lierde, C. van. *Doctrina sancti Augustini circa dona Spiritus Sancti ex textu Isaiae XI, 2–3.* Würzburg, 1935.

Linderbauer, B. *S. Benedicti Regula monachorum.* Metten, 1922.

Lippert, P. *Briefe in ein Kloster.* Munich, 1932.

Lohse, B. *Mönchtum und Reformation: Luthers Auseinandersetzung mit dem Mönchsideal des Mittelalters.* Göttingen, 1963.

Lorenz, R. "Die Anfänge des abendländischen Mönchtums im 4. Jahrhundert." *Zeitschrift für Kirchengeschichte,* 77 (1966), 1–61.

Madouze, M. A. "Où en est la question de la mystique augustinienne?" AM III. Pp. 103–63.

Madoz, J. "Una nueva transmisión del *Libellus de Institutione Virginum* de San Leandro de Sevilla." *Analecta Bollandiana,* 67 (1949), 407–24.

Mager, A. "Religiöses Leben in und mit der Gemeinschaft." BMS, 2 (1920), 294–306.

——. "Zur Psychologie der Orden." BMS, 6 (1924), 369–80.

Mandonnet, P. *Saint Dominique* II. Paris, 1938.

Manrique, A. *La vida monastica en San Agustín: Enchiridion historico-doctrinal y regla.* El Escorial & Salamanca, 1959.

——. "San Agustín y el monaquismo africano." CD, 173 (1960), 118–38.

——. "Orientación monastica de San Agustín: Acción o contemplación?" RAE, 1 (1960), 225–34.

——. "Concepto monastico de obediencia en San Agustín." RAE, 2 (1961), 18–40.

——. *Teología agustiniana de la vida religiosa.* El Escorial, 1964.
——. "Obediencia agustiniana y voluntad de Dios." RAE, 6 (1965), 177–84.
Marec, E. *Hippone la Royale, antique Hippo Regius.* 2nd ed. Algiers, 1954.
——. "Les dernières fouilles d'Hippo Regius." AM I. Pp. 1–18.
——. *Monuments chrétiens d'Hippone, ville épiscopale de Saint Augustin.* Algiers, 1958.
Mariani, U. "A New Critical Study on the *Rule* of St. Augustine." *The Tagastan*, 19 (1956), 44–47.
——. *Gli Agostiniani e la grande Unione del 1256.* Rome, 1957.
——. "The *Regula Secunda Ordo Monasterii.*" *The Tagastan*, 21 (1959), 38–40.
Marrou, H. J. *Saint Augustin et la fin de la culture antique.* 4th ed. Paris, 1958.
Marx, M. *Incessant Prayer in Ancient Monastic Literature.* Rome, 1946.
Mausbach, J. "Zur inneren Entwicklung des heiligen Augustinus." *Theologische Revue*, 25 (1926), 1ff.
——. *Die Ethik des heiligen Augustinus.* 2nd ed. 2 vols. Freiburg, 1929.
Maxsein, A. *Aurelius Augustinus: Das Gut der Ehe.* Würzburg, 1949.
——. *Aurelius Augustinus: Das Gut der Witwenschaft.* Würzburg, 1952.
Meda, F. "La controversia sul Rus Cassiciacum." MA II. Pp. 49–59.
Meer, F. van der. *Augustinus de Zielzorger.* Utrecht & Brussels, 1947.
Meijer, A. de, and Kuiters, R. "Licet Ecclesiae Catholicae." *Augustiniana*, 6 (1956), 9–36.
Meijer, M. *De Sapientia in de eerste geschriften van S. Augustinus.* Nijmegen, 1939.
Melchior (Beyenka), M. "Who Wrote the Rule of St. Augustine?" *Cross and Crown*, 8 (1956), 162–79.
Mellet, F. M. *L'Itinéraire et l'idéal monastiques de Saint Augustin.* Paris, 1934.
——. "Saint Augustin, prédicateur de la charité fraternelle dans ses commentaires sur Saint Jean." *La Vie Spirituelle*, 73 (1945), 304–25, 556–76; 75 (1946), 69–91.
Melli, R. *Il concetto di autorità negli scritti di S. Agostino.* Lecce, 1948.
Merlin, N. *Saint Augustin et la vie monastique: Etude historique et critique.* Albi, 1933.
——. "Exemple typique d'un préjugé littéraire." *Analecta Praemonstratensia*, 24 (1948), 5–19.

Monceaux, P. "Saint Augustin et Saint Antoine: Contribution à l'histoire du monachisme." MA II. Pp. 61–89.

——. "La formule 'Qui mecum sunt fratres' dans la correspondance de S. Augustin." In *Mélanges Paul Thomas.* Bruges, 1930.

Morán, J. "Filosofía y monacato en San Agustín." *Religión y Cultura,* 2 (1957), 625–54.

——. "Notas sobre el monacato agustiniano." CD, 175 (1962), 535–47.

——. *El hombre frente a Dios: El proceso humano de la ascensión a Dios segùn San Agustín.* Valladolid, 1963.

——. *El equilibrio: Ideal de la vida monastica en San Agustín.* Valladolid, 1964.

Morel, C. "La vie de prière de Saint Augustin d'après sa correspondance." In *Saint Augustin parmi nous.* Edd. H. Rondet et al. Le Puy & Paris, 1954. Pp. 57–87.

Morin, G. "L'ordre des heures canoniales dans les monastères de Cassiodore." *Revue Bénédictine,* 43 (1931), 145–52.

Mugnier, F. "Abstinence." *Dictionnaire de Spiritualité.* I, 112–33.

Mundó, A. "Mönchsregeln." LThK. VII², 540–42.

——. "Regula magistri." LThK. VIII², 1103f.

Murphy, F. X. "Melania die Ältere." LThK. VII², 249f.

——. "Melania the Elder: A Biographical Note." *Traditio,* 5 (1947), 59–77.

Murphy, M. G. *St. Basil and Monasticism.* Washington, 1930.

Mussner, F. "Ebed Jahwe." LThK. III², 622–25.

Nagel, P. *Die Motivierung der Askese in der alten Kirche und der Ursprung des Mönchtums.* Berlin, 1966.

Nathusius, M. von. *Zur Charakteristik der Circumcellionen des vierten und fünften Jahrhunderts in Afrika.* Greifswald, 1900.

Nédoncelle, M. "L'Intersubjectivité humaine est-elle pour Saint Augustin une image de la Trinité?" AM I. Pp. 595–602.

Nigg, W. "Augustin und das gemeinsame Leben der Kleriker." In *Vom Geheimnis der Mönche.* Ed. W. Nigg. Zürich & Stuttgart, 1953. Pp. 118–50.

Nock, A. D. "Bekehrung." *Reallexikon für Antike und Christentum.* II, 105–18.

Nolte, V. *Augustins Freundschaftsideal in seinen Briefen.* Würzburg, 1939.

Nörregaard, J. *Augustins Bekehrung.* Trans. A. Spelmeyer. Tübingen, 1923.

Nygren, A. *Eros und Agape.* 2nd ed. Gütersloh, 1954.
O'Meara, J. J. *The Young Augustine.* London, 1954.
——. "Augustine and Neo-Platonism." In *Recherches Augustiniennes* I. Paris, 1958. Pp. 91–111.
Oppenheim, P. *Das Mönchskleid im christlichen Altertum.* Freiburg, 1931.
——. *Symbolik und religiöse Wertung des Mönchskleides im christlichen Altertum.* Münster, 1932.
S. Pachomii Regulae monasticae. Ed. P. B. Albers. Bonn, 1923.
Pellegrino, M. *Verus sacerdos: Il sacerdozio nell' esperienza e nel pensiero di Sant' Agostino.* Fossano, 1965.
Penco, G. "La vita ascetica come 'filosofia' nell' antica tradizione monastica." *Studia Monastica,* 2 (1960), 79–93.
——. *Storia del monachesimo in Italia.* Rome, 1961.
——. "La vita monastica in Italia all'epoca di S. Martino di Tours." *Studia Anselmiana,* 46 (1961), 67–83.
Penna, A. "Lo studio della Bibbia nella spiritualità di S. Agostino." AVSM I. Pp. 147–68.
Pérez de Urbel, J. "Le monachisme en Espagne au temps de Saint Martin." *Studia Anselmiana,* 46 (1961), 45–65.
Perl, C. J. *Aurelius Augustinus: Die Ordnung.* 2nd ed. Paderborn, 1947.
Perler, O. "L'Eglise principale et les autres sanctuaires chrétiens d'Hippone-la-Royale d'après les textes de Saint Augustin." REA, 1 (1955), 299–343.
——. "La 'Memoria des Vingt Martyrs' d'Hippone-la-Royale." REA, 2 (1956), 435–46.
——. "Les voyages de Saint Augustin." In *Recherches Augustiniennes* I. Paris, 1958. Pp. 5–24.
——. "Hippo Regius." LThK. V^2, 376–78.
——. "Das Datum der Bischofsweihe des heiligen Augustinus." REA, 11 (1965), 25–37.
Pino, A. M. dal. "Autenticità della Regola di Sant' Agostino." *Studi storici dell' Ordine dei Servi di Maria,* 5 (1953), 5–36.
Pintard, J. *Le Sacerdoce selon Saint Augustin.* Paris, 1960.
Piolanti, A. "Il mistero del 'Cristo totale' in S. Agostino." AM III. Pp. 453–69.
Platz, P. *Der Römerbrief in der Gnadenlehre Augustins.* Würzburg, 1938.
Plenkers, H. *Untersuchungen zur Überlieferungsgeschichte der ältesten lateinischen Mönchsregeln.* Munich, 1906.
C. Plinius Secundus. *Naturalis historia.* Ed. C. Mayhoff. Leipzig, 1875.
Plinval, G. de. *Pélage: Ses écrits, sa vie et sa réforme.* Lausanne, 1943.

Popp, J. *Sankt Augustinus als Erzieher des Klerus und Volkes, als Seelenführer.* Munich, 1910.
Le Proust, A. *Traicté de la Règle de Saint Augustin.* Paris, 1963.
Puniet, J. "Abbé." *Dictionnaire de Spiritualité.* I, 49–57.
Quasten, J. "Julianus Pomerius." LThK. V², 1199.
Ranke-Heinemann, U. "Zum Ideal der Vita angelica im frühen Mönchtum." *Geist und Leben,* 29 (1956), 347–57.
Ratzinger, J. *Volk und Haus Gottes in Augustins Lehre von der Kirche.* Munich, 1954.
Reitzenstein, R. "Augustin als antiker und als mittelalterlicher Mensch." *Vorträge der Bibliothek Warburg 1922–1923.* Leipzig & Berlin, 1924. Pp. 28–65.
Rengstorf, K. "Δοῦλος, δουλεία, etc." *Theologisches Wörterbuch zum Neuen Testament.* II, 264–83.
Reul, A. *Die sittlichen Ideale des heiligen Augustinus.* Paderborn, 1928.
Reuter, A. *Sancti Aurelii Augustini doctrina de bonis matrimonii.* Rome, 1942.
Riccardi, D. *Verginità nella vita religiosa.* Rome, 1961.
Rodríguez, L. "La conversión de San Agustín a través de los diálogos de Casiciaco." CD, 176 (1963), 303–18.
Rodríguez, P. A. "Catálogo de las órdenes y congregaciónes religiosas, que militan o han militado bajo la apostólica regla del eximio doctor de la iglesia N. P. Agustín." ArA, 25 (1926), 89–101.
Roetzer, W. *Des heiligen Augustinus Schriften als liturgiegeschichtliche Quelle.* Munich, 1930.
Rondet, H. "Richesse et pauvreté dans la prédication de Saint Augustin." In *Saint Augustin parmi nous.* Edd. H. Rondet et al. Le Puy & Paris, 1954. Pp. 111–48.
Rössler, M. "Augustinus-Legenden." In *St. Augustin.* Würzburg, 1930.
Roth, F. "Cardinal Richard Annibaldi, First Protector of the Augustinian Order." *Augustiniana,* 2 (1952) – 4 (1954).
Rothenhäusler, M. "Hieronymus als Mönch." BMS, 2 (1920), 380–91.
——. "Die Anfänge der klösterlichen Profess." BMS, 4 (1922), 21–28.
——. "Der heilige Basilius der Grosse und die klösterliche Profess." BMS, 4 (1922), 280–89.
——. "Unter dem Geheimnis des Kreuzes: Die klösterliche Profess bei Kassian." BMS, 5 (1923), 91–96.
——. "Conversio morum." *Reallexikon für Antike und Christentum.* III, 422–24.

Sage, A. "Vie de perfection et conseils evangéliques dans les controverses pélagiennes." AVSM I. Pp. 195–220.

——. *La Règle de Saint Augustin, commentée par ses écrits.* Paris, 1961.

Salaville, S. "Une version grecque de la Règle de Saint Augustin." ΕΛΛΗΝΙΚΑ, 4 (1931), 81–110.

Sanchis, D. "Pauvreté monastique et charité fraternelle chez Saint Augustin: Note sur le plan de la *Regula.*" *Augustiniana,* 8 (1958), 5–21.

——. "Le Symbolisme communitaire du Temple chez Saint Augustin." *Revue d'Ascétique et de Mystique,* 37 (1961), 3–30, 137–47.

——. "Pauvreté monastique et charité fraternelle chez Saint Augustin: Le commentaire augustinien des Actes 4, 32–35 entre 393 et 403." *Studia Monastica,* 4 (1962), 7–33.

Sauer, J. "Der Kirchenbau Nordafrikas in den Tagen des heiligen Augustinus." In *Aurelius Augustinus.* Edd. M. Grabmann and J. Mausbach. Cologne, 1930. Pp. 243–300.

Schade, L. *Des heiligen Kirchenlehrers Eusebius Hieronymus ausgewählte Briefe* II. Munich, 1937.

Schaffner, O. *Christliche Demut: Des heiligen Augustinus Lehre von der Humilitas.* Würzburg, 1959.

Schiwietz, S. *Das morgenländische Mönchtum* I. Mainz, 1904.

——. *Das morgenländische Mönchtum* III. Mödling, 1938.

Schlund, R. "Diskretion." LThK. III², 418f.

Schmid, C. "Das Gottesbild der Benediktinerregel." In *Benedictus, der Vater des Abendlandes.* Ed. H. S. Brechter. Munich, 1947. Pp. 11–22.

Schmid, J. *Aurelius Augustinus: Die ehebrecherischen Verbindungen.* Würzburg, 1949.

Schmitt, A. "Vom Wesen des benediktinischen Mönchtums." BMS, 9 (1927), 91–107.

——. "Mathematik und Zahlenmystik." In *Aurelius Augustinus.* Edd. M. Grabman and J. Mausbach. Cologne, 1930. Pp. 353–66.

——. "Aus der Predigtwelt des heiligen Augustinus." BMS, 23 (1947), 210–15.

Schneider, R. *Welt und Kirche bei Augustin: Ein Beitrag zur Frage des christlichen Existentialismus.* Munich, 1949.

Schoeps, H. J. "Von der Imitatio Dei zur Nachfolge Christi." In *Aus frühchristlicher Zeit.* Tübingen, 1930. Pp. 286–301.

Schroeder, P. "Die Augustinerchorherrenregel, Entstehung, kritischer Text und Einführung der Regel." *Archiv für Urkundenforschung,* 9 (1926), 271–306.

Schulz, A. *Nachfolgen und Nachahmen im Neuen Testament.* Munich, 1962.

——, and Hofmann, R. "Nachfolge Christi." LThK. VII², 758–62.

Schuster, I. *Storia di San Benedetto e dei suoi tempi.* Milan, 1946.

Schwarz, R. "Die leib-seelische Existenz bei Augustinus." *Philosophisches Jahrbuch,* 63 (1955), 323–60.

Secundo de Jesús. "Las pasiones en la concepción agustiniana de la vida espiritual." *Revista de Espiritualidad,* 14 (1955), 251–80.

Seller, H. J. "Augustinus und seine Regel." In *St. Augustin: Festgabe der Deutschen Provinz der Augustinereremiten.* Würzburg, 1930. Pp. 89ff.

Sokolowski, P. von. *Der heilige Augustin und die christliche Zivilisation.* Schriften der königsberger Gelehrten Gesellschaft 4. Halle, 1927.

Somers, H. "Image de Dieu et illumination divine." AM I. Pp. 451–62.

Specht, T. *Die Lehre von der Kirche nach dem heiligen Augustin.* Paderborn, 1892.

Spreitzenhofer, E. *Die Entwicklung des alten Mönchtums in Italien.* Vienna, 1894.

Steggink, M. M. *Studie over de zelfverloochening en de versterving.* Utrecht, 1955.

Steidle, B. " 'Der Zweite' in Pachomiuskloster." BMS, 24 (1948), 97ff.

——. *Die Benediktusregel.* Beuron, 1963.

Stoeckle, B. *Die Lehre von der erbsündlichen Konkupiszenz in ihrer Bedeutung für das christliche Leibethos.* Ettal, 1954.

Stoop, J. A. A. *De deificatio hominis in de Sermones en Epistulae van Augustinus.* Leiden, 1952.

Thonnard, F. J. *Traité de vie spirituelle à l'école de Saint Augustin.* Paris, 1959.

Trapè, A. "Il principio fondamentale della spiritualità agostiniana e la vita monastica." AVSM I. Pp. 1–41.

——. "San Agustín y el monacato occidental." CD, 169 (1956), 400–24.

——. *San Agostino.* Rome, 1961.

Turrado, A. "El platonismo de San Agustín y su doctrina acerca de la inhabitación del Espíritu Santo." *Augustiniana,* 5 (1955), 471–86.

——. "El ideal monástico agustiniano en Santo Tomás de Villanueva." RAE, 1–6 (1960–1965).

——. "Eres templo de Dios: La inhabitación de la Ssma. Trinidad en los justos según S. Agustín." RAE, 7 (1966), 21–55, 203–27.

Urbana de N. Jesús. "Ensayo sobre los dones del Espíritu Santo en la espiritualidad agustiniana." *Revista de Espiritualidad,* 14 (1955), 227–50.

Vaca, C. *La vida religiosa en San Agustín.* 4 vols. Madrid, 1955, 1964.

Van Bavel, T. J. " '*Ante omnia*' et '*In Deum*' dans la *Regula Sancti Augustini.*" *Vigiliae Christianae,* 12 (1958), 157–65.

——. "Parallèles: Vocabulaire et citations bibliques de la *Regula Sancti Augustini.*" *Augustiniana,* 9 (1959), 12–77.

——. *Répertoire bibliographique de Saint Augustin.* The Hague, 1963.

Van Luijk, B. *Bullarium Ordinis Eremitarum S. Augustini: Periodus formationis, 1187–1256.* Würzburg, 1964.

Vathaire, J. de. "Les relations de Saint Augustin et de Saint Jérôme." In *Miscellanea Augustiniana.* Rotterdam, 1930. Pp. 484–99.

Vega, A. C. *La regla de San Agustín: Edición critica precedida de un estudio sobre la misma y los códices de Escorial.* El Escorial, 1933.

——. "Una adaptación de la *Informatio Regularis* de San Agustín, anterior al siglo IX, para unas vírgines españolas." In *Miscellanea G. Mercati* II. Vatican City, 1946. Pp. 34–56.

——. "Notas histórico-críticas en torno a los orígines de la *Regla de San Agustín.*" *Boletín de la Real Academia de la Historia,* 152 (1963), 13–94.

Verbeke, G. "Augustin et le stoïcisme." In *Recherches Augustiniennes* I. Paris, 1958. Pp. 67–89.

Verheijen, L. M. "Autour de la *Règle de S. Augustin.*" *L'Année Théologique,* 11 (1951), 345–48.

——. "Les manuscripts de la 'Lettre CCXI de saint Augustin.' " *Revue du Moyen Age Latin,* 8 (1952), 97–122.

——. "La *Regula Sancti Augustini.*" *Vigiliae Christianae,* 7 (1953), 27–56.

——. "Les sermons 355–356 de Saint Augustin et *Regula Sancti Augustini.*" *Recherches de Science Religieuse,* 41 (1953), 231–40.

——. "La *Regula Puellarum* et la *Regula Sancti Augustini.*" In *Augustiniana—sexto decimo exacto saeculo a die natali S. Aurelii Augustini.* Louvain, 1954. Pp. 42–52.

——. "Remarques sur le style de la Regula secunda de Saint Augustin: Son rédacteur." AM I. Pp. 255–63.

——. "Saint Augustin." In *Théologie de la vie monastique: Etudes sur la tradition patristique.* Paris, 1961. Pp. 201–12.

——. "La *Règle de Saint Augustin* et deux publications récentes." *Augustiniana,* 11 (1961), 412–20.

——. "La Vie de Saint Augustin par Possidius et la *Regula Sancti Augus-*

tini." In *Mélanges offerts à Mademoiselle Christine Mohrmann.* Utrecht & Antwerp, 1963. Pp. 270–79.

——. "La *Règle de S. Augustin.*" *Augustinianum,* 4 (1964), 109–22.

——. *La Règle de Saint Augustin.* 2 vols. Paris, 1967.

Vermeersch, A. "Le concept de la vie religieuse dans Saint Augustin." *Gregorianum,* 11 (1930), 92–130.

Vetter, J. *Der heilige Augustinus und das Geheimnis des Leibes Christi.* Mainz, 1929.

Vilanova, J. E. M. *Regula sanctorum Pauli et Stephani abbatum.* Montserrat, 1959.

Villegas, M. "La oración en San Agustín." CD, 175 (1962), 624–39.

Viller, M. *Aszese und Mystik in der Väterzeit.* Trans K. Rahner. Freiburg, 1939.

Vissers, H. "L'Esprît de la *Règle de Saint Augustin.*" In *Canonicorum Regularium Sodalitates XVI revoluto saeculo ab ortu S. Augustini.* Vorau, 1954. Pp. 19ff.

——. *Vie canoniale.* Vorau, 1957.

Vogels, H. J. "Die Heilige Schrift bei Augustinus." In *Aurelius Augustinus.* Edd. M. Grabmann and J. Mausbach. Cologne, 1930. Pp. 411–21.

Wagner, A. "Der klösterliche Haushalt des heiligen Benedikt." In *Benedictus, der Vater des Abendlandes.* Ed. H. S. Brechter. Munich, 1947. Pp. 77–102.

Wagner, P. "Über Psalmen und Psalmengesang im christlichen Altertum." *Römische Quartalschrift,* 12 (1898), 245–79.

Wallbrecht, E. *St. Augustins Regel in Wort und Sinn.* Würzburg, 1933.

Walter, H. "Die benediktinische *Discretio.*" In *Benedictus, der Vater des Abendlandes.* Ed. H. S. Brechter. Munich, 1947. Pp. 195–212.

Weinand, H. *Antike und moderne Gedanken über die Arbeit, dargestellt am Problem der Arbeit beim heiligen Augustinus.* Mönchen-Gladbach, 1911.

Weninger, F. *Die Regeln des heiligen Augustinus.* Innsbruck, 1929.

Wirges, K. "Über den Ursprung der Augustinerregel." *Theologisch-praktische Quartalschrift,* 80 (1927), 583–87.

——. *Die Anfänge der Augustinerchorherren und die Gründung des Augustinerchorherrenstiftes Ravengiersburg.* Betzdorf, 1928.

Wucherer-Huldenfeld, A. "Mönchtum und kirchlicher Dienst bei Augustinus nach dem Bild des Neubekehrten und des Bischofs." *Zeitschrift für katholische Theologie,* 82 (1960), 182–211.

Wunderle, G. *Einführung in Augustins Konfessionen.* Augsburg, 1930.

Wundt, M. "Ein Wendepunkt für Augustins Entwicklung." *Zeitschrift für neutestamentliche Wissenschaft,* 21 (1922), 53–64.

——. "Augustins Konfessionen." *Zeitschrift für neutestamentliche Wissenschaft,* 22 (1923), 161–206.

——. "Nachtrag zu 'Augustins Konfessionen." *Zeitschrift für neutestamentliche Wissenschaft,* 23 (1924), 154.

Zähringer, D. *Das kirchliche Priestertum nach dem heiligen Augustinus.* Paderborn, 1931.

Zellinger, J. *Augustin und die Volksfrömmigkeit.* Munich, 1933.

Zoepfl, F. "Regula sancta—Zum Benediktusjahr." *Geist und Leben,* 20 (1947), 306–309.

Zumkeller, A. "Das Charakterbild des Seelsorgers beim heiligen Kirchenvater Augustinus." *Anima,* 5 (1950), 63–74.

——. "Der klösterliche Gehorsam beim heiligen Augustinus." AM I. Pp. 265–76.

——. "Augustinus und das Mönchtum." *L'Année Théologique,* 14 (1954), 97–112.

——. "Zur handschriftlichen Überlieferung und ursprünglichen Textgestalt der Augustinusregel (aus dem Nachlass des P. Dr. Winfried Hümpfner OESA)." *Augustiniana,* 11 (1961), 425–33.

——. *Die Regel des heiligen Augustinus, mit Einführung und Erklärung.* 2nd ed. Würzburg, 1962.

——. *Aurelius Augustinus: Schriften gegen die Pelagianer* II. Würzburg, 1964.

——, and Hümpfner, W. "Die Regeln des heiligen Augustinus." In *Die grossen Ordensregeln.* Ed. H. U. von Balthasar. 2nd ed. Einsiedeln, Zürich, & Cologne, 1961. Pp. 135–71.

AUGUSTINE

This is in no sense a comprehensive list of editions of Augustine's Latin writings, though such an instrument is an urgent necessity. Few of the Church Fathers wrote more prolifically; during the Middle Ages his works were constantly being copied by scribes, and since the invention of printing, his editions have seldom ceased to appear. Instead, this is a list of the works mentioned by Adolar Zumkeller in his text and his copious footnotes, showing where the most modern editions are to be found.—Translators.

Adulterous Marriages (*De coniugiis adulterinis*) CSEL 41
The Advantage of Believing (*De utilitate credendi*) CSEL 25
Against an Adversary of the Law and the Prophets (*Contra adversarium legis et prophetarum*) PL 42
Against Faustus (*Contra Faustum*) CSEL 25
Against Fortunatus (*Contra Fortunatum*) CSEL 25
Against Julian (*Contra Julianum*) PL 44
Against Maximinus (*Contra Maximinum*) PL 42
Against the Academics (*Contra Academicos*) CSEL 63
Against the Writings of Petilian the Donatist (*Contra litteras Petiliani donatistae*) CSEL 52
The Catechizing of the Uninstructed (*De catechizandis rudibus*) PL 40
The Christian Combat (*De agone christiano*) CSEL 41
Christian Instruction (*De doctrina christiana*) CSEL 80, CCL 32
The City of God (*De civitate Dei*) CSEL 40 (Parts I and II), CCL 47, 48
Commentary on the Epistle to the Galatians (*Expositio Epistolae ad Galatas*) PL 35
Confessions (*Confessiones*) CSEL 33
Continence (*De continentia*) CSEL 44
The Creed for Catechumens (*Sermo de symbolo ad catechumenos*) PL 40
The Deeds of Pelagius (*De gestis Pelagii*) CSEL 42
The Eight Questions of Dulcitius (*De octo Dulcitii quaestionibus*) PL 40
The Excellence of Widowhood (*De bono viduitatis*) CSEL 41
An Exposition of Certain Propositions from the Epistle to the Romans (*Expositio quarundam propositionum ex Epistola ad Romanos*) PL 35
Expositions on the Psalms (*Enarrationes in Psalmos*) CCL 38, 39, 40
Faith and the Creed (*De fide et symbolo*) CSEL 41
Faith, Hope, and Charity (*Enchiridion ad Laurentium sive De fide, spe, et caritate*) PL 40

Forgiveness of Sin and Baptism (*De peccatorum meritis et remissione et de baptismo parvulorum*) CSEL 60

The Freedom of the Will (*De libero arbitrio*) CSEL 74

The Gift of Perseverance (*De dono perseverantiae*) PL 45

The Good of Marriage (*De bono coniugali*) CSEL 41

Grace and Free Will (*De gratia et libero arbitrio*) PL 44

The Grace of Christ and Original Sin (*De gratia Christi et peccato originali*) CSEL 42

The Greatness of the Soul (*De quantitate animae*) PL 32

The Happy Life (*De beata vita*) CSEL 63

Holy Virginity (*De sancta virginitate*) CSEL 41

Homilies on St. John's Epistle to the Parthi (*Tractatus in Joannis Epistolam I*) PL 35

Homilies on St. John's Gospel (*Tractatus in Joannis Evangelium*) CCL 36

The Immortality of the Soul (*De immortalitate animae*) PL 32

The Incomplete Book on the Literal Meaning of Genesis (*De Genesi ad litteram imperfectus liber*) CSEL 28

The Incomplete Work against Julian (*Contra Julianum opus imperfectum*) PL 45

In Reply to Two Letters of the Pelagians (*Contra duas epistolas Pelagianorum*) CSEL 60

A Letter to the Catholics against the Donatists, Commonly Called "The Unity of the Church" (*Ad catholicos epistola contra Donatistas, vulgo De unitate ecclesiae*) CSEL 52

Letters (*Epistolae*) CSEL 34 (Parts I and II), 44, 57

The Literal Meaning of Genesis (*De Genesi ad litteram*) CSEL 28

The Lord's Sermon on the Mount (*De sermone Domini in monte*) PL 34

Lying (*De mendacio*) CSEL 41

Man's Perfection in Righteousness (*De perfectione iustitiae hominis*) CSEL 42

Marriage and Concupiscence (*De nuptiis et concupiscentia*) CSEL 42

Nature and Grace (*De natura et gratia*) CSEL 60

Of Order (*De ordine*) CSEL 63

On 83 Various Questions (*De diversis quaestionibus LXXXIII*) PL 40

On Genesis against the Manichaeans (*De Genesi contra Manichaeos*) PL 34

On Heresies (*De haeresibus*) PL 42

On Music (*De musica*) PL 32

On the Cataclysm (*Sermo de cataclysmo*) PL 40

On Various Questions to Simplicianus (*De diversis quaestionibus ad Simplicianum*) PL 40
Problems in the Gospels (*Quaestiones Evangeliorum*) PL 35
Questions about the Heptateuch (*Quaestiones in Heptateuchum*) CSEL 28, CCL 33
Rebuke and Grace (*De correptione et gratia*) PL 44
Retractations (*Retractationes*) CSEL 36
Rule (*Regula*) Verheijen
Sermons (*Sermones*) CCL 41, PL 38, 39, Lambot, Morin
Soliloquies (*Soliloquia*) PL 32
The Spirit and the Letter (*De spiritu et littera*) CSEL 60
The Trinity (*De Trinitate*) PL 42
True Religion (*De vera religione*) CSEL 77, CCL 32
The Two Souls (*De duabus animabus*) CSEL 25
The Usefulness of Fasting (*De utilitate ieiunii*) PL 40
The Ways of the Catholic Church (*De moribus ecclesiae catholicae*) PL 32
The Work of Monks (*De opere monachorum*) CSEL 41

INDEX

Compiled by Joseph W. Sprug